MW00440387

FINDING BIRDS IN CONNECTICUT

A HABITAT-BASED GUIDE
TO 450 SITES

DAVE ROSGEN
and
GENE BILLINGS

1996

FINDING BIRDS IN CONNECTICUT

FINDING BIRDS IN CONNECTICUT

A HABITAT-BASED GUIDE
TO 450 SITES

DAVE ROSGEN
and
GENE BILLINGS

1996

This book has been printed on recycled paper.

Copyright @ 1996 Dave Rosgen and Gene Billings.

All rights reserved. No part of this work may be reproduced or transmitted in any form by any means, electronic or mechanical, including photocopying and recording, or by any information storage or retrieval system, without permission in writing from the authors.

Design, typography and printing, Rainbow Press, Torrington, Connecticut.
Printed in the United States of America

Library of Congress Catalog Card Number 96-068691   ISBN: 0-9652708-0-7

That there are well over 400 places open to the public that have good habitat in a state as small and populous as Connecticut is due to the generosity, effort, skill and foresight of many individuals, working on their own or through organizations. This guide is gratefully dedicated to them, with the promise that we shall be good stewards of the land they have protected.

CONTENTS

MAPS

CONTENTS (2)

CONTENTS (3)

ACKNOWLEDGMENTS

One of the pleasures of birding is the willingness of other birders to share their knowledge - about the arrival of an early migrant, the occurrence of an uncommon species, or the location of a good birding site. We have benefited greatly from that willingness, and the guide has been enriched by the information and insights of many other birders - through conversations with friends, and from the newsletters of birding and conservation organizations. The process of sharing is so common and taken for granted, that to list even a fraction of the people who have contributed information to this guide would be a daunting task.

However, one group of birders can be identified and should be mentioned. They are the individuals (some 520) and organizations (over 20) that contributed their time and skills in the development of <u>The Atlas of Breeding Birds of Connecticut.</u> We all owe them our gratitude for the significant contribution of that project to long-term conservation of birds in our state. In addition, the authors of this guide are indebted to them in a more specific way, because the information about species that nest at sites in the guide is based on records of the Breeding Bird Atlas project, updated through 1995.

INTRODUCTION

This guide contains information for 450 sites in Connecticut, every one of which is open to the public at least part of the year. We believe that these sites are the best publicly accessible places in the state for finding birds. Each of them has been visited by one or both of the authors.

However, this guide is intended to be more than a directory of places to go, with directions how to get there. Rather, it is intended to enable the reader to become more effective at finding birds, by providing information about types of habitat, and the bird species that occur in each type.

Still another goal is to increase the sensitivity of birders to the need to protect certain types of habitat, in order to protect the birds that depend on them. As people who enjoy birds, it is our responsibility and to our self interest to work for this protection. We can do so as individuals by having our conduct in the field set an example for others, and by working for habitat protection through conservation organizations such as those listed in Chapter 12: "Sources of Additional Information".

It was our hope that we could include at least one site in each of Connecticut's 169 towns. Unfortunately, this proved not to be feasible, since it was also our resolve to include only sites that we could recommend that birders visit. Such sites have to meet several criteria:

> have sufficient diversity or abundance of birds to make a visit worthwhile;
> be open to the public;
> not present serious problems of personal safety.

As any experienced birder knows, most sites have drawbacks of some kind - ticks, poison ivy, wet trails, degraded surroundings, and so on. Up to a point, such flaws can be regarded as inconveniences. However, when the negatives outweigh the pleasures, or when there is a significant threat to personal safety or to property, the site is better not entered, and better omitted from a guide such as this.

As time goes by, birding sites change. Sometimes changes have to do with public access - current sites are closed, or new ones acquired. Habitats within sites change - through natural succession or human intervention - in ways that affect the occurrence of birds within the site. We would appreciate your taking the trouble to let us know when you are aware of such changes, so that they may be taken into account in future editions of this guide. Also, you may know of additional good sites that you would be willing to share with readers of future editions. Please mail or telephone your comments to either:

Dave Rosgen	or	Gene Billings
84 D Falls Terrace		28 Sunset Ridge
Oakville, CT 06779		Norfolk, CT 06058
Tel: 860-274-6728		Tel: 860-542-5177

How To Use This Guide

HOW TO USE THIS GUIDE

Purpose of the Guide

This is a guide to the birding sites that are considered to be the best in Connecticut. It is not intended to be a complete directory of all of the good birding sites in the state - space does not permit. Rather, our intent is to include sites that are rewarding places in which to look for birds, are open to the public, and which contain high quality examples of the most important types of avian habitat found in Connecticut. The guide describes 450 sites considered to be worthy of your consideration. No matter where you live or are visiting in Connecticut, you are near several good sites that are described in this guide.

Organization of the Guide

Chapter 1: Birding in Connecticut provides an overview of birds and birding in the state.

Chapter 2: Using Habitats to Find Birds. An understanding of birds' relationship to their habitat is the starting point for developing effective bird finding strategies. The purpose of this chapter is to provide the information and understanding that will help you to develop effective strategies for finding birds.

Chapter 3: Finding Uncommon Birds in Connecticut is a list of bird species that occur on a regular basis, but only in a small number of sites. For each species, the list states the best habitats, sites and time of year in which to look.

Chapters 4 through 11 contain site descriptions of birding areas in each of Connecticut's eight counties. Each county chapter starts with a map of the county and a table that shows the habitats and seasons at each site.

Chapter 12: Sources of Additional Information contains lists of organizations, references and maps that are helpful to birders in Connecticut.

Glossary and Abbreviations: defines terms and abbreviations used in the guide that are not in common usage.

Indexes. There are three indexes to this guide. **Index 1** lists sites alphabetically by name of site. **Index 2** lists tours by county, and **Index 3** lists towns alphabetically, showing the county.

Site Descriptions

The description of each site does not attempt to provide information as to exactly where in the site to look in order to find certain bird species - space does not permit that degree of detail for the number of sites included in the guide. Instead, the guide attempts to develop in the reader an understanding of the distribution of birds among types of habitat. Such an understanding makes it possible for the reader to locate particular bird species at a site - a more rewarding process than being told exactly where to look.

The format and arrangement of information is intended to make it easy to skim, and to seek specific types of information. For this purpose, the site descriptions contain headlines that summarize information about the site. These headlines tell you at a glance what habitats are at the site, which birds groups occur at the site, the seasons when they are there, and the methods of getting around within the site. Upper-case letters indicate high quality or above average significance. Thus, by skimming you can quickly answer such questions as:

What sites contain a certain type of habitat?
At what sites do shore birds occur?
What are good sites to go to in winter?
What sites can be birded from a car?
Which sites are good to walk? bike? use a boat?

More detailed information is provided in the text that follows the headlines.

Birding sites within each county are listed alphabetically by town. For each site, the following information is provided:

Habitats

For quick reference, this section starts with headlines of the habitat groups (such as "forest") and the specific habitat types within each group (such as "hardwoods") that occur at the site. When the name of a habitat group is in capital letters, it means that there is a very good example of habitats within the group at the site; lower case means that the habitat is present, but is less important. The text that follows these headlines provides more detailed information about the habitats at the site. (Chapter 2: "Using Habitats to Find Birds" defines each type of habitat, and discusses the bird species that occur in each type.)

Seasons/Birds

Seasons. For quick reference, this section starts with headlines of the four seasons and of the bird groups that occur at the site during each season. When a season is in upper case letters, it means that birding is especially good at the site during that season.

The seasons listed are "spring migration", "nesting season", "fall migration" and "winter". These seasons refer to patterns of bird activity, and do not necessarily track with the calendar seasons of spring, summer, fall and winter. (For example, the spring migration of some species through Connecticut starts in February, the fall migration of others starts in July, and so on.)

Birds. For each season, bird groups that occur at the site during that season are stated. Examples of bird groups are "water birds", "land birds", etc. These bird groups are defined in the Glossary. When a bird group appears in upper case letters, it means that birding for species within that bird group during that season is particularly good. Lower case letters indicate that bird species within that group are present, but less important. When there is no entry for a particular bird group during a certain season, it means that species within the group are not present in significant numbers and / or diversity.

When a bird group is listed under "nesting season", it means that species within the group occur at the site during the nesting season. In most cases, such species nest at the site, but this is not always true. For example, during the nesting season, gulls and terns can be seen from many beaches as they feed, but they often nest elsewhere; great blue heron feeds in marshes that may be some distance from their nest; great egret may occur as a post breeding wanderer at sites in which it does not nest.

The text that follows these headlines provides more detailed information about seasons and birds at the site. If certain seasons are especially good, that is stated. The species that are mentioned in connection with a season include a representative group of interesting species. Very common species that one would expect to see in the types of habitat that are at the site are not individually identified. Bird species that are said to nest at a site have been documented as confirmed or probable nesters at the site in the records of the Connecticut Breeding Bird Atlas, updated through 1995.

The birds that are included in the site descriptions are species that occur in Connecticut on a regular or somewhat regular basis, but not species that only occur rarely or very infrequently. Information in the guide about the distribution of bird species among sites and habitats in Connecticut is based on information from records of the Connecticut Breeding Bird Atlas, and also on recent observations in the field. It is not based on information from textbooks or other field guides. There are cases where data in this guide contradicts existing perceptions of distribution; however, we believe that it does reflect current reality.

Getting Around

This section of each site description provides information about the characteristics of a site that facilitate or impede your ability to get around within it.

For quick reference, this section starts with a headline (**"Birding methods:"**) followed by words that indicate what methods can be used to get around at the site - car, walk, bike, boat, ski, wheelchair. When a method is in upper case letters, it means that the site is a good area in which to use that method. "Car" means that a significant part of the site can be seen from your car or near to it. "Bike" refers to the use of bicycles that are suitable for use on dirt roads - that is, cross or mountain bikes, but not touring bikes. "Boat" refers to canoe or other non-motorized boat. "Ski" refers to use of cross-country skis on reasonably level terrain.

A number of sites are wheelchair -accessible. In most cases, this consists of wheelchair ramps to observation platforms that overlook tidal wetlands. However, several, including Babcock Pond, Canal Park and Hammonasset Park have trail systems for wheelchairs.

The text that follows the "Birding methods" headline provides more detailed information about getting around at the site, and also about any special equipment that is required or special conditions that exist at the site. Conditions that occur at many sites, such as proximity to private property, poison ivy, ticks, etc. are considered to be routine conditions that call for the discretion of each birder, and they are not mentioned for specific sites unless they are considered to be especially important at the site. (They are discussed in general terms in the next chapter, "Birding in Connecticut".) The term "woods road" refers to a pathway that is wider than a trail, and can be easily walked but not driven by members of the public.

Directions

Directions are given from some easy-to-find starting point, such as a major route intersection, an interstate highway exit, or a town center. It is intended that this guide and a state highway map will be all that you need to reach each site and to explore the habitats within it. However, some sites - particularly those that are in state forests - are large and complex, so that more information would be useful. There are a number of county atlases, trail guides and maps which are helpful, and some of these are listed in Chapter 12: "Sources of Additional Information".

Tours

There are several cases in which a number of sites are close together and can conveniently be visited in sequence. When this is the case, directions for linking them are given under the heading of "tours". Such tours are listed first in each county chapter. When a tour includes sites that are particularly good or complex, such sites are also described separately in greater detail than is given in the tour description. Tours can be birded in large part from your car and do not require much walking, although most tours also include sites that can be birded on foot.

Maps

There are 82 maps in this guide. At the beginning of Chapter 1: "Birding in Connecticut", there is a map of the state that shows the eight counties within it. At the beginning of each county chapter, there is a map that shows the towns within the county. Tours that link several sites are displayed on maps, in order to give an overview of the tour. Sites that are especially important or complex are displayed on maps.

The maps are inteded to be simple tools to help you orient yourself on a tour or reach a site; they contain only enough detail to accomplish this purpose and mileages are approximate. For detailed directions and precise distances, refer to the "Directions" section of the site or tour description.

The following symbols are used in the maps:

━━━━━━━━━ main highway

───────── smaller auto road

- - - - - - - - - woods road or trail, not for use by autos

| P | a place to park, which in some cases also serves as the entrance to a site or a trailhead

water

wetland; marsh, swamp or bog

When place names are underlined on a map, it means that they are mentioned in the site description.

Terms That are Used in the Guide:

The intent of the guide is to provide the average birder with practical information that will be easy to use in the field. Scientific terms are avoided when it is possible to provide accurate information without using them. Terms that are not part of our daily vocabulary are defined in the Glossary.

Bird species are referred to by their common English names, rather than by the scientific Latin name including genus and species. Common names are sometimes shortened when doing so does not result in ambiguity. For example, American robin is referred to simply as "robin", but "common goldeneye" is always named in full, to avoid confusion with Barrow's goldeneye, which also occurs in Connecticut.

Bird groups. Throughout the guide, terms are used that refer to groups of birds. These groups are composed of species that occur in similar types of habitat, as they are usually seen by birders. The groups that are used are: water birds, marsh birds, shore birds, land birds. Each of these groups is defined in the Glossary.

Seasonal occurrence, abundance and distribution of bird species. There are terms that refer to the time of year during which bird species occur in Connecticut, to their abundance and to their residential status. These terms are defined in the Glossary.

Building on the Information in the Guide

This guide does not include all the sites in Connecticut at which there is good habitat for birds; space did not permit. There are additional areas to which you may gain access with some investigation and effort, (and, if the areas are private, with the permission of the land-owner).

Many additional areas are open to the public. These include additional state parks and state forests, other parts of state forests that are listed in the guide, and additional wildlife areas managed by DEP. Sources of information about such areas are listed in Chapter 12: "Sources of Additional Information".

There are over 100 local land trusts in Connecticut, and many of them manage land that is open to the public. There probably is at least one land trust near you. To find out, contact the Land Trust Service Bureau (see Chapter 12).

In addition, many areas of private land contain good avian habitat that may be accessible to you. Some streambelts and edges can be seen from public roads. If you ask, you may receive permission to look for birds in farmland, woods, open areas such as golf courses, and other such properties.

Probably the best - and most enjoyable - way to find good birding sites is to join a bird organization - either a local bird club or a state organization. This puts you in a network of information about birds - both background ornithological information, and also information about current events such as the occurrence in Connecticut of a rare species. It will also enable you to participate in activities that protect birds and develop our knowledge about them. See Chapter 12: "Sources of Additional Information" for a list of birding organizations in Connecticut.

Chapter 1

Birding In Connecticut

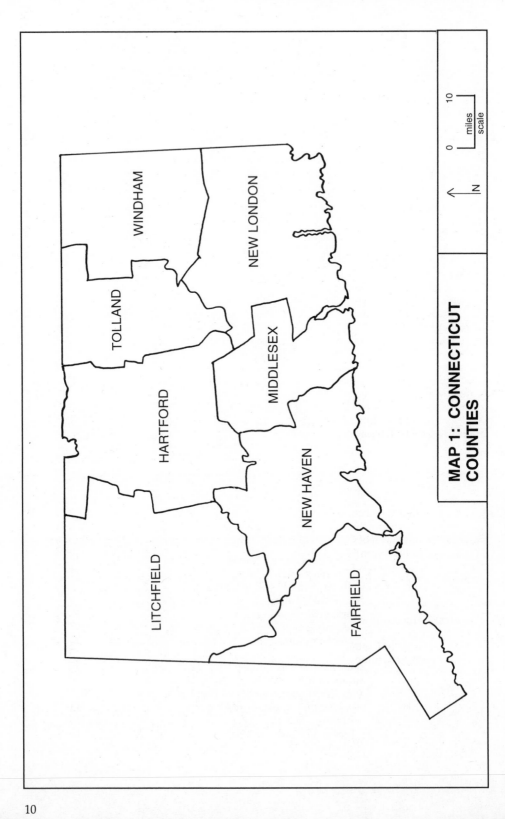

MAP 1: CONNECTICUT COUNTIES

BIRDING IN CONNECTICUT

Connecticut does not have a national reputation as a top birding state, but there are several good reasons why people who like birding and other aspects of nature should be glad that we live here. The bird life within the state is rich and varied. There are many good birding sites that are easily reached and open to the public. And there is a highly developed birding infrastructure - organizations that can facilitate the enjoyment of birds by providing information and guidance on trips.

The People and the Land

Connecticut has a population of 3,275,251 and a population density of 677 people per square mile — it is the 4th most crowded of the fifty states. Connecticut is a state of great geographical diversity, especially considering its small area. It is composed of five ecoregions - the Western Uplands, the Central Valley, the Eastern Uplands, the Coastal Slope, and the coast of Long Island Sound. Each of these areas has distinctive and diverse characteristics, habitats and patterns of occurrence by birds. Between the northwestern part of the state and along the coast, elevations range from 2,300' to sea level, mean annual temperatures from 45 degrees to 51 degrees, and average annual snowfall from 100 inches to 30 inches. These five regions are discussed in detail at the beginning of the county chapters (Chapters 4-11).

Connecticut is 60% forested, primarily by oaks and other hardwoods, mixed with white pine and hemlock. The specific characteristics of forest communities vary throughout the state in ways that are significant for the occurrence of birds. Within the state are numerous marshes and swamps, 6,000 lakes and ponds, 8,400 miles of rivers and streams. Connecticut has 253 miles of coastline along Long Island Sound - a succession of rocky headlands, sandy beaches, harbors, bays and estuaries.

These characteristics provide Connecticut with a rich mix of the bird species that one would expect to occur in these varied habitats at this latitude. However, there are additional factors that enrich this mix of bird species.

One factor is that Connecticut's geographical position and characteristics place it at the meeting place of two distinctly different zones of bird life. Bird species with breeding ranges that lie mainly to the south of Connecticut (such as red-bellied woodpecker, tufted titmouse, fish crow and Carolina wren), historically have expanded their nesting ranges into Connecticut by moving into habitats in the mild areas along the coast and up the major river valleys - and such species are most numerous in these areas today. At the same time, species with nesting ranges that are mainly north of Connecticut (such as solitary vireo, hermit thrush and black-throated blue warbler) have moved south into compatible nesting environments in the higher elevations of the northwestern and northeastern parts of the state.

A second reason for Connecticut's avian diversity is that the state lies along a major migration flyway (the coastline of Long Island Sound), and at its intersection with two important tributaries to it - the valleys of the Connecticut and Housatonic Rivers. This assures birders of exciting times during the spring and fall.

A third factor that benefits birders in Connecticut is the sheltered open water of Long Island Sound that provides a winter haven for water birds, during a period when inland lakes and ponds are frozen, and when other parts of the north Atlantic coast are more exposed to winter storms.

Public Areas And Birding Sites

Connecticut ranks 49th of the 50 states in terms of the amount of publicly owned open space and recreation lands available to each state resident. However, this does not really tell the story in terms that are meaningful to birders. What our state lacks in total acres of public open space, it makes up for in the number of individual parcels of public land that are within easy reach of anyone wishing to bird in the state.

Within our relatively small state, there are 91 state parks with a total of 29,856 acres, 30 state forests with 138,682 acres, 36 state wildldlife management areas with 17,356 acres, 110 local land trusts most of which manage public open space, as well as many nature centers, sanctuaries and private properties that are open to the public. Many of these areas include good avian habitat, and many of them are included as sites in this guide. Considering Connecticut's level of development, it's surprising how many really good birding areas there are in the state. And since Connecticut is such a small state, any of these areas can be visited by making a short day trip.

Seasons for Birding

In Connecticut, you can find good birding during any season, if you know where to go - each season is interesting in some part of the state. As a generalization, in the summer the best birding is in the northern areas of Connecticut; during the winter the birding is best along the coast and in mild areas near the coast; in the spring and fall, you can find good birding anywhere - choose your destination according to the species you want to see.

What follow are very general recommendations as to where to go in each season; more detailed summaries are given in the first section of each county chapter; details for each site are given in each site description.

Spring migration. The earliest spring birding occurs in early March at sites along the coast and inland on larger rivers, when water birds that have spent the winter in Connecticut are joined by the first spring migrants. During March, as inland lakes and ponds become ice-free, migrating water birds stop briefly at them on their way north. Next, a broad wave of land bird migrants passes through Connecticut, starting in early March along the coast, and then progressing inland throughout April and on into May. In inland areas, the early land bird migrants tend to follow rivers, but during May at the height of the migration, almost any site with suitable habitat can be good. Marsh birds can be seen at coastal and inland wetlands during March, April and May, as they migrate through the state or arrive to nest. The peak of the shore bird migration also occurs during May, and the largest numbers can be seen at intertidal flats and bars along the coast.

Nesting season. You have many good choices, so first decide what species you want to see, and visit sites with appropriate habitat. If you want to see nesting land bird species with northern affinities, go to forested sites at higher elevations in the northwestern or northeastern parts of the state. If southern land birds are your goal, go to sites with flood plain forest or other suitable habitats in central or southern Connecticut. For marsh birds, there are lots of inland and coastal wetland sites that are great places to observe birds and other wildlife of wetlands, and that are away from the crowds that descend on the beaches.

Fall migration. Don't wait for fall to start your fall birding. The shore bird fall migration starts in July, and August is the best month to watch it, especially at sites along the western Connecticut coast that have intertidal flats and bars. In September, land bird and marsh bird migrations reach their peaks. September is the best month to watch for migrating hawks; sites near and along the coast are the most reliable. In October, sparrows arrive at sites throughout Connecticut that have shrubby fields and edges. Also in October, migrating water birds start to drop in at lakes, ponds and rivers, with peak numbers present during November. As inland lakes and ponds become ice-covered, migrating water birds move to large rivers and tidal areas along the coast, where transient migrants and winter visitors can both be seen.

Winter. Most of the winter birding in Connecticut takes place at sites along the coast. Water birds from northern areas can be seen on Long Island Sound and in coastal bays and estuaries. Winter is also the best time to see bald eagles, along the lower Connecticut River and on the Housatonic. Winter is also an excellent time to look for hawks and owls at sites on the coast that have open marshes or woods with cedars. Open habitat land birds such as horned lark and Lapland longspur feed on beaches and fields along the coast, and lingering berry-eaters at shrubs just inland. In interior Connecticut, in addition to looking for resident species in their normal habitats, look along shrubby edges for lingering berry-eaters. Also, in some years there is the possibility of finding winter finches at forest habitats at higher elevations in northwestern and northeastern parts of the state. The best time for "owl prowls" is during late winter (February and March), anywhere in the state at sites with appropriate habitat.

Connecticut's Best Birding Sites

Any list of "best" birding sites is certain to be challenged, because there are so many different quality factors involved (During which season? For what bird species? etc.). However, having said that, here are our candidates:

Coastal:
Hammonasset Beach State Park, Madison
Milford Point and Nells Island, Milford
Sherwood Island State Park, Westport
Great Island area, Old Lyme
Bluff Point State Park, Groton
Barn Island Wildlife Management Area, Stonington

Inland:
White Memorial Foundation, Litchfield
Mohawk State Forest, Cornwall
Barkhamsted/upper Farmington River complex
    Barkhamsted Reservoir, Barkhamsted
    American Legion/Peoples State Forests, Barkhamsted
    Tunxis State Forest, Hartland
    Upper Greenwoods Recreation Area, Barkhamsted
    Lower Greenwoods Recreation Area, Barkhamsted/New Hartford
Nepaug Reservoir and Nepaug State Forest, New Hartford
Lower Connecticut River complex
    Sites on the river in Haddam, Deep River, Essex, Old Saybrook, Old Lyme, Lyme, East Haddam.

Mansfield cluster
UConn Parking Lot W, Horse Barn Hill, Mansfield Hollow State Park, Fenton River (Pumping Station Road)
Station 43, South Windsor
Cromwell Meadows Wildlife Management Area, Cromwell
McLean Game Refuge, Granby/Simsbury
Canaan Mountain Range, Canaan
Shepaug Dam area, Southbury/Newtown
Hurd State Park, East Hampton

Sources of Information and Help

There are a number of sources of information and help for birders in Connecticut.

Statewide organizations include The Connecticut Ornithological Association, the Connecticut Audubon Society and the Hartford Audubon Society. They are membership organizations that focus on the study and protection of birds in Connecticut, issue periodicals, conduct meetings and lead trips. In addition, there are a number of local bird clubs that provide a range of birding-oriented activities. The Nature Conservancy Connecticut Chapter has as its mission preservation of natural diversity in Connecticut, including the protection of many avian habitats, with emphasis on the Connecticut River Tidelands and the Northwestern Highlands. The Land Trust Service Bureau, sponsored by The Nature Conservancy, can provide information about Connecticut's 110 local land trusts, many of which manage natural areas that are open to the public.

Nature Centers can provide lots of helpful information about the areas in which they are located. State Park and Forest offices also can be very helpful, and sometimes have trail maps of their areas.

Written sources of information about birds in Connecticut include: *The Atlas of Breeding Birds of Connecticut*, that documents nesting occurrence and distribution of species that breed in the state, and *Connecticut Birds*, that provides information about the occurrence and distribution of all species known to occur in the state.

A good highway map of Connecticut is essential; the Official Tourist Map is quite adequate. For larger scale, county atlases will do, but are frequently inaccurate in their details. Topo maps are far more accurate, although out of date in some instances.

For addresses and other specifics as to how to reach organizations or obtain references and maps, refer to Chapter 12: "Sources of Additional Information".

Other Considerations for Connecticut Birders

Restrictions on access to property. Many of the sites in this guide are contiguous to private property, or have access restrictions that apply to parts of the site or to certain seasons (examples are eagle wintering areas, and town parks that are restricted to town residents during the warm months). Every birder must obey such restrictions, and be sensitive to the needs of wildlife to be free of disturbance, and to the needs and rights of property owners and local residents to enjoy their property without encountering trespassers. Remember, by Connecticut law, if it's not your property, you have no right to be on it, unless you are invited.

Hunting. In Connecticut, it is legal to hunt for a variety of birds and other animals: deer, turkey, ruffed grouse, pheasant, chukar, bobwhite, sora, Virginia, clapper and king rails, ducks, mergansers, coot, Canada and snow geese, woodcock, snipe, squirrel, rabbit, hare, woodchuck, raccoon, opossum, red and grey foxes and coyote) with various weapons (bow, shotgun, rifle, muzzleloader); in a variety of areas (state land - especially state forests and wildlife management areas - private land, tidal areas); at various times during the year (there are many different legal seasons, depending on the weapon and the target). Most hunting seasons occur at some time during the fall and early winter, but others occur in the spring, and still others are in effect all year. However, no hunting of any kind is allowed on Sunday. Sites that are known to be popular hunting areas are so noted in the site description under "Getting Around". To be on the safe side, go on Sunday to sites where hunting is permitted, especially during the fall.

Natural hazards. There are certain hazards and inconveniences that are an inevitable part of birding. In Connecticut, probably the most serious and one of the most common is the deer tick. Lyme disease, which is carried by these ticks, is serious, and worth making an effort to avoid. The best practical avoidance techniques are to wear long pants tucked into your socks, use of a tick spray, and close inspection of your body after an outing (the ticks are tiny, so look carefully). Other natural hazards include other insects and poison ivy. Copperhead snakes are a potential hazard, but they are rarely encountered (and then most often on rocky slopes). The site descriptions assume that you are aware of these hazards, and they are not mentioned unless they are especially significant at the site.

Equipment. Fortunately, birding is an activity that does not require a lot of special equipment. However, four items are essential: binoculars, a scope, a tripod and a field identification guide. In each case, good choices are available, and it is largely a matter of personal preference which is right for you. Start by asking your birding friends what they use and like; if possible, try their equipment. Then go to a store that specializes in optics or birding equipment, that is willing to let you try out items before purchase. Get the highest quality that you can afford - you will probably use it for many years.

Chapter 2

Using Habitats To Find Birds

SOME HABITAT BASICS

The purpose of this guide is to help you find birds in Connecticut. However, it is intended to do more than simply tell you where and when to look for birds. The purpose of this chapter is to help you develop your own strategies for finding birds, because that is far more interesting than simply going to a site that has been listed in a guide.

The most important element in any bird finding strategy is understanding the relationships between birds and the habitats in which they occur. Anyone who has been birding for a while uses habitat-based strategies, without giving it much thought. If you want to find waders, you head for a tidal marsh; for most warblers, you go into a woodland, and so on. You have only to read several of the site descriptions in this guide to be aware that bird species tend to occur in groups, depending on what habitats are at the site. There is the edge/shrubby field species group (prairie warbler, indigo bunting, et. al.), the northern forest group (solitary vireo, Blackburnian warbler, et al.), and so on.

However, to be effective, a habitat-based bird finding strategy must go well beyond the general knowledge that egrets occur in marshes, and warblers in forests. Each type of habitat has potential value for a certain group of bird species. But the degree to which that value is realized, and the ways that birds use the habitat, depend on a number of factors. And it is these factors that cause one habitat (such as a hardwood forest) to be a birding hot spot and attract uncommon bird species, while another nearby and seemingly identical hardwood forest is relatively barren, and attracts only a few common species.

Each kind of habitat occurs in many variations, and there are many factors, both inside the habitat and external to it, that influence the use birds make of the habitat, and the exact species that occur in it.

This chapter will begin by defining some terms and discussing some basics about habitat. It will then set forth a habitat-based bird finding strategy that is structured and explicit, and includes detailed questions that need to be answered about bird-habitat relationships in order to evaluate a habitat. The chapter will then apply this approach specifically to each major type of habitat, with details about habitat features and the individual bird species that those features attract.

Habitat Terms and Definitions

Habitat. It is helpful to think of the natural world in which plants and animals live in terms of units, and of systems that operate within the units. Habitat is the most important of those units for a birder to understand.

Each bird (and every other animal) lives in a specific part of the natural environment in which it can satisfy its needs for food, water, shelter for nesting and safety from predators. Each bird species has a set of such needs that is unique to that species. As a result, each species lives in a certain part of the environment; that is, in a specific type of habitat.

Habitat group. A group of similar types of habitat that have many common characteristics are lumped together in this guide as a habitat group. The habitat groups that occur in Connecticut are:
Forest
Open terrestrial
Marsh, swamp, bog

Lake/pond
River/stream
Coastal
Other

Each of these habitat groups, and the types of habitat that occur within each group, will be discussed later in this chapter.

Types of habitat as they typically occur in nature are not separate entities, but rather they are parts of a spectrum of continuous gradients in which habitat types intermingle and blend with one another. However, it is useful in organizing and expressing information about habitats to deal with them as if they are discrete units. This is a useful convenience - but keep in mind that the real natural world is far more complex.

Microhabitat is a kind of sub-unit of a habitat. Bird species typically do not occur uniformly throughout a habitat. Rather, in order to reduce competition from other bird species for the resources of the habitat, the space (and therefore the resources) of a habitat is divided among different species of birds into specific areas. Each such area includes a distinguishable subset of the physical and biotic characteristics of the habitat. For example, the hardwood forest habitat includes several such areas - ground, the shrub layer, the canopy, and others. Each such area is used by a distinguishable subgroup of the bird species that occur in the habitat. This guide refers to such areas as "microhabitats"

Community. Each type of habitat consists of a community of plants and animals - a group of interacting plant and animal populations that share a common environment. This environment also includes such elements as climate, slope, water, soil and rocks. But it is the plant community - trees, shrubs and herbaceous plants - by which each type of habitat is most easily recognized and by which it is commonly known. Thus, among habitat types are "hardwood forest", "cattail marsh", "short grass field", and so on. Each such type of habitat is used by a distinguishable group of bird species.

Land form is a large area which may contain a number of habitats. Certain types of land form affect the habitats that lie within them, as well as the abundance and distribution of birds within those habitats. For example, a river valley is a land form, and the varied habitats that occur in the river valley - streams, forests, wetlands, and others - may be affected by certain conditions that are associated with river valleys. A river valley typically has a milder climate than upland areas, and it may serve as a migration corridor. Other examples of land forms that occur in Connecticut are ridge (also a possible avenue for migration), coastal peninsula (a possible land trap during migration), and tidal estuary (in which nearby tidal habitats within the estuary may support one another).

Evaluating Sites and Habitats: Factors That Affect Birds' Use Of A Habitat

In order to understand why some habitats are so productive, and others that look the same are relatively barren, it is necessary to identify factors that may not seem obvious, but which may affect the usefulness of a habitat to birds. This examination should take into account the habitat type itself, its location within Connecticut, the land form in which it occurs, and numerous conditions within the habitat.

An evaluation of a site and of the habitats within it can be expressed as a series of questions that need to be answered. Those questions are listed below. The questions are applicable to all habitats to some degree, but the importance and relevance of each varies from one habitat to another.

Habitat types. What habitat types are in the site? Each habitat type is typically used by a distinctive group of bird species (though the exact members of the group will vary according to the factors discussed below).

Location in Connecticut. Where is the site located? Sites that are inland in the colder climate of northern Connecticut may be used by different species than sites that are near the coast in a milder climate.

Land form effect. Is the site within or near a land form that may affect birds' use of habitats in the site? Certain land forms are used as migration flyways (the coastline, major river valleys, ridgelines). Coastal peninsulas may act as land traps or landfalls during migration. Estuaries may contain other habitats that support or enrich the habitats within the site.

Microhabitats that are present or absent within a habitat can have a significant effect on the bird species that occur in it. For example, dead trees in a swamp attract cavity nesters, and species that hunt from perches; open air over a marsh provides an attractive feeding area to aerial hunters.

Size. How large is the site and the habitats within it? Size may be a limiting factor for species that might otherwise use the habitat. A forest habitat must be very large to be used successfully as a nesting habitat for certain interior-forest neotropical migrant species, including Blackburnian and black-throated green warblers. Tall grass fields must be quite large to be used successfully as nesting habitat by certain grassland species including bobolink and meadowlark.

Edges and interfaces. What type of edges are there? What species might they attract? What species might they threaten? Birds are abundant and diverse at the interface of natural communities, where they can use the resources of the habitats on either side of the interface. An interface between habitat types that serve different needs increases the usefulness of a habitat - such as a field in which certain hawks and owls can hunt, next to a forest in which they roost or nest. Little pockets of wetland within a forest attract additional species to those that would otherwise use the forest. In edge and interface areas, there is an inherent biological richness, known as the "edge effect". In the case of some habitat types and some species, edges are beneficial - the edge of a forest by a wetland benefits wood duck and red-shouldered hawk. However, a forest by a farm field or other open land subjects many forest nesters to nest parasitism by cowbird, and to predation by raccoon and other mammals.

Vegetation diversity. How diverse is the vegetation in the habitat? Diversity of vegetation tends to produce diversity of resources such as food and cover, and this attracts a diversity of bird species. For example, a pure hemlock forest has very little diversity of vegetation and is used by few bird species, compared with the many bird species in a hardwoods/hemlock forest, that typically has good diversity of both trees and shrubs.

Vegetation species composition. What plant species make up the vegetation in the habitats? Are any of these species significant for birds? For example, Canada and black-throated blue warblers typically occur in the mountain laurel shrub layer of a hemlock forest; and hooded warblers also are attracted to mountain laurel, but in hardwoods forest. Black-throated green warblers must have hemlocks in which to nest.

Corridors. Are there streams, roads or other avenues for movement? Streams that run through forests are used in the spring and fall by a variety of migrating land birds, for movement and also for feeding along the streambelt. Corridors are also used by goshawk and many other land bird species for local movement between resting and feeding areas.

Topographical and physical features. A wide variety of topographical and physical features may have a significant effect on birds' use of a habitat. The features that are significant will vary from one type of habitat to another. Topography may produce a microclimate (a hemlock ravine may act as a cold trap and provide habitat for northern species). The direction that a slope faces may also create a microclimate. Boulders on a forested slope provides nesting habitat for worm-eating warbler. Branches over a stream provide hunting perches for kingfisher and flycatchers; hemlock branches over a stream provide nest sites for Acadian flycatcher; open air over a river provides a hunting opportunity for osprey and bald eagle.

These general considerations are applied specifically to each habitat type in the discussion that follows. At the end of the discussion of each type, several sites that include good examples of the habitat are mentioned, except in the case of habitats that occur at a large number of sites.

FOREST HABITATS

Roughly 60% of Connecticut is covered by forest - more than at any other time during the past 200 to 300 years. Since forests occupy most of the land area of Connecticut, it is the habitat type that birders can reach most easily.

A forest is a growth of trees; lower layers of shrubs and herbaceous plants may vary from dense to absent. In Connecticut, forest habitat often occurs in the form of small woodlots. The trees, shrubs and herbs of a forest provide birds with nest sites, shelter, and food in the form of seeds and berries, small invertebrates and other animals.

Forest habitats are used by about half of the bird species that regularly occur in Connecticut (139 of about 280 species), including all or most of the raptors, woodpeckers, flycatchers, thrushes, vireos and warblers, as well as species from several other families.

Types of Forest Habitat

Hardwoods. Deciduous tree species - typically oaks, hickories, birches and cherries - make up most of this forest community. The shrub and herb layers are usually well developed. In Connecticut, hardwood forests are used by more than 100 species of "woodland" birds, of which over half nest in them. Among the most common of these species are wood thrush, red-eyed vireo, ovenbird and scarlet tanager. There are many sites in this guide that include hardwood forest.

Hardwoods/white pine. Deciduous trees make up roughly half of this forest community, and white pine all or most of the other half. This type of forest attracts the greatest number of bird species of any type except flood plain. Hardwoods and white pine in combination are used by basically the same species as hardwoods forest, plus such additional species as raven, red-breasted nuthatch, solitary vireo, yellow-rumped, Blackburnian and pine warblers. There are many sites in this guide that include hardwoods/white pine forest.

Hardwoods/hemlock. Deciduous trees make up about half of this forest community, and hemlock all or most of the other half. Bird species diversity is a bit lower than hardwoods/white pine forest, and about the same as hardwoods forest. It attracts basically the same species as hardwoods forest, plus such conifer specialists as magnolia and black-throated green warblers. There are many sites in this guide that include hardwoods/hemlock forest.

White pine. All or most of the trees are white pine. This forest type usually has a somewhat lower species diversity than forests in which hardwoods are an important component. This is due to the poor shrub and herb development typical of most white pine forests. However, some managed white pine forests have a well-developed understory of seedlings, saplings, shrubs and/or herbs. Species that typically occur in white pine forests include red-breasted nuthatch, brown creeper, solitary vireo, Blackburnian, yellow-rumped and pine warblers. American Legion State Forest, White Memorial and Mansfield Hollow State Park include good examples of white pine forest.

Hemlock. All or most of the trees in this forest community are hemlock. This forest type usually has a somewhat lower species diversity than forests in which hardwoods are an important component. This is due to the poor shrub and herb development typical of most hemlock forests. Species that typically occur in hemlock forests include solitary vireo, black-throated green and magnolia warblers. Sites that have areas of hemlock forest include Peoples State Forest, White Memorial, and Bigelow Hollow State Park.

Conifer plantations. In Connecticut, this forest type consists of artificially planted groves of conifers - usually a single species, typically red pine or one of the spruces. Such plantings have the lowest bird species diversity of any forest type, because of the lack of vegetative diversity and poorly developed shrub and herb layers. However, they are valuable as sheltered winter feeding habitat for golden-crowned kinglet, purple finch, both crossbills, pine and evening grosbeaks. They also serve as protected resting areas for saw-whet, great horned, barred and long-eared owls. The White Memorial Foundation includes plantations of spruces and other conifers.

Sand plain forest. Forest communities that grow on sand plains consist of pitch pine, white pine, any of several oak species, or a combination of pine and oak. These trees often appear to be stunted. Shrub and herb layers usually have little diversity, but may be quite dense. This type of forest supports a moderate diversity of bird species for both feeding and nesting. Pine warbler is especially common as a nester. Red-breasted nuthatch, crossbill and siskin find this habitat quite attractive in winter. There is a sand plain forest at Hopeville State Park.

Flood plain forest. This habitat type, also known as riparian forest, lies alongside rivers and occupies the lowland area that is subject to periodic flooding. Flood plain forests are usually composed almost entirely of hardwood species that can tolerate immersion in water, such as red maple, shagbark hickory and a number of species that typically occur south of Connecticut, such as sycamore, silver maple, several cottonwoods and willows. Flood plain forests are characterized by a dense shrub layer (poison ivy is often abundant) and the presence of dead trees. Flood plain forests have the greatest bird species diversity of any forest habitat, including some species not usually found in other forest habitats. In addition to most of Connecticut's common woodland species, nesters include wood duck, red-bellied woodpecker, Acadian flycatcher, Carolina wren, warbling vireo, cerulean, Kentucky and hooded warblers. In addition, several species of dabbling ducks occur during periods of flooding. There are areas of flood plain forest along the Connecticut River, including those at Wangunk Meadows in Glastonbury and at Cromwell Meadows.

Cedars, (usually northern red cedar) occur sometimes as groves but more often as scattered individual trees. They have dense foliage and produce berries that persist into winter. The presence of even a few scattered cedars in a forest or field adds diversity in terms of cover and food supply. Cedar waxwing, brown thrasher and mockingbird are frequently attracted by the presence of cedars, both for food and for nesting sites. Prairie warbler also readily nests at the base of cedars. Saw-whet owl often roosts in cedars in the winter. Colonial Park is a good example of a site in which cedars are important.

Factors That Affect Birds' Use of Forest Habitats

The location in Connecticut of a forest influences the bird species that inhabit the forest. At one extreme are woodlands at high elevations in the Northwest Highlands such as the Mohawk State Forest, in which nesters include species that have ranges mainly north of Connecticut, including Blackburnian and Canada warblers and northern waterthrush. At the other extreme are woodlands at low elevations near the coast such as the Fairchild Garden, in which nesters often include Carolina wren, red-bellied woodpecker and hooded warbler.

Land form effect. A number of forest habitats in Connecticut are influenced by the land forms in which they lie. Examples include river valleys with their typically southern forest habitat types, ridges and mountaintops with their typically northern forests types.

The size of a forest can be important for many bird species. One group is forest-interior land birds that require nesting sites that are far removed from the nest parasitism and predation that is concentrated along forest edges. (While forest-interior species are declining overall, they are doing well in the large area of Catlin Woods at White Memorial). Another group that needs large forest areas is made up of species such as goshawk, barred owl and pileated woodpecker that require large nesting territories. These species find suitable nesting habitat in large state forests, such as Patchaug, Natchaug, Tunxis, American Legion and Peoples.

Edges and interfaces with other types of habitat may contribute to the value of a forest, or may be a negative factor, depending on the bird species, the season, and on what is on the other side of the edge. Edges are a positive factor during the spring and fall, for migrating birds that stop briefly along forest edges to feed and rest. A stream running through a forest, or a pond within it, greatly enhance the value of the forest for birds by providing a migration corridor, serving as a place to drink and bathe, and as an additional source of food in the form of aquatic invertebrates. Such interfaces exist at Boston Hollow (stream), and White Memorial (ponds). A wetland within or next to a forest provides the same functions, and also provides a hunting area for woodland raptors such as barred owl and red-shouldered hawk. An open field near a forest provides a hunting area for other forest-dwelling raptors including red-tailed hawk, screech and great horned owls. White Memorial also has these kinds of interfaces. The negative side of edges is that they can be extremely harmful to a host of forest-nesting species that are vulnerable to nest parasitism by cowbirds and to predation by mammals. This can be a major problem in forests that border on farm fields and developed areas.

Corridors in the form of roads, trails, rivers, streams, lakes, ponds and power lines allow for movement by birds, and this is especially important during migration. They also create edges, which diversify the food supply.

Diversity of vegetation. In general, forests with diverse vegetation and well developed shrub and herb layers tend to attract the greatest diversity of bird species. Diversity of vegetation provides a variety of small invertebrates and other sources of food, and also affords varied forms of cover for protection and nesting.

Species composition of vegetation. The value of a forest for birds also depends on what particular species of trees, shrubs and herbs are in it, and how useful these are to birds. Pure hardwood forests provide nesting habitat for a mix of species that is typical for Connecticut, including red-eyed vireo, scarlet tanager, wood thrush and ovenbird. The presence of evergreen trees in a hardwood forest enhances both the cover and food value of the forest. Hemlock, cedar and white pine contribute branches to both the canopy and the understory layer of the forest and add protective cover that is used by owls and numerous other species of land birds.

The presence of white pine in a forest attracts red-breasted nuthatch, solitary vireo, Blackburnian, yellow-rumped and magnolia warblers (all mostly in northern Connecticut forests such as American Legion State Forest), and pine warbler, red-tailed hawk and great horned owl (throughout the state). The presence of hemlock attracts solitary vireo and magnolia warbler, and is a prerequisite for nesting by black-throated green warbler. Spruces are a favorite of red-breasted nuthatch and magnolia warbler. Many species of forest trees bear seeds or fruit that is eaten by a variety of birds. The most important berry-producers are black cherry, red cedar, apple and crabapple; the most important seed producers are white ash, tulip tree, white pine and hemlock; the most important catkin-bearers are birches; and the most important nut producers are American beech and several oak species. In years of

25

southward irruption by winter finches, look for crossbills and siskin in spruce stands, pine grosbeak in tamaracks and apple trees, and redpoll in birch and tamarack trees. Good sites in which to look for winter finches include the Barkhamsted Reservoir and Goshen East Street.

A well-developed and diverse shrub layer may contain valuable sources of food. Important sources are mast-producing shrubs such as witch hazel, catkin producers such as ironwood, as well as a few berry producers. Certain shrubs in a forest are important as shelter or cover for nesting. Mountain laurel is sought as a nest site by black-throated blue and Canada warblers (in northern Connecticut at sites such as Peoples State Forest, Mohawk State Forest and Mt. Riga), hooded warbler (in southern Connecticut at sites such as Putnam Park), and to a lesser extent by towhee, junco and white-throated sparrow. Herbaceous plants are also important. For example, fern clumps attract black-and-white warbler and ovenbird, and many of the flowering plants produce seeds and berries that are eaten by birds.

Ravines may act as cold traps which contain northern types of habitat (as does Campbell Falls State Park).

Slopes, and the direction they face, may create warm or cold microclimates that affect the composition of vegetation, and therefore the occurrence of birds.

Rocks on slopes in a forest (in the form of talus, slides or boulder fields) is a microhabitat that is used for nesting by winter wren and worm-eating warbler (as at Devil's Den and Dripps Road). Stone walls can be similarly useful.

Dying or dead trees, whether they are standing or have fallen, create reservoirs of small invertebrates, and thus provide an important source of food for woodpeckers and many other birds. They also serve as nest sites for many cavity nesters, including chickadee, woodpeckers, owls and others.

Birding in Forest Habitats

Birding in Connecticut woodlands is a seasonal activity. During the spring migration, forest edges, especially along rivers and streams, and corridors within forests, tend to be most productive, as birds stop to feed and rest briefly on their long journeys. As spring progresses, the forest-dwelling species that stay to nest move in from the edge and go deeper into the forest. During the breeding season, the best way to see birds is to stay on woods roads or trails, and look for them as they forage for food. Different species of birds forage at various levels of the forest, from the canopy down to the ground, so all levels should frequently be scanned. During the nesting season, one should be very careful not to harass nesting birds in any way - by stepping on ground nests, walking through shrubs that may contain nests, or getting too close to nests, thus leaving a scent trail for predators to follow later. During the fall migration, forest edges again become important, especially those with shrubs that carry seeds and berries (often near open fields). In winter, birding in forest habitats is generally limited to looking for a few resident species (these do include owls if you know just where to look). However, in years of winter finch irruption, birding in habitats with evergreens can be quite rewarding.

OPEN TERRESTRIAL HABITATS.

This habitat group includes fields of crops, grass and shrubs, the edges of such open areas, and hedgerows that go through them. Two-thirds of the bird species that regularly occur in Connecticut can be found at open terrestrial habitats (185 of about 280 species).

For a number of species, such areas are the primary habitat, and there are many additional species that reside in other types of habitat, but are attracted by the excellent feeding or hunting opportunities within open habitats or in the air above them.

Types of Open Terrestrial Habitat

Tilled field is an open area that is under agricultural management to grow crops other than hay, clover or alfalfa (those are classified as tall grass or herbaceous fields). In Connecticut, most tilled fields are used to grow corn (the best crop for birds), while some fields are used for truck gardens or community garden plots (the next best use for birds), and some to grow soybeans or tobacco.

Not as many bird species occur in tilled fields as in other types of field, because of frequent disturbance from agricultural management, and lack of vegetation diversity. In spring, tilled fields that are still bare may have waste grain from the previous year, and also a source of small invertebrates. This attracts killdeer that are coming to nest, and, if there are seasonal pools, migrating dabbling ducks, geese and shore birds. In summer, when crops have developed, small invertebrates on the vegetation attract a variety of flycatchers, warblers and other species. The crops themselves attract blackbirds, crows, jays, sparrows and finches. The usefulness of tilled fields as a nesting area is diminished by frequent disturbance that comes from agricultural management, but killdeer does nest on bare areas of tilled fields. Fall is prime time at tilled fields. Geese, dabbling ducks, sparrows, blackbirds, horned lark, pipit and other migrants are attracted to waste grain, invertebrates, and also seeds and berries in any weed growth or shrubby edges. In winter, fields on which manure has been applied attract winter visitors such as horned lark and snow bunting, which come to eat the seeds in the manure. Those same seeds attract rodents that provide food for a variety of raptors. Sites in this guide that have tilled field habitat include Farmington Meadows, Bear Hill and Pease Brook.

Short grass fields are covered by grasses less than six inches high, and are periodically mowed for use as lawns, public parks, golf courses, highway edges, airports and the like. These also include pastures and hay fields in the early stage of growth. The vegetation of short grass fields is not diverse, so that the food potential of this habitat type is somewhat limited. However, a variety of migrants feed in them in the spring and fall. Land bird species include meadowlark and Savannah sparrow. A variety of migrating shore birds also stop at short grass fields, especially at sites near the coast, and especially if there are seasonal pools within the field. Shore bird species often include black-bellied plover, sometimes lesser golden plover, and occasionally upland and buff-breasted sandpipers. Nesting is usually limited by the frequent mowing that is part of the management of short grass fields. However, grasshopper sparrow nests at one or two large fields in Connecticut; Savannah sparrow and meadowlark can nest in somewhat smaller fields. Bobolink comes to short grass fields to feed during the nesting season. Raptors that hunt over short grass fields include kestrel, red-tailed hawk, rough-legged hawk, short-eared and snowy owls (mainly in winter). Sites that include large areas of short grass field include Hammonasset Park and Haddam Meadows.

Tall grass fields are covered by grasses over six inches high, and are frequently used to grow hay. Tall grass fields do not exist as such in the spring before the grass has grown, nor in the fall if they have been mowed, nor in winter, if any remaining tall grass is matted down by snow. The primary value to birds of a tall grass field occurs during the summer, when it serves as nesting habitat, provided it is not mowed during the incubation and nestling periods. As such, tall grass field benefits only a few species. However, survival of bobolink and meadowlark as nesting species in Connecticut depends on this type of habitat. The height of the vegetation in tall grass fields provides protective cover, to the benefit of the nesters and their fledglings, and to the frustration of hunting raptors. If tall grass fields are not mowed, they provide a good source of seeds for migrating sparrows in the late fall. Horse Barn Hill and Topsmead State Forest have areas of tall grass field.

Mixed herbaceous fields consist of a variety of herbs, often including alfalfa, clover and vetches, and are usually harvested once or twice a year. Herbaceous fields that are not mowed for a year or two start the early stages of vegetative succession, and this soon results in the addition of wild herb species such as goldenrods and eventually woody vegetation. Because of the diversity of vegetation, mixed herbaceous fields can be really good for birds throughout the year. In the early spring, before vegetation has developed, the food value is modest, but these fields are used by a variety of land birds searching for seeds left over from the previous year and for early-season invertebrates. Raptors hunt these fields for rodents and for small birds that are feeding on the seeds. The diversity of leafy plants produces a great variety of insects, and this food source increases during the late spring and summer, drawing in such insectivores as flycatchers, swallows and bluebird. In the late spring, as the herbs grow and the protective cover becomes more dense, the value as a nesting habitat increases. There may be a nice diversity of nesters, but the species mix is variable, depending on the composition of vegetation. Field sparrow is a common nesting species, and grasshopper sparrow is possible, if the habitat is just right. In late summer, when the population of insects diminishes, the seeds borne by the various herbs become the primary food source, and this continues into early winter, providing an attractive feeding area for sparrows that migrate during the late fall and on into the winter, as long as the snow isn't too deep. There are good examples of mixed herbaceous fields at White Memorial and Skiff Mountain.

Shrubby field is a type of habitat that is usually in a state of natural succession, typically starting as abandoned farmland and eventually ending as some type of forest. However, in powerline rights-of-way, the process of succession is arrested by mowing every several years, thus maintaining the shrubby field habitat indefinitely. The vegetative content is quite variable, and may include a wide variety of herbs, shrubs, vines, and saplings of pioneer tree species. This diversity produces a wide variety of animal and plant food for birds throughout the seasons - insects and their larvae, seeds, catkins, berries, nuts and cones. Shrubby fields are enriched by the presence of scattered evergreens and of shrubs that produce berries. This bountiful food supply attracts large numbers and a good variety of birds during most of the year. In addition, throughout the year, dense shrub growth, vine tangles and thickets afford valuable protection from predators and from the winter weather.

The species that occur in shrubby fields are of the "shrub and edge" group - the habitat in shrubby fields is too dense for grassland species, and not yet mature enough for forest-dwelling species. In the early spring, most of the birds that feed in shrubby fields are insectivorous migrants that are attracted by the small invertebrates that are starting to become available on the vegetation. As the spring progresses, species that will nest start to arrive. The dense structure of the vegetation provides ideal protection for nest sites, and some 70 species nest in this habitat. Included among these nesters are: cardinal, towhee, catbird, robin, chipping and song sparrows, Carolina wren, brown thrasher, cedar waxwing, white-eyed vireo, blue-winged, golden-winged, chestnut-sided and yellow warblers, common yellowthroat and chat. In the late summer and fall, shrubby fields provide migrants with an abundance of seeds and berries, and also protective cover. By the time winter arrives, most of this food has been eaten, but seeds and berries that are less well liked often remain, and are available when the birds become less choosy. There are extensive areas of shrubby field habitat at White Memorial and Amnestied Hollow State Park.

Edge/Hedgerow. An edge is a transition zone between two or more habitats - often between a field and a forest. Many miles of edge habitat are created by roads, powerline and pipeline rights-of-way. Edges are usually long and narrow, and include an intermixing of the plant and animal species of the contiguous habitats, and often also certain species of plants and animals that use edge as their primary habitat. A hedgerow is typically a row of trees, shrubs and/or herbs only a few feet wide that divides two open fields.

The edge/hedgerow habitat type is used by more than half of the bird species that regularly occur in Connecticut (145 of about 280) These species are typically of three groups: species that occur primarily in shrubby fields, including catbird, yellowthroat, song sparrow and goldfinch; forest-dwellers (if the edge borders on a forest), including chickadee, titmouse, white-breasted nuthatch, black-and-white warbler and redstart; and edge species, including warbling vireo, blue-winged warbler and cardinal. This coming together of species that occur in three types of habitat causes edges and hedgerows to be very productive areas in which to look for birds.

The principal value of edges and hedgerows is as feeding habitat: the abundance of small invertebrates produced by the vegetation, and the ease with which they can be captured, makes them especially important during the spring migration for insectivorous passerines and also the raptors that prey on them, particularly sharp-shinned and Cooper's hawks. In addition, many species that nest in nearby habitats use edges as feeding areas. The value of edges and hedgerows as a nesting habitat is limited by the lack of depth, but the real drawback is that birds in edges are vulnerable to predation by other birds, snakes and mammals, and to nest parasitism by cowbirds. In the fall, berries, seeds and other food produced by shrubs, trees and herbs cause edges and hedgerows to be a prime feeding area for a multitude of migrating land birds. In winter, some of this food may still be left for lingering and resident land bird species, and the protective value of the dense vegetation of edges becomes vitally important.

Edges and hedgerows add to the overall productivity of the nearby habitats at a number of sites, including Upper County Road, Fenton River (Pumping Station Road), UConn Parking Lot W, Horse Barn Hill, and White Memorial.

Factors That Affect Birds' Use of Open Terrestrial Habitats

Location in Connecticut does have somewhat of an influence on which bird species use open habitats. This influence is most evident in the case of short grass fields and shrubby fields.

Short grass fields near the coast are most likely to draw in shore bird migrants in the spring and fall, as well as raptors during the fall, winter and spring. This is vividly demonstrated at Sherwood Island State Park and Hammonasset State Park.

Several of the many species that nest in shrubby fields occur mainly in specific areas of Connecticut:
> bobwhite, in southeastern Connecticut,
> white-eyed vireo, in southern Connecticut,
> golden-winged warbler, locally in Western Uplands,
> Nashville warbler, in northwest and northeast hills,
> chat, in southeast and southwest corners.

Land form effect. Open habitats that are located in river valleys or near the coastline have significantly milder climate than do similar habitats in other areas, and this affects their vegetation, seasons and occurrence of bird species. In addition, sites in river valleys or along the coast are better positioned for passing migrants than are similar sites in other areas. They are also more apt to hold lingering half-hardy land birds during the winter.

Size. The main importance of the size of open terrestrial habitats is for nesting, to place a spatial buffer between the nest and the edge of the field, where mammalian predation and brood parasitism by cowbirds is most apt to occur. Tall grass fields must be quite large in order to have successful nesting by bobolink and meadowlark. Short grass and mixed herbaceous fields must be very large to enable grasshopper sparrow to nest successfully.

Interfaces with other types of habitat, or among open habitats. For example, the presence of water, especially in form of a perennial stream that flows through an open habitat, greatly increases the diversity of birds, and is especially beneficial in winter. An example of a site that benefits from interfaces between terrestrial habitats is Tarrywile Park.

Vegetation diversity. Dense and varied vegetation tends to support the greatest avian species diversity. Shrubby field is by its nature the type of open habitat with the greatest diversity of vegetation.

Vegetation species composition. Among the crops in tilled fields, corn is best for birds, and mixed vegetables is next best. Shrubby fields, edges and hedgerows are enriched by the presence of shrubs that produce berries, and by scattered evergreens, especially northern red cedar and juniper, for both food and cover. They attract prairie warbler, brown thrasher and numerous other land bird species as nesters. The most important berry producing shrubs are: barberry, multiflora rose, hawthorn, chokecherry, autumn olive, and silky and gray dogwoods. The principal berry-producing vines are wildgrape, foxgrape, Virginia creeper, poison ivy and bittersweet.

Corridors are not especially important in open habitats where movement is generally unimpeded. In a way, hedgerows serve as corridors; by following hedgerows, passerines can avoid flying over open areas where they are vulnerable to avian predators.

Powerline rights-of-way are typically mowed every 3-5 years, so that they are maintained as shrubby fields. Hartman Park is a good example. In contrast, pipeline rights-of-way are typically mowed every year, so that they are maintained in a short grass/tall grass field condition.

Dead trees and branches within an open field or along its edges makes the hunting especially favorable by providing perches for kestrel, swallows, kingbird and other flycatchers, as well as providing nest sites for kestrel, screech owl, flicker, tree swallow, bluebird and others. Utility lines, either overland or along roads also serve as perch sites.

Seasonal pools that occur in the spring in open fields attract migrating dabbling ducks, geese and shore birds.

Manure spread on fields as fertilizer or dropped by animals in a pasture enriches the food production of the ecosystems. Manure also carries undigested seeds that attract winter visitors such as horned lark, snow bunting, pipit and sparrows. The seeds also attract rodents that draw in various raptors. Horse Barn Hill is a good site to visit in winter for these reasons.

Birding in Open Terrestrial Habitats

The bare ground of tilled fields is a good place to start your early spring birding, as killdeer, gulls and other birds come in to feed on earthworms and other invertebrates. Use a scope to scan from the edges of these fields. Next, try shrubby fields and edges, when the first activity by insects and their larvae brings in a variety of spring migrants. Grassy and herbaceous fields are not productive until later in the spring, when their vegetation has developed. During the nesting season, avoid walking into tilled or grassy fields; settle for what you can see from the edges. However, in the fall, (if it is permitted) walk about in shrubby fields and along edges in order to see the migrants that are feeding on seeds, berries and other food. In winter, you have two choices, and both are excellent. Shrubby field is about the most productive type of inland habitat for winter birding, especially if a stream passes through it. Look for lingering land bird migrants, as well as residents that come to feed from other types of habitat nearby. The other fine winter habitat is tilled field, now bare, especially if manure has been applied. Look for winter visitors such as snow bunting and horned lark, as well as raptors, including red-tailed and rough-legged hawks.

MARSH SWAMP AND BOG HABITATS

Fresh water marshes and swamps are among the most productive ecosystems in the world - they are twice as productive as temperate mixed forests, equal in productivity to tropical rain forests, and nearly as productive as salt water marshes. Marshes and swamps are natural collectors of nutrients, both organic and mineral, that flow in from surrounding higher areas, especially during periodic seasonal flooding. This concentration of nutrients supports a wide diversity and high density of plant and animal species. Among wetlands, bogs are different - they have harsh and relatively sterile ecosystems that lack the diversity of marshes and swamps; however, bogs support a unique group of plant and animal species that make them worthy of any birder's study.

Wetlands are normally in a process of succession - from water-saturated to drier, and from low herbs to higher shrubs and eventually trees. In this manner, bogs typically become marshes, which become swamps and eventually bottomland forests. And as these changes in the habitats occur, so does the mix of bird species that use the habitats.

The marsh, swamp and bog habitats discussed in this chapter are used by three-fourths of the bird species that occur regularly in Connecticut (207 out of about 280 species). Wetlands are sources of a wide range of food for a great diversity of bird species, many of which come in to feed from other habitats. Dabbling ducks feed from the surface of open water on vegetable matter and aquatic invertebrates. Herons and rails prey on invertebrates, amphibians and small fish. Shore birds also feed along the water's edge for invertebrates. A variety of land birds glean insects and other small invertebrates from vegetation. Aerial hunters such as swallows and flycatchers feed on flying insects in the air over the wetland. During cold weather, many species of land birds depend on berries and seeds on the shrubs in wetlands. And many forest-dwelling species find the trees of a swamp ideally situated for feeding, nesting and resting.

Types of Marsh, Swamp and Bog Habitat.

This group of inland wetlands is composed of the types of habitat discussed below, each one of which is visually recognizable and is used by a somewhat different group of bird species. However, even more than is the case with most types of habitat, types of wetland tend not to occur as discrete entities, but rather to blend with one another and to occur as patches or zones among other types of wetland, so that distinguishing among them is sometimes difficult.

Marshes are wetlands that are typically composed of emergent herbaceous plants and/or emergent shrubs. Marshes that have areas of open water amid herbaceous vegetation attract many species of water birds and marsh birds, while marshes that are dominated by shrubs host a wider variety of land birds. The air above all marshes provides good feeding opportunities for land birds that are aerial hunters, such as swallows and flycatchers.

Wet meadow is a wetland that is seasonally flooded. The dominant vegetation is emergent plants, principally grasses, sedges and rushes. A wet meadow is not as wet as other types of marsh, is usually quite dry in summer, and often resembles a grassland rather than a marsh. During the spring migration, wet meadows are used for feeding by a variety of dabbling ducks, rails, and shore birds (especially snipe). Sites that have wet meadow habitat include Wangunk Meadows in Portland and Haddam Meadows State Park.

Sedge marsh is a wetland that is flooded (except during dry spells) with standing water that may be shallow or deep. The dominant vegetation is emergent plants, principally sedges, grasses and rushes. Sedge marshes are used for feeding and nesting by a variety of dabbling ducks, as well as several species of shore birds, rails, blackbirds and sparrows. Ibis Swale at Horse Barn Hill is a sedge marsh.

Cattail marsh is a wetland that is permanently flooded with water that may be shallow or deep. The dominant vegetation is cattails, typically mixed with sedges and bulrushes. This is a highly productive type of inland wetland, for it provides many bird species with all of their needs - food even into winter, nest sites for a number of species, and protected resting areas throughout the year. Regular nesters include several dabbling ducks, both bitterns, sora, Virginia and king rails, moorhen, marsh wren, swamp sparrow, and other land birds. Mallard Marsh in White Memorial is a good example of a cattail marsh.

Mixed herbaceous marsh is a wetland that is permanently flooded with water that may be shallow or deep. It is a kind of blend that includes elements of cattail and sedge marshes. The vegetation is composed of a mixture of both broad-leafed and narrow-leafed herbaceous aquatic plants, typically including grasses, sedges, rushes and/or cattails. The mix of bird species that occur in it depends on the composition of the vegetation blend. If emergent vegetation is dense, it is attractive to American bittern. If there is lots of broad-leafed emergent vegetation, it attracts least bittern. Sora is attracted by the combination of broad- and narrow-leafed emergent vegetation. Dabbling ducks are most likely to use this wetland type if open water is within it or nearby. Roy Swamp includes areas of mixed herbaceous marsh.

Fresh water tidal marsh is a wetland that is flooded by water that fluctuates in level because of daily tidal action. Such marshes lie along sections of rivers that are reached by tides, but are above the reach of salt or brackish water. A number of these marshes occur on the tidal fresh water portion of the Connecticut River from where brackish water ends - about five miles upstream from Long Island Sound - to Windsor Locks, 40 miles upstream.

This type of wetland includes very diverse ecosystems that are enriched by nutrients brought into the marshes by the tides. The vegetation is quite variable, and occurs in zones that are determined by elevation and frequency of flooding. The low marsh is flooded twice daily, and typically includes emergent herbaceous plants such as wild rice, bulrushes, pickerelweed and other low growing vegetation. High marsh areas are flooded less often, may include some shrubs such as alders, as well as a variety of herbs such as cattails, sedges, bulrushes and ferns. Fresh water tidal marshes are likely to have open water during the winter when other fresh water wetlands are ice-covered.

Birds that use fresh water tidal marshes include a wide variety of water birds, waders, rails, shore birds and land birds - the exact species mix within these groups depends on the composition of the vegetation in each marsh. Fresh water tidal marshes along the lower Connecticut River include: Chester Creek, Pratt Cove, Chapman Pond, Selden Cove and Whalebone Creek.

Shrub marsh is a wetland that is normally flooded. The dominant vegetation is aquatic emergent shrubs usually less than six feet tall, and typically includes species such as buttonbush, water willow and marsh rose. In drier areas, red osier dogwood and elderberry may also occur. These shrubs may be accompanied by herbaceous vegetation.

Shrub marshes provide excellent food and cover for a variety of migrating and breeding water birds and marsh birds, including several dabbling ducks and Virginia rail. The presence of buttonbush and other shrubs make this type of wetland suitable as nesting habitat for a number of land bird species, including alder and willow flycatchers, kingbird, common yellowthroat and yellow warbler. Shrub marshes can be found at John A. Minetto State Park, Turnip Meadow in Mansfield Hollow State Park, and Little Pond in White Memorial.

Swamps are wetlands that are dominated by taller woody plants - shrubs such as alder, blueberry and spicebush, and/or trees such as maple, white pine or hemlock. This vegetation is more terrestrial than aquatic - it typically grows on moist, intermittently flooded ground rather than in permanent standing water. The vegetation usually forms a canopy. A great variety of birds come to swamps to feed - these include all the warblers and most other land bird species, including uncommon species such as rusty blackbird.

Shrub swamp is a wetland that is seasonally flooded; it is drier than a shrub marsh, and the shrubs grow in moist soil rather than out of water, as in a shrub marsh. A significant portion of the vegetation consists of larger shrubs - often blueberries, alders, silky dogwood, willows, sweet pepperbush, chokeberries, and tree saplings - typically red maple or white ash.

Birds that occur in shrub swamps include a wide variety of berry- and seed-eaters, as well as gleaners of invertebrates and hunters of flying insects. When there is open water, dabbling ducks may be present. Nesters include willow and alder flycatchers, kingbird, and a number of warblers - yellow, yellowthroat and chestnut-sided. Shrub swamps provide a source of both food and cover for birds in winter. John A. Minetto State Park and the Little Pond/Whites Woods Road area of White Memorial both contain areas of shrub swamp.

Shrubby hardwood swamp is a seasonally flooded wetland in which the largest plants are hardwood trees 15 to 30 feet high with trunks three to five inches in diameter, that are starting to develop a canopy. This tree community is often dominated by red maple. There is always a well developed understory of shrubs such as blueberry, spicebush, various alders and mountain laurel, along with tree seedlings and saplings.

The avian species diversity is less than that in shrub swamps, because the canopy of a typical shrubby hardwood swamp interferes with aerial hunting by swallows and flycatchers, and there is not enough open water to attract ducks. However, this is a habitat used by a wide variety of land bird migrants. Among the nesters are catbird, northern waterthrush and common yellowthroat. The trail along the north side of Bantam Lake in White Memorial passes through areas of shrubby hardwood swamp.

Hardwood swamp occurs in poorly-drained depressions, and is characterized by persistently wet conditions with minimal seasonal fluctuation in water level. The dominant vegetation is hardwood trees, typically red maple mixed with tulip tree, white and black ash, white oak, black birch and black cherry. These trees are usually over 20 feet tall and form a dense canopy that precludes a well-developed shrub layer.

The dense canopy, poorly-developed shrub layer, and lack of open water make hardwood swamps less attractive than shrub swamps or shrubby hardwood swamps to aerial feeders, seed- and berry-eaters and water birds. However, hardwood swamps are a good habitat for species that glean invertebrates from trees, such as vireos, warblers and tanager, and also for ground feeders such as thrushes and ovenbird. Hardwood swamps are a good birding habitat in the spring, summer and early fall, but unlike wetlands with an important shrub component, do not offer a good food supply in cold weather. There are many sites in Connecticut that include hardwood swamps.

Hemlock swamp is a wetland that is seasonally flooded, but is usually drier than a hardwood swamp. There is a well developed canopy dominated by hemlock trees, sometimes mixed with white pine, yellow and black birch. The understory is variable, usually not well developed, but may include mountain laurel. Hemlock swamps usually occur at higher elevations, in the Western Uplands or Eastern Uplands.

Hemlock swamps, due to their lower vegetation diversity and lack of much open water within them, and attract a less diverse group of bird species than hardwood swamps. However, for a limited number of species it is a very important habitat. During the spring migration and the nesting season, foliage gleaners including warblers and vireos feed among the hemlocks. Nesters include species that are not common in Connecticut, such as red-shouldered hawk, Acadian flycatcher, winter wren, solitary vireo, magnolia, black-throated green, Blackburnian and Canada warblers and northern waterthrush. In late fall and winter, chickadees, nuthatches, brown creepers and golden-crowned kinglets feed here; barred and saw-whet owls can sometimes be found roosting among the hemlocks. There are areas of hemlock swamp in Peoples State Forest and at White Memorial along the south side of Cranberry Pond.

White pine swamp is the driest of the wooded swamps; it has occasional seasonal areas of standing water. White pine swamps have well developed canopies dominated by white pine trees; the shrub layer is typically poorly developed. They are the least common of the wooded swamps, and typically occur at higher elevations in the Western and Eastern Uplands.

Unless flooded by beavers, white pine swamps do not attract water birds, nor do they have a diversity of shrubs for seed- and berry-eaters. However, they are a good food source for a number of insect-gleaners, during the spring and fall migrations, and the nesting season. In winter, chickadee, red-breasted nuthatch, brown creeper and golden-crowned kinglet feed here, and in some years, crossbills as well. White pine swamps are frequently flooded by beavers, and this changes the whole nature of the habitat. Typically, the pines die but remain standing for many years, and provide good nesting habitat for great blue heron and a host of cavity nesters. The dead pines overlooking open water provides an ideal hunting situation for aerial feeders. There are areas of white pine swamp in the Pine Island area at White Memorial.

Bogs are wetlands characterized by a ground cover of sphagnum moss together with herbaceous and shrubby vegetation of the heath family. Two quite different types occur in Connecticut - the black spruce bog and the Atlantic white cedar bog, sometimes called "cedar swamp".

Black spruce bog is a wetland that occurs in cool, poorly-drained depressions; most of those in Connecticut occur at higher elevations in the Western Uplands. Trees, often black spruce or tamarack, may be present as scattered individuals or forming a canopy. When there is not a dense canopy, there is a well-developed shrub layer dominated by leatherleaf or sweet gale. The ground cover is composed largely of sphagnum mosses.

Species diversity of plants and animals in bogs is quite narrow, but those that do occur are very interesting. Bogs are good places to look during both migrations and the nesting season for northern species, such as olive-sided flycatcher, solitary vireo, Nashville, black-throated green and yellow-rumped warblers, northern waterthrush, golden-crowned kinglet, junco and white-throated sparrow. In winter, bogs are a good place to look for saw-whet and barred owls, and winter finches in some years. There is a black spruce Bog in the Mohawk State Forest.

White cedar bog is a wetland that occurs along streams or in poorly-drained depressions; most of the few in Connecticut occur in the eastern part of the state - on the Coastal Slope or in the Eastern Uplands. The dominant tree species is Atlantic white cedar, often accompanied by red maple or gray birch. There may also be a well developed shrub layer, often including sweet pepperbush, rhododendron, mountain laurel, winterberry or greenbrier. The ground cover is composed largely of sphagnum mosses.

The birds that feed and nest in this habitat include southern species such as hooded warbler and Carolina wren, one northerner (northern waterthrush), and a few other species including catbird and common yellowthroat. In winter, saw-whet owl is possible, along with lingering berry-eaters. One of the few white cedar bogs in Connecticut is the Windham Bog; another is at the Middle Reservoir; still another is near the Rhododendron Sanctuary in the Patchaug State Forest.

Factors That Affect Birds' Use of Inland Wetlands

Land form effect. Wetlands that are associated with river or stream systems are likely to have greater use by migrants than those that are not within a migration corridor. Good examples are Haddam Meadows, and Station 43, both located along the Connecticut River.

Interfaces with other types of habitat. By their very nature, all wetlands interface with other types of habitat. The most common interface is with streams or rivers that run through most wetlands, and add to the diversity of species using the wetland. Isolated wetlands - especially if they are small - support fewer species than wetlands in complexes that have other nearby aquatic habitats. However, even small isolated wetlands are more productive than most terrestrial habitats.

Edge of a wetland may be composed of herbs, shrubs or trees, alone or in any combination. Wetland edges are usually more thickly vegetated than the habitats on either side, and usually include plants that are rich in food. At almost any time of year, wetland edges are the focus of high levels of feeding activity, by species that occur in the wetland or in the terrestrial habitat on the other side of the edge, plus "edge-dwelling" species such as catbird, least flycatcher, common yellowthroat, blue-winged and yellow warblers and song sparrow.

Diversity of vegetation, in the form of a variety of aquatic and emergent plants together with shrubs, produces a variety of food sources that are available during different seasons. Wetlands that contain the greatest variety of herbs, shrubs and trees are usually the ones in which the greatest diversity of bird species occur.

Species composition of vegetation. Marshes with dense herbaceous vegetation (cattails, sedges or grasses) are good places to look for marsh birds such as rails and bitterns. Marshes and swamps that have a significant shrub component (shrub marsh, shrub swamp, shrubby hardwood swamp, and wetlands with shrubby edges) provide a better source of food, nest sites and shelter for a wide variety of land birds than do marshes that are dominated by herbaceous vegetation. A mountain laurel shrub layer, especially under hemlock, attracts Canada and black-throated blue warblers. If berry- or seed-producing shrubs are present, both marshes and swamps are a good source of food for birds during the fall migration and into winter. Certain shrub species, such as winterberry holly, provide berries for birds during the winter. The presence of trees in a swamp attracts forest-dwelling land birds, but a tree canopy usually reduces the shrub and herb layers, and thus lowers productivity.

Areas of open water in marshes and swamps provide transportation corridors and a foraging area for water bird species such as dabbling ducks, hooded merganser and pied-billed grebe. An optimum condition is a 50/50 mix of open water and vegetation, with a diversity of aquatic vegetation around the edges of the water.

Deadwood may occur in almost any type of wetland in the form of dead and dying trees around the edges, or standing out in the middle of the wetland, often in open water that has been backed up by a beaver dam. The dead trees enrich the diversity of bird species that occur in the wetland in several ways. First, they draw in birds that hunt from a perch, such as kestrel, red-shouldered hawk, kingfisher, flycatchers, certain warblers and cedar waxwing. They also provide nest sites for cavity nesters including wood duck, hooded merganser, screech owl, woodpeckers, tree swallow and bluebird. Dead white pine is a favored nest site of great blue heron.

Open air above herbaceous or shrubby vegetation attracts aerial hunters such as nighthawk, swallows and flycatchers.

A variety of water depths increases the diversity of water, marsh and shore bird species that use a wetland.

A stream flowing through a marsh or swamp adds a productive type of habitat (for many species, including Louisiana waterthrush), and can continue to provide open water when other areas of the wetland are ice-covered.

Beavers, by rapidly changing water levels in wetlands, exert a significant effect on the plants and animals that occur within the wetland - an effect that benefits some species and is detrimental to others. In fact, beavers, through their dam-building abilities, can even create wetlands out of upland habitats.

Birding in Marsh, Swamp and Bog Habitats

Inland wetlands, together with coastal wetlands, are Connecticut's most rewarding habitats in which to look for birds. Birds use wetlands at all times of year - some seasons are better than others, but at any given season, wetlands are likely to be more rewarding to the birder than any of the terrestrial habitats.

Generally, the open types of inland wetland are more diverse and more productive throughout the year than the wooded types, which tend to slow down in winter. However, a wooded wetland is better than a wooded upland habitat at any season - water is the key. Because of their rich food supply, wetlands draw birds in from other nearby habitats; often, a wetland is associated with a river, stream, lake or pond, and these combinations are especially productive.

How to get a look at the birds is an important aspect of birding wetlands, because many wetland birds stay hidden within the vegetation (rails are the ultimate example). Some wetlands have roads, trails or boardwalks that go through them or beside them, and these walkways may provide enough elevation to give you a good view. Chatfield Hollow State Park has a boardwalk, as do Little Pond, Duck Pond and Laurel Hill Swamp, all in White Memorial. Stay on these walkways to avoid disturbing wildlife in the wetland. A spotting scope can be helpful in finding birds without entering the wetland. Some wetlands can be explored by canoe (Roy Swamp in Sharon, for example).

Springtime avian activity usually starts in fresh water marshes and swamps somewhat later than at rivers and streams, but earlier than at lakes and ponds. This is determined by when there is open water at each of these types of habitat, because it is open water that triggers activity by flying insects. The earliest spring bird activity at marshes and swamps occurs at the open types (marshes and shrub swamps), and at sites in southern Connecticut that are along rivers or near the coast.

The first water bird and land bird migrants and a few nesters arrive at fresh water wetlands in March, and they are followed in April and May by marsh birds, shore birds, and the later-migrating land birds. The peak of the spring activity in wetlands occurs during May. If you enjoy birding by ear, wetlands are an ideal habitat to do so; a May morning at a marsh is an unforgettable experience.

In summer, marshes and swamps offer quiet sites in which to study birds during the nesting season; many of these sites are overlooked by the crowds that descend on state parks in the warm weather. During the nesting season, all types of marshes, swamps and bogs have a good diversity of birds - the species mix depends on the wetland type and the vegetation. But, any wetland has greater diversity and abundance of nesters than any upland habitat. The greatest species diversity occurs at open types of wetland that have open water and shrubs. The presence of standing dead trees attracts cavity nesters; herbaceous vegetation attracts marsh birds, possibly including rails or waders. Shrubs - both aquatic and terrestrial - attract a variety of land birds.

Inland wetlands can provide very good birding throughout the fall - they include a great diversity of habitats and a high level of activity during migration. The species composition depends on the time of year and on the wetland type. Starting in August, shore birds are the first migrants to appear - at marshes that have mud along the shore, or shallow water over a muddy bottom. Waders and other marsh birds follow, at marshes that have shallows and herbaceous vegetation. Migrating water birds - mostly dabbling ducks and hooded merganser - drop in to marshes with open water starting in September. Starting early in the migration (late August) and continuing throughout the fall, land birds stop to feed along the shrubby and wooded edges of marshes and swamps. Many of these edges have a diversity of shrub species that produce sequential crops of berries throughout the fall. In addition, early in the fall there is still enough activity by flying insects over open water to attract flycatchers and other aerial feeders.

In winter, there is less action at wetlands, but they are still worth visiting - open marshes are better than wooded swamps. Much of the activity at marshes and swamps is food-oriented, and much of this food is aquatic in origin. Therefore, open water is needed for this food to be available to birds, so that in winter open water is a magnet for any birds that are around. Most ponds are frozen, but some marshes may still have open water (those that have springs or seeps, and especially those with a stream running through them). In addition, shrubs along wetland edges may still have berries through the winter, particularly if the shrubs includes winterberry holly. Land birds come to the edges to feed and for shelter.

LAKE, POND AND POOL HABITATS

Lakes, ponds and seasonal pools are bodies of non-flowing fresh water that lack persistent emergent vegetation except around the perimeter. There are about 6,000 lakes and ponds in Connecticut. The largest lake is Candlewood Lake in Fairfield and Litchfield Counties, and the largest natural lake is Bantam Lake in Litchfield County.

Lake, pond and pool habitats provide birds with an abundant source of both plant and animal food. Their shorelines and islands provide sheltered and concealed nesting sites, with safe areas in which to rest. About two-thirds of the bird species that regularly occur in Connecticut (177 of about 280 species) use lakes, ponds or pools, their shores or the air above the water for some purpose - all of them for feeding, and 59 species for nesting (about one-third of the state's total nesting species).

Thirty-four species of water birds occur at lakes, ponds or pools - many of them migrants that are travelling between distant breeding and winter ranges. Six species of marsh birds and 17 shore bird species use these habitats. Two-thirds of the birds that occur at them - 120 of 177 species - are land birds, including a number of forest-interior species. Clearly, as avian habitats, lakes, ponds and pools are more than just bodies of water; they also offer birds the fertile interface between aquatic and terrestrial environments, and productive hunting in the air over the water. Thus, these water bodies serve as an important focus for a wide variety of bird life.

Types of Lake and Pond Habitat

Lake, for the purpose of this guide, is a body of open water that is larger than 100 acres, and usually has extensive areas more than six feet deep. By this definition, the term "lake" includes most, but not all water bodies in Connecticut that are called lakes, most reservoirs, and some water bodies that are called ponds. Lakes may have submergent or emergent vegetation, and may occur with other types of wetland around their periphery.

The best lakes for birds are those that do not suffer from excessive human disturbance, and contain water that has not been polluted or entered a late stage of eutrophication. Lakes that are rich in plant and/or animal foods are attractive to the bird species that feed on those plants. Shallow lakes tend to be richer in food than deep lakes, but they do not have the deep water that attracts some water birds.

Large lakes with areas of deep water offer an attractive food supply to water birds that are able to catch fish (including common merganser and common loon), and to water birds that are able to dive for animal food on the bottom (including redhead, canvasback, common goldeneye and bufflehead). Gulls also occur on the deep water of inland lakes.

Another group of species usually feed at water of intermediate depth, but sometimes at deep water. These include horned grebe, ring-necked duck, both scaups and hooded merganser.

Some lakes have coves - sheltered indentations in the shore, in which the water is usually shallow. Coves on a lake offer a slightly different environment from the main part of the lake, and attract yet another group of water birds: pied-billed grebe, mute swan, Canada and snow goose, various dabbling ducks, hooded and common mergansers, coot, great blue heron and kingfisher.

Bantam Lake and the Nepaug Reservoir are both large lakes at which a wide diversity of bird species occur.

Pond in this guide is defined as a body of open water smaller than 100 acres, and mostly less than six feet deep. In Connecticut, ponds are more likely than lakes to have undeveloped shores and be free of excessive human disturbance.

Many bird species occur at both ponds and lakes, but the overlap is not complete. Most ponds lack deep water and do not have coves, so that ponds do not attract all of the water bird species that occur on larger lakes that have those characteristics. However, ponds typically have extensive areas of shallow water (defined as extending out from shore as far as there are submergent rooted plants). Shallow water is the most productive part of a water body, and supports the greatest number of plants and animals, including aquatic insects, other invertebrate animals, amphibians, reptiles and small fish. Much of the food supply in shallow water is available to species of water birds that do not normally dive, including a variety of dabbling ducks.

The air over lakes and ponds provides a rather narrow range of food, but at times does so in great abundance. Air over the shallow water that is typical of ponds provides a more bountiful supply of flying insects than does air over the deep water that is typical of lakes. Birds that feed on flying insects include aerial hunters (such as swallows and nighthawks), and "hawkers" that hunt from perches and make short flights to capture their prey (kingbird, waxwing and certain warblers hunt in this manner).

In addition, ponds are more attractive than most lakes to species that require marshy shores which are not disturbed by wave action or human activity - species such as snipe, woodcock, American bittern, Virginia rail and moorhen. Also, hooded merganser occurs more frequently at ponds than lakes.

Beavers can cause changes in the level of the water in ponds. Such changes may be quite rapid, and affect - for better or worse - almost any of the bird species that are using the pond. Beavers also create ponds through their damming abilities.

Sites with productive ponds include Great Pond State Forest, Cemetery Pond at White Memorial, and Knowlton Pond.

Seasonal Pool is an area of water that collects intermittently in a shallow depression, and is usually formed by melting snow or rainfall in the spring and fall. It usually dries up in summer, and is dry or frozen solid in winter.

The temporary nature of the water in seasonal pools precludes many types of aquatic foods found in lakes and ponds, but their shores and bottoms can be a source of some aquatic insects and other invertebrates on which birds feed, especially during mid-spring. The primary purpose served by seasonal pools in Connecticut is as short-term feeding and resting areas during the spring migration for water birds and shorebirds. The type of habitat that surrounds a seasonal pool largely determines the bird species that use it. Pools that are surrounded by farm fields, sand or gravel are typically used by geese, dabbling ducks, shore birds and a few land birds. Most of this activity is early in the spring (March and April). Pools that have shrubs or woods around them become important a little later in the spring as a feeding area for a wide variety of insect-eating land birds, including flycatchers, swallows, vireos, warblers and blackbirds.

Factors That Affect Birds' Use Of Lake, Pond and Pool Habitats

The location in Connecticut, and the land form effect. Lakes and ponds that lie near the coast in southern Connecticut have open water later in the fall, and become ice-free earlier in the spring. Water bodies that lie along a migration route (near the coast, or in a major river valley) have an advantage during the spring and fall migrations. Rain pools in grassy areas at coastal sites can attract a great diversity of shore birds especially in the fall.

Edges and interfaces with other types of habitat. The shore of a lake, pond or pool is an edge that provides a very productive interface between the aquatic habitat of the water body and some type of terrestrial habitat on the surrounding land. Shores offer a great variety of uses to a great number of bird species. The mix of species that are drawn to this interface depends partly on the nature of the water body, but primarily on the nature of the surrounding terrestrial habitats.

Lakes and ponds that have barren shores (mud, sand or gravel) attract shore bird migrants, including yellowlegs, solitary and least sandpipers. Barren shores also serve as resting areas for geese, dabbling ducks, hooded and common mergansers. Sand, gravel and rocks along a shore attract snow bunting and pipit in the late fall. Reservoirs that have been drawn down and have a strip of mud along their shores can retain migrating shore birds even into November. Lakes and ponds with grassy shores attract killdeer. Spotted sandpiper feeds at the water's edge of almost any type of shore.

Lakes and ponds that have marshy shores are the most attractive to waders. Great blue heron feeds on fish and other aquatic animals in shallow water near the marshy shore, but nests elsewhere. Green-backed heron feeds in similar areas, and nests in trees or shrubs near the shore. Great egret sometimes comes inland to feed at lakes and ponds in August and September.

A great variety of land birds feed at the shores of lakes, ponds and pools. The species mix depends on the shoreline habitat; shrubby, wooded and marshy shores are attractive to many species. Because shores attract so many small land birds, avian predators are also drawn to them - red-tailed hawk, great horned and barred owls hunt shores throughout the year, and saw-whet owl in winter; screech owl both hunts and nests along shores. Raven and crows scavenge along shores.

The proximity of a marsh or swamp increases the attractiveness of a lake or pond for all birds, especially water and marsh birds.

Species composition of vegetation. Vegetation types around lakes, ponds and pools are highly variable.

The vegetation species composition of marshy shores determines what bird species occur there. Areas of tussock sedge and cattail are used by Virginia rail and moorhen for nesting, and when more cattail is present, pied-billed grebe, American and least bitterns are possible nesting species. Canada goose, black duck and mallard also nest in sedges and cattails, if there is sufficient water among the vegetation. Marshy shores that are dominated by phragmites are not productive, and their use is pretty much confined to red-winged blackbird, grackle, song and swamp sparrows. In contrast, sedge marsh shore is very productive, especially in terms of food supply. Nesting species include kingbird, yellow warbler and common yellowthroat.

Certain shrubs on the shores of lakes and ponds are especially good providers of food in the form of berries and seeds, as well as insects and other small invertebrates; these include red osier dogwood, elderberry and winterberry. Shrubs that grow over or into the water, such as alders, buttonbush and water willow, are important because of the shelter they provide for water birds.

Wooded shores produce food in the form of terrestrial insects, and also seeds and nuts that fall into the water next to the shore. Tall trees overlooking water are used as hunting or resting sites by bald eagle (they prefer white pine), osprey, great blue heron (high in trees), and green-backed heron (lower in trees). Many species of land birds forage along wooded shores.

Birding at Lake and Pond Habitats

Start birding at lakes and ponds as soon as there is open water - usually in March, and earliest in southern Connecticut near the coast. As the spring goes on and water bodies continue to become ice-free, the number and diversity of migrating water birds increases until mid-April. At about this time, water birds that will stay to nest are arriving, and marsh, shore and land bird migrants start to pass through or arrive to nest. As soon as there is open water at lakes and ponds, the aquatic insect activity begins, and it remains a real drawing card for land bird migrants and nesters. Most migrating shore birds pass northward through Connecticut from late April through May; during this period, search for seasonal pools in farm fields - they are magnets for shore bird migrants.

During the nesting season, the best birding is at smaller ponds that are not highly developed or heavily used for swimming and boating. Some shallow-water species of water birds (mainly dabbling ducks and hooded merganser) nest at such ponds, and usually feed with their young near the shore. A variety of nesting land birds can also be seen along the shore.

Fall is the time to bird at lakes and ponds. Post-breeding wandering waders can be seen in August and September. Shore birds move through during July through late August, but may stay on even into November at reservoirs that have been drawn down, exposing mud at which to feed. Water bird migrants drop in starting in early September, and peak in November. Migrating land birds feed along lake and pond shores from September through the end of autumn.

In winter, search for lakes that have areas of open water, where there are sometimes large groups of water birds. Lingering land bird migrants and residents feed in shrubs along the shore, especially where the lake or pond is near a wetland.

RIVER AND STREAM HABITATS

Connecticut has about 8,400 miles of rivers and streams, in watersheds that tend to flow southward. There are three major rivers in the state - The Housatonic drains the Western Uplands, the Thames drains the Eastern Uplands, and the Connecticut flows between them, through the upper part of the Central Valley. (The Connecticut is the largest river in the Northeast, and has a total length and volume of water flow considerably greater than the Hudson.) These three rivers broaden and deepen as they approach Long Island Sound, and two of them (the Housatonic and the Connecticut) have large estuaries where they enter the Sound.

Smaller rivers, most of which are tributaries to the three major rivers, include the Shepaug, Naugatuck, Quinnipiac, Farmington, Shetucket and Quinebaug. In addition, there are hundreds of smaller streams throughout the state.

From the perspective of avian habitat, it is useful to think of rivers and streams as including their immediate shores, together with associated islands, bars of mud, sand or gravel, rocks, and also the air above them.

Of the roughly 280 bird species that occur regularly in Connecticut, 242 species (over 85%) use rivers and streams for some purpose - feeding, nesting, bathing or resting. This total includes most of the species in each of the major bird groups - water, marsh, shore and land birds.

Types of River and Stream Habitat

River. A river is a body of flowing water that is generally more than 20' wide and typically 50' or more. Rivers are usually at lower elevations than streams, and flow through broader valleys. Rivers serve as a source of aquatic food, and also provide birds with water for drinking, bathing and on which to rest. Rivers also enrich the value of the terrestrial habitats on their immediate shores, as well as the air above the water.

Many of the same bird species occur at rivers as at streams, but the diversity is greater on rivers. Species that commonly occur on both rivers and streams include: great blue and green-backed herons, spotted sandpiper, woodcock, kingfisher, plus various vireos, warblers, swallows and flycatchers. Among the species that are more common on rivers than streams are: a greater variety of water birds, including Canada goose, mallard, black duck, ring-necked duck, both scaups, common goldeneye, common and hooded mergansers, and occasionally green-winged teal and pintail; a greater variety of shore birds, including solitary and pectoral sandpiper, killdeer and snipe; and a greater variety of land birds, including bald eagle and osprey.

The air above rivers often contains great diversity and numbers of flying insects - even more than is the case over lakes and ponds. Species that feed on this bounty include swallows, swift, nighthawk, flycatchers, several vireos and warblers, and cedar waxwing. Other hunters that use the air over rivers include the fish eaters (osprey and bald eagle), and hunters of the birds that hunt insects (Cooper's and sharp-shinned hawks).

Examples of river habitats in this guide include Kings Island/Parsons Road, and also three River Road sites - in Canaan, Kent and New Milford.

Perennial stream is a body of water that flows year-round, and is less than 20' wide. Streams usually occur at higher elevations than rivers, and often flow in narrower, more steep-sided valleys. They can be highly variable in water depth and velocity, substrate, shoreline and streambelt. Streams, like rivers, are important to birds as a source of aquatic food and water for drinking, bathing and resting, and also because they enrich the food potential of the terrestrial habitats along their shores, and in the air above the water. They also serve as important corridors for movement.

Several species of water birds, marsh birds and shore birds feed and rest at streams. The variety of water birds that use streams diminishes as the size of the stream decreases. The most common species of water birds are wood duck and mallard. Spotted sandpiper regularly feeds and nests along streams in open areas. In years when the early arrival (in March) of woodcock in Connecticut is complicated by a late winter freeze or snowfall, their survival often depends on their ability to find bare ground along a stream. Kingfisher feeds on small fish in the shallow water of streams, and nests in embankments along the shore. Many swallows, flycatchers, vireos, and warblers feed on insects flying over streams. Acadian flycatcher and Louisiana waterthrush both feed and nest along small, fast-moving streams with steep embankments. Winter wren feeds along the edge of streams, especially in winter.

Sites in which perennial streams are important include Devil's Hopyard State Park and Macedonia Brook State Park.

Seasonal Stream. Seasonal, or intermittent streams do not usually have flowing water throughout the year. Typically, they flow in the spring, dry up in summer, may or may not have water in the fall, and are dry or ice-covered in winter. Because they are dry for periods, the avian food that they produce is limited. Seasonal streams are usually small and lack clearly defined shore habitats, so that they tend to blend into the habitat that surrounds them. A number of land bird species may come to seasonal streams when they are flowing during the spring migration. The most common nesting species are winter wren and Louisiana waterthrush, both of which use overhanging embankments as their nest site.

Factors That Affect Birds' Use of River and Stream Habitats

Location in Connecticut. Rivers and streams in the northwestern and northeastern parts of the state tend to have a swifter current and pass through narrower, more steep-sided valleys (the streams at Mt Riga and Boston Hollow are good examples). Streams that flow through the more level Central Valley or the Coastal Slope in the southern part of the state tend to have slower current and flow through broader valleys (as does the Mill River at East Rock Park).

Land form effect (valley). Rivers and streams all flow through some kind of a valley that affects the climate around them, and influences the plants and animals that occur near them.

At one extreme of this valley effect are hemlock ravines, that most often occur where the streams are still quite small. Such ravines are deeply shaded and contain a cool, damp microclimate characteristic of areas to our north (an example is Campbell Falls State Park). Hemlock ravines do not attract a wide diversity of bird species, but they are the best places in which to look for certain specialists that prefer this unique northern type of microhabitat. Louisiana waterthrush, winter wren, phoebe and Acadian flycatcher are all species that nest in hemlock ravines.

At the other extreme of the valley effect are the broad valleys through which large rivers flow. Connecticut's major river valleys are formed by the Connecticut River and its main tributaries (the Farmington and the Salmon), the Housatonic River and its main tributaries (the Naugatuck and the Shepaug), and the Thames River and its main tributaries (the Shetucket and the Quinebaug). These river valleys have more moderate climate than nearby upland areas, and contain many plant and animal species that are common south of Connecticut.

During the spring migration, birds that are arriving in Connecticut or passing through on their way north, tend to occur earliest in river valleys - days or even weeks before they are seen in upland areas.

Species that expand their nesting ranges north into Connecticut seem to follow avenues of moderate climate, and enter Connecticut initially along the coast, and later penetrate inland areas by extending their ranges up major river valleys. Even after they have become established in many parts of the state, these species continue to be most numerous in river valleys. Examples include cerulean and yellow-throated warblers, both of which occur at River Road along the Housatonic River in Kent. Other species that have expanded their ranges north into Connecticut include red-bellied woodpecker, fish crow, tufted titmouse, blue-gray gnatcatcher, Carolina wren, and orchard oriole, all of which now occur in many parts of the state, but still are most common along the coast and in major river valleys.

Size. Smaller and swifter streams have less diversity of water birds than larger, slower rivers and streams. Larger, swifter rivers attract common merganser and goldeneye, during the fall, winter and spring (as at Kings Island and Farmington River Park). Larger, slow rivers attract a wide variety of water birds in fall, winter and spring (as at sites along the lower Connecticut River, including the Deep River Town Dock and the Essex Steamboat Dock), and a variety of waders in spring, summer and fall (as at Selden Cove and Whalebone Creek). Bald eagle and osprey prefer larger rivers, in which the air above the river is open and free of overhanging branches (as at the Salmon Cove Boat Landing).

Streambelts (interface with other habitats, edges, diversity of vegetation and species composition of vegetation). By their very nature, rivers and streams can flow through almost any other habitat type - and most pass through a multitude of different habitats, which may include forest, open terrestrial and wetlands. One of the strengths of rivers and streams as avian habitat is that they have built in to them this dimension of habitat interfaces, edges, and vegetative diversity. One aspect of this interface dimension is particularly important - the interface between aquatic and terrestrial habitats. Where land meets water, wildlife finds its richest sources of food.

An important step in evaluating a river or stream is to ask, "What is its streambelt? What is along the immediate shore? And what habitats does it go through?" Different types of shore and different adjacent habitats greatly affect the bird species that occur at rivers and streams:

Embankment. Kingfisher and bank swallow excavate nest cavities in steep dirt banks, and rough-winged swallow will reuse these cavities for their own nests. Louisiana waterthrush and phoebe don't excavate, but place their nests under overhangs or roots on embankments.

Barren shore (a low, flat strip along the shore composed of mud, sand, gravel or rocks). Herons, spotted sandpiper and Louisiana waterthrush all use this strip as a hunting place.

Herbaceous shore. A great diversity of species feed here, depending on the type, density and height of the vegetation. Time of year is also a factor, as it determines seed and berry production of the plants.

Shrubby shore: in spring, shrubs along a river or stream are an early source of invertebrate food; start your birding here to find flycatchers, swallows, cedar waxwing, warblers and ruby-crowned kinglet. Shrubs along the shore are also used for nesting by yellow and chestnut-sided warblers, song sparrow and catbird. In the fall, berries on the shrubs attract robin, bluebird, cedar waxwing and yellow-rumped warbler. In winter, such shrubs provide food for lingering frugivores. And all year they provide protection and shelter for a multitude of species.

Hardwood shore is a good source of small invertebrates - especially in the spring and through the nesting season; it is less productive during the winter. But at any season hardwoods by a river or stream are better than an inland hardwood forest - they have more food and more birds. Starting early in the spring, mixed bands of insect-eating vireos, warblers, kinglets and gnatcatcher feed in hardwoods along rivers and streams. Hardwood tree branches that hang over the river or stream are sought as nest sites by least flycatcher, gnatcatcher, waxwing, northern oriole, yellow-throated and warbling vireos.

White pine shore: during the spring migration, mixed flocks of vireos, warblers and kinglets feed on caterpillars and other invertebrates in the tops of white pines. During the winter, mixed feeding bands of chickadees, titmouse, downy woodpecker, golden-crowned kinglet, creeper and both nuthatches feed in white pines by a river or stream.

Corridors. By their very nature, rivers and streams are corridors, and this is an important function. During migration, rivers and streams provide avenues of easy movement; moreover, these avenues contain rich sources of food that can be reached without deviating from the route of the migration. At other times, rivers and streams provide an easy way to travel between local feeding or resting sites.

Water Depth and rate of flow. Flat, deeper water usually has the greatest variety of food for birds, in the form of fish, aquatic insects, crustaceans and molluscs. Flat water is apt to freeze in winter, but areas of flat water that stay open become important feeding and resting areas for water birds. In spring, the flat water areas of rivers become ice-free before lakes, ponds, marshes and swamps, and provide the best early source of flying insects for swallows, vireos, warblers and other aerial hunters. Great blue heron prefers shallow backwaters. Louisiana waterthrush prefers swift water, in stream with steep banks.

Overhanging branches. Low overhanging branches make good hunting perches for green-backed heron; higher overhanging branches make good hunting perches for flycatchers.

Branches for perching by the side of a stream or river, but with open space above the water, are best for hunting by kingfisher. Open air above a river, free of overhanging branches, provides the best hunting opportunities for osprey and bald eagle. Overhanging branches are used as a nest site by hummingbird; overhanging hemlock branches are used as a nest site by Acadian flycatcher, especially over swift water in hemlock ravines.

Bottom. Mud in shallow water provides a good feeding area for spotted sandpiper and other shore birds. A gravel substrate is especially important as a breeding area for stone flies, caddis flies, and other insects that birds eat.

Mud, sand and gravel bars provide birds with places from which to hunt, or on which to rest, preen and bathe. All three types are used by herons, crows, blackbirds, killdeer and a host of other species. Mud bars are preferred by both yellowlegs, spotted, solitary, western, white-rumped, least and pectoral sandpipers, woodcock and snipe. Any type of bar that is used by any of the above species draws in bird hunters - Cooper's and sharp-shinned hawks, merlin and peregrine falcon.

Rocks provide feeding and resting sites for a variety of water birds, especially fish-eating species (herons, common merganser, bald eagle, osprey). A variety of land birds use rocks as places to bathe and preen.

Islands generally attract a diversity of bird species, depending on the type, density and diversity of vegetation on the island. The size of the island is also important, as is the character of its shoreline. Islands can serve as very important nesting sites, safe from mammalian predators.

The air above rivers and streams often contains a high density of flying insects - even more than the air over lakes and ponds. This insect activity starts early in spring (March/early April, while most lakes and ponds are still ice-covered) and extends through late fall. Species that hunt these flying insects include swallows, nighthawk, flycatchers, cedar waxwing, vireos and warblers. Other aerial hunters include osprey and bald eagle (both hunt fish), Cooper's and sharp-shinned hawks (both hunt birds).

Birding at River and Stream Habitats

Your earliest inland spring birding can be along rivers and streams in March and April - begin on larger rivers near the coast and work your way up to smaller streams as the season progresses. Flat water areas of rivers generally become ice-free earlier in the spring than lakes and ponds. Rivers and streams are especially good during the spring migration, when they serve as migration corridors that are also good sources of early-season food. In the early spring, a variety of migrating water birds feed and rest on the open water of larger rivers. Also in the early spring, both rivers and streams attract early-arriving insect eaters such as phoebe and yellow-rumped warbler. During the nesting season, when young birds must be fed, a lot of foraging goes on along rivers and streams by species that nest in other habitats. They are also good during the fall migration; at this time they are less important as a migration route than they were in the Spring, but still attract a variety of migrating land birds because of the food value of shrubs along the banks. However, rivers are apt to have fewer water birds during the early part of the fall migration than lakes and ponds which during that period are a better source of food. In winter, do your birding at rivers and streams that are ice-free. A variety of water birds feed and rest on the water of larger rivers, bald eagle perches on trees on the shore, and lingering and resident land birds search for food in shrubs along the shores. A stream running through a shrubby field or wetland is a good place to look for birds at any time of year, but especially in the winter.

COASTAL HABITATS

Many birders in Connecticut would rank a site on the coast as their top choice for a birding trip. And for several good reasons.

Birds are abundant and diverse at the interface of natural communities, and certainly the greatest interface in Connecticut is the coast itself, where terrestrial and marine habitats come together along a coastal strip 253 miles long. Many of the habitats along this interface are the richest and most productive in the state.

The coastline of Connecticut is also one of North America's major migration routes, and this makes for excellent birding during the spring and fall. During the winter, Connecticut's coastal habitats provide open water that has an abundant marine food supply for water birds. In addition, the coast has a milder, more moderate climate than inland areas, and in winter provides a greater supply of terrestrial food than is available inland. The result of all of these considerations is that virtually all of the 280 bird species that occur regularly in Connecticut can be seen at coastal habitats.

Types of Coastal Habitat

Coastal habitats are defined as extending seaward over Long Island Sound as far as you can see and identify birds with a spotting scope, and extending inland as far as habitats are directly influenced by salt water.

Estuary is really not a habitat in itself, but rather is a cluster of habitats. An estuary forms at the mouth of a river, and is a semi-enclosed body of water that has a free connection to a larger body of water (in this context, Long Island Sound). An estuary consists of tidal waters and contiguous wetlands, and it extends upstream in coastal rivers to where no salt water can be detected. The habitats within an estuary typically include a barrier beach, tidal marshes and intertidal flats. The overriding feature of an estuary that affects all life within it, is the mixing of salt water from the Sound with fresh water from the river that drains into it. The most saline water tends to be at the lower end near Long Island Sound, with decreasing salinity upstream in the river. Typically, salt water marshes occur near the Sound, brackish marshes in the lower section of the river, and fresh water marshes farther upstream. However, the action of the tides against the flow of the river produces a very complex mixture of salinities which varies continuously. The sheltered water of an estuary and the input of sediments from the river encourage the development of mud and sand flats - solid substrates are rare. Nutrients are brought in both by the tides and also by the river, and tend to accumulate in an estuary. As a result, estuaries are among the richest and most productive ecosystems in the world, and support large numbers of molluscs, crustaceans, other invertebrates, fish and birds.

Estuaries are attractive to birds for several reasons. First, they are unsurpassed as feeding areas - they provide a year-round food supply with types of food that vary by season. In addition, estuaries typically include a mutually-supporting cluster of feeding and roosting habitats that lie within an area that is sheltered from severe weather. The combination of these features causes a wide diversity and large numbers of birds to occur in estuaries through-out most of the year. Waders hunt in shallows for fish, crustaceans, gastropods. Shore birds hunt in mud flats for invertebrates. Dabbling bucks, bay ducks and divers all feed in estuar-ies, at appropriate water depths. Terns, gulls and osprey hunt over the water. The occurrence of each species varies with season and tide stage.

There are several text-book type examples of estuaries along the Connecticut coast, and it is no coincidence that some of the state's finest birding sites are within these estuaries. The largest of them are at the mouths of the Connecticut and the Housatonic Rivers - at Great Island, Griswold Point and other sites on the Connecticut River; and Milford Point, Nells Island, Great Meadows and other sites on the Housatonic River.

Long Island Sound is actually a large estuary - tides enter at the east end of the Sound near Stonington, and fresh water enters from three major rivers - the Housatonic, Connecticut and Thames - and many smaller rivers and streams. It covers an area of 1,600 square miles, is 110 miles long and up to 25 miles wide. Long Island Sound differs from the open ocean in several important respects. Its water is somewhat protected from severe conditions of the ocean, particularly wave action. Salinity is similar to that of the ocean at the eastern end (about 30 parts per thousand), but much less salty at the western end (about 20ppt on aver-age). Being largely enclosed, foreign substances that enter it tend to stay within it and con-centrate at the west end, with results that can be both harmful and beneficial. The harmful effects result from input from rivers of toxic industrial wastes, and of fertilizer and other nutrients, which in excessive amounts cause oxygen depletion of the water to occur. How-ever, when these conditions are within tolerable levels, conditions on Long Island Sound can be very good for many bird species.

Birds that feed or rest on the Sound include almost all of the terns, gulls, and water birds that occur in these latitudes of Eastern North America. Probably the most spectacular sight on the Sound is the many thousands of greater scaup that spend the winter on its fertile, shel-tered waters. In addition, by serving as a kind of migration barrier, the Sound greatly en-riches the mix of species that migrate along the coast, over sites such as Hammonasset and Lighthouse Point. Species that are normally missing from the Sound are the birds of the open ocean, such as fulmer, shearwaters, storm petrels and alcids.

Long Island Sound can be seen well from many coastal sites, especially those on peninsulas, such as Sherwood Island, Hammonasset Park and Harkness Park.

Peninsula, like an estuary, is a group of habitats rather than a single type of habitat. It juts out into a body of water (in this context, Long Island Sound), and is surrounded on three sides by water. A peninsula may contain a variety of habitats; often, there is a wetland at the upper end, and a rocky shore at the lower end. There is usually a windy side and a sheltered side, and the habitats on a peninsula are affected by the action of wind, tides and waves.

During the fall migration, peninsulas act as land traps, and often acquire impressive num-bers (and sometimes uncommon species) of migrants that pause on their southward journey before they take flight over Long Island Sound or continue along the coast. In the spring, peninsulas act as a land fall, for migrants that have flown over water and need to pause on land to rest and feed, before they resume their migration.

Peninsulas along the Connecticut coast provide excellent birding, at sites such as Greenwich Point, Hammonasset and Lighthouse Point.

Island is a body of land surrounded by water. There are 143 islands in Long Island Sound near the Connecticut coast, most of which are small and uninhabited. They are of three general types: some have a rocky substrate (such as those in the Thimble Island group), others are formed of glacial till - gravel and cobbles (such as those in the Norwalk Island group), and still others are coastal barrier islands - sandy deposits created and maintained by wave action (such as Griswold Point, which has recently lost its connection to the mainland). Connecticut's smallest islands are barren rocks, while larger ones that have some elevation contain vegetation of shrubs and in some cases coastal forest. Many contain other coastal habitats, such as intertidal zones, marshes, beaches and dunes. Some of the islands formed of glacial till have cobble or "shingle" beaches, relatively uncommon elsewhere in Connecticut. Several of the islands have been given legal protection from development, but many are subject to occasional disturbance from recreational activities.

For birds, the most important aspect of Connecticut's islands is that some of them provide protected, sheltered habitats for nesting. The wooded glacial islands, such as Chimon and Charles, have supported nesting colonies of virtually all of the waders that breed in Connecticut, plus double-crested cormorant (which unfortunately has been taking over some of the rookeries). Islands with open, rocky, gravelly or sandy areas (such as Faulkner's) are being used for nesting by roseate and common terns, gulls, oystercatcher, and piping plover.

Coastal islands that can be seen or visited are discussed in several site descriptions, including the Norwalk Islands, Calf Pasture Beach, Charles Island off Silver Sands Park, and Griswold Point.

Bars are deposits of mud, sand or gravel that lie fairly close to shore. They are formed by the deposition of this material by river currents, tides or waves. They are above water during normal high tides, but may be inundated by high spring or storm tides. Bars are dynamic by nature, and are frequently altered by wave action. High bars usually develop vegetation, and eventually may become islands.

At high tide, bars may become crowded with roosting gulls, terns and shore birds. At low tide, bars are used by a variety of shore birds and waders as a base from which to feed on the contiguous intertidal flat. Bars are also a nesting habitat, but a very perilous one, since they are subject to flooding. Terns and plovers nest on sandy bars, oystercatcher on gravel bars, and gulls and terns on gravel or cobble bars. Milford Point has the most spectacular display of bars in Connecticut. Bluff Point is another good example.

Rocky coast can be the shore of the mainland, of a peninsula or of an island. The eastern section of the Connecticut coast in New London County is almost entirely rocky, but the rocky portions become intermittent as you go west. In Connecticut, rocky coasts are usually composed of broken rocks, rather than cliffs or headlands. Breakwaters and jetties can replicate on a small scale the ecosystems of a rocky coast. The terrestrial portion of a rocky coast is not an important habitat, but the intertidal areas and nearby water provide a wide variety of microhabitats - most are exposed to direct wave action, while some may be relatively sheltered. Aquatic plants typically include seaweeds, rockweeds, Irish moss and algae. Many small animals live here, including killifish and other small fish, crabs, barnacles, limpets, shrimps, mussels, jellyfish, snails and worms.

For birds, the water next to a rocky coast provides an abundant food supply - in a shallow foraging area at high tide, and on exposed rocks at low tide. Because of the rocky substrate, the food in this habitat is on the surface of the rocks, rather than buried in mud or sand, so this habitat does not attract many of the shore birds that probe in soft material for their food. The species that do feed in the rocky intertidal zone include oystercatcher and turnstone in the spring, summer and fall, and purple sandpiper in winter. Species that feed in the water next to a rocky coast include brant, dabbling ducks, red-necked grebe (occasional), all in late fall, winter and early spring. In the rare occasions when they occur in Connecticut, harlequin duck and both eiders use this habitat. During spring, summer and fall, additional species feed here including terns and osprey over the water, egrets and black-crowned night-heron in the intertidal zone. Gulls occur all year.

Sites that have a rocky coast include Hammonasset Beach, Eastern Point, Bluff Point and Harkness Park.

Intertidal flats lie next to the shore between the mean low tide line and the mean high tide line, so that they are covered at high tide, and exposed at low tide. This intertidal zone is typically almost flat and composed of mud, sand, gravel, or cobbles. Such areas are formed by the deposition of material by river currents, tides or waves. (There are also intertidal zones composed of rocks, discussed above under "Rocky Shore", and sloping intertidal zones composed of sand that form the lower part of beaches, discussed below under "Beach".) Intertidal flats are usually contiguous to another coastal habitat - commonly a bar, beach or marsh. Over time, a sheltered mud flat may develop into a low salt marsh. Intertidal flats are the richest of Connecticut's habitats - they teem with invertebrates at all tides, and with small fish at high tide. The species mix of animal life differs in each type of substrate (mud, sand or gravel).

Intertidal flats are an important feeding habitat for a great diversity of birds. Lots of species feed at low tide in all types of intertidal flat, including both yellowlegs, black-bellied plover and dunlin. Waders feed in a few inches of water on any type of flat. Mud flats (with or without shallow water) are preferred by dabbling ducks and the worm feeders among shore birds - both yellowlegs, semipalmated and least sandpipers, and semipalmated plover. Sand flats are preferred by sanderling, and gravel flats by turnstone.

Several coastal sites provide good views of intertidal flats, including Milford Point, Sherwood Island and sites along the west shore of New Haven Harbor.

Beach is a coastal habitat composed of sand, shell fragments, gravel or cobbles. For the purposes of this guide, the beach habitat is defined as lying between the mean low tide line and the line of frontal dunes at the back of the beach. The dynamic, mobile nature of the beach substrate means that beaches are constantly moving and changing from the action of waves and wind. This produces a very unstable habitat, in which there are very few higher plants, and an animal community of little diversity. However, there are many individuals of the few animal species that are adapted to and present in this environment. All of these animals are small, and most are minute. Many of them live in the sloping intertidal zone of beaches that lies between the mean low tide line and the mean high tide line. This area is also known as the "wave wash" zone of the beach, because it is constantly washed by incoming waves. (The lower intertidal zone of a beach may be a flat - a nearly horizontal and sometimes extensive area composed of mud, sand or gravel. Flats are discussed above under "Intertidal flats".) The animals that live in the wave wash zone among the grains of sand include mole crab, ghost shrimp, burrowing worms, snails and a host of other small invertebrates. The upper end of this area is delineated by the tide line - a line of plant and animal material carried in and left by a recent high tide. Above it is the tide wrack, a more substantial line of material that has accumulated over time from higher than average tides. Both of these tide lines are rich rows of compost, within which live multitudes of amphipods, beach fleas and other tiny animals. The upper part of the beach that lies above the tide wrack and extends back to the frontal dunes supports relatively little life, but may have a sparse growth of grasses.

Beaches are primarily a feeding area for birds, to which they come from other nesting or resting habitats. Much of the feeding takes place in the wave wash zone, where a variety of sandpipers, plovers and waders hunt for the prey that abounds in this part of the beach. Much feeding activity also takes place at the tide line and tide wrack, especially if they are fresh. All peeps hunt for invertebrates in the wrack; least sandpiper and turnstone are specialists in this foraging area; crows and grackle come here to scavenge. Piping plover hunts in the tide wrack and also in the higher, dry sand above the wrack. Only a few species nest on the open beach - piping plover, least tern and horned lark nest on the higher part of the beach, above the mean high tide line. Beaches are used for roosting by a number of species.

Many coastal sites have beaches, including Milford Point, Hammonasset, Sherwood Island and Bluff Point.

Dune is a deposition of sand on higher, drier land just behind a beach. Dunes are generally covered by beach grasses and other pioneering plants that serve to hold the sand and stabilize the dune. However, dunes are subject to wind action, and sometimes to tidal and wave action, so that they are quite unstable and even mobile over time. Dunes protect the area behind them, where typically there are shrub thickets, pioneering tree species and often a wetland.

Compared with beaches, dunes are less important for feeding, but more important for nesting. Dune vegetation discourages species of the open beach including most shore birds, but other species depend on the vegetation of dunes for nesting. The principal nesters are horned lark, Savannah sparrow and song sparrow. Also, look in dunes for Ipswich sparrow during winter. Dunes and their vegetation provides both roosting and foraging areas for harrier and short-eared owl.

Sites that have dunes include Hammonasset, Bluff Point and Waterford Beach.

Cove is an indentation on the coast; its water is somewhat protected from wave and wind action of Long Island Sound by surrounding land, but is less protected than a salt pond. The largest coves are usually called harbors or bays. A cove may or may not be fed by a stream and have a current, its water may be salt or brackish, and often there is a low salt marsh at the sheltered upper end. Many coves contain intertidal flats of mud, sand or gravel.

Birds use coves principally as sheltered feeding areas. In late fall, winter and early spring, dabbling ducks feed in coves with shallow water; bay ducks including common goldeneye, bufflehead and greater scaup feed in coves with deeper water. During the spring, summer and fall, waders feed in coves. However, in summer, coves are a less important habitat than at other times of year. Jordan Cove in Waterford is a good example.

Salt pond is a body of salt water that is subject to tidal action, and connected to Long Island Sound by a narrow creek or channel. A salt pond is more sheltered from wind and waves than a cove. Salt ponds are typically fully covered by water during high tide, but at low tide almost the entire area of the pond may be an exposed mud flat. Salt ponds generally are richly supplied with nutrients - by the tides, and in some cases, by a stream entering from inland. As a result, they are highly productive sources of both plant and animal food for birds. Most salt ponds have an abundant supply of crustaceans, molluscs and other inverte-brates; and some are breeding areas for fish. The shores of salt ponds may include almost any type of coastal habitat - low and high salt marsh, beach, shrubby edges, or coastal forest.

Salt ponds are prime feeding and resting areas for waders, shore birds, dabbling ducks, and in some ponds with deeper water, bay ducks as well. Osprey frequently hunts over salt ponds. Depending on the habitats along the shore of the pond, there may also be feeding activity by a variety of land birds. Good examples of salt ponds are: Gulf Pond, Sherwood Millpond at Sherwood Island State Park, and Goshen Cove at Harkness Park.

Low salt water marsh lies just above the mid-tide level, but below the mean high tide level. This position means that its vegetation is immersed in salt water twice each day, and is above the water twice each day. Relatively few plant species are adapted to these harsh conditions, so that low salt marsh vegetation is less diverse than that of brackish or fresh water marshes. The dominant vegetation of a low salt marsh is spartina alterniflora or smooth cordgrass, which grows taller than spartina patens, the dominant plant of a high salt marsh. However, there is great diversity and large numbers of animals present in these marshes, including snails, crabs, periwinkle, mussels, many species of insects and small fish.

Low salt water marshes are a very important feeding area for waders; also for shore birds, if the spartina is not too dense. It is good habitat for clapper rail, if the spartina vegetation is dense. Dabbling ducks and Canada goose also feed here. Seaside and sharp-tailed sparrows both nest and feed in low salt marshes in the higher grassy areas.

Sites that have low salt water marshes include Milford Point (Nells Island), Hammonasset and Great Island.

High salt water marsh lies just above the mean high tide level, so that it is flooded by salt water only by spring tides each month at full moon and new moon, and occasionally by storm tides. The vegetation is somewhat more diverse than that of low salt water marsh. The dominant vegetation is spartina patens, or salt hay, which grows shorter than the spartina alterniflora of low salt water marshes. The vegetation often includes spike grass, black grass, sea lavender and salt marsh aster. Sometimes, a few shrubs also are present. Water some-times collects in shallow depressions, called pannes. As sea water evaporates, the water in a panne becomes increasingly salty. There is abundant animal life in high salt marshes, in the form of myriads of crustaceans, molluscs, and insects. High salt marshes include productive interfaces - with a coastal forest, a low salt water marsh, tidal creeks or ditches.

Birds use this habitat in a variety of ways. Dabbling ducks come in to feed at high tide. Waders also feed here, especially in the pannes which typically have a mud bottom under shallow water. Shore birds also feed in pannes and other areas of high salt marshes - especially black-bellied and American golden plovers, and buff-breasted sandpiper. Waders and shore birds also roost in high salt marshes - almost any species, but especially greater yellowlegs. Some land birds regularly feed here - species such as sharp-tailed and seaside sparrows. The vegetation of high salt marshes is short and dense, and does not attract much nesting activity, but willet is a regular nester. This habitat provides an excellent hunting area for harrier, short-eared owl and other raptors.

The East River Marsh in Guilford is a large high salt water marsh that can be seen well from several points.

Brackish Marsh occurs in the upper portion of coastal estuaries, and a short distance upstream in rivers - situations in which the marsh is inundated partly by salt water, and partly by fresh water. Brackish marshes are typically exposed to a very wide range of salinity - from almost salt water to almost fresh. This variation can be both daily and seasonal. It depends on the amount of sea water brought in by the tides, and the amount of fresh water entering the marsh from inland sources. Typically the fresh water input is high in the spring, and low in late summer. In addition, within a given brackish marsh, there may be a significant positional variation - from more saline in the lower portion to more fresh in the upper portion. Reflecting this, the vegetation in a brackish marsh is often transitional, with spartinas and other salt water species in the lower end, blending in the upper end with fresh water species such as water smartweed, cattails, bulrushes and wild rice. During the winter, brackish marshes are more likely to become ice-covered than salt water marshes, and less likely than fresh water marshes. Brackish marshes have a wide variety of food, in the form of many species of molluscs, crustaceans, other invertebrates, and numerous fish which come to these marshes to breed.

Bird species that occur in brackish marshes include a variety of dabbling ducks and waders, as well as clapper rail (in more saline parts of the marsh), king and Virginia rails, sora, least and American bitterns. In addition, a diversity of land birds feed around the edges of the marsh.

Brackish marshes in Connecticut lie in a narrow band in the lower sections of tidal rivers. Lord Cove is a good example - Great Island just downstream is a salt water tidal marsh, and Selden Cove just upstream is a fresh water tidal marsh.

Tidal Creek is a flowing body of water that is subject to tidal action and is highly variable. Some creeks are all tidal; others are coastal extensions of inland streams; therefore they may be highly saline, or somewhat fresh. Some tidal creeks are shallow, while others are very deep at high tide - especially those along the western Connecticut coast where the tide range is greatest. The current in tidal creeks can be mild, or strong and swift. Some creeks are almost dry at low tide, while others maintain a flow of water; the banks are often steep and muddy. Most have intertidal areas that are exposed at low tide. There are also lots of variables along the shore - tidal creeks frequently flow through high or low salt marshes, but the shores can also be shrubs or coastal forest. All of these variables - of the creek itself and its shore - influence the type of use of the creek by birds, and the species that use it. But almost all tidal creeks are important avian feeding habitats; although the creek itself usually has little vegetation, it supports lots of invertebrate animals and fish - over 60 species of fish, of which the more common are killifish, silversides and sticklebacks.

A wide variety of bird species feed at tidal creeks. When there is deeper water in the creek, canvasback and goldeneye feed on invertebrates, and red-breasted merganser hunts fish.

When the water is shallower, dabbling ducks come in. Waders feed along the shore at any level. Lots of shore bird species feed in creeks that have exposed mud at low tide. Terns and osprey also hunt tidal creeks from the air overhead.

Sites that have tidal creeks include Milford Point (Nells Island at Court Street), Sherwood Island and Barn Island.

Edge can occur at the interface of almost any combination of the coastal habitat types. In the coastal context, typically an edge occurs between a marsh, tidal pond or tidal creek and some type of upland habitat. The edge may be the wooded edge of a coastal forest, but most often it is composed largely of shrubs. Coastal edges are usually dense, and often include greenbrier, poison ivy and other salt-tolerant shrubs. The upland edge of a salt marsh typically also includes herbaceous vegetation such as switch grass, phragmites, sea myrtle and seaside goldenrod.

Shrubby coastal edges are very important to land birds - for cover, nesting and feeding. In the fall and winter, shrubby edges along the coast are important because they provide food and shelter in a mild climate for species such as towhee, winter wren and various sparrows. Wooded coastal edges are also a food source - primarily of insects and other small invertebrates in spring and summer. Wooded edges of coastal habitats also provide nest sites for a variety of land birds. The species of nesting land birds depends on the vegetative composition. In general, the number and diversity of nesting species that use coastal edges is less than at comparable inland edges; however, there still are a fair number of species that nest at coastal edges. Black-crowned night heron is one such species - it typically nests in wooded edges that overlook a tidal wetland.

Coastal forest is a woodland that is right on the shoreline, or is separated from the shoreline by some other type of coastal habitat - often a salt water marsh. In addition, a coastal forest may be on an island in Long Island Sound. In any of these positions, coastal forests are subject to coastal climate conditions, including wind and salt air. They are composed mainly of hardwoods - principally oaks, cherries and sassafras, and may also include scattered red cedar and pitch pine. Usually there are lots of dead and wind-damaged trees in the forest, and many fallen trees and limbs on the ground. There usually is a dense shrub layer, characterized by vine tangles and thickets that include greenbrier. Coastal forests have a good variety of food for birds.

Coastal forests get a good general diversity of land bird migrants - especially in the fall, and especially if the forest is on a peninsula. Nesters include white-eyed vireo and lots of standard forest species. There is also the potential for nesting by waders; black-crowned night-heron is the most likely. If the forest is on an island, other possible nesters include snowy and great egrets, little blue heron and yellow-crowned night-heron. Because of the mild climate and abundance of food-bearing shrubs, a variety of land bird species such as winter wren and hermit thrush stay through the winter.

One of the best examples of a coastal forest is at Salt Meadow.

Factors That Affect Birds' Use of Coastal Habitats

Location in Connecticut. As you go west along the coast, the tides become greater, the intertidal zones larger, the tidal creeks deeper.

Land form effect. Several land forms contribute to good birding at the coast. First, the coast itself is a major migration route. The major river valleys that intersect with the coast are also migration routes, and the intersections are especially productive during migration. The estuaries at these intersections provide rich habitats in symbiotic clusters. Peninsulas on the coast act as migration land traps in the fall and land falls in the spring.

Size is important to minimize the effect of disturbance from the intense recreational activity that occurs along the coast especially during the nesting season. Also, the larger the habitat, the more diversity and quantity it offers in the way of food and cover.

Water depth influences the species of water birds that use coastal wetlands.

Birding at Coastal Habitats

There is no down time for birders at the coast. Pick your sites right, and you will have good birding throughout the year. The birding at coastal sites during the spring and fall migrations is superb. In summer, you need to avoid sites that get crowded, such as coastal beaches, but you have lots of good alternatives, since most of the birding action during the summer is behind the beaches in marshes and other habitats that don't get crowded. Winter, for many birders, is the high season at the coast - at a time when inland areas are pretty quiet. Severity of winter weather at coastal sites is the only negative; pick your trip days carefully.

Water birds - migrants or winter visitors - are present all year, but the greatest diversity and number occur from September through May, and especially from November through April. Focus on Long Island Sound, coves and tidal creeks. Ducks feed in marshes at high tide, especially spring tides. In summer there is less activity - but there are some nesters in the marshes, especially black duck and gadwall.

Marsh birds pass through or arrive to nest starting in early April. Most nesting occurs during the period May-July. In August the greatest number and diversity of marsh birds are present, as young of the year are joined by post-breeding wanderers. The action starts to taper off in September.

The shore bird northward migration is compressed - it starts late in March with the arrival of a few early migrants. The peak runs from late April to early June, after which the activity tapers off. The southward migration is spread out over a longer period; adults and males of some species tend to pass through first, followed later by juveniles and females. July is inconsistent, but in mid-July the numbers start to build. August is the peak of the "fall" migration, and it diminishes in September. In October and even into November there are still a few of the later migrants. But don't stop looking for shore birds in winter; this is the best time to find dunlin and sanderling, and the only time to find purple sandpiper.

Looking for land birds on the coast can be rewarding. Many migrants follow the coast, in both spring and fall. Depending on the species, look in coastal forests, edges or open habitats. Nesting osprey and sparrows can be found in marshes from May through August. The fall hawk migration at sites on or near the coast can be spectacular, and is more reliable than at inland sites. In winter, look in open habitats for ground feeders such as horned lark, snow bunting and Lapland longspur, and for raptors, including short-eared owl and rough-legged hawk.

Birding by the tides. Birding effectively in tidal habitats on the Connecticut coast requires that you make a plan that takes the tides into account in deciding when and where you will go.

Long Island Sound is a large estuary; incoming tides enter it at the eastern end near Stonington, and flow westward toward Greenwich. It takes about two and a half hours for a given tide stage to travel the length of the Connecticut coast. In addition, it takes more than an hour for the tide to travel from the estuary of the Connecticut River at Saybrook Point upstream to some of the sites along the lower Connecticut River. Each high tide is followed in about six hours and twelve minutes by the next low tide, which is followed in about six hours and twelve minutes by the next high tide. In order to determine tide times at sites along the coast and on the lower Connecticut River, refer to Table 1: "Tide Times in Connecticut".

As tides travel westward in Long Island Sound, the tidal range (the difference in height between mean low tide and mean high tide) increases, from an average of about two and a half feet at Stonington at the eastern end of the coast, to about seven and a half feet at Greenwich at the western end. Twice each month, during the periods of full moon and new moon, high tides are higher and low tides are lower than average (these are called "spring tides").

Water birds, marsh birds and shore birds time their periods of feeding and roosting with the tides; effective birding strategies are based on this timing. The birding can be rewarding at any tide stage, if you are at the right site and habitat for that tide stage.

Low tide, when intertidal areas are exposed, is feeding time for most waders, rails and shore birds. Dabbling ducks also move in to feed on the exposed intertidal zone or in nearby shallow water. However, at very large intertidal areas, at dead low tide, birds that are feeding may be too far away from shore for you to see them well, unless you have a scope. Sites that have visible intertidal areas include Milford Point (mud, sand and gravel flats), and Sandy Point (sand and mud flats).

High tide, when the intertidal feeding areas are covered by water, is roosting or resting time for many waders and shore birds. Many of these species rest in concentrated groups on gravel bars or sand spits, while others go to high salt marshes. In winter, deep water species of water birds are apt to be closer to shore at high tide. Sites in which gravel bars, sand spit and high salt marsh can be seen well include Milford Point (gravel bars, sand spit), and Great Harbor (high salt marsh).

Falling tide can be an excellent time to look for waders and shore birds. The birds are hungry, and come to the first appropriate intertidal areas that are exposed, which may be quite close to you if you have positioned yourself well. As the tide continues to fall, the birds may move farther away or go to other better areas.

Rising tide can also be a good time to look for waders and shore birds, because the rising tide forces them to move closer to where you can see them well. Also, they begin to move to roosting areas where you can watch them arrive, especially at sites where the feeding areas are close to sand spits or gravel bars used for roosting, as is the case at Milford Point and Sandy Point.

Boating in tidal waters requires careful timing, to avoid getting stranded by an adverse tide. Check tide times using a newspaper or tide table, together with Table 1: "Tide Times in Connecticut".

TABLE 1: TIDE TIMES IN CONNECTICUT

The tables that follow show the average tide time intervals for points along the Connecticut coast, and are roughly correct for either high tide or low tide. To determine when a given tide stage will reach a point on the coast, first determine the tide times for some known location along the coast. Most daily newspapers carry tide information for the current day in the weather section; many marinas along the coast provide tide tables for the current year. Typically, information is given for high tide at New London or Bridgeport - low tide occurs about six hours and twelve minutes later. Then, from the table below, determine the time difference between the location given in the newspaper or tide table and the location you plan to visit. For example: you plan to visit Milford Point, and the newspaper gives times for New London. From the table below, you can determine that a given stage of the tide will occur one hour forty minutes later at Milford Point than at New London (two hours fifteen minutes munus thirty five minutes equals one hour forty minutes). For coastal sites that are between the locations on the table, tide times can be estimated.

Locations (from east to west)	Time difference (fr Stonington)
New London County	
Stonington	0:00
New London	0:35
Middlesex County	
Saybrook Point	1:35
New Haven County	
Madison	2:05
Guilford	2:05
Branford	2:15
New Haven	2:15
Milford	2:15
Fairfield County	
Stratford	2:20
Bridgeport	2:25
Fairfield	2:25
Stamford	2:30
Greenwich	2:25

To determine when a given tide stage will reach a point along the lower Connecticut River, first determine the tide time at Saybrook Point (the Saybrook Jetty). Then add the indicated time intervals for the locations on the table, for both rising and falling tides. These times differences are not exact, and vary with other variable factors, primarily the velocity of current in the river.

Locations	Time Difference (fr Saybrook Point)
New London County	
Old Lyme (NL Cty): Great Island Area	0:10
Old Lyme (NL Cty): Lieutenant River	0:20
Lyme (NL Cty): Lords Cove	0:45
Deep River (MI Cty): Pratt Cove	1:30
Chester (MI Cty): Chester Creek	1:35
Lyme (NL Cty): Selden Cove / Creek	1:35
Lyme (NL Cty): Whalebone Creek	1:40
Lyme / Chester (NL / MI Cty): Chester / Hadlyme Ferry	1:40
East Haddam (MI Cty): Chapman Pond	2:00

OTHER TYPES OF HABITAT

The "Other" habitat category includes other physical features, some of which may not be habitats in the usual sense, but which have some significance for birds. Some of these are natural, and others are man-made structures of some kind.

Cliffs and ledges. This habitat consists of exposed bedrock, usually with a face that is near vertical, and often includes ledges, caves and outcroppings. Often, there is a talus slope at the base. Cliffs and ledges usually have very little food for birds, but are important as nest sites for birds that specialize in this habitat type. Fourteen species occur here, of which eight nest here, including turkey vulture and raven for which this is the principal nesting habitat. Cliff and rough-winged swallows nest in nooks in the rock face, phoebe on small ledges, and, in northern Connecticut, junco on herb-covered ledges.

Areas of sand or gravel are usually the result of excavation; may be a pit, mound or hillside, may contain water or be dry, may be bare or have vegetation, may be steep-sided or gently sloping. Sixty-six species of birds occur in such areas, of which 64 feed and 32 nest - the species mix depends on the characteristics of the area. If such areas have shrub growth, the open air above them provides flying insects for aerial feeders. Such areas provide nest sites for a limited number of species that are specialists in using this type of habitat: kingfisher and bank swallow excavate burrows in steep banks, which are later used by rough-winged swallow. Exposed tree roots attract phoebe.

Dams, spillways, drainpipes, bridges: used for nesting by rough-winged swallow (in drain-pipes), by barn swallow, cliff swallow and phoebe (on beams and girders of dams and bridges). Spotted sandpiper feeds on dam spillways. Dams often make good watching sites for hawks and other migrants during the spring and fall.

Mountain tops with or without observation towers, or farmland hilltops often make good watching sites for hawks and other migrants during the spring and fall.

Buildings, silos, water towers and similar structures especially if abandoned provide nesting sites for such species as barn owl, kestrel, barn and cliff swallows, purple martin and phoebe, especially if abandoned.

Nesting boxes, nesting platforms: boxes are often used by such species as bluebird, tree swallow, wood duck and kestrel, depending on the design. Platforms are used by osprey.

Breakwaters, piers, docks and navigation aids provide places on which to roost, or along which to forage, for species that are present in nearby habitats, including gulls, cormorants and a variety of other species.

Chapter 3

Finding Uncommon Birds in Connecticut

FINDING UNCOMMON BIRDS IN CONNECTICUT

A number of bird species occur in Connecticut on a regular basis, but their occurrence is not necessarily widespread or common. Some are restricted by habitat, others by seasonal times of occurrence, and still others by both of these factors. If you know exactly where and when to go, you have a good chance of seeing these birds, but you are not as likely to find them if you look elsewhere. Such species are listed below, together with the sites and times at which they are most likely to occur, and habitats in which they are most likely to occur at the sites that are listed.

The list does not include species that are very irregular in their occurrence (for news of their presence in Connecticut stay in touch with the Connecticut Rare Bird Alert), or species that are quite widespread, and can be found at a large number of sites.

All sites on the list are included and described in this guide. Refer to the "Index of Sites by Site Name" to locate the description of the site. For each species, sites are listed in order of probability of occurrence.

Red-throated Loon, Horned Grebe, Great Cormorant
Habitats: Long Island Sound; major river estuaries.
Sites: Hammonasset, western New Haven Harbor, Milford Point, Sherwood Island, Saybrook Point.
Times: late November through mid-April.

Common Loon
Habitats: Long Island Sound, large inland lakes.
Sites and times: Hammonasset, western New Haven Harbor, Sherwood Island, late November to mid-April; Nepaug Reservoir, April; Bantam Lake, November.

Pied-billed Grebe
Habitats: lake (cove), pond.
Sites: White Memorial (Bantam Lake, Cemetery Pond).
Times: early September-late November.

Northern Gannet
Habitats: Long Island Sound, well offshore.
Sites: Hammonasset, Harkness Memorial Park.
Times: late October-late November.

American Bittern
Habitats: high salt marsh, fresh water tidal marsh, cattail and mixed herbaceous marsh.
Sites and times: Hammonasset, Great Island, October-November; White Memorial (Mallard Marsh and Little Pond), April-May.

Least Bittern
Habitats: cattail marsh.
Sites: Station 43.
Times: May-June.

Little Blue Heron
Habitats: high and low salt marsh, in creek edges and salt pannes.
Sites: Manresa, Sherwood Island, Bluff Point.
Times: May-August (especially May).

Black-crowned Night Heron
Habitats: high and low salt marshes, along tidal creeks, on edge of salt ponds, perched in trees of coastal forest.
Sites: Milford Point (Nells Island), Sherwood Island, Oyster River Marsh, Sandy Point, Great Harbor, Gulf Pond, Manresa.
Times: early May-late September.

Yellow-crowned Night Heron
Habitats: high and low salt marshes, along tidal creeks, on edge of salt ponds, perched in trees of coastal forest.
Sites: Milford Point (Nells Island), Gulf Pond, Manresa, Sherwood Island.
Times: early May-late September.

Glossy Ibis
Habitats: high salt marsh, coastal island.
Sites: Manresa, Sherwood Island, Silver Sands Beach (Charles Island), Hammonasset, Plum Bank Marsh, Great Island, Barn Island.
Times: late April-late August.

Snow Goose
Habitats: on water of lakes and ponds; overhead along coast and over major river valleys; in tilled (corn) fields.
Sites and times: on water at White Memorial (Bantam Lake) and Southbury Training School Pond, March-April and October-November; in flight over Station 43, April and October; over Lighthouse Point, October; in corn fields at Horse Barn Hill, March-April, October-November.

Brant
Habitats: Long Island Sound off rocky shore, on gravel bars, in high salt marshes.
Sites: Sherwood Island, Milford Point, Middle Beach, Hammonasset, Eastern Point, Avery Point, Sandy Point.
Times: November-April.

Green-winged Teal
Habitats: salt and brackish ponds, tidal creeks, mud flats, fresh ponds, cattail marshes.
Sites: Gulf Pond, Milford Point, Watch Rock (Great Island), White Memorial (Cemetery Pond, Bantam Lake).
Times: September-November, March-April.

Northern Pintail
Habitats: salt ponds, tidal creeks, brackish coves; fresh lakes and ponds, marshy edges.
Sites and times: Old Saybrook South Cove, Milford Point, Gulf Pond, November-March; White Memorial (Bantam Lake, Cemetery Pond), September-late November, late March to mid-April.

Blue-winged Teal
Habitats: fresh water pond close to marshy edge; cattail marsh.
Sites: White Memorial (Cemetery Pond, Little Pond).
Times: mid-August to mid-September.

Northern Shoveler
Habitats: tidal creeks, mud flats within high or low salt marshes; fresh water lakes and ponds with marshy edges.

Sites: Milford Point (Nells Island), White Memorial (Bantam Lake, Cemetery Pond).
Times: September-November, March-April.

Gadwall
Habitats: tidal creeks, high and low salt marshes, brackish marsh, fresh water tidal marsh, cove, salt pond, Long Island Sound.
Sites: Oyster River, western New Haven Harbor, Milford Point (Nells Island), Gulf Pond, Great Island, South Cove, Sherwood Island (Mill Pond).
Times: October-November and March-April are best; all other months possible.

Eurasian Wigeon
Habitats: Long Island Sound offshore from rocky coast, gravel and cobble beaches, cove, tidal creek.
Sites: western New Haven Harbor from Oyster River through West Haven.
Times: late November-late March.

American Wigeon
Habitats: wide range of coastal habitats; inland on lakes and ponds along marshy shores.
Sites and times: western New Haven Harbor from Oyster River through West Haven, plus Milford Point, Gulf Pond, Great Island, South Cove, early September-end of April; White Memorial (Bantam Lake, Cemetery Pond), September-November, March-April.

Canvasback
Habitats: coastal coves, tidal rivers, salt ponds, tidal creeks, high salt marshes at high tide; inland lakes and coves;
Sites: Milford Point (Nells Island), Frash Pond, Gulf Pond, West River, South Cove; White Memorial (Bantam Lake).
Times: coastal: November-March; inland: November and March.

Redhead
Habitats: tidal river.
Sites: West River.
Times: November-March.

Greater Scaup
Habitats: Long Island Sound, coastal harbors and coves.
Sites: New Haven Harbor, South Cove, Milford Point.
Times: early November-late March.

Lesser Scaup
Habitats: coastal rivers and coves, fresh water lakes, ponds and rivers.
Sites and Times: West River, lower Connecticut River, November-late March; White Memorial (Bantam Lake), November and March.

Oldsquaw
Habitats: Long Island Sound.
Sites: Hammonasset, Milford Point, Gulf Beach, Silver Sands, Sherwood Island, western New Haven Harbor.
Times: November-March.

Surf Scoter, Black Scoter, White-winged Scoter
Habitats: Long Island Sound.
Sites: Middle Beach, Hammonasset, western New Haven Harbor, Sherwood Island.
Times: November-March.

Barrow's Goldeneye
Habitats: fast water of river.
Sites: Kings Island (Enfield Rapids).
Times: January-February.

Hooded Merganser
Habitats: various inland river, pond and lake habitats, in open water or along shore.
Sites and times: White Memorial (Bantam Lake), Shepaug Dam/River Road, November and March; Mystic River, November-March.

Ruddy Duck
Habitats: lake, cove.
Sites: White Memorial (Bantam Lake)
Times: November-December.

Black Vulture
Habitats: tilled and short grass fields.
Sites: Sunny Valley.
Times: all year.

Osprey
Habitats: high and low salt marsh, tidal creeks, rivers, coves, salt and fresh water ponds, Long Island Sound.
Sites and times: Great Island and other marshes along the central and eastern Connecticut coast April-September; Lighthouse Point September-October.

Bald Eagle
Habitats: open water of rivers and lakes with wooded shores.
Sites: Shepaug Dam, Connecticut River (especially sites in East Haddam, Chester, Deep River and Essex.
Times: December-March.

Northern Harrier
Habitats: high and low salt marsh, open fields.
Sites and times: Hammonasset and Great Island, October-April; Milford Point (Nells Island) and Great Meadows, September-April; Lighthouse Point, October-November.

Sharp-shinned and Cooper's Hawks
Habitats: coastal habitats.
Sites: Lighthouse Point, Hammonasset.
Times: September-November.

Northern Goshawk
Habitats: hardwoods/hemlock and hardwoods/white pine forests.
Sites: White Memorial, Mohawk State Forest, American Legion State Forest, Steep Rock Reservation.
Times: April-July

Red-shouldered Hawk
Habitats: hardwoods/hemlock forest.
Sites and Times: Sunnybrook Park, April-September; Shepaug Dam and George C. Waldo Park, March-September.

Rough-legged Hawk
Habitats: low and high salt marshes, short grass fields.
Sites: Great Island, Essex Steamboat Dock, Silver Sands State Park.
Times: January-February.

Golden Eagle
Habitats: flying, often near rocky outcrops, ledges;
Sites and Times: Canaan Mountain, December-March; Quaker Ridge, October-November.

Merlin
Habitats: open coastal habitats.
Sites: Lighthouse Point, Haley Farm, Bluff Point, Hammonasset.
Times: October-November.

Peregrine Falcon
Habitats: open coastal habitats.
Sites: Lighthouse Point, Milford Point, Hammonasset.
Times: October-November

Bobwhite
Habitats: shrubby fields.
Sites: Haley Farm, Bluff Point, Barn Island, Flaherty Field Trial Area, Nod Brook WMA.
Times: all year.

Clapper Rail
Habitats: low and high salt marshes, edges of tidal creeks, intertidal mud flats.
Sites: Milford Point (Nells Island), Gulf Pond, Great Island, Barn Island, Sherwood Island, Sandy Point, Hammonasset.
Times: April-November.

King Rail
Habitats: brackish or salt marshes, especially at interface of low and high marsh; fresh water marshes with mixture of cattail, sedge and mixed herbaceous vegetation.
Sites: White Memorial (Mallard Marsh), Durham Meadows.
Times: May/June.

Virginia Rail
Habitats: cattail and mixed herbaceous marshes.
Sites: White Memorial (Mallard Marsh, Little Pond, Cranberry Pond), Station 43.
Times: April-late September.

Sora
Habitats: cattail and mixed herbaceous marshes.
Sites: White Memorial (Mallard Marsh, Little Pond).
Times: May-late September, dawn and evening.

Common Moorhen
Habitats: ponds bordered by cattail marsh.
Sites and times: Roy Swamp (May); White Memorial (Cemetery Pond, Little Pond (August-September).

American Coot
Habitats: pond, cove of lake.
Sites and times: White Memorial (Bantam Lake), October until freeze-up, and ice-out through March; Lake Zoar, November-March.

American Golden Plover
Habitats: coastal short grass fields, seasonal pools, high salt marsh, gravel bar, sand bar.
Sites: Hammonasset, Milford Point and Nells Island.
Times: September-November.

Piping Plover
Habitats: sandy beach, dunes, gravel bar.
Sites: Milford Point, Short Beach, Long Beach, Sandy Point.
Times: April-August.

American Oystercatcher
Habitats: rocky shore, breakwater, gravel bar, sandy, gravel or cobble beach, high salt marsh.
Sites: Bluff Point, Milford Point, Hammonasset, Stonington Point.
Times: April-October; August is best.

Willet
Habitats: high salt marsh, low salt marsh, edges of tidal creeks, intertidal mud flats, gravel bars.
Sites: Hammonasset, Milford Point and Nells Island, Hammock River Marsh, Barn Island, Great Island, East River Marsh.
Times: April-September.

Whimbrel
Habitats: high salt marsh, gravel bar.
Sites: Hammonasset, Milford Point, Barn Island, Great Island.
Times: August-September.

Red Knot
Habitats: gravel bar.
Sites: Milford Point.
Times: August.

Western Sandpiper
Habitats: gravel bar, sand or gravel beach, intertidal mud flat.
Sites: Milford Point.
Times: August.

White-rumped Sandpiper
Habitats: gravel bar, sand or gravel beach, intertidal mud flat.
Sites: Milford Point.
Times: August-September.

Pectoral Sandpiper
Habitats, sites and times: seasonal pools in short grass field, pannes in high salt marsh: Hammonasset, April-May, August-September; beach, gravel bar: Milford Point, August-September.

Purple Sandpiper
Habitats: rocky coast, breakwater.
Sites: Avery Point, Eastern Point, Middle Beach.
Times: December-March.

Common Snipe
Habitats: wet meadow.
Sites and times: Wangunk Meadows in Portland, April; Horse Barn Hill (Ibis Swale), April, October-November.

American Woodcock
Habitats: short grass, mixed herbaceous and shrubby fields, shrubby edges of wetlands.
Sites: White Memorial (Little Pond, field by Museum, Apple Hill), Enders State Forest, Horse Barn Hill and UConn Parking Lot W.
Times: March-April, sunset to dark.

Bonaparte's Gull
Habitats: coves of Long Island Sound.
Sites: South Cove, Oyster River, Hammonasset.
Times: March-April.

Roseate Tern
Habitats: gravel bar.
Sites: Milford Point.
Times: August.

Forster's Tern
Habitats: gravel bar, high salt marsh, tidal creeks.
Sites: Milford Point and Nells Island.
Times: August.

Least Tern
Habitats: sandy beach, gravel bar.
Sites: Milford Point, Sandy Point.
Times: May-August.

Black Tern
Habitats: gravel bar, high salt marsh, tidal creeks.
Sites: Milford Point, Harkness.
Times: August-September.

Black Skimmer
Habitats: gravel bar, tidal creeks, Long Island Sound.
Sites: Milford Point.
Times: August.

Monk Parakeet
Habitats: groves of conifers or deciduous trees.
Sites: Milford Point (Court Street).
Times: all year.

Screech Owl
Habitats: groves of hardwoods, especially near wetlands and rivers.
Sites: widespread; boat launch by Kings Island; Wangunk Meadows, Glastonbury, White Memorial (South Lake Street by Little Pond), Ferry Park.
Times: October-May; March is best.

Great Horned Owl
Habitats: variety of mature hardwood and evergreen forests, especially those adjacent to open terrestrial or wetland habitats.
Sites: widespread; White Memorial (anywhere, but especially near Museum), Fenton River near Pumping Station Road/back of Horse Barn Hill, Northeast Audubon Center, Talcott Mountain Reservoirs # 1 and 6, Hammonasset.
Times: vocal October-May, January-March is best.

Barred Owl
Habitats: hardwoods/hemlock swamp, hardwoods/hemlock forest, hardwoods/white pine forest.
Sites: White Memorial (Duck Pond near Bissell Road), Tunxis State Forest and Barkhamsted Reservoir (along Routes 20 and 181), Fenton River (along Old Turnpike Road and Nipmuck Trail), Mohawk State Forest, Roaring Brook Nature Center.
Times: vocal February-July.

Long-eared Owl
Habitats: groves of cedars.
Sites: Hammonasset, Greenwich Point.
Times: November-February.

Short-eared Owl
Habitats: marshes and other open coastal areas.
Sites: Hammonasset, Great Island, Great Meadows, Milford Point.
Times: November-March.

Saw-whet Owl
Habitats: cedars, mixed conifer (spruces) forest, hemlock forest, hemlock swamp.
Sites: Hammonasset, Greenwich Point, Waldo State Park, Colonial Park, Sperry Sanctuary.
Times: November-March.

Common Nighthawk
Habitats: feeds over water bodies, open wetlands, open terrestrial habitats, city streets.
Sites: White Memorial (Little Pond and Mallard Marsh), Farmington Meadows, Station 43.
Times: May and August, sunrise and sunset.

Whip-poor-will
Habitats: shrubby fields, edges of hardwoods, hardwoods/white pine, or sand plain forests.
Sites: Scoville Road, Blue Swamp.
Times: Evenings in May.

Red-headed Woodpecker
Habitats: hardwoods forests, hardwood swamps.
Sites and times: Stanley Quarter Park, calling during May-July; Lighthouse Point and Hammonasset, migrant fly-by during October.

Yellow-bellied Sapsucker
Habitats: hardwoods forests, hardwoods swamps, wooded streambelts.
Sites: Mohawk State Forest, Miles Sanctuary (including Eggleston Road), White Memorial (Five Pond Natural Area), Tunxis/Peoples/American Legion State Forests, Sunnybrook State Park, John A. Minetto State Park.
Times: April-July.

Acadian Flycatcher
Habitats: hemlock ravine.
Sites: River Road in Kent, Northeast Audubon Center, Devil's Hopyard State Park.
Times: May-June.

Alder and Willow Flycatchers
Habitats: shrub marsh; willow flycatcher prefers willows and drier areas, alder flycatcher prefers alders and wetter areas.
Sites: White Memorial (Little Pond, Cranberry Pond), Lower Greenwoods Recreation Area, Miles Sanctuary/Roy Swamp.
Times: May-June.

Horned Lark
Habitats: short grass field, tilled field (especially when manured), sandy beach, dunes.
Sites: Hammonasset, Horse Barn Hill, UConn Parking Lot W, Milford Point, Sherwood Island, Sandy Point, Short Beach, Farmington Meadows, Station 43.
Times: October-April.

Purple Martin
Habitats: around martin houses in open terrestrial and high salt marsh habitats.
Sites: Hammonasset, Barn Island, Milford Point (Nells Island).
Times: May-July.

Rough-winged Swallow
Habitats: drain pipes at dams; bridges.
Sites: Shepaug Dam, Talcott Mountain Reservoir #1, Nepaug Reservoir.
Times: May-July.

Bank Swallow
Habitats: steep embankments, gravel pits; feeding over lakes, ponds and rivers.
Sites: Lower Greenwoods Recreation Area, Shepaug Dam, White Memorial (feeding over Little Pond, Cemetery Pond), Station 43.
Times: May-early August.

Cliff Swallow
Habitats: bridges, dams.
Sites: Shepaug Dam, River Road in Kent, Colebrook River Reservoir Dam.
Times: May-early August.

Fish Crow
Habitats: all coastal habitats; white pine forests, short grass fields, lakes and ponds; shores and overhead at rivers.
Sites: western New Haven Harbor, Sherwood Island, Milford Point (Court Street), Talcott Mountain Reservoir #1, Bantam Lake.
Times: all year.

Common Raven
Habitats: cliffs and ledges, flying over most other inland habitats.
Sites: Canaan Mountain (from Route 63, Undermountain Road and Cobble Road), Barkhamsted Reservoir (Route 20 overlook, Saville Dam and along Route 181), Miles Sanctuary (Eggleston Road, West Cornwall Road), Upper and Lower Greenwoods Recreation Areas.
Times: all year.

Red-breasted Nuthatch
Habitats: white pine, hemlock, mixed conifer forests.
Sites: White Memorial (everywhere, but easiest to see at feeder by Museum), Tunxis/American Legion/Peoples State Forests, Nepaug Reservoir, Nepaug State Forest, McLean Game Refuge, Mohawk State Forest.
Times: all year.

Brown Creeper
Habitats: white pine, hardwoods/white pine and hardwoods/hemlock forests.
Sites: White Memorial, Tunxis/American Legion/Peoples State Forests, Nepaug Reservoir, Nepaug State Forest.
Times: all year.

Winter Wren
Habitats: hemlock forest, hemlock ravine, rocky slope.
Sites: Mohawk State Forest, Tunxis/American Legion/Peoples State Forests, River Road in Kent, White Memorial (Five Pond Natural Area), Northeast Audubon Center.
Times: sings late April-June.

Marsh Wren
Habitats: cattail and mixed herbaceous marshes, fresh water marshes, tidal, brackish and high salt marshes.
Sites: White Memorial (Little Pond, Mallard Marsh, Cemetery Pond), Great Island, Great Meadows.
Times: May-September.

Swainson's Thrush
Habitats: hardwoods/hemlock and hardwoods/white pine forests.
Sites: River Road in Kent, White Memorial, Mohawk State Forest, American Legion/Peoples State Forests.
Times: May.

Brown Thrasher
Habitats: shrubby fields and edges.
Sites: Shepaug Dam, Upper Greenwoods Recreation Area, White Memorial (Apple Hill), Talcott Mountain Reservoir Area.
Times: May-August.

American Pipit
Habitats: tilled field, short grass field, sandy beach.
Sites: Station 43 (Vibert Road), UConn Parking Lot W, Horse Barn Hill, Hammonasset, Milford Point, Farmington Meadows, Fisher Meadow Park.
Times: October-November, late March-April; October is best.

Northern Shrike
Habitats: interfaces - open habitats (especially shrubby field and shrub marsh) with edges that have perch sites.
Sites: Lyman Orchards, Durham Meadows, Station 43.
Times: November-February.

White-eyed Vireo
Habitats: shrubby field, shrub marsh, shrubby edge.
Sites: Haley Farm, Bluff Point, Kellogg Environmental Center/Osborndale State Park.
Times: May-July.

Golden-winged Warbler
Habitats: shrubby field, especially with cedars, shrub marsh and shrub swamp.
Sites: River Road in Canaan/Cornwall; River Road in Kent, Miles Sanctuary.
Times: May-June.

Black-throated Blue Warbler
Habitats: mountain laurel in any forest habitat in NW or NE CT.
Sites: Mohawk State Forest, Tunxis/American Legion/Peoples State Forests, Mt. Riga, Nipmuck State Forest (Laurel Sanctuary), Enders State Forest, Sunnybrook State Park.
Times: May-July.

Blackburnian Warbler
Habitats: white pine/hemlock forest.
Sites: White Memorial (Museum area, Catlin Woods), Tunxis/American Legion/Peoples State Forests, McLean Game Refuge, Nepaug Reservoir and State Forest.
Times: May-July.

Yellow-throated Warbler
Habitats: riparian forest (sycamores) interface with white pine and mixed conifers.
Sites and times: River Road in Kent (May-June, nesting), East Rock Park (late April, migrating).

Cerulean Warbler
Habitats: riparian forest, hardwoods streambelt.
Sites: River Road in Kent, Stanley WMA Northern Block, Devil's Hopyard State Park, Gillette Castle State Park.
Times: May.

Worm-eating Warbler
Habitats: nests on rocky slopes in hardwoods or hardwoods/hemlock forests (same habitat as copperheads!), family groups at same habitats or at base of slope in shrub swamp or shrubby hardwood swamp.
Sites: Devil's Den, River Road in Kent, Talcott Mountain Reservoirs #1 and #6.
Times: May-July.

Northern Waterthrush
Habitats: shrubby hardwood swamp, shrubby hardwood/hemlock swamp.
Sites: White Memorial (Duck Pond area, other wetlands), Boston Hollow.
Times: May-June.

Kentucky Warbler
Habitats: young hardwoods with dense understory, interspersed with more open areas.

Sites: Fairchild Garden.
Times: May-June.

Hooded Warbler
Habitats: mountain laurel, sweet pepperbush, rhododendron or greenbrier in shrubby hardwood swamp or hardwoods forest.
Sites: Putnam Memorial State Park, Naugatuck State Forest, Hartman Park.
Times: May-June.

Canada Warbler
Habitats: mountain laurel in a forest (hardwoods/white pine or hardwoods/hemlock) or in a swamp (shrubby hardwood swamp, hardwoods or hemlock swamp).
Sites: Tunxis/American Legion/Peoples State Forests, Mohawk State Forest, White Memorial (Duck Pond, Cranberry Pond), Mt. Riga, Nepaug State Forest.
Times: May-July.

Yellow-breasted Chat
Habitats: shrubby field.
Sites: Haley Farm, Bluff Point, Barn Island.
Times: May-June.

Vesper Sparrow
Habitats: interface of tilled and mixed herbaceous fields.
Sites: UConn Parking Lot W (gardens), Horse Barn Hill, Hammonasset, Lighthouse Point, Station 43.
Times: April-May, October-November (April and October are best).

Savannah Sparrow
Habitats: short grass, tall grass and mixed herbaceous fields, shrubby edges.
Sites: UConn Parking Lot W, Horse Barn Hill, Hammonasset, Station 43.
Times: April-November; late April and October are best.

Ipswich Sparrow
Habitats: barrier beaches, dunes.
Sites: Milford Point, Long Beach, Short Beach.
Times: early December-late March.

Grasshopper Sparrow
Habitats: short grass field with scattered shrubs or weeds, short mixed herbaceous field.
Sites: Northwest Park.
Times: May-June (singing).

Sharp-tailed Sparrow
Habitats: low salt marsh.
Sites: Hammonasset, Great Meadows, Great Island, Milford Point (Nells Island).
Times: May-September.

Seaside Sparrow
Habitats: high and low salt marsh.
Sites: Hammonasset, Great Island, Great Meadows.
Times: May-September.

Lincoln's Sparrow
Habitats: tilled and mixed herbaceous fields, edges.
Sites: UConn Parking Lot W, Horse Barn Hill, Station 43.
Times: October.

White-crowned Sparrow
Habitats: tilled, short grass and mixed herbaceous fields, edges.
Sites: UConn Parking Lot W, Horse Barn Hill, Hammonasset, Lighthouse Point, Station 43.
Times: October-November.

Lapland Longspur
Habitats: tilled and short grass fields, barrier beach.
Sites: Hammonasset, Lighthouse Point, Milford Point.
Times: November-March.

Snow Bunting
Habitats: tilled and short grass fields, sand and gravel beach, dunes.
Sites: Hammonasset, Sandy Point, Milford Point, UConn Parking Lot W.
Times: November-March.

Bobolink
Habitats: short grass, tall grass and mixed herbaceous fields.
Sites: Skiff Mountain, Topsmead State Forest, UConn Parking Lot W, Horse Barn Hill.
Times: May-August (May and June are best).

Meadowlark
Habitats: short grass, tall grass and mixed herbaceous fields.
Sites: Topsmead State Forest, UConn Parking Lot W, Horse Barn Hill, Hammonasset.
Times: April-November.

Rusty Blackbird
Habitats: shrub swamp, shrubby hardwood swamp.
Sites: White Memorial (Little Pond, area between Museum and Bantam Lake, Mallard Marsh), Station 43, Farmington Meadows, Maple Hollow.
Times: April and October.

Orchard Oriole
Habitats: scattered trees in short grass field; riparian forest.
Sites: Shepaug Dam, Kellogg Environmental Center/Osborndale State Park, Haley Farm.
Times: May-August (May and June are best).

Pine Grosbeak
Habitats: crabapple and apple trees, often in shrubby field.
Sites: Goshen East Street North, Barkhamsted Reservoir (Routes 20 and 181), Canaan Mountain.
Times: late October-March (some years).

Red Crossbill, White-winged Crossbill
Habitats: mixed conifer (spruce or tamarack) forest, white pine forest.
Sites: Barkhamsted Reservoir/Tunxis State Forest (Routes 181 and 20), Goshen East Street North, White Memorial (spruce groves), Patchaug State Forest.
Times: September-May (some years).

Common Redpoll
Habitats: feeders, mixed herbaceous field, birch trees in hardwood forest or shrubby field, mixed conifer (tamarack) forest.
Sites: UConn Parking Lot W (open areas along edges), Barkhamsted Reservoir (Routes 181 and 20), White Memorial, Goshen East Street North, Canaan Mountain.
Times: November-March (some years).

Pine Siskin
Habitats: feeders, any forest edge with conifers or birch trees.
Sites: White Memorial, Barkhamsted Reservoir (Routes 181 and 20), Canaan Mountain, Goshen East Street North, Nepaug Reservoir and State Forest.
Times: September-May (some years).

Evening Grosbeak
Habitats: feeders, mixed conifer (tamarack and spruce) forest, edges and plantings.
Sites: White Memorial, Canaan Mountain, Barkhamsted Reservoir (Routes 181 and 20), Goshen East Street North.
Times: October-April (some years).

Chapter 4

Fairfield County

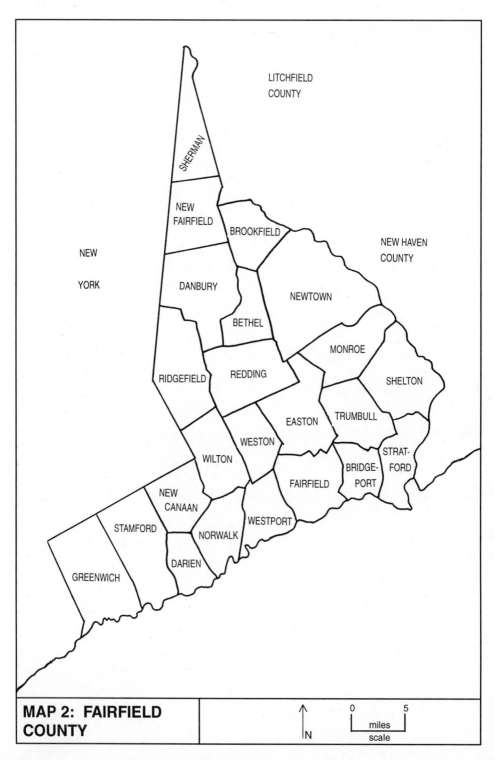

LITCHFIELD
COUNTY

SHERMAN

NEW
FAIRFIELD

BROOKFIELD

NEW
HAVEN
COUNTY

NEW

YORK

DANBURY

NEWTOWN

BETHEL

MONROE

RIDGEFIELD

REDDING

SHELTON

EASTON

TRUMBULL

WESTON

STRAT-
FORD

WILTON

BRIDGE-
PORT

FAIRFIELD

NEW
CANAAN

STAMFORD

NORWALK

WESTPORT

DARIEN

GREENWICH

**MAP 2: FAIRFIELD
COUNTY**

0   5
miles
scale

N

FAIRFIELD COUNTY

TABLE 2: HABITATS AND SEASONS AT FAIRFIELD COUNTY SITES

Habitats
- ● very good example
- ○ present, but not as significant

Seasons
- ● excellent during this season
- ○ less good during this season

	HABITATS							SEASONS			
	FOREST	OPEN	MARSH	LAKE	RIVER	COAST	OTHER	SPRING	NEST	FALL	WINTER
Tour of Housatonic River Sites	●	●	○	●	●		○	●	●	●	●
Bethel: East Swam Wildlife Mgmt. Area	○	○	●		○		○	●	○	●	○
Bridgeport: Seaside Park		○				●		○	○	○	●
Brookfield: Lillinonah Woods Sanctuary	○	○		○	○			○	○	○	○
Brookfield: Williams Park	○		○		○			○	○	○	○
Danbury: Bear Mountain Reservation	○	●	○		○			●	●	●	●
Danbury: Tarrywile Park	○	●	○	○				●	●	●	○
Easton: Aspetuck Reservoir/Hemlock Reservoir				●				○	○	○	○
Easton: Easton Reservoir				●				○	○	○	○
Fairfield: Larsen Sanctuary	●	●	○	○	○			●	○	●	○
Fairfield: Pine Creek Open Space Area		○				●		●	○	●	○
Fairfield: Southport Beach						●		●	○	●	●
Greenwich: Audubon Center/Quaker Ridge	●	●	●	○			●	●	●	●	○
Greenwich: Byram Park	○	○				●		●	●	●	○
Greenwich: Fairchild Garden	●	○	○	○	○			●	●	●	○
Greenwich: Greenwich Point Park	○	○	○	○		●	○	●	●	●	●
Greenwich/Stamford: Mianus River Park	●		○		●		○	●	●	○	○
Monroe: Webb Mountain Park	●	○			○		○	●	○	○	○
New Canaan: New Canaan Nature Center	○	○	●	○				●	●	○	○
New Fairfield: Pootatuck SF/Squantz Pond SP	●	○		●	○		○	●	○	●	○
New Fairfield/Sherman/Brookfield: Candlewood Lake				●				○	○	○	●
Newtown: NU Shepaug Dam Area (S. Side)	○	●		○				●	●	●	○
Newtown: Paugusset State Forest (N. Block)	●		○	●	○		○	●	●	●	○
Newtown: Paugusset State Forest (S. Block)	●			●	○		○	●	●	●	○
Newtown: Pootatuck Open Space Area	○	○	○		●			●	○	●	●
Newtown: Nature Conserv. Shepaug Dam Pres.	●	○	○		○		○	●	●	●	
Norwalk: Calf Pasture Beach/City Park		○				●		●	○	●	●
Norwalk: Manresa Island						●		●	●	●	●
Norwalk: Norwalk Islands						●		○	●	○	○
Norwalk: Veterans Memorial Park		○		○		●		●	○	●	●
Redding: Huckleberry Swamp (Steichen Preserve)	○		●		○			●	●	○	○
Redding: Saugatuck Falls Natural Area	○	○	○		○		○	○	○	○	○
Redding: Topstone Park	○	○	○	○	○		○	○	○	○	○
Redding: Valley Road	●		○		○		○	●	●	○	○
Redding/Bethel: Collis P. Huntington State Park	○	●	○	○				●	●	●	○
Redding/Bethel: Putname Memorial State Park	●	○	○	○			○	●	●	○	○
Ridgefield/Wilton: Woodcock Nature Center	○		●	○	○			●	●	●	○
Shelton: Indian Well State Park	○	○			○			○	○	○	○
Sherman: Colonial Park	○	●	○		○			○	○	○	○
Sherman: Wimisink Preserve		○	●	○	○			●	●	●	●

TABLE 2: HABITATS AND SEASONS AT FAIRFIELD COUNTY SITES CONT.

Habitats ● very good example ○ present, but not as significant Seasons ● excellent during this season ○ less good during this season	HABITATS							SEASONS			
	FOREST	OPEN	MARSH	LAKE	RIVER	COAST	OTHER	SPRING	NEST	FALL	WINTER
Stamford: Cummings Park/West Beach Park		○				●		●	○	●	○
Stamford/Darien: Holly Pd./Cove Is. /Weed Bch. Pk.	○	○				●		●	○	●	●
Stamford/New Canaan: Laurel Reservoir				●				●	○	●	○
Stratford: Frash Pond				●				●	○	●	●
Stratford: Great Meadows/Long Beach						●		●	●	●	●
Stratford: Short Beach/Veterans Park		○				●		●	●	●	●
Trumbull: Trumbull Basin	○		○		○			○	○	○	○
Weston: Devil's Den	●		○	○	○		○	●	●	○	○
Weston: Saugatuck Reservoir				●				●	○	●	○
Westport: Saugatuck River					○			○	○	○	○
Westport: Sherwood Island State Park	○	●		○		●	○	●	●	●	●
Westport: Smith Richardson Preserve	○	○						○	○	●	○
Westport: Longshore Pk./Compo Bch./Compo Cv.	○	○				●		●	○	●	●
Wilton: Weir Nature Preserve	○	○	○		○		○	○	○	○	○

BIRDING IN FAIRFIELD COUNTY

Fairfield County occupies the southwest corner of Connecticut; it is bounded by New York State on the west, Litchfield County on the north, New Haven County on the east, and, in the south, the westernmost portion of Connecticut's coast on Long Island Sound. It is crossed by four major highways: I-84, I-95, Route 8 and the Merritt Parkway.

The People

Fairfield County has a population of 857,000 (ranks second behind Hartford), and a land area of 632 square miles, giving it a population density of 1,356 per square mile. This is about twice the density of Connecticut overall, and makes Fairfield County the most densely populated county in the state, with New Haven County a close second. Population growth has been moderate in recent decades. Fairfield is Connecticut's most affluent county - of its 23 towns, 17 are among the state's wealthier towns.

The Land

The inland areas of Fairfield County lie in Connecticut's Western Uplands Ecoregion, which is characterized by hilly terrain, a series of north/south ridge systems, and the narrow, steep-sided valley of the Housatonic River. Most of the region is forested, with central hardwoods communities mixed with hemlock and white pine.

The southern portion of the county lies in Connecticut's Coastal Slope, and the southern edge includes a portion of the Connecticut shoreline. This part of the coast lies at the upper (western) end of Long Island Sound, where tides are greater and the intertidal zone more extensive than along the coast to the east. This produces more extensive mud flats and other types of intertidal areas, and greater development of the tide wrack on barrier beaches. In spite of intense coastline development, Fairfield County still possesses a few excellent salt marshes, that are among the best in Connecticut.

There are significant elevational differences south to north, and within the northern part. Elevations range from sea level and near sea level at and near the coast, up to about 1,000' inland. This variation makes for great habitat diversity, with both southern and northern types of habitat within the county.

Fairfield County includes Connecticut's largest lake (Candlewood - 5,420 acres). Only about 3% of the county is in farmland, the result of topography characterized by steep profiles, and of widespread development.

Public Areas and Birding Sites

Among Connecticut's eight counties, Fairfield County best exemplifies the impact of intense human activity on avian habitats and other natural areas, as well as the importance of creative conservation in response to such activity.

Much of Fairfield County's population and intensive development is concentrated in the southern portion of the county, especially along the shoreline and within commuting distance of New York City. Many former areas of tidal wetland have been drained for commercial uses, but several areas have been protected against further degradation.

Inland areas are still largely wooded and include several large tracts of undisturbed habitat, but areas that are not protected are being lost to development. As development continues, both inland and coastal areas are becoming isolated islands of natural habitat amid vast areas of intense development.

Within Fairfield County, there are eight state parks, three blocks of state forests, three large private sanctuaries, and also numerous smaller sanctuaries, town parks and reservoirs. These public areas are well distributed throughout the county, and encompass a wide variety of habitat types. Those that contain the best avian habitat and are open to the general public are included in this guide.

Taken together, these many areas place public open space and birding opportunities within a short distance of anyone who is in Fairfield County. Despite development, there are still quite a few really good places to look for birds.

Fairfield County offers first-class birding at both coastal and inland sites. The best site, measured in terms of the species diversity that occurs there throughout the year, is the Great Meadows/Long Beach/Short Beach complex in the estuary of the Housatonic River at Stratford. This site offers great birding throughout the year, but with drawbacks: nearby industrial development, parking, security and seasonally limited access. Some of these problems may be reduced as the site is incorporated into the McKinney National Wildlife Refuge. Another prime coastal site is Sherwood Island State Park, that is also good throughout the year (but excellent in March/April and September/October). Its only drawback is that it gets crowded during the warm months. Greenwich Point Park is the third of the fine coastal sites; access is restricted to town residents except during winter (when it is the most interesting).

Inland, the Audubon Center and nearby Fairchild Garden, both in Greenwich, contain fine habitat and provide excellent birding almost all year. Farther inland, Devil's Den in Weston and Huntington State Park in Redding both provide large areas of relatively undisturbed forest habitat. Valley Road, also in Redding, offers exciting birding on a smaller scale.

Seasons for Birding

One can find good birding in Fairfield County at any time of year. Both migrations are good - in the early spring and late fall for water birds along the coast and on the Housatonic River, and, later in the spring and earlier in the fall, for land birds at inland terrestrial habitats. During the nesting season, even in built-up Fairfield County there are large forested areas in which to bird quietly for breeding species. In winter, coastal and Housatonic River sites offer the most activity.

Spring migration. The first action of the spring migration begins along the coast. Coastal sites in Fairfield County offer a chance to see a wide variety of water birds and marsh birds early in the spring (March and April). Great Meadows in Stratford and Sherwood Island in Westport are the best bets. Inland, look for water bird migrants at sites along the Housatonic River (see Tour of Housatonic River Sites), and on reservoirs such as those in Easton and Weston. Later in the spring (April and May), land bird migrants come through in a broad wave over inland areas; try the Greenwich Audubon Center, Fairchild Garden, Devil's Den, Huntington State Park and Valley Road. The peak of the shore bird migration occurs during May at coastal sites.

Nesting season. The same inland sites as those mentioned above offer interesting birding during the nesting season. In addition to the typical mix of Connecticut nesting species, southern land bird species nest with some regularity in Fairfield County. Kentucky warbler nests in young hardwood/edge habitat at Fairchild Garden in Greenwich. Hooded warbler nests in sweet pepperbush and other wooded wetland habitat, also at Fairchild Garden, as well as in the mountain laurel thickets in Putnam Park in Redding. Orchard oriole nests in flood plain forest, open groves of hardwoods, and wooded edges of fields at sites scattered throughout Fairfield County. A nice variety of forest-dwelling species can be seen at the Northern and Southern Blocks of the Paugusset State Forest in Newtown. Several of Fairfield County's coastal salt marshes are among the best places in the state during the summer to look for a wide variety of nesting or feeding waders and other marsh birds. Among species that nest at Great Meadows are: shoveler, pied-billed grebe, harrier, moorhen, clapper and king rails, least bittern, willet, marsh wren, sharp-tailed and seaside sparrows. Sherwood Island, Great Meadows/Long Beach and Manresa in Norwalk are sites at which to see little blue heron, yellow-crowned night heron, glossy ibis, a variety of other waders and clapper rail. Black skimmer occurs at Sherwood Island, Great Meadows and Short Beach. Cattle egret can be found at several sites in Fairfield, Norwalk and Westport.

Fall migration. The first fall migrants are shore birds along the coast. Start your fall migration birding at Sherwood Island in August; it's also a top site for marsh birds and land birds in September and October. One of the best places in the Northeast for watching migrating hawks is Quaker Ridge at the Audubon Center in Greenwich; you might also try Huntington State Park in Redding. September is the best month at both sites. Good sites at which to see migrating land birds are Greenwich Audubon, Fairchild Garden, Huntington State Park and Devil's Den. In the late fall (especially November), migrating water birds pass by sites along the coast (Great Meadows, Sherwood Island, Greenwich Point), along the lower Housatonic River (see "Tour of Housatonic River Sites"), and at inland reservoirs (in Easton and Weston).

Winter. Most of the action in winter (during the period November-March) is at sites along the coast, and some of Connecticut's best are in Fairfield County. Go to Stratford Great Meadows/Long Beach, for wintering water birds, raptors and other land birds; to Short Beach for horned lark, snow bunting, and other wintering open-country land birds; to Sherwood Island for water birds and lingering land birds; to Greenwich Point for water birds, owls and other land birds. Inland sites are also worth a visit, because the mild climate in Fairfield County causes a variety of land birds to linger or winter over.

Sources of Information and Help

There are several excellent sources of information and help for birders in Fairfield County. The Audubon Center at Greenwich has an extensive collection of guide books, and professional naturalists are often at the visitor center. The New Canaan Nature Center can provide the same kind of help on a smaller scale. At Devil's Den, professional ornithologists conduct field studies on breeding birds, and can be very informative. The Connecticut Audubon Society has a sanctuary and visitor center, as well as the Birdcraft Museum and bird banding station, all in Fairfield. And there are several local bird clubs based in Fairfield County - the Audubon Societies of Darien, Greenwich, Lillinonah, New Canaan and Saugatuck Valley.

There is no problem finding places to eat, sleep or whatever in southern Fairfield County; up north, things get pretty rural, and support facilities are fewer.

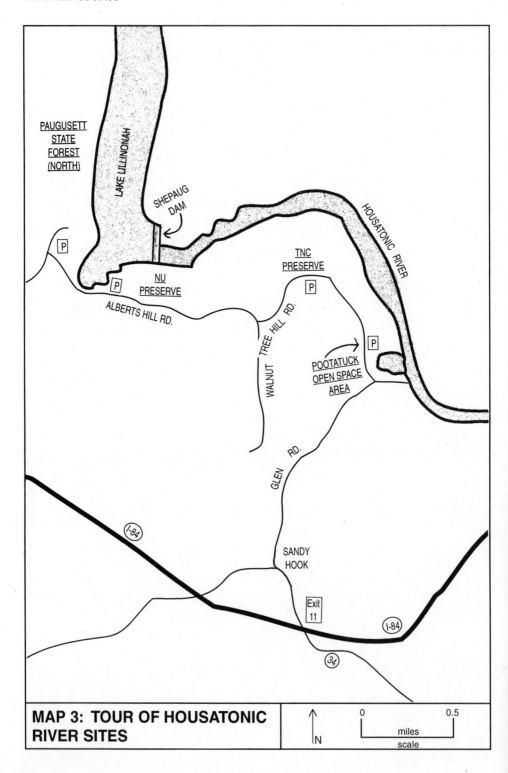

MAP 3: TOUR OF HOUSATONIC RIVER SITES

TOUR OF HOUSATONIC RIVER SITES

THE TOUR: This tour includes four sites that are near one another in Newtown along the west side of the Housatonic River, across from the Shepaug Dam Eagle Observation Area. These sites offer an excellent alternative to the habitats near the Area, during the periods when it is closed to the public (in the spring before Memorial Day, and in the fall after Labor Day). In addition, the sites on the tour are a convenient add-on to a trip to the Area in summer or winter when it is open. The sites on the tour, in the order in which they are reached, are:

> Pootatuck Open Space Area
> The Nature Conservancy Shepaug Dam Preserve
> Northeast Utilities Shepaug Dam Area (south side)
> Paugusset State Forest (Northern Block)

Details for each of these sites are included in separate site descriptions that appear elsewhere in this chapter under Newtown.

HABITATS
> **RIVER/STREAM:** river, cove, shores that are marshy, swampy, shrubby and wooded; perennial and seasonal streams, shrubby and wooded streambelts;
> **FOREST:** hardwoods, hardwoods/white pine, hardwoods/hemlock, hemlock, flood plain;
> **OPEN TERRESTRIAL:** short grass field, shrubby field, scattered cedars, shrubby edges;
> **LAKE/POND:** lake, cove, deep water, hardwoods/hemlock shore;
> **Marsh/swamp/bog:** shrub marsh; shrub and shrubby hardwood swamps; shrubby and wooded edges;
> **Other:** ledges, rocky slopes.

Each of these four sites offers a distinctive assemblage of habitats:

Pootatuck Open Space Area is composed of a mowed playing field that borders on the Pootatuck River at its confluence with a cove of the Housatonic River in the dammed section called Lake Zoar. The habitats at this site include open water, wetlands, shrubby edges, and flood plain forest.

The Nature Conservancy Shepaug Dam Preserve is largely forested by hardwoods, white pine and hemlock; there are shrubby edges along a powerline, a shrubby hardwood swamp, small streams with wooded streambelts, Lake Zoar and its wooded shore, rocky slopes and ledges.

Northeast Utilities Shepaug Dam Area (south side) lies on the south shore of the Housatonic River directly across from the Shepaug Dam Eagle Observation Area. Most of it is forested, and goes down to a cove of Lake Lillinonah, a dammed section of the Housatonic just upstream from Lake Zoar. A power line provides an abundance of shrubby field and edge habitats.

Paugusset State Forest (Northern Block) is an 850-acre area that occupies a peninsula which juts into Lake Lillinonah. It includes extensive shoreline which is largely composed of hardwoods and hemlock forest. Several small streams flow through the forest. The land is hilly, rocky and rugged.

SEASONS/BIRDS
> **SPRING MIGRATION:** WATER BIRDS, marsh birds, shore birds, LAND BIRDS;
> **NESTING SEASON:** water birds, marsh birds, shore birds, LAND BIRDS;

FALL MIGRATION: gulls, WATER BIRDS, marsh birds, shore birds, LAND BIRDS; **WINTER:** gulls, WATER BIRDS, LAND BIRDS.

These sites are good places to look for land birds during migrations and the nesting season, and, subject to access restrictions, for migrating and wintering water birds.

Pootatuck Open Space Area is best during the spring and fall migrations. In the late fall, winter and early spring, look for water birds on the cove. Later in the spring and earlier in the fall, this is a good site for land birds, especially edge-dwellers, and, later in the fall, berry-eaters.

The Nature Conservancy Shepaug Dam Preserve is worth visiting during the spring, summer and fall. While there is the possibility of seeing water birds on Lake Zoar, the real draw at this site is land birds. There is a good variety of both migrants and nesting species.

Northeast Utilities Shepaug Dam (south side) is a good site to visit any time in the spring, summer and fall, but it is best during April/May and September/October (just when the Shepaug Dam Eagle Observation Area across the river is closed). Both migrations are good, especially the fall, because of the large areas of berry-carrying shrubs at the power line. That edge habitat also produces an interesting nesting season. Although this site is smaller than the nearby Paugusset State Forest, it contains greater habitat diversity.

Paugusset State Forest (Northern Block) offers the possibility of seeing a nice mix of typical migrating and nesting forest-dwelling and edge-habitat land birds during the period late April through late September.

GETTING AROUND

Birding methods: car, WALK, boat.

This tour offers ample opportunities for birding on foot. In addition, parts of some of the areas can be seen from your car, and there is one place from which a boat can be launched. Parts of three of these sites are not open to the public in winter, and the fourth gets crowded in summer. However, among the four sites, it is possible to find good places to bird at any time of year.

Pootatuck Open Space Area is relatively small and easily covered on foot. Walk along the edges of the playing field, looking through the edge at the river, cove and wetland as opportunities occur. This site is open all year, but in summer the park is crowded and heavily used for recreation.

The Nature Conservancy Shepaug Dam Preserve has several trails that lead through the preserve and down to the shore of Lake Zoar. During the period December 1 through March 31, the preserve is closed to the public to protect the bald eagles, but is open for birding the rest of the year.

Northeast Utilities Shepaug Dam (south side) has one main trail that leads to the south end of the Shepaug Dam, and two side trails that go to the shore of Lake Lillinonah. It is best not to come here in winter, when parts of the area are closed to the public to avoid disturbance to bald eagles that perch on this hillside.

Paugusset State Forest (Northern Block) has woods roads and trails that lead to some parts of the forest and river shore; other parts are difficult to reach. Alberts Hill Road provides easy and good birding on foot, or in a car. There is a place by the road where you can easily launch a canoe into the cove of Lake Lillinonah. Access to some parts of the forest is prohibited from December through March to prevent disturbance to wintering bald eagles.

DIRECTIONS (see Map 3): The sites on this tour are in Newtown on the west (or south) bank of the Housatonic River northeast of Danbury. **Start at I-84 exit 11, and go west on Route 34 for 1.0 mile to the traffic light in the center of Sandy Hook.**

To get to the Pootatuck Open Space Area, go north (straight ahead) on Glen Road for 1.4 miles, left on Walnut Tree Hill Road for 0.2 miles, and right on Bridge End Road for 0.1 mile to a parking area on the right.

To get to The Nature Conservancy Shepaug Dam Preserve, retrace your route on Bridge End Road to Walnut Tree Hill Road, right for 0.7 mile to where a gas pipeline crosses the road, and there is a gate on the right. Park on the left side of the road, and follow the pipeline to the right for a hundred feet or so to a trail on the right marked "The Nature Conservancy". This trail leads to other trails within the preserve.

To get to Northeast Utilities Shepaug Dam (south side), continue on Walnut Tree Hill Road for another 0.3 miles, right on Alberts Hill Road for 1.1 miles to the entrance on the right (opposite Valley Field Road on the left). Park where you do not block the gate.

To get to the Paugusset State Forest (Northern Block), continue on Alberts Hill Road for another 0.2 mile to the entrance on the right, or walk for another 0.4 mile to a woods road on the right.

BETHEL: EAST SWAMP WILDLIFE MANAGEMENT AREA

HABITATS
MARSH/SWAMP/BOG: cattail, mixed herbaceous and shrub marsh, shrub swamp, shrubby hardwood swamp, hardwood swamp, dead wood, open water, edge of shrubs, vines, thickets;
Forest: hardwoods;
Open terrestrial: shrubby field, scattered apple and aspen trees, shrubby and wooded edge;
River/stream: perennial and seasonal streams;
Other: rocky slope.

This 79-acre parcel of the East Swamp Wildlife Management Area has a wide variety of habitat types, including large stretches of productive shrubby edges. Wetland habitats include varied marshes and swamps that are fed by East Swamp Brook. Other habitats include an old field with apple trees, fruiting shrubs and clumps of aspen trees, lots of edges that are dense with thickets of shrubs and vines, all backed by a rocky hillside covered by mature oak-hickory forest. This site is under active habitat management that seeks to encourage the growth of shrubs, and also to maintain shrubby fields.

SEASONS/BIRDS
SPRING MIGRATION: water birds, LAND BIRDS;
Nesting season: water birds, land birds;
FALL MIGRATION: water birds, LAND BIRDS;
Winter: land birds.

Standard water bird species occur at this site, and the land bird species that you would expect in these edge, wetland and forest habitats are here in abundance during the spring and fall migrations. Fall is especially good, because the edges contain large areas of spicebush, grape vine, silky dogwood and other berry-producing shrubs. A large number of land birds nest here, including a variety of edge-dwelling species such as brown thrasher and warbling vireo, along with woodland species like pileated and red-bellied woodpeckers, and wetland users like northern waterthrush and wood duck. In addition, there is suitable habitat for worm-eating and hooded warblers. The wetland has too little open water to induce many marsh birds to nest or feed here, and there is little suitable habitat for shore birds.

GETTING AROUND
Birding methods: WALK.
Walking at this site is confined to a single woods road, but it provides easy walking, and goes from one end of the area to the other, past excellent edge habitat, along the edge of the wetland, and near the hillside - a one-way distance of about 0.8 mile. Hunting is permitted.

DIRECTIONS: This area is in Bethel, about a mile east of Danbury. In Bethel at the intersection of Routes 302 and 53, go east on Route 302 for 0.7 mile, left on P. T. Barnum Street for 0.1 mile, right on Main Street for 0.2 mile, left on Maple Avenue for 0.5 mile, and left on Ballfield Road for 0.2 mile to the entrance on the left.

BRIDGEPORT: SEASIDE PARK

HABITATS
COASTAL: Long Island Sound, rocky point, rocky shore, breakwater, sand and gravel beach, salt water tidal cove, tidal creek, intertidal flats of mud, sand and gravel, offshore gravel bar.
Open terrestrial: short grass and shrubby fields, brushy field, groves of hardwood trees.
The centerpiece of Seaside Park is a wide sandy beach that occupies over two miles of coastline. It overlooks Long Island Sound, and has extensive intertidal areas. There is also a cove that provides a sheltered feeding and rest area for water birds in winter.

SEASONS/BIRDS
Spring migration: gulls, terns, water birds, marsh birds, shore birds;
Nesting season: gulls, terns, marsh birds;
Fall migration: gulls, terns, water birds, shore birds;
WINTER: gulls, WATER BIRDS, land birds.
This site is especially good in winter, when it affords the opportunity to see both deep water birds such as loons, grebes and scoters, and also shallow water species such as brant, gadwall, American wigeon and occasionally Eurasian wigeon. Snowy owl is sometimes here in winter. In summer, waders come to the beach to feed. Fish crows are present all year.

GETTING AROUND
Birding methods: CAR, walk, bike.
An important plus for this area is that in severe winter weather, much of it can be birded from within your car. In better conditions, you can walk or bike along the beach for over a mile. The park is crowded in summer. Don't leave valuables in your car.

DIRECTIONS: This park comprises much of the waterfront of the city of Bridgeport. From I-95 exit 27, go south on Lafayette Street for 0.7 mile, right on Waldemere Avenue for 0.1 mile to park entrance on left. Or, to get to the western end of the park, continue west on Waldemere Avenue for about two miles, following signs to the beach.

BROOKFIELD: LILLINONAH WOODS SANCTUARY

HABITATS
Forest: hardwoods, hardwoods/hemlock;
Open terrestrial: short grass field, shrubby and wooded edge;
Lake/pond: lake, deep water, wooded shore;
River/stream: stream, wooded streambelt;
This is a wooded area that includes a small stream, and slopes down to the shore of Lake Lillinonah (a dammed section of the Housatonic River).

SEASONS/BIRDS
Spring migration: water birds, land birds;
Nesting season: land birds;
Fall migration: water birds, land birds;
Winter: land birds.
During the late fall, winter (when there is open water) and early spring, water birds, including goldeneye and common merganser, occur on Lake Lillinonah. Bald eagle occasionally hunts the river during the period December through March. In the later spring, through the summer and into early fall, a good mix of land bird migrants and nesters can be seen in the woods on the way down to the lake shore. Pileated woodpecker is one of the more visible of the nesting species.

GETTING AROUND
Birding methods: WALK.
There is a parking area by the highway, and from here a woods road leads down to the edge of Lake Lillinonah, a distance of about one quarter mile. It provides a way to reach the shore, with good birding as you go.

DIRECTIONS: This site is on the west (or south) bank of the Housatonic River northeast of Danbury. Start at the west (or south) end of the Route 133 bridge across the Housatonic River, and go west on Route 133 for 0.2 mile to the park entrance on the left, just before the intersection with Obtuse Rocks Road, also on the left.

BROOKFIELD: WILLIAMS PARK

HABITATS
Forest: hardwoods, vine tangles, thickets;
River/stream: perennial and seasonal streams, hardwood streambelts;
Marsh/swamp/bog: mixed herbaceous and shrub marsh, shrub, shrubby hardwood and hardwood swamp.
This town park is virtually in the center of Brookfield, but is quiet and secluded. The park occupies the valley of a small stream. The upper end of the valley near the park entrance is composed of a moist bottomland forest of hardwoods with a dense understory of shrubs and thickets. As the valley gradually slopes downward toward the northern end of the park, the forest grades into a shrub and hardwood swamp.

SEASONS/BIRDS
Spring migration: land birds;
Nesting season: land birds;

Fall migration: land birds;
Winter: land birds.
You can see the standard mix of forest land bird species here, in a very nice setting.

GETTING AROUND
Birding methods: WALK.
There is a network of well-maintained trails and woods roads that provide easy and pleasant birding on foot.

DIRECTIONS: This park is at Brookfield Center, about five miles northeast of Danbury. From Brookfield Center, at the intersection of Routes 25 and 133, go north on Route 25 for 0.3 mile to Long Meadow Hill Road and the park entrance, both on the right (opposite the library).

DANBURY: BEAR MOUNTAIN RESERVATION

HABITATS
OPEN TERRESTRIAL: mixed herbaceous, tall grass and shrubby fields, edges.
Forest: hardwoods, white pine, hemlock, mixed conifers, tamarack;
River/stream: seasonal stream, wooded streambelts;
Marsh/swamp/bog: small patches of shrubby hardwood swamp.
The overall productivity of this site is enhanced by the fact that there are lots of interfaces between the open, wooded and wetland habitats.

SEASONS/BIRDS
SPRING MIGRATION: LAND BIRDS;
NESTING SEASON: LAND BIRDS;
FALL MIGRATION: LAND BIRDS;
Winter: land birds.
Although this is not one of Connecticut's top birding sites, it is quite good throughout most of the year, and can be really good for land bird migrants. The best period is late April through October, with May being the most interesting month. A nice assortment of both migrants and nesters occur in the park. Because the trail travels where woods and fields meet, it is possible to see both forest-dwelling and open country species as you walk.

GETTING AROUND
Birding methods: WALK, ski.
A trail makes a loop through the park. It would be suitable for cross-country skiing in winter.

DIRECTIONS: This park is about five miles north of Danbury. From I-84 westbound: take exit 6, go north on Route 37 for 2.9 miles, right on Bear Mountain Road for 0.3 miles to the entrance on the right. From I-84 eastbound: take exit 5, go north on Route 37 for 3.6 miles, right on Bear Mountain Road for 0.3 miles to the park entrance on the right.

DANBURY: TARRYWILE PARK

HABITATS
OPEN TERRESTRIAL: short grass, tall grass and shrubby fields, edges and hedgerows;
Forest: hardwoods, white pine, hemlock, vine tangles and thickets;
Lake/pond: pond, shrubby and wooded shores;
Marsh/swamp/bog: wet meadow.
These habitat types are intermingled, and there are lots of interfaces between the types.

SEASONS/BIRDS
SPRING MIGRATION: LAND BIRDS;
NESTING SEASON: LAND BIRDS;
FALL MIGRATION: LAND BIRDS;
Winter: land birds.
A good variety of the standard species for these types of habitat (especially open terrestrial species and raptors) can be seen at this site. Nesting species include bobolink, indigo bunting and a variety of warblers.

GETTING AROUND
Birding methods: walk.
There are a number of trails that go through the park, starting at the main entrance. The trail network interconnects all of the habitat types in the park, making "edge birding" easy and productive.

DIRECTIONS: This park is in the southeast part of the city of Danbury. The simplest approach is from the south at the intersection of Routes 53 and 302. Go north on Route 53 for 1.8 miles at which point Route 53 turns sharp right. Go straight onto South Street for 0.2 mile, left on Mountainville Road for 0.2 mile, right on Southern Boulevard for 0.2 mile to the main entrance and parking area on the left.

EASTON: ASPETUCK RESERVOIR/HEMLOCK RESERVOIR

HABITATS
LAKE/POND: lakes, deep water, shallow water, shore of hardwoods, white pine, hemlock and mixed forest types.
These two reservoirs lie in the same narrow valley, one (Aspetuck) upstream from the other (Hemlock). Their position near the Connecticut coast minimizes freeze-over periods in winter.

SEASONS/BIRDS
Spring migration: water birds, land birds;
Nesting season: land birds;
Fall migration: water birds, land birds;
Winter: water birds, land birds.
This is a good site at which to look for water birds during the spring and fall migrations; the position of the reservoirs in southern Connecticut causes them to attract migrants that are travelling along the coast. It can also be good in winter because there are usually periods

when there is open water (again, because of the location near the coast). The best period is early November through early April, and the best months are November and March. In spring, summer and fall, there are land birds to look for along the shores, and osprey is sometimes present in spring and fall.

GETTING AROUND
Birding methods: CAR.
A road (Route 58) follows the west shore of both reservoirs. It provides intermittent, somewhat obscured views of the Hemlock Reservoir, and parking is difficult. However, the views of the Aspetuck Reservoir are clear and close, and parking is not a problem. The land along the shore of both reservoirs is posted by the water company, so stay on the road shoulders and parking areas. Beware of speeding traffic.

DIRECTIONS: These reservoirs are immediately northwest of the city of Bridgeport. From the Merritt Parkway, take exit 44/45 and go north on Route 58. Starting almost immediately and continuing for 3.3 miles, the Hemlock Reservoir can be seen intermittently on the right side of the road. At 3.3 miles, Route 58 intersects with Route 136 which passes between the Hemlock and the Aspetuck Reservoirs. Continue north on Route 58 for another 1.3 miles; the Aspetuck Reservoir can be seen on the right.

EASTON: EASTON RESERVOIR

HABITATS
LAKE/POND: lake, deep water, shore of hardwoods, white pine and hemlock in various combinations.
This is a long, narrow reservoir. Its position near the shore minimizes freeze-over periods in winter.

SEASONS/BIRDS
Spring migration: water birds, land birds;
Nesting season: land birds;
Fall migration: water birds, land birds;
Winter: water birds, land birds.
This is a site at which to look for water birds during the spring and fall migrations, and, when there is open water, in winter. The position of the reservoir in the southern part of the state attracts water birds that are migrating along the coast. The best period is early November through early April, and the best months are November and March. Osprey is often present in spring and fall.

GETTING AROUND
Birding methods: car
A road that goes near (about 50 yards distant) the south shore of the reservoir provides intermittent and somewhat obscured views of the water. There is a better view of an area of water near the dam from the road shoulder at the dam. Stay on the road - the land near the reservoir is posted by the water company. Parking is difficult.

DIRECTIONS: This reservoir is located a few miles northwest of the city of Bridgeport. From the Merritt Parkway, take exit 46, go north on Route 59 for 2.3 miles, right on Old Oak Road for 0.6 mile. From here to the dam, at 1.0 mile, there are intermittent views of the water

FAIRFIELD: LARSEN SANCTUARY

HABITATS
      FOREST: hardwoods;
      OPEN TERRESTRIAL: shrubby field, edges;
      Lake/pond: ponds, wooded and shrubby edges;
      River/stream: stream, wooded streambelt;
      Marsh/swamp/bog: wet meadow, shrub swamp, hardwood swamp;
The Connecticut Audubon Society's Larsen Sanctuary is located within several miles of the coast, and has 152 acres of managed habitat including woods, open areas, wetlands and several small ponds.

SEASONS/BIRDS
      SPRING MIGRATION: LAND BIRDS;
      Nesting season: land birds;
      FALL MIGRATION: LAND BIRDS;
      Winter: land birds.
This is a good site at almost any time of year, but especially during the spring migration of land birds and during the fall hawk migration.

GETTING AROUND
      Birding methods: WALK.
There is a network of well-maintained trails throughout the sanctuary; a trail map and directions may be obtained at the visitor center located at the entrance. There is an entrance fee.

DIRECTIONS: The Larsen Sanctuary is located at 2325 Burr Street in Fairfield. To get there from I-95, take exit 21 and go north on Mill Plain Road (which becomes Burr Street) for 4.4 miles to the Sanctuary entrance on the left.

FAIRFIELD: PINE CREEK OPEN SPACE AREA

HABITATS
      COASTAL: low salt water marsh, tidal creek, mud flats and tide pools;
      Open Terrestrial: short grass field, shrubby edges, thickets.
This is a little-known area owned by the Town of Fairfield. It is 220 acres in size, occupies the site of a former landfill, and now includes a restored tidal marsh and creek, surrounded by shrubby edges and thickets.

SEASONS/BIRDS
      SPRING MIGRATION: gulls, water birds, MARSH BIRDS, SHORE BIRDS, land birds;
      Nesting season: MARSH BIRDS, land birds;
      FALL MIGRATION: gulls, water birds, MARSH BIRDS, SHORE BIRDS; land birds;
      Winter: gulls, water birds, land birds.
This is an all-season birding area, with something happening at any time of year. During the spring, there are lots of the standard water bird, shore bird and land bird migrants. In summer, nesters include some interesting species (such as clapper rail, sharp-tailed and seaside sparrows) and a variety of waders come in to feed. Also, this is a place that is not overrun by

crowds in which to do your summer birding. The fall migration sometimes brings uncommon shore birds such as lesser golden plover and buff-breasted sandpiper, plus a variety of raptors and sparrows. In winter, look for harrier and short-eared owl.

GETTING AROUND
Birding methods: WALK.
There are three trails that provide views over the marsh.

DIRECTIONS: This area is on the coast at Fairfield. From I-95, take exit 21, go south on Mill Plain Road for 0.3 mile, right on Route 1 for 0.3 mile, left on South Pine Creek Road for 1.1 miles, left on Old Dam Road for 0.3 mile to a point just past the ballfields to the entrance of the area on the left.

FAIRFIELD: SOUTHPORT BEACH

HABITATS
COASTAL: Long Island Sound, rocky coast, sand and gravel beach, tidal creek, small estuary, breakwater, intertidal flats of mud, sand and gravel.
This is a beach that looks out on Long Island Sound, and has offshore intertidal areas. It is a good example, on a small scale, of the richness of estuaries where rivers or streams enter salt water.

SEASONS/BIRDS
SPRING MIGRATION: GULLS, TERNS, WATER BIRDS, marsh birds, shore birds;
Nesting season: marsh birds;
FALL MIGRATION: GULLS, TERNS, WATER BIRDS, marsh birds, shore birds;
WINTER: GULLS, WATER BIRDS.
From September to late April, this is a good site from which to look for water birds and gulls on the Sound and areas near the creek mouth. There are also a few shore birds during the spring and fall migrations, and occasionally waders come in to feed in the spring, summer and fall.

GETTING AROUND
Birding methods: CAR.
All there is to see at this site can be seen from near your car. In summer, access to the beach and parking is restricted to town residents.

DIRECTIONS: This beach lies on the coast just on the Fairfield side of the town line with Westport. From I-95 exit 19, at the end of the ramp, go south on Center Street for 0.3 mile, right on Pequot Avenue for 0.8 mile to entrance to the beach on the left.

GREENWICH: AUDUBON CENTER/QUAKER RIDGE

HABITATS
FOREST: mixed hardwoods, hardwoods/hemlock, flood plain;
OPEN TERRESTRIAL: shrubby field, edge;
MARSH/SWAMP/BOG: shrub swamp, hardwood swamp;
Lake/pond: several ponds, shrubby and wooded shores;
OTHER: hawk watching site.
This is a National Audubon Sanctuary that includes 288 acres of managed habitat, including woodland, wetlands, two ponds, streams and reverting shrubby fields. Within the Sanctuary is Quaker Ridge, one of the premiere hawk watching sites in the Northeast.

SEASONS/BIRDS
SPRING MIGRATION: water birds, LAND BIRDS
NESTING SEASON: LAND BIRDS
FALL MIGRATION: water birds, LAND BIRDS;
Winter: land birds.
The spring migration is especially good at this sanctuary. During the nesting season, there are varied habitats in which to bird without encountering summertime crowds. Watching the fall hawk migration from Quaker Ridge can be a memorable experience.

GETTING AROUND
Birding methods: car, WALK.
Trails lead throughout the sanctuary; a trail map is available at the visitor center. There is an entrance fee. The Quaker Ridge hawk watching site is near the parking area at the entrance. There is a visitor center also near the entrance that has a bookstore with one of the most comprehensive selections of natural history and environmental books in Connecticut.

DIRECTIONS: The Greenwich Audubon Center is located about five miles north of the city of Greenwich. To get there from the Merritt Parkway, take exit 28 and go north on Round Hill Road for 1.4 miles, and left on John Street for 1.5 miles to Riversville Road. The sanctuary entrance is located on the right at this intersection. Ask at the visitor center for directions to Quaker Ridge.

GREENWICH: BYRAM PARK

HABITATS
COASTAL: cove, Long Island Sound.
Forest: groves of hardwoods;
Open terrestrial: short grass field, shrubby edges.
This little park lies in a sheltered cove of western Long Island Sound. Its grounds consist of well tended lawns, groves of hardwoods and shrubs.

SEASONS/BIRDS
SPRING MIGRATION: WATER BIRDS, land birds;
Nesting season: land birds;
FALL MIGRATION: WATER BIRDS, land birds;
WINTER: WATER BIRDS, land birds.
This is a good site at which to see a wide variety of water birds during the period October

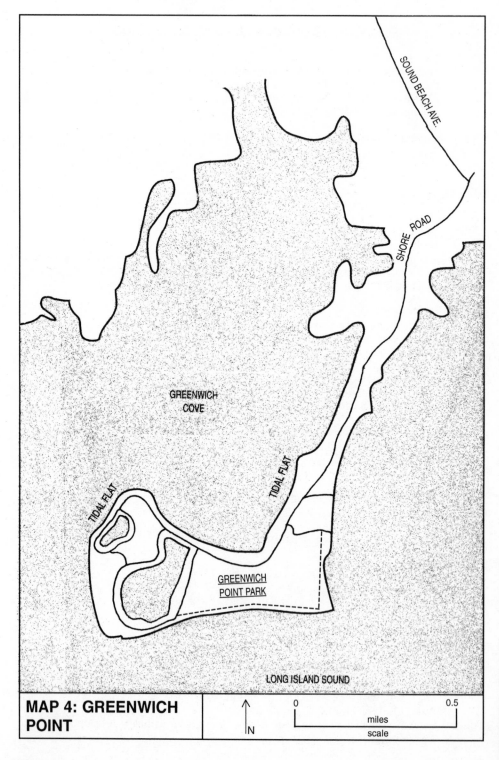

SOUND BEACH AVE.

SHORE ROAD

GREENWICH
COVE

TIDAL FLAT

TIDAL FLAT

GREENWICH
POINT PARK

LONG ISLAND SOUND

**MAP 4: GREENWICH
POINT**

N

0   0.5

miles
scale

through April. A tufted duck was once seen among the greater scaup that commonly occur in this cove, and a black-throated gray warbler was reported among the shrubs one fall.

GETTING AROUND
Birding methods: CAR, walk.
You can park at the water's edge. During the warm months, the park is crowded, and admission is restricted to town residents.

DIRECTIONS: This site is the westernmost harbor on the Connecticut coast. From I-95 southbound: take the exit 2 ramp to the first traffic light, left at the light for 0.1 mile, bear left at another light for 0.1 mile to the park entrance on the right. From I-95 northbound: take the exit 2 ramp to a stop sign, left for 0.1 mile, right at the light for 0.1 mile to the park entrance on the right.

GREENWICH: FAIRCHILD GARDEN

HABITATS
FOREST: hardwoods;
Open terrestrial: shrubby field, edges;
Lake/pond: two small ponds, wooded and shrubby shore;
River/stream: stream, hardwood streanbelt;
Marsh/swamp/bog: wet meadow, mixed herbaceous marsh.
This 127-acre wildflower sanctuary, despite its small size, has a wide variety of inland habitats, including deciduous forest, a pond, a section of the Byram River, a stream, and areas of herbaceous wetlands.

SEASONS/BIRDS
SPRING MIGRATION: LAND BIRDS;
NESTING SEASON: LAND BIRDS;
FALL MIGRATION: LAND BIRDS;
Winter: land birds.
This is a beautiful area in which to go birding, particularly in May, when migrating land birds can be seen along with a wealth of wildflowers for which the garden is justly famous. Over the years, a number of uncommon land bird species have been seen here. Nesting species have included worm-eating, Kentucky, hooded, and Lawrence's warblers.

GETTING AROUND
Birding methods: walk.
There is a network of trails that are well maintained but sometimes wet in places. A trail map be obtained at the nearby Greenwich Audubon Center, also described in this guide.

DIRECTIONS: Fairchild Garden is located about five miles north of the city of Greenwich. To get there from the Merritt Parkway, take exit 28, go north on Round Hill Road for 1.4 miles, left on John Street for 1.5 miles, left on Riversville Road for 0.4 mile, and left on North Porchuck Road for 0.5 mile to the preserve entrance on the right.

GREENWICH: GREENWICH POINT PARK

HABITATS
COASTAL: peninsula, tidal cove, Long Island Sound, rocky shore, cobble, gravel and sand beach, tidal pond, mud flat, sand bar, low salt marsh;
Open Terrestrial: short grass and shrubby fields, wooded and shrubby edges;
Forest: hardwoods, conifer groves, cedars;
Lake/pond: ponds;
Marsh/swamp/bog: herbaceous marsh.
Other: hawk watching site.
Greenwich Point Park is a long, narrow peninsula that extends 1.7 miles into Long Island Sound, and acts as a land trap during migration. On this peninsula, there is a wide variety of habitat types - cobble and sand beaches, mud flats, a sand bar, two small ponds, two small marshes, open terrestrial habitats, groves of conifers and other wooded areas.

SEASONS/BIRDS
SPRING MIGRATION: GULLS, TERNS, WATER BIRDS, MARSH BIRDS, SHORE BIRDS, LAND BIRDS;
Nesting season: marsh birds, land birds;
FALL MIGRATION: GULLS, TERNS, WATER BIRDS, MARSH BIRDS, SHORE BIRDS, LAND BIRDS;
WINTER: GULLS, WATER BIRDS, LAND BIRDS.
This is one of the most interesting birding sites on the western Connecticut coast, especially during the period late November to early April. The variety of habitat types together with the "land trap" effect of the peninsula makes it very productive during the fall migration and winter. On a visit during this period, it is normal to see a wide variety of water birds and land birds; in the fall, there are interesting marsh birds and shore birds. The entrance to the park has been used as a fall hawk watching site. Over the years, an impressive number of uncommon species have been seen here, including lesser black-backed gull, king eider, Wilson's plover, snowy, long-eared and saw-whet owls, chuck-wills-widow, chat, blue grosbeak, grasshopper sparrow and many others.

GETTING AROUND
Birding methods: CAR, WALK.
A road goes through the park and passes near most of the habitat areas; short trails provide access to the others. The town park occupies the entire peninsula, and it is closed to non-residents of Greenwich between April and November. Fortunately, the most interesting birding occurs outside of this period.

DIRECTIONS (see Map 4): This point is on the coast of Long Island Sound immediately south of Old Greenwich. To get there from I-95, take exit 5 to Route 1 which is 100 yards north of I-95; go right on Route 1 for 0.2 mile; right on Sound Beach Avenue for 1.7 miles; right on Shore Road for 0.9 mile the park entrance.

GREENWICH/STAMFORD: MIANUS RIVER PARK

HABITATS
RIVER/STREAM: river, slow water, shrubby and wooded streambelt;
FOREST: hardwoods, hemlock, mountain laurel;

Marsh/swamp/bog: wet meadow, shrub marsh, shrub swamp;
Other: rocky slope.

This is an undeveloped local park that consists of rocky, hilly terrain covered by mature hardwood and hemlock forest, thickets of mountain laurel, a wet meadow surrounded by shrubs, a buttonbush marsh, and a section of the Mianus River.

SEASONS/BIRDS

SPRING MIGRATION: LAND BIRDS;
NESTING SEASON: LAND BIRDS;
Fall migration: land birds;
Winter: land birds.

This is a good site during the spring land bird migration. Nesting species include red-shouldered hawk and hooded warbler (look for the latter in the mountain laurel).

GETTING AROUND

Birding methods: walk.

A wide, well-kept trail goes past the wetlands to the Mianus River at the north end of the park. Several side trails make loops through different habitat areas.

DIRECTIONS: This park is located in the eastern part of Greenwich, near the Stamford line. To get there from I-95, take exit 4, go north on Indian Field Road for 0.6 mile across Route 1, left on Stanwich Road for 3.6 miles, right on Cognewaugh Road for 0.5 mile to the park entrance on the left.

MONROE: WEBB MOUNTAIN PARK

HABITATS

FOREST: hardwoods, hardwoods/white pine, hardwoods/hemlock, hemlock, conifer groves;
Open terrestrial: short grass field, wooded edge, shrub field, shrubby and wooded edge;
River/stream: river, deep and shallow water, wooded streambelt; stream, wooded streambelt, hemlock ravine;
Other: rock outcrops, ledges, rocky slope.

This town park occupies a steep-sided stream valley that drops down to the Housatonic River. It includes large areas of hemlock and spruces, sections of hemlock ravine, and steep, boulder-strewn slopes. A pipeline right-of-way provides shrub and edge habitat. Much of this site is rugged country which has a wilderness character that makes it feel more like an undeveloped state forest than a town park.

SEASONS/BIRDS

SPRING MIGRATION: water birds, LAND BIRDS;
Nesting season: land birds;
Fall migration: water birds, land birds;
Winter: water birds, land birds.

Land birds are the real draw at this site. Both migrations bring a nice variety of standard woodland species. The downstate, river valley location of this site may account for the southerners among the nesting species: red-bellied woodpecker, Carolina wren, worm-eating warbler and orchard oriole. Pileated woodpecker is also a resident. The habitat along the pipe line right-of-way provides good nesting habitat for edge-dwellers such as prairie warbler. Water birds can be seen on the Housatonic River during the late fall, winter (when it is ice-free) and early spring. Bald eagles, foraging at the nearby Stevenson Dam, can sometimes be seen circling overhead during this same period.

GETTING AROUND
Birding methods: car, WALK.
A driveway goes through this park for 1.4 miles; it follows the slope along the stream and ends at the Housatonic River. It can be driven, but is rough and may be impassable at times. However, it provides good birding on foot at any time. There are also several trails, and a trail map is posted near the park entrance.

DIRECTIONS: This park is on the west bank of the Housatonic River several miles northwest of Shelton. To get to it from the intersection of Routes 111 and 34, go south on Route 111 for 2.4 miles, left on East Village Road for 0.8 mile; at the three-way intersection, bear right to stay on East Village Road for another 0.8 mile, left on Webb Circle Road for 0.6 mile to the park entrance on the right.

NEW CANAAN: NEW CANAAN NATURE CENTER

HABITATS
MARSH/SWAMP/BOG: shrub marsh, hardwood swamp;
Forest: hardwoods, mixed conifers;
Open Terrestrial: shrubby field, shrubby and wooded edge;
Lake/pond: pond, wooded and shrubby shoreline.
The New Canaan Nature Center is located on one of several small areas of managed habitat owned by the town of New Canaan and open to the public. This 40-acre parcel is the largest.

SEASONS/BIRDS
SPRING MIGRATION: LAND BIRDS;
Nesting season: land birds;
Fall migration: land birds;
Winter: land birds.
Although this area is small and is surrounded by miles of intensive suburban development, the habitats are sufficiently varied to attract a reasonable variety of standard species of birds during migration and the nesting season.

GETTING AROUND
Birding methods: walk.
The nature center is located at the entrance, and can provide trail maps and directions to this and the several nearby areas that are also under its management.

DIRECTIONS: The nature center and this habitat area are located less than a mile north of the center of New Canaan. To get there from the northern intersection of Routes 124 and 106, go north on Route 124 for about 0.5 mile to the entrance of the nature center on the left. The other town-owned areas are nearby; directions to them can be obtained at the nature center.

NEW FAIRFIELD: POOTATUCK STATE FOREST/SQUANTZ POND STATE PARK

HABITATS
LAKE/POND: lake, wooded shore;
FOREST: hardwoods, hemlock/hardwoods;
River/stream: perennial and seasonal streams, wooded streambelts;
Open terrestrial: short grass field, cedar stands, shrubby edges;
Other: cliffs and ledges, rocky slopes.

Squantz Pond Park (172 acres) lies along the shore of Squantz Pond (really an arm of Candlewood Lake), and is contiguous to the state forest. Much of the park is developed for swimming and picnicking. Pootatuck State Forest consists of 1,066 largely wooded acres of rugged, rocky terrain, with cliffs and ledges.

SEASONS/BIRDS
SPRING MIGRATION: WATER BIRDS, LAND BIRDS;
Nesting season: land birds;
FALL MIGRATION: WATER BIRDS, LAND BIRDS;
Winter: water birds, land birds.

Squantz Pond and the causeway where Route 39 crosses the outlet just north of the park entrance are worth checking during the early spring and late fall for migrating water birds and some land birds including osprey. In winter, there is a chance to see a bald eagle and, if there is open water, a few water birds. Pootatuck State Forest provides an area in which to look for land birds during the spring and fall migrations, and during the nesting season. A nice assortment of standard migrating and nesting species can be seen here. The best times are May, early June and September.

GETTING AROUND
Birding methods: car, WALK.

The Squantz Pond Park driveway goes near the shore of the pond. The park is usually crowded in summer and on warm weekends, and an entrance fee is charged during the period May-September. Pootatuck State Forest has a network of trails and woods roads, is seldom crowded, and there is no fee.

DIRECTIONS: This area is about ten miles north of Danbury, just west of Candlewood Lake. To get to Squantz Pond State Park from I-84, take exit 6, go north on Route 37 for 4.6 miles, right on Route 39 for 3.9 miles, left on Shortwoods Road for 0.1 mile to the entrance to Squantz Pond Park on the right. (Just beyond Shortwoods Road, Route 39 passes over the causeway that provides views of the lower end of Squantz Pond to the north (on the left) and of Squantz Cove of Candlewood Lake to the south (on the right). Do not park or stop your car on the causeway. To get to Pootatuck State Forest, continue on Shortwoods Road (becomes Pine Hill Road) for 0.4 mile to a woods road on the right that goes into the forest.

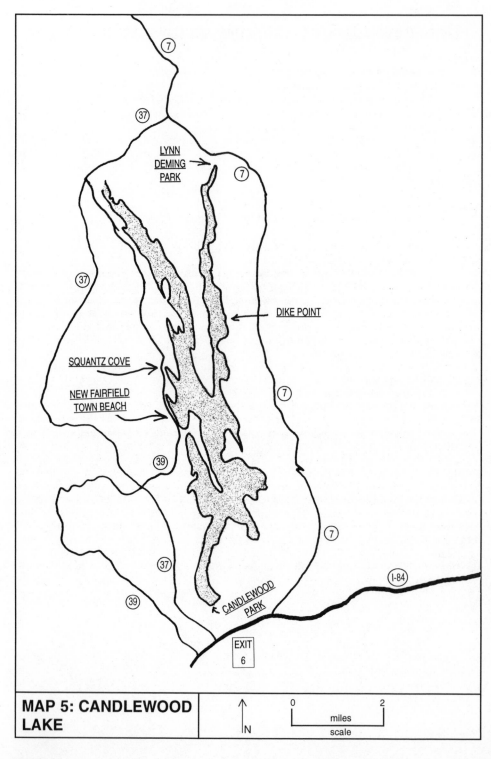

LYNN DEMING PARK

DIKE POINT

SQUANTZ COVE

NEW FAIRFIELD TOWN BEACH

CANDLEWOOD PARK

EXIT 6

I-84

MAP 5: CANDLEWOOD LAKE

0 miles 2
scale

N

NEW FAIRFIELD/SHERMAN/BROOKFIELD: CANDLEWOOD LAKE

HABITATS
LAKE/POND: lake, deep water, coves, islands, wooded shoreline.
This long lake (Connecticut's largest) occupies a steep-sided valley, and lies in the towns of New Fairfield, Sherman, Brookfield and New Milford. Most of the shoreline is occupied by small vacation properties. The valley and the lake within it serve as a flyway for water birds and certain land birds.

SEASONS/BIRDS
Spring migration: gulls, water birds, land birds;
Nesting season: water birds, land birds;
FALL MIGRATION: gulls, WATER BIRDS, land birds;
WINTER: gulls, WATER BIRDS, land birds.
Most of the water bird species that occur on Connecticut's inland lakes and rivers can be found at Candlewood Lake during the fall, winter and spring. There are several areas of the lake that usually stay ice-free in the winter. Interesting gull species, including lesser black-backed and Iceland have been seen at Lynn Deming Park. Osprey occurs in spring and fall. This lake is also a good site at which to look for migrating or wintering bald eagles. Overall, the best periods are November, December and March. Don't bother going here from May through October, because heavy boating activity precludes birding.

GETTING AROUND
Birding methods: CAR.
The main problem at Candlewood is to get to where there is a view of the water, since so much of the shoreline is privately owned. The route suggested below takes you to the five points that are open to the public and provide good views of the lake. The route goes entirely around the lake, and passes several other parks, launch areas and marinas. These other areas provide views of the water, but may be closed at times to non-town residents or to non-customers.

DIRECTIONS (see Map 5): Candlewood Lake lies immediately north of the city of Danbury. The route described below starts at the south end of the lake, and goes clockwise entirely around it, up the west side, over the north end and down the east side. This route passes five public access points to the lake shore.

To get to Candlewood Park at the very south end of Candlewood Lake, from I-84 exit 6, go north on Route 37 for 0.1 mile, right on Hayestown Avenue for 0.3 mile to the intersection, left on East Hayestown Road for 0.8 mile to the park.

To get to to New Fairfield Town Beach on the west shore of the lake, go back to Route 37 the way you came, and go up the west side of the lake by turning north (a right turn) on Route 37 for 4.4 miles, right on Route 39 for 2.4 miles to the park on the right. At this park, there is a view of an area of the lake that often stays ice-free into January, and also a view to the northeast across the lake to the shore of Vaughn's Neck, on which bald eagles often rest in winter.

To get to the causeway over Squantz Cove, go back to Route 39 and continue north on Route 39 (by turning right) for 1.5 miles to the causeway. Squantz Pond State Park is on the left, and a boat landing on the right. Both provide places from which areas of water can be seen. (See also "New Fairfield: Pootatuck State Forest and Squantz Pond State Park" elsewhere in this chapter).

To get to Lynn Deming Park on the east side of the lake, continue north on Route 39 for 4.8 miles until Route 39 intersects with Route 37 again, go right on Route 37 for 3.0 miles over the north end of the lake, right on Route 7 for 1.8 miles, right on North Candlewood Lake Road for 1.1 miles to the park entrance on the right. Look for gulls; lesser black-backed and Iceland have been seen here.

To get to the Dike Point Recreation Area, continue south on North Candlewood Lake Road down the east side of the lake for 2.4 miles; right on Old Town Park Road for 0.2 mile to the recreation area on the left. This area lies on the east shore and provides a view of an area of the lake that often stays ice-free into January. There is a trail that makes a 0.8 mile loop in part along and near the shore. (See separate description under "New Milford: Dyke Point Recreation Area" in the Litchfield County chapter.)

To return to Route 7, go back out Old Town Park Road and across North Candlewood Lake Road.

NEWTOWN: NORTHEAST UTILITIES SHEPAUG DAM AREA (SOUTH SIDE)

HABITATS
OPEN TERRESTRIAL: shrubby field, scattered cedars, edge;
Forest: hardwoods, hardwoods/hemlock;
Lake/pond: lake, cove, deep water, hardwood/hemlock shore.
This site lies on the south shore of the Housatonic River directly across from the Shepaug Dam Eagle Observation Area. A power line right of way crosses the site, and provides an abundance of shrubby field and edge habitats, together with scattered cedar trees. A forest of hardwoods and hemlock occupies most of the area, and goes down to a cove of Lake Lillinonah, a dammed section of the Housatonic (as habitat, it is more like a lake than a river).

SEASONS/BIRDS
SPRING MIGRATION: water birds, LAND BIRDS;
NESTING SEASON: LAND BIRDS;
FALL MIGRATION: water birds, LAND BIRDS;
Winter: land birds.
This is a good site to visit any time in the spring, summer and fall, but it is best during April/May and September/October (just when the Shepaug Dam Eagle Observation Area across the river is closed). It is best not to come here in winter, when parts of the area are closed to the public to avoid disturbance to the bald eagles that winter here. Both migrations are good, especially the fall, because of the large areas of berry-carrying shrubs at the power line. That edge habitat also produces an interesting nesting season; nesting species include wild turkey, woodcock, both cuckoos, barred and great horned owls, brown thrasher, gnatcatcher, yellow-throated and warbling vireos, chestnut-sided and prairie warblers, indigo bunting and field sparrow. Although this site is smaller than the nearby Paugusset State Forest, it contains greater habitat diversity.

GETTING AROUND
Birding methods: walk.

There is one main trail that leads to the south end of the Shepaug Dam (this trail is closed between December 1 and March 31 to avoid disturbance to wintering bald eagles), and two side trails that go to the shore of Lake Lillinonah.

DIRECTIONS (see Map 3): This site is in Newtown, on the west (or south) bank of the Housatonic River, immediately across from the Shepaug Dam Eagle Observation Area, and about one mile north of Newtown. To get there from I-84 exit 11, go west on Route 34 to the traffic light in the center of Sandy Hook, north (straight ahead) on Glen Road for 1.4 miles, left on Walnut Tree Hill Road for 1.3 miles, right on Alberts Hill Road for 1.1 miles to the entrance on the right, opposite Valley Field Road on the left. (This preserve is also part of the "Tour of Housatonic River Sites".)

NEWTOWN: PAUGUSSET STATE FOREST (NORTHERN BLOCK)

HABITATS
FOREST: hardwoods, hardwoods/hemlock, hemlock;
LAKE/POND: lake, cove, deep water, wooded shore, several small streams, wooded streambelts;
River/stream: perennial stream, seasonal streams, wooded streambelts;
Marsh/swamp/bog: small shrub swamp.
Other: rocky slope.
This is an 850-acre area which occupies a peninsula that juts into Lake Lillinonah - a dammed section of the Housatonic River below its confluence with the Shepaug River. Lake Lillinonah is defined here as lake rather than river habitat. It includes extensive shoreline, and is almost entirely wooded, hilly, rocky and rugged. Several small streams flow through the forest.

SEASONS/BIRDS
SPRING MIGRATION: WATER BIRDS, LAND BIRDS;
NESTING SEASON: LAND BIRDS;
FALL MIGRATION: WATER BIRDS, LAND BIRDS;
Winter: land birds.
This site offers the possibility of seeing migrating water birds, as well as a nice mix of typical migrating and nesting forest-dwelling land birds. Nesting species include goshawk, red-shouldered hawk, barred owl, pileated woodpecker, solitary vireo, black-throated green and worm-eating warblers. The best periods are from late April to late September for land birds, March and November for water birds.

GETTING AROUND
Birding methods: car, WALK, boat.
Woods roads and trails lead to some parts of the forest and river shore; other parts are difficult to reach. Alberts Hill Road provides easy and good birding on foot, or in a car. There is a place by the road where you can easily launch a canoe into the cove of Lake Lillinonah. Access to some parts of the forest is prohibited from December through March to prevent disturbance to wintering bald eagles. Access roads may be in poor condition in winter and spring.

DIRECTIONS (see Map 3): This part of the Paugusset State Forest is on the west (or south) bank of the Housatonic River, one or two miles north of Newtown. To get there from I-84 exit 11, go west Route 34 for 1.0 mile to the traffic light in the center of Sandy Hook, north (straight ahead) on Glen Road for 1.4 miles, left on Walnut Tree Hill Road for 1.3 miles, right on Alberts Hill Road for 1.3 miles to the entrance on the right, or walk for another 0.4 mile to a woods road on the right. (This preserve is also part of the "Tour of Housatonic River Sites".)

NEWTOWN: PAUGUSSET STATE FOREST (SOUTHERN BLOCK)

HABITATS
    FOREST: hardwoods, hardwoods/white pine, hardwoods/hemlock, hemlock;
    LAKE/POND: lake, deep water, wooded shore;
    River/stream: several small streams, shrubby and wooded streambelts;
    Other: slope with debris.
This southern block is the larger part (1,044-acres) of the Paugusset State Forest, and is separate from the northern block. This area lies on the west shore of the Housatonic River, at a section that is dammed and called Lake Zoar. It is largely wooded, with varied deciduous, conifer and mixed forest types, and it also includes streambelt habitats associated with several streams that go through the forest. (At the time this was written the hemlocks of this forest were being hit hard by the wooly adelgid, and this will certainly change its character.)

SEASONS/BIRDS
    SPRING MIGRATION: water birds, LAND BIRDS;
    NESTING SEASON: LAND BIRDS;
    FALL MIGRATION: water birds, LAND BIRDS;
    Winter: land birds.
The spring and fall migration periods are best at this site, mainly for the land birds that occur in the terrestrial habitats and along the shoreline. Land bird species that nest in the forest include great horned owl, pileated and red-bellied woodpeckers, great crested flycatcher, hermit thrush, yellow-throated vireo and worm-eating warbler. Lake Zoar itself can be pretty good for water birds, once cold weather has stopped the boating activity.

GETTING AROUND
    Birding methods: walk, boat.
There are several trails and woods roads that lead through the forest and to Lake Zoar. Access to Lake Zoar is prohibited from December through March to prevent disturbance to wintering bald eagles.

DIRECTIONS: This area is about ten miles east of Danbury. To get there from I-84, take exit 11, go south on Route 34 for 5.1 miles, left on Great Quarter Road for 1.3 miles to a dead end at the forest. Starting at 0.8 mile from Route 34, the forest lies along the left side of Great Quarter Road.

NEWTOWN: POOTATUCK OPEN SPACE AREA

HABITATS

RIVER/STREAM: river, cove, marshy, swampy, shrubby and wooded streambelt; stream, shrubby and wooded streambelt;
Forest: hardwoods, hardwoods/white pine, hardwoods/hemlock, flood plain;
Open terrestrial: short grass field, shrubby edge;
Marsh/swamp/bog: shrub marsh, shrub swamp, shrubby and wooded edge;
The Pootatuck Open Space Area is a recreation area that centers around mowed playing fields. These fields border on three water bodies: on the Housatonic River (called Lake Zoar in this dammed section), on a backwater cove of the Housatonic, and on the Pootatuck River (a stream really) that flows into the cove. This section of Lake Zoar has enough current to be considered river, rather than lake habitat. The cove includes open water, shrub marsh, shrub swamp, and a shrubby and hardwood edge. The edges of the field are made up of dense shrub growth composed of lots of berry-producing shrubs and scattered cedars. This edge is backed by a narrow strip of flood plain deciduous forest. Across the Housatonic River and easily seen is a forest of hardwoods and hardwoods/hemlock.

SEASONS/BIRDS

SPRING MIGRATION: WATER BIRDS, marsh birds, shore birds, LAND BIRDS;
Nesting season: water birds, land birds;
FALL MIGRATION: WATER BIRDS, marsh birds, shore birds, LAND BIRDS;
WINTER: gulls, WATER BIRDS, LAND BIRDS.
This is a small area, easy to cover, and you will see a lot of birds. It is best during the spring and fall migrations. In the late fall, winter and early spring, look for water birds on the cove, including mallard, black duck, ring-necked duck, lesser scaup, bufflehead, common golden-eye, hooded merganser. Interesting species of gulls sometimes occur here in winter - Iceland gull has been reported. Later in the spring and earlier in the fall, this is a good site for land birds, especially edge-dwellers, and, in the late fall, berry-eaters. Osprey occur here in spring and fall. Nesting species include green-backed heron, wood duck, red-bellied woodpecker, willow flycatcher, Carolina wren, warbling and yellow-throated vireos, orchard oriole and swamp sparrow. In winter, both Carolina and winter wrens occur here. Bald eagle also occurs in winter, so be careful to avoid disturbance.

GETTING AROUND

Birding methods: walk.
This is a relatively small area, and is easily covered on foot. Walk along the edges of the playing field, looking through the edge at the river, cove and wetland as opportunities occur. In summer, the park is crowded and heavily used for recreation. This site is open all year, and is an alternative to the nearby Shepaug Dam site, which is closed in the spring and fall.

DIRECTIONS(see Map 3): This site is in Newtown, on the west (or south) bank of the Housatonic River, and about a mile north of Newtown. To get there from I-84 exit 11, go west on Route 34 for 1.0 mile to the traffic light in the center of Sandy Hook, north (straight ahead) on Glen Road for 1.4 miles, left on Walnut Tree Hill Road for 0.2 miles, and right on Bridge End Road for 0.1 mile to a parking area on the right. (This site is also part of the "Tour of Housatonic River Sites".)

NEWTOWN: THE NATURE CONSERVANCY SHEPAUG DAM PRESERVE

HABITATS
      FOREST: hardwoods, hardwoods/white pine, hardwoods/hemlock;
      Open terrestrial: shrubby edge;
      River/stream: river, wooded shore, perennial stream, wooded streambelt;
      Marsh/swamp/bog: shrubby hardwood swamp;
      Other: ledge, rocky slope.
This Nature Conservancy preserve is bounded on the north by the Housatonic River (here called Lake Zoar) and on the west by a pipeline right of way. It is hilly and rocky, largely forested by hardwoods, white pine and hemlock in various combinations. There are shrubby edges along the pipeline, a shrubby hardwood swamp, and small streams with wooded streambelts.

SEASONS/BIRDS
      SPRING MIGRATION: water birds, LAND BIRDS;
      NESTING SEASON: water birds, LAND BIRDS;
      FALL MIGRATION: water birds, LAND BIRDS;
      Winter: (not open to public).
This preserve is worth visiting during the spring, summer and fall. While there is the possibility of seeing water birds on Lake Zoar, the real draw at this site is land birds. There is a good variety of migrants - all the species you would expect to see in these habitats. Nesting species include wild turkey, great horned owl, pileated and red-bellied woodpeckers, crested flycatcher, hermit thrush, yellow-throated vireo, gnatcatcher, black-throated green and worm-eating warblers, and Louisiana waterthrush. Sharp-shinned hawk has been seen feeding here, but nesting is not confirmed. In the fall, the berries on shrubs along the pipeline edge produce a lot of feeding activity.

GETTING AROUND
      Birding methods: walk.
Several trails lead through this preserve and down to the shore of Lake Zoar. During the period December 1 through March 31, this preserve is closed to the public to protect the bald eagles that winter here. However, it is open for birding the rest of the year, so that it offers an alternative to the nearby Shepaug Dam Eagle Observation Area while that site is closed during the spring and fall.

DIRECTIONS(see Map3): This site is in the town of Newtown, on the west (or south) bank of the Housatonic River about a mile northeast of Newtown center. To get there from I-84 exit 11, go west on Route 34 for 1.0 mile to the traffic light in the center of Sandy Hook, north (straight ahead) on Glen Road for 1.4 miles, left on Walnut Tree Hill Road for 1.0 mile to where a gas pipeline crosses the road, and there is an iron gate on the right. Park on the left side of the road, and follow the pipeline to the right for a hundred feet or so to a trail on the right marked "The Nature Conservancy". This trail leads to other trails within the preserve. (This preserve is also part of the "Tour of Housatonic River Sites".)

NORWALK: CALF PASTURE BEACH/CITY PARK

HABITATS

COASTAL: peninsula, tidal cove, Long Island Sound, islands, offshore rocks, sand bar, sandy beach;
Open terrestrial: short grass field.
This park occupies the end of the point that forms the eastern side of Norwalk Harbor. The sandy beach of the park overlooks Norwalk Harbor and the Sound, and provides distant views of several of the Norwalk Islands.

SEASONS/BIRDS

SPRING MIGRATION: GULLS, TERNS, WATER BIRDS, marsh birds, shore birds, land birds;
Nesting season: gulls, terns, shore birds;
FALL MIGRATION: GULLS, TERNS, WATER BIRDS, SHORE BIRDS, land birds;
WINTER: GULLS, WATER BIRDS, LAND BIRDS.
This site is best from October through April, when water birds can be seen on nearby waters of the harbor. During the warm months, oystercatchers nest on offshore sand bars and rocks, and black skimmers feed at the sandbars. Also, in late fall, winter and early spring, open-country land bird species such as snow bunting and horned lark occur on the mowed lawns and beach. Over the years, uncommon species including gannet, harlequin duck, tricolored heron and snowy owl have been seen here.

GETTING AROUND

Birding methods: CAR.
The park driveway provides a view of the main habitat areas. Bring a scope to look for oystercatchers on the offshore rocks and islands. Public access to this park is restricted during the warm months.

DIRECTIONS: This site is on the coast at Norwalk. From I-95 exit 16, go south on East Street for 0.4 mile, bear left on Cemetery Street (which becomes Gregory Boulevard) for 0.7 mile, bear left on Calf Pasture Road for 1.0 mile to the park entrance.

NORWALK: MANRESA ISLAND

HABITATS

COASTAL: high salt marsh, low salt marsh, tidal creek, intertidal flats, herbaceous and shrubby edges;
Manresa Island is owned by Northeast Utilities and operated as a power plant. It is really not an island, but a peninsula that extends into Long Island Sound. It is a land trap that contains a rich variety of coastal habitats, including a tidal marsh, tide pools and mud flats. Unfortunately, these habitats are all closely surrounded by industrial, residential and commercial development.

SEASONS/BIRDS

SPRING MIGRATION: gulls, terns, WATER BIRDS, MARSH BIRDS, SHORE BIRDS, land birds;
NESTING SEASON: MARSH BIRDS, land birds;
FALL MIGRATION: gulls, terns, WATER BIRDS, MARSH BIRDS, SHORE BIRDS, land birds;
WINTER: gulls, WATER BIRDS, LAND BIRDS.

This site has certain drawbacks as a birding area, but a number of uncommon species have been seen here over the years, including marsh birds such as glossy ibis, tricolored heron, little blue heron and yellow-crowned night heron; shore birds such as whimbrel, Hudsonian and marbled godwits, and stilt sandpiper. Species that have nested here include clapper and king rails, seaside and sharp-tailed sparrows. During the spring migration - especially in May - look at low tide for shore birds and waders, and at mid- and high tide for waders and water birds. During the spring, summer and fall, the marshes at this site are used as a feeding area by herons from rookeries on the Norwalk Islands. In winter, the marsh is hunted by raptors including rough-legged hawk and short-eared owl; snowy owl has been seen here a few times.

GETTING AROUND
Birding methods: car, walk.
It is difficult to get to places from which this marsh can be seen, since the land next to it is almost all private and heavily developed. Parts of the marsh can be seen by walking from the power plant entrance (see below) along Woodward/Longshore Avenue. Parking anywhere in this area can be a problem; be sure to obey current regulations. The Northeast Utilities property itself is off-limits to the public; it might be worthwhile to write to NU Public Relations to ask for a permit to enter.

DIRECTIONS: Manresa Island is immediately south of the city of Norwalk. To get there from I-95, take exit 16, go south on East Avenue for 0.5 mile, right on Route 136 for 1.4 miles, (following Route 136 as it makes several turns), to a point where Route 136 goes right; here, go straight on Woodward Avenue (which becomes Longshore Avenue) for 0.8 mile to the power plant entrance.

NORWALK: NORWALK ISLANDS

HABITATS
COASTAL: islands, rocky shore, cobble, gravel and sand beach, coastal forest, shrubby and herbaceous edge, salt marsh, mud flat, dune.
A cluster of islands lies off the coast of Norwalk and Westport, near the mouth of the Norwalk River. The four largest are Chimon, Sheffield, Cockenoe and Shea; in addition, there are nine smaller islands and numerous rocks. Most have the important island attribute of being relatively protected from mammalian predation and human disturbance. In other respects, their habitats vary somewhat, but those islands that are most important for birds share certain characteristics - they are covered by dense shrub thickets and some areas of coastal forest.

SEASONS/BIRDS
Spring migration: gulls, terns, water birds, marsh birds, shore birds, land birds;
NESTING SEASON: GULLS, TERNS, WATER BIRDS, MARSH BIRDS, SHORE BIRDS, land birds;
Fall migration: gulls, terns, water birds, marsh birds, shore birds, land birds;
Winter: gulls, water birds, land birds.
Several of these islands were once among the most important heron rookeries along the entire Northeast coast. However, in recent years, double-crested cormorants have taken over several of the islands for nesting, and the herons have moved elsewhere. The Norwalk Islands are also important as protected nesting and resting areas for a variety of other species,

including gulls, terns and shore birds. Historically, many of the waders and several shore bird species that are seen as they feed in marshes and on mudflats along the western Connecticut coast have been dependent on the protected nesting areas and rookeries afforded by the Norwalk Islands. The principal species that have nested on one or more of these islands are: gulls including herring and great black-backed; terns including common and least; double-crested cormorant; oystercatcher, and nine species of waders, including great and snowy egrets, little blue and green-backed herons, yellow-crowned and black-crowned night herons.

GETTING AROUND
Birding methods: BOAT.
It is necessary to use a boat in order to get close enough to see birds on these islands. The islands are protected during the nesting season, and must not be landed on or approached too closely.

DIRECTIONS: The Norwalk Islands are now part of the Stuart B. McKinney National Wildlife Refuge, and subject to certain management regulations. A boat from Norwalk Harbor takes individuals and groups to some of the islands with a naturalist during the period July 1 through Labor Day. For details, contact the Maritime Center, 10 N Water Street, Norwalk CT 06854, tel. (203) 852-0700.

NORWALK: VETERANS MEMORIAL PARK

HABITATS
COASTAL: salt water tidal cove, mud flat, mixed herbaceous shore;
Open Terrestrial: short grass field.
Lake/pond: seasonal pools.
This park occupies a small peninsula that extends into Norwalk Harbor. It provides a good view of the upper end of the harbor, and of extensive mud flats just offshore. Within the park are playing fields with mowed lawns.

SEASONS/BIRDS
SPRING MIGRATION: GULLS, TERNS, WATER BIRDS, MARSH BIRDS, SHORE BIRDS, land birds;
Nesting season: gulls, terns, marsh birds;
FALL MIGRATION: GULLS, TERNS, WATER BIRDS, MARSH BIRDS, SHORE BIRDS, LAND BIRDS;
WINTER: GULLS, WATER BIRDS, land birds.
The mud flats that the park overlooks at low tide are used as a feeding area by a wide variety of water birds (fall, winter and spring), marsh birds (spring, summer and fall), and shore birds. Shore birds gather at pools of rain water on the lawns after storms. A variety of hawks - buteos, accipiters and falcons - occur here during the fall migration. Numerous uncommon species have been seen at the mud flat, including stilt, pectoral and buff-breasted sandpipers, Hudsonian godwit and black skimmer.

GETTING AROUND
Birding methods: CAR.
Park driveways go near or through the main habitat areas. The park is open to the public all year; it is crowded in summer.

DIRECTIONS: This site is on the coast at Norwalk. From I-95 exit 16, go south on East Avenue for 0.5 mile, right on Van Zant Street (Route 136) for 0.3 mile, left on Veterans Park Road into the park.

REDDING: HUCKLEBERRY SWAMP (STEICHEN PRESERVE)

HABITATS
MARSH/SWAMP/BOG: sedge and mixed herbaceous marsh, shrub swamp with some cattails, shrubby hardwood swamp, hardwood swamp, dead wood;
Forest: hardwoods, hardwoods/white pine;
River/stream: stream, slow water, wooded shore.
The centerpiece of this 54-acre Connecticut Audubon Society preserve is a shrub and wooded swamp fed by a slow-moving stream. It lies at the southern end of the Northeastern Lime Belt, a long, narrow limestone area that extends south from Vermont. This position causes the swamp to lie over calcareous (alkaline) bedrock that counteracts the normal acidity of the wetland, and permits several unusual plant species to grow here. These include dwarf birch, hoary willow and rush aster. A hardwoods forest covers the hillsides that surround the wetland. Unfortunately, phragmites is taking over much of the marsh area.

SEASONS/BIRDS
SPRING MIGRATION: water birds, marsh birds, LAND BIRDS;
NESTING SEASON: water birds, marsh birds, LAND BIRDS;
Fall migration: marsh birds, land birds;
Winter: land birds.
This site was once a prime wetland area in which to bird, because a boardwalk permitted quiet passage through the wetland. Unfortunately, at the time of writing, the boardwalk is not usable; however, most of the birds are still there (phragmites notwithstanding), and it is still worth a visit. Over the years, Virginia rail has nested here, and it has been one of the few places in Connecticut where whip-poor-will could be heard singing from a nearby hillside. In addition, a nice variety of wetland-oriented land birds occur here as migrants and nesters. Mallard and wood ducks are about the only water bird species you can expect to see. Overall, May and June are the best months to come here.

GETTING AROUND
Birding methods: walk.
A portion of the marsh and swamp can be seen from the road. The beginning of the former trail can still be walked for a few yards. Parking is limited.

DIRECTIONS: This preserve is about ten miles south of Danbury. To get there from Ridgefield at the intersection of Routes 7 and 35, go south on Route 7 for 2.0 miles, left on Topstone Road for 1.0 mile (straight across an intersection), and left on Chestnut Woods Road for 0.1 mile to the wetland on the right, and for 0.2 mile to a small parking area at the start of the trail and former boardwalk.

REDDING: SAUGATUCK FALLS NATURAL AREA

HABITATS
Forest: hardwoods, hemlock, floodplain, mountain laurel.
Open terrestrial: shrubby field, shrubby edge.
River/stream: stream, fast water, wooded streambelt, hemlock ravine;
Marsh/swamp/bog: hardwood swamp. shrubby hardwood swamp,
Other: cliff, rocky slope.
This 312-acre area contains a nice diversity of habitats in rocky, hilly terrain - varied woodlands, a stream, and some open and edge areas created by a power line.

SEASONS/BIRDS
Spring migration: land birds;
Nesting season: land birds;
Fall migration: land birds;
Winter: land birds.
You can expect to find a standard mix of woodland and edge species throughout the spring, summer and fall. A few residents are present in winter.

GETTING AROUND
Birding methods: WALK.
A network of trails goes throughout this area; it is possible to do a variety of short loop walks (total distance of all the trails is about five miles). A map is posted at the entrance.

DIRECTIONS: This area is close to the center of Redding, midway between Danbury and Bridgeport. From the intersection of Routes 53 and 107, go north on Route 53 for 0.9 mile to the entrance on the left, across the road from the John Reed Middle School.

REDDING: TOPSTONE PARK

HABITATS
Forest: hardwoods, hardwoods/hemlock, cedar, shrubby edges;
Open terrestrial: short grass field, shrubby edges, vine tangles and thickets;
Lake/pond: ponds, deep and shallow water, grassy, shrubby and wooded shores;
River/stream: streams, wooded streambelts;
Marsh/swamp/bog: hardwood swamp;
Other: rocky hilltop, rocky slope.
This 274-acre town park includes two ponds - one developed for swimming - a wetland, and a rocky hilltop with a distant view of Long Island Sound. Most of the area is forested.

SEASONS/BIRDS
Spring migration: land birds;
Nesting season: land birds;
Fall migration: land birds;
Winter: land birds.
This is a nice site in which to look for a typical mix of both woodland and edge birds, during both migrations and the nesting season. Screech owl nests in the park.

GETTING AROUND
Birding methods: walk.

The main woods road provides easy birding along forest edges of shrubs and thickets. There are a number of trails that make loop trips possible along the ponds and wetland, and over Topstone Mountain. Access to the park is restricted to town residents during the warm months.

DIRECTIONS: This preserve is about ten miles south of Danbury. To get there from Ridgefield at the intersection of Routes 7 and 35, go south on Route 7 for 2.0 miles, left on Topstone Road for 1.2 miles to the entrance on the right.

REDDING: VALLEY ROAD

HABITATS
FOREST: mixed hardwoods, hardwoods/hemlock;
River/stream: stream, fast and slow water, wooded streambelt, hemlock ravine;
Marsh/swamp/bog: shrubby hardwood swamp, hardwood swamp;
Other: rocky slope.

This is a quiet rural road that passes through good habitat. It goes through the valley formed by one of the tributaries of the Aspetuck River - here a small stream with a streambelt that includes a hemlock ravine and a hardwood swamp, and lies between wooded and rocky hillsides.

SEASONS/BIRDS
SPRING MIGRATION: LAND BIRDS
NESTING SEASON: LAND BIRDS
Fall migration: land birds
Winter: land birds.

The spring migration, especially of warblers, is very good in this lovely valley. Nesting species include Acadian flycatcher (in the hemlock ravine) and worm-eating warbler (on the rocky slopes).

GETTING AROUND
Birding methods: car, WALK.

This section of Valley Road is rough for driving, but passable in dry weather. However, it does provide easy walking. Stay on the road; the surrounding land is private.

DIRECTIONS: This area is about ten miles southeast of Danbury. To get there from the intersection of Routes 58 and 107 (at Putnam Memorial State Park) go south on Route 58 for 6.3 miles, and left on Valley Road for 1.5 miles to Rock House Road. At this point, Valley Road becomes dirt, and continues for another 1.5 miles to Stepney Road. It is this stretch of Valley Road between Rock House Road and Stepney Road that goes through the habitats described above. However, other sections of Valley Road are also good.

REDDING/BETHEL: COLLIS P. HUNTINGTON STATE PARK

HABITATS
OPEN TERRESTRIAL: mixed herbaceous and shrubby fields; hedgerows, shrubby and wooded edges;
Lake/pond: four ponds, shrubby and wooded shores;
Forest: hardwoods, hardwoods/white pine
Marsh/swamp/bog: shrub marsh, shrub swamp;
Other: hawk watching site.

This 900-acre park is a former estate that now includes reverting farmland, extensive areas of shrubs and vine-choked thickets, four ponds, several swamps and varied deciduous forest, including a stately grove of mature oaks. This is a good area in which to see habitat types undergoing the process of succession.

SEASONS/BIRDS
SPRING MIGRATION: LAND BIRDS;
NESTING SEASON: LAND BIRDS;
FALL MIGRATION: LAND BIRDS;
Winter: land birds.

The large size of this site combined with the variety of habitats within it make for decent birding during migrations and the nesting period. Both migrations are good, with a variety of warblers in the spring and fall, hawks in September, and sparrows in October and November. Nesting species include yellow-bellied flycatcher, great horned owl, pileated woodpecker, brown thrasher, white-eyed and warbling vireos, worm-eating, prairie and hooded warblers, orchard oriole and indigo bunting.

GETTING AROUND
Birding methods: WALK.
There are seven miles of trails that go throughout the park.

DIRECTIONS: This park is in Redding, about five miles southeast of Danbury. To get there from Bethel at the intersection of Routes 58 and 302, go south on Route 58 for 1.4 miles, left on Sunset Hill Road for 2.4 miles to the park entrance on the left.

REDDING/BETHEL: PUTNAM MEMORIAL STATE PARK

HABITATS:
FOREST: hardwoods, hardwoods/hemlock, mountain laurel;
Marsh/swamp/bog: shrub and wooded swamp;
Open terrestrial: short grass field;
Lake/pond: pond, shrubby edge.
Other: rocky slope, ledge.

All of this small (183 acre) park is somewhat developed for human use, but it includes a rich variety of habitats - mostly woods with a well-developed understory of mountain laurel, and also small areas of swamp, patches of lawn and a pond.

SEASONS/BIRDS
SPRING MIGRATION: water birds, LAND BIRDS;
NESTING SEASON: water birds, LAND BIRDS;
Fall migration: land birds;
Winter: land birds.

Spring and early summer are the best times to visit this park. The spring migration, especially of warblers, is very good. In addition, hooded warbler nests in the laurel understory of the woods east of Route 58, and worm-eating warbler on rocky slopes west of Route 58.

GETTING AROUND
Birding methods: car, walk.

Park driveways and trails go through most areas of the park.

DIRECTIONS: This park is about five miles southeast of Danbury. The intersection of Routes 58 and 107 (just south of the Redding/Bethel town line) is at the entrance to the main part of the park. Route 58 goes north from this intersection past another part of the park (on your right as you head north).

RIDGEFIELD/WILTON: WOODCOCK NATURE CENTER

HABITATS
MARSH/SWAMP/BOG: shrub swamp, shrubby hardwood swamp, hardwood swamp, deadwood swamp, shrubby edges;
Forest: hardwoods, mountain laurel;
Lake/pond: pond, shrubby and hardwood shore;
River/stream: perennial stream, seasonal stream, hardwood streambelts.

This small (146-acre) site lies in the midst of suburban development, but seems completely isolated from it. Much of it is woodland, and it also includes a pond, several streams (tributaries of the Norwalk River), and a good-sized wooded and shrubby swamp.

SEASONS/BIRDS
SPRING MIGRATION: water birds, marsh birds, shore birds, LAND BIRDS;
NESTING SEASON: water birds, LAND BIRDS;
FALL MIGRATION: water birds, marsh birds, shore birds, LAND BIRDS;
Winter: land birds.

This site is a nice place to do some birding if you are nearby. It has a good mix of the species you would expect in these habitats. Spring migrants include a wide variety of warblers, and nesters include red-shouldered hawk, barred owl, pileated woodpecker and southern species such as red-bellied woodpecker, Carolina wren and worm-eating warbler.

GETTING AROUND
Birding methods: WALK.

There are two miles of well-maintained trails that reach all the main habitat areas. A boardwalk goes through the swamp.

DIRECTIONS: This site lies on the border between Ridgefield and Wilton, about ten miles south of Danbury. From the intersection of Routes 33 and 35 in the southern part of Ridgefield center, go south on Route 33 for 3.3 miles, left on Millstone Road for 0.7 mile, and left on Deer Run Road for 0.9 mile to the entrance on the left.

SHELTON: INDIAN WELL STATE PARK

HABITATS

River/stream: river; wooded, shrubby and herbaceous streambelt; stream, hemlock ravine;
Forest: hardwoods, hardwoods/hemlock, hemlock;
Open terrestrial: short grass and shrubby fields, edges.

This long, narrow park lies on a river terrace along the western shore of the Housatonic River. In addition to the river itself, habitats include a stream that flows through a hemlock ravine, wooded areas of hardwoods and hemlock in various combinations, a mowed playing field and a small shrubby field.

SEASONS/BIRDS

Spring migration: water birds, land birds;
Nesting season: water birds, land birds;
Fall migration: water birds, marsh birds, land birds;
Winter: water birds, land birds.

The best birding at this site is for land birds, especially in the spring and fall during the warbler migration. During the fall, several species of marsh birds may appear as migrants or post-breeding season wanderers - black-crowned night heron, great egret, great blue heron. In late fall, winter and early spring, there are often water birds on the Housatonic River, sometimes including lesser scaup. Nesters include a mix of typical species, plus orchard oriole.

GETTING AROUND

Birding methods: car, WALK.

There are several short paths and a section of the Paugussett Trail within this site. The park gets crowded and an admission fee is charged during the warm months. Do not leave valuables in your car.

DIRECTIONS: This park lies immediately north of the city of Shelton. The easiest way to get there is from the west, by starting at the intersection of Routes 110 and 111. Go east on Route 110 for 4.9 miles, sharp left on Indian Well Road for 0.8 mile to the park entrance on the right.

SHERMAN: COLONIAL PARK

HABITATS

OPEN TERRESTRIAL: short grass and shrubby field, cedars, shrubby and wooded edge;
Forest: hardwoods, cedar;
River/stream: seasonal streams, hardwood streambelts;
Marsh/swamp/bog: shrubby hardwood swamp.

The outstanding feature of this park is a large stand of maturing cedar trees, that vary in height from 3' to 18'. Some of them are scattered in an open field, and others have matured into a forest habitat.

SEASONS/BIRDS
Spring migration: land birds;
Nesting season: land birds;
Fall migration: land birds;
Winter: land birds.

During the spring and fall migrations, a nice variety of land birds passes through this site. In October and November, bird the edges of the field for sparrows. Nesters include such edge species as prairie warbler, indigo bunting and brown thrasher. In winter, this is an excellent site at which to look for saw-whet owl; long-eared owl has also been seen here on an irregular basis. Also in winter, look in the shrubs and edges for berry-eating land bird species such as flicker, robin, bluebird and cedar waxwing.

GETTING AROUND
Birding methods: walk, ski.

There are several trails that make loops of different lengths, and provide easy walking.

DIRECTIONS: This park is in the town of Sherman, which lies in the northern tip of Fairfield County. To get there from the village of Sherman at the northern intersection of Routes 37 and 39, go southwest on these two Routes for 0.4 mile and left on the park driveway.

SHERMAN: WIMISINK PRESERVE

HABITATS
MARSH/SWAMP/BOG: sedge, cattail and shrub marsh, shrub swamp, dead trees, herbaceous, shrubby and wooded edges;
Open Terrestrial: mixed herbaceous and shrubby fields;
Lake/pond: small beaver pond;
River/stream: stream, herbaceous and shrubby streambelt.

This wetland has a good mix of habitat types. It is a sanctuary of the Naromi Land Trust.

SEASONS/BIRDS
SPRING MIGRATION: water birds, shore birds, land birds;
NESTING SEASON: water birds, LAND BIRDS;
FALL MIGRATION: water birds, marsh birds, shore birds, LAND BIRDS;
WINTER: LAND BIRDS.

This site has something to offer at every season. During the spring migration, species of interest include snipe (April), woodcock (March-May), solitary and spotted sandpipers, and harrier (March and April). Nesting species include red-tailed hawk, Virginia rail and willow flycatcher; red-shouldered and Cooper's hawks nest nearby and come to this wetland to feed. The fall migration brings a similar species mix to that in the spring, plus sparrows in October. In winter, habitats at this site attract several raptor species, sparrows and other lingering land birds such as hermit thrush. Great horned, screech and barred owls are here throughout the year.

GETTING AROUND
Birding methods: car, walk.

As yet there are no trails through this site. However, the habitat areas can be reached by walking across fields. Parts of the area can be seen by walking along Routes 39 and 55, but go in the early morning to avoid the heavy traffic later in the day.

DIRECTIONS: This site is at the northern tip of Fairfield County, a mile or two west of Gaylordsville. In Gaylordsville at the intersection of Routes 7 and 55, go west on Route 55 for 1.1 mile, left on Route 39 for 0.1 mile to a pulloff on the right. The wildlife area is on the right, and is bounded on the east by Route 39 and on the north by Route 55.

STAMFORD: CUMMINGS PARK/WEST BEACH PARK

HABITATS
COASTAL: sandy beach, breakwater, Long Island Sound, tidal cove, islands, off-shore rocks;
Open Terrestrial: short grass field.
Both of these two contiguous parks have sandy beaches on the upper shoreline of Westcott Cove, in which there are offshore rocks and an island.

SEASONS/BIRDS
SPRING MIGRATION: gulls, terns, WATER BIRDS, marsh birds, shore birds;
Nesting season: gulls, terns, shore birds;
FALL MIGRATION: gulls, terns, WATER BIRDS, marsh birds, shore birds;
Winter: gulls, WATER BIRDS, land birds
The greatest variety of birds to be seen here are water birds on Long Island Sound during the period October through March. During the nesting season, oystercatchers can be seen (by using a scope) on rocks out in the cove, where they are believed to be nesting.

GETTING AROUND
Birding methods: car.
Driveways in each of these parks lead to the beach and views of Long Island Sound. The parks are crowded in summer, and access may be limited to town residents.

DIRECTIONS (see Map 6): These two parks are on the coast at Stamford. To get to Cummings Park, from I-95 exit 8, go south on Elm Street for 0.4 mile, right on Shippen Avenue for 0.3 mile to the park entrance on the left. To get to West Beach Park, continue on Shippen Avenue for another 0.2 mile, left on Seaview Avenue for 0.1 mile to the park entrance on the left.

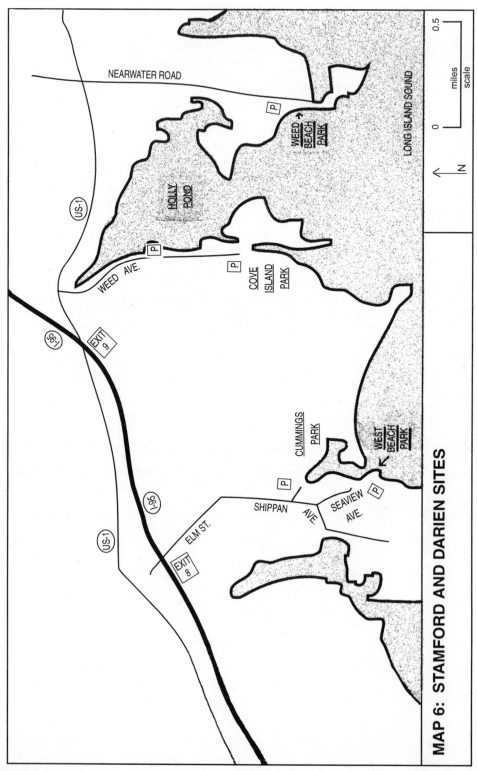

MAP 6: STAMFORD AND DARIEN SITES

STAMFORD/DARIEN: HOLLY POND/COVE ISLAND PARK/WEED BEACH

HABITATS
COASTAL: peninsula, Long Island Sound, tidal cove, salt pond, tidal creek, mud flat, high saltwater marsh, cobble and gravel beach, rocky shore, offshore rocks, coastal forest.
Open terrestrial: short grass field, shrubby edge;
Forest: hardwoods, cedars.
Holly Pond lies where the Noroton River enters Long Island Sound. It is sheltered and shallow with mud flats and a marshy shore. Cove Island Park occupies the end of the point on the west side of Holly Pond. It overlooks Holly Pond and a cove of Long Island Sound, and has open fields and shrubby areas. Weed Beach Park occupies the end of the point on the east side of Holly Pond, and it, too, overlooks Long Island Sound and a small cove.

SEASONS/BIRDS
SPRING MIGRATION: WATER BIRDS, marsh birds, shore birds, land birds;
Nesting season: marsh birds, land birds;
FALL MIGRATION: WATER BIRDS, marsh birds, shore birds, land birds.
WINTER: WATER BIRDS, land birds.
This is a good area in which to see a variety of water birds in fall, winter and spring, as well as some waders and shore birds during the spring and fall migrations. Waders also feed in Holly Pond during the summer. The open areas and groves of cedars at Cove Island Park attract land birds migrants during the period September through November (look for sparrows in the shrubby areas) and again in April. Also, during the winter, look in open areas for horned lark, snow bunting and (occasional) Lapland longspur.

GETTING AROUND
Birding methods: car.
Holly Pond can be seen from several points on Weed Avenue (see below). Cove Island Park and Weed Beach Park provide views of Long Island Sound, but have restrictions for non-residents during the warm months.

DIRECTIONS (see Map 6): These areas are on the coast in Stamford and Darien between the cities of Stamford and Norwalk. To get to Holly Pond, start at I-95 exit 9, go north (east) on Route 1 for 0.3 mile, and right on Weed Avenue. During the next 0.9 mile, there are two places at which it is possible to stop and look at Holly Pond. To get to Cove Island Park, continue on Weed Avenue for another 0.6 mile to the park entrance on the right. To get to Weed Beach Park, go back up Weed Avenue to Route 1, right for 1.0 mile, right on Nearwater Road for 1.0 mile to the park entrance.

STAMFORD/NEW CANAAN: LAUREL RESERVOIR

HABITATS
LAKE/POND: lake, wooded and shrubby shore.
This is a deep water reservoir with a largely wooded shore.

SEASONS/BIRDS
SPRING MIGRATION: WATER BIRDS, marsh birds, land birds;
Nesting season: water birds, marsh birds, land birds;
FALL MIGRATION: WATER BIRDS, marsh birds, land birds;
Winter: water birds.

There is often a good variety of water birds at this reservoir during the late fall, winter (if there is open water) and early spring. For water birds, the best months are November and March. In addition, during the spring and fall migrations, a variety of land birds feed in the trees and shrubs along the shoreline.

GETTING AROUND
Birding methods: car, walk.
Unfortunately, in order to see birds at this site, it is necessary to stay on town roads that carry heavy traffic, and have limited opportunities to pull off.

DIRECTIONS: This reservoir straddles the Stamford/New Canaan town line, almost at the New York State border. The following route goes around the reservoir clockwise, and provides intermittent and often obscured views of the water. From the Merritt Parkway, take exit 35 and go north on Route 137 for 4.9 miles, right on Trinity Pass Road for 1.1 miles, right on Ponus Ridge Road for 1.2 miles, right on Reservoir Lane for 0.4 mile, and right on Laurel Road for 0.7 mile back to Route 137.

STRATFORD: FRASH POND

HABITATS
LAKE/POND: pond, shore of herbs (mostly phragmites) and shrubs.
This is a small, shallow pond that is very near the Housatonic River, directly across the river from Milford Point and Nells Island. Frash Pond is surrounded by industrial and commercial development.

SEASONS/BIRDS
SPRING MIGRATION: gulls, WATER BIRDS, marsh birds;
Nesting season: gulls, water birds, marsh birds;
FALL MIGRATION: gulls, WATER BIRDS, marsh birds;
WINTER: gulls, WATER BIRDS.
This is a good site at which to look for water birds during the period September through April, especially November and March. During the summer, black-crowned night heron, snowy and great egrets come here to feed.

GETTING AROUND
Birding methods: car.
A shopping area on the southeast shore provides a view of the water.

DIRECTIONS (see Map 7): This pond is located in the city of Stratford very near the west shore of the Housatonic River and not far from Short Beach. **From I-95 southbound,** take exit 32, and immediately make two left turns onto West Broad Street. **From I-95 northbound,** take exit 32, go to the rotary and turn right onto West Broad Street. Once on West Broad Street, go southeast (toward Long Island Sound) for 0.1 mile, right on Main Street (Route 113) for 1.3 miles, right on Access Road and immediately right into a shopping area that is on the shore of Frash Pond.

STRATFORD: GREAT MEADOWS/LONG BEACH

HABITATS

COASTAL: Long Island Sound, tidal cove, sand and gravel beach, dunes, herbs and shrubs on both the beach and the dunes, extensive high salt marsh and patches of low saltwater marsh, brackish marsh, fresh water marsh, patches of shrubs within the marsh, intertidal areas of mud and sand, tidal creeks, coastal forest, shrubby edges.

Several of connecticut's finest coastal birding areas lie in the estuary of the Housatonic River. They are Great Meadows (aka Lordship), Long Beach and Short Beach on the west side in Stratford; Milford Point and Nells Island Marsh across the river in Milford; and Charles Island not far offshore. Together, these sites demonstrate how a cluster of differing habitats within an estuary support and enrich one another.

Great Meadows is the largest unditched high salt marsh in Connecticut. It provides one of the most important habitats for marsh birds, shore birds and water birds in Southern New England, even though it has been seriously degraded and constricted by filling, draining and pollution associated with industrial development. Together with Long Beach, this large area contains a wide variety of rich coastal habitats. The western part of the site is dry much of the time, and includes upland habitats. The eastern portion is a high saltwater marsh cut through by a number of tidal creeks. There are brackish and fresh water marshes in the higher, upstream portions of the area. Inside the barrier beach on the south side is a tidal cove , tidal creek and areas of mud flats. The open water of Long Island Sound lies on the other side of the beach.

SEASONS/BIRDS

SPRING MIGRATION: GULLS, TERNS, WATER BIRDS, MARSH BIRDS, SHORE BIRDS, LAND BIRDS;
NESTING SEASON: GULLS, TERNS, WATER BIRDS, MARSH BIRDS, SHORE BIRDS, LAND BIRDS;
FALL MIGRATION: GULLS, TERNS, WATER BIRDS, MARSH BIRDS, SHORE BIRDS, LAND BIRDS;
WINTER: WATER BIRDS, LAND BIRDS.

This is a fantastic site throughout the year for almost any species that might occur in these types of habitat - over the years, 270 species of birds have been seen here. May and August are the best months for migrating waders and shore birds. May through September are best for nesting species. Nesting species include: least tern, pied-billed grebe, gadwall, green-winged teal, blue-winged teal, shoveler, clapper and king rails, common moorhen and least bittern, piping plover and willet, marsh wren, sharp-tailed and seaside sparrows. In addition, during the summer a variety of waders feed here, including black-crowned night heron, great and snowy egrets. A wide variety of water birds occur here from late October through late April. This is also a good period for seeing raptors including harrier and occasionally short-eared and snowy owls, as well as various lingering land bird species.

GETTING AROUND

Birding methods: car, walk.

At the time of writing, this site is in the process of acquisition by the U. S. Fish and Wildlife Service to become part of the Stuart B. McKinney National Wildlife Refuge. Hopefully, this will result in more satisfactory public access than now exists - currently, parking is a real problem.

At present, there is no real public access to the western side of this area. In order to bird the eastern side, find a place to park and view the marsh by walking along Oak Bluff Avenue and Lordship Boulevard. In order to bird the south portion, it is necessary to enter Long Beach, which is restricted to town residents during the warm months.

DIRECTIONS (see Map 7): Great Meadows is in Stratford, immediately southeast of Bridgeport. **From I-95 northbound,** take exit 30 and go right onto Lordship Boulvard at the end of the ramp. **From I-95 southbound,** take exit 30 to Surf Avenue; left on Surf Avenue for 0.1 mile; left on Lordship Boulevard. This road goes along the northern portion of the marsh and at 2.3 miles from I-95, intersects with Oak Bluff Avenue. **To reach Long Beach** (the barrier beach between the marsh and Long Island Sound), turn south (right) on Oak Bruff Avenue to the entrance to Long Beach.

STRATFORD: SHORT BEACH/VETERANS PARK

HABITATS
COASTAL: Long Island Sound, tidal cove, tidal creek, sandy beach, intertidal areas of mud, sand and gravel, sand and gravel bars offshore, dunes, low salt marsh, high salt marsh;
Open terrestrial: short grass and shrubby field, shrubby edge.
These two contiguous parks contain a wide variety of coastal habitat, especially considering their relatively small size. There is a sandy crescent beach backed by dunes, with a small tidal marsh and creek, and extensive intertidal flats offshore. In addition, this area lies within the estuary of the Housatonic River, and receives the benefit (in terms of bird species variety) of other nearby rich coastal habitats (Great Meadows and Long Beach also on the west side of the river, and Milford Point and Nells Island over on the eastern side).

SEASONS/BIRDS
SPRING MIGRATION: gulls, terns, WATER BIRDS, MARSH BIRDS, SHORE BIRDS, land birds;
NESTING SEASON: gulls, TERNS, MARSH BIRDS, SHORE BIRDS, land birds;
FALL MIGRATION: gulls, terns, WATER BIRDS, MARSH BIRDS, SHORE BIRDS, LAND BIRDS;
WINTER: gulls, WATER BIRDS, LAND BIRDS.
The best seasons here are the spring and fall, when migrating shore birds can be seen feeding on the intertidal flats at low tide. Waders feed here at mid-tide during spring, summer and fall - species such as black-crowned night heron, great and snowy egrets. Several uncommon species nest here, including least tern, piping plover and horned lark. In addition, from October through April, a variety of water birds can be seen. During this same period, a number of interesting open-habitat land bird species occur here occasionally - harrier, rough-legged hawk, short-eared owl, snow bunting, Lapland longspur, horned lark, pipit (fall and spring), and snowy owl (winter).

GETTING AROUND
Birding methods: car, walk.
The parking area is within a few yards of the beach, and the other habitats are nearby. The area is crowded and there is a parking charge during the warm months.

DIRECTIONS (see Map 7): These two contiguous parks are on Long Island Sound, south of the city of Stratford, and just east of Great Meadows and Long Beach. **From I-95 southbound:** take exit 32 and immediately make two left turns onto West Broad Street. **From I-95 northbound:** take exit 32, go to the rotary and turn right onto West Broad Street. Once on West Broad Street, go southeast (toward Long Island Sound) for 0.1 mile, right on Main Street (route 113) for 2.0 miles, left on Short Beach Road for 0.2 mile, and left on Dorne Drive to a parking area.

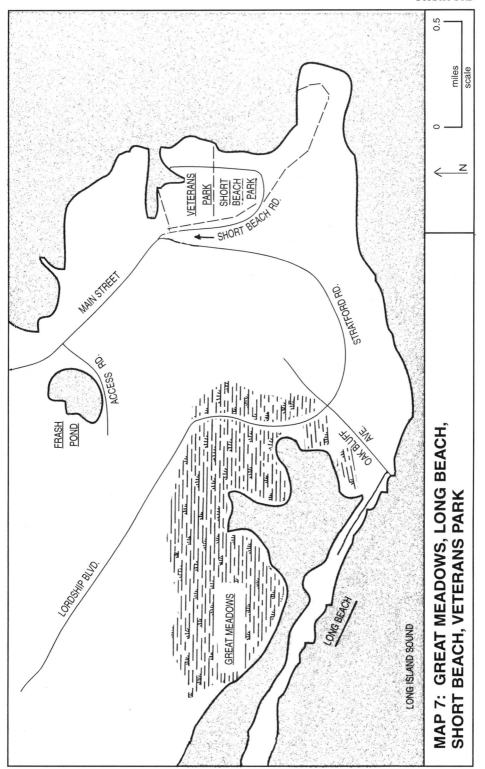

MAP 7: GREAT MEADOWS, LONG BEACH, SHORT BEACH, VETERANS PARK

TRUMBULL: TRUMBULL BASIN

HABITATS
Marsh/swamp/bog: shrub marsh, shrub swamp, shrubby hardwood swamp, hardwood swamp, shrubby edge;
Forest: hardwoods;
River/stream: stream, shrubby streambelt.
This 335-acre wetland lies along the Pequonnock River. It is leased to the State by the Bridgeport Hydraulic Company.

SEASONS/BIRDS
Spring migration: water birds, land birds;
Nesting season: water birds, land birds;
Fall migration: water birds, land birds;
Winter: land birds.
This site has all the standard species that you would expect in these types of habitat. During both the spring and fall migrations, the species diversity and the number of individual birds is quite good.

GETTING AROUND
Birding methods: walk.
Walk the abandoned railroad bed, which provides views over the wetland.

DIRECTIONS: This site is immediately north of the village of Trumbull, and lies between Routes 111 and 25. From the intersection of Routes 111 and 25, go south on Route 111 for 0.8 mile, left on Whitney Avenue for 0.4 mile, and right on the inconspicuous access road.

WESTON: DEVIL'S DEN

HABITATS
FOREST: hardwoods, hardwoods/white pine, hardwoods/hemlock, mountain laurel;
Lake/pond: pond, shrubby and wooded edge;
River/stream: river, stream, shrubby and wooded streambelts;
Marsh/swamp/bog: shrubby hardwood swamp, hardwood swamp, shrubby edge.
Other: cliff/ledge, rocky slope.
Devil's Den is one of the largest undeveloped areas in southwestern Connecticut; it includes 1,720 acres of woodland, varied wetlands, a river, numerous small streams, open knolls and rocky ridges. It contains enough undisturbed interior space for forest-dwelling species that require extensive areas for nesting.

SEASONS/BIRDS
SPRING MIGRATION: LAND BIRDS
NESTING SEASON: LAND BIRDS;
Fall migration: land birds;
Winter: land birds.
An impressive species variety occurs in this large area throughout the spring, summer and fall. The spring migration of forest-dwelling species is very good. Over 80 species have shown

evidence of nesting; these species include broad-winged hawk, barred owl, red-bellied and pileated woodpeckers, gnatcatcher, yellow-throated vireo, worm-eating and hooded warblers, Louisiana waterthrush, and a host of more common woodland species.

GETTING AROUND
Birding methods: WALK.
There are 22 miles of trails within this large preserve. A trail map is posted at the entrance, and maps may also be obtained from the nearby preserve directors' house. Many people visit this area, but it is large enough to provide solitude even on summer weekends.

DIRECTIONS: This preserve is in Weston, about five miles north of the city of Westport. From the Merritt Parkway, take exit 42 and go north on Route 57 for 5.0 miles, right on Godfrey Road for 0.5 mile, left on Pent Road to the preserve entrance.

WESTON: SAUGATUCK RESERVOIR

HABITATS
LAKE/POND: lake, deep water, hardwood and hemlock shore;
This is a reservoir with largely wooded shores.

SEASONS/BIRDS
SPRING MIGRATION: WATER BIRDS, land birds;
Nesting season: land birds;
FALL MIGRATION: WATER BIRDS, marsh birds, land birds;
WINTER: water birds, land birds.
This is a good site at which to look for water birds in the spring and fall, and during periods in the winter when there is open water (the position of the reservoir in the southern part of the state minimizes periods of freeze-over). The best period is from early November through early April. Land birds occur in the woods along the shore in spring, summer and fall, and bald eagle is a possibility in winter.

GETTING AROUND
Birding methods: car.
State and town roads follow the west shore of the reservoir, providing intermittent and sometimes obscured views of the water. Parking is difficult. The land along the shore of the reservoir is posted by the water company.

DIRECTIONS: This reservoir is about ten miles south of Danbury. In Redding, at the intersection of Routes 53 and 107, go south on Route 53 for 0.7 mile to the point where the reservoir is visible on the left. Route 53 follows the shoreline for 2.3 miles, at which point, go left on Valley Forge Road, which follows the shoreline for another 1.9 miles.

WESTPORT: SAUGATUCK RIVER

HABITATS
River/stream: tidal river, slow water, mud flat, shrubby and developed shore.
This is an overlook point on a section of the Saugatuck River that is still tidal. Intertidal mud is exposed at low tide.

SEASONS/BIRDS

Spring migration: gulls, water birds, marsh birds, shore birds, land birds;
Nesting season: water birds, marsh birds, land birds;
Fall migration: gulls, water birds, marsh birds, shore birds, land birds;
Winter: gulls, water birds, land birds.

The main attraction of this site is that it provides close looks at water birds during the late fall, winter and early spring - sometimes including lesser scaup, canvasback and bufflehead.

GETTING AROUND

Birding methods: car.

You can drive to the viewing point.

DIRECTIONS (see Map 9): This overlook point is on the west shore of the Saugatuck River, within a couple of miles of Long Island Sound. From I-95 exit 17, go north on Route 33 for one mile to the overlook point on the right by the river.

WESTPORT: SHERWOOD ISLAND STATE PARK

HABITATS

COASTAL: Long Island Sound, rocky point, sand and gravel beach, dunes, salt water tidal pond, high and low salt marshes, salt water tidal creek, intertidal areas of mud, sand and cobble, edges of herbs, shrubs and hardwoods.
OPEN TERRESTRIAL: short grass field, edge;
Lake/pond: seasonal rain pools in the shortgrass field;
Forest: hardwoods, white pine, mixed conifers;
Other: hawk watching site.

This popular state park is situated on a 218-acre island that extends into Long Island Sound (in effect, it is a peninsula). There are four areas that are of interest to birders. The south side of the island is a mile-long shoreline composed of sand and gravel beach and a rocky point with good views of Long Island Sound. Sherwood Millpond is a tidal pond that lies on the west side of the island, and has exposed mudflats at low tide. There are also two areas of tidal marsh, along the northeast and west edges of the park. In between these habitats are large areas of lawn and groves of trees.

SEASONS/BIRDS

SPRING MIGRATION: GULLS, TERNS, WATER BIRDS, MARSH BIRDS, SHORE BIRDS, LAND BIRDS;
NESTING SEASON: GULLS, TERNS, MARSH BIRDS, LAND BIRDS;
FALL MIGRATION: GULLS, TERNS, WATER BIRDS, MARSH BIRDS, SHORE BIRDS, LAND BIRDS;
WINTER: GULLS, WATER BIRDS, LAND BIRDS.

This is one of the two finest coastal sites in Fairfield County (Stratford Great Meadows Marsh/ Long Beach is the other), and it offers something of interest to birders at any time of year. The best time to see water birds is November through March - look in Sherwood Mill Pond and at the nearby water of Long Island Sound, where both loon species, red-necked and horned grebes, old squaw and scoters have often been seen. The best time to see shore birds is April/ May and August/September - look in mudflats and also pools in the mowed areas after rains. Sherwood Mill Pond is a prime feeding area during the spring, summer and fall for the waders that nest on the islands offshore in Long Island Sound. A wide variety of land birds also occur here. Meadowlarks are confirmed as nesters. This is a good site at which to watch the fall hawk migration. From October through March it is worthwhile to look in open areas for such land bird species as horned lark, snow bunting, Lapland longspur and pipit. In some winters, short-eared and even long-eared owls have been seen in the park.

GETTING AROUND
Birding methods: CAR, WALK, BIKE, boat.
Park driveways lead to many of the habitats, and short walks over open ground will get you to most of the rest. During the warm months, the park is crowded, and there is an admission fee.

DIRECTIONS(see Map 8): This park lies on the shore of Long Island Sound in Westport. From I-95, take exit 18 which leads to the park entrance in 0.2 mile.

WESTPORT: SMITH RICHARDSON PRESERVE

HABITATS
Forest: mixed conifers;
Open terrestrial: short grass, tall grass, mixed herbaceous and shrubby fields, shrubby and wooded edges, vine tangles and thickets.
A large part of this site is managed as a tree farm, with spruces and other conifers planted throughout a field that is mowed sporadically. The resulting open field and edge habitat lies within a very short distance of the coast.

SEASONS/BIRDS
Spring migration: land birds;
Nesting season: land birds;
FALL MIGRATION: LAND BIRDS;
Winter: land birds.
This is a good place to go to find open field and edge species. In both migrations, but especially the fall (during October and November), look for a variety of sparrows; Lincoln's, white-crowned and white-throated all have occurred here. Meadowlark has also been seen in migration. Migrating warblers and kinglets are attracted by the conifers. Nesters include brown thrasher and numerous common edge species. In winter, this is a good site at which to look for winter finches feeding in the spruce trees. And it has good winter habitat for long-eared and saw-whet owls.

GETTING AROUND
Birding methods: walk.
The habitats within the preserve can be walked by staying in the more open areas.

DIRECTIONS: This site is very close to the shore, and one mile east of Sherwood Island State Park. To get there from I-95, take exit 19 to Route 1 at the end of the ramp. Go south (westward) on Route 1 for 0.2 mile, left on Kings Highway West (which becomes Greens Farms Road) for 1.0 miles, left on Sasco Creek Road for 0.2 mile to the entrance on the left.

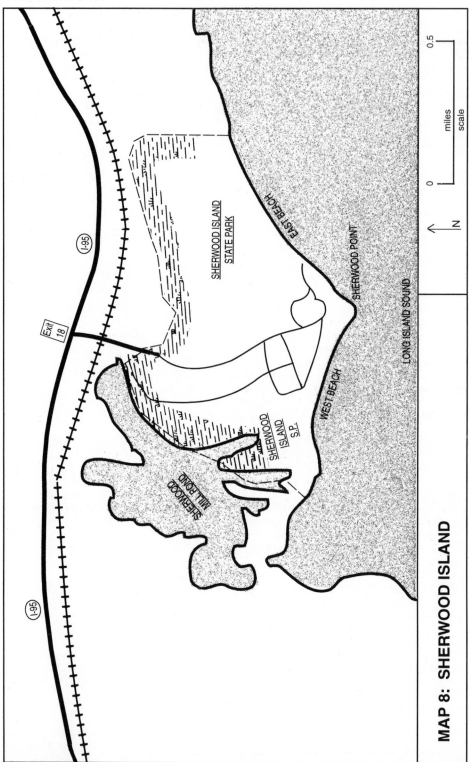

MAP 8: SHERWOOD ISLAND

WESTPORT: WESTPORT LONGSHORE PARK/COMPO BEACH/COMPO COVE

HABITATS

COASTAL: Long Island Sound, rocky point, rocky shore, tidal cove, sandy beach, mud and sand flats, low saltwater marsh, coastal forest;
Open terrestrial: short grass field, shrubby edges;
Forest: hardwoods, hemlock, white pine.

These areas lie next to each other along the coast, and together contain a variety of coastal, open terrestrial and forest habitats. Longshore Park includes a golf course, varied woods, shrubby edges and a low salt marsh. Compo Beach and the road to Compo Cove provide an extensive look at Long Island Sound over nearby sand flats, while Compo Cove itself is a shallow and sheltered feeding area.

SEASONS/BIRDS

SPRING MIGRATION: gulls, terns, WATER BIRDS, marsh birds, shore birds, land birds;
Nesting season: marsh birds, land birds;
FALL MIGRATION: gulls, terns, WATER BIRDS, marsh birds, shore birds, LAND BIRDS;
WINTER: gulls, WATER BIRDS, land birds.

This is a good site in which to look for a wide variety of bird species that occur in coastal, open country and forest habitats. The best period is from October through March, when water birds occur on the Sound and in Compo Cove, and when migrating and lingering land birds can be seen in the open and edge habitats. During the late fall, look in shrubby areas for sparrows, and in open areas for horned lark and snow bunting.

GETTING AROUND

Birding methods: CAR.

Roads and park driveways get you to or very near all of the habitat areas. Compo Beach is restricted to use by town residents during the warm months.

DIRECTIONS (see Map 9): This site is on the coast between the cities of Westport and Norwalk. Start at I-95 exit 17. **To get to Longshore Beach Park,** go north on Route 136 for 0.8 mile, and right on Compo Road for 0.6 mile to the park entrance. **To get to Compo Beach,** continue on Compo Road for another 0.3 mile, right on Compo Beach Road for 0.5 mile to the entrance to the beach. **To get to Compo Cove,** continue on the road along the shore (named Compo Beach Road, then Sound View Drive, then Hills Point Road) for an additional 0.7 mile.

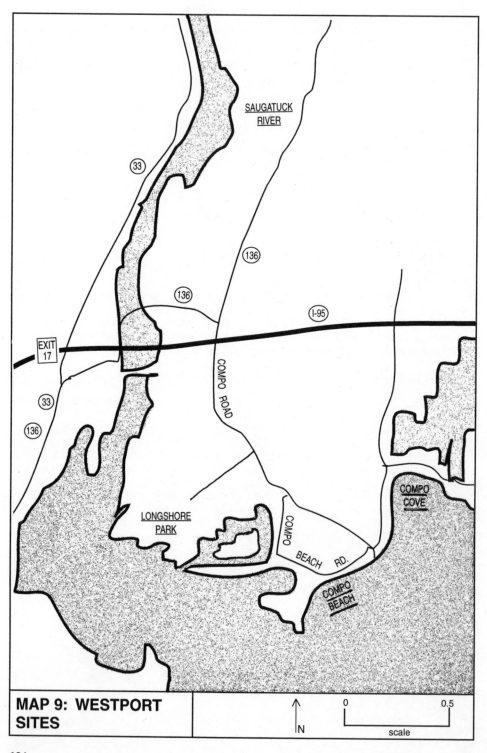

MAP 9: WESTPORT SITES

N

scale   0   0.5

WILTON: WEIR NATURE PRESERVE

HABITATS
Forest: hardwoods, mountain laurel;
Open terrestrial: mixed herbaceous and shrubby fields, scattered cedars, vine tangles and thickets, edges;
River/stream: streams, shrubby and wooded streambelts;
Marsh/swamp/bog: shrub swamp, shrubby hardwood swamp, hardwood swamp;
Other: ledges, rock outcrops.

This 110-acre preserve was once farmland that has now reverted to varied post-agricultural habitats. There are fields in various stages of succession - some have become young hardwoods, others are covered by shrubs, and a few are still mowed. In addition, there are mature hardwoods, swamps, streams, and thickets of mountain laurel and sweet pepperbush. Bedrock lies close to the surface throughout the area, and there are numerous ledges and rock outcrops.

SEASONS/BIRDS
Spring migration: land birds;
Nesting season: land birds;
Fall migration: land birds;
Winter: land birds.

Come to this preserve to see a nice variety of the standard forest- and edge-affinity land bird species. In addition, hooded warbler is among the nesters (look in the sweet pepperbush).

GETTING AROUND
Birding methods: WALK.
About two miles of good trails make several loops through the main habitat areas.

DIRECTIONS: This site is about five miles north of the center of Wilton. From the center, go north on Route 33 for 2.0 miles, right on Nod Hill Road for 3.3 miles to the entrance on the left.

Chapter 5

Hartford County

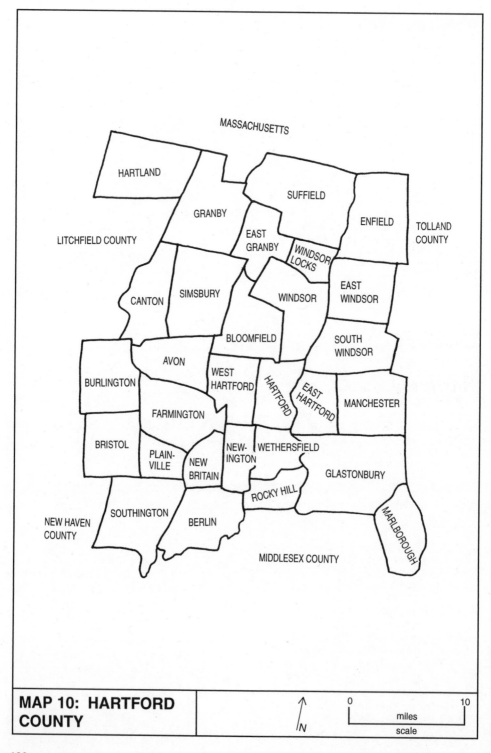

MAP 10: HARTFORD COUNTY

N

0   miles   10

scale

HARTFORD COUNTY

HARTFORD COUNTY   PAGE

TABLE 3: HABITATS AND SEASONS AT HARTFORD COUNTY SITES

Habitats ● very good example ○ present, but not as significant Seasons ● excellent during this season ○ less good during this season	FOREST	OPEN	MARSH	LAKE	RIVER	COAST	OTHER	SPRING	NEST	FALL	WINTER
Tour of Simsbury	●	○	●	○	○		○	●	●	●	○
Avon: Fisher Meadow Park/Spring Lake	●	●		●	●			●	●	●	○
Avon: River Park	○	○	○	○	○			●	●	●	○
Berlin: Silver Lake	○	○		●			○	●	○	●	○
Bloomfield: Penwood Park/Talcott Mtn. Park	●	○		○			○	●	○	●	○
Bristol et al: Marsh Pond	○	○	○	●				●	○	●	○
Burlington: Nassahegan SF	○	○	○		○			●	●	●	○
Burlington: Punch Brook	○				●			●	○	○	○
Burlington: Scoville Road	○	○	●	○	○			●	●	●	○
Burlington: Sessions Woods WMA	●		●	○	○			●	●	●	○
Burlington: Upson Road	○	●	○	○				●	●	●	○
Canton: Breezy Hill Pres.	○	○	○	○	○		○	●	●	○	○
Canton: Ratlum Mountain Pres.	●				●		○	●	●	○	○
Canton: Roaring Brook NC	●	●	○	○	●			●	●	●	○
Canton et al: Smith Tree Farm Preserve	●	○			●		○	●	●	●	○
East Granby: Newgate WMA	○	●	●	○				●	●	●	○
East Windsor: Flaherty Area	○	●	○		○			●	●	●	○
Enfield: Kings Island WMA/Parsons Road	●	○			●			●	○	●	●
Farmington: Farmington Mdws/Shade Swamp	●	●	●	○	●			●	●	●	○
Farmington: Memorial Town Forest	●							○	○	○	○
Glastonbury: Wangunk Meadows (Upper)	○	●	●	○	●			●	○	●	○
Granby: Enders SF	●	●	●	○	●			●	●	●	○
Granby: McLean Game Refuge	●	●	●	●	●			●	●	●	○
Hartland/Barkhamsted: Tunxis SF	●	○	●	○	○		○	●	●	●	○
Manchester: Union Pond Park	○	○		○	○			○	○	○	○
Marlborough: Salmon River SF	●		○		○			○	○	○	○
New Britain: Stanley Park/Stanley Qtr. Park	○	○	○	○	○			○	○	○	○
New Britain: Batterson Park Pond	○			●				●	○	●	○
Rocky Hill: Ferry Park	○	●	○	○	●		○	○	○	○	○
Simsbury: Curtis Park	○	○			●			○	○	○	○
Simsbury: Great Pond SF	●	○	○	●	○			●	●	●	○
Simsbury: Nod Brook WMA	○	●	●	○	●		○	●	●	●	○
Simsbury: Simsbury WMA	○	●	○	○	●			○	○	○	○
South Windsor: S. Windsor Sanctuary/Idlenot	○	●	○				○	●	●	●	○
South Windsor: Station 43	○	●	●	○	●			●	●	●	●
Suffield: Lewis Farm Sanctuary	○	○	○		○			○	○	○	○
Suffield: Stony Brook Park	○	●	○	○	○			○	○	○	○
West Hartford: Spice Bush Swamp	○	○	○	○	○			●	○	○	○
West Hartford: et al: Talcott Mountain Rsvrs.	●	●	○	●	○		○	●	●	●	○
Wethersfield: Cove Park	○	○			○			○	○	○	○

TABLE 3: HABITATS AND SEASONS AT HARTFORD COUNTY SITES (2)

Habitats ● very good example ○ present, but not as significant Seasons ● excellent during this season ○ less good during this season	HABITATS								SEASONS			
	F O R E S T	O P E N	M A R S H	L A K E	R I V E R	C O A S T	O T H E R		S P R I N G	N E S T	F A L L	W I N T E R
Wethersfield: Mill Woods Park	○	○	○	○	○				●	○	●	○
Wethersfield: Wintergreen Woods Park	○	●	○	○	○				●	○	●	○
Wethersfield et al: Cedar Hill Cemetary	○	○	○	○	○		○		●	○	●	○
Windsor: Farmington River Town Park	○	○			●				○	○	○	○
Windsor: Northwest Park	●	●	○	○	●				●	●	●	○
Windsor: Rainbow Dam Boat Landing	○				●				○	○	○	○

BIRDING IN HARTFORD COUNTY

Hartford lies in the north-central part of Connecticut. It is bounded on the west by Litchfield County, on the north by Massachusetts, on the east by Tolland County, and on the south by Middlesex and New Haven Counties. It is crossed by three major highways - I-84, I-91 and Routes 5 and 15.

The People

Hartford County has a population of 870,980 (it is the most populous of Connecticut's eight counties), and an area of 739 square miles, giving it an average population density of 1,179 people per square mile (third among Connecticut counties, behind Fairfield and New Haven). Population growth has been slower than most other Connecticut counties in recent decades. Affluence is about average among Connecticut counties.

The Land

Most of Hartford County lies in Connecticut's Central Valley. The western portion lies on the edge of the Western Uplands, and a small area in the southeastern corner lies on the edge of the Eastern Uplands. Elevations range from near sea level on the floor of the Central Valley, to about 1,250" in the portion that lies in the Western Uplands.

The main topographical feature in Hartford County is the Central Valley, and the Connecticut River within it - the largest and longest river in the Northeastern United States. The soils of the Central Valley are deep and rich, and most of the successful farming in Connecticut takes place in this lowland area (13% of Hartford County's total area is active farmland). The nearly level to gently sloping lowlands in the Central Valley are broken by a series of north/south trap rock ridges with steep, hilly slopes. Rivers and streams have broad flood plains in which there are many large marshes and meadows.

The western part of the county that lies in the Western Uplands includes the towns of Hartland, Granby, Canton, Burlington and Bristol. In this higher, more hilly area, the climate and habitats more closely resemble Litchfield County than other parts of Hartford County. Compared with the Central Valley, the summers are cooler, the winters colder, and the habitats have a more northern character.

Public Areas and Birding Sites

Most of Hartford County's population is concentrated in the Greater Hartford area, with lower-density suburban development throughout most of the outlying areas. Many of the public open areas occur within this rural/suburban landscape, and as a general rule, are quite heavily used by the public. Finding solitude is difficult, and traffic noise may be a problem in the smaller public areas.

Within Hartford County, there are seven state parks, four state forests, two large blocks of water supply property, a large wildlife preserve, and a number of DEP wildlife management areas, sanctuaries, nature centers, town parks and cemeteries.

Among these areas there is a nice diversity of habitat types, with a greater proportion of sites that have open- and edge-habitats than is the case in other counties.

There are many high quality birding sites within Hartford County, so that it is difficult to select a handful that everyone would agree are the top sites. However, our candidates would be: Station 43 in South Windsor, the McLean Game Refuge and Enders State Forest, both in Granby, the Talcott Mountain Reservoir Area in West Hartford and Bloomfield, Fisher Meadow in Avon and the Sessions Woods WMA in Burlington. Among them, these sites include open and edge habitats, wetlands, lakes, ponds, a major river, flood plain and up-land forests - all within areas that are quite large considering the population density of the county overall.

Seasons for Birding

Many of the sites in Hartford County lie in the path of the Central Valley migration corridor, and contain edges and open habitats that attract migrants, especially in the fall. Among these sites, there is ample variety to attract a nice mix of nesting species from most of the major bird groups. Hartford County does not have a coastline to provide birding excitement during the winter, but the broad diversity of habitats within the county make for interesting winter birding, provided you know just where to go.

Spring migration. Start your spring birding early (in March or as soon as there is open water), by looking for water bird migrants along the Connecticut River at Station 43, along the Farmington River at Farmington Meadows in Farmington, and on the lakes and ponds of the Talcott Mountain Reservoir Area. In April and May, focus on land bird migrants, at sites such as McLean, the Talcott Mountain Reservoir Area, Sessions Woods and the Roaring Brook Nature Center in Canton. A wide variety of water birds and marsh birds can be seen at Station 43 throughout the migration period.

Nesting season. There are many sites to choose from as birding destinations during the nesting season. McLean is excellent, in its combination of northern forest, open and wetland habitats, in a large area that is accessible by well maintained trails. Enders State Forest, nearby in Granby, also has species that nest in northern forest and edge/open habitats. The Talcott Mountain Reservoir Area offers habitat diversity, large size and good trails. Species that nest here include pine-associated species such as red-breasted nuthatch and pine warbler, north-ern forest species such as solitary vireo and black-throated green warbler, open and edge species such as prairie warbler, plus worm-eating warbler and a host of more common nest-ers. Other sites worth visiting during the nesting season are: Sessions Woods (northern for-est species, good trails, easy birding), Roaring Brook Nature Center (lots of habitat types, good trails), Nod Brook WMA in Simsbury (open habitats - willow flycatcher, prairie war-bler, green-backed heron), and Great Pond, also in Simsbury (forest and wetland habitats, nice species variety, good trails).

Fall migration. Many of the sites in Hartford County contain habitats with open areas and shrubby edges that are especially good during the fall migration. Early in the fall (Septem-ber), focus on the migration of hawks and warblers. The Talcott Mountain end of Penwood Park/Talcott Mountain has a good hawk watching spot, and Sessions Woods is good for migration of warblers and other forest species. McLean is good early for migrating forest species, and later for sparrows. Nod Brook offers marsh birds, shore birds and land birds in the early part of the migration, and a wide variety of water birds and land birds later (Octo-ber and November). Station 43 is outstanding, especially in the late fall when it is possible to see pipit, white-crowned and other sparrows, plus a whole gamut of other species. Other sites that are good late in the fall for terrestrial species are Farmington Meadows, Fisher Meadow Park, Wangunk Meadows in Glastonbury, and Northwest Park in Windsor. A good late fall water bird site is Batterson Park Pond in New Britain.

Winter. Since Hartford County does not have a coast on Long Island Sound, in order to find interesting birding during the winter, you should visit sites that have open water, or tilled fields, or edges with shrubs that carry berries or seeds into winter - habitats that occur at a number of sites described in this chapter. However, the occurrence of birds at such sites is inconsistent, with one major exception - Station 43 is one area where you can almost always count on seeing something interesting. In winter, the possibilities include rough-legged hawk, bald eagle and northern shrike.

Sources of Information and Help

Probably the best source of information about birding in Hartford County is the Hartford Audubon Society, which now has a bird information line. Also, if you are in the area and would like immediate help, try the Roaring Brook Nature Center in Canton. DEP has an office at Sessions Woods in Burlington, staffed by people who can answer your questions. The headquarters of the Talcott Mountain Reservoir Area in West Hartford sells maps of that large open space area.

There are places to eat in almost all of the larger towns in Hartford County, and lodging is not hard to find.

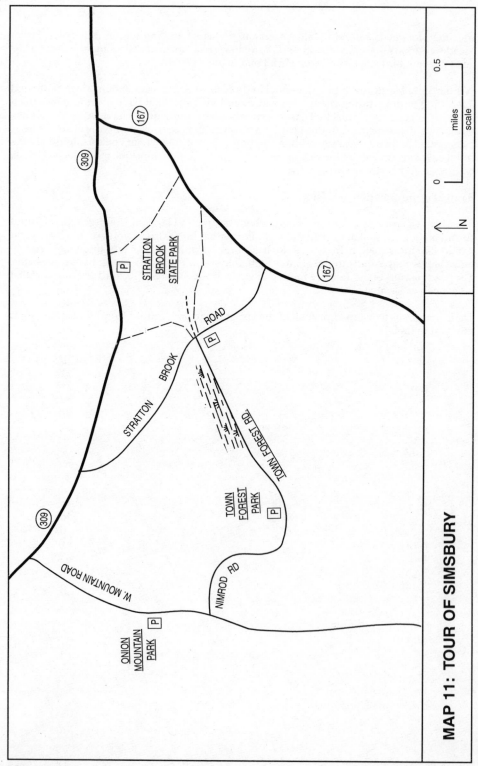

MAP 11: TOUR OF SIMSBURY

TOUR OF SIMSBURY

THE TOUR. This is a fairly short tour - a little over six miles. It includes four sites connected by roads that pass through additional interesting and productive habitats. The tour includes:

Town Forest Road
Town Forest Park
Onion Mountain Park
Stratton Brook State Park

These sites are not covered by separate site descriptions.

HABITATS

FOREST: sand plain (comprised of white pine, pitch pine, hardwoods); hardwoods/white pine forest, hardwoods/hemlock forest;
MARSH/SWAMP/BOG: sedge, cattail and shrub marsh; shrub, shrubby hardwood, hardwood and hardwood/white pine swamp; dead wood; open water;
Lake/pond: ponds; grassy, marshy, shrubby and wooded shores;
River/stream: perennial and seasonal streams, marshy, shrubby and wooded shores;
Open terrestrial: short grass and shrubby fields, shrubby edges;
Other: sand bank.

Much of the area included in this tour is sand plain, covered by forest communities of white pine and pitch pine, mixed with hardwoods (mostly oaks). Stratton Brook and several smaller perennial and seasonal streams feed two ponds and various wetlands.

Town Forest Road goes past small perennial streams with wooded streambelts, two wetlands composed of small ponds with wooded and grassy shores; cattail, sedge, mixed herbaceous and shrub marsh, shrub and shrubby hardwood/white pine swamp - all within the sand plain forest.

Town Forest Park is also within the sand plain forest of pitch pine and white pine mixed with oak and other hardwoods, and includes a sand and gravel bank.

Onion Mountain Park is forested with hardwoods/hemlock and hardwoods/white pine.

Stratton Brook State Park is largely covered by a typical sand plain forest of pitch pine and white pine mixed with oaks and other hardwoods. It also includes two ponds, a perennial stream and a marsh.

SEASONS/BIRDS

SPRING MIGRATION: water birds, marsh birds, shore birds, LAND BIRDS;
NESTING SEASON: water birds, marsh birds, LAND BIRDS;
FALL MIGRATION: water birds, marsh birds, shore birds, LAND BIRDS;
Winter: land birds.

Because of the variety of habitats, this tour is good at almost any season, especially for land birds, and to a lesser extent, water and marsh birds. Land bird species that are seen during migration and the nesting season include forest-dwellers, species that are drawn to wetlands, shrubby fields and edges. Also present are common species of water birds and marsh birds.

Town Forest Road is excellent, especially during the spring and fall migrations for wetland-oriented land birds. The habitat also has the potential for rails and shorebirds. Pine warbler and gnatcatcher are among the nesters.

Town Forest Park features nesting bank swallows (behind the highway department garage), as well as many of the same forest-dwelling species as other parts of this tour.

Onion Mountain Park has a typical mix of forest land bird species, with a few northerners, including winter wren, solitary vireo, black-throated green and black-throated blue warblers.

Stratton Brook Park is worth a visit during both migrations and the nesting season. It offers the possibility of seeing a few marsh birds (great blue and green-backed herons), shrub and edge-affinity land birds (brown thrasher, cedar waxwing, warbling vireo, blue-winged, prairie and chestnut-sided warblers, as well as pine warbler (lots of them!), Louisiana waterthrush, pileated and red-bellied woodpeckers.

GETTING AROUND
Birding methods: CAR, WALK, BIKE.
This is basically a driving tour in which most of the main habitat areas can be seen from your car. However, it also includes several opportunities to bird on foot. In addition, it provides access to the network of bike paths that go through much of Simsbury.

Town Forest Road offers excellent birding from your car, walking, or on a bike.

Town Forest Park: some of the habitat can be seen from your car, but most can best be seen by using the network of trails within the park.

Onion Mountain Park can best be birded by using the trails within the park.

Stratton Brook Park offers a network of trails, as well as a bike path that connects to other parts of Simsbury.

DIRECTIONS (see Map 11): The tour covers an area that is a mile or two southwest of the center of Simsbury. The starting point is the intersection of Routes 167 and 309. From here, go south on Route 167 (Bushy Hill Road) for 1.1 miles (along the way you pass a trail into **Stratton Brook Park**), right on Stratton Brook Road for 0.6 mile, left onto **Town Forest Road** and park at this intersection on the wide shoulder. From here, you can walk or bike on the bike path that starts on the opposite side of Stratton Brook Road. Also, you can walk or drive on Town Forest Road past two wetlands within the sand plain forest. To continue the tour, follow Town Forest Road (which becomes Nimrod Road) for 1.6 mile (along the way you pass **Town Forest Park** and a sand bank), right on West Mountain Road for 0.3 mile to the entrance to **Onion Mountain Park** on the left. To complete the tour, continue on West Mountain Road for 0.4 mile, right on Route 309 for 1.2 miles to **Stratton Brook State Park** and more sand plain forest on the right. To return to your starting point, continue on Route 309 for a short distance to its intersection with Route 167.

AVON: FISHER MEADOW PARK/SPRING LAKE

HABITATS
FOREST: flood plain, hardwoods/white pine;
OPEN TERRESTRIAL: tilled, short grass and shrubby field; edge;
LAKE/POND: pond with shrubby and hardwood shore;
RIVER/STREAM: river, slow water, hardwood streambelt, stream, shrubby and wooded streambelt.
This site occupies an area along the Farmington River. It contains a rich variety of habitats, including a riparian forest of sycamore, silver maple, cottonwood and other hardwoods along the river. There is a nearby pond (Spring Lake) and also large open areas.

SEASONS/BIRDS
SPRING MIGRATION: water birds, shore birds, LAND BIRDS;
NESTING SEASON: LAND BIRDS;
FALL MIGRATION: water birds, shore birds, LAND BIRDS;
Winter: land birds.
This site has something to offer during every season. There are usually a few water birds (including pied-billed grebe and wood duck) on the river during the spring and fall. During the spring and fall migrations a good variety of land birds pass along the river and the nearby forest - osprey is often present. Fall migration is especially good around the fields for sparrows, horned lark and pipit. A number of species nest in the flood plain forest and along the river, including wood duck, red-bellied woodpecker, northern oriole (lots), great crested flycatcher and warbling vireo. The shrubby fields provide nesting habitat for willow flycatcher, brown thrasher, prairie warbler, indigo bunting and field sparrow. Green-backed heron and screech owl are probable nesters. In winter, there is the possibility of seeing a bald eagle over or near the river. Snow bunting and longspur have been seen in the fields during the period November-early March.

GETTING AROUND
Birding methods: walk.
There are several trails that follow the shores of the Farmington River and Spring Lake, and go along the edges of the fields.

DIRECTIONS: In Avon, at the eastern intersection of Routes 10 and 44, go south on Route 10 for 2.4 miles, and right on Old Farms Road for 0.2 mile to the park entrance on the right.

AVON: RIVER PARK

HABITATS
River/stream: river, slow water, hardwood shore;
Open terrestrial: short grass field, shrubby edge;
Forest: flood plain;
Lake/pond: pond, grassy and shrubby shore.
Marsh/swamp/bog: small pockets of mixed herbaceous and shrub marsh; shrub swamp;
This site is a small park on the shore of the Farmington River. Its habitats include a section of the river itself, hardwood flood plain forest (including a grove of impressive sycamore by the river), mowed areas with shrubby edges, and a small artificial pond. Although it is within

a few yards of Route 44, it seems isolated from the activity and noise of the highway.

SEASONS/BIRDS
    SPRING MIGRATION: water birds, LAND BIRDS;
    NESTING SEASON: land birds;
    FALL MIGRATION: water birds, LAND BIRDS;
    Winter: land birds.

The best period at this site is from early May to late July. You can get good looks at a variety of the standard species, so that this is a good site for beginning birders. During the spring and fall migrations, there is a chance to see a few water birds on the river, and a mix of land birds that is typical for these habitats. Nesting species include red-eyed, yellow-throated and warbling vireos, indigo bunting and scarlet tanager. (A few years ago, a yellow-throated warbler was observed singing in the sycamore trees throughout the month of June.)

GETTING AROUND
    Birding methods: walk.

From the parking area for the shopping center (see below) it is a short walk down into this park. There are short paths that lead to the river and go through all of the other habitat areas. At the time of writing, this park was poorly maintained (trails not mowed, trash cans not emptied).

DIRECTIONS: This park is in the center of Avon, about ten miles west of Hartford. From the western intersection of Routes 44, 10 and 202, go east on Route 44 for 0.3 mile and right, into the parking area for River Park Shopping Center. The path into the park is near the entrance to the shopping center.

BERLIN: SILVER LAKE

HABITATS
    LAKE/POND: lake, deep water, shallow water, shrubby and hardwood shore;
    Open terrestrial: shrubby field, shrubby edge, vine tangles and thickets;
    Forest: hardwoods;
    Other: cliff, ledge, talus slope, hawk watching site.

From two overlook points, you look down on this lake, and across the lake at the cliffs of Lamentation Mountain.

SEASONS/BIRDS
    SPRING MIGRATION: WATER BIRDS, marsh birds, land birds;
    Nesting season: water birds, land birds;
    FALL MIGRATION: WATER BIRDS, marsh birds, land birds;
    Winter: water birds, land birds.

The spring and fall migrations are the best seasons at this site. Early in the spring (March/April) and late in the fall (November), you may see good numbers of water birds; often present are pied-billed grebe, mute swan, ring-necked duck, wood duck, common and hooded mergansers; and there is always the possibility of wigeon, gadwall, pintail and goldeneye. The lake usually stays ice-free and water birds continue to be present into December. In the later spring (April/May), you may see Osprey and a variety of edge-habitat land birds. In the early fall (September), there is the added interest provided by hawks (mostly broad-wings) that follow the updrafts along the cliffs of Lamentation Mountain across the lake as they migrate southward. And, continuing into November, migrating sparrows feed on the seeds and fruits of the shrubs in the edges and thickets. Nesters include orchard oriole, and edge species such as prairie warbler, field sparrow and indigo bunting. In winter, after the lake has frozen, there may be a few lingering land birds in the shrubs and thickets.

GETTING AROUND
Can be birded by: car, walk, boat.
It is possible to reach two overlook points by car from Norton Lane. In addition, the shrubs and thickets on either side of Norton Lane make it rewarding to bird on foot. Do not cross the railroad tracks, which are in use.

DIRECTIONS: This site is in Berlin. To get there from the intersection of Route 5-15 (the Berlin Turnpike) and Route 9, go south on Route 5-15 for 3.0 miles, right of Toll Gate Road for 0.2 mile, and left on Norton Lane for 0.6 mile to a boat launch on the shore of Silver Lake. If you continue on Norton Lane, you pass through good edge habitat and reach a second point that overlooks the lake.

BLOOMFIELD/SIMSBURY: PENWOOD PARK/TALCOTT MOUNTAIN PARK

HABITATS
FOREST: hardwoods, hardwoods/hemlock;
Open terrestrial: short grass field, shrubby and wooded edge;
Lake/pond: pond, wooded shore;
Other: cliff/ledge.
These two parks lie next to each other along the high ground of a trap rock ridge. Much of its area is covered by mature hardwoods forest. There are also groves of hemlock and some mowed grassy areas. The western edge of the parks is on the edge of the ridge, and over-looks the broad valley of the Farmington River.

SEASONS/BIRDS
SPRING MIGRATION: LAND BIRDS;
Nesting season: land birds;
FALL MIGRATION: LAND BIRDS;
Winter: land birds.
These two parks are especially good during the spring and fall migrations, when they are probably the best area in central Connecticut for watching hawks and other land birds as they travel along the ridge.

GETTING AROUND
Birding methods: car, walk.
There are several trails, including short ones to the hawk watching points. The driveways may be closed in winter.

DIRECTIONS: These parks lie along the Bloomfield/Simsbury town line. From Simsbury at the intersection of Routes 202 and 185, go east on Route 185 for 1.6 miles to the entrance of Talcott Mountain Park on the right, or for another 0.2 mile to the entrance of Penwood Park on the left.

BRISTOL/PLYMOUTH/BURLINGTON: MARSH POND

HABITATS

LAKE/POND: lake, shallow water, deep water, shore of hardwoods, hardwoods/white pine, hardwoods/hemlock, mixed conifers, shrubs;

Open terrestrial: short grass, mixed herbaceous and shrubby fields, shrubby and wooded edges, scattered apple trees;

Forest: white pine, hardwoods/white pine, hardwoods, hardwoods/hemlock, cedar, shrubby edges;

Marsh/swamp/bog: wet meadow, shrub marsh.

This site has a nice mix of pond, open and wooded habitats. The shrub areas include many blueberry and blackberry bushes.

SEASONS/BIRDS

SPRING MIGRATION: WATER BIRDS, LAND BIRDS;
Nesting season: water birds, land birds;
FALL MIGRATION: WATER BIRDS, marsh birds, LAND BIRDS;
Winter: land birds.

The spring migration is good at this site. Water bird species include ring-necked duck, bufflehead, common goldeneye, common and hooded merganser. In addition, there are great blue and green-backed herons, and a nice variety of land birds. In summer, there are some of the common water bird species, green-backed heron, and a mix of the land bird species that you would expect to nest in these open and forested habitats. The fall migration is largely a replay of the spring migration; in the early fall (September), there is usually a good flight of migrating warblers, and later - during October and November - a variety of sparrows come through. Bald eagle occurs occasionally during the late fall, winter and early spring. Also in winter, there is usually a scattering of other land birds, trying to get by on any berries that have not already been eaten.

GETTING AROUND

Birding methods: car, walk.

A town road passes the southern end of Marsh Pond and goes by a portion of the terrestrial habitats. Do your birding from this road - the land around the lake is not open to the public because Marsh Pond is a reservoir. However, 0.3 mile to the east, on the south side of the road, is Nature Conservancy land that is open to the public.

DIRECTIONS: This pond (also known as Bristol Reservoir #7) lies across the Bristol, Plymouth and Burlington town lines, about four miles north of the city of Bristol. To get there from the intersection of Routes 72 and 6 in Plymouth, go north on Route 72 for 0.7 mile, and right on East Plymouth Road for 0.8 mile. (This section of East Plymouth Road includes two confusing intersections; the first at 0.3 mile from the intersection with Route 72 where staying on East Plymouth Road requires bearing up to the left; and the second in another 0.1 mile, where staying on East Plymouth Road requires bearing a little left, not sharp left.) When you have gone 0.8 mile on East Plymouth Road, turn right on Marsh Road for 0.1 mile to the point at which the pond is visible on the left. Park by the road beyond the pond.

BURLINGTON: NASSAHEGAN STATE FOREST

HABITATS
Forest: hardwoods, hardwoods/white pine, hardwoods/hemlock; hardwoods/white pine sand plain; mountain laurel;
Open terrestrial: short grass, mixed herbaceous and shrubby fields including apple and cedar trees; shrubby and wooded edges;
River/stream: stream, wooded streambelt;
Marsh/swamp/bog: shrubby hardwood swamp.
The main part of the Nassahegan State Forest consists of 1,226 acres in an irregularly-shaped parcel. Its habitats include typical central hardwood forest, sand plain communities, laurel thickets, swamps, wooded streambelts and shrubby fields.

SEASONS/BIRDS
SPRING MIGRATION: LAND BIRDS;
NESTING SEASON: LAND BIRDS;
FALL MIGRATION: LAND BIRDS;
Winter: land birds.
This is a good site in which to look for the standard variety of land bird species in the spring, summer and fall, and a few typical resident species in winter. Among the migrants and nesters are species such as pine warbler (in the sand plain), and northerners including black-throated blue warbler (in the mountain laurel), solitary vireo and yellow-bellied sapsucker.

GETTING AROUND
Birding methods: car, WALK.
The road that goes through the central part of this forest (George Washington Turnpike) carries frequent and fast traffic, so that it is not safe for birding by car, but it does cross many woods roads and trails that provide good ways to bird interior areas of the forest on foot.

DIRECTIONS (see Map 12): This state forest lies immediately east of the Burlington village center. In Burlington, from the intersection of Routes 4 and 69, go east on Route 4 for 0.3 mile and bear right onto the George Washington Turnpike. During the next one to two miles, this road goes through the main part of the forest. In addition, it leads to other roads that go through smaller parts of the forest - at 0.4 mile from the intersection of Route 4 and George Washington Turnpike, Cornwall Road goes off to the right, and at 0.5 mile from the intersection, Belden Road goes off to the left. Both of these roads lead to parts of the forest. At 0.6 mile from the intersection of Route 4 and the George Washington Turnpike, George Washington Turnpike crosses the Tunxis Trail, which can be walked in either direction into the forest. At 1.0 mile from the intersection, on the right there is an area of mowed playing fields, and on the left a woods road that goes into an area of sand plain forest.

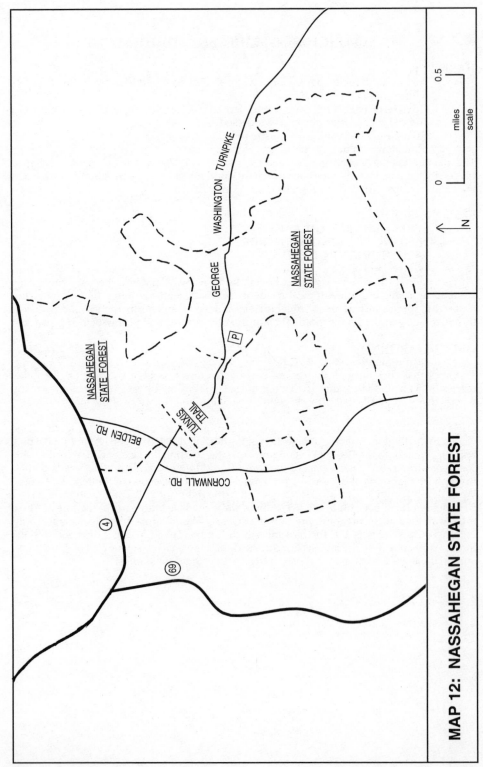

MAP 12: NASSAHEGAN STATE FOREST

BURLINGTON: PUNCH BROOK ACCESS AREA

HABITATS
    RIVER/STREAM: river, fast and slow water, hardwood shore;
    Forest: flood plain.
This site lies along a section of the Farmington River between the Collinsville Dam and Unionville. Habitats include the river itself, and hardwoods forest along the shore.

SEASONS/BIRDS
    SPRING MIGRATION: water birds, LAND BIRDS;
    Nesting season: land birds;
    Fall migration: water birds, land birds;
    Winter: water birds, land birds.
This site is worth stopping at during the spring and fall migrations. The water birds that can be seen here include pied-billed grebe, common and hooded merganser, common golden-eye and ring-necked duck. Also during the migrations, osprey move along the river, and a variety of warblers pass through the woods by the shore. Winter can be worthwhile if the river is not frozen, for water birds and occasionally bald eagle.

GETTING AROUND:
    Birding methods: car, walk.
The first two points described below can be reached by car; the third is a very short walk. Avoid rush hour, when there is traffic noise from the highway.

DIRECTIONS: This site is in Burlington, about fifteen miles west of Hartford. There are three points from which the river can be reached.

1. To get to the river from the intersection of Routes 4 and 179, go east (or south) on Route 4 for a few yards, and left on a small road that goes down to the shore of the river.

2. From the same intersection, go north on Route 179 for 0.3 mile to another small road on the right that goes down to the river.

3. Continue north on Route 179 for another 0.6 mile to a paved parking area on the right, from which point the river is a short downhill walk.

BURLINGTON: SCOVILLE ROAD

HABITATS
    MARSH/SWAMP/BOG: sedge and shrub marsh; shrub, shrubby hardwood and hardwood swamp, dead wood; open water, shrubby and wooded edges;
    Forest: hardwoods, hardwoods/white pine, sand plain of hardwoods/white pine, mixed conifers;
    Open terrestrial: tall grass, mixed herbaceous and shrubby fields; shrubby and wooded hedgerows and edges;
    River/stream: stream, marshy shore.
    Lake/pond: pond, marshy shore.
This site consists of a 0.7 mile stretch of Scoville Road that passes by some very nice habitat.

At the beginning (east end) of the road, there is a cemetery that has an edge of mixed coni-fers, and overlooks a wetland with areas of shrub marsh and shrub swamp, and the vestiges of a bog. At this point there is also an access to the Tunxis Trail that can be walked through a sand plain forest of hardwoods and white pine. About midway down Scoville Road (going west) is another wetland - on one side of the road there is shrub swamp and shrubby hard-wood swamp, while on the other there are areas of sedge and shrub marsh and some open water. At the far (west) end of Scoville Road are various types of fields with shrubby and wooded hedgerows and edges.

SEASONS/BIRDS
SPRING MIGRATION: water birds, marsh birds, shore birds, LAND BIRDS;
NESTING SEASON: water birds, marsh birds, LAND BIRDS;
FALL MIGRATION: water birds, marsh birds, shore birds, LAND BIRDS;
Winter: land birds;
This site provides an easy way to bird several nice habitats, and offers the possibility of seeing (or hearing) a variety of common (and several uncommon) species that inhabit open fields, edges, wetlands and woodlands. Spring, summer and fall are all very good.

In the early spring (March and April) listen at the open fields at the west end of Scoville Road for woodcock, barred and great horned owls. A little later (May, June and July), these same fields and edges are likely to have migrant and / or nesting indigo bunting, yellowthroat, chestnut-sided and blue-winged warblers. Also, listen here for whip-poor-will on June eve-nings. The wetland midway along Scoville Road is a good place to look for ducks, marsh birds and shore birds, especially in the spring. The water level fluctuates from beaver activ-ity, and if it is low during migration, several species of shore birds come here to feed on the exposed mud. The wetland is also a good place to observe four flycatcher species near one another, but each occupying its distinctive type of habitat. Olive-sided flycatcher sometimes passes by in migration, doubtless attracted by the standing dead trees. Least, willow and alder flycatchers stay to nest, and can be heard singing in the different habitats that they select within the wetland.

During the summer, many of the species seen in the spring along Scoville Road stay on to nest. Wetland-oriented land birds are the specialty: flycatchers, and other species such as yellow warbler and swamp sparrow. Pine warbler nests in and sings from the white pines. The fall migration is much like the spring migration. In winter, most of the activity is by year-round residents, including pileated woodpecker, barred and great horned owls. Also, northern shrike has been seen here in winter.

GETTING AROUND
Birding methods: CAR, WALK.
Scoville Road itself provides good birding on foot or from your car, as there are places to pull off where there is habitat to look at. Stay on the road, the surrounding land is private. Unfor-tunately, the traffic can be fast and heavy during weekday afternoons - mornings and week-ends are a better time to bird here. The cemetery at the east end of Scoville Road can be walked, in order to bird along the conifers on the edge, and to look into the nearby wetland. The Tunxis Trail, which passes near the cemetery, provides an easy walk, of whatever dis-tance you choose, through a sand plain forest of hardwoods and white pine.

DIRECTIONS: This site is in Burlington, about two miles south of the village center. From the center of Burlington at the intersection of Routes 69 and 4, go south on Route 69 for 2.1 miles to the intersection with Scoville Road on the right. At this intersection, the cemetery and the access to the Tunxis Trail are on the east (left) side of Route 69. Scoville Road, to the right, runs west for 0.7 mile, through the habitats described above to its end at the intersec-tion with Chippens Hill Road.

BURLINGTON: SESSIONS WOODS WILDLIFE MANAGEMENT AREA

HABITATS
FOREST: mixed hardwoods, hardwoods/white pine, hardwoods/hemlock, hemlock, sand plain;
MARSH/SWAMP/BOG: mixed herbaceous and shrub marsh, shrub swamp, hardwood swamp and dead trees;
Lake/pond: pond, seasonal pools;
River/stream: streams, wooded streambelts.
This 455-acre wildlife management area contains a nice assembly of habitats, including all the common forest habitat types, together with beaver ponds, other beaver-controlled wetlands, and a stream.

SEASONS/BIRDS
SPRING MIGRATION: water birds, marsh birds, LAND BIRDS;
NESTING SEASON: water birds, marsh birds, LAND BIRDS;
FALL MIGRATION: water birds, marsh birds, LAND BIRDS;
Winter: land birds.
Forest-dwelling land birds are the main attraction here, during both migrations and also the nesting season (upwards of 100 species have nested here). This site can be highly productive for birding during the spring, summer and fall.

GETTING AROUND:
Birding methods: WALK.
There are over three miles of well maintained woods roads and trails through the area. This site does not become crowded even during summer weekends. Trail maps are available at trailheads and at the office.

DIRECTIONS: This area is in Burlington, about 15 miles west of Hartford. To get to it from the village of Burlington at the intersection of Routes 69 and 4, go south on Route 69 for 3.3 miles, and right for 0.1 mile up a short hill to the entrance of the wildlife management area on the left. The wetland can be reached by going straight back from the office building. A woods road that also leads into the area can be reached by continuing on Route 69 for another 0.6 mile to a barway on the right.

BURLINGTON: UPSON ROAD

HABITATS
OPEN TERRESTRIAL: short grass and shrubby field, shrubby edge;
Forest: hardwoods/white pine, sand plain of hardwoods/white pine;
Marsh/swamp/bog: wet meadow, mixed herbaceous marsh, shrub swamp and shrubby hardwood swamp;
River/stream: stream, shrubby and wooded streambelt;
Lake/pond: pond, seasonal pools, shrubby and wooded edges.
This is a nice, quiet country road that passes through a variety of good habitats: a sand plain forest, a pond and pools, several types of field and a wetland that is in the process of succession from wet meadow to shrubby hardwood swamp.

SEASONS/BIRDS
SPRING MIGRATION: water birds, marsh birds, LAND BIRDS;

NESTING SEASON: water birds, marsh birds, LAND BIRDS;
FALL MIGRATION: water birds, marsh birds, LAND BIRDS;
Winter: land birds.

Come here to enjoy a nice variety of standard land bird migrants and nesters in a quiet setting. Species that are present in the spring and summer include wetland-oriented species such as yellow warbler; open and edge habitat species such as kestrel, brown thrasher, indigo bunting and prairie warbler, and a variety of woodland species, including (in recent years) whip-poor-will. In addition, common species of water and marsh birds occur in spring, summer and fall.

GETTING AROUND
Birding methods: CAR, WALK, BIKE.

This road is suitable for birding from your car, on foot, or by bike. Traffic is not a problem. But stay on the road - the surrounding land is private.

DIRECTIONS: This site is in Burlington, less than a mile northwest of the village center. From the center of Burlington at the intersection of Routes 4 and 69, go west on Route 4 for 0.7 mile to Upson Road on the right. This road passes through the habitats described above for the next 0.7 mile to its end.

CANTON: BREEZY HILL PRESERVE

HABITATS
Forest: hardwoods, white pine;
River/stream: stream; shrubby, wetland and wooded streambelt;
Marsh/swamp/bog: shrub marsh, shrub swamp.
Lake/pond: ponds, wooded shores;
Open terrestrial: short grass field, shrubby edges;
Other: ledges.

This 232-acre preserve is former farmland that now contains a diversity of typical post-agricultural habitats including young mixed hardwoods forest, ponds, shrubby wetlands and exposed ledges.

SEASONS/BIRDS
SPRING MIGRATION: LAND BIRDS;
NESTING SEASON: LAND BIRDS;
Fall Migration: land birds;
Winter: land birds.

At this preserve, you can see a good mix of standard land bird species, plus both Louisiana and northern waterthrushes.

GETTING AROUND
Can be birded by: walk.

The 1.5 mile Breezy Hill Farm Trail starts from the parking area described below, and makes a loop through hardwoods forest, a white pine plantation and along the edge of several pastures.

DIRECTIONS: This preserve is in the northwestern part of Canton. From the western intersection of Routes 44 and 179, go west on Route 44 for 1.4 miles, right on Indian Hill Road for 1.4 miles to a trailhead and parking on the left, just past the intersection with Breezy Hill Road.

CANTON: RATLUM MOUNTAIN PRESERVE

HABITATS
FOREST: hardwoods, hardwoods/white pine, hardwoods/hemlock, white pine, hemlock, mountain laurel;
RIVER/STREAM: stream, wooded streambelt, hemlock ravine;
Other: ledges.
This 170-acre preserve contains a variety of deciduous and evergreen forest communities, with areas of mountain laurel thickets, and a hemlock ravine.

SEASONS/BIRDS
SPRING MIGRATION: LAND BIRDS;
NESTING SEASON: LAND BIRDS;
Fall Migration: land birds;
Winter: land birds.
A good mix of species occur at this preserve, as both migrants and nesters - and the spring migration is especially good. Among the nesters are such standard species as gnatcatcher, scarlet tanager, wood thrush and red-eyed vireo, plus a number of northerners such as yellow-bellied sapsucker, brown creeper, winter wren, hermit thrush, black-throated blue, yellow-rumped, Canada and black-throated green warblers. Louisiana waterthrush and Acadian flycatcher nest by the stream.

GETTING AROUND
Can be birded by: walk.
The Ted Wright Trail leads from the parking area north (right) for 1.5 miles through the preserve, and can be walked to the Smith Tree Farm Preserve, also described under Canton. In addition, the continuation of Breezy Hill Road past the parking area provides good birding on foot (but is rough for a car).

DIRECTIONS: This preserve is in the northwestern part of Canton. From the western intersection of Routes 179 and 44, go north on Route 179 for 1.8 miles, left on Barbourtown Road for 1.7 miles, and left on Breezy Hill Road for 0.4 mile, with the preserve on the right side of the road, to a small parking area, also on the right, at the point where Breezy Hill Road becomes dirt.

CANTON: ROARING BROOK NATURE CENTER

HABITATS
FOREST: hardwoods, hardwoods/white pine, white pine, hardwoods/hemlock, hemlock, conifer plantation;
OPEN TERRESTRIAL: short grass, tall grass, mixed herbaceous and shrubby fields, edges;
RIVER/STREAM: stream, wooded shore including hemlock;
Lake/pond: pond, wooded shore, seasonal pools.
Marsh/swamp/bog: shrubby hardwood swamp.
This site is only 115 acres in size, but it includes a nice variety of habitats.

SEASONS/BIRDS
SPRING MIGRATION: water birds, LAND BIRDS;
NESTING SEASON: LAND BIRDS;
FALL MIGRATION: LAND BIRDS;
Winter: land birds.

There is birding here at all seasons. The spring migration brings a nice mix of the standard species for these habitats, including lots of warblers. The fall migration is also good - early fall (September) for warblers, and later (October/November) for sparrows. Nesters include both northern species such as solitary vireo and black-throated green warbler, and southerners such as red-bellied woodpecker and worm-eating warbler. In winter, there are usually birds to see near the visitor center; they are attracted by bird feeders and ornamental berry-producing shrubs.

GETTING AROUND:
Birding methods: WALK.

Six miles of trails go through the area. There is a visitor center at the entrance.

DIRECTIONS: This nature center is about 15 miles west of Hartford. In Canton, at the intersection of Routes 44 and 177 (Lawton Road), go north on Lawton Road for 1.0 mile, bear left on Gracey Road for 0.5 mile to the entrance on the left.

CANTON/BARKHAMSTED: SMITH TREE FARM PRESERVE

HABITATS
FOREST: hardwoods, hardwoods/white pine, hardwoods/hemlock, white pine, hemlock, mixed conifers, mountain laurel;
RIVER/STREAM: streams, wooded streambelts;
Open terrestrial: short grass field, mixed conifers, wooded edges;
Other: ledges.

This 90-acre preserve is located in the back country of Canton, with little evidence of the suburbs that are not far away. An open field is used as a Christmas tree farm, and surrounded by a mixed forest of hardwoods, hemlock, white pine and spruces. A small stream passes nearby.

SEASONS/BIRDS
SPRING MIGRATION: LAND BIRDS;
NESTING SEASON: LAND BIRDS;
FALL MIGRATION: LAND BIRDS;
Winter: land birds.

An interesting mix of land birds occur here, including wild turkey, great horned owl, red-breasted nuthatch, yellow-rumped, black-throated blue, blue-winged, chestnut-sided and prairie warblers.

GETTING AROUND
Can be birded by: walk.

A gravel road into the preserve is rough but usually passable by auto. This road, together with its extension past the tree farm, plus several trails, provide good albeit hilly birding on foot. One of the trails leads north to the ridge of Ratlum Mountain, and another trail leads south to the Breezy Hill Preserve.

DIRECTIONS: This preserve is in the northwestern part of Canton. From the western intersection of Routes 179 and 44, go north on Route 179 for 3.8 miles, left on Wright Road for 2.1 miles, and left on Doyle Road for 0.5 mile to a farm house and the preserve on the right.

EAST GRANBY: NEWGATE WILDLIFE MANAGEMENT AREA

HABITATS
OPEN TERRESTRIAL: mixed herbaceous and shrubby fields, shrubby and wooded edges;
MARSH, SWAMP/BOG: mixed herbaceous and shrub marsh, shrub swamp, shrubby hardwood swamp, hardwood swamp;
Forest: hardwoods, hardwoods/white pine, cedar;
Lake/pond: pond, shrubby and wooded shore.
This wildlife management area of 429 acres includes a variety of open terrestrial and marsh/swamp habitats, with some forested areas.

SEASONS/BIRDS
SPRING MIGRATION: water birds, marsh birds, LAND BIRDS;
NESTING SEASON: water birds, marsh birds, LAND BIRDS;
FALL MIGRATION: water birds, marsh birds, LAND BIRDS;
Winter: land birds.
This area is good in spring, summer and fall. The shrubby fields and edges attract a nice variety of open and edge species, both in migration and for nesting, including: indigo bunting, willow flycatcher, prairie, blue-winged and chestnut-sided warblers. Woodlands at this site attract other nesting species: red-tailed, red-shouldered and broad-winged hawks, several vireos (yellow-throated, warbling, solitary and red-eyed), and other warblers (including pine, black-throated green and Blackburnian). During migration, a variety of swallows feed over the wetland - rough-winged, bank, barn and tree). The late part of the fall migration is marked by the presence of seed and berry eaters - a variety of sparrows, cedar waxwing, and thrushes including robin, veery, hermit thrush, wood thrush and bluebird. In winter, there may still be a few of these species searching among the shrubs for any remaining food, as well as residents such as pileated woodpecker. Water birds and marsh birds also occur here during the spring, summer and fall, but the species are usually confined to Canada goose, mallard, wood duck, great blue and green-backed herons; however, Virginia rail and sora have also been seen.

GETTING AROUND:
Birding methods: WALK.
There are good trails and maintenance roads to walk. This is a popular hunting area in the fall.

DIRECTIONS: This area is in East Granby, about five miles northwest of Bradley Airport. It has two access points. To get to one of them from the village of Granby at the intersection of Routes 20 and 202, go east on Route 20 for 1.2 miles to the area entrance on the left. To reach the other access point, continue east on Route 20 for another 1.6 miles and go left on Newgate Road for 0.3 mile to the entrance on the left.

EAST WINDSOR: FLAHERTY FIELD TRIAL AND WILDLIFE AREA

HABITATS
OPEN TERRESTRIAL: tilled, short grass, tall grass, mixed herbaceous and shrubby fields, shrubby and wooded hedgerows and edges;
Forest: hardwoods, scattered conifers;
River/stream: seasonal stream;
Marsh/swamp/bog: patches of shrub swamp.
This 398-acre wildlife area is where to come for a variety of open habitats. Large fields are bordered by shrubby and wooded edges, and include scattered conifers and deciduous trees.

SEASONS/BIRDS
SPRING MIGRATION: LAND BIRDS;
NESTING SEASON: LAND BIRDS;
FALL MIGRATION: LAND BIRDS;
Winter: land birds.
The specialty here is open-habitat species - during the migrations and winter, but particularly during the nesting season. Nesters include bobwhite, indigo bunting, brown thrasher, prairie warbler and field sparrow. The fall migration is the time to see a variety of sparrows. A bonus, usually during the fall, are bobwhite and pheasant, both of which are released for field trials.

GETTING AROUND:
Birding methods: walk.
Walking about in this area is easy - there are large open fields, and marked trails. Field trials are held here, and the area is closed to other activities while they are in progress. Dates of the current field trial schedule are posted near the entrance. Many of the trials occur during October and November. In addition, this is a popular hunting area.

DIRECTIONS: This area is about ten miles north of Hartford, just east of the Connecticut River. To get there from I-91 exit 44, go south on Route 5 for 1.1 miles, and left on Tromley Road for 0.7 mile to the entrance on the left.

ENFIELD: KINGS ISLAND WMA/PARSONS ROAD

HABITATS
RIVER/STREAM: river, fast water, hardwood shore; wooded island with hardwood shore, perennial stream;
FOREST: hardwoods, flood plain;
Open terrestrial: shrubby field, shrubby and wooded edges.
This site provides views of a stretch of the Connecticut River which stays open in winter because of the Enfield rapids that are just upstream. It also provides a view of a wooded and protected island in the river (Kings Island).

SEASONS/BIRDS
SPRING MIGRATION: gulls, WATER BIRDS, land birds;
Nesting season: water birds, land birds;
FALL MIGRATION: gulls, WATER BIRDS, land birds;
WINTER: gulls, WATER BIRDS; land birds.
The late fall, winter and early spring are the best times at this site. During that period, sev-

eral bald eagles can often be seen resting or hunting from the trees on Kings Island and on the nearby wooded river shoreline (Kings Island provides an area that is relatively free from disturbance). In addition, during the same period, a variety of water birds can be seen on the river, and this is one of the few sites in Connecticut at which the occurrence of Barrow's goldeneye has been a repeated event. In winter, gulls are often also present, and have included glaucous and Iceland. A variety of land birds can be seen throughout the year. Screech owl has been regular near the driveway. Osprey occurs over the river in spring and fall. Double-crested cormorant has nested on the island in the past few years.

GETTING AROUND:
Birding methods: car, walk.
It is possible to drive to the shore of the river at the boat landing, and the river can be seen from several other points as you drive north on Parsons Road. In addition, there is a trail that goes south from the landing through the woods along the river; however, it is closed during the winter in order to protect the bald eagles from disturbance.

DIRECTIONS: This section of the Connecticut River is about fifteen miles north of Hartford. From I-91 exit 46, go north on Route 5 for 0.4 mile, left on Old King Street for 0.3 mile, and left again on Parsons Road. The boat landing is on the left side of Parsons Road in 0.3 mile; for 1.0 mile after that, Parsons Road goes near the river and provides several opportunities to pull off on a shoulder and scan the water.

FARMINGTON: FARMINGTON MEADOWS/SHADE SWAMP SANCTUARY

HABITATS
OPEN TERRESTRIAL: tilled, short grass, tall grass, mixed herbaceous and shrubby fields; shrubby and wooded edges;
RIVER/STREAM: river and stream; slow and fast water; herbaceous, marshy, shrubby and hardwood streambelts; seasonal streams;
MARSH, SWAMP/BOG: sedge, cattail, mixed herbaceous and shrub marsh; shrub and hardwood swamp; edges of shrubs, hardwoods and white pine;
FOREST: sand plain, flood plain, white pine, hardwoods/white pine;
Lake/pond: ponds, shores that are marshy, shrubby and wooded; seasonal pools.
Farmington Meadows and the Shade Swamp Sanctuary lie side by side on the fertile bottomland of the Farmington River Valley. These two contiguous areas, taken together, contain a wide variety of habitat types.

Farmington Meadows, immediately north and east of the Shade Swamp Sanctuary, includes a section of the Pequabuck River (a small, winding tributary of the Farmington River), the confluence of the Pequabuck and Farmington Rivers, a section of the Farmington, seasonal backwater areas, flood plain forest communities, and open fields of various types.

The Shade Swamp Sanctuary, immediately south and west of Farmington Meadows, includes another section of the Pequabuck River, and also a large wetland system around the Pequabuck that is made up of sedge, cattail and shrub marsh, and surrounded by hardwoods and white pine forest, much of it sand plain.

SEASONS/BIRDS

SPRING MIGRATION: WATER BIRDS, marsh birds, SHORE BIRDS, LAND BIRDS;

NESTING SEASON: water birds, marsh birds, shore birds, LAND BIRDS;

FALL MIGRATION: WATER BIRDS, marsh birds, SHORE BIRDS, LAND BIRDS;

Winter: water birds, land birds.

The wide variety of habitats in these two areas is reflected in the interesting species diversity that occurs in them. The best times to go there are the spring migration (March, April and early May), and the fall migration (especially October and November). In the spring, it is possible to see a nice variety of water birds (including wood duck, ringneck, common goldeneye, common and hooded mergansers); and shore birds (including snipe, spotted, solitary and least sandpipers, greater and lesser yellowlegs). In addition, many land bird species are present. The fall migration brings such land bird species as harrier, red-tailed hawk, swallows, white-crowned and various other sparrows, pipit and snow bunting. Nesters include common merganser (an uncommon nester in Connecticut), green-backed heron, Virginia rail, alder and willow flycatchers, warbling and yellow-throated vireos, pine and blue-winged warblers, swamp sparrow, orchard and northern orioles. In winter, look for Cooper's and rough-legged hawks, horned lark and snow bunting.

GETTING AROUND

Birding methods: car, walk, bike, boat.

These two areas can be entered, and the major habitats reached, from several points on Meadow Road, Red Oak Hill Road, New Britain Avenue, Route 4 and Route 6 (see below). A sidewalk runs beside Meadow Road and Red Oak Hill Road, and can be used for walking or biking. In addition, there are several trails - one along the Farmington River, a two that go north from Route 6. The Pequabuck River can be canoed.

DIRECTIONS (see Map 13): This site is in Farmington, about eight miles southwest of Hartford.

Farmington Meadows: In Farmington, from the intersection of Routes 10 and 4, go south on Route 10 for 0.9 mile, and right on Meadow Road. Follow Meadow Road as it crosses the Pequabuck River, (Farmington Meadows is on both sides of the road at this point), and then goes along the open fields of Farmington Meadows on the right side of the road. After following Meadow Road for 0.9 mile, bear right on Red Oak Hill Road and follow it for 0.3 mile to the entrance of Tunxis Meade Park on the right. The river and other habitats can be reached by crossing the fields to the right of Meadow Road and Red Oak Hill Road, or by entering Tunxis Mead Park and going through playing fields to a parking area near the Farmington River.

Another part of Farmington Meadows can be reached by starting in Farmington at the intersection of Routes 10 and 4, and going west on Route 4 for 0.3 mile to the bridge over the Farmington River. There is a parking area on the south (left) side of the bridge, and the beginning of a trail that follows the edge of the river.

Shade Swamp Sanctuary: Start in Farmington at the intersection of Routes 6 and 177. Go east on Route 6 for 0.7 mile to a DEP sign at a trailhead on the left, and for another 0.4 mile (just past New Britain Avenue) to a second trailhead, also on the left. Trails from these two points lead north into the Shade Swamp Sanctuary.

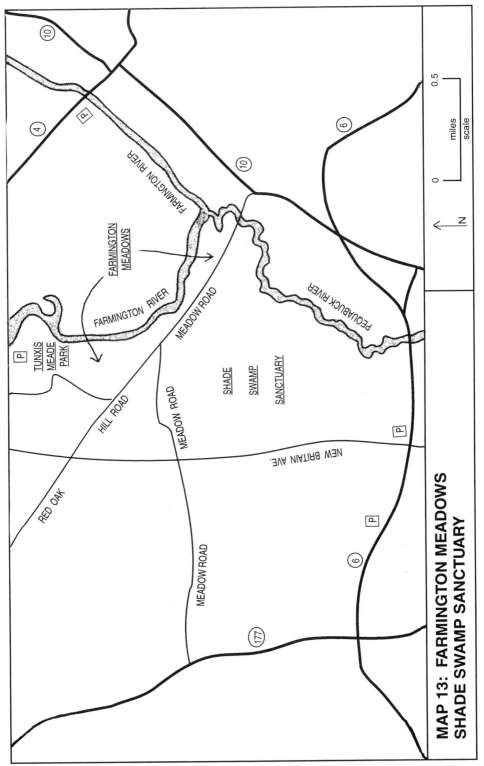

**MAP 13: FARMINGTON MEADOWS
SHADE SWAMP SANCTUARY**

FARMINGTON: MEMORIAL TOWN FOREST

HABITATS
FOREST: hardwoods, hardwoods/white pine.
This town forest lies amid scattered suburban development, and is composed almost entirely of young hardwood forest.

SEASONS/BIRDS
Spring migration: land birds;
Nesting season: land birds;
Fall migration: land birds;
Winter: land birds.
This site attracts a nice mix of the standard Connecticut forest species - both migrants and nesters. The best time is May through October. Nesters include a typical mix of woodland species, such as great crested flycatcher, pileated woodpecker, redstart, red-eyed vireo, scarlet tanager, rose-breasted grosbeak and towhee. In winter, there are a few forest-dwelling residents.

GETTING AROUND
Birding methods: walk.
Several woods roads go through most of the area.

DIRECTIONS: This area is in Farmington, about eight miles southwest of Hartford. To get there from the intersection of Routes 177 and 6 in Farmington, go north on Route 177 for 1.4 miles to one entrance to the forest on the right, and for another 0.4 mile to a second entrance on the right. Still another entrance can be reached by continuing north on Route 177, right on Copper Mine Road which becomes Red Oak Hill Road and passes an entrance to the forest on the right.

GLASTONBURY: WANGUNK MEADOWS (UPPER SECTION)

HABITATS
MARSH/SWAMP/BOG: wet meadow, mixed herbaceous and shrub marshes, fresh water tidal marsh, shrub, shrubby hardwood and hardwood swamps;
OPEN TERRESTRIAL: tilled, mixed herbaceous, short grass, tall grass and shrubby fields; shrubby and hardwood edges;
RIVER/STREAM: river, perennial and seasonal streams, shrubby and wooded edges;
Lake/pond: pond, seasonal pools, shrubby and hardwood edges;
Forest: hardwoods, flood plain.
Wangunk Meadows is a large bottomland that lies along the east shore of the Connecticut River. It is made up of alluvial marshes, tilled and reverting fields, flood plain hardwood forest, and a mosaic of shrubby and wooded edges. At times, especially in the spring, there are rain pools scattered in the marshes and fields. The banks of the river run along the western edge of the site.

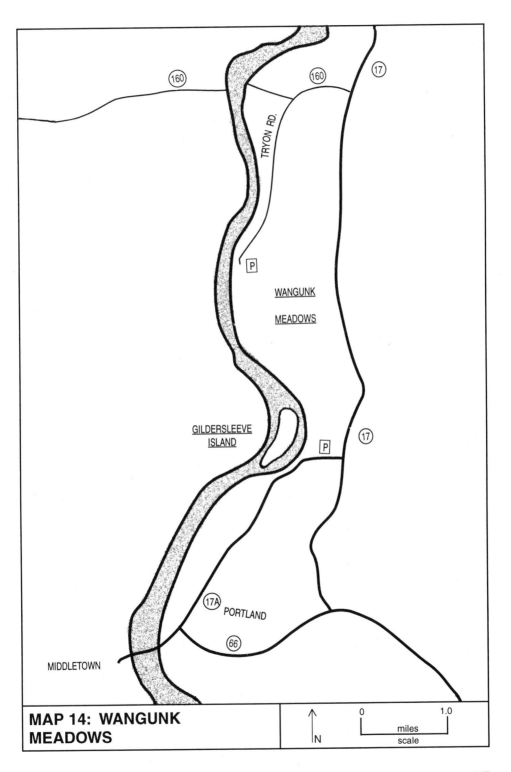

MAP 14: WANGUNK MEADOWS

SEASONS/BIRDS

SPRING MIGRATION: WATER BIRDS, marsh birds, SHORE BIRDS, LAND BIRDS;

Nesting season: water birds, land birds;

FALL MIGRATION: water birds, marsh birds, shore birds, LAND BIRDS;

Winter: land birds.

This is one of the outstanding birding areas in Connecticut's Central Valley. To a great extent, the species variety that this bottomland offers depends on the presence of rain pools that attract dabbling ducks, marsh and shore birds.

Spring migration is the best period. In the early spring (March and April), look in the pools for dabbling ducks - green-winged teal, wigeon, gadwall, pintail, wood duck and ring-necked duck. Later in the spring, a variety of shore birds can be seen, often including spotted, solitary, least and pectoral sandpipers, snipe (in April), greater and lesser yellowlegs, killdeer and woodcock. Throughout the spring and the nesting season, a standard mix of wetland- and shrub-oriented land birds occur in appropriate habitats within this bottomland, as well as occasional great blue and green-backed herons.

Early in the fall migration (in September), look for a variety of land birds. Then, in October and November, the shrubby areas within this site are especially good for sparrows (sometimes including grasshopper), and the fields for pipit, horned lark and snow bunting. If there are pools during the fall, dabbling ducks are also likely. Kestrel is usually present, and if you are lucky, you may see red-shouldered hawk, merlin or peregrine falcon.

Winter can also be interesting here. There are usually the open-habitat land birds that you would expect, including horned lark and snow bunting, and also from time to time, harrier, rough-legged hawk and short-eared owl. Screech owls (quite a few of them) are here throughout the year.

GETTING AROUND:

Birding methods: car, WALK.

A network of trails goes through this area - some are easy, others are rough or wet. The Wangunk Wildlife Management Area includes 500 acres of this wetland/field complex. Although it lies in Portland, Middlesex County, it is best approached from the north, as described here. The approach from the south is described in the Middlesex County chapter, under "Portland: Wangunk Meadows (Lower Section)/Gildersleeve Island". There is public access to the north end of the area; public access from the south is currently in dispute, so that reaching habitats in the southern part of this area should be done by walking down from the north on trails within the area. It is also possible to look down at some of the part of the site (distantly) through a spotting scope from Route 17.

DIRECTIONS (see Map 14): This area lies along the east shore of the Connecticut River, about ten miles south of Hartford. In Glastonbury from Route 2 exit 7, go south on Route 17 for 2.9 miles, right on Route 160 for 0.8 mile to a point where it turns right toward the Glastonbury ferry. At this point, keep going straight (south) on Tryon Road, which passes through farm fields for over two miles, and ends at a parking area. From this point, it is possible to walk south through the area for about three miles.

GRANBY: ENDERS STATE FOREST

HABITATS
FOREST: hardwoods, hardwoods/white pine, hardwoods/hemlock, white pine, hemlock, spruce, mountain laurel;
OPEN TERRESTRIAL: tilled, short grass, tall grass, mixed herbaceous and shrubby fields; junipers, shrubby and wooded edges;
RIVER/STREAM: streams, slow water, fast water, shrubby, marshy and hardwood streambelts, hemlock ravine;
MARSH/SWAMP/BOG: sedge, mixed herbaceous and shrub marsh, shrub swamp, shrubby hardwood swamp, hardwood swamp, dead wood, beaver-controlled wetlands;
Lake/pond: small pond, shrubby and wooded shore.
This 1,434-acre state forest contains a very productive assortment of almost every type of inland habitat, including a fine wetland (see directions).

SEASONS/BIRDS
SPRING MIGRATION: water birds, marsh birds, shore birds, LAND BIRDS;
NESTING SEASON: water birds, marsh birds, LAND BIRDS;
FALL MIGRATION: water birds, marsh birds, shore birds, LAND BIRDS;
Winter: land birds;
This site is tops as a birding area; it offers great species diversity during the entire period from late April through late October. The spring and fall migrations bring a nice mix of the species you would expect in this wide range of habitats. Water birds include Canada goose, mallard and wood duck; marsh birds include great blue and green-backed heron and Virginia rail (the latter two species are nesters); shore birds include snipe, spotted and solitary sandpipers; land birds include a variety of forest and open habitat species. About 90 species nest here; they include a number of northern forest species - hermit thrush, solitary vireo, black-throated green, black-throated blue, magnolia and Blackburnian warblers, northern waterthrush and golden-crowned kinglet (one of the few nesting occurrences of this species in Connecticut). Other nesters are Louisiana waterthrush, great horned and barred owls, red-tailed and broad-winged hawks. Many open habitat species also nest here - blue-winged, Brewster's and prairie warblers, field sparrow, indigo bunting, and brown thrasher, among others. Winter produces the standard mix of land birds, plus (during incursion years) winter finches - especially redpoll feeding on birch catkins. Northern shrike has also been seen.

GETTING AROUND
Birding methods: CAR, WALK, BIKE.
There are several quiet country roads that go through this area (see "Directions" below) that can be driven, walked or biked, and woods roads and trails that can be walked. Moreover, like many other state forests, Enders does not get crowded during the summer, and unlike many others, hunting is not permitted - an ideal situation for birders. Black bears frequent this area, especially the cornfields, so be alert, and maybe you'll see one of these magnificent creatures.

DIRECTIONS (see Map 15): This state forest is about five miles west of Granby. To get there from the intersection of Routes 219 and 20 near Granby, go west on Route 219 for 1.5 miles to a parking area on the left that provides access to a hemlock ravine and the section of the forest that extends westward to Case Road. Then continue on Route 219 for another 0.1 mile to Enders Road on the right. You can park here, and walk up Enders Road, or drive Enders Road for 0.7 miles to its intersection with LeGeyt Road. Here again, you have the choice of walking or driving: right on LeGeyt Road for 0.4 miles, or straight on LeGeyt Road for 0.5 miles (this takes you past a high quality marsh/swamp wetland). Woods roads and trails lead into habitat areas from both Enders and LeGeyt Roads.

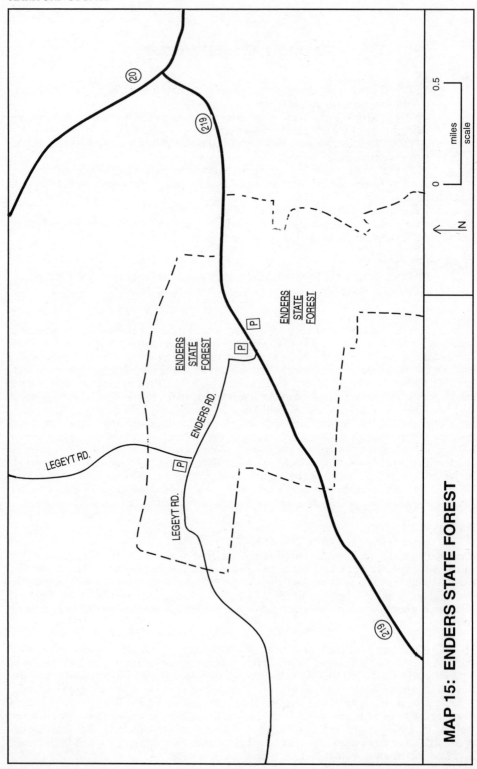

MAP 15: ENDERS STATE FOREST

GRANBY: MCLEAN GAME REFUGE

HABITATS
FOREST: hardwoods, hardwoods/white pine, hardwoods/ hemlock, white pine/ hemlock, sand plain, flood plain, cedar;
OPEN TERRESTRIAL: tilled, short grass, tall grass, mixed herbaceous and shrubby fields; shrubby and hardwood edges;
RIVER/STREAM: stream, shrubby and wooded streambelt;
LAKE/POND: pond, marshy, shrubby and wooded shore; seasonal pools;
MARSH, SWAMP/BOG: sedge marsh, shrub marsh, shrub swamp, shrubby/hardwood swamp, hardwood swamp, shrubby edges, black spruce bog.

One can get a feeling of near-wilderness within an otherwise suburban countryside on the trails of this sanctuary that occupies over 4,000 acres. This refuge is really diverse - within it are high quality examples of most of the forest and inland wetland habitat types that occur in Connecticut.

SEASONS/BIRDS
SPRING MIGRATION: water birds, shore birds, LAND BIRDS;
NESTING SEASON: water birds, shore birds, LAND BIRDS;
FALL MIGRATION: water birds, marsh birds, shore birds, LAND BIRDS;
Winter: land birds.

This is an excellent area at any season in which to look for a wide variety of migrating, nesting and year-round resident species. The spring and fall migrations are excellent, with a wide variety of sparrows present in October and November. Nesters include such northern species as solitary vireo, magnolia, black-throated green, yellow-rumped, blackburnian, black-throated blue warblers and northern waterthrush; also open-habitat species including prairie warbler and indigo bunting in shrubby fields and edges, and bobolink in grassy fields. Winter finches are likely to be found here in years of incursion.

GETTING AROUND
Birding methods: WALK.
There are many miles of good trails that pass through forest, open country and wetland habitats, and provide an easy way to see a variety of species. Maps are available at the main entrances.

DIRECTIONS (see map 16): The preserve is about five miles west of Bradley Airport. To get there from the center of Granby at the intersection of Routes 20, 202 and 10, go south on Routes 202 and 10 for 1.0 mile to the refuge entrance on the right. Another entrance of the preserve can be reached from the center of Granby by going west on Route 20 for 1.3 miles, and left on Barn Door Hills Road for 1.0 mile to the preserve entrance on the left. Trails lead into the preserve from several area roads. In addition to the eastern section described here, there is also a large western section, included on the trail map available at the refuge.

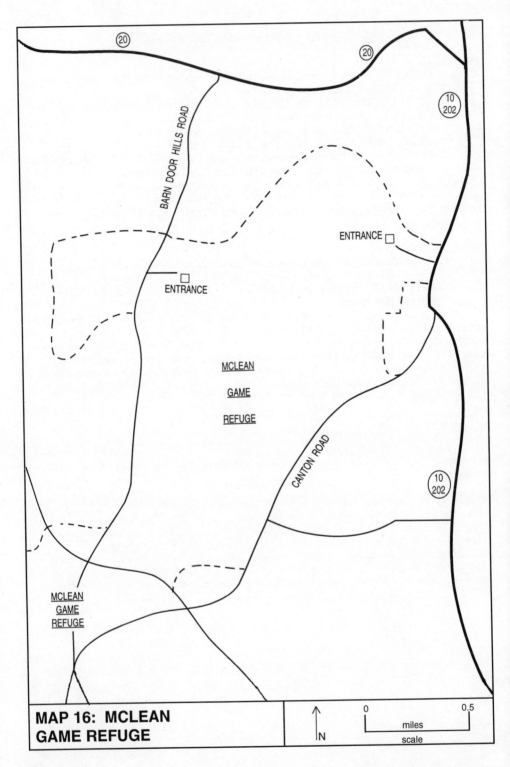

MAP 16: MCLEAN GAME REFUGE

HARTLAND/BARKHAMSTED: TUNXIS STATE FOREST

HABITATS

FOREST: hardwoods, hardwoods/white pine, white pine, hardwoods/hemlock, white pine/hemlock, hemlock, mixed conifers, mountain laurel;
MARSH, SWAMP/BOG: sedge, cattail, mixed herbaceous and shrub marshes; shrub swamp, shrubby hardwood swamp, dead wood, spruce bog;
Open terrestrial: shrubby fields;
Lake/pond: pond; marshy, shrubby and wooded shore, seasonal pools;
River/stream: streams, marshy, shrubby and wooded streambelts; hemlock ravine;
Other: ledge, cliff, rocky slope.

This 8,692-acre state forest has a wild, remote quality that reminds one of northern New England. The area it contains is one of Connecticut's best examples of an extensive northern forest habitat complex; it is more typical of Vermont, New Hampshire or Maine than of anywhere in Southern New England. This is largely the result of altitude - much of this area lies at elevations up to 1,200 feet. There is a bog in which black and red spruce trees grow, and a pristine pond (Emmons Pond) with a distinctly boreal character and a marsh at its north end. Throughout the forest the trees also have a northern character - the most common species are hemlock, white pine, beech, yellow and white birch in various combinations. There are extensive areas of mountain laurel. Occasional clearcut lumbering operations over time have left patches of forest of varying ages, and clearings that are in early stages of regrowth.

SEASONS/BIRDS

SPRING MIGRATION: water birds, marsh birds, LAND BIRDS;
NESTING SEASON: water birds, marsh birds, LAND BIRDS;
FALL MIGRATION: water birds, marsh birds, LAND BIRDS;
Winter: land birds.

This should be one of your top choices during the period May through early September for forest-dwelling land birds, especially species that normally occur in areas to our north. The spring and fall migrations are excellent for a great diversity of forest dwelling species, including many of the species that nest at this site. Nesters include goshawk, red-shouldered hawk, saw-whet owl, winter wren, red-breasted nuthatch, Acadian flycatcher, hermit thrush, solitary and yellow-throated vireos, black-throated green, black-throated blue, Blackburnian, yellow-rumped, Canada and magnolia warblers, northern waterthrush, white-throated sparrow, junco, golden-crowned kinglet and purple finch. Nesters also include a number of edge and reverting-field species such as chestnut-sided warbler and towhee. American bittern was heard calling at Emmons Pond in 1994, and great blue heron regularly feeds at the pond. In years of southward irruption by winter finches, look for crossbills and siskins in the spruce stands, pine grosbeak in tamaracks and apple trees, and redpolls in birch and tamarack trees.

GETTING AROUND

Birding methods: CAR, WALK, BIKE, SKI.

There are miles of hardtop and dirt road that can be driven through or along parts of this forest. In addition, there are many dirt roads that are rough to drive but easy to walk. Numerous woods roads and trails make it possible to reach still more areas of habitat. In some areas, state forest land, water company land, land trust property and small residential holdings are intermingled, so that it is necessary to look for signs and be certain of your position in order to avoid trespassing. Most parts of this large area are open for hunting.

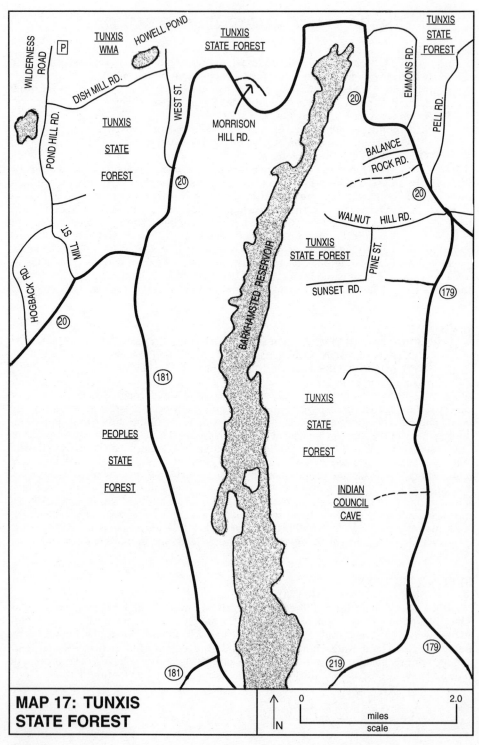

MAP 17: TUNXIS STATE FOREST

DIRECTIONS (see Map 17): There are three main blocks of the Tunxis State Forest, all of them lying on either side of the Barkhamsted Reservoir within a few miles of the Connecticut/Massachusetts state line. The directions that follow take you into avian habitats in each of these three blocks. Some of the side roads lack road signs, so rely on the mileages stated in the directions.

To get to habitats in and near the southeastern block, from the intersection of Routes 20 and 179:

1. Go south on Route 179 for 2.6 miles, turn right on an unnamed road that goes through parts of the forest and leads to other roads through the forest. The Tunxis Trail can be walked from here north into the northeastern block of the forest, and can also be followed southward.

2. Go back to Route 179, and continue south for another 0.8 mile (a total of 3.4 miles from the intersection of Routes 179 and 20) to a woods road on the right. This road can be walked into the Indian Council Cave area of the forest.

3. Continue south on Route 179 for another 1.1 miles (a total of 4.5 miles from the intersection of Routes 179 and 20), right (straight, really) on Route 219 for 1.5 miles, left on Ratlum Road for 0.2 mile to the point at which the Tunxis Trail crosses the road. From here you can walk south (right) on the trail, over Ratlum Mountain to the Sundown Ski Area, a distance of 2.8 miles. (This area is not within the Tunxis State Forest, so that only the trail is public.)

To get to habitats in the northeastern block, from the intersection of Routes 20 and 179:

4. Go a few yards north on Route 20, right on Old Town Road for 0.5 mile, and right on Pell Road, which goes through hardwood/hemlock and hemlock forest for more than a mile. The road is dirt, and better walked than driven in some seasons.

5. Return to the intersection of Routes 20 and 179, go west on Walnut Hill Road for 0.9 mile to the intersection with Pine Street. Go straight ahead on Walnut Hill Road for a short distance to a barway. Woods roads and trails lead through hardwoods/hemlock forest.

6. Go back to the intersection of Walnut Hill Road and Pine Street, go south on Pine Street for 0.6 mile, right on Sunset Road for 0.5 through northern hardwoods/hemlock/ white pine/ mountain laurel to the edge of the state forest and the beginning of private property.

To get to more habitats in the northeastern block, from the intersection of Routes 20 and 179:

7. Go west on Route 20 for 0.8 mile to a woods road on the left. This road and others it leads to can be walked through hardwoods, hardwoods/white pine, hardwoods/hemlock, a small pond, clearings, and a bog (quite far in).

8. Return to Route 20, continue west for another 0.2 mile, left on Balance Rock Road for 0.4 mile to a barway and a woods road straight ahead. This road can be walked through northern hardwoods and mixed conifers.

9. Return to Route 20 and continue west for another 0.3 mile and go right on Emmons Road (which becomes Hurricane Brook Road). This road passes near Emmons Pond and descends steeply through a hemlock ravine along a brook with a wooded streambelt. In 1.9 miles it rejoins Route 20. It is rough and better walked than driven.

To get to habitats in the western block of the forest, start in Hartland, on the west side of the Barkhamsted Reservoir, at the intersection of Routes 20 and 181. (To reach that point from the end of the dirt road described in the preceding paragraph, continue west on Route 20 over the north end of the Reservoir).

10. From the intersection of Routes 20 and 181 in Hartland, go west (or south) on Route 20 for 2.8 miles, right on Hogback Road for 2.6 miles (much of it along the Farmington River with frequent pulloffs), left on Mill Street for 0.5 mile, left on Pond Hill Road for 1.1 miles to a fork, at which Wilderness Road goes straight ahead, and Dish Mill Road goes right. Go straight on Wilderness Road for 0.3 mile to a parking area and the beginning of a woods road that goes into the Tunxis Wildlife Managament Area. (Note: you can easily enter the Colebrook River and Goodwin Reservoirs site, described under Colebrook in Litchfield County, by turning left from Hogback Road onto the road over the Goodwin Dam, visible as you pass.)

11. From the Tunxis WMA parking area (see 10), go back on Wilderness Road for 0.3 mile, east on Dish Mill Road for 0.7 mile to Howell Pond which is surrounded by hemlock forest and is just above a hemlock ravine. Continue on Dish Mill Road for another 0.2 mile, right on West Street for 1.4 mile to Route 20.

12. Turn left on Route 20 in order to go east (north) for another 1.8 miles to Morrison Hill Road on the left. It can be walked (or sometimes driven) through hemlock/mixed conifers forest and clearcut openings.

13. Return once again to Route 20 and continue east (north) for another 1.1 miles, much of it through state forest, to the overlook on the right. It provides a spectacular view of the northern portion of the Barkhamsted Reservoir, and offers the possibility of seeing bald eagle and other raptors. It is a fitting climax to your tour of this magnificent forest.

See also: Barkhamsted: Barkhamsted Reservoir, in the Litchfield County chapter.

MANCHESTER: UNION POND PARK

HABITATS
Lake/pond: lake, grassy, shrubby and hardwood shore with pockets of marsh, seasonal pools;
Forest: hardwoods;
Open terrestrial: short grass field, shrubby edge;
River/stream: stream, hardwood streambelt.
This town park lies within a developed area near Manchester, and is centered around Union Pond, a small lake that is surrounded by a deciduous woodland through which the Hockanum River flows. The entrance area is maintained as mowed lawn.

SEASONS/BIRDS
Spring migration: gulls, water birds, land birds;
Nesting season: land birds;
Fall migration: gulls, water birds, land birds;
Winter: land birds.
The main attraction at this site is water birds during the spring and fall migrations - there is some variety, but usually the mix is confined to common species. Gulls are also present in the spring and fall, again common species. A typical mix of hardwood forest land birds can be found in the woods around the lake in spring, summer and fall.

GETTING AROUND
Birding methods: car, WALK, BIKE.
It is possible to see most of the pond from the parking area (a scope is helpful). In addition, there is a wide trail that connects to a trail network that provides easy birding on foot with excellent views of the lake. The main trail follows the Hockanum River for a considerable distance.

DIRECTIONS: This site lies a mile or two north of the center of Manchester. From the western intersection of Routes 83 and 30, go south on Route 83 for 0.9 mile, right on North School Street for 0.1 mile to the park entrance on the right.

MARLBOROUGH: SALMON RIVER STATE FOREST (DICKINSON CREEK AREA)

HABITATS
FOREST: hardwoods, hardwoods/white pine, hardwoods/hemlock, flood plain;
River/stream: stream, hardwood streambelt;
Marsh/swamp/bog: hardwood swamp.
This is the largest of several separate tracts of the Salmon River State Forest. It is 1,000 acres in size, and lies in a three mile section of the shallow valley that is formed by Dickinson Creek. Habitats in the streambelt of the creek include bottomland hardwood forest and some areas of hardwood swamp.

SEASONS/BIRDS
Spring migration: water birds, land birds;
Nesting season: water birds, land birds
Fall migration: water birds, land birds;
Winter: land birds.

This area offers a typical mix of woodland species during the spring and fall migrations, and in the nesting season. In addition, a nice variety of hawks and owls occur here, especially in spring, summer and fall. Nesting species include black duck, wood duck, broad-winged and red-shouldered hawks, great horned and barred owls, woodcock, pileated and red-bellied woodpeckers, and worm-eating warbler.

GETTING AROUND:
Birding methods: car, walk.

There are woods roads through parts of the forest; it is also possible to see edges of it from your car on Flood Road, and also from several other town roads that skirt the forest.

DIRECTIONS: This block of the forest lies in the southwest portion of Marlborough, about 15 miles southeast of Hartford. From the intersection of Routes 66 and 2 in Marlborough, go south on Route 66 for 1.7 miles, left on Flood Road for 0.5 mile, left at the fork for 0.2 mile to a barway and woods road leading into the forest on the right. The state forest lies on both sides of the road at this point, with the larger part on the right side.

NEW BRITAIN: A. W. STANLEY PARK/STANLEY QUARTER PARK

HABITATS
Forest: hardwoods, hardwoods/white pine, cedar groves;
Open terrestrial: short grass, mixed herbaceous and shrubby fields, shrubby edges;
Lake/pond: two ponds, shores of grass, wetlands and woods;
River/stream: perennial stream, shrubby and wooded streambelt;
Marsh/swamp/bog: mixed herbaceous and shrub marsh, shrubby hardwood and hardwood swamp.

These two parks contain nice natural areas within the city of New Britain.

SEASONS/BIRDS
Spring migration: gulls, water birds, marsh birds, shore birds, land birds;
Nesting season: water birds, land birds;
Fall Migration: gulls, water birds, marsh birds, shore birds, land birds;
Winter: land birds.

Common species of water birds occur in the ponds of both parks during the spring, summer and fall. During migration, the species often include double-crested cormorant, ring-necked duck, common and hooded mergansers. In the fall, great egret, great blue and green-backed herons sometimes stop by the wetlands. Land birds occur here all year; during the spring and fall, look for migrants along the wooded edges. A pair of red-headed woodpeckers have nested in Stanley Quarter park for several years (see "Directions" below). Other nesting species include scarlet tanager and great crested flycatcher.

GETTING AROUND
Can be birded by: car, WALK, bike.

Driveways lead to many parts of both parks, and there are also trails and woods roads.

DIRECTIONS: These two parks are near one another seven or eight miles southwest of Hartford. To get to A. W. Stanley Park, from I-84 exit 37, go south on Fienemann Road for 0.3

mile, left on Alexander Road for 1.1 miles (past Batterson Park Pond) to the entrance to A. W. Stamnley Park which is straight ahead, directly across Stanley Street. To get to Stanley Quarter Park, exit from A. W. Stanley Park through that same entrance, and turn south (left) on Stanley Street (which merges with Route 71) and go for 0.7 mile to the entrance to Stanley Quarter Park straight ahead. To reach the red-headed woodpecker nest site, follow the park driveway past the pond for 0.3 mile, then turn hard right and follow another driveway for 0.1 mile to a parking area on the left. A trail starts here, and leads in the direction of the nesting area, and to a trail network.

NEW BRITAIN: BATTERSON PARK POND

HABITATS
LAKE/POND: lake, deep water, shallow water, cove; shore composed of grass, shrubs, hardwood swamp, hardwoods.
Forest: hardwoods.
This is a large lake that has a shore that is partly developed, partly wooded, with sections of mowed grass, shrubs and small pockets of wetland.

SEASONS/BIRDS
SPRING MIGRATION: gulls, WATER BIRDS, land birds;
Nesting season: land birds
FALL MIGRATION: gulls, WATER BIRDS, water birds, land birds;
Winter: gulls, water birds, land birds.
Migrating water birds are the major interest at this site, and it sometimes has an interesting diversity. There are usually large numbers of geese - commonly Canada, sometimes snow, and once in a while white-fronted. Other regular species are pied-billed grebe, common goldeneye, wigeon, ring-necked duck, bufflehead, common and hooded mergansers. Gulls are often present - commonly herring and ring-billed, but Iceland has been seen here more than once. Some of the more common land bird species can be seen in the shrubs and edges near the landing during spring, summer and fall.

GETTING AROUND:
Birding methods: car, walk.
There is a parking area on the shore of the lake, and a short driveway down to it (about 100 yards). The driveway is blocked off in cold weather. All the property around the landing is private. The lake is large, so a scope is helpful. Boating on the lake is very active during warm weather.

DIRECTIONS: This lake is seven or eight miles southwest of Hartford. From I-84 exit 37, go south on Fienemann Road for 0.3 mile, left on Alexander Road for 0.2 mile to the driveway down to the state boat landing at the lake.

ROCKY HILL: FERRY PARK

HABITATS
> **RIVER/STREAM:** river, slow water, mud flat, hardwood shore, seasonal stream;
> **OPEN TERRESTRIAL:** shrubby field;
> **Lake/pond:** pond, rocky and shrubby shore;
> **Marsh/swamp/bog:** mixed herbaceous and shrub marsh, hardwood swamp;
> **Forest:** flood plain.
> **Other:** cliff, ledge.

This site has a good view of the Connecticut River, in a section that is still affected by tides, but far above the reach of salt water. Also within the park are a shrubby field, a small quarry pond and areas of flood plain forest.

SEASONS/BIRDS
> **Spring migration:** gulls, water birds, shore birds, land birds;
> **Nesting season:** land birds;
> **FALL MIGRATION:** gulls, water birds, marsh birds, shore birds, LAND BIRDS;
> **Winter:** gulls, water birds, land birds;

The spring and fall migrations are both good, for water birds on the river, a few shore birds in the mud near the shore, osprey moving along the river, and a variety of land birds in the terrestrial habitats within the park. The most productive of these are the shrubby fields, the seeds and berries of which attract migrating sparrows during October and November. Nesters include those species that are partial to reverting-field type habitat. A variety of land birds occur here during the winter, as they come to feed on the seeds and berries that are still on the shrubs. Bald eagle occurs here during the fall, winter and spring, and screech owl all year.

GETTING AROUND
> **Birding methods:** car, walk.

The river can be seen from the parking area. There is a trail from the parking area into the park, and several trails within it. At the time of writing, there was some question of public access, so be sure to observe any posted restrictions. Hunting is allowed during the fall.

DIRECTIONS: This site is on the west bank of the Connecticut River, about ten miles south of Hartford. To get there from Rocky Hill at the intersection of Routes 160 and 99, go east on Route 160 for 0.6 mile to the ferry dock. Ferry Park is immediately to the north, by the river.

SIMSBURY: CURTIS PARK

HABITATS
> **RIVER/STREAM:** river, slow water, streambelt of hardwoods, shrubs and herbs;
> **Open terrestrial:** short grass field, shrubby edge.
> **Forest:** flood plain.

This site is a recreational area located next to an oxbow of the Farmington River; it has large mowed fields, shrubby edges and flood plain forest by the river. There are some really nice, stately old sycamores here.

SEASONS/BIRDS

Spring migration: water birds, land birds;
Nesting season: water birds, land birds;
Fall migration: water birds, land birds;
Winter: water birds, land birds.

This is one of several sites in the Farmington River valley that are quite good at all seasons. During the spring and fall migrations, osprey and a variety of other land bird species travel along the river and through the woods of its streambelt. Warbling vireo is among the species that nest within the park. In winter, look for bald eagle and screech owl, as well as water birds if there is open water.

GETTING AROUND:

Birding methods: car, walk.

All the habitats in this park, including the shore of the river, can be reached or seen from your car, or by easy walking over the open areas.

DIRECTIONS (see Map 18):This area is a mile or two north of the center of Simsbury, fifteen miles northwest of Hartford. From the intersection of Routes 315, 10 and 202, go east on Route 315 across the river for 0.5 mile to the park entrance on the left.

SIMSBURY: GREAT POND STATE FOREST

HABITATS

FOREST: hardwoods, white pine and hemlock alone and in combination; sand plain of pitch pine, white pine and oak.
LAKE/POND: pond, shallow water; shrubby islands; shore of shrubs, forest, shrub marsh, shrub swamp and shrubby hardwood swamp;
Open terrestrial: shrubby field, shrubby and wooded edges;
River/stream: perennial stream, wooded shore;
Marsh/swamp/bog: mixed herbaceous and shrub marsh, shrub and shrubby hardwood swamp.

This relatively small state forest includes a pond, managed and natural woodlands, as well as open areas and edges associated with a power line and logging. The forest occupies a sand plain, and is composed largely of white pine and hemlock together with some hardwoods.

SEASONS/BIRDS

SPRING MIGRATION: WATER BIRDS, marsh birds, shore birds, LAND BIRDS;
NESTING SEASON: WATER BIRDS, marsh birds, LAND BIRDS;
FALL MIGRATION: WATER BIRDS, marsh birds, shore birds, LAND BIRDS;
Winter: land birds.

This is a good area in which to look for a variety of common water birds. It is also a good site for land bird species that are drawn to conifer-dominated sand plain forest, as well as some shrub and edge species that occur in the power line clearing. Both migrations are good. Look on the pond for pied-billed grebe, ring-necked duck, goldeneye, hooded merganser and great blue heron. Also come during the nesting season - within the area in which this forest is located, 101 bird species have shown evidence of nesting, and of these, 56 are confirmed. Among the nesters are: common merganser, green-backed heron, red-shouldered and broad-winged hawks, great horned and barred owls, pileated woodpecker, pine warbler (especially in the sand plain community), Louisiana waterthrush, and a number of northern species - red-breasted nuthatch, brown creeper, solitary vireo, black-throated blue, black-throated green, Canada, Blackburnian, yellow-rumped warblers and northern waterthrush. In winter, fewer species are present, but this is still a nice place to do some birding. Winter finches are a possibility in years of incursion.

GETTING AROUND
Birding methods: WALK, BIKE, SKI.
A short driveway leads from the entrance to a parking area and the beginning of several trails, one of which goes to the pond. In addition, from the park it is possible to get on a bike path that is part of the extensive network in Simsbury. The driveway from the park entrance is closed to cars in winter, but is can be walked or skied.

DIRECTIONS This area is about two miles northwest of the center of Simsbury. From Simsbury, at the intersection of Routes 167, 10 and 202, go west on Route 167 for 0.2 mile, right on Firetown Road for 0.8 mile, and bear left on Great Pond Road for 1.6 miles to the entrance on the right.

SIMSBURY: NOD BROOK WILDLIFE MANAGEMENT AREA

HABITATS
OPEN TERRESTRIAL: tilled, short grass, tall grass, mixed herbaceous and shrubby fields; shrubby and hardwood edges;
RIVER/STREAM: river, slow water, streambelt of hardwoods, shrubs and herbs;
MARSH/SWAMP/BOG: backwater of the Farmington River: wet meadow, sedge marsh, shrub marsh;
Lake/pond: ponds; grassy, marshy and shrubby shores;
Forest: hardwoods, flood plain.
Other: cliff.
This area of river bottomland includes a very productive mix of all five major groups of inland habitat - open terrestrial, river, ponds (in the form of artificial impoundments), marsh and forest. The cliffs of Talcott Mountain are visible in the distance.

SEASONS/BIRDS
SPRING MIGRATION: WATER BIRDS, marsh birds, SHORE BIRDS, LAND BIRDS;
NESTING SEASON: water birds; marsh birds, shore birds, LAND BIRDS;
FALL MIGRATION: WATER BIRDS, MARSH BIRDS, SHORE BIRDS, LAND BIRDS;
Winter: water birds, land birds.
As a result of the wide variety of habitats and the productive interfaces between them, an exciting diversity of birds can be seen at this site, and it is an exceptional birding area in the early fall. The spring migration usually includes snipe, spotted and solitary sandpipers, both yellowlegs, osprey, bald eagle, harrier and other hawks. The fall migration commonly brings these same species, plus pied-billed grebe, least sandpiper, additional hawk species, night-hawk (in August), various blackbirds including rusty, numerous sparrows and pipit. In addition to the fall migrants, great egrets occur here as post-breeding wanderers. The many species that nest here include spotted sandpiper, bobolink, bobwhite, willow flycatcher and indigo bunting. During the winter, shrubby fields and edges provide shelter for lingering land birds (including bobwhite that is stocked in the fall); also there is the chance of seeing a bald eagle and (infrequently) northern shrike. If there is open water, ducks may be present.

GETTING AROUND
Birding methods: CAR, WALK.
A dirt road with several branches reaches most of the habitats. (It is somewhat rough, and may not be usable by cars during the cold months and early spring; however, it always provides good walking.) In addition, there are several trails. The area is regularly used for hunting and dog field trials.

DIRECTIONS: This area is located about midway between the centers of Simsbury and Avon, about fifteen miles northwest of Hartford. In Avon, at the western intersection of Routes 10, 202 and 44, go north on Routes 10 and 202 for 1.4 miles, and turn right into a business park. Follow the road within the park for 0.1 mile to the entrance to the wildlife management area on the right. The dirt road through the area begins here.

SIMSBURY: SIMSBURY WILDLIFE MANAGEMENT AREA

HABITATS
RIVER/STREAM: river, slow water, hardwood streambelt;
OPEN TERRESTRIAL: tilled, tall grass, mixed herbaceous and shrubby fields, vine tangles and thickets;
Marsh/swamp/bog: mixed herbaceous and shrub marsh, shrub swamp;
Forest: flood plain, hardwoods;
Lake/pond: ponds, shrubby and wooded shores.
This area includes 223 acres of rich bottomland along both sides of the Farmington River. It contains several small artificial ponds, and a variety of good streambelt, wetland and open terrestrial habitats.

SEASONS/BIRDS
Spring migration: water birds, marsh birds, land birds;
Nesting season: marsh birds, land birds;
Fall migration: water birds, marsh birds, land birds;
Winter: land birds.
The mix of habitats at this site provides interesting birding throughout the spring, summer and fall. During both migrations and the nesting season, it is a good place to look for land bird species that are drawn to shrubby edges and thickets. In the fall, you can expect to see numerous sparrow species. Nesters include a nice variety of shrub and edge-dwellers. Water birds are present on the river during the spring and fall, and in winter as well, when there is open water. Also in winter, bald eagle is sometimes present.

GETTING AROUND
Birding methods: walk.
There are trails through some parts of this area. This site is mosquito heaven, so come prepared!

DIRECTIONS (see Map 18): This area lies on both sides of the Farmington River a mile or two north of the center of Simsbury and fifteen miles northwest of Hartford. **To get to the part of the area on the east side of the Farmington River,** from the intersection of Routes 315, 202 and 10, go east on Route 315 for 0.2 mile, right on Terrys Plain Road for 0.5 mile, and right on Goodrich Road for 0.3 mile to the entrance on the right. **To get to the part of the area on the west side of the Farmington River,** from the intersection of Routes 315, 202 and 10, go south on Routes 202 and 10 for 0.5 mile. The entrance to the area is on the left side of the road at this point, but difficult to see. There is a place to park a few yards farther south on the right side of the highway.

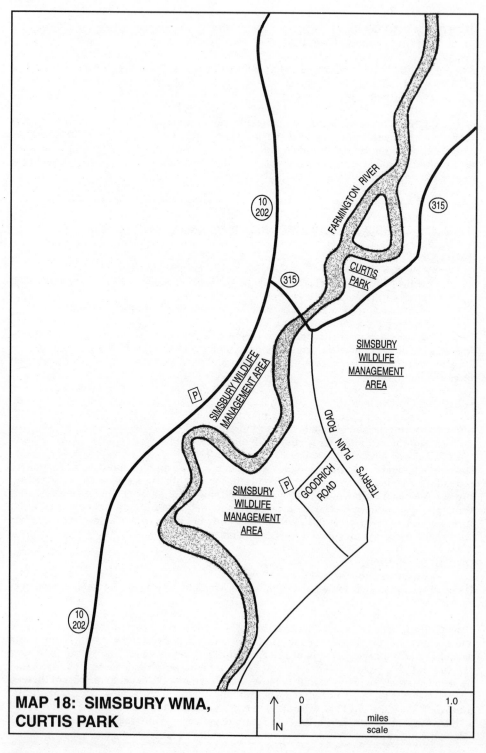

MAP 18: SIMSBURY WMA, CURTIS PARK

N

0   1.0

miles
scale

SOUTH WINDSOR: SOUTH WINDSOR WILDLIFE SANCTUARY/IDLENOT FARM

HABITATS
OPEN TERRESTRIAL: tilled, short grass, tall grass, mixed herbaceous and shrubby fields; shrubby and hardwood edges, hedgerows;
Marsh/swamp/bog: wet meadow, seasonal pools, shrub swamp, shrubby hardwood swamp;
Forest: hardwoods, white pine;
Other: hawk watching site.

The South Windsor Wildlife Sanctuary is a 117-acre former farm that occupies a gentle hill-top. It is surrounded by the flat country of Connecticut's Central Valley, and has views of Hartford and southern Massachusetts, and you can see as far south as Sleeping Giant in Hamden. Habitats include tilled fields, as well as untilled fields and edges in various stages of post-agricultural succession, bordered by areas of young hardwood forest with some white pine. A small sanctuary of the Hartford Audubon Society (Idlenot Farm) is across the road; it has open fields, managed conifers and shrubby edges.

SEASONS/BIRDS
SPRING MIGRATION: LAND BIRDS;
NESTING SEASON: LAND BIRDS;
FALL MIGRATION: LAND BIRDS;
Winter: land birds.

This is an excellent site at which to look for open field, shrub and edge species, during both migrations and the nesting season. Species that occur both as migrants and nesters include: woodcock, bobolink, meadowlark, indigo bunting, prairie warbler and field sparrow, in addition to many more common species. Both migrations are very good - and in the fall, there are some bonuses. During the early fall (September and October), the open fields and clear views provide a good place from which to watch migrating hawks (particularly broad-winged, sharp-shinned and Cooper's hawks, and harrier). Also in September, among the shrubs you are likely to see berry-eaters, including cedar waxwing, robin, hermit thrush and bluebird. A little later (in October and November), many sparrows are present, including white-throated, white-crowned, Savannah, Lincoln's, and sometimes even vesper. In the late fall, horned lark and snow bunting are possibilities. In winter, there are common land bird species, plus a few lingering berry- and seed-eaters. In years of incursion, redpolls have been seen.

GETTING AROUND
Birding methods: walk, ski.

These two sanctuaries are on opposite sides of Niederwerfer Road - the South Windsor Sanctuary on the west, and Idlenot Farm on the East. There are trails (sometimes wet in places) that make loops through both areas. Park on the west side of the road.

DIRECTIONS: This area is located about 15 miles northeast of Hartford. From the center of South Windsor at the intersection of Routes 74 and 30, go northeast on Route 74 for 2.6 miles, left on Neiderwerfer Road for 0.4 mile to the entrance to the South Windsor Wildlife Sanctuary on the left. Idlenot Farm is on the right, 0.1 mile before you reach the wildlife sanctuary.

SOUTH WINDSOR: STATION 43

HABITATS

OPEN TERRESTRIAL: tilled, short grass, tall grass, mixed herbaceous and shrubby fields, shrubby and wooded edges and hedgerows;

RIVER/STREAM: river, slow water, mud bar, hardwood streambelt; stream, slow water, shrubby and marshy streambelt;

MARSH, SWAMP/BOG: sedge, cattail and shrub marsh; shrub and hardwood swamp; standing dead wood.

Forest: hardwoods, flood plain;

Lake/pond: pond, shallow water, marshy shore.

Station 43 is justly famous throughout Connecticut for its extraordinary productivity throughout the year. The high quality of this site is due to its position along the east shore of the Connecticut River, an important avenue of migration through the state, and also to the richness and diversity of the habitats within the area, including: a stretch of the Connecticut River and its flood plain, a variety of tilled, mowed and reverting fields, numerous types of marsh and swamp, a pond, a stream, shrubby edges and thickets, shrubby and wooded hedgerows.

This area is generally known as "Station 43". The term survives from the era of inter-urban trolley lines; on the trolley line that followed the Connecticut River north from Hartford, Station 43 was within the area included in this site. Considered as a birding site, Station 43 is bounded by the Connecticut River on the west, Main Street of South Windsor on the east, Strong Road on the north, and Vibert Road on the south. The heart of the avian habitats lie in the southern part of the area near Vibert Road, and near Newberry Road which passes (as a path) from east to west through the middle of the area.

SEASONS/BIRDS

SPRING MIGRATION: WATER BIRDS, MARSH BIRDS, SHORE BIRDS, LAND BIRDS;

NESTING SEASON: water birds, MARSH BIRDS, shore birds, LAND BIRDS;

FALL MIGRATION: WATER BIRDS, MARSH BIRDS, SHORE BIRDS, LAND BIRDS;

WINTER: water birds, LAND BIRDS;

This is one of the prime birding sites in all of inland Connecticut. Over the years, a long list of rare and uncommon species have been seen here. There have been reports of white pelican, wood stork, purple gallinule, sandhill crane, hawk owl, western kingbird and clay-colored sparrow. But of greater interest to the average birder is the wide variety of interesting species that can be seen here on a somewhat regular basis. There is no real down time at Station 43, because all of the major bird groups are represented by a variety of species. (In the paragraphs that follow, only a few of the many standard species that occur at Station 43 are mentioned.)

The spring migration starts in March, with the arrival of water birds, including common merganser, common and sometimes Barrow's goldeneyes on the river, and, in the pond and wetlands, pied-billed grebe, Canada and snow geese, black duck, green-winged and blue-winged teal, pintail, shoveler, wigeon, ring-necked duck and hooded merganser. Later in the spring, a variety of shore birds pass through, including both yellowlegs, snipe, woodcock, pectoral, least, solitary and spotted sandpipers. Among the many land bird migrants are a variety of blackbirds including rusty.

The extraordinary productivity of this site is perhaps most evident during the nesting season, when many species that are uncommon elsewhere in Connecticut can be found here.

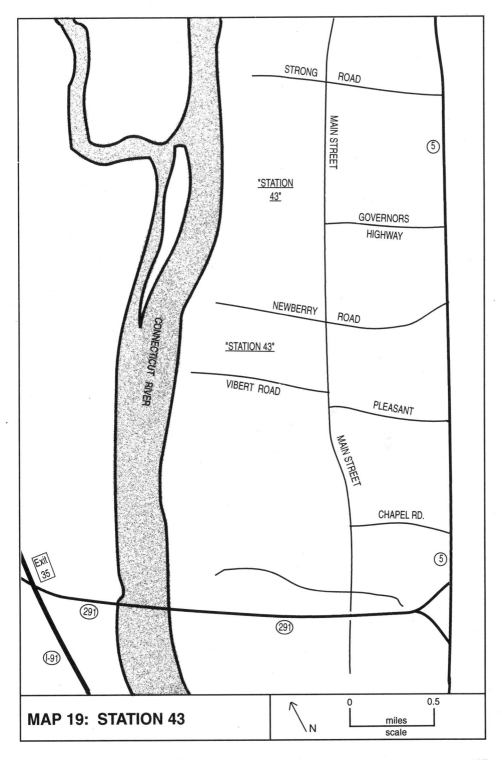

MAP 19: STATION 43

Water bird nesting species include blue-winged teal; marsh birds include American and least bitterns, moorhen, sora and Virginia rails; and there are many interesting land bird nesters such as red-bellied woodpecker, Carolina wren, warbling vireo, swamp sparrow, bobolink, meadowlark, indigo bunting, orchard oriole, rough-winged and bank swallows.

The fall migration produces a return of the species that were seen in the spring, plus the possibility of additional shore birds such as lesser golden plover, upland, Baird's and buff-breasted sandpipers, pipit, and a variety of sparrows, including Savannah, field, Lincoln's (occurs regularly!), white-crowned, white-throated, fox and vesper.

Even winter can be exciting at Station 43; there are water birds on the river (most of the species that occur on the river in fall and spring), lingering land birds such as winter wren, hermit thrush and other berry-eaters, horned lark, snow bunting, common redpoll, and a variety of raptors including red-tailed and rough-legged hawks, harrier, great horned, screech and short-eared owls, bald eagle and sometimes northern shrike.

GETTING AROUND
Can be birded by: car, WALK.
The best way to bird this area is to walk both Newberry and Vibert Roads, which pass by or come within sight of most of the good habitats. The walking may be very wet, especially during the spring, when areas of Newberry Road and the surrounding habitats are often flooded. In addition, it is possible to drive Vibert Road to its end at the landing on the river. Much of the land at this site is private and actively farmed; respect the rights of the owners while birding here. The area is used for hunting, so that visits in the fall are best scheduled for Sunday.

DIRECTIONS (see Map 19): Station 43 lies on the east shore of the Connecticut River, about five miles north of Hartford. From I-91 exit 35, go east on Route 291 for 2.5 miles across the Connecticut River, left on Route 5 for 2.3 miles, left on Newberry Road for 0.6 mile to a stop sign at Main Street in South Windsor. **Newberry Road:** Directly across Main Street is the continuation of Newberry Road which goes through the middle of the Station 43 area toward the Connecticut River. This road can be walked (but not driven - park on Main Street) along shrubby edges, hedgerows and thickets, past wetlands, seasonal pools and a small pond, to open fields near the river. **Vibert Road:** From the intersection of Newberry Road and Main Street, go south (left) on Main Street for 0.6 mile to Vibert Road on the right. This road can be driven through the southern part of the area for 0.8 mile to the Connecticut River. On the way, you pass a small stream, a marsh, various types of fields, many shrubby edges, and end at the shore of the river.

SUFFIELD: LEWIS FARM SANCTUARY

HABITATS
> **Forest:** young hardwoods, hardwoods/white pine;
> **Open terrestrial:** mixed herbaceous and shrubby fields; shrubby edges, vine tangles and thickets;
> **River/stream:** seasonal streams, shrubby and wooded streambelts;
> **Marsh/swamp/bog:** small shrubby hardwood swamp.

This site is composed of reverting farmland, with various types of successional habitats.

SEASONS/BIRDS
> **Spring migration:** land birds;
> **Nesting season:** land birds;
> **Fall Migration:** land birds;
> **Winter:** land birds.

During the spring and fall, there is a nice mix of standard land bird migrants; a variety of sparrows pass through during October and November. Nesters include screech owl, brown thrasher, chestnut-sided warbler (lots of them!), and other standard species that you would expect in these habitats. In winter, a few of the typical resident land bird species occur here.

GETTING AROUND
> **Can be birded by:** walk.

There is one main path, from which several secondary trails make loops.

DIRECTIONS: This site is in Suffield, about two miles north of the village center. To get there from the intersection of Routes 168 and 75, go west on Route 168 for 0.7 mile, right on Hill Street for 2.0 miles to the entrance sign (inconspicuous) on the left. Park on the right opposite the entrance.

SUFFIELD: STONY BROOK PARK

HABITATS
> **OPEN TERRESTRIAL:** short grass, mixed herbaceous and shrubby fields, shrubby and wooded edges;
> **River/stream:** stream, shrubby and wooded streambelt;
> **Lake/pond:** pond, shrubby and hardwood shore;
> **Marsh/swamp/bog:** shrubby hardwood and hardwood swamp;
> **Forest:** hardwoods, hemlock, white pine, flood plain;

This town open space area includes a variety of maintained and reverting fields that surround a stream with a wooded streambelt. An oxbow of Stony Brook produces a pond habitat.

SEASONS/BIRDS
> **Spring migration:** land birds;
> **Nesting season:** land birds;
> **Fall migration:** land birds;
> **Winter:** land birds.

This site has a nice mix of the species that you would expect in these habitats. The spring and fall migrations are both good, with the highlight being the passage of sparrows in October and November. Nesters include several open and edge habitat species, among them are indigo bunting and brown thrasher; prairie warbler has not been confirmed, but the habitat is just right.

GETTING AROUND
Birding methods: WALK.
A woods road leads into the area from each entrance, and there are additional trails within the park.

DIRECTIONS: This site is near the center of Suffield, about five miles north of Bradley Airport. To get to the western entrance from Suffield at the intersection of Routes 168 and 75, go west on Route 168 for 0.7 miles, left on Remington Road for 0.1 mile to the park entrance on the left. To get to the eastern entrance, from the intersection of Routes 75 and 168, go south on Route 75 for 0.8 mile to the entrance on the right (nothing fancy - just the start of a woods road).

WEST HARTFORD: SPICE BUSH SWAMP

HABITATS
Forest: hardwoods, cedar;
Open terrestrial: short grass, mixed herbaceous and shrubby fields, shrubby and wooded edges, thickets;
Lake/pond: pond, grassy, shrubby and wooded shore;
River/stream: stream, shrubby streambelt;
Marsh/swamp/bog: shrubby hardwood swamp, hardwood swamp.
This is an attractive little suburban park that is tucked in between busy Mountain Road and Talcott Mountain. In a small area, it offers a good mix of habitats that are intermingled, and thus present many productive interfaces.

SEASONS/BIRDS
SPRING MIGRATION: LAND BIRDS;
Nesting season: land birds;
Fall migration: land birds;
Winter: land birds.
This small site is especially good during the spring migration. During spring and summer, you will find a typical mix of edge and forest land bird species here - such as hummingbird, wood thrush, warbling and white-eyed vireos, redstart, yellowthroat, yellow warbler and screech owl.

GETTING AROUND
Birding methods: walk.
Several trails with frequent intersections wind through the park, and make it easy to see all of the habitats in a relatively short time. These trails are muddy at times.

DIRECTIONS: This park is in the western part of West Hartford. From the intersection of Routes 44 and 218 (at Bishop's Corner), go west on Route 44 for 1.0 mile, and left on Mountain Road for 2.0 miles to the park entrance on the right.

WEST HARTFORD/BLOOMFIELD: TALCOTT MOUNTAIN RESERVOIR AREA

HABITATS

FOREST: hardwoods, hardwoods/white pine, hardwoods/hemlock, white pine/ hemlock, white pine, hemlock, mixed conifers, mountain laurel;

OPEN TERRESTRIAL: short grass, tall grass and shrubby fields, shrubby and wooded edges;

LAKE/POND: lakes, pond, grassy, shrubby and wooded shores;

River/stream: perennial and seasonal streams, marshy, shrubby and wooded streambelts;

Marsh/swamp/bog: shrub marsh, shrub, shrubby hardwood and hardwood swamps;

Other: cliff, rocky slope.

This is an extraordinary block of open space, considering that it lies within five miles of two major metropolitan areas - Hartford and New Britain. It measures about one mile by five miles, and lies on the east side of Talcott Mountain. Included within it are five reservoirs and a wide variety of habitat types - forests composed mainly of hardwood/hemlock and hardwood/white pine, shrubby fields within a power line, a marsh, shrub and hardwood swamps, ponds and several streams.

SEASONS/BIRDS

SPRING MIGRATION: WATER BIRDS, marsh birds, shore birds, LAND BIRDS;

NESTING SEASON: water birds, LAND BIRDS;

FALL MIGRATION: WATER BIRDS, marsh birds, shore birds, LAND BIRDS

Winter: water birds, land birds

The size of this area, and the variety of habitats within it, make a visit worthwhile at any time of year. Although the reservoirs do not attract a great variety of water birds, they often have species such as bufflehead, goldeneye and ringneck. The woods around the reservoirs and the open areas nearby attract interesting land bird species, including a wide variety of migrants. The many nesting species include all three accipiters, three buteos, kestrel and three owl species, as well as pileated woodpecker, red-breasted nuthatch, brown creeper, golden-crowned kinglet, brown thrasher, bluebird, black-throated green, worm-eating and prairie warblers, Louisiana waterthrush and indigo bunting.

GETTING AROUND

Birding methods: car, WALK, BIKE, ski.

This is a wonderful site for those who like to combine birding with walking. There is an extensive system of gravel roads and trails throughout this area that are not open to vehicles. (Trail maps are available at the administration building, on the left as you enter the southern part of the area from Route 4.) However, Reservoirs 1 and 6 can be reached by car or bike, and some of the habitats near them are visible from the driveways. Parking is restricted to certain areas.

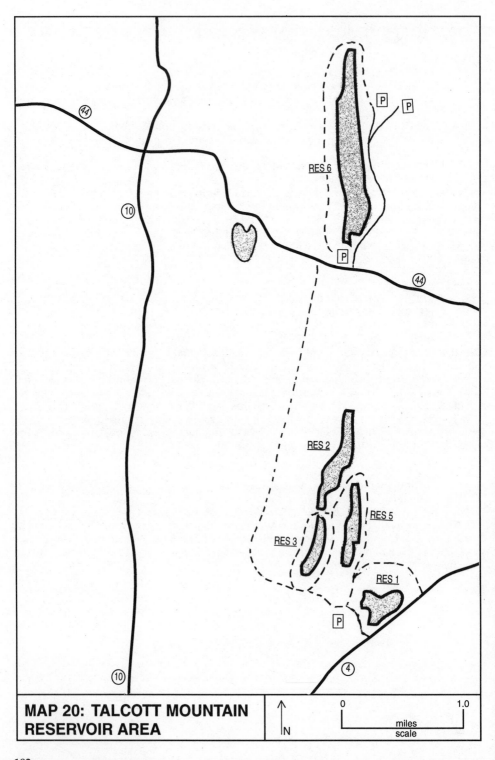

MAP 20: TALCOTT MOUNTAIN RESERVOIR AREA

N

0   1.0

miles
scale

DIRECTIONS (see Map 20): This area lies in the western parts of West Hartford and Bloomfield, next to the Avon Town Line.

To get to the southern part of the area and Reservoirs 1, 2, 3, and 5: From I-84, take exit 39, go east on Route 4 for 2.5 miles, left into the driveway of the West Hartford Water Treatment Plant. There is one parking lot on the left at 0.1 mile, a second on the right at 0.2 mile, and a third straight ahead at 0.5 mile. Trails into the area start from all of these lots.

To get to the northern part of the area and Reservoir 6: from I-84 take exit 39, go east on Route 4 for 3.1 miles, left on Mountain Road for 2.0 miles, left on Route 44 for 1.3 miles to the Metropolitan District area entrance and parking lot on the right. A driveway and trail start at the back of the parking lot and lead to Reservoir 6 and the northern portion of the area. Trails to the southern part of the area start on the other side of Route 44 0.2 mile to the west (up the hill).

WETHERSFIELD: COVE PARK

HABITATS
RIVER/STREAM: fresh water tidal cove, mud and sand flats, grassy and shrubby streambelt; river, deep slow water, wooded streambelt;
Forest: hardwoods, flood plain;
Open terrestrial: short grass field, shrubby edge;
This is a cove of the Connecticut River, well above the reach of salt water, and in the upper part of the tidal portion of the river. The cove itself is the centerpiece of this site; around it are small areas of flood plain forest, shrubby edges and mowed lawns. It also affords access to the Connecticut River.

SEASONS/BIRDS
Spring migration: gulls, water birds, shore birds, land birds;
Nesting season: water birds, land birds;
Fall migration: gulls, water birds, marsh birds, shore birds, land birds;
Winter: gulls, water birds, land birds.
There is something here during most of the year (but in summer, there are more people at the cove than birds). The spring migration brings some water birds (usually mallard, pintail, gadwall and common merganser), and a few shore birds (spotted and solitary sandpipers, killdeer), as well as some land birds. The fall migration is a replay of spring. In winter, look for water birds and the occasional bald eagle. Gulls are present all year, and in winter the common species are sometimes joined by Iceland and glaucous.

GETTING AROUND
Birding methods: car, walk, boat.
You can take your car to the shore of the cove, and the shrubby edges can be explored on foot. All of the cove can be seen from the parking area, and a scope is helpful. A tunnel under the highway leads to the Connecticut River.

DIRECTIONS (see Map 21): This park is not far from the center of Wethersfield. To get to it from the center at the intersection of Route 99 (Silas Deane Highway), Route 175 (which goes west) and Main Street (which goes east), go east on Main Street for 1.5 miles - past some of Wethersfield's beautiful old houses - to Cove Park.

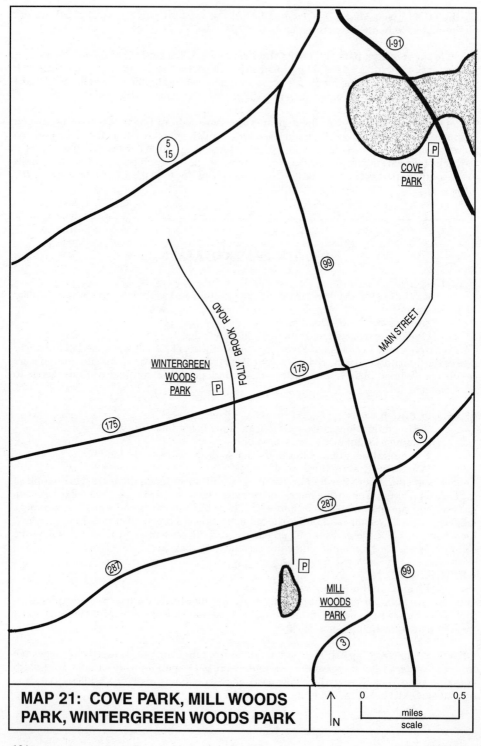

MAP 21: COVE PARK, MILL WOODS PARK, WINTERGREEN WOODS PARK

WETHERSFIELD: MILL WOODS PARK

HABITATS
>**Forest:** hardwoods, white pine grove;
>**Open terrestrial:** short grass field, shrubby and wooded edges;
>**Lake/pond:** ponds, cattail, shrubby and wooded shores;
>**River/stream:** stream, wooded streambelt;
>**Marsh/swamp/bog:** shrubby hardwood swamp, hardwood swamp.

This is a small (30-acre) town park, but is has a nice diversity of habitats - three small ponds, woods, a small swamp and open areas (lawns and edges).

SEASONS/BIRDS
>**SPRING MIGRATION:** water birds, LAND BIRDS;
>**Nesting season:** water birds, land birds;
>**FALL MIGRATION:** water birds, marsh birds, LAND BIRDS;
>**Winter:** water birds, land birds.

Look here throughout the year for the standard land bird species, including southerners such as Carolina wren and red-bellied woodpecker. The spring migration is good, and the fall even better, bringing a variety of warblers and sparrows including white-crowned and fox. Great blue heron occurs in migration, and great horned owl is a resident. Winter is also pretty good; the park benefits from the abundance of bird feeders at surrounding suburban homes. Mallard is the dominant water bird species, and is present all year except when the ponds are frozen.

GETTING AROUND
>**Birding methods:** car, walk, wheelchair.

Almost all of this park can be reached by driveways that can be driven or walked. And much of the park is accessible by wheelchair.

DIRECTIONS (see Map 21): This park is near the center of Wethersfield. To get to it from the center at the intersection of Route 99 (Silas Deane Highway) and Route 3, go west on Route 3 for 0.2 mile, right on Route 287 for 0.4 mile, and left on the park driveway for 0.2 mile to the parking area.

WETHERSFIELD: WINTERGREEN WOODS PARK

HABITATS
>**OPEN TERRESTRIAL:** short grass and shrubby fields, shrubby and wooded edges;
>**Forest:** hardwoods;
>**Lake/pond:** seasonal pool;
>**River/stream:** perennial stream, seasonal streams;
>**Marsh/swamp/bog:** mixed herbaceous and shrub marsh, shrub, shrubby hardwood and hardwood swamp.

This park has a nice mix of habitats, including woods, a marsh/swamp complex, a perennial stream, several seasonal streams and pools, shrubby fields and lots of edges.

SEASONS/BIRDS
SPRING MIGRATION: LAND BIRDS;
Nesting season: land birds;
FALL MIGRATION: LAND BIRDS;
Winter: land birds.

Large numbers and a nice variety of land birds occur here throughout the year. The migrations are good, especially the fall migration that brings a variety of warblers in September and sparrows in October and November. Berry- and seed-producing shrubs, together with the open water of the stream, cause many birds to stay here through the late fall and into winter. Nesters and residents include screech owl and southerners such as Carolina wren and red-bellied woodpecker.

GETTING AROUND
Birding methods: walk.

There are several trails that provide easy walking, but they are wet in the spring.

DIRECTIONS (see Map 21): This park is near the center of Wethersfield. To get to it from the center at the intersection of Route 99 (Silas Deane Highway) and Route 175, go west on Route 175 for 0.6 mile, and right on Folly Brook Road for 0.2 mile to the Wintergreen Woods parking area.

WETHERSFIELD/NEWINGTON/HARTFORD: CEDAR HILL CEMETERY

HABITATS
Forest: groves of hardwoods, mixed conifers, scattered cedar;
Open terrestrial: short grass and shrubby fields, hedgerows, shrubby edges, vine tangles and thickets;
Lake/pond: ponds, short grass, shrubby, white pine and hardwood shores;
River/stream: perennial streams, streambelts composed of short grass, shrub swamp, shrubby hardwood swamp, shrubs and woods;
Marsh/swamp/bog: shrub and shrubby hardwood swamps;
Other: brush dump.

This is a large cemetery that has all the habitats that are typical of burying grounds: large expanses of lawn, groves of hardwoods, spruces and other conifers, hedgerows, lots of edges of various types, and two ponds. Around the periphery there are shrubby fields and thickets.

SEASONS/BIRDS
SPRING MIGRATION: gulls, water birds, marsh birds, LAND BIRDS;
Nesting season: water birds, land birds;
FALL MIGRATION: gulls, water birds, marsh birds, LAND BIRDS;
Winter: land birds.

The abundance of groves, hedgerows and edges attracts migrating warblers and other land birds that come here to feed. Residents include red-tailed hawk, great horned owl, red-bellied woodpecker and wild turkey. Great blue heron feeds here during the warm months, and great egret comes in late summer and fall.

GETTING AROUND
Can be birded by: car, walk.
There is a network of driveways throughout the cemetery, and the open nature of the habitat makes birding the edges on foot easy. The cemetery closes at 5 PM.

DIRECTIONS: Most of this cemetery lies in the northwestern corner of Wethersfield, and small parts cross town lines into Newington and Hartford. From the intersection of Route 5/15 (Berlin Turnpike) and Route 175, go north on Route 5/15 for 0.9 mile to where Route 5/15 bends to the right. At this point, go straight onto Maple Avenue for 0.6 mile, and left on Jordan Lane into the cemetery grounds, through edges and thickets and past a brush dump to a dead end in about 0.5 mile. To get to a second entrance (actually the main entrance), return to Maple Avenue and continue north for another 0.5 mile to the cemetery entrance on the left.

WINDSOR: FARMINGTON RIVER TOWN PARK

HABITATS
RIVER/STREAM: river, fast water, slow water, short grass, shrubby and wooded streambelt;
Forest: hardwoods, flood plain;
Open terrestrial: short grass field, scattered hardwoods, shrubby and wooded edge.
This is a small town park that has a mowed lawn by the shore of the Farmington River at a section that has rapids and riffles.

SEASONS/BIRDS
Spring migration: water birds, land birds;
Nesting season: land birds;
Fall migration: water birds, land birds;
Winter: water birds, land birds.
This is a good place from which to see water birds during migration and in winter, especially common goldeneye and common merganser. Land birds are present in the surrounding woods and edges throughout the year. Bald eagle is fairly regular in winter, and osprey in spring and fall.

GETTING AROUND
Birding methods: car, walk.
It is possible to see the river from where you park, but a better view can be had by walking a few yards to the shore.

DIRECTIONS (see Map 22): This park is about a mile south of Bradley Airport. From the intersection of Routes 75 and 20 near Bradley Airport, go south on Route 75 for 1.0 mile, left on River Road for 0.4 mile, right on Old River Road for 0.2 mile to the park on the right.

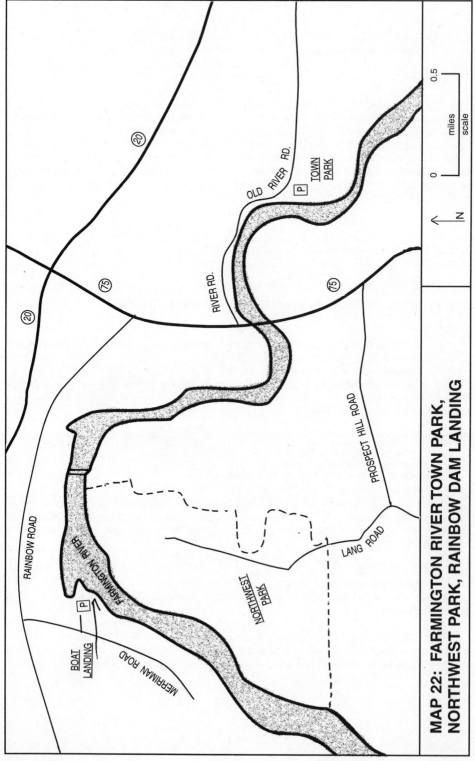

MAP 22: FARMINGTON RIVER TOWN PARK, NORTHWEST PARK, RAINBOW DAM LANDING

WINDSOR: NORTHWEST PARK

HABITATS
FOREST: hardwoods, hardwoods / white pine, hardwoods / hemlock;
OPEN TERRESTRIAL: tilled, short grass, tall grass, mixed herbaceous and shrubby fields; shrubby and wooded edges;
RIVER/STREAM: river, slow water, hardwood, hardwood / white pine, hardwoods / hemlock streambelt;
Lake/pond: pond, marshy, shrubby and wooded shore;
Marsh/swamp/bog: mixed herbaceous marsh, shrub marsh, shrub swamp.
This park occupies a section of shoreline of the Farmington River, and includes a productive combination of riverine, forest, open, and wetland habitats. Part of it is developed with mowed playing fields, and the rest left in a more or less natural state for hiking, skiing and wildlife.

SEASONS/BIRDS
SPRING MIGRATION: water birds, marsh birds, LAND BIRDS;
NESTING SEASON: water birds, marsh birds, LAND BIRDS;
FALL MIGRATION: water birds, marsh birds, LAND BIRDS;
Winter: water birds, land birds;
Because of the variety of habitat types, a large number of bird species occur here - over 130 are on the park's bird list, and from time to time, a rare or uncommon species is reported (clay-colored sparrow and blue grosbeak were seen here in the spring of 1995). Species that occur on a regular basis include most of the land birds you would expect in this combination of habitats, including prairie warbler, field sparrow and indigo bunting. Grasshopper sparrow and orchard oriole nest here. The spring migration is very good, and the fall even better, especially for pipit and a wide variety of sparrows.

GETTING AROUND
Birding methods: WALK, bike, ski.
This park has a network of trails and woods roads, some of which are open to biking. Expect the park to be crowded during weekends in warm weather (and even in winter).

DIRECTIONS (see Map 22): This park is in Windsor, about a mile south of Bradley Airport. From the intersection of Routes 75 and 20 near Bradley Airport, go south on Route 75 for 1.7 miles, right on Prospect Hill Road for 1.1 miles, right on Lang Road for 0.6 mile to the park.

WINDSOR: RAINBOW DAM BOAT LANDING

HABITATS

RIVER/STREAM: river, slow water, cove, hardwood, hardwood/white pine and hardwood/hemlock streambelt;
Forest: hardwoods, hardwoods/white pine, hardwoods/hemlock, flood plain.
This site provides a look at the Farmington River where it is wide and slow-moving. It is directly across the river from Northwest Park.

SEASONS/BIRDS

Spring migration: gulls, water birds, land birds;
Nesting season: land birds;
Fall migration: gulls, water birds, land birds;
Winter: land birds.
This site is a good place from which to look for water birds - including common goldeneye and common merganser - as they migrate along the Farmington River, especially just after ice-out in the early spring. Bald eagle sometimes occurs here in the late fall, winter and early spring. The warbler migration can also be pretty good in May.

GETTING AROUND

Birding methods: car, walk.
It is possible to take your car almost to the water's edge.

DIRECTIONS (see Map 22): This landing is on the west shore of the Farmington River, across from Northwest Park. From the intersection of Routes 75 and 20, near Bradley Airport, go south on Route 75 for 0.5 mile, right on Rainbow Road for 1.7 miles (following Rainbow Road to the left at a stop sign), left on Merriman Road for 0.3 mile to the driveway to the landing on the left.

Chapter 6

Litchfield County

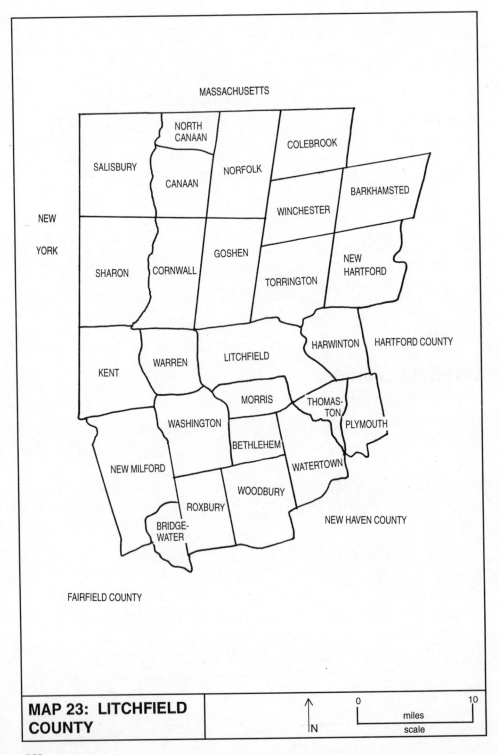

MASSACHUSETTS

NORTH
CANAAN

COLEBROOK

SALISBURY

NORFOLK

CANAAN

BARKHAMSTED

NEW

WINCHESTER

YORK

GOSHEN

NEW
HARTFORD

SHARON

CORNWALL

TORRINGTON

HARWINTON

HARTFORD COUNTY

WARREN

LITCHFIELD

KENT

MORRIS

THOMAS-
TON

WASHINGTON

PLYMOUTH

BETHLEHEM

WATERTOWN

NEW MILFORD

WOODBURY

ROXBURY

NEW HAVEN COUNTY

BRIDGE-
WATER

FAIRFIELD COUNTY

**MAP 23: LITCHFIELD
COUNTY**

↑
N

0

10

miles
scale

LITCHFIELD COUNTY

LITCHFIELD COUNTY (3)   PAGE

TABLE 4: HABITATS AND SEASONS AT LITCHFIELD COUNTY SITES

Habitats ● very good example ○ present, but not as significant Seasons ● excellent during this season ○ less good during this season	HABITATS							SEASONS			
	FOREST	OPEN	MARSH	LAKE	RIVER	COAST	OTHER	SPRING	NEST	FALL	WINTER
Tour of Litchfield et al	●	○	●	●	○			●	●	○	○
Tour of Salisbury/Sharon	○	●	○	●	○			●	○	●	○
Tour of the Upper Housatonic River	○	○			●			●	○	●	●
Barkhamsted: American Legion/Peoples SF	●	○	●	○	●		○	●	●	●	○
Barkhamsted: Barkhamsted Reservoir	●	○	○	●	○		○	●	●	●	○
Barkhamsted: Upper Greenwoods	○	●			●			●	●	●	○
Barkhamsted et al: Lower Greenwoods	○	●	○	○	●			●	●	●	○
Bethlehem: Bellamy Preserve	○	○	○	○	○			○	○	○	○
Bridgewater: Rocky Hill Preserve	○	●	○	○	○			●	●	●	●
Canaan: Amesville Power Plant	○	○			●			○	○	○	○
Canaan/Cornwall: Housatonic SF	●	○	○	○	○			●	●	●	○
Canaan/Cornwall: River Road	○	●			●		○	●	●	●	○
Canaan/North Canaan: Canaan Mountain	●	●	●	●	●		●	●	●	●	●
Canaan/North Canaan: Robbins Swamp	○	●	●		●			●	●	●	○
Colebrook: Colebrook River/Goodwin Res	●	●	○	●	○		○	●	●	●	○
Cornwall: Furnace Brook	○				●			○	○	○	○
Cornwall: Hollenbeck Wetlands	○	○	●	○	○			●	●	●	○
Cornwall/Goshen: Hart Pond WMA	○	○	●	●				●	●	●	○
Cornwall/Goshen: Mohawk SF	●	○	●	○	○		○	●	●	●	○
Goshen: East Street North	○	○	●	○				●	●	●	○
Goshen: Long Swamp	○	○	●	○	○			●	●	●	○
Goshen: Peat Swamp			●					●	●	●	○
Goshen: Tyler Lake			○	○				○	○	○	○
Harwinton: Harwinton Conservation Area	○	○		○	○			●	●	●	○
Harwinton: Kalmia Sanctuary	○	○	○	○	○			●	○	●	○
Harwinton: Roraback WMA	●	●	○	○	○			●	●	●	○
Harwinton: Valley Road	○	●	○		●			●	●	●	○
Kent: Bulls Bridge Road	○				●			●	●	○	○
Kent: Iron Mountain Reservation	●		○	○	○			●	●	●	○
Kent: Kent Falls SP	○	○			●			●	○	○	○
Kent: Macedonia Brook SP	●	○	○		●		○	●	●	○	○
Kent: River Road	●	●			●		○	●	●	○	○
Kent: Schaghticoke Road	●	○	○		●		○	●	●	●	○
Litchfield: Boyd Woods	●	●	○	○	○		○	●	●	●	○
Litchfield: East Cemetery	○	○	○	○	○			○	○	○	○
Litchfield: Mt. Tom SP	○			●			○	○	○	○	○
Litchfield: Topsmead SF	○	●	○	○	○			●	○	○	○
Litchfield et al: White Memorial	●	●	●	●	●		○	●	●	●	●
Morris: Jones Pond				○				●	○	●	○
Morris et al: Wigwam/Morris/Pitch Reservoir	●	○	○	●	○			●	●	●	○

TABLE 4: HABITATS AND SEASONS AT LITCHFIELD COUNTY SITES (2)

Habitats ● very good example ○ present, but not as significant Seasons ● excellent during this season ○ less good during this season	HABITATS							SEASONS			
	FOREST	OPEN	MARSH	LAKE	RIVER	COAST	OTHER	SPRING	NEST	FALL	WINTER
New Hartford: Maple Hollow	○	○	●	○	○		○	●	●	●	○
New Hartford: Nepaug SF	●	○			○		○	●	●	●	○
New Hartford et al: Nepaug Reservoir	●	○	○	●	○			●	●	●	○
New Milford: Dyke Point Rec Area	●			●	○		●	○	○	○	○
New Milford: River Road/Boardman Road	●	○			●			●	●	●	●
New Milford: Sunny Valley	○	●	○	○	○			●	○	●	○
New Milford/Kent: Bulls Bridge	○	○	○		●			●	●	●	○
Norfolk: Campbell Falls SP	●	○	○		●			○	○	○	○
Norfolk: Dennis Hill SP	○	○	○				○	○	●	○	○
Norfolk: Haystack Mountain SP	●	○		○	○			○	○	●	○
Norfolk: North Swamp FCA	○	○	●	○	○			●	●	●	○
Norfolk: Wood Creek FCA	○	○	●	○	○			○	●	○	○
Norfolk: Wood Creek Pond	○		○	●	○			○	○	○	○
Plymouth: Hancock Brook FCA	○	○	●	○	○			●	●	●	○
Roxbury: Hemlock Cemetery	○	●	○		○			●	●	●	○
Roxbury: Judds Bridge Road	●	●	○		●		○	●	●	●	○
Roxbury: Lilly Preserve	●	●	●		○		○	●	●	●	○
Roxbury: Mine Hill Preserve	●	○	○		○		○	●	●	●	○
Roxbury: River Road Preserve	○	○		○	●			●	●	●	○
Roxbury: Upper County Road	●	●	○		○		○	●	●	●	○
Salisbury: Housatonic River Road	○	○	○	○	○			●	○	○	○
Salisbury: Lond Pond	●	●		●	○			●	○	●	○
Salisbury: Mt. Riga	●		●	○	●		○	●	●	●	○
Salisbury: Railroad Path	○	○	●	○	○			●	●	○	○
Salisbury: Weatogue Road	○	●	○		●			●	○	○	○
Salisbury: Wononscopomuc Lake	○	○		●	○			●	●	●	○
Sharon: Guinea Brook Wetland	○		●	○	○			●	●	●	○
Sharon: Housatonic Meadows SP	●	○			●		○	●	●	○	○
Sharon: Mudge Pond	○	○	○	●	○			●	○	●	●
Sharon: Northeast Audubon Center	●	●	●	●	●			●	●	●	○
Sharon: Roy Swamp/Miles Sanct/Housatonic SF	●	●	●	●	●		○	●	●	●	○
Sharon: Skiff Mountain WMA	○	●	○	●	○			●	●	○	○
Sharon: Stanley WMA	○	●			●			●	●	●	○
Thomaston: Northfield Brook FCA	○	●		○	○		○	●	○	●	○
Thomaston: Thomaston Dam/Leadmine Brook	●	●	●	○	●		○	●	●	●	○
Thomaston: Thomaston Nature Trail	○	○	○		○		○	○	○	○	○
Thomaston et al: Black Rock SP/FCA	●	●	○	●	●		○	●	●	●	○
Torrington: John A. Minetto SP	○	●	●	○	○			●	●	●	○
Torrington: Stillwater Pond	●		○	○	○		○	○	○	○	○
Torrington: Sunnybrook SP/Paugnut SF	●	●	●	○	●			●	●	●	○

TABLE 4: HABITATS AND SEASONS AT LITCHFIELD COUNTY SITES (3)

Habitats ● very good example ○ present, but not as significant Seasons ● excellent during this season ○ less good during this season	HABITATS							SEASONS			
	FOREST	OPEN	MARSH	LAKE	RIVER	COAST	OTHER	SPRING	NEST	FALL	WINTER
Torrington/Winchester: Burr Pond SP	●	○	○	○	○		○	●	●	●	○
Warren: Eel Pond			●	○				○	○	○	○
Warren: Wyantenock State Forest	●	○	●	○	○		○	●	●	●	○
Washington: Hidden Valley	●	○			○		○	●	●	●	○
Washington: Shepaug River Loop	●	○	○		●		○	●	●	●	○
Washington: Steep Rock	●	○			●		○	●	●	●	○
Washington: Weantinogue LT Wetland	●	●	●		○			●	●	●	○
Washington et al: Lake Waramaug	○	○	●	●	○			●	○	●	○
Winchester: Crystal Lake	○			○	○			○	○	○	○
Winchester: Highland Lake				●				○	○	●	○
Winchester: Mad River Dam/FCA	○	●	●	○	●		○	●	●	●	○
Winchester: Platt Hill SP	○	●					○	●	●	●	○
Winchester: Rugg Brook	●	○	●	○	●		○	●	●	●	○
Winchester: Silas Hall Pond	●		●	○	○		○	●	●	○	○
Winchester: Sucker Brook Dam/FCA	○	●	○	○	○		○	●	○	●	○
Woodbury: Van Vleck Sanctuary	●	●	●	●	○			●	●	●	○
Woodbury: Whittemore Sanctuary	●		○	○	○			●	●	●	○

BIRDING IN LITCHFIELD COUNTY

Litchfield County occupies the northwest corner of Connecticut; its western border is the New York State line, and its northern border is the Massachusetts line. On the east, it is bounded by Hartford County, on the southeast by New Haven County, and on the southwest by Fairfield County. Route 8 is the only limited-access highway that crosses it.

The People

Litchfield County has a population of 175,550, and a land area of 921 square miles (it is Connecticut's largest county), giving it a population density of 190 people per square mile, the lowest density of any county in the state. In recent decades, it has been growing at a rate slightly faster than Connecticut overall. In terms of affluence, Litchfield County overall is about average for Connecticut.

The Land

All of Litchfield County lies in Connecticut's Western Upland ecoregion, an area characterized by hilly terrain, most of which is forested, but some of which is cleared for farming (16% of Litchfield County is farmland). Elevations range from about 250' to 2,380' above sea level, with the higher elevations occurring in the northern part of the county. The terrain, especially in the north, is characterized by sharp profiles - great elevation diversity, steep mountains, high-energy streams, deep ravines, and rolling hills even in the most level areas. A major river (the Housatonic) and two smaller rivers (the Shepaug and Naugatuck), pass from north to south through steep-sided valleys. The Farmington River flows from north to southeast through a more moderate valley.

Within Litchfield County is Connecticut's Northwest Plateau; it the southern extension of the Berkshire and Taconic Plateaus, and is Connecticut's highest, coldest, wettest and most mountainous area. Average annual snowfall is 100", compared with 45-50" in the rest of the state. It is in this northern part of Litchfield County that most of Connecticut's northern types of habitat occur - hemlock ravines, mountain summits and ridges, spruce bogs and other wetlands, often located in large tracts of remote, wilderness-like land. Forest communities over most of this area are transition zone hardwoods mixed with white pine and hemlock, but at the highest elevations, there are areas of northern hardwoods, together with white pine and hemlock.

Also within Litchfield County is the southern end of the Marble Valley, a long, narrow area of surficial limestone that extends southward from Vermont through western Massachusetts and into the northwestern part of Connecticut. Such limestone is not found elsewhere in Connecticut, and it supports plant communities that are unique to Litchfield County.

The southern half of Litchfield County lies at somewhat lower elevations, is rolling, hilly country, and has a climate more nearly like the rest of the state. This area is within the central hardwoods/white pine forest zone, and much of this part of the county is farmed.

Public Areas and Birding Sites

Litchfield County is favored by a combination of topographic and habitat diversity, low population density, and an active birding network. More well-known public areas of open space occur here than in any other Connecticut county. Within the county, there are 19 state parks, 10 state forests, a very large privately-funded wildlife conservation area, numerous smaller conservation areas managed by organizations such as The Nature Conservancy, local land trusts and bird clubs, several water supply areas, a number of DEP wildlife management areas, plus town parks, cemeteries and other areas open to the public. Litchfield County has the greatest number and largest total area of birding sites that are open to the public of any county in Connecticut. Among these public areas there is an abundance of forest, open, wetland, riverine and pond habitats. And among these areas there are large tracts of forest; as a result, the populations of several neotropical migrant species that require undisturbed interior forest habitat are actually increasing at several sites in Litchfield County, at a time when they are declining throughout most of North America. Overall, the diversity of birds that occurs in Litchfield County is greater than in any other inland county of Connecticut, and the number of species that breed in Litchfield County is greater than in any other county - of the 185 bird species confirmed as breeding in Connecticut, 150 are found in Litchfield County; most of the rest are species that require tidal habitats. It is for these reasons that Litchfield County is represented in this guide by more sites (over 90) than any other county in Connecticut.

Litchfield County has within it the top five birding areas in Connecticut, as measured by number of species that have shown evidence of nesting:
> Litchfield: White Memorial
> New Hartford: Nepaug Reservoir
> Barkhamsted: Barkhamsted Reservoir/Peoples State Forest
> Sharon: Northeast Audubon Center
> Cornwall: Mohawk State Forest

These and numerous other sites have forested habitats. There are also fine wetlands to be found, at such sites as White Memorial, Roy Swamp and the Miles Sanctuary in Sharon. Riverine and flood plain habitats occur along the Housatonic River at sites such as River Road in Kent. Lakes and ponds occur at many sites, including the Barkhamsted and Nepaug Reservoirs.

Seasons for Birding

The birding during the spring, summer and fall are exceptional. Probably the most distinctive aspect of Litchfield County during the nesting season is the large number of sites at which northern forest-dwelling species can be found. The Housatonic and Farmington Rivers act as migration coridors, especially in the spring. In winter, even though Litchfield County has a severe climate and lacks a coastline, it is possible to find reasonably good birding, if you choose your sites carefully.

Spring Migration. Spring comes to Litchfield County later than elsewhere in Connecticut, so if you want to get an early start in the spring, try areas along the coast in other counties. But by late March, you can start your Litchfield County birding by looking for water birds at White Memorial, where the outlet to Bantam Lake is generally open. Also try sites along the Farmington River such as American Legion/Peoples State Forests and the Lower Greenwoods Recreation Area, all in Barkhamsted. As soon as there is open water on the Nepaug Reservoir, migrating water birds start to drop in. Later in the spring, go back to White for marsh birds, and later still for land birds. The Northeast Audubon Center is a good bet for water birds in April, and warblers in May. Habitats at Roy Swamp/ Miles Sanctuary/ Housatonic State Forest are excellent throughout the spring, for water birds early, marsh birds later, and warblers and other land birds in May. During April and May, go back to American Legion/Peoples State Forests and the Lower Greenwoods Recreation Area for land birds that use the Farmington River as a migration corridor. The Canaan Mountain Range offers good birding - early spring in the surrounding valleys, and later in higher areas up the mountain. For many birders, River Road in Kent is the Mecca of the spring migration - it is best starting in early May. Other good sites during the latter half of the spring migration are Minetto Park in Torrington (water and land birds), the Van Vleck Sanctuary in Woodbury and Mohawk State Forest in Cornwall (both for land birds).

Nesting Season. During the nesting season, once again White Memorial is the hands-down best site. Among water, marsh and land birds that breed in Connecticut, you name it, and it probably nests at White. For a variety of northern species, go to American Legion/Peoples State Forests, or to Mohawk State Forest, where there is a black spruce bog, and nesting golden-crowned kinglet and Nashville warbler. For pine-oriented land bird species such as red-breasted nuthatch, solitary vireo, pine and Blackburnian warblers, the Nepaug State Forest and Nepaug Reservoir are good sites. For riverine-habitat land birds such as Acadian flycatcher and cerulean warbler, go to the River Road complexes in Canaan, Sharon, Kent and New Milford. Roy Swamp/Miles Sanctuary/ Housatonic State Forest and the Northeast Audubon Center are excellent for a variety of nesting marsh and land bird species. Minetto State Park in Torrington is good for wetland-oriented land birds, and provides easy birding. Nearby Sunnybrook State Park is also good for woodland and edge species of land birds, as is Steep Rock Reservation in Washington. The specialty at Sunny Valley in New Milford and Topsmead State Forest in Litchfield is edge and grassland species.

Fall Migration. There are some differences between the fall and spring migrations in Litchfield County, and they call for different birding strategies. There are fewer hot spots in the fall than in the spring - in this respect Litchfield County is just the opposite of Hartford County. In the fall, migrants tend to follow ridge lines, and to feed along edges of open areas and water bodies. Rivers are not as important as migration corridors, so don't spend a lot of time at the several River Road sites. To get an early start on the fall migration, go to the Nepaug Reservoir; in August and September, there is often a strip of exposed mud along the shore that attracts shore birds and waders. The edges of the forest along the public roadway at the east end of the reservoir provide good habitat for migrating land birds, and as the fall progresses, increasing diversity and numbers of water birds feed and rest on the water of the reservoir, and bald eagle sometimes comes here to hunt. Early in the fall, Bald Peak at Mount Riga in Salisbury can be a good site for watching the migration of hawks and other land birds. (Hawk watching sites in Litchfield County such as Bald Peak and Chestnut Hill in Litchfield do have exciting days, but flights at these inland sites are unpredictable compared with sites along the coast.) White Memorial is excellent throughout the fall migration - go to its wetlands, ponds, woods, open habitats and their edges during the early and middle parts of the migration, and then focus on Bantam Lake from November until winter. Northeast Audubon provides good fall birding - mainly for land birds in September and October. The Roy Swamp/Miles Sanctuary/Housatonic State Forest area provides a variety of land, marsh and water birds during the early and middle periods of the migration. The Black Rock and Thomaston Dams are very good sites for migrating land birds. Sunny Valley and the Lower Greenwoods Recreation Area are both good for sparrows during October and November. Minetto and Sunnybrook State Parks are also worth a visit in the fall. The Canaan Mountain Range, with its great variety of habitats, can offer something at almost any time, but the highlight occurs late in the fall and into winter, when raven, bald eagle, and sometimes golden eagle can be seen soaring against the cliffs on the western side of the mountain.

Winter. Severe cold, together with ice and snow cover on food sources sharply limit the species diversity and number of birds that are present in Litchfield County during the winter. It becomes necessary to target your birding trips to those sites that have specific habitats or conditions that escape this winter bottleneck. Bantam Lake at White Memorial almost always has open water by the outlet, and there are usually water birds there. The cliffs along the western side of Canaan Mountain have been consistently good in recent winters for raven, bald eagle and sometimes golden eagle. In years of winter finch irruption, go to the Barkhamsted Reservoir area, following Routes 181 and 20 around the reservoir. Beyond that - look for sites with shrubby edges (such as Rocky Hill in Bridgewater) that may still have food for lingering land bird berry-eaters.

Sources of Information and Help

The best places to go for on-site information during a birding trip are the museum at White Memorial, the Northeast Audubon visitor center and the office at Sunny Valley. There are also several bird clubs that can be reached by mail:

> Litchfield Hills Audubon Society
> Housatonic Audubon Society
> Western Connecticut Bird Club

Places to eat and lodging are not difficult to find in the larger towns in Litchfield County, and such towns are distributed throughout most of the county.

TOUR OF LITCHFIELD, GOSHEN, WARREN AND CORNWALL

THE TOUR. This tour starts near the center of Litchfield, and ends near the center of Cornwall Bridge. Most of the sites on the route are in the western part of Litchfield; however, the end of the route extends for a short distance into Goshen, Warren and Cornwall, at the corner where these towns meet. The distance from start to finish is about twenty miles, almost entirely on back roads. The sites on the tour, in the order in which they are reached, are:

> **Litchfield: Prospect Mountain Sanctuary**
> **Litchfield: Milton Cemetery**
> **Litchfield: Blue Swamp**
> **Cornwall/Goshen: Hart Pond***
> **Cornwall: Wyantenock State Forest**
> **Warren: Melius Road wetlands**

*This site is also covered by a separate description.

HABITATS

> **MARSH/SWAMP/BOG:** cattail, sedge and mixed herbaceous marshes; shrub, shrubby hardwood, white pine and hemlock swamps; dead wood; shrubby, hardwood and hemlock edges;
> **FOREST:** hardwoods, hardwoods/white pine, hardwoods/hemlock, white pine, hemlock, spruce plantation, mountain laurel;
> **LAKE/POND:** ponds, shrubby and wooded edges;
> **Open terrestrial:** tilled, short grass, tall grass, mixed herbaceous and shrubby fields; shrubby, hardwood and conifer edges; hedgerows;
> **River/stream:** river, streams, shrubby and wooded streambelts.

The back roads of this route pass by a tremendous variety of habitats, including almost every type of inland wetland that occurs in Connecticut. The major sites along the route and the habitats that occur at them are:

Prospect Mountain Sanctuary. A forest dominated by hemlock, together with hardwoods, white pine, red pine and mountain laurel, is on either side of the road; the pond down the hill to the left is beaver-controlled and surrounded by various types of swamp. Nearby, there are tilled, short grass, tall grass and mixed herbaceous fields.

Milton Cemetery includes short grass field, wooded and shrubby edges. It is surrounded on three sides by a wetland that consists of several types of marsh and swamp. A stream runs through this wetland system, and joins a branch of the Shepaug River a few yards away.

Blue Swamp. This huge wetland contains almost the entire spectrum of Connecticut's inland marsh and swamp types, including the uncommon white pine and hemlock swamps. Nearby, there is farmland and open fields.

Several other wetlands lie further along on the route (e. g. on Melius Road); they are mainly beaver-controlled pond / marsh / swamp systems.

The woods along the route contain a variety of forest habitats, with hemlock often being the dominant species. There are extensive areas of mountain laurel at several points (e. g. on Flat Rock Road).

SEASONS/BIRDS
> **SPRING MIGRATION:** water birds, marsh birds, shore birds, LAND BIRDS;
> **NESTING SEASON:** water birds, marsh birds, shore birds, LAND BIRDS;
> **Fall Migration:** water birds, marsh birds, shore birds, LAND BIRDS;
> **Winter:** land birds.

Land birds are the main attraction of the habitats along this route, especially near the wetlands. Throughout the route there is an abundance of common species appropriate to each type of habitat, during both migrations and in the nesting season.

Prospect Mountain Sanctuary. There are some water, marsh and shore birds in this area, but land birds are the main draw, especially during the nesting season. Among the nesters are solitary vireo and black-throated green warbler in the forest, black-throated blue and Canada warblers in areas of mountain laurel. Barred owl can be counted on to respond to calling.

Milton Cemetery provides a good look at wetland and edge species in the surrounding marshes.

Blue Swamp. Here again, land birds provide the most action, especially during the spring and summer. Many of these are wetland-oriented and edge species, including yellow warbler, northern waterthrush, least flycatcher, and possibly (but not confirmed as nesting species) willow and alder flycatchers. Whip-poor-will can be heard calling in the evening, and is believed to nest here. Both great horned and barred owls are resident. During the warm months, great blue and green-backed herons are often present, and sometimes Virginia rail.

Some of the habitats along other parts of the roads are also very good, and it is worth stopping frequently whenever the habitat appears promising.

GETTING AROUND
> **Birding methods:** CAR, WALK.

It is possible to see all of the habitats described here from within or near your car. The route follows little traveled back roads, some of which are paved, but many are dirt and may be soft and muddy in the early spring. All are ideal for birding on foot, and most of the time are good for birding from your car. Some of the land along the roads is public, but much is private.

DIRECTIONS (see Map 24): **The starting point is the intersection of Routes 202 and 209 about three miles west of the center of Litchfield.**

To get to the Prospect Mountain Sanctuary, go west on Route 202 for 1.3 miles, right on Old Turnpike Road for 0.2 mile, right on Prospect Mountain Road for 1.5 miles to where there is a pulloff on the right, and a pond down the hill on the left. The Mattatuck Trail crosses the road here.

To get to Milton Cemetery and Blue Swamp, continue on Prospect Mountain Road for another 1.1 miles to a four-way intersection. Go straight through the intersection onto Head-quarters Road for 0.7 mile, left on Sawmill Road for 0.8 mile, left on Blue Swamp Road for 0.3 mile to Milton Cemetery on the right. Continue on Blue Swamp Road for another 0.5 mile to a pulloff on the right, and the eastern edge of Blue Swamp on the left. Continue for another 0.3 to where the west side of Blue Swamp is visible on the right from the road.

To get to additional birding areas, continue on Blue Swamp Road (which becomes Milton Road, then South Road) for 2.0 miles to the intersection with Flat Rock Road and College Street. Here a right turn onto College Street takes you to nearby Hart Pond (described in this chapter under Cornwall/Goshen). Turn left onto Flat Rock Road for 1.1 mile to a pulloff along the Wyantenock State Forest. (The mountain laurel here is a good place to look for Canada and black-throated blue warblers.) Continue for another 0.4 mile to another pulloff. (This is a good area in which to bird along the road.)

To get to still more birding areas, continue on Flat Rock Road for another 0.3 mile, left on Melius Road for 1.7 miles to a wetland, for another 0.4 mile to a second wetland.

To get out to main highways, continue on Melius Road for 0.5 mile, right on Route 45 for 5.0 miles to Route 7, and right for 1.0 mile to Cornwall Bridge at the intersection of Routes 7 and 4.

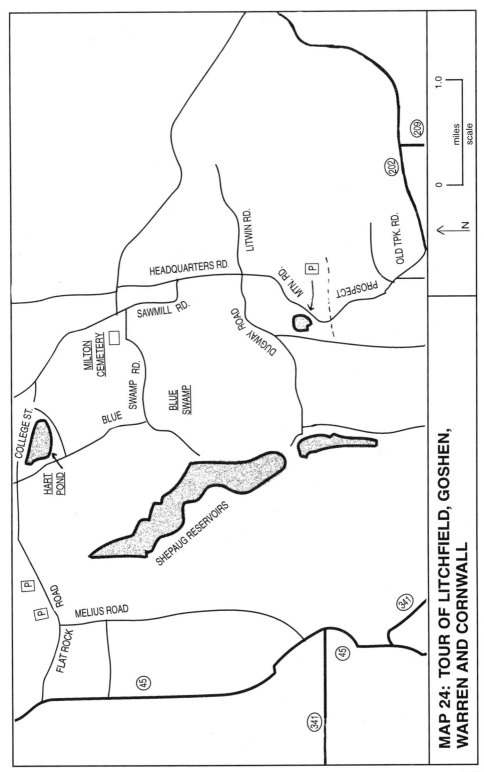

MAP 24: TOUR OF LITCHFIELD, GOSHEN, WARREN AND CORNWALL

N

0   miles   1.0
scale

202

209

OLD TPK. RD.

LITWIN RD.

PROSPECT

MTN. RD.

HEADQUARTERS RD.

SAWMILL RD.

DUGWAY ROAD

MILTON CEMETERY

BLUE SWAMP RD.

BLUE SWAMP

COLLEGE ST.

HART POND

SHEPAUG RESERVOIRS

FLAT ROCK ROAD

MELIUS ROAD

45

341

45

341

TOUR OF SALISBURY AND SHARON

THE TOUR. This is a sixteen mile driving tour which passes by a lake and a variety of forested and open habitats, including some of Connecticut's most beautiful farm land. The centerpiece of the tour is Mudge Pond in Sharon, for which there is also a separate site description.

HABITATS
> **OPEN TERRESTRIAL:** tilled, short grass, tall grass, mixed herbaceous and shrubby fields, shrubby and wooded edges, hedgerows, scattered cedars;
> **LAKE/POND:** lake, deep water, shallow water, shrubby shore;
> **Forest:** hardwoods, hardwoods/white pine, hardwoods/hemlock, cedar;
> **River/stream:** perennial and seasonal streams, shrubby and wooded streambelts;
> **Marsh/swamp/bog:** wet meadow, cattail, sedge, mixed herbaceous and shrub marsh, shrub swamp.

There is a great variety of avian habitat on this rather short driving tour. The main attractions are Mudge Pond and various open and edge habitats. There are also several types of forest, and small areas of wetland.

SEASONS/BIRDS
> **SPRING MIGRATION:** WATER BIRDS, marsh birds, shore birds, LAND BIRDS;
> **Nesting season:** water birds, marsh birds, land birds;
> **FALL MIGRATION:** WATER BIRDS, marsh birds, shore birds, LAND BIRDS;
> **Winter:** land birds.

Given the combination of habitats on this route - open terrestrial, forest and aquatic - there is something to look for throughout the year.

In the early spring (March), look on Mudge Pond for ducks and Canada goose, often with snow goose and sometimes white-fronted goose among them. Common loon and pied-billed grebe are often present. Also in March, raptors start to move through the area, and horned lark and snow bunting may still be in the fields. In March and April, snipe may be seen in wet meadows. In April and May, there is a good chance of seeing kestrel, bobolink, meadowlark and Savannah sparrow in the fields. Still later, prairie warbler and indigo bunting may be seen in the shrubby open areas. In May, greater yellowlegs and solitary sandpiper occur as migrants.

Many of those species also occur in those same habitats as nesters, as well as sora and Virginia rail in the marshes. Harrier has exhibited breeding behavior, but nesting has not yet been confirmed.

In the early fall (August and September) greater yellowlegs and other shore birds come through again, and in September and October there are migrating hawks to see. In October and November, look for migrating sparrows among the shrubby open areas. In November, snipe occasionally move through. In November and December, geese, ducks and coot are present on Mudge Pond once again, and there may be some newly arrived snow buntings in the fields.

In winter, snow bunting continues to be a possibility, together with horned lark, rough-legged hawk and snowy owl - all in or near open field areas. Bald eagle may occasionally be seen hunting from the shore of Mudge Pond or feeding on the ice. Turkey is present all year.

GETTING AROUND
Birding methods: CAR.
The habitats described above can all be seen from the road. In addition, it is necessary to stay on the road, since the land on either side of it is private, and houses occur intermittently.

DIRECTIONS (see Map 25): This driving tour starts and ends at the intersection of Routes 41 and 112, a couple of miles south of Lakeville. Go south on Route 41 for 4.7 miles, right at the Sharon post office on Low Street for 2.5 miles, left on Dug Road for 0.3 mile, left on Mudgetown Road for 0.8 mile, left on Mudge Pond Road for 1.8 miles along the west shore of Mudge Pond, left on Route 361 for 1.1 miles, left on Route 41 and follow it north to its intersection with Route 112 and your starting point.

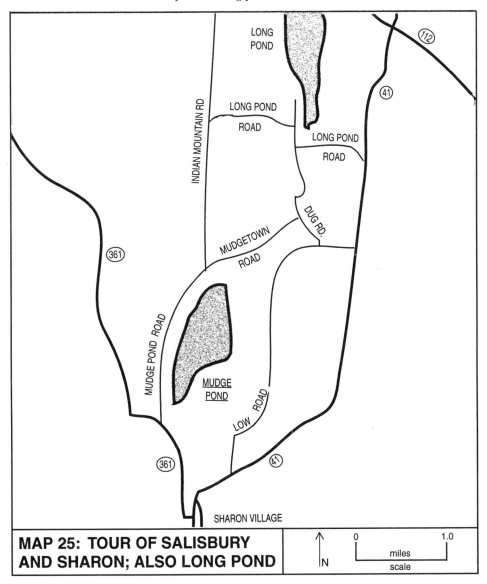

MAP 25: TOUR OF SALISBURY AND SHARON; ALSO LONG POND

0   1.0
miles
scale

N

TOUR OF THE UPPER HOUSATONIC RIVER

THE TOUR. The following driving tour of the Housatonic River covers the section of the river that runs from the Massachusetts line in Salisbury down to below New Milford, where the river leaves Litchfield County and forms the border between Fairfield and New Haven Counties. The tour provides access to points from which the river can be seen, access to varied habitats along the shores of the river, and takes you to several of Connecticut's best inland birding areas. This tour can be productive throughout the year for different groups of birds.

The tour is long - about 70 road miles one way from the starting point in Ashley Falls Massachusetts to the end near New Milford - and it is slow going, with numerous stops. Therefore you may not want to do the whole tour in one day. However, it is described in a way that permits you to start or stop at any point, and continue on another day. The sites that are part of the tour are listed below, in the order in which they occur on the tour (from north to south):

> **Salisbury: Weatogue Road***
> **Salisbury: Housatonic River Road***
> **Canaan: Amesville Power Plant***
> **Canaan/Cornwall: River Road***
> **Sharon: Housatonic Meadows State Park***
> **Sharon: Stanley WMA (Northern Block)***
> **Kent: Kent Falls State Park***
> **Kent: River Road (Stanley WMA - Southern Block)***
> **Kent: Schaghticoke Road***
> **Kent: Bulls Bridge Road (Appalachian Trail)***
> **New Milford: Bulls Bridge Recreation Area***
> **New Milford: River Road/Boardman Road***
> **New Milford: Fishing Access**
> **New Milford: Harry Brook Park**
> **New Milford: Lovers Leap Park**
> **New Milford: Addis Park**
> **New Milford: Clatter Valley Park**

*These sites are discussed in greater detail in separate site descriptions.

HABITATS

> **RIVER/STREAM:** river, fast water, slow water, perennial streams, seasonal streams; streambelts of shrubs and various combinations of hardwoods, white pine and hemlock;
> **Open terrestrial:** tilled, short grass and shrubby fields, edges and hedgerows;
> **Forest:** various combinations of hardwoods, white pine and hemlock; flood plain.

This tour includes extensive sections of the Housatonic River, its associated flood plain, and a wide variety of terrestrial habitats nearby in the river valley. Details about many of the habitats are included in separate site descriptions.

SEASONS/BIRDS

> **SPRING MIGRATION:** WATER BIRDS, shore birds, LAND BIRDS;
> **Nesting season:** water birds, land birds;
> **FALL MIGRATION:** WATER BIRDS, marsh birds, shore birds, LAND BIRDS;
> **WINTER:** WATER BIRDS, land birds.

This tour is worthwhile during any season, because of the wide variety of habitats that it goes through. During the early spring and late fall, there are migrating water birds on the river itself. Later in the spring and earlier in the fall, land bird migrants move through terrestrial habitats along the river valley. Osprey uses the river as a migration corridor. In winter, water birds and gulls congregate where there is open water, and bald eagle frequently can be seen hunting or resting on trees along the shore.

GETTING AROUND
Birding methods: CAR, WALK.

This is basically a driving tour, but there are opportunities for birding on foot, walking a nature trail, and for hikes of several miles on trails and woods roads that go along the river. There are sections of dirt road that, in the fall, winter and spring, require cars with good road clearance; and there are sections that are not maintained in winter.

DIRECTIONS (see Map 26): The starting point for this tour is in the center of Ashley Falls in southwestern Massachusetts at the intersection of Route 7A and Rannapo Road.

To get to Salisbury: Weatogue Road, go west on Rannapo Road (along the Housatonic River) for 0.9 mile, left on Weatogue Road for 0.8 mile to the Massachusetts/Connecticut state line. Now in Connecticut, continue on Weatogue Road along the river for 2.7 miles, left on Twin Lakes Road for 0.8 mile to Route 44.

To get to Salisbury: Housatonic River Road from the intersection of Route 44 and Twin Lakes Road, go right on Route 44 for 0.5 mile, and left on Housatonic River Road. Follow this road along or near the Housatonic River for 3.5 miles to Amesville, and turn left on Falls Village Road.

To get to the Amesville Power Plant Nature Trail, follow Falls Village Road for 0.3 mile across the bridge to the parking area for the nature trail on the right.

To continue down along the Housatonic River, go back across the bridge on Falls Village Road, and turn south (left) on Dugway Road which goes down the valley and intermittently near the river for another 2.2 miles to its junction with Route 112.

To get to Canaan/Cornwall: River Road, go left on Route 112 for 0.8 mile, left on Route 7 for 0.3 mile, to the north (far) end of the bridge over the Housatonic River. At this point, turn right on a small, paved road (Lime Rock Station Road) that will become the Warren Turnpike and then River Road. In 1.0 mile, bear right at a fork. Now the road will follow the river for 4.8 miles to the intersection with Route 128 in the center of West Cornwall. To continue on South River Road, go west (right) on Route 128 for less than 0.1 mile, and left on South River Road. It passes near the river at one point, and in 0.7 mile, ends at the beginning of a woods road that can be walked into the Housatonic State Forest.

To get to Housatonic Meadows State Park, go back up South River Road to the center of West Cornwall, go west (left) on Route 128 for 0.1 mile, through the covered bridge, and left on Route 7. Follow Route 7 as it goes along the river (with occasional opportunities to pull of the highway) for 2.6 miles to the entrance to Housatonic Meadows State Park on the left.

To get to Sharon: Stanley WMA (Northern Block), from the entrance of Housatonic Meadows State park, go south (left) on Route 7 for 1.3 miles to just before you reach the west (near) end of the bridge over which Route 7 crosses the Housatonic River. At this point, make a sharp turn left onto River Road, and follow River Road as it loops around clockwise until it runs south along the river and passes under the Route 7 bridge. Drive this road for 1.6 miles to a fork at which there is a small parking area. A trail starts here, follows the river south and leads to the Stanley WMA (Northern Block) and eventually to the Southern Block in Kent (aka "River Road").

To get to Kent: Kent Falls State Park, return to Route 7 and go south for about five miles to a grassy parking area on the right by a stone chimney. It is a short walk down to the river from here. (The main part of the park is 0.2 miles south and on the east side of Route 7).

To get to Kent: Stanley WMA (Southern Block) aka Kent River Road, return to Route 7 and go south for about four miles into the village of Kent. From the intersection of Routes 7 and 341, go right (west) on Route 341 for 0.3 mile across the Housatonic River, right on Skiff Mountain Road for 1.2 miles, and right again on River Road which continues for 2.7 miles along the river through riverine habitats to its end at a barrier (this dirt road can be birded on foot or from your car). At this point, the Appalachian Trail continues north along the river, and leads to the Stanley WMA Northern Block in Sharon. To continue the driving tour, return to the intersection of Skiff Mountain Road and Route 341.

To get to Kent: Schaghticoke Road, from the intersection of Skiff Mountain Road and Route 341, go right (west) on Route 341 for 0.4 mile, and left on Shaghticoke Road. This road follows the west bank of the Housatonic River for 4.3 miles to its intersection with Bulls Bridge Road.

To get to Kent: Bulls Bridge Road (Appalachian Trail), go left (east) on Bulls Bridge Road for 0.2 mile to where the Appalachian Trail crosses the road, with parking areas on either side. This trail can be walked along the river either north or south.

To get to New Milford: Bulls Bridge Recreation Area, continue east on Bulls Bridge Road for 0.1 mile through the covered bridge, right on Route 7 for 4.9 miles (along the river for part of the way, but with only two pulloffs) to an entrance to the recreation area on the right.

To get to New Milford: River Road/Boardman Road, continue south on Route 7 for another 1.3 miles, left on River View Road for 0.4 mile, and right on River Road. This road follows the river for 4.4 miles until it reaches Boardman Road. Go left on Boardman Road for 2.3 miles to a wide pulloff on the right, 0.1 mile upstream from the Route 202 bridge that goes across the river. To return to Route 7, continue south on Boardman Road for 0.1 mile, go right on Route 202 for 0.2 mile across the bridge to Route 7.

To get to a fishing access to the Housatonic River further downstream, go south (left) on Route 7 for 0.7 mile to the second light; left on Pickett District Road for 0.1 mile to a dirt parking/loading area on the left. At the back of this area, there is a State of Connecticut right-of-way path that leads to a fishing access at the river.

To get to Harry Brook Park and a look at a backwater of the river, continue south on Pickett District Road for another 1.9 miles, left on Still River Drive for 0.2 mile to the park entrance on the right at the far end of the bridge.

To get to Lovers Leap Park and still another look at the river, from the entrance to Harry Brook Park, turn right onto Still River Drive (aka Lower Grove Street) for 0.4 mile to the entrance to the park on the right.

To get to Addis Park (a boat landing on the river), continue north on Lower Grove Street (which becomes Grove Street) for 0.8 mile to the landing on the left.

To get to another part of Lovers Leap Park that also overlooks the river, go back the way you came on Grove Street for 0.4 mile, left on Hine Hill Road for 0.7 mile, right on Clatter Valley Road (aka Town Farm Road) for 0.3 mile, right on Lovers Leap Road for 0.7 mile to a woods road into the park on the right.

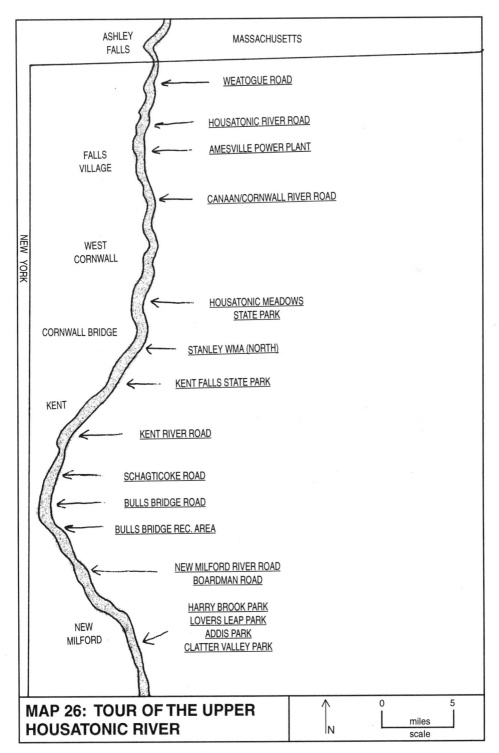

ASHLEY FALLS

MASSACHUSETTS

← WEATOGUE ROAD

← HOUSATONIC RIVER ROAD

← AMESVILLE POWER PLANT

FALLS VILLAGE

← CANAAN/CORNWALL RIVER ROAD

WEST CORNWALL

← HOUSATONIC MEADOWS STATE PARK

CORNWALL BRIDGE

← STANLEY WMA (NORTH)

← KENT FALLS STATE PARK

KENT

← KENT RIVER ROAD

← SCHAGTICOKE ROAD

← BULLS BRIDGE ROAD

← BULLS BRIDGE REC. AREA

← NEW MILFORD RIVER ROAD
BOARDMAN ROAD

HARRY BROOK PARK
LOVERS LEAP PARK
ADDIS PARK
CLATTER VALLEY PARK

NEW MILFORD

NEW YORK

MAP 26: TOUR OF THE UPPER HOUSATONIC RIVER

N

0   miles   5
scale

To get to the Clatter Valley Park (a nearby town recreation area that you pass on the way to Lovers Leap; it is not on the river but has open fields, shrubby and hardwood edges), go back on Lovers Leap Road for 0.7 mile to the intersection with Town Farm Road, and turn hard right into the Clatter Valley Park driveway.

BARKHAMSTED: AMERICAN LEGION STATE FOREST/PEOPLES STATE FOREST

HABITATS

FOREST: hardwoods, white pine and hemlock, alone and in combination; mixed conifer plantations; mountain laurel;

RIVER/STREAM: river, fast water, slow water, shrubby, hardwood, white pine and hemlock streambelt; numerous perennial and seasonal streams, various streambelts;

MARSH/SWAMP/BOG: sedge, cattail mixed herbaceous and shrub marsh, shrub swamp, dead trees, edges of hardwoods, white pine and hemlock;

Lake/pond: beaver pond, seasonal pools;

Open terrestrial: short grass field, shrubby and wooded edge;

Other: ledge, cliff, rocky slope, gravel pit.

These two state forests lie opposite each other along the upper Farmington River - American Legion State Forest (782 acres) on the west side, and Peoples State Forest (2,954 acres)is on the east side. Together, they include deciduous and conifer woods with a distinctly northern character, a five mile stretch of the Farmington River, and some open playing fields. In addition, perched high in remote parts of each of these two forests are fine wetlands that includes various marsh, swamp and edge habitats. The elevation of these wetlands (750') and of the surrounding forest causes them to have a distinctly northern character.

SEASONS/BIRDS

SPRING MIGRATION: water birds, marsh birds, shore birds, LAND BIRDS;

NESTING SEASON: water birds, marsh birds, LAND BIRDS;

FALL MIGRATION: water birds, marsh birds, LAND BIRDS;

Winter: land birds.

This site is a pleasant and rewarding place to do your birding. In the forested areas, both the spring and fall migrations are very good, especially May and September for warblers and other land birds. In the laurel thickets that occur throughout these parks, nesting black-throated blue and Canada warblers are abundant. Among the many other nesting species are sapsucker, solitary vireo, Blackburnian and black-throated green warblers. In winter, expect to see common forest-dwelling residents, plus winter finches in some years. Bald eagle, raven and common merganser occur throughout the year.

The two marshes within the forests are good places to study life in a wetland even during a summer weekend. Spring, summer and fall are all good here. During both the spring and fall migrations, warblers and a variety of other land birds feed along the edges of the marshes. Olive-sided flycatcher can sometimes be seen hunting over the wetland. During the nesting season, a number of species that nest in the forest nearby also come to the wetlands to feed. These include: yellow-bellied sapsucker, solitary vireo, magnolia and yellow-rumped warblers, junco, white-throated sparrow, brown creeper, and red-breasted nuthatch, all species that are characteristic of northern forests. In addition, swamp sparrow nests in the wetlands, and great blue heron feeds in them, with nests in their trees or at nearby swamps. The wetland in American Legion State Park is a good place to look for olive-sided flycatcher during migration, and yellow-bellied sapsucker at any time.

GETTING AROUND
Birding methods: car, WALK, bike, ski, boat.
In the parts of these parks that are near the Farmington River, hardtop roads follow both banks of the river, and lead to wood roads and trails. This is a good area in which to bird from your car or on foot. This stretch of river makes a nice canoe trip if you can arrange to be picked up downstream. But don't do this boat trip in the early spring - there is heavy white water during the spring run-off.

Birding at either of the two wetlands may or may not require walking, depending on whether the vehicle roads are barred - 1.6 miles (one way) to the wetland in American Legion State Forest, and about 1.0 mile to the wetland in Peoples State Forest. However, it is worth the effort; you will be in fine habitat and away from the crowds even on a summer weekend.

DIRECTIONS (see Map 27): These two parks are about five miles northeast of Winsted.

To get to the parts of the parks that lie along either side of the Farmington River, from the intersection of Routes 44 and 318 between Winsted and New Hartford, go east on Route 318 for 0.7 mile to a bridge across the Farmington River. At both ends of this bridge are roads (West River Road and East River Road) which go north along the river through the parks. Both roads end in the village of Riverton, about five miles to the north.

To get to the wetland in American Legion State Forest, start at the west end of the Route 318 bridge over the Farmington River, go north on West River Road for 2.4 miles, left on Legion Road past a gravel pit to a gate that may or may not be barred. The wetland is 1.1 miles farther up Legion Road.

To get to the wetland in Peoples State Forest (Beaver Brook Meadow), start at the east end of the bridge over the Farmington River (see above), go north on East River Road for 0.8 mile, and right on Greenwoods Road. Follow Greenwoods Road for 1.7 miles, at which point Beaver Brook Road (which may or may not be barred) goes off to the right and passes the wetland. Just before this intersection, there are several trails on the right side of Greenwoods Road that lead down the hill to the wetland and to a Blue Trail that follows the west edge of it. Several other trails start from Greenwoods Road and go through nearby forest habitats.

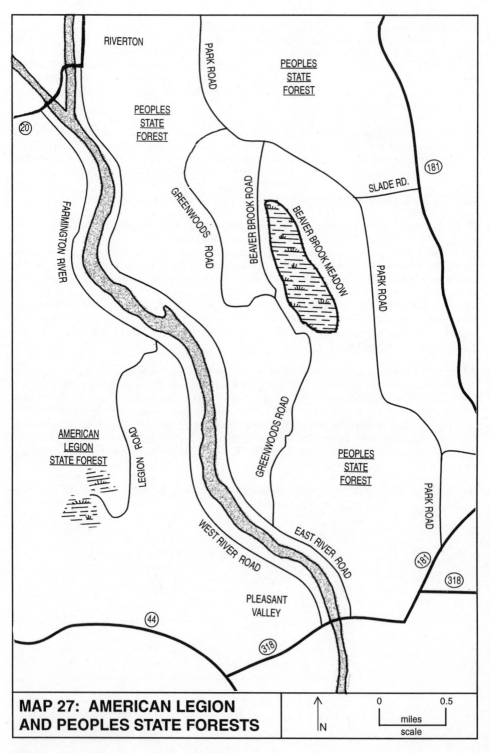

RIVERTON

PARK ROAD

PEOPLES
STATE
FOREST

PEOPLES
STATE
FOREST

20

FARMINGTON RIVER

GREENWOODS ROAD

BEAVER BROOK ROAD

BEAVER BROOK MEADOW

SLADE RD.

181

PARK ROAD

AMERICAN
LEGION
STATE FOREST

LEGION ROAD

GREENWOODS ROAD

PEOPLES
STATE
FOREST

PARK ROAD

WEST RIVER ROAD

EAST RIVER ROAD

181

318

PLEASANT
VALLEY

44

318

**MAP 27: AMERICAN LEGION
AND PEOPLES STATE FORESTS**

N

0   0.5

miles
scale

BARKHAMSTED: BARKHAMSTED RESERVOIR

HABITATS

FOREST: hardwoods, white pine and hemlock, alone and in combination, mixed conifers, cedar, mountain laurel;
LAKE/POND: lake, deep water; shores of marshes, shrubs, hardwoods, white pine and hemlock; seasonally barren shore (gravel, rocks); islands with steep dirt shores; pond, marshy and shrubby shore;
Open terrestrial: short grass, mixed herbaceous and shrubby fields;
River/stream: river, fast and slow water, perennial and seasonal streams, varied streambelts;
Marsh/swamp/bog: mixed herbaceous and shrub marsh, shrub swamp;
Other: dam, rocky slopes, cliffs and ledges.

This is a varied and rich area in which just about every type of inland habitat is represented. The main feature is a narrow, nine mile long reservoir which lies in an undeveloped valley with steep, wooded sides. The forest types are mostly of a northern character, composed largely of northern hardwoods, white pine and hemlock in various combinations. Within this woodland are cliffs, ledges, rock outcrops and rocky slopes. The reservoir itself is long, narrow and deep. There is usually open water into the early winter, and areas that are ice-free periodically during the winter. The shore of the reservoir is composed mainly of hardwoods, white pine and hemlock forest. In periods when the water level is low, there is an exposed strip of sand and gravel along the shore. The reservoir has seven islands of which one has steep dirt banks on its shore. The Farmington River enters the reservoir at its north end, and leaves via the Saville Dam at the south end. In addition there are numerous perennial and seasonal streams that flow into the reservoir. There is also a variety of marshes, swamps and a beaver pond, but these are in areas not open to the public.

SEASONS/BIRDS

SPRING MIGRATION: WATER BIRDS, marsh birds, shore birds, LAND BIRDS;
NESTING SEASON: WATER BIRDS, marsh birds, shore birds, LAND BIRDS;
FALL MIGRATION: WATER BIRDS, marsh birds, shore birds, LAND BIRDS;
WINTER: WATER BIRDS, LAND BIRDS.

This is one of Connecticut's top inland birding areas, even though only parts of it are open to the public.

The spring and fall migrations are incredible, and it is possible to see virtually every species that occurs inland in Connecticut. Water birds on the reservoir are certainly one of the highlights: all of the divers that occur in Connecticut have been seen here, as well as all of the dabbling ducks except blue-winged teal. When the water level is low during the shore bird migration, it is not uncommon to see greater yellow-legs and solitary sandpiper. During the fall migration, Saville Dam at the southern end of the reservoir is a good site from which to look for hawks moving down the valley.

More than 120 species are known to nest in this area; in this respect, the Barkhamsted Reservoir ranks third in Connecticut, behind only White Memorial in Litchfield and the Nepaug Reservoir area in New Hartford. Nesters at Barkhamsted include virtually all the land birds that are standard nesters in Connecticut, plus northern species such as black-throated blue, Canada and magnolia warblers. Bank swallows nest on the steep dirt shore of one of the islands, and can be seen from the dam as they feed. Nesting raptors include all three accipiters, red-tailed, red-shouldered and broad-winged hawks, great horned, barred and saw-whet owls. Raven nests on rock outcrops on the west side of the reservoir. Perhaps the best known nesting species is bald eagle, which started successfully fledging young near the reservoir in 1992 - the only known bald eagle nest in Connecticut since the early 1950s. (The nest is in a remote area that is off-limits to the public.)

In winter also, this is an outstanding area. When there are ice-free areas on the reservoir, look for water birds. In years of winter finch irruption, this is one of the best areas in the state to search for these elusive species. Other uncommon species have occurred here in winter, including northern shrike and rough-legged hawk. And bald eagle is a good possibility any time during the fall, winter and spring.

GETTING AROUND
Birding methods: car, walk.

Unfortunately, the interior of this large area is owned by the Metropolitan District Commission (MDC) and is not open to the public. However, the edges of public roads and other areas around the periphery that are open to the public all provide good birding, either from your car or on foot. These areas are:

the Saville Dam at the south end of the reservoir;
Beech Rock Road;
Beech Rock and the trail to it;
Route 181;
Route 20;
the Tunxis Trail from where it crosses Routes 20 and 219 (see "Hartford County: Hartland: Tunxis State Forest").

Taken together, the areas listed above make it possible to see virtually all of the species that occur at this site. Most of the land on either side of these roads and trails is private or MDC-owned, and must not be entered.

DIRECTIONS (see Map 28): The Barkhamsted Reservoir lies five to ten miles east and northeast of Winsted.

To reach the Saville Dam, from the intersection of Routes 44 and 318 between Winsted and New Hartford, go east on Route 318 for 3.2 miles to the dam. This dam at the south end of the reservoir provides expansive views of the valley to both north and south, and is a good place from which to look for water birds on the south end of the reservoir and for flying migrants.

To reach Beech Rock from the Saville Dam, take Beech Rock Road which starts from Route 318 at a point 0.3 miles west of the dam. Go north on Beech Rock Road 0.2 miles to a small parking area on the west side of the road. The trail to Beech Rock starts from the east side of the road, and goes south along a rock ridge for 0.1 mile. Beech Rock is a ridge on the west side of the valley just north of the dam, and it provides much the same views as the Saville Dam but from a secluded point away from the highway.

To bird along the highways around the reservoir, continue north on Beech Rock Road. This road first joins Route 181 and then joins Route 20. Together, these roads go clockwise up through the forest habitats on the west side of the reservoir and over the north end of it. The reservoir itself cannot be seen, except for one spectacular overlook point on Route 20 near the north end of the reservoir. The woods and fields along these roads are very good for a variety of land bird species.

To complete the circle around the reservoir, continue on Route 20 and make right turns on Route 179 and then Route 219. This takes you down the east side of the reservoir (but not within sight of it) and completes the clockwise circle around it.

See also Hartford County: Hartland: Tunxis State Forest.

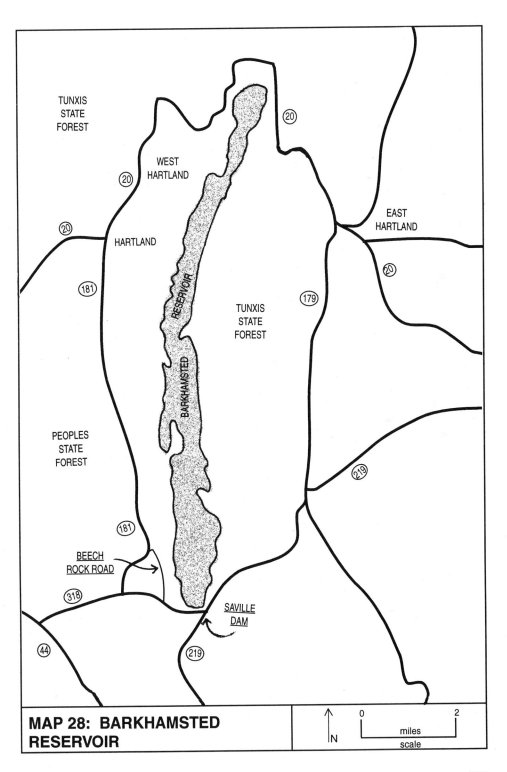

MAP 28: BARKHAMSTED RESERVOIR

TUNXIS STATE FOREST

WEST HARTLAND

EAST HARTLAND

HARTLAND

TUNXIS STATE FOREST

RESERVOIR

BARKHAMSTED

PEOPLES STATE FOREST

BEECH ROCK ROAD

SAVILLE DAM

0 miles 2
scale

N

227

BARKHAMSTED: UPPER GREENWOODS RECREATION AREA

HABITATS:
>**RIVER/STREAM:** river, slow water, fast water, shrubby and hardwood streambelt, backwater pond, shrubby edge;
>**OPEN TERRESTRIAL:** mixed herbaceous and shrubby fields, shrubby and hardwood edges;
>**Forest:** hardwoods, hardwoods/white pine, white pine, flood plain.

This site lies along the eastern shore of the Farmington River. It includes a section of the river itself, together with a strip of prime streambelt, open and wooded habitats.

SEASONS/BIRDS
>**SPRING MIGRATION:** water birds, shore birds, LAND BIRDS;
>**NESTING SEASON:** water birds, shore birds, LAND BIRDS;
>**FALL MIGRATION:** water birds, shore birds, LAND BIRDS;
>**Winter:** water birds, land birds.

The Farmington River is a migration corridor, and both spring (especially May) and fall (especially September) are good times to see migrants here. In the spring, look on and along the river for common and hooded mergansers, spotted sandpiper and osprey, and in the woods along the shore for a nice variety of warblers. Nesters include pine and prairie warblers, indigo bunting, field sparrow, brown thrasher and Louisiana waterthrush. The fall migration is similar to spring. Common merganser is apt to be present at any time of year, as are (less frequently) raven and bald eagle.

GETTING AROUND
>**Birding methods:** car, WALK.

A dirt road and trail follow the east shore of the river. This area is a popular hunting spot in the fall.

DIRECTIONS: This site is about five miles east of Winsted. From the intersection of Routes 318 and 44, go east on Route 318 for 0.9 mile to the far end of the bridge over the Farmington River. A dirt road follows the river for 0.5 mile to a barrier, where a trail continues.

BARKHAMSTED/NEW HARTFORD: LOWER GREENWOODS RECREATION AREA

HABITATS
>**RIVER/STREAM:** river, slow water, fast water, herbaceous, shrubby and wooded streambelt;
>**OPEN TERRESTRIAL:** mixed herbaceous, tall grass and shrubby fields, shrubby and wooded edges;
>**Forest:** young hardwoods, flood plain.;
>**Lake/pond:** seasonal pools;
>**Marsh/swamp/bog:** wet meadow, sedge, herbaceous and shrub marshes.

This is a very productive strip of streambelt habitat that lies along the western shore of the Farmington River.

SEASONS/BIRDS
SPRING MIGRATION: water birds, shore birds, LAND BIRDS;
NESTING SEASON: LAND BIRDS;
FALL MIGRATION: water birds, shore birds, LAND BIRDS;
Winter: water birds, land birds.

The spring migration (especially May to early June) is excellent for land birds (including olive-sided flycatcher and a variety of swallows) that are migrating up the Farmington River Valley. Nesting species include alder and willow flycatchers, brown thrasher and indigo bunting. The fall is also very good for migrating land birds, including many sparrows in the late fall. Osprey migrates along the river in spring and fall. Bald eagle and raven occur in this area at any time of year.

GETTING AROUND
Birding methods: car, WALK.
Rough dirt roads and trails go along the river and through nearby habitats.

DIRECTIONS: This area is about six miles east of Winsted and three miles west of New Hartford. From the intersection of Routes 181 and 44, go north on 181 for 0.2 mile and turn right on a dirt road into the area (there is no sign).

BETHLEHEM: BELLAMY PRESERVE

HABITATS
Forest: hardwoods, hardwoods/white pine, hemlock, cedar, mixed conifers;
Open terrestrial: tilled, short grass, tall grass and shrubby fields, orchard, shrubby and wooded edges;
Lake/pond: pond, shore of shrubs;
River/stream: stream, hardwood/hemlock streambelt;
Marsh/swamp/bog: shrubby hardwood swamp.

This rather small preserve (some 90 acres) occupies the site of an old farm, now mostly in various stages of succession. It has a nice variety of inland habitats - a mixture of young and mature hardwoods, a tilled field, several hayfields, shrubby former farm fields, the remnants of an orchard, a stream that goes through a miniature hemlock ravine, and a small pond surrounded by shrubs and hardwoods.

SEASONS/BIRDS
Spring migration: land birds;
Nesting Season: land birds;
Fall Migration: land birds;
Winter: land birds.

While not large or especially notable as a birding site, the Bellamy Preserve offers a nice variety of the standard land bird species that you would expect in these habitats during the spring and fall migrations and the nesting season.

GETTING AROUND
Birding methods: WALK.
There is a matrix of old farm roads and trails that make walking easy. It is possible to cover the entire area by making a walking loop of about a mile.

DIRECTIONS: This preserve is in Bethlehem, about eight miles northwest of Waterbury. In Bethlehem at the intersection of Routes 132 and 61, go west on Route 132 for 0.1 mile, right on Munger Lane for 0.1 mile to the preserve entrance on the right.

BRIDGEWATER: ROCKY HILL PRESERVE

HABITATS
> **OPEN TERRESTRIAL:** tilled, short grass, mixed herbaceous and shrubby fields; shrubby and hardwood edges; vine tangles, cedar;
> **Forest:** hardwoods, hardwoods/hemlock, hemlock, cedar;
> **River/stream:** perennial stream, several seasonal streams;
> **Marsh/swamp/bog:** mixed herbaceous and shrub marsh, shrubby hardwood swamp;
> **Lake/pond:** pond, mixed herbaceous and shrubby shore.

This preserve lies inconspicuously among the hills along the eastern side of the Housatonic River Valley, amid quiet rural-residential countryside. It contains a rich combination of open, forest and wetland habitats. There is a profusion of berry-producing shrubs and vines.

SEASONS/BIRDS
> **SPRING MIGRATION:** LAND BIRDS;
> **NESTING SEASON:** LAND BIRDS;
> **FALL MIGRATION:** LAND BIRDS;
> **WINTER:** LAND BIRDS.

This site is very good at every season, including winter. The spring migration includes a nice variety of both open-country species and forest-dwellers. Nesting species also reflect the presence of high quality open and edge habitats: bobolink, meadowlark, indigo bunting, field sparrow, prairie, blue-winged, chestnut-sided, yellow and yellowthroat warblers, towhee, cedar waxwing, bluebird and tree swallow. Other interesting nesting species are goshawk, barred and great horned owls, brown creeper and acadian flycatcher. The fall migration is also good, with the highlight being the passage of a variety of sparrows during October and November. In winter, berry-producing shrubs attract lingering migrants such as robin, bluebird, yellow-rumped warbler and fox sparrow. Saw-whet owl has been found in the cedar trees; Cooper's and sharp-shinned hawks also occur here in winter.

GETTING AROUND
> **Birding methods:** WALK.

A network of trails leads through the preserve. Parking is tight in winter; sometimes it is difficult to find a safe place to pull off the road.

DIRECTIONS: The Rocky Hill Preserve is in western Connecticut, about five miles south of New Milford. To get there from New Milford at the eastern intersection of Routes 67 and 202, go east on Route 67 for 3.2 miles, right on Route 133 for 1.4 miles, right on Sarah Sanford Road West for 0.3 mile, and left on Northrop Street for 0.7 mile to the start of a trail into the preserve on the right side of the road by a small stream. A second trail can be reached by continuing on the same road for another 0.5 mile to an intersection, and turning right on Benson Road for 0.4 mile to the start of a trail into the preserve on the right side of the road, also by a small stream.

CANAAN: AMESVILLE POWER PLANT

HABITATS
RIVER/STREAM: river; slow water, fast water, hardwood and hemlock streambelt;
Forest: hardwoods, hardwoods/hemlock;
Open terrestrial: short grass and shrubby fields, shrubby edges.
This is the section of the Housatonic River that is immediately above and below a hydro-power dam. Above the dam, the river is slow and deep; below it there are rapids over a rocky bottom.

SEASONS/BIRDS
Spring migration: land birds;
Nesting season: land birds;
Fall migration: land birds;
Winter: land birds.
This is a pleasant site at which to look for land birds over the river and along its shore. During the spring and fall, osprey, warblers and other migrants can be seen from this area. During the nesting season, look for the standard woodland and edge species, including yellow-throated and warbling vireos. In August, this is a good place to see all of the swallow species that occur in Connecticut (except for purple martin) as they engage in pre-migration staging over the river. During the winter, bald eagle is a possibility.

GETTING AROUND
Birding methods: car, walk.
The picnic area overlooking the river can be reached by car. In addition, there is a 0.8 mile nature trail that goes through woods and past remains of a canal and other human works.

DIRECTIONS: This area is at Falls Village, about five miles south of Canaan. From the intersection of Routes 126 and 7, go west on Route 126 for 0.5 mile, left at the stop sign and immediately right onto Water Street, for 0.1 mile to the parking area on the left. The nature trail starts here. To get to the picnic area, continue for 0.3 mile beyond the parking area to the far end of the bridge, and left on Dugway Road.

CANAAN/CORNWALL: HOUSATONIC STATE FOREST

HABITATS
FOREST: hardwoods, hardwoods/white pine, hardwoods/hemlock, hemlock, mixed conifers;
River/stream: perennial and seasonal streams, shrubby and wooded streambelts, hemlock ravine;
Marsh/swamp/bog: wet meadow, mixed herbaceous and shrub marsh; shrub and shrubby hardwood swamp, dead wood;
Lake/pond: ponds, marshy, shrubby and wooded shores;
Open terrestrial: tilled, mixed herbaceous and shrubby fields, shrubby clearings and edges, cedars.
This state forest consists of a number of separate blocks in the towns of Canaan, Sharon and Cornwall, with a total area of 9,492 acres. The Cream Hill Block, described here, lies on the Canaan/Cornwall town line. This area is extensive, largely unspoiled, and includes many of the inland habitat types that occur in Connecticut. Most of the area included in this site is

forested with a variety of woodland communities, including extensive hardwood forest and areas of hemlock. There are several wetlands, including a variety of marshes and swamps, as well as beaver ponds with marshy edges. There are numerous seasonal and perennial streams, including one that flows through a spectacular hemlock ravine (Deane Ravine). This is a classic example of a hemlock ravine, with steep sides and a rocky brook, complete with falls and pools. Within the ravine is a cool, moist microclimate which supports plant and animal communities more typical of northern New England.

SEASONS/BIRDS
SPRING MIGRATION: water birds, marsh birds, LAND BIRDS;
NESTING SEASON: LAND BIRDS;
FALL MIGRATION: water birds, marsh birds, LAND BIRDS;
Winter: land birds;

Both migrations and the nesting season are all good, especially for forest-dwelling land birds. These include northern species such as yellow-bellied sapsucker, yellow-rumped warbler and junco. Some interesting raptors are present as probable nesters - kestrel, Goshawk, Cooper's, red-tailed, red-shouldered and broad-winged hawks, great horned, barred, screech and saw-whet owls. The Housatonic River is used as a flyway by water bird and land bird migrants, including merlin (in March and April). Dean Ravine is one of the relatively few places in Connecticut in which a public trail goes through a hemlock ravine. In parts of it, the roar of the waterfall makes it difficult to hear singing birds, but it is still a good place to look for Acadian flycatcher, Louisiana waterthrush, solitary vireo and black-throated green warbler.

GETTING AROUND
Birding methods: car, WALK, ski.

Lower Barrack Road, Yelping Hill Road and several other roads that go through parts of the forest are dirt, sometimes in good condition, but impassable at other times, and often require four wheel drive vehicles that have high road clearance. However, all of these roads and the trails and woods roads that they lead to provide excellent birding on foot. The trail through Dean Ravine is steep in places - it descends 250 feet in 0.7 mile. Much of the land that the roads described here go through is public, but some is private, so watch for posting.

DIRECTIONS (see Map 29): This area lies along the Canaan/Cornwall town line. The following areas are considered to be among the best in this large state forest:

Lower Barrack Road. In Falls Village at the intersection of Routes 63 and 126, go south on Route 63 for 50 yards, right on Music Mountain Road for 0.4 mile and right on Lower Barrack Road, which becomes dirt and rough. It ends in 1.4 miles when it rejoins Music Mountain Road, after passing through a forest of hardwoods and hemlock, and past a small stream.

Trails in the Music Mountain Area. Start as above, but continue on Music Mountain Road for another 1.6 miles past Lower Barrack Road (a total of 2.0 miles from Route 63), and turn left on Yelping Hill Road. It runs for 1.0 mile past several trails and woods roads, through a forest that is mostly hardwoods, some hardwoods/white pine, with some shrubby clearings and a mixed herbaceous marsh with dead wood. If you continue on Music Mountain Road for 0.1 mile past the turn onto Yelping Hill Road, you come to a mixed herbaceous marsh/wet meadow on the left.

Dean Ravine. Start as above, but continue on Music Mountain Road for 3.7 miles from Route 63 to the point at which Cream Hill Road comes in from the left. The trail through Dean Ravine starts here on the right side of Music Mountain Road.

More trails in the Music Mountain area. From the intersection of Music Mountain Road and Cream Hill Road (see "Dean Ravine" above), go south (left) on Cream Hill Road; starting almost immediately, trails enter the state forest from either side of the road.

River Road. (See also separate description under "Litchfield County: Canaan/Cornwall: River Road".) From the intersection of Music Mountain Road and Cream Hill Road (see "Dean Ravine" above), continue on Music Mountain Road (bear right at the intersection) for another 0.9 mile, and turn left on Warren Turnpike. This road becomes River Road and follows the east bank of the Housatonic River for several miles to the village of West Cornwall.

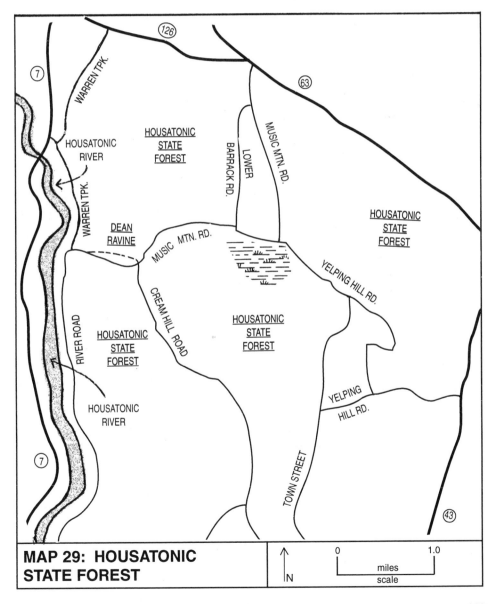

MAP 29: HOUSATONIC STATE FOREST

CANAAN/CORNWALL: RIVER ROAD

HABITATS

RIVER/STREAM: river, fast and slow water, streams, streambelts of shrubs, hardwoods, white pine, hemlock, and mixes of them;

OPEN TERRESTRIAL: short grass, tall grass, mixed herbaceous and shrubby fields; shrubby, hardwood and white pine edges; cedar;

Forest: hardwoods, hardwoods/white pine, white pine, flood plain;

Other: cliff.

A dirt road closely follows the east bank of the Housatonic River, along a wooded and sparsely settled part of the valley. The little-used road provides good looks at the river, as well as the varied woodlands and reverting fields through which it flows. Much of this section of the river has rapids or water that moves right along, so that there are always ice-free areas in winter.

SEASONS/BIRDS

SPRING MIGRATION: WATER BIRDS, shore birds, LAND BIRDS;

NESTING SEASON: LAND BIRDS;

FALL MIGRATION: WATER BIRDS, shore birds, LAND BIRDS;

Winter: water birds, land birds.

This is a good area to bird when you want both good habitat and solitude. The river and the water birds that occur on it in the spring, fall and winter (principally black duck, mallard, common merganser) make this a worthwhile trip, but the area offers an even more interesting variety of land birds. The spring land bird migration is very good, especially during the period mid-April through late May. The Housatonic River Valley is an important migration corridor for many species of land birds including various vireos and warblers (especially in the spring), and sparrows, (especially in the fall). Marsh birds (great blue and green-backed herons) and shore birds (principally spotted and solitary sandpipers) occur along the river during migration. Osprey uses the river as a migration route in spring (especially April) and fall (especially September). Many land bird species nest in this river valley, including a variety of open country/edge habitat species such as prairie warbler and the uncommon golden-winged warbler, and forest-dwellers such as black-throated green and Blackburnian warblers. (At least ten warbler species nest at this site.) This is a good site during the fall migration for seeing raptors and sparrows. There is far less action in winter, but open water on the river attracts a few water birds, and bald eagle can sometimes be seen perched on trees overlooking the water.

GETTING AROUND

Birding methods: CAR, WALK, BIKE.

The dirt road may become impassable for cars during the winter and early spring, but can be walked at any time. The woods road at the south end of Lower River Road provides good walking. The railroad near River Road is used, and should not be walked.

DIRECTIONS: This section of the Housatonic River runs from near the village of Lime Rock in Canaan to the village of West Cornwall in the town of Cornwall. To get to the north end of it from the intersection of Routes 7 and 112, go north on Route 7 for 0.3 miles; at the north (far) end of the bridge over the Housatonic River, turn right on Lime Rock Station Road that will become the Warren Turnpike and then River Road. In 1.0 mile, bear right at a fork. Now the road will follow the river for 4.8 miles to its intersection with Route 128 in the center of West Cornwall. To continue on South River Road, go right on Route 128 for less than 0.1 mile, and left on South River Road. It passes near the river at one point, and in 0.7 mile, ends at the beginning of a woods road that can be walked into the Housatonic State Forest.

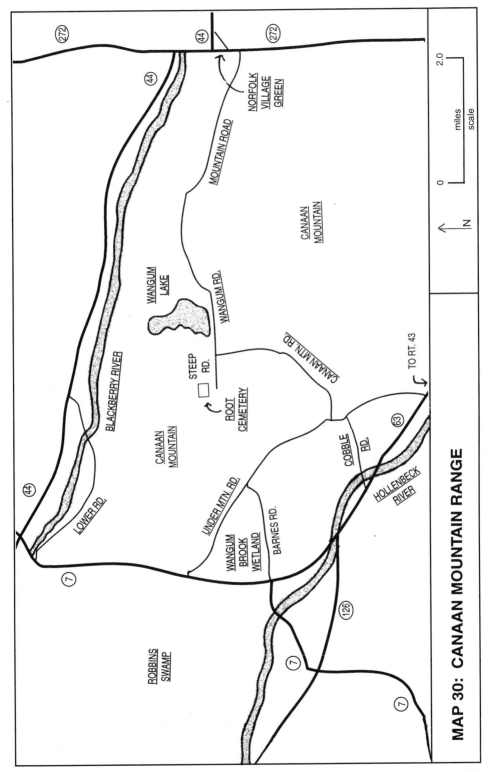

MAP 30: CANAAN MOUNTAIN RANGE

CANAAN/NORTH CANAAN: CANAAN MOUNTAIN RANGE

HABITATS

FOREST: hardwoods, white pine and hemlock, alone and in various combinations; native red pine; plantations of mixed conifers; cedar; mountain laurel;
OPEN TERRESTRIAL: fields of every type, from actively farmed fields to old pastures that have become almost totally forested; miles of shrubby and wooded edges; many areas of thickets;
LAKE/POND: lake, deep water, grassy, shrubby and wooded shore; farm ponds, seasonal pools;
RIVER/STREAM: numerous perennial and seasonal streams, mostly fast water; marshy, swampy, shrubby and wooded streambelts, hemlock ravines;
MARSH/SWAMP/BOG: wet meadow, sedge, cattail, mixed herbaceous and shrub marshes; shrub, shrubby hardwood, hardwood and hemlock swamps, dead wood;
OTHER: cliff, ledge, rocky slope.

This is a huge land mass that lies in Canaan and North Canaan. Commonly referred to as "Canaan Mountain", it is actually a high plateau that contains a series of mountains, cliffs and gorges, with elevations that go up to nearly 2,000'. It is bounded on the north and west by river valleys and farmland. Taken together, the Canaan Mountain Range and the valleys that surround it contain almost every type of terrestrial and wetland habitat that occurs in inland Connecticut.

Almost all of the Canaan Mountain plateau is covered by a northern hardwood and conifer forest, and includes a lake, pockets of wetlands and a number of streams that pass through wooded gorges as they descend to the surrounding lowlands. This area is wild and remote, and much of it is inaccessible.

The Canaan Mountain Range is bounded on the north by the valley of the Blackberry River, and on the west by the valley of the Hollenbeck River. These lowlands are characterized by streams with wooded and shrubby streambelts, active and reverting farmland with a wide variety of fields, ranging from areas that are currently managed to old pastures that have been invaded by cedars, white pines and other forest pioneers. There is an abundance of shrubby thickets and edges.

SEASONS/BIRDS

SPRING MIGRATION: water birds, marsh birds, shore birds, LAND BIRDS;
NESTING SEASON: water birds, marsh birds, shore birds, LAND BIRDS;
FALL MIGRATION: WATER BIRDS, marsh birds, shore birds, LAND BIRDS;
WINTER: LAND BIRDS;

The wide variation of habitat types support a great diversity of bird species at almost any season.

During the spring migration, look on Wangum Lake for water birds, usually including ring-necked duck and hooded merganser (lots of them!). Great blue and green-backed herons are present at several of the wetlands; woodcock and snipe at the wetland by Barnes Road. Numerous warblers feed at the edges along Under Mountain Road and other roads. The fall migration brings many of the same species that passed through in the spring, plus a greater variety of water birds, additional sparrows and hawks. The warbler migration in early September can be really impressive.

Eighty-nine species have shown evidence of nesting somewhere at this large site. These include open- and edge-habitat species in the valleys and farmland at the base of the mountain range, and forest-species up on the plateau. Raven nests on the ledges along the western side of the mountain range, great blue heron and hooded merganser at wetlands, and a host of species within the forest, including Cooper's hawk, goshawk, saw-whet owl, yellow-bellied sapsucker, hermit thrush, solitary vireo, and many warblers: magnolia, black-throated blue, yellow-rumped, black-throated green, Canada, and both waterthrushes; also junco and white-throated sparrow. Golden-winged warbler has nested at Root Cemetery on Steep Road.

This is one of the few sites in inland Connecticut that is better known for birding in the winter than at any other time of year. In large part, this is due to the presence in recent years of ravens, several bald eagles and up to three golden eagles, all seen soaring near the cliffs at the western end of Canaan Mountain, and best seen from Under Mountain Road. Cooper's hawk, goshawk, rough-legged hawk and northern shrike have all been seen during recent winters. Also in winter, conifers in forests on the plateau offer lots of winter finch potential, and the thickets and edges in the valleys usually have lingering fruit- and seed-eaters.

GETTING AROUND
Birding methods: CAR, WALK.
The route discussed below that goes through the valleys of the Blackberry and Hollenbeck Rivers uses state and town roads that are well maintained and have occasional places to pull off for birding. The route over the plateau uses small town roads that are partly paved, partly dirt, but almost always in good condition for use by autos. In addition, these same roads can be birded on foot - Routes 44, 7 and 63 carry frequent through traffic, but all of the other roads are lightly used by local traffic. Most of the land on either side of the roads is private, but the roads themselves provide opportunities for fine birding. A scope is helpful for looking at water birds on Wangum Lake and raptors at the western cliffs.

DIRECTIONS: Map 30 shows the auto roads that go around and across Canaan Mountain. The directions that follow suggest a route that follows the valleys along the northern and western sides of the Canaan Mountain Range, and also goes up and over the range. These roads can be linked in a number of ways to make a birding trip; each road segment is described separately, so that you can make up your own route.

The starting point is the Norfolk Village Green, at the southern intersection of Routes 44 and 272.

Route 44: the valley of the Blackberry River. From the Norfolk Village Green, go west on Route 44 for 7.3 miles to the intersection of Routes 44 and 7 in Canaan. During this stretch Route 44 goes parallel to the Blackberry River along its valley, and provides broad views of the farmland in the valley, and of the steep northern side of Canaan Mountain.

Lower Road: the valley of the Blackberry River, (a variation of the above). Westbound on Route 44, 5.0 miles west of the Norfolk Village Green, turn left (south) on Lower Road for 2.6 miles to its intersection with Route 7 just south of the Route 7/Route 44 intersection. For much of its length, Lower Road is close to the shrubby and wooded streambelt of the Blackberry River, and goes past a mix of tilled, mowed and reverting fields, shrubby thickets, wooded areas, and interfaces among these habitat types.

Route 7: Robbins Swamp, Wangum Brook wetland. At the intersection of Routes 7 and 44 in Canaan, go south on Route 7 for 4.6 miles to the intersection of Routes 7 and 63. As you go south on Route 7, the cliffs and rocky hillside of Canaan Mountain are on the left, and a hardwood swamp along the eastern edge of the Robbins Swamp Wildlife Management Area is on the right (see site description of Robbins Swamp under Canaan/North Canaan). Route 7 then passes through active and reverting farmland and drops down to the Wangum Brook wetland, a large marsh and swamp complex.

Route 63: the valley of the Hollenbeck River. At the intersection of Routes 63 and 7, bear left on Route 63 for 4.9 miles to the intersection of Routes 63 and 43. As you go south on Route 63, the Hollenbeck River and its wooded and shrubby streambelt is on the right, as well as a cattail marsh. As you proceed south, Route 63 passes just about every type of open and edge habitat, from tilled fields to reverting pastures that have been invaded by cedar, white pine and other forest pioneer tree species. There is an abundance of thickets and shrubby edges. The steep western side of Canaan Mountain is visible on the left (but more easily seen driving north - see below).

Under Mountain Road: the western cliffs of Canaan Mountain. When you reach the intersection of Routes 63 and 43, turn around and go back north up Route 63 for 1.1 miles, and turn right on Under Mountain Road. As you go north on Under Mountain Road, you get excellent views of the western cliffs of Canaan Mountain, especially at 0.4 mile, where there is a cemetery on the right. In winter, scan the mountainside for raven, bald eagle and golden eagle. Under Mountain Road also passes through active and reverting farmland, forest (mostly hardwoods), and rocky hillsides. In addition, it is how you get to the three roads described in the following paragraphs: Cobble Road, Canaan Mountain Road and Barnes Road. If you follow Under Mountain Road for all of its 4.8 mile length, you end up back at Route 7.

Cobble Road goes left from Undermountain Road 1.4 miles from the Undermountain Road / Route 63 intersection, and runs for 1.1 miles between Under Mountain Road and Route 63. It crosses the Hollenbeck River, passes a marsh and farm pond, goes through farmland and across a power line, and provides a panoramic view of the western end of Canaan Mountain. Look from Cobble Road in spring and summer for kestrel, meadowlark and bobolink.

Barnes Road goes left from Undermountain Road at a point 3.3 miles north of the Undermountain Road/Route 63 intersection, and runs for 1.6 miles between Under Mountain Road and Route 63. It passes through farmland and a wetland including wet meadow habitat, where snipe has occurred in migration, and woodcock has nested.

Canaan Mountain Road/Steep Road/Wangum Road/Mountain Road. This sequence of country roads goes right over the Canaan Mountain Range, running for just over seven miles between Under Mountain Road and the Norfolk Village Green where this trip started. From Under Mountain Road, at a point 1.7 miles north of the intersection of Under Mountain Road and Route 63, turn east (right) on Canaan Mountain Road. It climbs up the western side of Canaan Mountain range, following the side of a ravine, gaining 800' in 2.5 miles to its intersection with Steep Road on the left, and Wangum Road on the right. Steep Road is short, but soon passes a wetland and the Root Cemetery, where golden-winged warbler has nested. To continue the trip, turn onto Wangum Road. During its 4.5 mile length across the plateau, this road passes another wetland, goes along the shore of Wangum Lake, through several miles of forest, passes a hardwood/hemlock swamp, becomes known as Mountain Road, and finally ends at Route 272 in Norfolk. Go north (left) on Route 272 for 0.1 mile to reach the Norfolk Village Green, the starting point of this trip.

CANAAN/NORTH CANAAN: ROBBINS SWAMP WMA/HOLLENBECK PRESERVE

HABITATS
OPEN TERRESTRIAL: tilled, tall grass, mixed herbaceous and shrubby fields, shrubby and hardwood edges, seasonal pools;
RIVER/STREAM: river, stream, shrubby and hardwood streambelts;
MARSH/SWAMP/BOG: wet meadow, shrubby hardwood swamp, hardwood swamp, white pine swamp, hemlock swamp; edges;
Forest: hardwoods, hardwoods/white pine, flood plain.

Robbins Swamp is the largest inland wetland in Connecticut, and includes a great diversity of habitats and species. It is a calcareous wetland (it lies in the Limestone Belt that extends south from Vermont); this produces an alkaline soil and results in the occurrence of uncommon and rare plant species. The habitats listed above are in a small part of this large wetland, in the area where the Hollenbeck River flows into the Housatonic River. This part of Robbins Swamp is a bottomland that includes a wide variety of habitats - woodlands, fields, streambelt habitats, swamps and other wetlands. The Robbins Swamp Wildlife Management Area includes a large part of this wetland, and consists of a number of separate parcels that have a total area of 1024 acres. The Hollenbeck Preserve is a contiguous 182-acre area that includes fields and a wooded swamp.

SEASONS/BIRDS
SPRING MIGRATION: water birds, marsh birds, shore birds LAND BIRDS;
NESTING SEASON: water birds, marsh birds, shore birds, LAND BIRDS;
FALL MIGRATION: water birds, marsh birds, shore birds, LAND BIRDS;
Winter: land birds.

The best times to visit this site are May and September. The spring migration is especially good; during that period look for water birds on the backwaters of the Housatonic and Hollenbeck Rivers - pintail, blue-winged and green-winged teal occur here on a regular basis. Marsh bird migrants include great blue and green-backed herons. Snipe occur as uncommon migrants. And there are lots of land bird migrants, including osprey, vireos, many warblers, white-throated sparrow and meadowlark. During the nesting season, look for spotted sandpiper and Virginia rail, as well as bobolink, meadowlark and bluebird in the nearby fields. This area also has a lot to offer during the fall migration, especially hawks (osprey, broad-winged, red-tailed, goshawk, kestrel and harrier), as well as sparrows (white-throated, white-crowned and Lincoln's). Pileated woodpecker is among the many all-year resident species.

GETTING AROUND
Birding methods: car, walk.

Getting about within the wetland is difficult. However, some of the habitats can be scanned from the parking area at the entrance from Route 126, and also from Routes 126 and Page Road (don't bird from Route 7 - the traffic is heavy and fast). It is also possible to walk to the back of the cornfields that lie across Route 126 from the entrance, in order to reach additional edge and wetland habitats.

DIRECTIONS (see Map 31): This part of Robbins Swamp lies about a mile north of Falls Village, along the east side of the Housatonic River. To get there from Falls Village at the intersection of Routes 126 and 7, go north (really west at this point) on Route 126 for 1.5 miles to a small parking area on the west (left) side of Route 126. The habitats described above lie on both sides of Route 126 above and below this entrance. In addition, to see the fields in the southern part of the Hollenbeck Preserve, from the intersection of Routes 7 and

Preserve lies on the right side of Page Road. (Other parcels of the Robbins Swamp Wildlife Management Area lie a short distance to the north, between Routes 126, 7 and 44, with several access points, one of which is on the west side of Route 7, 4.4 miles north of the Route 7 / Route 126 intersection.)

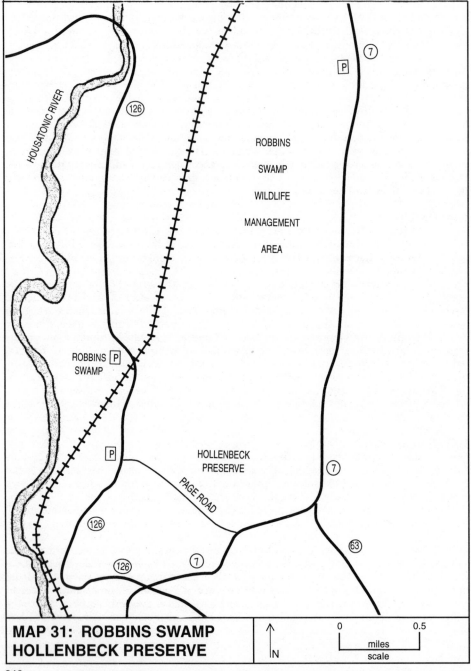

MAP 31: ROBBINS SWAMP HOLLENBECK PRESERVE

0   0.5
miles
scale

N

COLEBROOK: COLEBROOK RIVER AND GOODWIN RESERVOIRS

HABITATS

FOREST: hardwoods, hardwoods/white pine, hardwoods/hemlock, white pine, hemlock, mixed conifers; mountain laurel;

OPEN TERRESTRIAL: short grass, tall grass, mixed herbaceous and shrubby fields, reverting clearcut areas, hedgerows, shrubby and wooded edges;

LAKE/POND: lakes, deep water; wooded shore (hardwoods, white pine, hemlock, alone and in combination); shrubby shore; exposed gravel bottom, ponds, seasonal pools, a variety of shores;

River/stream: river, fast shallow water; perennial and seasonal streams; wooded streambelts (hardwoods, white pine, hemlock); hemlock ravine;

Marsh/swamp/bog: mixed herbaceous and shrub marsh, shrub swamp, shrubby hardwood/hemlock swamp, dead wood;

Other: hawk watching site, dam, ledge, rocky slope, cliff.

This vast area (1,400 acres), encloses two reservoirs (the larger Colebrook River Reservoir upstream and the smaller Goodwin/West Branch Reservoir downstream), both formed when the West Branch of the Farmington River was dammed. The shores of the reservoirs are 85% forested, 15% shrubs; in late summer the water is often drawn down enough to expose a strip of gravel bottom along the shoreline. The steep hills on both sides of both reservoirs are largely forested by various combinations of northern hardwoods, white pine and hemlock. A number of small perennial streams flows through a hemlock ravine before reaching the reservoir. Along the driveway to the Colebrook River Reservoir dam, there are also a shrub swamp, a wooded swamp, and some open areas - tall grass field, shrubby field and edges - that include many autumn olive and honeysuckle bushes. The Colebrook River Burying Ground lies near the reservoirs, and provides short grass field, hedgerow and edge habitats. Below the lower dam there is a section of the West Branch of the Farmington River, with shallow water, riffles and rapids, and a shrubby and wooded streambelt. The Wilderness Area is a remote area on the east side of the Colebrook River Reservoir that is forested by hardwoods, white pine and hemlock, and includes a fast water stream that goes through a hemlock ravine.

SEASONS/BIRDS

SPRING MIGRATION: water birds, marsh birds, shore birds, LAND BIRDS;

NESTING SEASON: water birds, marsh birds, shore birds, LAND BIRDS;

FALL MIGRATION: water birds, marsh birds, shore birds, LAND BIRDS;

Winter: water birds, land birds.

This large area is a great place to bird at any time of year. The northern vegetation, plus the large areas of undisturbed habitat cause the bird species list to read more like something from northern New England than from Connecticut.

The spring migration is excellent. Water birds that occur with some regularity (but in low numbers) on the reservoirs early in the spring include common loon, horned grebe, bufflehead, goldeneye, ring-necked duck, and common merganser. Later, species that start to arrive or to move through include: great blue and green-backed herons, killdeer, spotted and solitary sandpipers, osprey, many warblers and a host of other land bird species.

Birds that nest somewhere within this area include many of the standard species for Connecticut, plus: hooded merganser, common merganser, great blue heron, goshawk, barred owl, raven, kingfisher, pileated woodpecker, yellow-bellied sapsucker, brown creeper, Acadian flycatcher (in the hemlock ravine), various swallows including cliff swallow (at the dam), hermit thrush, yellow-throated, warbling and solitary vireos, Nashville, magnolia, yellow-rumped, black-throated green, black-throated blue and Canada warblers, Louisiana waterthrush, junco, swamp sparrow and purple finch. Common loon and Swainson's thrush have been seen here in summer, but are considered as only possible nesters.

In many respects, the fall migration is a replay of spring, but with some additions. In years when the water level in the reservoirs is low in late August and September, both yellowlegs, pectoral and least sandpipers have all been seen feeding on the exposed strip of bottom along the shoreline. Also during the early fall, many warblers, swallows, osprey and other land birds pass through. In September, the dam provides a good place from which to watch hawks migrating down this valley. Later, berries and seeds on the shrubs attract robin, hermit thrush, bluebird, cedar waxwing and a variety of sparrows. In October and November, a fairly good variety of water birds pass through, but in relatively low numbers.

In winter, this is a good area in which to look for red-breasted nuthatch, golden-crowned kinglet, brown creeper, and in some years, winter finches. Bald eagle is in the area all year, but is most evident in winter. When the water is not ice-covered, water birds may be present.

GETTING AROUND
Birding methods: CAR, WALK, BIKE, SKI.
Much of this large area can be reached by car, but some of the roads are rough, and several not maintained in winter. In addition, much of the area cannot be reached by auto roads. However, there are many woods roads and trails that provide wonderful birding on foot.

DIRECTIONS (see Map 32): This area occupies the northeast corner of Litchfield County, and is five or six miles north of Winsted.

To get to the Colebrook River Burying Ground, Arnold Park, the Goodwin Reservoir Dam and a free-flowing section of the West Branch of the Farmington River, from Winsted at the western intersection of Routes 8 and 44, go north on Route 8 for 4.5 miles, right on Eno Hill Road for 0.5 mile to the intersection with Durst Road. The entrance to the Colebrook River Burying Ground and Arnold Park is a pull-off on the left. To reach the Goodwin Dam, go left on Durst Road for 0.9 mile (with good birding along several trails that the road passes). The overlook at the dam provides a spectacular view of the valley of the West Branch of the Farmington River. To go through that valley, continue across the Goodwin Dam, and turn right on Hogback Road. This road runs beside the river, and in 1.4 miles intersects with Route 20 at Riverton. (Note: you can easily enter the Tunxis State Forest site, described under Hartland in Hartford County, from Hogback Road.)

To get to the pond, marsh and swamp, as well as the shrub swamp, wooded swamp and the Colebrook River Reservoir Dam, start at the same place as above (in Winsted at the western intersection of Routes 8 and 44), go north on Route 8 for 5.6 miles (1.1 miles past Eno Hill Road), right on the dam driveway for 1.1 miles to the dam. On the way in, you pass the pond, marsh and swamp on the left. (This driveway is closed to cars on weekends, but open during the week; when it is closed, park in the area provided on Route 8. The driveway can be walked anytime.)

To get to the boat landing on the shore of the reservoir, continue north on Route 8 for another 1.5 miles to the boat landing driveway and parking area on the right.

To get to the hemlock ravine, continue north on Route 8 for another 0.1 mile, to Beech Hill Road on the left. This road (officially closed from December to May and rough at any time) follows the edge of the ravine for 1.2 miles.

To pass by more northern hardwood/white pine/hemlock forest, continue north on Route 8 for another 1.8 miles through this forest to a parking area in Massachusetts.

To get to the wilderness area on the east side of the Colebrook River Reservoir, (not shown on Map 32), continue north on Route 8 for another 3.7 miles (a total distance of 12.7 miles from the starting point in Winsted at the western intersection of Routes 8 and 44); right (east) on Route 57 for 2.9 miles, right on Burt Hill Road for 2.9 miles to Colebrook River Road; at this intersection, continue straight (south) for another 0.7 mile to the Massachusetts/Connecticut state line, at which point there is a parking area, a barway and a woods road that leads straight ahead into the wilderness area of MDC land on the east side of the Colebrook Reservoir. These roads split and go in several directions, so a compass and topo map are important to have with you.

CORNWALL: FURNACE BROOK

HABITATS
RIVER/STREAM: stream, fast, shallow water; streambelt of hardwoods/hemlock and hemlock;
Forest: hardwoods/hemlock;
This is a classic little mountain brook, with a steady drop and fast, shallow water. The shore is composed largely of mature hemlock, with branches that overhang and shade the stream.

SEASONS/BIRDS
Spring migration: land birds;
Nesting season: land birds;
Fall migration: land birds;
Winter: land birds.
This stream has a distinctly northern quality, and that is reflected in the bird species that occur here. Nesters include solitary and yellow-throated vireos, black-throated green warbler and other northern forest-dwellers. It looks like ideal habitat for Louisiana waterthrush and Acadian flycatcher, and in fact both species nest near the stream. The spring migration is especially good; May and June are the best months.

GETTING AROUND
Birding methods: car.
Route 4 goes right along this stream, and there are several places to park. This makes it ideal for birders with limited mobility, but there are drawbacks. The traffic on the highway is fast and frequent; between the road noise and that of the stream itself, birding by ear is difficult. This site is best visited early in the morning when there are fewer cars using Route 4.

DIRECTIONS: This site is just north of the center of Cornwall Bridge (that is where Route 7 and 4 cross the Housatonic River, and is not the covered bridge, which is in West Cornwall). From the eastern intersection of Routes 4 and 7, go east on Route 4 for 0.1 mile. Starting at this point, and continuing for the next two miles, Route 4 runs next to Furnace Brook.

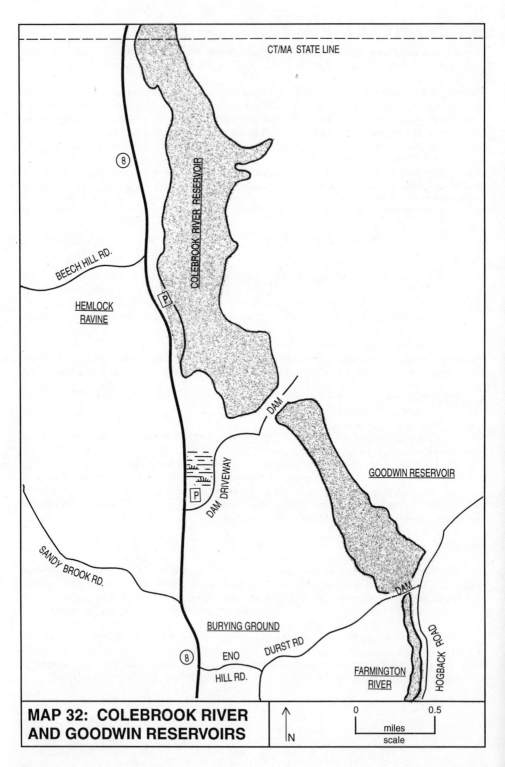

CT/MA STATE LINE

⑧

COLEBROOK RIVER RESERVOIR

BEECH HILL RD.

HEMLOCK
RAVINE

P

DAM

DAM DRIVEWAY

P

GOODWIN RESERVOIR

SANDY BROOK RD.

BURYING GROUND

DURST RD

⑧

ENO

HILL RD.

FARMINGTON
RIVER

HOGBACK ROAD

DAM

**MAP 32: COLEBROOK RIVER
AND GOODWIN RESERVOIRS**

↑
N

0   0.5
miles
scale

CORNWALL: HOLLENBECK WETLANDS

HABITATS
MARSH/SWAMP/BOG: cattail, sedge, mixed herbaceous and shrub marshes; shrub swamp, shrubby hardwood swamp, hardwood, white pine and hemlock swamps; dead wood;
Forest: hardwoods, white pine and hemlock in various combinations;
Open terrestrial: short grass, tall grass and shrubby fields; shrubby edges;
Lake/pond: pond, grassy shore;
River/stream: stream, slow and fast water, herbaceous, shrubby and wooded streambelt.
This wetland system is associated with the headwaters of the Hollenbeck River, and is extraordinary in its extent and variety. Almost the entire spectrum of Connecticut inland wetland types lies on either side of a five mile stretch of highway. Included among these types are white pine swamp and hemlock swamp, both of which are uncommon in Connecticut. The streambelt passes through farmland with hay fields and pastures.

SEASONS/BIRDS
SPRING MIGRATION: water birds, MARSH BIRDS, shore birds, LAND BIRDS;
NESTING SEASON: water birds, MARSH BIRDS, shore birds, LAND BIRDS;
FALL MIGRATION: water birds, MARSH BIRDS, shore birds, LAND BIRDS;
Winter: land birds.
A very satisfying variety and abundance of wetland-oriented bird species occurs in this riverine/wetland system. The spring and fall migrations are both very good, with a nice variety of land birds that includes olive-sided flycatcher. One plus in the spring is the arrival of many of the species that stay to nest - including American bittern (a probable nester), Virginia rail and green-backed heron. There are also many yellow warblers and swamp sparrows, as well as least flycatcher. The fall migration brings a return of the spring species, plus, in the late fall, many berry-eating species such as robin, cedar waxwing and hermit thrush. Winter offers some interesting possibilities - northern shrike, rough-legged hawk and golden eagle have all been seen here in recent years. Raven is present all year.

GETTING AROUND
Birding methods: car, walk.
The logistics of birding at this site are not ideal. The wetland system lies along Route 43, and while the traffic is not heavy, those who use it seem bent on reaching their destinations quickly. The road shoulder is narrow, and there are very few good places to pull off. There is one good viewing place, however, on Johnson Road; it is little traveled, and overlooks a section of the wetland. You could park there, and walk Route 43.

DIRECTIONS: This site lies in Cornwall, about ten miles west of Torrington. Start at the intersection of Routes 43 and 4, and follow Route 43 north. Most of the wetlands are on the east (right) side of the road. Johnson Road joins Route 43 from the east 0.5 mile north of the Route 43/Route 4 intersection.

CORNWALL/GOSHEN: HART POND WILDLIFE MANAGEMENT AREA

HABITATS

MARSH, SWAMP, BOG: sedge, cattail, mixed herbaceous and shrub marsh; shrub swamp, tall grass, shrubby and wooded edges;

LAKE/POND: pond; wetland, grassy, shrubby and wooded shore;

Open terrestrial: short grass, tall grass and shrubby fields, shrubby edges;

Forest: hardwoods, wooded edges.

This is a pond that lies in farm country. The pond itself and its associated marshes are the attraction at this site. One side of the pond grades into pasture. There are patches of hardwoods together with shubbby / hardwoods hedgerows among the surrounding fields.

SEASONS/BIRDS

SPRING MIGRATION: water birds, MARSH BIRDS, shore birds, LAND BIRDS,

NESTING SEASON: water birds, MARSH BIRDS, LAND BIRDS,

FALL MIGRATION: water birds, marsh birds, LAND BIRDS,

Winter: land birds.

The pond at this site is really great, although only visible from a couple of places. Spring and early summer are the best times. During the spring and fall migrations, land birds move along the edges of the wetland as they feed. Nesting species include a few water birds: pied-billed grebe, Canada goose, mallard, wood duck and hooded merganser. Nesting marsh birds include both least and American bitterns, Virginia rail, sora and moorhen; great blue heron nests somewhere else and comes here to feed. There are lots of nesting land birds - all of the species you would expect plus several woodpeckers (yellow-bellied sapsucker, pileated, downy and hairy), kestrel, both alder and willow flycatchers, northern waterthrush, and, just west of the management area, golden-winged warbler.

GETTING AROUND

Birding methods: car, walk.

There are not many options for viewing the pond, but from those that there are, you can see and hear a lot. You can stop on the town road that runs past the pond at two places from which the pond and its shore can be seen. In addition, you can walk (don't try to drive it!) on Seeley road that runs in back (southwest) of the pond.

DIRECTIONS: This site is in the southeast part of Cornwall, very near the corner of Cornwall, Goshen, Warren and Litchfield. To get there from the center of Litchfield at the intersection of Routes 202 and 63, go west on Route 202 for 0.8 mile, right on Milton Road for 5.4 miles, and bear left on Seeley Road. Hart Pond becomes visible in 0.7 mile. The dirt road (Seely Road) that runs behind (southeast of) the pond can be reached by turning left just before the pond, or by going past the pond and going left on South Road for 0.5 mile.

CORNWALL/GOSHEN: MOHAWK STATE FOREST

HABITATS

FOREST: hardwoods, hardwoods/white pine, hardwoods/hemlock, white pine/hemlock, white pine, hemlock, mixed conifers, mountain laurel;

MARSH/SWAMP/BOG: black spruce bog, shrub, shrubby hardwood and hardwood swamps, dead wood;

Open terrestrial: short grass, tall grass and shrubby fields, various edges;

Lake/pond: ponds, with wetland, grassy, shrubby and wooded shores; seasonal pools;

River/stream: numerous perennial and seasonal streams with wooded streambelts;

Other: hawk watching site (tower), rocky slopes, ledges and rock outcrops.

Mohawk State Forest's 3,505 acres includes virtually every type of inland terrestrial habitat found in Connecticut. The country is mountainous, and has elevations that reach over 1,600 feet above sea level. Most of its area is wooded, much of it with forest communities typical of northern New England, including a black spruce bog in a late stage of succession. There is also a variety of successional communities under active forest management - clearcutting, hardwood thinning and replanting, as well as a power line right-of-way. Throughout the forest, there are little pockets of shrubby and wooded swamp. Mohawk Mountain has a tower on the summit with a view in all directions.

SEASONS/BIRDS

SPRING MIGRATION: LAND BIRDS;

NESTING SEASON: LAND BIRDS;

FALL MIGRATION: LAND BIRDS;

Winter: land birds

The large expanses of relatively undisturbed forest and the variety of woodland habitat types make this a good area for forest-interior land bird species. The spring migration is exceptional - every Connecticut birder should plan a visit during May when it is possible to see 28 warbler species, including bay-breasted, Cape May and mourning. Many other land birds, such as yellow-bellied flycatcher, Swainson's thrush and Lincoln's sparrow, regularly occur as spring migrants. Come back during June and July, because 120 species have exhibited breeding behavior in Mohawk State Forest, placing it fourth in the state - not far behind White Memorial, Nepaug Reservoir and Barkhamsted Reservoir. A number of the nesting species are northerners: goshawk, saw-whet owl, yellow-bellied sapsucker, golden-crowned kinglet, hermit thrush, solitary vireo, Blackburnian and black-throated green warbler, black-throated blue warbler (there are lots of them!) and Canada warbler, both of the latter species in areas of mountain laurel. In 1990, yellow-bellied flycatcher, mourning warbler and white-winged crossbill all exhibited breeding behavior at or near the black spruce bog (none have been confirmed as nesters). The fall migration is also very good, and similar to that in the spring. Winter is a good time (in some years) to see such visitors as pine siskin, redpoll, white-winged and red crossbills.

GETTING AROUND

Birding methods: CAR, WALK, BIKE, SKI.

Several country roads go through or alongside the forest. In addition, there are numerous trails through the forest, including the blue-blazed Mohawk Trail, so that much of it can be seen by car or by relatively easy walking. The auto roads are not maintained in winter. Unlike many state forests, hunting is not allowed.

DIRECTIONS (see Map 33): This state forest straddles the Cornwall/Goshen town line, in the southern half of both towns. It is irregular in shape, longer north/south than it is wide east/west. The following route goes through most of the forest through good habitats and past numerous woods roads and trails.

1. From the village of Cornwall, at the intersection of Routes 128, 4 and 43, go east on Route 4 for 1.3 miles to Toumey Road and the entrance to the state forest on the right. A trail on the left of Route 4 can be walked a short distance to the top of Red Mountain.

2. Go south (right) on Toumey Road (the right fork as you start out) for 1.4 miles to the intersection with Mohawk Mountain Road. This stretch of road passes through good mixed hardwoods/white pine habitat and several woods roads and trails.

3. At the intersection of Toumey and Mohawk Mountain Roads (see 2 above), turn right (west) on Mohawk Mountain Road and go for 1.3 miles through good woodland habitat and shrubby fields to the lookout tower at the top of Mohawk Mountain. This location can be used for hawk watching during the fall migration. There are other lookouts and several trails along the way.

4. From the intersection of Toumey Road and Mohawk Mountain Road (see 2 above), go left (east) on Mohawk Mountain Road for 0.2 mile to the intersection with Wadhams Road. One trail leads left from Mohawk Mountain Road at this intersection to the black spruce bog. Another leads to a pond/swamp complex and shrubby fields/clearcut areas.

5. From the intersection of Mohawk Mountain and Wadhams Roads (see 4 above), Wadhams Road goes south for 2.9 miles to the junction with Eli Bunker Road. At the time of writing, Wadhams Road was barred to autos but could be walked or skied past a number of trails and more wetlands.

6. From the intersection of Mohawk Mountain and Wadhams Roads, (see 4 above), continue east on Mohawk Mountain Road for 0.4 mile to a spruce stand. From this point, it is possible to reach Route 4 by continuing east on Mohawk Mountain Road; this road leaves the state forest in 0.7 mile, becomes Allyn Road and goes through farm country with short and tall grass fields before intersecting with Route 4 at a point 2.5 miles east of the intersection of Routes 4, 43 and 128, where the trip started.

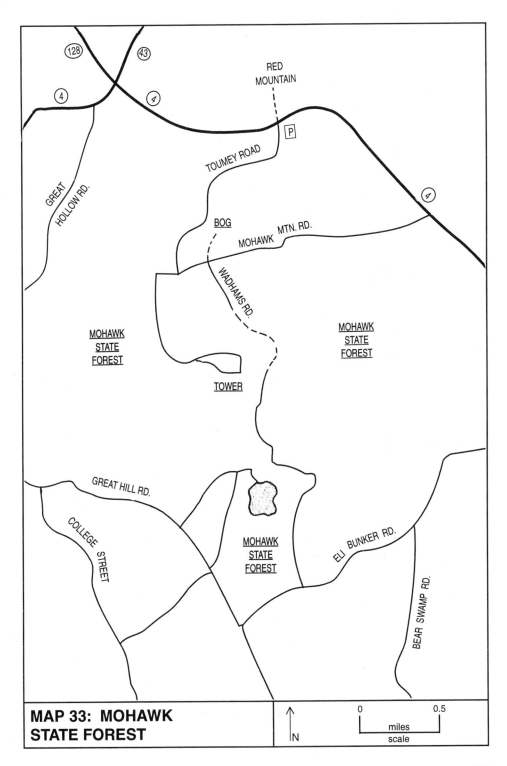

MAP 33: MOHAWK STATE FOREST

GOSHEN: EAST STREET NORTH

HABITATS
MARSH/SWAMP/BOG: shrub swamp, shrubby hardwood swamp, hardwood swamp, dead trees;
Forest: hardwoods, hardwoods/white pine, hardwoods/hemlock, white pine, mixed conifers;
Open terrestrial: short grass, tall grass and shrubby fields, shrubby and hardwood edges;
Lake/pond: a large pond with herbacous, shrubby, hardwood and conifer shore; a smaller beaver pond with shrubby and hardwood shore.

A town road passes by several swamps and two ponds, as well as open terrestrial habitats associated with small farms and a clear-cutting operation. Many berry-producing shrubs occur along the edges of the road.

SEASONS/BIRDS
SPRING MIGRATION: water birds, marsh birds, shore birds, LAND BIRDS;
NESTING SEASON: water birds, marsh birds, LAND BIRDS;
FALL MIGRATION: water birds, marsh birds, shore birds, LAND BIRDS;
Winter: land birds.

There is almost always something to look for among the various habitats at this site. The spring and fall migrations are quite good, and can be enjoyed by walking along the road. The pond near the northern end of the road almost always has some water bird migrants in March and November, and great blue and green-backed herons in the spring, summer and fall. During the nesting season, it is possible to look down on several small wetlands from the road, and observe life in a marsh. At this time, there is an abundance of yellow and chestnut-sided warblers, as well as indigo bunting, least, alder and willow flycatchers, and hooded merganser. In late fall and winter, the shrubs and crabapple trees along the road provide a good source of food for cedar waxwing, robin and other frugivores. In winter, look for cross-bills in the pines, and for pine grosbeak in the crabapples. One year there were Bohemian waxwings among the cedar waxwings, also feeding on the crabapples.

GETTING AROUND
Birding methods: CAR, WALK, BIKE.

All of these habitats can be seen from a car. It is possible, in fact necessary, to bird this area from the town road, since the surrounding land is private. The road is not heavily used, and is a pleasant walk.

DIRECTIONS: This stretch of road lies five to ten miles northwest of Torrington. In Torrington at the intersection of Routes 4 and 8, go west on Route 4 for 5.0 miles and turn right on East Street North. This road continues north for several miles and passes by the habitats described above until it intersects with Route 272 north of Torrington.

GOSHEN: LONG SWAMP

HABITATS

MARSH/SWAMP/BOG: wet meadow, sedge, cattail and shrub marsh, wooded edge, dead trees.
Lake/pond: pond;
River/stream: stream, mixed herbaceous streambelt;
Forest: hardwoods/white pine;
Open terrestrial: short grass field, shrubby edge.

At this site, a small stream meanders through a marsh of varied composition, and feeds a small pond within the marsh. Nearby is the edge of a wooded area. This wetland is an extraordinarily rich habitat.

SEASONS/BIRDS

SPRING MIGRATION: water birds, MARSH BIRDS, shore birds, LAND BIRDS;
NESTING SEASON: water birds, MARSH BIRDS, shore birds, LAND BIRDS;
FALL MIGRATION: water birds, marsh birds, shore birds, LAND BIRDS;
Winter: land birds.

A wide diversity of species have been seen at this wetland. The spring migration brings all of the edge and wetland-oriented species you would expect, plus usually a few surprises, such as snipe, seen here in April a number of times. During the nesting season, it is not unusual to see moorhen, Virginia rail and sora. King rail has also occurred here, along with least and American bitterns. Great blue and green-backed herons come in to feed. Among the land bird species usually seen are swamp sparrow and five flycatchers: willow, alder, great crested, least and kingbird. In addition, a variety of other land birds come in from nearby upland habitats to feed at the edges of the wetland. The fall migration is good too, but more oriented toward land birds, especially sparrows. In winter, there are the usual residents, plus the possibility of harrier, rough-legged hawk, northern shrike and common redpoll.

GETTING AROUND:

Birding methods: CAR, walk, bike.

The marsh can be viewed from a quiet town road (a nice contrast to the wetland at nearby Peat Swamp). Do not leave the road - all the land around it is private property.

DIRECTIONS: Long Swamp is located in Goshen, about five miles northwest of Torrington. From Goshen at the intersection of Routes 4 and 63, go south on Route 63 for 1.4 miles, and right on Nielsen Road for 0.2 mile to the wetland.

GOSHEN: PEAT SWAMP

HABITATS

MARSH/SWAMP/BOG: sedge, cattail and shrub marsh, deadwood swamp, shrubby and wooded edge.

This is a varied wetland, most notable for the standing dead white pines in it.

SEASONS/BIRDS

SPRING MIGRATION: water birds, MARSH BIRDS, shore birds, land birds;
NESTING SEASON: water birds, MARSH BIRDS, land birds;
FALL MIGRATION: water birds, MARSH BIRDS, shore birds, land birds;

Winter: land birds.

Some uncommon species have occurred at this wetland. During the spring, in addition to the migrants that you would expect, olive-sided flycatcher has been seen. During the nesting season, Virginia rail, sora, and American bittern have occurred here. The only confirmed nesting of sedge wren in Connecticut occurred in this marsh. Both alder and willow flycatchers nest here on a regular basis.

GETTING AROUND
Birding methods: car.

This wetland can be viewed from Route 4. Do not leave the road (the surrounding land is private), but be careful of the heavy, fast and noisy traffic. The only hope of avoiding this unpleasantness is to bird very early in the morning.

DIRECTIONS: Peat Swamp is located in Goshen, about five miles northwest of Torrington. From the intersection of Routes 4 and 63, go west on Route 4 for 0.7 mile, at which point the wetland is visible on both sides of the road.

GOSHEN: TYLER LAKE

HABITATS
Lake/pond: lake, deep water, shallow water, shore of hardwoods, shrub marsh and residential development;
Marsh/swamp/bog: small mixed herbaceous and shrub marsh.

This is a fairly large lake with a shoreline that is partly developed with second homes, partly undeveloped and covered by shrubs and young hardwood forest. On the north shore, directly across the lake from the one public access, there is a nice wetland.

SEASONS/BIRDS
Spring migration: water birds, marsh birds, land birds;
Nesting season: water birds, marsh birds, land birds;
Fall migration: water birds, marsh birds, land birds;
Winter: land birds.

There are often some water birds on the lake in November and again in late March. The number is usually not great, nor is the species variety predictable, but over the years, some interesting species have been seen here: common loon, pied-billed and horned grebes, ring-necked duck, common goldeneye, bufflehead, black scoter, canvasback, common and hooded mergansers and coot. During the spring, summer and early fall, the marsh across the lake is likely to have green-backed heron, Virginia rail, marsh wren, swamp sparrow and wood duck. In winter, if there is open water, bald eagle is sometimes present.

GETTING AROUND:
Birding methods: car, boat.

There is only one public access and viewpoint - the state launching area, from which most of the open water of the lake can be seen, with the aid of a spotting scope. However, the marsh across the lake is too far away to be seen well from the landing - for that, a boat is necessary.

DIRECTIONS: Tyler Lake is located in Goshen, about eight miles northwest of Torrington. From the intersection of Routes 4 and 63, go west on Route 4 for 2.9 miles, and right on

Dohren Drive for 0.2 mile to the state boat launch on the shore of the lake.

HARWINTON: HARWINTON CONSERVATION AREA

HABITATS
River/stream: stream, fast water, slow water, shrubby and wooded streambelt;
Forest: hardwoods, hardwoods/white pine, hardwoods/hemlock, cedar;
Lake/pond: pond, grassy, shrubby and wooded shore;
Open terrestrial: short grass and shrubby field, edge.
This area includes the streambelt of Leadmine Brook and contains a rich variety of habitats. The stream is bordered by shrubs, hardwoods and white pine. Nearby there is a reverting field with scattered crabapple and cedar trees, backed by a mixed forest of hardwoods, white pine and hemlock.

SEASONS/BIRDS
SPRING MIGRATION: LAND BIRDS;
NESTING SEASON: LAND BIRDS;
FALL MIGRATION: LAND BIRDS;
Winter: land birds.
A wide variety of both nesting and migrating land birds have been seen in this area. One hundred nine species are confirmed or probable nesters at this site; the group includes northerners as well as a variety of standard Connecticut breeders. Among the nesters are 12 species of warbler, blue-gray gnatcatcher, yellow-throated vireo, pileated woodpecker, Cooper's and red-shouldered hawks, great horned and barred owls. The most memorable impression of a visit here during the nesting season is the large number of redstarts, chestnut-sided and blue-winged warblers. During migration, most of the warbler species that occur in Connecticut can be seen here. In some winters, pine grosbeaks can be seen feeding in the crabapple trees.

GETTING AROUND:
Birding methods: WALK.
There are three trails within the area that make loops of a half mile or more.

DIRECTIONS: This area is in Harwinton, about three miles southeast of Torrington. To get there from Route 8 exit 42, go east on Route 118 for 2.6 miles. The entrance to the area is on the right side of Route 118 at its intersection with Route 4.

HARWINTON: KALMIA SANCTUARY

HABITATS
Forest: hardwoods, hardwoods/white pine, hardwoods/hemlock, white pine, mixed conifers, sand plain, mountain laurel;
Open terrestrial: short grass field, shrubby and wooded edge, apple orchard;
Lake/pond: ponds, shallow water, shrubby island, shores of shrub marsh, shrubs and woods;
Marsh/swamp/bog: mixed herbaceous and shrub marsh, shrub swamp;
River/stream: perennial stream, wooded streambelt.
There are really four parts to this site: the two ponds that you pass on the way to the Kalmia Sanctuary, the sanctuary itself, and the dirt section of Laurel Road that is past the sanctuary entrance.

Bull Pond is shallow, has large areas of emergent plants, a shore that is partly marshy and swampy, partly wooded and partly developed.

Wilson Pond has a shrubby island, a shore that is wooded with areas of shrub marsh and shrubs. There is a wetland across the road composed of mixed herbaceous and shrub marsh. The surrounding forest includes hardwoods, white pine and hemlock in various combinations, and areas of sand plain.

The Kalmia Sanctuary includes an open field, an apple orchard, and a forest of hardwoods, white pine, hemlock and extensive areas of mountain laurel (hence the name of the sanctuary, from Kalmia latifolia).

Laurel Road is surrounded by a forest of similar composition.

SEASONS/BIRDS
> **SPRING MIGRATION:** water birds, marsh birds, LAND BIRDS;
> **Nesting Season:** water birds, marsh birds, land birds;
> **FALL MIGRATION:** water birds, marsh birds, LAND BIRDS;
> **Winter:** land birds.

A nice variety of warblers and other land birds pass through the habitats in this area during the spring and fall migrations. Water bird migrants include pied-billed grebe, wood duck, ring-necked duck, hooded and common mergansers and coot. Great blue and green-backed herons are present during the spring and summer, and are joined by great egret in the late summer and fall. Nesting species of land birds include such northerners as yellow-bellied sapsucker, solitary vireo, black-throated green, yellow-rumped and black-throated blue warblers.

GETTING AROUND
> **Birding methods:** car, WALK.

Parts of both Bull Pond and Wilson Pond can be seen from near your car. There is a loop trail through the Kalmia Preserve, and you can walk along the edges of the field. You can also get good birding by walking on down Laurel Road past the parking area. (The land on either side of this part of Laurel Road is private.) Check in with the Kalmia Sanctuary caretaker before you enter (his house is on Laurel Road opposite the parking area).

DIRECTIONS: This preserve is in Harwinton, about five miles southeast of Torrington. From the intersection of Routes 4 and 118, go east on Route 4 for 1.1 miles, right on Locust Road for 1.6 miles to Bull Pond and the Bull Pond Sanctuary on the right. In another 0.2 mile, bear left at a fork in order to stay on Locust Road. After going on Locust Road for a total of 2.7 miles, go straight (rightish) on Laurel Road for 0.4 mile to Wilson Pond on right. Then continue on Laurel Road for another 0.5 mile (a total of 0.9 mile from the intersection of Locust and Laurel Roads) to a small parking area on the left, opposite the Kalmia Sanctuary on the right. (It is OK to park here, in spite of the "no parking" sign.)

HARWINTON: RORABACK WILDLIFE MANAGEMENT AREA

HABITATS
OPEN TERRESTRIAL: tilled, short grass, tall grass and shrubby fields; edges;
FOREST: hardwoods, hardwoods/white pine, hardwoods/hemlock, white pine, hemlock, sand plain;
River/stream: perennial stream, fast water, seasonal streams, wooded streambelts;
Marsh/swamp/bog: hardwood swamp;
Lake/pond: seasonal pools.
This 2,222-acre wildlife area is predominently wooded upland habitat, with scattered wetlands in the form of small pockets of hardwood swamp among the woods.

SEASONS/BIRDS
SPRING MIGRATION: LAND BIRDS;
NESTING SEASON: LAND BIRDS;
FALL MIGRATION: LAND BIRDS;
Winter: land birds.
This is an excellent site in which to look for forest-dwelling land birds, both in migration and during the nesting season. The roads that go through the area create avenues along which migrants travel. The relatively high elevation of this inland forest seems to attract a variety of northern species. Among the 103 species believed to nest in the area are: yellow-bellied sapsucker, red-breasted nuthatch, brown creeper, hermit thrush, solitary vireo, yellow-rumped, black-throated green and black-throated blue warblers; also, Cooper's, red-tailed, broad-winged and red-shouldered hawks, great horned and barred owls, whip-poor-will and pine warbler.

GETTING AROUND
Birding methods: car, walk.
South Road and Plymouth Road both go through good habitat, are lightly travelled, and are good for birding by car or on foot. In addition, there is a network of trails that go through most parts of the area. Hunting is permitted.

DIRECTIONS: This site is in Harwinton, about five miles southeast of Torrington. To go through the site on South Road, from the intersection of Routes 4 and 118, go east on Route 4 for 0.4 mile, and right on South Road. Starting in 1.7 miles and continuing for 1.8 miles, South Road goes through the wildlife area, and past trails that go into it. To go through the site on Plymouth Road, starting again back at the intersection of Routes 4 and 118, go east on Route 4 for 1.1 miles, right on Locust Road for 0.8 mile, and right (straight, really) on Plymouth Road. Starting in about a mile, and continuing for about a mile, Plymouth Road goes through a part of the wildlife area, and also through good habitat that is not within the site. (Stay on the road to avoid trespassing.)

HARWINTON: VALLEY ROAD

HABITATS
RIVER/STREAM: river; slow water, fast water, backwater areas, islands, varied streambelts - hardwood, hardwood/white pine, shrubby and herbaceous; small perennial streams, seasonal streams;
OPEN TERRESTRIAL: shrubby field, edge;
Forest: hardwoods, hardwoods/white pine;

Marsh/swamp/bog: shrub marsh, shrub swamp, shrubby hardwood swamp.
This site includes a rich variety of riverine habitats along the Naugatuck River, together with small patches of varied wetlands that are interspersed among the upland habitats.

SEASONS/BIRDS

SPRING MIGRATION: water birds, LAND BIRDS;
Nesting season: LAND BIRDS;
FALL MIGRATION: water birds, LAND BIRDS;
Winter: land birds.

This site offers good birding, especially during migration. Open- and edge-habitat species are the specialty here, especially among nesters: brown thrasher, catbird, cardinal, indigo bunting, white-eyed vireo, chestnut-sided, prairie and blue-winged warblers. In addition, kingfisher, green-backed heron and rough-winged swallow nest near the river. During the fall migration, a nice variety of sparrows can be seen.

GETTING AROUND

Birding methods: CAR, walk.

(First, read "Directions" below.) From the first barway a trail leads down to the west shore of the river, and from the second barway another trail goes along the east shore of the river. These two trails, as well as Campville and Valley Roads, and a nearby power line all lead through a rich variety of streambelt and open terrestrial habitats. Hunting is allowed. There is lots of noise from Route 8.

DIRECTIONS: This site is in Harwinton, about five miles south of Torrington. To get there from Route 8, take exit 41. **Southbound:** At the end of the exit ramp, left on Marsh Road for 0.1 mile, and left on Campville Road. Follow Campville Road (passing a barway and trail on the right at 0.6 mile), for 0.8 mile to a bridge over the Naugatuck River and the intersection with River Road. Turn left, and go 0.2 mile to a second barway at a small parking area; or, turn right and follow Valley Road along the river for 1.4 miles, in part through private property. **Northbound:** At the end of the exit ramp, go right on Campville Road and proceed as above.

KENT: BULLS BRIDGE ROAD (APPALACHIAN TRAIL)

HABITATS

RIVER/STREAM: river, slow water, fast water, streambelt of hardwoods, hardwoods/white pine, hardwoods/ hemlock;
Forest: hardwoods, hardwoods/white pine, hardwoods/hemlock.

This stretch of the Housatonic illustrates how variable this river can be - within a short distance it goes from relatively still water to rapids. The forest along its shore is equally variable - from flat flood plain to steep-sided hemlock and white pine communities.

SEASONS/BIRDS

SPRING MIGRATION: water birds, LAND BIRDS;
NESTING SEASON: LAND BIRDS;
Fall migration: water birds, land birds;
Winter: land birds.

The spring migration is best here; the whole assortment of standard land bird migrants pass up the valley, plus some water birds, primarily wood duck and hooded merganser. A nice variety of land birds nest here. The fall migration is not as good as the spring migration, and

things get pretty quiet in winter.
GETTING AROUND
Birding methods: WALK.
The Appalachian Trail provides an excellent way to bird this area on foot. It is well used and well maintained, and goes through very productive riverine habitats.

DIRECTIONS: This site is about five miles south of the village of Kent. To get there from Kent at the intersection of Routes 7 and 341, go south on Route 7 for 3.9 miles, right on Bulls Bridge Road for 0.1 mile to a parking area on the right. The Appalachian Trail goes north from this parking area; it goes south from the left side of the road 0.1 mile farther west, at another parking area.

KENT: IRON MOUNTAIN RESERVATION

HABITATS
FOREST: hardwoods, hardwoods / hemlock;
Lake/pond: pond, hardwood shore;
River/stream: two small perennial streams, many seasonal streams, wooded streambelts;
Marsh/swamp/bog: shrubby hardwood swamp, hardwood swamp.
This 257-acre preserve occupies Ore Hill, one of the many hills on the east side of the Housatonic Valley in Kent. It contains areas of rich habitat, including northern hardwood forest communities on the higher ground, together with moist bottomlands, a hardwood swamp and Irving Pond.

SEASONS/BIRDS
SPRING MIGRATION: LAND BIRDS;
NESTING SEASON: water birds, LAND BIRDS;
FALL MIGRATION: LAND BIRDS;
Winter: land birds.
The spring migration is really good for warblers and other land birds. Early in the spring, resident barred owls may be heard calling. Nesting species include wood duck, broad-winged hawk, grouse, turkey, yellow-bellied sapsucker, pileated and red-bellied woodpeckers, hermit thrush, great crested flycatcher, Louisiana waterthrush, scarlet tanager, rose-breasted grosbeak, plus many redstarts and other common species. The fall migration is also very good, during late August and September. After that, things quiet down for the winter.

GETTING AROUND
Birding methods: walk.
A trail makes a loop through the preserve and over the top of Ore Hill.

DIRECTIONS: The preserve is about five miles southeast of the village of Kent. To get there from the village center at the intersection of Routes 341 and 7, go east on Route 341 for 3.3 miles, right on South Road for 0.9 mile, left on Flat Rock Road for 0.4 mile, and right on Treasure Hill Road for 0.1 mile to the preserve entrance and parking area on the right.

KENT: KENT FALLS STATE PARK

HABITATS

RIVER/STREAM: stream, fast water, hemlock streambelt; river, hardwood streambelt;

Forest: hardwoods, white pine and hemlock, alone and in combination; flood plain;

Open terrestrial: short grass field.

This park lies on both sides of Route 7. The centerpiece of the better-known east side of the park is a hemlock ravine, through which a brook descends over a series of waterfalls. Above the ravine, there is a mature stand of hemlock and an upper-slope forest of sugar maple, white ash and chestnut oak. On the west side of the park, in back of the mowed field, there are white pines and, near the Housatonic River, a flood plain forest.

SEASONS/BIRDS

SPRING MIGRATION: LAND BIRDS;

Nesting season: LAND BIRDS;

Fall migration: land birds;

Winter: land birds.

This is a good site in which to see migrating warblers, especially along the woodland edges in May. In the spring and during the summer, a number of interesting species nest here. East of Route 7, Acadian flycatcher, winter wren and Louisiana waterthrush nest in the area of hemlocks in the ravine and hillside, and, west of Route 7, nesters include Blackburnian warbler in the white pines, and cerulean warbler in the flood plain forest near the river.

GETTING AROUND

Birding methods: car, walk.

On the east side of Route 7, the lower part of the ravine can be reached by walking 0.2 mile across the open fields of the park. The upper part of the ravine and the hill above it can be reached and birded from a dirt road, which may not be usable by car during the winter and early spring. On the west side of Route 7, it is a short walk from the parking area by Route 7 into the white pines and flood plain forest near the river. This park (especially the part east of Route 7 near the main entrance) gets crowded during warm weather; it is best to visit here in the early morning and on weekdays. An fee is charged during the period May-September for entry into the main part of the park.

DIRECTIONS: This park is located in western Connecticut near Kent.

To get to the main park entrance on the east side of Route 7, from the center of Kent at the intersection of Routes 7 and 341, go north on Route 7 for about four miles to the park entrance on the right. The lower part of the ravine and the waterfall in it are visible across the fields of the park.

To reach the upper part of the ravine from the park entrance, go south on Route 7 for 0.5 mile, left on Carter Road for 0.1 mile, and left on Dugan Road for 0.1 mile to the parking area. The upper part of the ravine is visible from here. Dugan Road continues up the hill, and from this point on, is best birded on foot.

To get to the part of the park on the west side of Route 7, from the main park entrance, go north on Route 7 for 0.2 mile to the grassy parking area on the left by the stone chimney.

KENT: MACEDONIA BROOK STATE PARK

HABITATS
RIVER/STREAM: stream, fast water, hardwoods and hemlock streambelt;
FOREST: hardwoods, hardwoods/white pine, hardwoods/
hemlock, white pine, mountain laurel;
Open terrestrial: short grass field, shrubby and wooded edges;
Marsh/swamp/bog: shrub swamp;
Other: rocky slope.

This 2,300-acre park includes four miles of a swift mountain stream (Macedonia Brook), the valley through which it flows, steep ridges along either side of the valley, and Cobble Mountain, elevation 1,390 feet. Most of the area is covered with mid- and upper-slope hardwood/conifer forest. The valley also includes a small shrub swamp, small cleared areas, and edges of shrubs and saplings.

SEASONS/BIRDS
SPRING MIGRATION: LAND BIRDS;
NESTING SEASON: LAND BIRDS;
Fall migration: land birds;
Winter: land birds.

The spring, summer and early fall are great in this park. May and June are the best months, and the best birding area is the northern portion of the park. For the spring migration, take advantage of the valley effect and look along Macedonia Brook and the park driveway beside it. In the fall, look for migrants up on the ridges and hillsides. Among the nesters, there are a number of northern species, including yellow-bellied sapsucker and solitary vireo. Look in the big white pines for nesting hermit thrush, Blackburnian and black-throated green warblers. Nesting Canada and black-throated blue warblers can be found in the mountain laurel. Louisiana waterthrush nests near Macedonia Brook and feeds along its shore. In winter, there are a few resident red-breasted nuthatches, brown creepers and chickadees.

GETTING AROUND
Birding methods: CAR, WALK.

A small road goes through the length of the park, following the brook most of the way. There is a network of trails, including a section of the Appalachian Trail. A trail map is available at the ranger building.

DIRECTIONS: This park is about two miles west of the village of Kent. To get there from the center of Kent at the intersection of Routes 341 and 7, go west on Route 341 for 1.9 miles, and right on Macedonia Brook Road for 0.8 mile to the park entrance. This road continues through the park.

KENT: RIVER ROAD (STANLEY WMA - SOUTHERN BLOCK)

HABITATS
FOREST: all types except sand plain;
OPEN TERRESTRIAL: short grass, tall grass, mixed herbaceous and shrubby fields; edges;
RIVER/STREAM: river, fast and slow water, rocks, sand and gravel bars, islands with shrubby shores; streambelt of shrubs, hardwoods, hardwoods/white pine, hardwoods/hemlock; perennial and seasonal streams, hemlock ravine;
Other: cliffs and ledges.

This site consists of a dirt road that follows the west bank of the Housatonic River for almost three miles. A narrow strip of riparian forest lies between the road and the river. The hillside west of the road consists of mid- and lower-slope deciduous forest interspersed with overgrown clearings and small hemlock ravines formed by brooks coming down the hillside. At the end of the road, there is an area of overgrown fields and shrubby edges, surrounded by white pine and mixed conifer forest.

SEASONS/BIRDS
SPRING MIGRATION: water birds, shore birds, LAND BIRDS;
NESTING SEASON: water birds, LAND BIRDS;
Fall migration: water birds, shore birds, land birds;
Winter: land birds.

River Road in Kent is one of Connecticut's finest inland birding sites, at which a wide variety of birds may be seen, including a number of uncommon species. It is particularly good during the spring migration, because the Housatonic River is an important migration route through western Connecticut. During the spring migration (mid-April through late May) many feel that River Road offers the most exciting birding in the state - as many as 80 species have been seen in a single day. Look for water birds (certainly Canada goose, common merganser, maybe others) on the river, and shore birds on mud along the shore, and on mud, sand or gravel bars. Land birds are abundant in the flood plain forest or in nearby upland forests. Nesting species include both southerners attracted to the flood plain forest and shrubs (Acadian flycatcher, cerulean, hooded, Kentucky, worm-eating and the uncommon yellow-throated warblers), and northern species that inhabit other nearby terrestrial habitats (hermit thrush, winter wren and Canada warbler). In addition, both blue-winged and golden-winged warblers are regular nesters in the reverting field just north of the barway at the end of the road. While not visible from River Road, the cliffs of St. John's Ledges tower above it, and provide nesting habitat for turkey vultures. Other raptors that nest here include red-shouldered and red-tailed hawks and barred owls. The fall migration is good, but does not quite match that of spring. In winter, bald eagle is possible.

GETTING AROUND
Birding methods: CAR, WALK.

Most of the best of these habitats can be seen simply by driving the three-mile dirt road along the river, and stopping frequently to look and listen. Just north of the barway at the northern end of the road, there is a very productive area of reverting fields that can be explored on foot. The road is often in very poor condition during the winter. For those inclined to add a hike and some additional birding, an extension of this trip is possible. It involves continuing north past the barway for 3.5 miles on the Appalachian Trail as it follows the Housatonic River and leads to River Road in Sharon and the upper section of the Stanley Wildlife Management Area (described under Sharon).

DIRECTIONS: River Road is in Kent, in western Connecticut. From the village of Kent, at the intersection of Routes 7 and 341, go west on Route 341 for 0.3 mile across the Housatonic River, right on Skiff Mountain Road for 1.2 miles, and right again on River Road. This dirt road provides good birding for its entire 2.7 mile length to the barrier. At this point, the Appalachian Trail continues north along the river through more good habitat.

KENT: SCHAGHTICOKE ROAD

HABITATS
RIVER/STREAM: river, slow water, islands, coves, streambelts of herbs, shrubs, hardwoods, hardwoods/hemlock; perennial and seasonal streams;
FOREST: hardwoods, white pine, hardwoods/hemlock, mixed conifers, flood plain, mountain laurel;
Open terrestrial: short grass, tall grass, mixed herbaceous and shrubby fields, shrubby and wooded edges;
Marsh/swamp/bog: hardwood swamp;
Other: ledge, cliff, rocky slope.
This is a quiet section of the Housatonic River - the banks are low, and there are occasional islands, coves and swampy areas. There is a flood plain forest along the river, and a typical mixed hardwoods forest on higher ground. There are several small plantations of spruce trees.

SEASONS/BIRDS
SPRING MIGRATION: water birds, marsh birds, shore birds, LAND BIRDS;
NESTING SEASON: water birds, shore birds, land birds;
FALL MIGRATION: water birds, marsh birds, shore birds, land birds;
Winter: land birds.
This is an excellent area during the spring, summer and fall. The spring migration of land birds includes a wide species variety, and there are usually a few water birds (commonly ring-necked duck, wood duck and common merganser), marsh birds (great blue and green-backed herons), and shore birds (spotted and solitary sandpipers) to add to the interest. Species that nest in the habitats near this road include Canada goose, wood duck, mallard, killdeer, spotted sandpiper, great horned owl, kingfisher, least flycatcher, pileated and red-bellied woodpeckers, brown creeper, gnatcatcher, Acadian flycatcher, yellow-throated and warbling vireos, winter wren and orchard oriole. The fall migration of land birds starts in August when various swallow species begin their pre-migration congregating, and peaks in September. Shore birds go through in August and September, and water birds in October and November. Osprey occurs in September, and bald eagle any time from early fall through spring. Other than the occasional bald eagle, winter is pretty quiet along this road.

GETTING AROUND
Birding methods: CAR, walk.
The land on either side of the road is private and heavily posted, so stay in your car or on the road near it.

DIRECTIONS: This road is in Kent, and runs along the Housatonic River between Route 341 and Bulls Bridge Road, a distance of 4.3 miles. It can be approached from either end. **To get to the north end,** from Kent at the intersection of Routes 7 and 341, go west on Route 341 for 0.7 mile, and left on Schaghticoke Road. **To get to the south end** from the intersection of Route 7 and Bulls Bridge Road (at the traffic light on Route 7 about four miles south of Kent), go west on Bulls Bridge Road for 0.4 mile, and right on Schaghticoke Road.

LITCHFIELD: BOYD WOODS

HABITATS
FOREST: hardwoods. hardwoods/hemlock;
OPEN TERRESTRIAL: short grass, tall grass, mixed herbaceous and shrubby fields, shrubby and wooded edges;
Lake/pond: pond, shallow water, shore of mixed herbaceous marsh, shrub swamp, and woods; seasonal pools;
River/stream: perennial stream, fast water, wooded streambelt, seasonal streams, streambelts of shrubby hardwood and hardwood swamps;
Marsh/swamp/bog: shrubby hardwood and hardwood swamp;
Other: rocky outcrop.
This is a 102-acre parcel made up of about 80 acres of former farmland that has reverted to forest, and about 20 acres near the highway that is actively farmed as a hay field.

SEASONS/BIRDS
SPRING MIGRATION: water birds, LAND BIRDS;
NESTING SEASON: water birds, LAND BIRDS;
FALL MIGRATION: water birds, LAND BIRDS;
Winter: land birds.
This site has a nice diversity of the land bird species that you would expect to find in these habitat types. There are lots of migrating warblers in May and again in late August and September. Sparrows pass through in April and October-November. About 80 species nest here, including broad-winged hawk, screech and great horned owls, pileated woodpecker, yellow-bellied sapsucker, brown creeper, hermit thrush and indigo bunting. Common species of water birds (Canada goose, wood duck and mallard) are present in spring, summer and fall.

GETTING AROUND
Birding methods: walk.
At present in this new preserve there is one loop trail that starts at the back of the hay field (it's apt to be wet in the spring). More trails are planned.

DIRECTIONS: This preserve is three miles southeast of the center of Litchfield. From the intersection of Routes 254 and 118, go south on Route 254 for 1.7 miles to the preserve and parking on the right, just past Jefferson Hill Road on the left.

LITCHFIELD: EAST CEMETERY

HABITATS
Forest: hardwoods, white pine, spruces;
Open terrestrial: short grass, mixed herbaceous and shrubby fields; shrubby and wooded edges;
Lake/pond: pond, short grass shore;
River/stream: stream, shrubby and wooded streambelt;
Marsh/swamp/bog: shrub, shrubby hardwood and hardwood swamp.
This is a town cemetery that extends a considerable distance in from the road. The cemetery itself has a typical cemetery habitat structure - mowed lawn with a wooded edge (in this case, hardwoods and mature spruces). However, if you stand at the back edge, you look down on a swamp, a pond, a shrubby field, and a section of the Bantam River.

SEASONS/BIRDS

Spring migration: water birds, marsh birds, shore birds, LAND BIRDS;
Nesting Season: water birds, marsh birds, shore birds, LAND BIRDS;
Fall Migration: water birds, marsh birds, shore birds, LAND BIRDS;
Winter: land birds.

This is basically a site in which to look for land birds, although green heron and killdeer are sometimes also present. In the spring and fall migrations there is a nice variety of warblers and other land birds. May and especially September are the best months. Nesters include a typical mix of standard species. In winter, the mature spruces provide the potential for winter finches.

GETTING AROUND

Birding methods: CAR, WALK.

This is an easy place in which to do your birding. When the entrance gate is open (May 1 to November 30), you can reach all of the habitats and viewpoints in your car by using the network of driveways within the cemetery. In addition, you can walk in the cemetery and along its edges at any time.

DIRECTIONS: This cemetery is within the center of Litchfield. From the intersection of Routes 118 and 202, go east on Route 118 for 0.3 mile to the cemetery entrance on the left.

LITCHFIELD: MT. TOM STATE PARK

HABITATS

LAKE/POND: lake, deep water, wooded shore;
Forest: hardwoods, hardwoods/white pine, hardwoods/hemlock, mountain laurel;
Other: hawk watching site.

This is a relatively small park (233 acres) that occupies one side of 1,291 foot Mount Tom and the southern shore of Mount Tom Pond. Most of the park is wooded with mid-slope mixed hardwood forest. There is an observation tower on the summit of Mount Tom. Mt. Tom pond has a partly developed wooded shore.

SEASONS/BIRDS

Spring migration: water birds, land birds;
Nesting season: land birds;
Fall migration: water birds, land birds;
Winter: land birds.

During the spring and fall migrations, this site has a nice variety of land birds along with some water birds. Most often, the water birds are limited to common species, but sometimes in November some uncommon species show up (for example, over the years, all three scoter species have been seen here). Some interesting land birds nest here, including northerners such as black-throated blue warbler and yellow-bellied sapsucker. In winter, there are only a few year-round residents. All things considered, September is probably the best month to bird here, especially for the hawk migration.

GETTING AROUND
Birding methods: car, walk.

The park driveway leads through a part of the park and to the shore of a cove of the pond (the rest of the pond can be seen from Route 202). Trails lead to the tower and to other parts of the park. A fee is charged during the summer, and the park gets quite crowded.

DIRECTIONS: This park is about six miles west of the village of Litchfield. In Litchfield, at the intersection of Routes 202 and 63, go west on Route 202 for 6.6 miles to the park entrance on the left.

LITCHFIELD: TOPSMEAD STATE FOREST

HABITATS
OPEN TERRESTRIAL: tilled, short grass, tall grass and shrubby fields; shrubby and hardwood edges;

Forest: hardwoods, mixed conifers;

Lake/pond: pond, shallow water, short grass and wooded shore;

Marsh/swamp/bog: mixed herbaceous and shrub marsh, shrubby hardwood and hardwood swamp;

River/stream: perennial stream, wooded streambelt.

This nature preserve of about 100 acres includes a moist forest of mixed hardwoods and scattered groups of conifers, a small pond, wetlands, and open fields.

SEASONS/BIRDS
SPRING MIGRATION: LAND BIRDS;

Nesting season: land birds;

Fall migration: land birds;

Winter: land birds.

The spring and fall migrations are highlighted by waves of warblers as well as other land birds. The nesters include a variety of warblers, and species with an affinity for open fields, including bobolink, meadowlark and kestrel. May and September are the best times to come here.

GETTING AROUND
Birding methods: WALK.

A 0.7 mile self-guiding nature trail makes a loop through the center of the preserve, and there are other trails as well. The walking is easy.

DIRECTIONS: This preserve is about two miles east of the center of Litchfield. To get there from Litchfield at the intersection of Routes 118 and 202, go east on Route 118 for 2.0 miles, right on East Litchfield Road for 0.4 miles, right on Buell Road for 0.4 miles to the entrance on the right.

LITCHFIELD/MORRIS: WHITE MEMORIAL FOUNDATION

HABITATS
FOREST: all types;
MARSH/SWAMP/BOG: all types;
LAKE/POND: a lake and several ponds, shallow and deep water; marshy, shrubby and wooded shores; seasonal pools;
RIVER/STREAM: a river and several streams; marshy, shrubby and wooded streambelts;
OPEN TERRESTRIAL: all types;
Other: hawk watching site; cliff, ledge, rocky slope.

This is a very large (4,440 acre) preserve that consists of several parcels in the towns of Litchfield and Morris. Almost every type of inland habitat that exists in Connecticut can be found here. The variety of habitat types and its large size make it one of Connecticut's most interesting and productive natural areas.

Three quarters of the preserve is forested, and it is contiguous to another large tract of undeveloped forest land (the Waterbury Reservoir property). Within the White preserve, there is almost every type of forest community that occurs in southern New England, including areas of undisturbed interior forest habitat.

Also within the preserve, there is an incredible quantity and variety of marshes and swamps. In addition, there are water bodies of all sizes, ranging from the large Bantam Lake down to small beaver-controlled ponds. The Bantam River is the largest of many watercourses that connect lakes and ponds, and flow through the swamps and marshes.

An important reason for the productivity of the preserve as a whole is the fact that these different types of habitat are intermingled, with pockets of one type in the midst of contrasting types. This is certainly beneficial for wildlife, but is bewildering to the birder planning a visit to the preserve. The information that follows oversimplifies the rich complexities of the preserve by describing only several examples of habitats within it. The many others can best be found by using the preserve map (available at the museum) to explore on your own. Good places to start are the following (directions to each are given later in this site description):

The Museum Area has a nice mix of woodland, wetland and open habitats.

The Mallard Marsh, Pine Island Duck Pond complex includes a rich mosaic of woods and wetlands.

Little Pond, Cranberry Pond and Cemetery Pond are rich, shallow ponds with associated marshes and swamps, the vestiges of a black spruce bog (at Cranberry Pond), and surrounding woodlands.

Catlin Woods contains white pine and hemlock old-growth forest, with distinctly "northern" characteristics.

The Laurel Hill/Apple Hill area is covered by a younger forest with a mountain laurel understory more typical of Connecticut. There is a tower on the top of Apple Hill that can be used to watch the fall hawk migration. Just south of Apple Hill is an area of tall grass fields, an apple orchard, bottomland forest and a hardwood swamp.

Bantam Lake is a large, rather shallow eutrophic lake that produces great quantities of aquatic plant life.

The Bantam River is a small river of moderate water flow, that has a streambelt of varied marshes and swamps, shrubs and hardwoods.

The Five Ponds Natural Area is a diverse mix of ponds, wetlands and woodlands.

SEASONS/BIRDS

SPRING MIGRATION: WATER BIRDS, MARSH BIRDS, SHORE BIRDS, LAND BIRDS;
NESTING SEASON: WATER BIRDS, MARSH BIRDS SHORE BIRDS, LAND BIRDS;
FALL MIGRATION: WATER BIRDS, MARSH BIRDS, SHORE BIRDS, LAND BIRDS;
WINTER: WATER BIRDS, LAND BIRDS.

246 bird species have been recorded on the preserve, of which 140 have shown evidence of nesting (of these, 116 are confirmed nesters). The other species are migrants, residents or winter visitors. The preserve bird list includes all of the species that occur with any frequency in inland Connecticut, plus an impressive list of uncommon species.

Among the species that are probable or confirmed nesters at White Memorial are: pied-billed grebe, green-winged teal, blue-winged teal, wood duck (abundant), hooded merganser, great blue and green-backed herons, Virginia rail, sora and moorhen, goshawk, Cooper's and sharp-shinned hawks, alder and willow flycatchers, golden-crowned kinglet, fish crow, marsh wren, white-eyed vireo, northern waterthrush and many other warblers. King rail is a possible nester. Saw-whet owl is present all year, and considered a possible breeding species.

Migrant species include: snipe (April and late fall), solitary and least sandpipers, greater and lesser yellowlegs; American and least bittern, olive-sided flycatcher, rusty blackbird, all the swallows that occur in Connecticut, and a great variety of vireos, warblers and other land birds.

All year is good at the White preserve; the best times are March through June and September through November.

The Museum Area is very good for seeing a variety of migrating and breeding land birds.

The Mallard Marsh, Pine Island, Duck Pond complex is an especially good area for seeing breeding wood duck, marsh birds, northern waterthrush and other warblers, as well as many migrating land birds, especially warblers.

Little Pond and its associated marshes is a nesting area for both alder and willow flycatchers, marsh wren and a variety of marsh birds including Virginia rail and moorhen. Feeding nighthawks and swallows can be seen here in May and August, osprey and American bittern during the periods April/May and August/October.

Catlin Woods is a nesting area for forest-interior species usually found north of Connecticut, including Blackburnian, black-throated green, magnolia and yellow-rumped warblers.

Cranberry Pond has interesting nesting species, including Virginia rail, Canada warbler, northern and Louisiana waterthrushes.

Laurel Hill/Apple Hill is a good area during migration and the nesting season for a variety of warblers, vireos and other land birds. The bottomland and fields a short distance south of Apple Hill is also good for a variety of land birds.

Cemetery Pond is especially good in the spring and fall for its variety of migrating dabbling ducks and other water birds.

Bantam Lake is famous among birders in Connecticut as a place to see migrating water birds. There are usually large numbers and a good variety of species in March just after ice-out, and again in November until the lake freezes over.

The Bantam River and the shrubby, marshy streambelt through which it flows provides habitat for a variety of water, marsh and land birds, both in migration and during the nesting season.

The Five Ponds Natural Area is very good for migrant land birds in the spring and fall, and such breeders as wood duck, hooded merganser, sapsucker, hermit thrush, black-throated blue and Canada warblers, northern and Louisiana waterthrushes.

GETTING AROUND:
Birding methods: CAR, WALK, BIKE, SKI, BOAT.
The preserve is complex, with several outlying areas, 25 miles of woodland roads and 12 miles of hiking trails. There is a visitor center, museum and book store near the main entrance. A map of the preserve is posted at the parking area, and a map is also sold in the visitors' center. Use of the map is strongly recommended; it will make it possible to explore many good habitats in addition to the few that are discussed in this site description.

The Museum Area has several driveways, woods roads and trails that provide easy access to nearby habitats.

The Mallard Marsh, Pine Island, Duck Pond area can be explored by several trails and can be done as a one to two mile loop.

Little Pond: there is a raised boardwalk that provides a good way to see and hear the birds in the pond and surrounding marsh. A loop around the pond on the boardwalk and trails is 1.8 miles long.

Catlin Woods: a town road goes along one side of this area; a woods road and several trails go through it.

Cranberry Pond can be reached by a woods road with a round-trip distance of about one mile.

Laurel Hill/Apple Hill: there is a trail that leads over Laurel Hill and Apple Hill, a distance of about a mile and a half. The fields and bottomland woods just south of Apple Hill can be seen from East Shore Road.

Cemetery Pond can be seen well from nearby town roads (Constitution Way and White Woods Road).

Bantam Lake: there are two observation platforms from which Bantam Lake can be seen. Each requires a walk - 0.3 miles to the one on the shore of North Bay, and about 100 yards to the one at Point Folly. A scope is helpful.

The Bantam River can be seen from several land points, but can best be explored by canoe, and is worth the effort. From the put-in point (see "Directions" below), it is possible to paddle upstream for over a mile through Little Pond and its marshes, or downstream for about a mile to the marshy delta where the river enters Bantam Lake.

The Five Ponds Natural Area is covered by a network of trails and woods roads that provide access to all of the habitat areas.

DIRECTIONS (see Map 34): **The main section of this preserve** lies about two miles southeast of the center of Litchfield. To get there from Litchfield at the intersection of Routes 202 and 63, go west on Route 202 for 2.0 miles to the entrance on the left.

Museum: Go through the entrance and follow the driveway for 0.5 mile to a parking area at the museum. (And, please, get a preserve map here! The directions that follow lack the detail you will need.)

Mallard Marsh, Pine Island, Duck Pond: at the preserve entrance, instead of taking the driveway into the preserve, go left on Bissell Road for 0.1 mile to a woods road on the left. This leads to a network of woods roads and trails that go through the Mallard Marsh/Pine Island/Duck Pond area. Or, continue on Bissell Road for 0.7 mile, left on Whites Woods Road for 0.4 mile to the start of two trails on the left by parking areas.

Little Pond: at the preserve entrance, instead of taking the driveway into the preserve, go left on Bissell Road for 0.8 mile, left on Whites Woods Road for 0.1 mile to a woods road into Little Pond on the right.

Catlin Woods: at the preserve entrance, instead of taking the driveway into the preserve, go left on Bissell Road for 0.8 mile, right on Whites Woods Road for 0.4 mile, left on Webster Road for 0.4 mile to a woods road into Catlin Woods on the left.

Cranberry Pond: the woods road into Cranberry Pond is directly across Webster Road from the woods road into Catlin Woods (see above).

Laurel Hill/Apple Hill: at the preserve entrance, instead of taking the driveway into the preserve, go left on Bissell Road for 0.8 mile, right on Whites Woods Road (which becomes Alain White Road) for 1.2 miles, right on East Shore Road for 0.7 mile to a woods road to Laurel Hill on the left, opposite Marsh Point Road on the right. This trail goes over Laurel Hill and Apple Hill and ends on the East Shore Road 1.0 mile south of the starting point. Starting 0.1 mile still further south on East Shore Road is the beginning of the area of open fields, bottomland woods and the wooded swamp.

Cemetery Pond: From the preserve entrance, go east on Route 202 (toward Litchfield center) for 1.3 miles, right on Constitution Way for 0.3 mile to where Cemetery Pond is visible on the left, and two small ponds on the right.

Bantam Lake: The Lake Trail to the observation platform on the north shore of Bantam Lake starts from the parking area at the museum. There is a second observation platform at Folly Point. To get there, starting at the preserve entrance, go west on Route 202 for 0.5 mile, left on North Shore Road for 1.0 mile, and left into the parking area on the shore of the lake. The

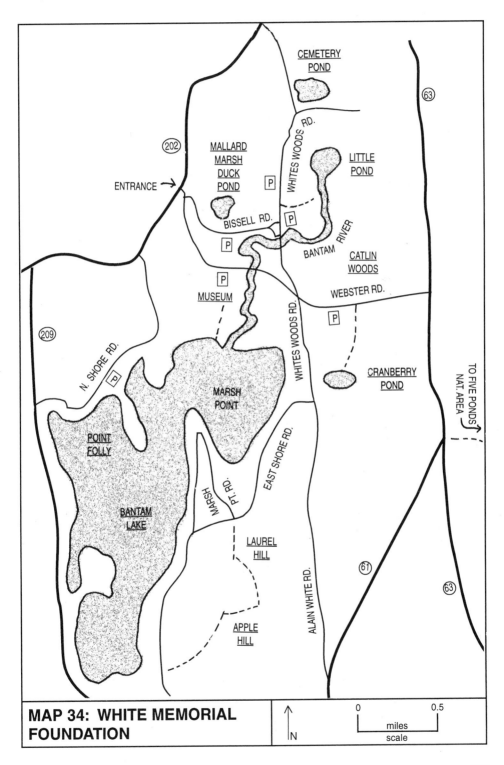

MAP 34: WHITE MEMORIAL FOUNDATION

observation platform is about 100 yards down the driveway that starts at the parking area.

The Bantam River: Starting just outside the preserve entrance, go east on Bissell Road for 0.7 mile, right on a preserve driveway for 0.2 mile to where the river is close to the driveway on the left, and a small parking area is on the right. It is possible to park and launch your canoe near here. Upstream (left as you face the river) leads to Little Pond, and downstream (right) leads to Bantam Lake.

The Five Ponds Natural Area: From the center of Litchfield at the intersection of Routes 63 and 202, go south on Route 63 for 2.8 miles to a woods road on the left (at the intersection of Routes 63 and 61). The woods road leads into The Five Ponds Narural Area.

MORRIS: JONES POND

HABITATS

Lake/pond: pond, shallow water, shore of cattail and mixed herbaceous marsh, shrubs, hardwoods, white pine and mixed conifers.

This is a shallow pond in a quiet setting, in spite of the fact that a state road runs along one side. The rest of the shore is privately owned residential property.

SEASONS/BIRDS

SPRING MIGRATION: WATER BIRDS;
Nesting Season: water birds;
FALL MIGRATION: WATER BIRDS, marsh birds;
Winter:

This pond is a good place to look for migrating water birds - ring-necked and wood ducks are the specialty. The best periods are March/April and September/October/November.

GETTING AROUND

Birding methods: car.

There are two places where you can pull off the highway and view the pond - the cemetery on the north side and a wide shoulder on the state road at the southwest corner. All of the surrounding land is private.

DIRECTIONS: Jones Pond is in Morris, near the south end of Bantam Lake. To get there from the intersection of Routes 109 and 209, go west on Route 109 for 0.5 mile to a cemetery on the left, from which the pond can be viewed. For another view, continue west on Route 109 for another 0.3 mile to a pulloff on the left.

MORRIS/WATERTOWN/THOMASTON: WIGWAM/MORRIS/PITCH RESERVOIRS

HABITATS

LAKE/POND: lakes, deep and shallow water, seasonal pools, shores of hardwoods, shrubs, short grass;
FOREST: hardwoods, hardwoods/white pine, hardwoods/hemlock, white pine, hemlock, mixed conifers, red pine plantations;
Open terrestrial: short grass, mixed herbaceous and shrubby fields;
River/stream: perennial streams, seasonal streams, wooded streambelts;
Marsh/swamp/bog: shrub marsh, shrub swamp, shrubby hardwood swamp, hard-

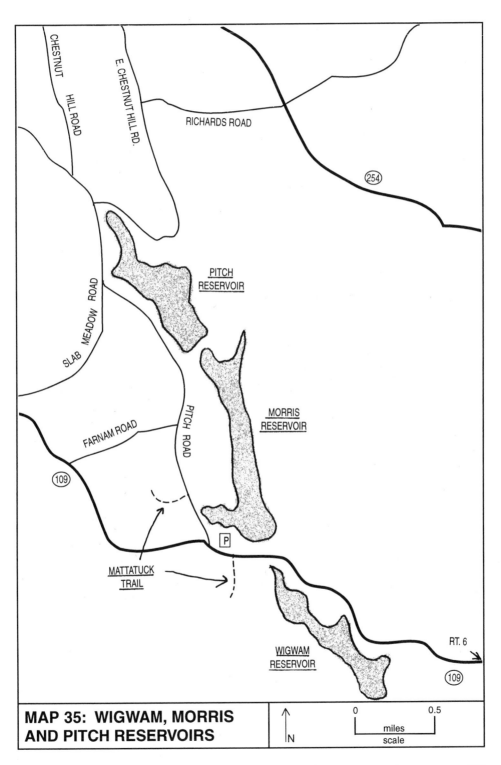

CHESTNUT HILL ROAD

E. CHESTNUT HILL RD.

RICHARDS ROAD

254

PITCH
RESERVOIR

SLAB MEADOW ROAD

PITCH ROAD

MORRIS
RESERVOIR

FARNAM ROAD

109

P

MATTATUCK
TRAIL

RT. 6

WIGWAM
RESERVOIR

109

**MAP 35: WIGWAM, MORRIS
AND PITCH RESERVOIRS**

N

0   0.5
miles
scale

wood swamp.

This site consists of three connecting reservoirs surrounded by varied woodlands and small areas of open habitats.

SEASONS/BIRDS

SPRING MIGRATION: water birds, marsh birds, shore birds, LAND BIRDS;
NESTING SEASON: water birds, LAND BIRDS;
FALL MIGRATION: water birds, marsh birds, shore birds, LAND BIRDS;
Winter: land birds.

Land birds are the draw at this site. The best period is late April through late October; May and September are excellent. During the spring migration, it is possible to see a good variety of warblers and other land birds, as well as various species of water birds, shore birds including solitary sandpiper and killdeer, and waders including great blue and green-backed herons. Nesters include the standard woodland variety of land birds plus northern species such as goshawk, solitary vireo and Blackburnian warbler. Woodcock and spotted sandpiper are also nesters. The fall migration has the variety of spring, plus some added attractions. Post-breeding season great egret may occur early in the fall. If the water in the reservoirs is low and exposes mud in August or September, a variety of shore bird migrants may stop in; over the years, species have included both yellowlegs, least and pectoral sandpipers. Later in the fall (September and October), the berry-eaters (including robin, hermit thrush, cedar waxwing) start to arrive. And the area continues to offer interest through the winter; resident great horned owls become quite vocal, and the habitats are good for winter finches in years when they are present in Connecticut.

GETTING AROUND:

Birding methods: car, WALK, bike, ski.

Pitch Road and the other dirt roads that go through this site are ideal for walking, at times for biking or skiing, but sometimes too muddy for driving. At times, it may be best to park at the beginning of Pitch Road and walk from there. The roads are public, but the surrounding land is owned by the Waterbury Water Department, and not open to the public, except for the Mattatuck Trail (which can provide good birding on foot).

DIRECTIONS (see Map 35): This area is about three miles west of Thomaston. To get there from the intersection of Routes 109 and 6, go west on Route 109 for 3.1 miles to a pulloff on the road shoulder by an overlook from which the Wigwam Reservoir can be seen. Continue west on Route 109 for another 0.6 mile to Pitch Road on the right. Pitch Road goes north from this point for 3.1 miles, past the Morris Reservoir to the south end of the Pitch Reservoir. This can be walked, driven, biked or skied depending on your inclination and the condition of the road. The dirt road continues north beyond Pitch Reservoir to a network of other dirt roads that can provide good birding. To get on The Mattatuck Trail southbound, from the intersection of Route 109 and Pitch Road, go east on Route 109 for about 100 feet to the trail on the right (south) side of Route 109. To get on the trail northbound, from the intersection of Route 109 and Pitch Road, go north on Pitch Road for 0.2 mile to the trail on the left.

NEW HARTFORD: MAPLE HOLLOW

HABITATS

MARSH/SWAMP/BOG: wet meadow, shrub marsh, shrub swamp, shrubby hardwood swamp;
Open terrestrial: short grass, tall grass, mixed herbaceous and shrubby fields, shrubby edges;
Lake/pond: pond, grassy shore;
River/stream: streams, shrub marsh and shrub swamp streambelt, shrubby and hardwood streambelt.
Forest: hardwoods;
Other: gravel bank.

This is a small shallow valley (a little over a mile by half a mile) occupied by several farms and residences. It contains a wetland that includes both marsh and swamp, and that is surrounded by farm fields and areas of hardwoods forest. There are several small streams and a farm pond that is surrounded by open fields. Shrubby edges lie among all of these habitats. There is a gravel bank nearby.

SEASONS/BIRDS

SPRING MIGRATION: water birds, marsh birds, shore birds, LAND BIRDS;
NESTING SEASON: marsh birds, shore birds, LAND BIRDS;
FALL MIGRATION: water birds, marsh birds, shore birds, LAND BIRDS;
Winter: land birds.

You can spend a pleasant hour birding along this country road, and expect to see or hear a variety of standard wetland-oriented species during the spring, summer and fall (May is the best month). During the period March/April and again in October, snipe and rusty blackbird occur here. During the spring and summer, look for wood duck, Virginia rail, green-backed heron, great blue heron (comes here to feed), spotted sandpiper, woodcock, killdeer, alder, willow and least flycatchers, and swamp sparrow. The nearby gravel pit and the proximity of water provide nesting habitat for bank and rough-winged swallows and kingfisher. Sparrows occur in abundance during October and November. Winter often yields a few lingering berry- and seed-eating land birds, and also screech owl (which is here all year).

GETTING AROUND

Birding methods: CAR, walk.

Maple Hollow Road is not heavily traveled, and provides a good opportunity either to bird from your car or on foot. The surrounding land is all private, so stay on the road.

DIRECTIONS: This valley is about four miles south of the center of New Hartford. From the intersection of Routes 219 and 44, go south on Route 219 for 3.8 miles, right on Bruning Road for 0.3 mile, and left on Maple Hollow Road. The latter goes through the valley and past the habitats described above for 0.9 mile.

NEW HARTFORD: NEPAUG STATE FOREST

HABITATS
FOREST: all types except flood plain; mountain laurel;
Open terrestrial: shrubby field;
River/stream: river, fast and slow water; perennial and seasonal streams, wooded streambelts; hemlock ravine;
Other: rocky slope.

This 1,094 acre state forest is composed of rugged, wooded terrain, and includes one bank of the Farmington River as it passes through the gorge known as Satan's Kingdom. The Nepaug State Forest contains a wide variety of forest communities (mostly white pine, hemlock and hardwoods/white pine), as well as varied wooded streambelts, shrubby fields and edges along a power line. In the southern part of this site, there is a large area of sand plain that supports pitch pine, white pine and hardwoods.

SEASONS/BIRDS
SPRING MIGRATION: LAND BIRDS;
NESTING SEASON: LAND BIRDS;
FALL MIGRATION: LAND BIRDS;
Winter: land birds.

A great variety of land bird migrants occur in this forest in both spring and fall. Among the many nesting species are a number of northern forest-dwellers (including magnolia warbler) and some open and edge habitat nesters, including indigo bunting, Nashville and prairie warblers and field sparrow (all of these in or near the power line). In some years, winter finches can be found here.

GETTING AROUND
Birding methods: walk, ski.

A number of trails and wood roads go through the forest. There is also a rough vehicle road that is better walked than driven.

DIRECTIONS (see Map 36): This forest lies about midway between Hartford and Torrington, just north of the Nepaug Reservoir. There are several ways to get in to different parts of the forest; here are two of them:

To enter the southern part of the forest, from Canton at the point at which Route 202 splits west from Route 44, go west on Route 202 for 2.0 miles to a point just past the causeway at the Nepaug Reservoir, and turn right on a short road. Just before you reach a barricade in 0.2 mile, there is a rough road (best walked) on the left; this road leads to other trails within the forest. Another trail enters the forest further west on Route 202, at a point which is 3.3 miles from the Route 202/44 intersection.

To enter the northern part of the forest, from Canton at the intersection of Routes 202 and 44, go west on Route 44 for 2.3 miles to the west end of the bridge over the Farmington River, and turn left on Satans Kingdom Road. Starting in 0.4 mile, this road goes through the forest for almost a mile, and trails go into the forest from the right side of the road. The road is steep and rough, and is best walked.

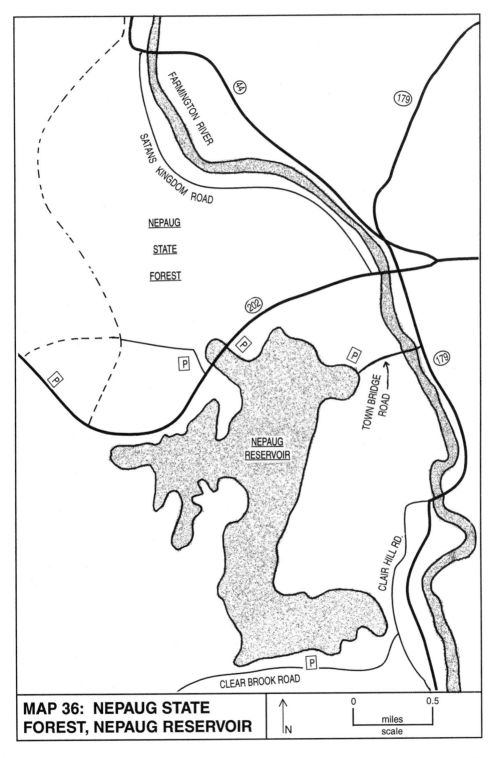

FARMINGTON RIVER

44

179

SATANS KINGDOM ROAD

NEPAUG

STATE

FOREST

202

179

P

P

P

P

TOWN BRIDGE ROAD

NEPAUG
RESERVOIR

CLAIR HILL RD.

P

CLEAR BROOK ROAD

**MAP 36: NEPAUG STATE
FOREST, NEPAUG RESERVOIR**

N

0   0.5
miles
scale

NEW HARTFORD/BURLINGTON/CANTON: NEPAUG RESERVOIR

HABITATS
LAKE/POND: lake, deep water, grassy, shrubby and wooded shore; ponds;
FOREST: hardwoods, white pine and hemlock alone and in various combinations, mixed conifers, pitch pine, sand plain, mountain laurel;
Open terrestrial: short grass and mixed herbaceous fields;
River/stream: river, perennial and seasonal streams, wooded streambelts, hemlock ravine;
Marsh/swamp/bog: shrub marsh.

This site includes the Nepaug Reservoir and the forest immediately around it. Nepaug is a large reservoir with a shore that is mostly wooded, and reflects the composition of the surrounding forest - hardwoods, white pine and hemlock in various combinations. At the southern end of the reservoir, there is a forest of mature mixed conifers - tamarack, hemlock, white pine, pitch pine, and various spruces. There is a river (the Nepaug), many perennial and seasonal streams, and also small areas of shrubs and marsh along the shore of the reservoir.

SEASONS/BIRDS
SPRING MIGRATION: gulls, WATER BIRDS, shore birds, LAND BIRDS;
NESTING SEASON: water birds, LAND BIRDS;
FALL MIGRATION: gulls, WATER BIRDS, marsh birds, shore birds, LAND BIRDS;
Winter: water birds, land birds.

The Nepaug Reservoir has become a destination for birders from all over the state, especially during the water bird migration in the early spring (March/April) and late fall (October/November). Almost any species may be seen here; common loon, hooded merganser, common goldeneye, bufflehead and ring-necked duck are common. In recent years sightings have also included red-necked and horned grebes, both scaup, all three scoters, and oldsquaw. What many birders do not realize is that the migration of land birds, a little later in the spring (May) and earlier in the fall (September) is also fantastic. And many of the species that are seen during the spring migration stay to nest. There are 130 species that have shown evidence of nesting at this site (of which 105 are confirmed), making the Nepaug Reservoir #2 in the state (White Memorial is #1). This species list r eads like a Who's Who of the Connecticut bird world: common loon, double-crested cormorant, common merganser, most of Connecticut's raptors; Acadian, willow and alder flycatchers, golden-crowned kinglet, whip-poor-will, junco, white-throated sparrow, all the vireos, and many warblers - worm-eating, golden-winged, Nashville, magnolia, black-throated green, black-throated blue, Blackburnian, pine, prairie, plus all the more common species. Winter is quiet by comparison, but this site is still worth a visit. All of the winter finches have been seen here, and bald eagle is frequently present.

GETTING AROUND
Birding methods: CAR, WALK, BIKE, SKI.

The northern part of the reservoir can be seen from overlook points at two parking areas that are connected by a pedestrian road a little over a mile long. The southern part of the reservoir can be seen from a quiet town road that goes for two miles along the shore or near it through a mixed conifer forest. This road can be birded from your car or by walking. All the land surrounding the vehicle and pedestrian roads is owned by the Metropolitan District Commission, and is off-limits to the public.

DIRECTIONS (see Map 36): The Nepaug Reservoir lies midway between Hartford and Torrington.

To get to the north end of the reservoir, from Canton at the western intersection of Routes 202 and 44, go west on Route 202 for 1.7 miles to where the reservoir is visible on the left. Just short of this point, there is an overlook at a parking area. This is also the western end of the pedestrian road that goes along the north shore of the reservoir, and ends at another overlook point and parking area. The east end of this road can be reached from the same starting point (Routes 202 and 44); go west on Route 202 for 0.2 mile, left on Route 179 for 0.6 mile, right on Town Bridge Road for 0.5 mile to its intersection with Freedom Road and Country Lane. Go straight ahead a few yards to reach the parking area, overlook point, and east end of the pedestrian road.

To get to the south end of the reservoir, go back to the intersection of Routes 179 and 202; go south on Route 179 for 2.5 miles, right on Sand Bank Hill Road for 0.1 mile, left on Claire Hill Road for 0.2 mile, right on Barns Hill Road for 0.2 mile, and right on Clear Brook Road. This is a quiet, little used road that runs along or near the south end of the reservoir for over two miles.

NEW MILFORD: DIKE POINT RECREATION AREA

HABITATS
> **FOREST:** hardwoods, hardwoods/hemlock, hemlock;
> **LAKE/POND:** lake, deep water, islands, wooded shore, seasonal pool;
> **River/stream:** seasonal stream, wooded streambelt;
> **OTHER:** ledge, cliff, rocky slope.

This Northeast Utilities recreation area lies on the east shore of Candlewood Lake, and provides a view of a part of the lake that often stays ice-free into January. Within the area there are woods that include a hemlock ravine, ledges and a rocky hillside.

SEASONS/BIRDS
> **Spring migration:** gulls, water birds, land birds;
> **Nesting Season:** gulls, water birds, land birds;
> **Fall Migration:** gulls, water birds, land birds;
> **Winter:** gulls, water birds, land birds.

This is a nice place to go birding at any time of year. In the spring and fall, you can see water birds and a good variety of land birds, including osprey and many warblers. Breeders include red-bellied woodpecker, worm-eating warbler, plus a variety of the species you would expect in these wooded habitats. In winter, look for water birds and bald eagle.

GETTING AROUND
> **Birding methods:** WALK.

A trail makes a 0.8 mile loop, partly along the lake shore, and partly through the wooded habitats. The gate and parking area are open only between Memorial Day and Labor Day, during which time the park becomes crowded especially on weekends and in the afternoon. At other times of year, you can enter the area on foot, after parking immediately to the right of the closed gate (but not blocking it, and not parking along the road or in the nearby marina - they tow violators).

DIRECTIONS: This park lies on the east shore of Candlewood Lake about three miles southwest of New Milford. To get there from the intersection of Routes 7 and 37, go south on Route 7 for 1.8 miles, right on North Candlewood Lake Road for 3.5 miles, right on Old Town Park Road for 0.2 mile to the recreation area on the left.

NEW MILFORD: RIVER ROAD/BOARDMAN ROAD

HABITATS
RIVER/STREAM: river; slow, moderate and fast water; shrubby, hardwoods, hardwoods/hemlock streambelt; perennial and seasonal streams, wooded streambelts;
FOREST: mixed hardwoods, hardwoods/hemlock, flood plain, dense understory of shrubs and vines;
Open terrestrial: short grass and shrubby fields, shrubby edges.
River Road runs along the Housatonic River through several miles of riparian forest habitat with a well developed understory. Boardman Road continues along the river farther downstream to a section that has deep, slow water, and often stays open in winter. Still farther downstream, there are other places from which the river can be seen.

SEASONS/BIRDS
SPRING MIGRATION: WATER BIRDS, LAND BIRDS
NESTING SEASON: LAND BIRDS
FALL MIGRATION: WATER BIRDS, LAND BIRDS;
WINTER: WATER BIRDS, land birds;
These roads are good places from which to see water and land birds as they use the Housatonic River Valley as a migration corridor. The spring is especially good - in March and April for water birds, and mid-April through May for land birds. Acadian flycatcher and cerulean warbler occur in this flood plain forest both as migrants and as nesters. The fall migration is less exciting, but in September there are vireos, warblers and other forest-dwelling land bird species, and later in the fall and into winter there are seed- and berry-eaters including thrushes, waxwing and sparrows, together with some water birds. Osprey is likely in April and September, and bald eagle in late fall, winter and early spring. In winter (January through March), the sections of the river by the Boardman Bridge and downstream just above the Route 202 bridge (see "Directions" below) can be very good for water birds, often including ring-necked duck, redhead, common goldeneye, common and hooded mergansers, and sometimes uncommon species such as Barrow's goldeneye. Bald eagle and interesting gull species also occur here.

GETTING AROUND
Birding methods: CAR, walk.
As River Road goes south, it follows the east bank of the Housatonic River for 4.5 miles. Most of it can either be driven or walked, except in winter and early spring when it is often impassible for vehicles. There are numerous places to pull off where the river is visible. The first half mile and the last mile are built up with residences, but the three miles in between are still undeveloped and open to the public. The parts of the river by Boardman Bridge and just above the Route 202 bridge can be reached by car in winter.

DIRECTIONS: River Road follows the east bank of the Housatonic River for about five miles between Gaylordsville and New Milford. **To get to River Road from Gaylordsville** at the intersection of Routes 7 and 55, go north on Route 7 a very short distance to the north end of the bridge, turn east on River View Road for 0.4 mile, and right on River Road. This road follows the river for 4.5 miles until it reaches Boardman Road (Boardman Bridge is a short distance to the right).

To continue south along the river, turn left on Boardman Road and follow it for 2.3 miles to a wide pulloff on the right, 0.1 mile upstream from the Route 202 bridge over the river. To get back on Route 7, turn right on Route 202 and cross the bridge.

NEW MILFORD: SUNNY VALLEY

HABITATS

OPEN TERRESTRIAL: tilled, mixed herbaceous, short grass, tall grass and shrubby fields; shrubby and hardwood edges and hedgerows;
Forest: hardwoods;
Lake/pond: small farm ponds; grassy, mixed herbaceous and shrubby shores;
River/stream: perennial and seasonal streams, grassy, shrubby and wooded streambelts;
Marsh/swamp/bog: wet meadow, mixed herbaceous and sedge marshes.

Most of this area is farmland that contains a variety of actively managed as well as reverting fields in association with several small farm ponds, pockets of marsh, hardwood forest on the periphery, and lots of shrubby edges and hedgerows.

SEASONS/BIRDS

SPRING MIGRATION: water birds, shore birds, LAND BIRDS;
Nesting Season: water birds, shore birds, land birds;
FALL MIGRATION: water birds, shore birds, LAND BIRDS;
Winter: water birds, land birds.

There is some activity here throughout the year, but the spring and fall migrations bring the greatest species diversity. In the spring, check the edges and hedgerows for a wide variety of land birds. As you would expect in this type of habitat, many of the nesters are open-country and edge species such as kestrel, killdeer,, woodcock, bobolink, meadowlark, indigo bunting, prairie warbler, Savannah and field sparrows. Screech owl is also a nester at the farm. In the late fall it is not uncommon to see migrating bobolink, pipit and a variety of sparrows, including white-crowned, Lincoln's and vesper. Common water bird species are present in spring and fall, including large flocks of Canada geese that stay through the winter. It is worth checking those flocks closely, because sometimes snow geese and once in a while a greater white-fronted goose is among the Canadas. In winter, you are apt to see several raptor species hunting over the fields - red-tailed hawk, bald eagle, turkey vulture, and occasionally black vulture. Horned lark and sparrows are usually also present.

GETTING AROUND

Birding methods: car, WALK.

There are several nature trails, one of which starts across the road from the preserve office. Several separate areas of this farm/preserve complex are open to the public; you'll need a map, and they are available to the office. Limited areas of the farm are visible from your car.

DIRECTIONS (see Map 37): The area in which the office is located is in New Milford, less than a mile south of the northern intersection of Routes 7 and 202. From that intersection, go south on Route 7 and 202 for 0.5 mile, right on Sunny Valley Road for 0.4 mile, turn left (in order to stay on Sunny Valley Road) for another 0.4 mile, and right on Sunny Valley Lane for 0.1 mile to the office on the right.

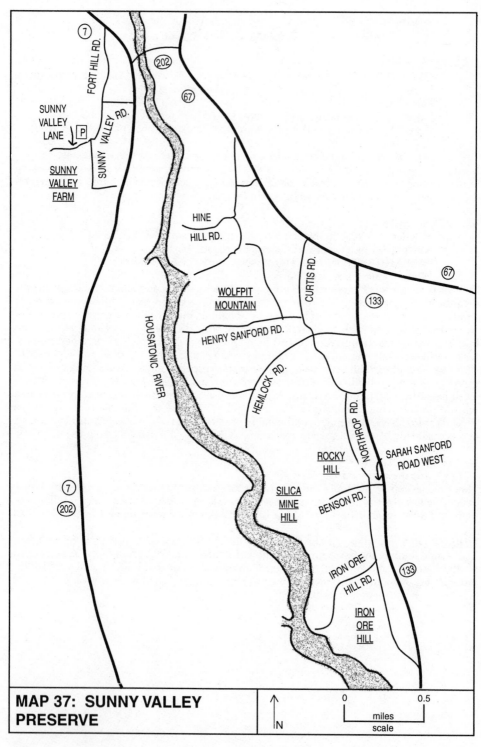

MAP 37: SUNNY VALLEY PRESERVE

N

0   0.5
miles
scale

NEW MILFORD/KENT: BULLS BRIDGE RECREATION AREA

HABITATS
RIVER/STREAM: river, fast water, streambelt of hardwoods, hardwoods/white pine and hardwoods/hemlock;

Forest: flood plain, hardwoods, hemlock, mixed conifers, cedar;

Open terrestrial: shrubby field with cedar and shrubby edges, vine tangles and thickets;

Marsh/swamp/bog: shrubby hardwood swamp.

This small area lies along the east bank of the Housatonic River at a point where there are rapids. It is composed of hardwoods in which there are isolated mature spruce trees, an understory of vine tangles and thickets, shrubby fields with scattered cedars, small shrubby openings, and a small shrubby swamp.

SEASONS/BIRDS
SPRING MIGRATION: water birds, LAND BIRDS;

NESTING SEASON: LAND BIRDS;

FALL MIGRATION: water birds, LAND BIRDS;

Winter: water birds, land birds.

This site benefits from the fact that the Housatonic River and its valley are an important migration route for both water birds and land birds. Look for land birds in the shrubs and woods near the river - a variety of woodland and edge species in the spring and fall, plus seed- and berry-eaters (sparrows, cedar waxwing, hermit thrush and robin) in the late fall and early winter. During the spring migration and also during the nesting season, look in and around the cedars and edges for brown thrasher, prairie warbler and indigo bunting. In winter, this is a good site for raptors: great horned, long-eared and saw-whet owls have all been seen here. Bald eagles sometimes perch on trees overlooking the river; be careful not to disturb them.

GETTING AROUND
Birding methods: walk.

There are several unmarked trails that provide easy walking through the habitats and to the river.

DIRECTIONS: This site is between Route 7 and the east bank of the Housatonic River, about nine miles south of the center of Kent. To get to the main entrance from the intersection of Routes 7 and 341 in Kent, go south on Route 7 for 8.8 miles to an iron gate at the entrance on the right.

NORFOLK: CAMPBELL FALLS STATE PARK

HABITATS
FOREST: hardwoods/hemlock, white pine/hemlock;

RIVER/STREAM: stream, fast water, wooded streambelt, hemlock ravine;

Open terrestrial: tall grass field, shrubby and wooded edge;

Marsh/swamp/bog: mixed herbaceous marsh, dead wood.

The shape of this steep-sided ravine, plus its high elevation (about 1,100 feet above sea level), cause it to contain a microclimate that supports flora and fauna more typical of northern

New England than Connecticut. Hemlock is the dominant tree in the ravine itself, while a mix of northern hardwoods, white pine and hemlock occurs in the forest above and below the ravine. The stream is a rocky, swift mountain brook in a wooded streambelt that continues for several miles until it emerges into farm country. Before the stream enters the park, it passes through a mixed herbaceous marsh with standing dead trees.

SEASONS/BIRDS
Spring migration: land birds;
NESTING SEASON: LAND BIRDS;
Fall migration: land birds;
Winter: land birds.

The spring and fall migrations are good, but not spectacular; the nesting season is interesting because of the occurence of northern species such as goshawk, solitary vireo, black-throated green and Blackburnian warblers.

GETTING AROUND
Birding methods: car, WALK.

There are two trails in this park - one from each entrance. Both are short (0.3 and 0.1 mile) but steep near the falls. When you are in the ravine, the sound of the falls makes birding by ear difficult. There are also opportunities to bird from your car along Campbell Falls Road. A map of trails at this and other sites in Norfolk is available at the Town Hall, Pharmacy and Library.

DIRECTIONS: This park is in Norfolk, about four miles north of the town center. **To get to the southern entrance of the park,** from the western (or northern) intersection of Routes 272 and 44, go north on Route 272 for 4.1 miles, and left on Old Spaulding Road for 0.2 mile to the park entrance on the right. If you continue on Old Spaulding Road for 0.1 mile, the marsh is visible on the left, and the stream on the right. **To get to the northern entrance,** continue north on Route 272 for another 0.2 mile, and left on Campbell Falls Road for 0.4 mile to the entrance on the left. Campbell Falls Road continues along the brook for several miles.

NORFOLK: DENNIS HILL STATE PARK

HABITATS
Forest: mixed hardwoods, hardwoods/white pine, hardwoods/ hemlock, mixed conifers, mountain laurel;
Open terrestrial: short and tall grass fields, shrubby and wooded edges;
Marsh/swamp/bog: hardwood swamp, wooded edge;
Other: hawk watching site.

This site is largely wooded with northern hardwoods, white pine and hemlocks in various combinations. The top of Dennis Hill is bare and rocky, and affords expansive views; according to local folklore, on clear days you can see Long Island Sound.

SEASONS/BIRDS
Spring migration: land birds;
NESTING SEASON: LAND BIRDS;
Fall migration: land birds;
Winter: land birds.

Although most of the action at this park occurs during the spring and fall migrations, the nesting season is especially interesting because, in addition to the usual woodland species, this park is a good place to see northern species, including black-throated blue and Canada warblers in mountain laurel along the trail, plus magnolia, black-throated green and blackburnian warblers in the conifers. Along the edges of the mowed area at the summit, there are usually several pairs of nesting chestnut-sided warblers.

GETTING AROUND:
Birding methods: car, WALK, SKI.

The park driveway (which is barred to autos in winter) leads to the summit. In addition, there is a trail off to the left as the driveway starts to climb to the summit, that makes a mile-plus loop through forest and swamp habitats. It is good for walking as well as skiing. A map of trails at this site and others in Norfolk is available at the Town Hall, Pharmacy and Library.

DIRECTIONS: This park is in Norfolk, two and a half miles south of the town center. From the eastern (or southern) intersection of Routes 272 and 44, go south on Route 272 for 2.5 miles to the park entrance on the left.

NORFOLK: HAYSTACK MOUNTAIN STATE PARK

HABITATS
FOREST: mixed hardwoods, hardwoods/white pine, hardwoods/ hemlock;
Open terrestrial: tall grass field, shrubby field, shrubby and wooded edges;
Lake/pond: pond, shallow water, wooded shore;
River/stream: stream, fast water, wooded streambelt.

This park is largely forested with hardwoods, white pine and hemlock in various combinations. There is a shallow pond with a wooded shore. On the top of Haystack Mountain, there is a tower with limited visibility.

SEASONS/BIRDS
Spring migration: land birds;
Nesting season: land birds;
FALL MIGRATION: LAND BIRDS;
Winter: land birds.

The spring land bird migration is good but not spectacular. Nesting species include the usual forest-dwellers plus some northerners. Nesting by Cooper's hawk was confirmed several years ago. The fall migration can be very good, especially for warblers in September. Pileated woodpecker is among the residents, along with red-breasted nuthatch and brown creeper.

GETTING AROUND
Birding methods: car, WALK, ski.

The park driveway (barred to autos in winter) goes from the entrance to a parking area several hundred yards below the summit. Several trails go to the summit and to other parts of the park. A map of trails at this site and others in Norfolk is available at the Town Hall, Pharmacy and Library.

DIRECTIONS: This park is in Norfolk, immediately north of the town center. From the western (or northern) intersection of Routes 272 and 44, go north on Route 272 for 0.2 mile to the park entrance on the left.

NORFOLK: NORTH SWAMP FLOOD CONTROL AREA

HABITATS

MARSH/SWAMP/BOG: sedge and shrub marsh, shrub swamp, dead wood.
Forest: hardwoods, white pine and hemlock in various combinations;
Open terrestrial: tall grass, shrubby field, shrub, hardwood, white pine and hemlock edges;
Lake/pond: ponds, mixed herbaceous, shrub, hardwoods and hemlock shores, dead wood;
River/stream: stream, fast water, slow water, shrubby, hardwood, white pine and hemlock streambelt.

The centerpiece of this area is a beaver-influenced wetland that includes a fairly large pond in which there are standing dead trees. Around the shore are pockets of herbaceous and shrub marsh, and shrub swamp. Nearby are smaller ponds, a shrubby field, and a tall grass field mowed seasonally as part of a flood control area. These habitats are surrounded by a forest that includes areas of hardwoods, white pine, hemlock, and various mixes of these species. The habitats have a northern quality, not surprising considering the high elevation of this area (1,300-1,400' above sea level).

SEASONS/BIRDS

SPRING MIGRATION: water birds, LAND BIRDS;
NESTING SEASON: water birds, LAND BIRDS;
FALL MIGRATION: water birds, LAND BIRDS;
Winter: land birds.

Spring, summer and fall are good at this area. The migrations, while not spectacular, do bring a nice variety of land birds, plus a few of the common water birds. The list of nesters is made up of wetland-oriented and woodland species, including some northerners: wood duck, yellow-bellied sapsucker, pileated woodpecker, red-breasted nuthatch, solitary vireo, yellow-rumped, Canada and black-throated green warblers, northern and Louisiana water-thrushes, and many other species. Olive-sided flycatcher has occurred here during the breeding season, but nesting is not confirmed. Activity in winter is confined to a few residents, the most visible being woodpeckers.

GETTING AROUND

Birding methods: WALK.

A trail makes a loop (about one and a half miles long) around the pond and past the habitats described above. A map to this and other areas in Norfolk is available at the Norfolk Town Hall, Pharmacy and the Library.

DIRECTIONS: This area is just east of the center of Norfolk. To get there from the eastern (or southern) intersection of Routes 44 and 272, go east on Route 44 for 0.5 mile, right on the lower of two driveways to the Botelle School; go past the school buildings and parking area down to the tennis courts in the field below the school and park here. The trail begins at the barway past the tennis courts.

NORFOLK: WOOD CREEK FLOOD CONTROL AREA

HABITATS

MARSH/SWAMP/BOG: wet meadow, sedge and shrub marsh; shrub and shrubby hardwood swamp, dead wood; edges of tall grass, shrubs, hardwoods, white pine and hemlock;

Forest: hardwoods, white pine and hemlock in various combinations;

Open terrestrial: tall grass and shrubby fields, shrubby, hardwood, white pine and hemlock edges;

Lake/pond: pond; mixed herbaceous, tall grass, shrubby, hardwood and hemlock shore;

River/stream: stream; fast and slow water; shrubby, hardwood, white pine and hemlock streambelt.

This area occupies a bottomland between two flood control dams. It includes a pond, a stream, and a large marsh of varied vegetation, all surrounded by woods. The areas around the dams are mowed and maintained as tall grass fields. Nearby are a wet meadow and shrubby fields. These habitats are surrounded by a forest that includes areas of northern hardwoods, white pine, hemlock, and various mixes of these species. In many ways, this site is a twin of the North Swamp Flood Control Area, a mile or two to the south (also in Norfolk). Like North Swamp, the elevation here is high - 1,100-1,200' above sea level - and this contributes to the northern character of the vegetation.

SEASONS/BIRDS

Spring migration: water birds, marsh birds, shore birds, land birds;

NESTING SEASON: water birds, marsh birds, LAND BIRDS;

Fall migration: water birds, marsh birds, shore birds, land birds;

Winter: land birds.

Spring, summer and fall are good at this area. The migrations bring a nice variety of land birds, plus a few common species of water, marsh and shore birds, including wood duck, hooded merganser, great blue heron, killdeer and spotted sandpiper . The list of nesters is made up of wetland-oriented and woodland species, including some northerners: wood duck, yellow-bellied sapsucker, pileated woodpecker, yellow-rumped, black-throated green, blue-winged and golden-winged warblers, and many other species. Olive-sided flycatcher has been heard here briefly during the breeding season, but nesting is not confirmed. There is good habitat for snipe, Virginia rail and sora, but their presence has not been confirmed.

GETTING AROUND

Birding methods: WALK.

A trail goes through this area, a distance of a little over a mile. A trail map to this and other areas in Norfolk is recommended, and is available at the Norfolk Town Hall, Pharmacy and Library.

DIRECTIONS: This area is less than a mile north of the center of Norfolk. To get there from the northern (or western) intersection of Routes 272 and 44, go north on Route 272 for 0.9 mile to a barway on the right, just before the state garage, also on the right. The trail starts at the barway; this trail ends on Route 272 0.6 mile south of your starting point (the trail distance is just over one mile).

NORFOLK: WOOD CREEK POND

HABITATS
LAKE/POND: lake, shallow water, shrubby islands, marshy and wooded shore;
Forest: hardwoods, hardwoods/white pine, hardwoods/hemlock;
River/stream: stream, fast water, slow water, marshy and wooded streambelt;
Marsh/swamp/bog: cattail, sedge, mixed herbaceous and shrub marsh, shrub swamp.

This is a rather large but shallow lake that has one hard island covered mainly by white pine, and several shrubby islands. Much of the shore is soft and marshy. There is a herbaceous and shrub marsh at the north end of the lake. The outlet stream has a wooded and marshy streambelt.

SEASONS/BIRDS
Spring migration: water birds, land birds;
Nesting season: water birds, land birds;
Fall migration: water birds, land birds;
Winter: land birds.

Spring, summer and fall are good on this lake and along its shore. There are usually some common water bird species during migration (principally Canada goose, wood duck and ringneck), but the real interest is land birds. Several warbler species can be seen around the outlet stream below the dam, and others in the forest habitats near the lake shore. Nesters include a typical mix of common water birds, and northern forest land bird species. In winter, there is very little activity.

GETTING AROUND
Birding methods: car, walk, BOAT.

You can drive to the state landing at the south end of the pond, which overlooks one bay and the outlet stream. Short trails start at the landing and across the dam. The marsh at the northern end of the pond and the entire shore are worth birding from a boat (the land is private).

DIRECTIONS: This area is a mile or two north of the center of Norfolk. To get there from the northern (or western) intersection of Routes 272 and 44, go north on Route 272 for 1.5 miles, right on Ashpohtag Road for 0.4 mile to the driveway on the left to the landing at the south end of the pond.

PLYMOUTH: HANCOCK BROOK FLOOD CONTROL AREA

HABITATS:
MARSH/SWAMP/BOG: herbaceous and shrub marsh, shrub swamp, shrubby/hardwood swamp, hardwood swamp;
Forest: hardwoods, hardwoods/white pine, hardwoods/hemlock;
Open terrestrial: shrubby field, sand plain;
Lake/pond: pond, shrubby and wooded shore;
River/stream: perennial and seasonal streams; marshy, shrubby and wooded streambelts;

This is a large flood control area in a shallow valley. The area is made up of a variety of bottomland and streambelt habitats, including varied wetlands and several small ponds (which become one large pond when the area is flooded). There is a sand plain that occurs as a shrubby field, rather than the more common forested form. Much of the bottomland and most of the hillsides are covered by various types of forest.

SEASONS/BIRDS
SPRING MIGRATION: water birds, marsh birds, shore birds, LAND BIRDS;
NESTING SEASON: LAND BIRDS;
FALL MIGRATION: water birds, marsh birds, shore birds, LAND BIRDS;
Winter: land birds.

This is an excellent site at which to see a nice variety and good numbers of standard species. The best birding is at the north end. The spring and fall land bird migrations are very good - for warblers in May and September, and for a variety of sparrows later in the fall. There is also a shore bird migration that sometimes includes yellowlegs, snipe and solitary sandpiper as well as the more common woodcock, killdeer and spotted sandpiper. In addition, some common water birds species may seen, and an occasional great blue heron. Nesters include a standard mix of land bird species, plus some southerners and open-habitat species: red-bellied woodpecker, white-eyed vireo, blue-gray gnatcatcher, brown thrasher, indigo bunting and prairie warbler. In past years, whip-poor-will has nested (at the south end). If it is present, it can be heard during evenings in May, June and July. Barred owl is a resident.

GETTING AROUND
Birding methods: WALK.

There are several trails, including a section of the Mattatuck Trail. Some of these trails are rough in places, but there is one mostly paved path that starts at the north end. There are ticks in warm weather, and hunters in the fall.

DIRECTIONS: This area is about six miles north of Waterbury and two to four miles southeast of the town of Plymouth. To get to the northern part of the area from Plymouth at the intersection of Route 6 (East Main Street) and Route 262, go east on Route 6 for 0.7 mile and right on Todd Hollow Road for 1.6 miles to an entrance to the area where the road goes sharply right. (On the way, Todd Hollow Road passes several ponds that are worth checking for dabbling ducks.) To get to the southern part of the area from the intersection of Routes 262 and 6, go south on Route 262 for 4.3 miles and left on South Main Street. Starting at 0.6 mile, the area is on the left side of the road.

ROXBURY: HEMLOCK CEMETERY

HABITATS

> **OPEN TERRESTRIAL:** short grass, tall grass and shrubby fields, cedars in field; shrubby edges;
> **Forest:** cedar, mixed conifers;
> **River/stream:** stream;
> **Marsh/swamp/bog:** mixed herbaceous and shrub marsh, shrub swamp.

This is a rather small cemetery that has red cedars, pitch pines and other conifers scattered about its lawn area. It is surrounded by shrubby woodland with more cedars and a shrubby edge.

SEASONS/BIRDS

> **SPRING MIGRATION:** LAND BIRDS;
> **NESTING SEASON:** LAND BIRDS;
> **FALL MIGRATION:** LAND BIRDS;
> **Winter:** land birds.

This cemetery is a miniature birding hotspot, especially during May and June, when migrants mix with newly arrived nesters. Shrubby edge nesters are the specialty here - brown thrasher, white-eyed vireo, blue-winged, prairie and chestnut-sided warblers, yellowthroat, indigo bunting and field sparrow. In fall and winter, it would be worth checking for saw-whet owl - the habitat is just right.

GETTING AROUND

> **Birding methods:** walk.

The walking is easy - around the periphery of the cemetery, and along Hemlock Road, past the cemetery entrance.

DIRECTIONS (see Map 38): This cemetery is in Roxbury, about five miles southeast of New Milford. From the intersection of Routes 67 and 199, go west on Route 67 for 0.1 mile, left on Hemlock Road for 0.2 mile to the cemetery entrance on the left.

ROXBURY: JUDDS BRIDGE ROAD

HABITATS

> **FOREST:** hardwoods, hardwoods/hemlock, hardwoods/white pine, hemlock, hemlock/white pine, mountain laurel;
> **RIVER/STREAM:** river, perennial and seasonal streams; streambelts of shrubs, hardwoods, hemlock and white pine;
> **OPEN TERRESTRIAL:** tilled, short grass and tall grass fields; shrubby and wooded edges, hedgerows;
> **Marsh/swamp/bog:** small hemlock and hardwood swamps;
> **Other:** rocky slope, ledges.

During the two miles of its length included in the site, this quiet dirt road passes through a mixed forest of hardwoods/hemlock/white pine, crosses a mountain brook and hemlock ravine, passes small pockets of hemlock and hardwood swamp, and emerges into open farmland where it runs along the Shepaug River.

SEASONS/BIRDS
SPRING MIGRATION: LAND BIRDS;
NESTING SEASON: LAND BIRDS;
FALL MIGRATION: LAND BIRDS;
Winter: land birds.

This two mile drive can produce an impressive variety of species, including both forest-dwellers and open country birds. Both the spring and fall migrations are good, and produce all of the species one would expect in this mix of forest, open and streambelt habitats. Nesters include species typical of northern forests, such as brown creeper, winter wren, hermit thrush, and solitary vireo; also screech owl, pileated woodpecker, yellow-throated and warbling vireos. Nesters in or near the open fields along the road include bobolink, meadowlark and indigo bunting.

GETTING AROUND
Birding methods: CAR, WALK.

This dirt road can be safely driven during most of the year, but be cautious about mud at times. It is ideal to walk, because it is used only by local traffic. At 1.2 miles from the start, where Judds Bridge Road crosses Battle Swamp Brook, there is a public trail that follows the brook through a ravine. Outside of that, the land surrounding the road is private.

DIRECTIONS (see Map 38): This area is in the northwest corner of Roxbury, a mile or two above the center of Roxbury Station. To get there from the intersection of Routes 199 and 67, go north on Route 199 for 0.2 mile, and left on Judds Bridge Road. This road goes through forest habitats for 1.2 miles, at which point it crosses Battle Swamp Brook with a trail and parking area on the right just beyond the bridge. The road then continues for another 0.7 mile, coming out of the woods, into open fields and along the Shepaug River. The trip ends in another 0.1 mile, by a bridge across the Shepaug River on the left.

ROXBURY: LILLY PRESERVE

HABITATS
MARSH/SWAMP/BOG: wet meadow; sedge, mixed herbaceous and shrub marsh; shrub, shrubby hardwood and hardwood swamp;
FOREST: hardwoods, hardwoods/hemlock, hemlock, mountain laurel;
OPEN TERRESTRIAL: short grass, tall grass, mixed herbaceous and shrubby fields; cedar, young hardwood edges;
River/stream: perennial and seasonal streams, shrubby and wooded streambelts;
Other: rocky slopes, rock outcrops.

The southern part of this preserve has most of the wetland habitats - wet meadow, various marshes and swamps, together with open areas: short grass and shrubby fields with scattered cedars. There is also some hardwood forest. The northern part is higher and drier, with hardwoods and hemlock forest, an understory of mountain laurel, rocky slopes and outcrops, and areas of reverting shrubby fields and young hardwoods. There is also a hardwood swamp, perennial and seasonal streams.

SEASONS/BIRDS
SPRING MIGRATION: marsh birds, shore birds, LAND BIRDS;
NESTING SEASON: marsh birds, LAND BIRDS;
FALL MIGRATION: marsh birds, shore birds, LAND BIRDS;
Winter: land birds.

The southern part of the Lilly Preserve has good habitat for marsh birds and wetland-oriented land birds, and spring, summer and fall are all good. Among the more interesting nesting species are: Virginia rail, green-backed heron, woodcock, willow and alder flycatchers, warbling vireo and swamp sparrow. The northern portion is also very good during the spring, summer and fall, and offers the chance to see a rather different group of nesting species, including: hooded, Canada and black-throated blue warblers in the mountain laurel understory, and worm-eating warbler on the rocky slopes. There is also an abundance of nesting redstarts and chestnut-sided warblers.

GETTING AROUND
Birding methods: car, WALK.
There are trails within the preserve that lead to all of the main habitat areas. To a limited extent, it is possible to bird from your car along Old Tophet Road and the preserve driveway.

DIRECTIONS (see Map 38): This preserve is about a mile east of the center of Roxbury. There are two access points to the preserve, one at the south side and the other at the north side. A trail within the preserve connects the two. To get to the southern part of the preserve, from the intersection of Routes 317 and 67, go east on Route 317 for 1.7 miles to a pulloff on the right. A trail leads into the preserve from the left side of the road. To get into the northern part of the preserve, continue east on Route 317 for 0.6 mile, left on Welton Road for 1.1 miles, left on Old Tophet Road for 0.2 mile to the preserve driveway on the left.

ROXBURY: MINE HILL PRESERVE

HABITATS
FOREST: hardwoods/hemlock;
Open terrestrial: tilled, short grass and tall grass fields, shrubby and wooded edges;
River/stream: river, shrubby and wooded streambelt, small perennial and seasonal streams, wooded streambelts;
Marsh/swamp/bog: mixed herbaceous and shrub marsh, shrubby hardwood swamp;
Other: rocky slope.
Several rather different areas of habitat occur at this site. As you approach it, Route 67 goes close to a section of the Shepaug River where it has a shrubby and wooded streambelt and flows past a tilled field and other farmland (See #1 below under "Directions"). Then, within the preserve, the parking area is surrounded by hardwoods/hemlock forest (see #2 below). Finally, Hodge Road on the edge of the preserve overlooks the Shepaug River, associated wetlands, farm fields, and also provides a way to bird through other forest habitats (see #3 below).

SEASONS/BIRDS
SPRING MIGRATION: water birds, marsh birds, shore birds, LAND BIRDS;
NESTING SEASON: water birds, LAND BIRDS;
FALL MIGRATION: water birds, marsh birds, shore birds, LAND BIRDS;
Winter: land birds.
A nice variety of bird species occurs at this site, reflecting the diversity of habitats within it and nearby. During the migrations, especially in the spring, it is possible to see a good mix of warblers and other standard species. Nesters include good variety of land bird species, such

as broad-winged hawk, turkey, screech owl, red-bellied woodpecker, least flycatcher, gnat-catcher, warbling vireo, worm-eating and black-throated green warblers, and Louisiana wa-terthrush.

GETTING AROUND
Birding methods: car, WALK.
Mine Hill Road, which passes by the southern edge of the preserve, can be driven or walked, but traffic is annoying at times. Hodge Road is rough, not suitable for driving for any dis-tance, but makes a nice walk.

DIRECTIONS (see Map 38): This area is in the northwest corner of Roxbury, a mile or two above the center of Roxbury Station. From the intersection of Routes 67 and 199, 1) go west on Route 67 to a pulloff on the right at a point where Route 67 is close to the Shepaug River that is also on the right. 2) Continue on Route 67 for a total distance from the intersection of Routes 67 and 199 of 2.3 miles, right on Mine Hill Road for 0.1 mile to a fork, go straight (west) on Mine Hill Road for 0.3 mile to the Mine Hill Preserve parking area on the right, at which there is the start of one trail. 3) Return on Mine Hill Road to the fork, and turn left (north) on Hodge Road for 0.2 mile. At this point the road becomes very rough. Pull over as best you can and park. From here, the road overlooks a backed-up section of the Shepaug River and associated wetlands. Hodge Road can be birded on foot northward from this point.

ROXBURY: RIVER ROAD PRESERVE

HABITATS
RIVER/STREAM: river, streambelt of shrubs, hardwoods, hemlock and tilled field, hemlock ravine; perennial and seasonal streams, wooded streambelts;
Forest: hardwoods, hardwoods/white pine, hardwoods/hemlock, white pine, hem-lock, flood plain;
Open terrestrial: tilled, short grass, tall grass and shrubby fields, wooded and shrubby edges;
Lake/pond: pond with grassy shore and beach.
This preserve lies on a hillside that overlooks the Shepaug River and the surrounding valley floor. Habitats include upland and flood plain forest, a hemlock ravine, the river and its streambelt, farm fields and a small pond.

SEASONS/BIRDS
SPRING MIGRATION: water birds, marsh birds, shore birds, LAND BIRDS;
NESTING SEASON: LAND BIRDS;
FALL MIGRATION: water birds, marsh birds, shore birds, LAND BIRDS;
Winter: land birds.
Both migrations and the nesting season are all good. The species that nest here reflect the varied habitats within the preserve: wetland-oriented birds include green-backed heron and spotted sandpiper; forest species include Acadian flycatcher (in the hemlocks along the west side of River Road), cerulean warbler (in the flood plain forest by the Shepaug River), brown creeper, screech and great horned owls; edge species include least flycatcher and warbling vireo; and open country species include bobolink, meadowlark and indigo bunting.

GETTING AROUND
Birding methods: WALK.

The best way to bird this area is to park at the Roxbury Land Trust parking area and walk from there. A woods road leads down to the Shepaug River, and there are other trails. In addition, you can continue south on River Road, birding on foot, with the preserve on your right (and private land on the left). It is better to walk this section of the road than to drive it, because it is narrow and there is no safe way to park a car.

DIRECTIONS (see Map 38): This site is in the western part of Roxbury, about two miles south of the center of Roxbury Station. To get there from the intersection of Routes 67 and 199, go west on Route 67 for 1.9 miles, left on Wellers Bridge Road for 0.1 mile, right on River Road for 0.6 mile to the Roxbury Land Trust parking area on the right.

ROXBURY: UPPER COUNTY ROAD

HABITATS
OPEN TERRESTRIAL: tilled, short grass, tall grass, mixed herbaceous and shrubby fields; shrubby and wooded hedgerows and edges; vine tangles and thickets; cedars;
FOREST: hardwoods, hemlock / hardwoods;
River/stream: perennial and seasonal streams;
Marsh/swamp/bog: seasonal pools, hardwood swamp;
Other: hawk watching site.

These quiet country roads pass through an extensive area of farm country. Some of it is currently active, and consists of large fields that are used for a variety of crops, and are bordered by hedgerows. Within this part of the site is a broad hilltop with views over very large farm fields. Much of the rest of the site is not actively farmed and consists of areas in various stages of succession - shrubby fields, vines and thickets, hardwoods of varied of ages, and cedars scattered about.

SEASONS/BIRDS
SPRING MIGRATION: LAND BIRDS;
NESTING SEASON: LAND BIRDS;
FALL MIGRATION: LAND BIRDS:
Winter: land birds.

There are birds to look for throughout the year along these roads, with a wide variety that includes open country species as well as forest-dwellers. In addition, some of these species are represented by impressive numbers of individual birds. The best period is late May and early June, when both migrants and nesters are present. During the spring migration, all of the habitats along these roads are filled with birds, either moving through or coming in to nest. Edge and shrub nesters are abundant along Upper County Road - indigo bunting, yellowthroat, chestnut-sided and blue-winged warblers. In summer, an especially interesting area is the moist hardwood forest at the intersection of Upper County and Painter Hill Roads, where there usually is a concentration of nesting forest species, including red-eyed and yellow-throated vireos, rose-breasted grosbeak, red-bellied woodpecker, least flycatcher and gnatcatcher. Another great area in summer is the high point on Painter Hill Road; it overlooks the surrounding farm fields, in or near which bobolink, meadowlark, kestrel and Savannah sparrow nest. This is also a good spot in the fall from which to look for migrating hawks, and, in winter, for horned lark, snow bunting, Lapland longspur, red-tailed and rough-legged hawks, all of which feed in the fields. Also in fall and winter, check the apple and crabapple trees, shrubby fields and thickets along Upper County and Booth Roads for sparrows, pine grosbeak and other seed- and berry- eaters. Turkey is abundant all year.

GETTING AROUND
Birding methods: CAR, WALK, BIKE.

This site is a quiet dirt road that can be birded from a car or on a bike during dry seasons, or on foot at any time of year. All the surrounding land is private, but the good habitats can be seen from the road.

DIRECTIONS (see Map 38): This road is in Roxbury, about five miles southeast of New Milford. From the intersection of Routes 317 and 67, go east on Route 317 for 1.0 mile, and turn left (north) on Upper County Road. The beginning of this road goes through farm country with fields and hedgerows. In 0.8 mile, stop at the intersection with Booth Hill Road on the right. Booth Hill Road is best birded on foot, through reverting shrubby fields and hardwoods/hemlock forest. Then, continue on Upper County Road for another 0.4 mile, and park at the intersection with Painter Hill Road, amid a moist hardwood forest that is good for nesting species. Next, go left on Painter Hill Road for 0.3 mile to a high point amid a large open area of farm fields. This is a good spot from which to look for grassland nesters, migrants and winter visitors, as well as migrating hawks in the fall. To get back to Route 317, continue on Painter Hill Road for another 1.1 miles.

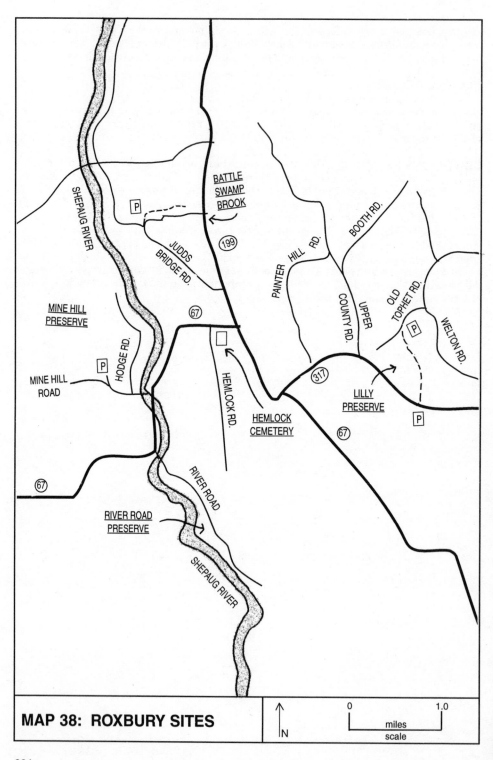

MAP 38: ROXBURY SITES

N

0   1.0

miles

scale

SALISBURY: HOUSATONIC RIVER ROAD

HABITATS
River/stream: river, slow and fast water, rocky rapids; streambelt of varied farm fields, shrubs, hardwoods, white pine and hemlock in various mixes;
Open terrestrial: tilled, short grass, tall grass and shrubby fields; shrubby and hardwood edges and hedgerows;
Forest: hardwoods, white pine, mixed conifers, cedar, flood plain;
Lake/pond: pond, herbaceous shore;
Marsh/swamp/bog: cattail marsh, hardwood and hardwood/white pine swamp.
In this section, the Housatonic River is slow and deep until it reaches the Amesville dam and power plant, below which it becomes rapid and rocky. The river valley contains a variety of farm-influenced terrestrial habitats - tilled fields, hay fields and pastures, sme of them containing scattered cedars, all bordered by shrubby and wooded edges. some of them containing scattered cedars. Next to the river are areas of flood plain forest, and away from the river, there are upland forests of hardwoods, white pine, hemlock and mixes of these species. The road also passes by two small wetlands separated from the river - a cattail marsh, and a hardwood/white pine swamp.

SEASONS/BIRDS
SPRING MIGRATION: water birds, marsh birds, shore birds, LAND BIRDS;
Nesting season: shore birds, land birds;
Fall migration: water birds, marsh birds, shore birds, land birds;
Winter: water birds, land birds.
The Housatonic River and the valley through which it passes serves as an important migration corridor in western Connecticut. The spring migration is especially good, with lots of land bird migrants; there is less variety in the fall. During both spring and fall, look for water birds on the river (including black duck, mallard, common merganser), and a variety of land birds in the terrestrial habitats nearby. Ruby-crowned kinglet often occurs in the cedars in the fields. Osprey migrates and hunts along the river in late spring and early fall, and sometimes bald eagle earlier in the spring and later in the fall. Nesting species are the usual mix, including a number that like edges and open areas. The wetlands are worth checking any time during the warm months. In winter, when there is some open water on the slow stretches of the river, there is a chance of seeing a few water birds. In addition, red-tailed hawk, wild turkey, bald eagle and raven regularly occur in this valley.

GETTING AROUND
Birding methods: CAR.
River Road provides only occasional views of the river, but passes through the varied terrestrial habitats. The surrounding land is all private.

DIRECTIONS: This section of river is several miles southeast of Canaan. To get there from the intersection of Routes 44 and 126, go west on Route 44 for 0.8 mile, and left on Housatonic River Road. This road goes through the valley described above for 3.5 miles to Amesville. Here, go left on Falls Village Road for less than 0.1 mile, and right on Dugway Road for another 2.2 miles down the valley to the intersection with Route 112.

SALISBURY: LONG POND

HABITATS
LAKE/POND: lake, shallow water, deep water, shore of hardwoods, hardwoods/ hemlock, and mixed herbaceous marsh;
OPEN TERRESTRIAL: short grass, tall grass, mixed herbaceous and shrubby fields, vine tangles and thickets, scattered cedars;
FOREST: hardwoods, hardwoods/hemlock, cedar;
River/stream: perennial and seasonal streams.

Long Pond, aka Wononpakook Lake, has a wooded, partly developed shore, with small pockets of marsh here and there. There is an undeveloped town recreation area at the south end of the lake. This area, and the driveway that leads to it, is surrounded by reverting fields, with scattered cedars, thickets, and patches of mixed hardwoods/conifer forest.

SEASONS/BIRDS
SPRING MIGRATION: WATER BIRDS, marsh birds, shore birds, LAND BIRDS;
Nesting season: land birds;
FALL MIGRATION: WATER BIRDS, marsh birds, shore birds, LAND BIRDS;
Winter: land birds.

The spring and fall are the most interesting times at this site. Migrating water bird species that are often seen here in the spring include common loon, ring-necked duck, common goldeneye, bufflehead, common and hooded mergansers. Also during the spring migration, you may expect to see great blue and green-backed herons, woodcock, spotted and solitary sandpipers. Notable among nesters are shrub and edge species that are attracted to the shrubby fields and thickets around the driveway and recreation area. These include brown thrasher, indigo bunting, prairie warbler and field sparrow. (However, see access restriction under "Getting Around", below.) Fall migrants include the species seen in the spring, plus an abundance of such berry-eaters as robin, hermit thrush and cedar waxwing.

GETTING AROUND
Birding methods: car, walk.

A dirt road leads to the shore of the lake and runs along it for a short distance; it provides views of the southern end of the lake. This is a town recreation area for residents of Salisbury, and should not be entered during the warm months when it is used for that purpose.

DIRECTIONS: (See Map 25): Long Pond is about five miles southwest of the center of Salisbury, and not far from Lake Wononskopomuk (described elsewhere in this chapter). From the intersection of Routes 41 and 112, go south on Route 41 for 1.2 miles, right on Long Pond Road for 0.7 mile, right on Valley Road for 0.2 mile, and right on the driveway to the town recreation area.

SALISBURY: MT. RIGA

HABITATS
FOREST: hardwoods, hardwoodsw/white pine, hardwoods/hemlock, hemlock, mixed conifers, mountain laurel;
RIVER/STREAM: stream, fast water, streambelts of hardwoods, hardwoods/hemlock and hemlock;
MARSH/SWAMP/BOG: black spruce bog, hemlock swamp, hardwood swamp;
Lake/pond: lake, pond, wooded shore;
Other: ledge, cliff, rocky slope, rocky summit.

This area lies in Connecticut's northwest plateau ecoregion. It is the highest and coldest part of the state, and has conditions and vegetation more typical of northern New England than of Connecticut. The vegetation of the hillsides is northern - hemlock, white pine, white and yellow birch, and other northern hardwoods with large areas of mountain laurel understory. Wachocastinook Brook drains the east side of the plateau, and forms a steep-sided ravine with a hardwood and hemlock streambelt. There are several mountains - Bald Peak and Bear Mountain among them - on this remote and unspoiled plateau, and their rocky summits offer views of the Catskill Mountains to the west, and of the lakes and farms in the Housatonic Valley to the east. Bingham Pond lies high on the plateau - at 1894 foot elevation, it is the highest pond in Connecticut. There is a bog around part of the shore that contains leatherleaf and other shrubs growing on a mat of sphagnum moss. Black spruce trees grow on the bog, and red spruce - rare as a natural species in Connecticut - occurs at the edge of the forest behind the bog.

SEASONS/BIRDS
SPRING MIGRATION: LAND BIRDS
NESTING SEASON: LAND BIRDS;
FALL MIGRATION: LAND BIRDS;
Winter: land birds.

The spring and fall migrations are quite good on this plateau, but the real reason for a visit is to look for nesting species - this area provides the type of large, undisturbed habitat required by some forest-interior land bird species for nesting. The best period is from April (when these species start to arrive) through August. Species known to nest in this area include: winter wren, solitary vireo, black-throated green, black-throated blue and Canada warblers (look for the latter two species in the mountain laurel understory of the hemlock forest), Louisiana waterthrush (look along the brook), and junco. In the fall, Bald Peak provides a scenic spot from which to watch the hawk migration.

GETTING AROUND
Birding methods: CAR, WALK.

A dirt road can be driven through much of the area. The road starts near the village of Salisbury at about 700 feet above sea level and climbs up to the plateau, reaching an altitude of about 1,900 feet. On the way, it follows the side of the deep ravine formed by Wachocastinook Brook. The dirt section of this road (most of it) is often impassable during the late fall, winter and early spring. Many trails start from points along the road, including one to the top of Bald Peak (0.2 mile, rough and steep), and one to Bingham Pond (0.2 mile, often wet).

DIRECTIONS: This large area occupies the northwest corner of Connecticut, and lies several miles northwest of the center of Salisbury. From Route 44 in the center of Salisbury, go north on Washinee Street (next to the town hall) for 0.7 mile, and left at the fork onto the road to Mt. Riga. This road immediately forks again - this time take the right fork, still following signs to Mt. Riga. From this point for the next several miles this road (now dirt) passes through forest habitats near the brook. At 3.6 miles from your starting point in Salisbury, there is an intersection with another dirt road at a dam. Turn right. **To get to Bald Peak,** follow this road for still another 0.4 mile to a grassy parking area on the left. The trail to the top of Bald Peak starts here, on the right. **To get to Bingham Pond,** follow the road for another 0.7 mile to a small parking area on the left. The trail to the pond starts here, on the right. From here, it is possible to follow the road for several more miles until it drops down from the plateau and intersects with a hardtop road near North Egremont in Massachusetts. (On the way, the road passes two trails on the right that can be taken to the summit of Bear Mountain.)

SALISBURY: RAILROAD PATH

HABITATS
MARSH/SWAMP/BOG: sedge and shrub marsh, shrub swamp;
Forest: hardwoods, white pine;
Open terrestrial: shrubby field, edge;
Lake/pond: pond, shallow water, shores of marsh, swamp and woods.
River/stream: perennial stream.
This former railroad line passes through varied forest and open terrestrial habitats, and close by a marsh, of which it affords excellent views from an elevation of eight or ten feet.

SEASONS/BIRDS
SPRING MIGRATION: water birds, marsh birds, shore birds, LAND BIRDS;
NESTING SEASON: water birds, marsh birds, LAND BIRDS;
Fall migration: water birds, marsh birds, shore birds, LAND BIRDS;
Winter: land birds.
This site is a pleasant place to see a typical variety of migrating and resident water, marsh and edge-dwelling land birds. The spring migration is good. Among the highlights of the nesting season are Virginia rail and green-backed heron. Great blue heron comes here to feed.

GETTING AROUND
Birding methods: WALK, BIKE, SKI.
The railroad tracks and ties have been removed, so this is now a broad and level walking/biking/skiing path, 1.3 miles in length. Because the path is elevated eight feet or so above the marsh, and is right next to it, it is an ideal place to observe life in a wetland.

DIRECTIONS: This path runs between the village centers of Salisbury and Lakeville. From the center of Salisbury at the eastern (or northern) intersection of Routes 44 and 41, go west on Route 44 for 0.4 mile, left on Lime Rock Road for 0.1 mile to the point at which the path intersects with the road. Park here and walk right (or west) toward Lakeville. From this point it is also possible to walk a shorter distance to the east.

SALISBURY: WEATOGUE ROAD

HABITATS
RIVER/STREAM: deep water, streambelt of shrubs, hardwoods, hardwoods/white pine, white pine;
OPEN TERRESTRIAL: tilled, short grass and tall grass fields, shrubby and hardwood edges and hedgerows;
Forest: hardwoods, hardwoods/white pine, white pine, flood plain, cedar;
Marsh/swamp/bog: shrub marsh, shrub swamp, shrubby hardwood swamp, hardwood swamp, open water.

This is the northernmost section of the Housatonic River in Connecticut. Here, the river is slow and deep, and runs through intermittent woods and farm country. The fields are varied - some are tilled, most to grow corn, others are used to grow hay, and still others are used as pasture. Shrubby edges and hedgerows separate them, and the river banks and hillsides are mostly wooded. In addition, there is a wetland a short distance from the river. There are occasional stretches where the road runs right along the river; elsewhere it is separated from it by fields and/or woods.

SEASONS/BIRDS
SPRING MIGRATION: water birds, marsh birds, shore birds, LAND BIRDS;
Nesting season: land birds;
Fall migration: water birds, marsh birds, shore birds, land birds;
Winter: water birds, land birds.

The spring migrations is best at this site. Ducks and geese (mostly Canada goose, black duck and mallard) feed on the river and nearby fields, and common merganser occurs on the river. The river is used as a migration corridor by lots of land birds including most of the standard mix of inland land bird species, as well as osprey in May and September, and occasionally bald eagle, earlier in the spring and later in the fall. Nesters include a variety of species with an affinity for fields, edges and hedgerows. In winter, there is usually some open water on the river, and this attracts a few water birds and an occasional bald eagle. Raven is sometimes also in the area. Red-tailed hawk is present all year. Marsh birds and land birds that are attracted to aquatic habitats can be found in spring, summer and fall at a nearby wetland.

GETTING AROUND
Birding methods: CAR, walk.
All of the areas described above can be seen from your car. The road can be walked, but the surrounding land is private.

DIRECTIONS: This site is a couple of miles northwest of Canaan. The best way to start is at the center of Ashley Falls in southwestern Massachusetts. From the intersection of Route 7A and Rannapo Road, go west on Rannapo Road (along the Housatonic River) for 0.9 mile, left on Weatogue Road for 0.8 mile to the Massachusetts/Connecticut state line. Follow Weatogue Road along the river for 2.7 miles, left on Twin Lakes Road for 0.8 mile to Route 44. The wetland is on both sides of Route 44 near the intersection of Route 44 and Twin Lakes Road.

SALISBURY: WONONSCOPOMUC LAKE

HABITATS
LAKE/POND: lake, deep and shallow water; short grass, shrubby, wooded, sandy and partly developed shore; pond with shallow water, short grass shore;
Forest: hardwoods;
Open terrestrial: short grass field;
River/stream: stream.

This lake has a shore with many residences among hardwoods. The lake itself has a very deep area, so that it freezes later than most other lakes in Litchfield County.

SEASONS/BIRDS
SPRING MIGRATION: WATER BIRDS, land birds;
Nesting season:
FALL MIGRATION: WATER BIRDS, shore birds, land birds;
Winter: gulls, water birds.

This is a site to visit in the early spring (March and early April), and late fall (November and early December) to see migrating water birds. Sometimes there is not much to see, but at other times ring-necked duck, common goldeneye, bufflehead and common merganser are present. In addition, if you put together all of the sightings over the years, you realize that a great diversity of water birds has occurred here, including just about every species that might occur in inland Connecticut.

GETTING AROUND
Birding methods: car.

The only access that can be used is the town recreation area, called the Town Grove. Off season, you can drive close to the shore of the lake, but the area is restricted to use by town residents during warm months.

DIRECTIONS: This lake is in Lakeville, a couple of miles west of the center of Salisbury. From the western (or southern) intersection of Routes 44 and 41, go west on Route 44 for less than 0.1 mile, left on Holly Street for 0.1 mile, and take the first right into the town recreation area.

SHARON: GUINEA BROOK WETLAND

HABITATS
MARSH/SWAMP/BOG: sedge, mixed herbaceous and shrub marsh; shrub swamp, shrubby hardwood swamp; dead wood, shrubby and hardwood edges;
Forest: hardwoods, hardwoods/hemlock, mountain laurel;
Lake/pond: pond, hardwoods shore;
River/stream: perennial stream, hardwoods streambelt.

This large, beaver-controlled wetland contains a rich and very productive pond and associated marsh and swamp. The dirt road that passes it continues through a forest of hardwoods and hemlock.

SEASONS/BIRDS
SPRING MIGRATION: WATER BIRDS, MARSH BIRDS, shore birds, LAND BIRDS;
NESTING SEASON: water birds, marsh birds, LAND BIRDS;
FALL MIGRATION: water birds, marsh birds, shore birds, LAND BIRDS;
Winter: land birds.

This fine wetland is good for birding in the spring, summer and fall. During the spring and fall, it is possible to see a good variety of wetland-oriented migrants. Highlights include olive-sided flycatcher and, in May and August, a large number of nighthawks. Numerous species nest in the wetland or come to it to feed from nest sites in nearby terrestrial habitats. These include: wood duck, great blue and green-backed herons, Virginia rail, red-shouldered hawk, screech owl, yellow-bellied sapsucker, pileated woodpecker, alder, willow, least and great crested flycatchers, northern waterthrush, black-throated blue and Canada warblers. In winter, there is much less diversity.

GETTING AROUND
Birding methods: CAR, WALK.

This is a good site for non-walkers to bird, because the wetland can be seen well from the road. In addition, West Woods Road beyond the wetland is little traveled, and is good for birding through forest habitats by car or on foot. It is sometimes not suitable for driving during the late fall, winter and early spring. Stay on the road - the surrounding land is private.

DIRECTIONS: This area is three or four miles west of the center of Cornwall Bridge, where Routes 4 and 7 cross the Housatonic. From the western intersection of Routes 4 and 7, go west on Route 4 for 2.5 miles, and left on West Woods Road #2 for 0.7 mile to the intersection with South Ellsworth Road. Bear right on West Woods Road for 0.1 mile to the wetland on the left. West Woods Road continues for about two miles past the wetland, and can be walked or (sometimes) driven.

SHARON: HOUSATONIC MEADOWS STATE PARK

HABITATS
FOREST: hardwoods, hardwoods/white pine, hardwoods/hemlock, white pine, flood plain;
RIVER/STREAM: river, fast water, islands, shrubby and wooded streambelt; perennial streams;
Open terrestrial: short grass field, wooded and shrubby edges;
Other: ledge, cliff, rocky slope.

This park occupies 451 acres along the west bank of the Housatonic River. It includes over two miles of river shore and also includes the steep west side of the valley that has a typical upland mixture of hardwoods and white pine.

SEASONS/BIRDS
SPRING MIGRATION: LAND BIRDS;
NESTING SEASON: LAND BIRDS;
Fall migration: land birds;
Winter: land birds.

This is a spring and summer site - the spring migration is great, and there are interesting nesting species. Lots of migrants come up the river in the spring, especially thrushes (gray-cheeked has been seen here), vireos and warblers. Nesters include several northern species (winter wren, black-throated green, black-throated blue and magnolia warblers), several that have an affinity for riverine habitats (rough-winged swallow, Acadian flycatcher, cerulean warbler and Louisiana waterthrush), and such others as broad-winged hawk and all of the vireos except white-eyed. The fall migration is pretty good. The main winter attraction is an occasional bald eagle on a tree overlooking the river.

GETTING AROUND
Birding methods: car, WALK.
There are trails that go along the river and up the hillside. These trails go through the western part of the state park and into the Housatonic State Forest, which is contiguous and lies just to the west. The part of the park near the river gets crowded in summer and on spring and fall weekends.

DIRECTIONS: This park lies along Route 7 just north of the village of Cornwall Bridge. To get there from the intersection of Routes 7 and 4 at the west end of the bridge over the Housatonic River, go north on Route 7, which runs through the park for the next 2.9 miles. The main park entrance is on the east side of Route 7, 1.3 miles north of the bridge. Trails up the western hillside start at the tent camping parking area on the west side of Route 7, 1.1 miles north of the intersection of Routes 7 and 4, and at other points within the park north of this parking area.

SHARON: MUDGE POND

HABITATS
LAKE/POND: lake, shallow water, deep water, shrubby and wooded shore;
Forest: hardwoods, white pine;
Open terrestrial: mixed herbaceous and shrubby field, edge/hedgerow;
River/stream: stream, shrubby streambelt;
Marsh/swamp/bog: shrub marsh, shrub swamp.
This is a mid-sized lake that has extensive areas of shallow water, and a deep area near the eastern shore, where there is usually open water throughout the winter. The shoreline is partly developed, partly wooded, and has an area of marsh and swamp at the north end.

SEASONS/BIRDS
SPRING MIGRATION: WATER BIRDS, marsh birds, shore birds, land birds;
Nesting season: land birds;
FALL MIGRATION: WATER BIRDS, marsh birds, shore birds, land birds;
WINTER: WATER BIRDS, land birds.
Migrating and wintering water birds are the main attraction at this site; the variety and numbers vary from fair to very good. The best periods are spring (especially March), fall (especially November) and winter, because there is usually open water.

Dabbling ducks feed in the shallow water at the south end of the lake - the species may include gadwall, pintail, green-winged teal, wigeon, and also coot. In the deep water area, there are often ring-necked duck, common goldeneye, bufflehead, hooded and common mergansers and pied-billed grebe. Canvasback, redhead and both scaup species have also been seen here. The land bird migrations make the habitats around the shore worth check-ing, especially in November for sparrows among the shrubby edges of the town beach. In April, several species of swallows feeding over the lake put on quite a show. Osprey occurs in spring and fall.

During winter, there often is a large group of Canada geese in and around the open water area. They are worth a careful look because there are sometimes snow geese among them, and occasionally one or two white-fronted geese. Bald eagle is sometimes present in late fall, winter and early spring.

GETTING AROUND:
Birding methods: CAR.
Stay on the town road and within the town beach area; the surrounding land is private. Do not come here in summer - the area is crowded and access to the town beach is restricted. When birding at other times, a scope is helpful.

DIRECTIONS: (See Map 25): Mudge Pond is about a mile north of the Sharon village green. From the green, at the intersection of Routes 361 and 41, go west (or north) on Route 361 for 1.0 mile, and right on Mudge Pond Road for 0.4 mile, at which point it starts going north along the west shore of the pond, providing views from almost all of it. The town beach is at the north end of the lake, to the right of Mudge Pond Road.

SHARON: NORTHEAST AUDUBON CENTER

HABITATS
FOREST: hardwoods, hardwoods/white pine, hardwoods/hemlock, hemlock;
OPEN TERRESTRIAL: short grass, tall grass, mixed herbeceous and shrubby fields, shrubby and wooded edges;
LAKE/POND: ponds; shores of hardwoods, mixed herbaceous and shrub marshes, shrub and shrubby hardwood swamps.
RIVER/STREAM: stream, fast water, shrubby, hardwood and hemlock streambelt, hemlock ravine;
MARSH/SWAMP/BOG: cattail, sedge, mixed herbaceous and shrub marshes, shrub, shrubby hardwood and hardwood swamps.
Almost every type of inland habitat is represented in this 684-acre sanctuary. Most of the area is wooded, and there are two large ponds with areas of marsh, swamp and hardwoods along their shores, streams, several clearings, and a hemlock ravine. The extensive lower- and mid-slope deciduous forest which covers most of the preserve provides areas of undisturbed interior forest habitat. Bog Meadow Pond, at the back of the preserve, has a remote, un-spoiled quality that is rare in Connecticut. There is a feeling of wilderness in this preserve, a sense confirmed by occasional sightings of bobcat, fox, coyote and otter.

SEASONS/BIRDS
SPRING MIGRATION: WATER BIRDS, marsh birds, shore birds, LAND BIRDS;
NESTING SEASON: WATER BIRDS, marsh birds, LAND BIRDS;
FALL MIGRATION: WATER BIRDS, marsh birds, shore birds, LAND BIRDS;
·**Winter:** land birds.
This is one of Connecticut's richest inland birding areas. It is an excellent place in which to look for almost any of the land bird species that commonly occur in Connecticut, and you

may see uncommon species among them. Over 190 species have been reported here over the years, including: 18 raptors, seven thrushes, five vireos, and 32 species of warblers (plus two subspecies). The total includes a number of species that are uncommon in interior Connecticut, such as northern shoveler, blue-winged teal and black-crowned night heron.

This sanctuary is especially good for spring and fall migrant warblers. In number of probable or confirmed nesting species, Northeast Audubon ranks fifth in the state, behind White Memorial, Nepaug Reservoir, Barkhamsted Reservoir and Mohawk State Forest. Among the nesters are a number of northern species: yellow-bellied sapsucker, hermit thrush, brown creeper, winter wren, solitary vireo, magnolia, Canada, black-throated blue and black-throated green warblers and pine siskin. Acadian flycatcher nests in hemlocks over the Ford Pond outlet stream.

GETTING AROUND
Birding methods: WALK, HANDICAP ACCESS.
Eleven miles of trails reach all the major habitats in the preserve. One nature trail is designed to be accessible to those who use walkers, wheelchairs, canes, or baby strollers. Parts of the sanctuary of particular interest to birders are the outlet to Ford Pond (a hardwoods/hemlock streambelt with a well developed understory), the Bog Meadow Trail (goes through excellent forest habitats), Bog Meadow Pond (open water, varied wetlands across the pond), and the outlet stream of Bog Meadow Pond (has a wooded streambelt). A trail map is available at the visitor center, which also has an excellent book store which specializes in natural history and environmental topics for adults and children. A fee is charged.

DIRECTIONS: This sanctuary is located two miles southeast of the village of Sharon. To get there from Sharon at the intersection of Routes 4 and 41, go east on Route 4 for 2.4 miles to the sanctuary entrance on the right.

SHARON: ROY SWAMP WMA/MILES SANCTUARY/HOUSATONIC STATE FOREST

HABITATS
MARSH/SWAMP/BOG: cattail, mixed herbaceous, sedge and shrub marsh; shrub, shrubby hardwood and white pine swamp, dead wood;
RIVER/STREAM: stream, fast water, slow water; streambelt of marshes, shrubs, hardwoods, hemlock;
LAKE/POND: pond, shallow water, marshy, shrubby and wooded shore;
OPEN TERRESTRIAL: mixed herbaceous and shrubby fields, shrubby and wooded edges;
FOREST: hardwoods, hardwoods/white pine, hardwoods/hemlock, hemlock;
Other: rocky slope, ledge.
This site includes a chain of connected habitats that lie in a three-mile-long valley that is perched high above the Housatonic River, into which the valley drains. The Roy Swamp Wildlife Management Area lies at the upper (northern) end of this valley; it is an extremely productive pond surrounded by sedge, cattail and shrub marsh. This pond drains into a gentle valley, with a bottomland that contains a series of rich streambelt habitats, including sedge and shrub marshes, shrub swamps, standing deadwood, Miles Pond and and other small ponds. These habitats are protected by National Audubon's Miles Sanctuary. The hillsides of the valley are covered by deciduous forest, and some of this area lies within the Housatonic State Forest. The road and ponds have edges of shrubs and saplings. The stream

that goes through the valley (Carse Brook) is slow and meandering for much of its length, but picks up energy at the south end of the valley as it drops down through a hemlock ravine into the larger, deeper valley of the Housatonic River.

SEASONS/BIRDS

SPRING MIGRATION: WATER BIRDS, MARSH BIRDS, SHORE BIRDS, LAND BIRDS;
NESTING SEASON: WATER BIRDS, MARSH BIRDS, LAND BIRDS;
FALL MIGRATION: WATER BIRDS, MARSH BIRDS, SHORE BIRDS, LAND BIRDS;
Winter: land birds.

This is an exceptionally good wetland site - in Litchfield County it is second only to White Memorial. The birding is excellent from mid-March to mid-October, and is fantastic in May. During the spring migration, it is possible to see a very wide variety of water, marsh, shore and (especially) land birds, including olive-sided flycatcher, osprey and a large number of warblers. Also during the spring migration, the many species that will nest in the area start to arrive. These include a number of water birds - such as pied-billed grebe, wood duck and hooded merganser. Nesting marsh and shore birds include least and American bitterns, green-backed heron, moorhen, Virginia rail, sora, spotted sandpiper, woodcock and great blue heron (feeding only). The list of nesting land birds is truly impressive: all of Connecticut's wood-peckers (except the rare red-headed, but including both the northern yellow-bellied sap-sucker and the southern red-bellied woodpecker); willow and alder flycatchers; various warblers including golden-winged; both waterthrushes; screech, barred and great horned owls; swamp sparrow; and (at least in past years) whip-poor-will. Additional northern spe-cies nest along the fast, lower end of Carse Brook: solitary vireo, black-throated green war-bler and junco, as well as Acadian flycatcher. The fall migration is also good, but the excite-ment subsides in winter.

GETTING AROUND:

Birding methods: CAR, WALK, BOAT.

Much of the Roy Swamp wetland can be seen from sections of the West Cornwall and Eggleston Roads, but it can be better explored from a canoe. The streambelt habitats and the hillsides of the valley can be viewed from the West Cornwall Road as it goes down the valley. The south-ern part of Carse Brook - the section that goes through the ravine - can be seen intermittently from Smith Hill Road. The nature of the habitat (much is marshy) and its ownership (some is private) makes it necessary to stay on the road when birding. The exception is Roy Swamp, to which there is public access.

DIRECTIONS (see Map 39): This area is located between the villages of Sharon and West Cornwall. The following directions start in Sharon and end in West Cornwall.

From Sharon at the intersection of Routes 41 and 4, go north on Route 41 for 0.9 mile and turn right onto Caulkinstown Road (which soon becomes West Cornwall Road). In 2.5 miles, Roy Swamp and an access to it by the outlet stream are on the left. In 0.1 mile further, Egglestown Road is on the left. It can be birded by car or on foot for about half a mile as it runs between the shrubby edge of Roy Swamp and the hardwoods of the Housatonic State Forest. Con-tinue on West Cornwall Road for another 0.5 mile to a dirt road on the left that leads into an extensive block of the Housatonic State Forest. Park here and walk this dirt road through hardwoods/white pine forest with a mountain laurel shrub layer, to a white pine swamp where great blue heron has nested. Return to West Cornwall Road and continue for another 2.4 miles down the valley along very nice wetland habitats, to the intersection with Surdan Mountain Road. (Continued on p. 307.)

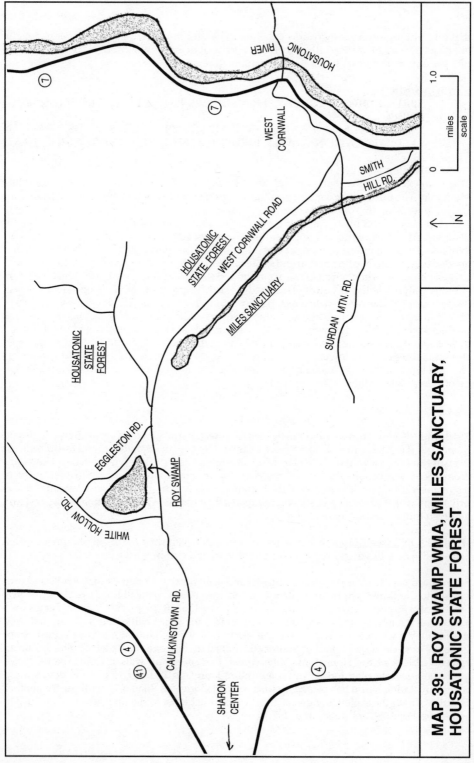

MAP 39: ROY SWAMP WMA, MILES SANCTUARY, HOUSATONIC STATE FOREST

At this point, one choice is to continue on West Cornwall Road for 1.3 miles and reach Route 7 at West Cornwall. Another choice is to go through the Carse Brook ravine by going right on Surdan Mountain Road for 0.1 mile, and left on Smith Hill Road. The latter goes steeply through the ravine for 0.9 mile and reaches Route 7 at a point 1.5 miles south of West Cornwall. Smith Hill Road is not maintained in winter, and is rough at any time of year; but the habitat is very good.

SHARON: SKIFF MOUNTAIN WILDLIFE MANAGEMENT AREA

HABITATS
OPEN TERRESTRIAL: tall grass, mixed herbaceous and shrubby fields, shrubby and wooded edges, shrubby and hardwood hedgerows;
LAKE/POND: pond, shallow water, marshy, shrubby and wooded shore;
Marsh/swamp/bog: cattail, mixed herbaceous and shrub marsh, shrub and hardwood swamp;
Forest: hardwoods, hardwoods/white pine, mixed conifers;
River/stream: perennial and seasonal streams.
This quiet and secluded area lies in the highlands on the west side of the Housatonic River Valley, 1,200 to 1,300 feet above sea level. It contains a variety of open terrestrial, forest and wetland habitats.

SEASONS/BIRDS
SPRING MIGRATION: water birds, marsh birds, shore birds, LAND BIRDS;
NESTING SEASON: water birds, LAND BIRDS;
Fall migration: water birds, marsh birds, shore birds, land birds.
Winter: land birds.
A nice range of bird species occurs at this site, reflecting the diversity of the habitats within it. During the spring migration, water birds include Canada goose and common species of dabbling ducks. Great blue and green-backed herons, spotted sandpiper, killdeer and woodcock can all be seen in the vicinity of the pond and the surrounding wetlands and fields. Land bird spring migrants include a variety of open and forest species. The list of nesters features open and edge species: there are lots of bobolinks and Savannah sparrows; also brown thrasher, indigo bunting, field sparrow, and warblers - prairie, chestnut-sided, blue-winged, golden-winged and both of their hybrids (Lawrence's and Brewster's). In the fall, look for many of the same species as in the spring. The best fall birding is for sparrows in October and November along the main road through the area. In winter, the open fields attract red-tailed hawk, rough-legged hawk (occasional), harrier (in fall, winter and spring), horned lark and snow bunting.

GETTING AROUND:
Birding methods: CAR, WALK.
A road goes through the area, and there are a number of woods roads that can be walked. This area is quite heavily used for hunting.

DIRECTIONS: This area is in Sharon, immediately north of the Sharon/Kent town line. The best way to get there is from the village of Kent, at the intersection of Routes 7 and 341. Go west on Route 341 for 0.3 mile across the Housatonic River, and right on Skiff Mountain Road. At 4.5 miles from Route 341, Skiff Mountain Road goes off to the right, but keep going straight ahead on West Woods Road. Starting at 4.8 miles from Route 341 and continuing until 6.2 miles, the road (once again called Skiff Mountain Road) goes through the wildlife management area.

SHARON: STANLEY WILDLIFE MANAGEMENT AREA (NORTHERN BLOCK)

HABITATS
OPEN TERRESTRIAL: tilled, short grass, tall grass, mixed herbaceous and shrubby fields; shrubby and hardwood edges;
RIVER/STREAM: river, slow and fast water, shrubby and hardwood streambelt; perennial and seasonal streams;
Forest: hardwoods, hardwoods/white pine, hardwoods/hemlock, flood plain.
This area lies along the west side of the Housatonic River, just north of the Kent River Road area (which is described under Kent). The habitats in this northern block include the shore of the Housatonic River, flood plain forest, mixed hardwoods on the hillsides west of the trail, and areas of tilled, grassy and reverting fields - quite similar to the Kent River Road area to the south, but parts of this northern area are still in agricultural use.

SEASONS/BIRDS
SPRING MIGRATION: water birds, LAND BIRDS;
NESTING SEASON: LAND BIRDS;
FALL MIGRATION: water birds, LAND BIRDS;
Winter: land birds.
Spring, summer and fall are all good on this road and trail. During the spring migration, there are water birds on the river, but the real attraction is the great variety of land birds that are moving up the valley, and also coming to this variety of habitats to nest. Interesting species among the many nesters are cliff swallow (under the Route 7 bridge), orchard oriole (usually in sycamore trees), cerulean warbler (in the flood plain forest), golden-winged warbler (on field edges), and bobolink (in tall grass fields).

GETTING AROUND:
Birding methods: car, WALK.
Starting at the west end of the bridge over the Housatonic, a road goes south along the west shore of the river for 1.6 miles to a small parking area. From this point, a three-mile section of the Appalachian Trail continues south through the wildlife management area, along the west bank of the Housatonic river, and eventually reaches River Road in Kent.

DIRECTIONS: This area is immediately south of the town of Cornwall Bridge. To get to it from Route 7 at the west end of the Route 7 bridge over the Housatonic River, make a sharp turn to the north off Route 7 onto River Road, and follow River Road as it loops around clockwise until it runs south along the river and passes under the Route 7 bridge . Drive this road for 1.6 miles to a fork at which there is a small parking area. A trail and woods road starts here, follows the river and eventually reaches River Road in Kent.

THOMASTON: NORTHFIELD BROOK FLOOD CONTROL AREA

HABITATS
OPEN TERRESTRIAL: short grass and shrubby fields, edges;
Forest: hardwoods, hardwoods/hemlock, hardwoods/white pine, hemlock;
River/stream: stream with wooded and shrubby shore;
Lake/pond: pond, shore of short grass field, shrubs;
Other: hawk watching site.

A dam lies across a tributary of the Naugatuck River, and the flood control area above the dam contains the bottomlands of a small valley. This valley includes a rich variety of streambelt habitats, shrubby fields, mixed hardwoods and hemlock/hardwoods forest. The top of the dam overlooks the valley.

SEASONS/BIRDS
SPRING MIGRATION: LAND BIRDS;
Nesting season: land birds;
FALL MIGRATION: LAND BIRDS;
Winter: land birds.

During migration, there is a nice variety of the land bird species that you would expect in these habitats, and in the nesting season, the standard mix of species, plus northern nesters including yellow-bellied sapsucker and solitary vireo.

GETTING AROUND
Birding methods: CAR, WALK, BIKE, SKI.

Most of the area can be seen from the access road, and other areas are visible from the open mowed fields. There is a paved road over a mile long within the site. This area gets crowded during the summer, and an admissions fee is charged.

DIRECTIONS: This area is about two miles northwest of Thomaston. To get there from the northern intersection of Routes 254 and 6 in Thomaston, go north on Route 254 for 2.3 miles to the dam on the right, and a total of 3.1 miles to the entrance road on the right.

THOMASTON: THOMASTON DAM/LEADMINE BROOK AREA

HABITATS
FOREST: hardwoods, hardwoods/white pine, hardwoods/hemlock, white pine/ hemlock, hemlock;
OPEN TERRESTRIAL: short grass, tall grass, mixed herbaceous and shrubby fields;
RIVER/STREAM: river, herbaceous, shrubby and hardwood streambelt, perennial and seasonal streams, pools, shrubby, hardwood and hemlock streambelt, hemlock ravine;
MARSH/SWAMP/BOG: wet meadow, mixed herbaceous marsh, shrub marsh, shrub swamp, shrubby hardwood swamp, hardwood swamp;
Lake/pond: seasonal pond, seasonal pool, edge;
Other: hawk watching site, rocky slope, ledge, cliff.

This site is includes a stretch of the Naugatuck River where it is dammed, and the confluence of Leadmine Brook with the Naugatuck River. The habitats are enriched by the presence of small pockets of varied wetlands among the woods and fields. The dam provides a panaramic view of the Naugatuck Valley, and is a good place from which to hatch hawks during the fall migration.

SEASONS/BIRDS
SPRING MIGRATION: WATER BIRDS, marsh birds, shore birds, LAND BIRDS;
NESTING SEASON: water birds, marsh birds, shore birds, LAND BIRDS;
FALL MIGRATION: water birds, marsh birds, shore birds, LAND BIRDS;
Winter: land birds.

The spring and fall migrations are very good at this site; a nice variety of land birds can be seen (including osprey), as well as great blue and green-backed herons, spotted and solitary sandpipers, greater yellowlegs, killdeer and a variety of water birds. During October and November, a wide variety of sparrows occur here. Nesting land birds include both northern species such as yellow-bellied sapsucker and southerners such as red-bellied woodpecker. There are also large numbers of red-eyed, yellow-throated and warbling vireos, as well as great crested flycatcher and gnatcatcher. Nesters also include edge species such as willow and least flycatchers, catbird, indigo bunting, yellowthroat, yellow, chestnut-sided and prairie warblers. Kingfisher and rough-winged swallows also nest here. Bald eagle can occasionally be seen during the fall, winter and early spring.

GETTING AROUND
Birding methods: CAR, WALK, BIKE.
There are roads and trails through this area, some of which are paved and can be driven, and also provide easy walking or biking. It is a popular hunting area.

DIRECTIONS: This site is on the east shore of the Naugatuck River, about a mile northeast of the center of Thomaston. **To get there from Route 8: southbound**, take exit 40, turn left and go north on Route 222 for 1.0 mile to the dam on the left. The road into the Leadmine Brook area is on the left side of Route 222 0.8 mile further north. **Northbound:** take exit 39, go west (left) on Route 6 for 0.4 mile, right on Route 222 for 1.6 miles to the dam on the left. The access road into the Leadmine Brook area is on the left side of Route 222 0.8 mile farther north.

THOMASTON: THOMASTON NATURE TRAIL

HABITATS
Open terrestrial: shrubby field;
Forest: hardwoods, hardwoods/hemlock, flood plain, cedar;
Marsh/swamp/bog: mixed herbaceous, cattail and shrub marsh, deadwood;
River/stream: stream, hardwood streambelt;
Other: gravel pit.
This site is contiguous to the Black Rock State Park, and consists mainly of shrubby overgrown gravel pit and a small wetland. There is also an overgrown gravel pit.

SEASONS/BIRDS
Spring migration: land birds;
Nesting season: land birds;
Fall migration: land birds;
Winter: land birds.
This site is good during the land bird migration - especially in the fall, when sparrows abound. It also has a nice variety of shrub and edge nesters, including brown thrasher, prairie warbler and indigo bunting. If there are still berries on the shrubs in winter, robins, flickers and other frugivores come in to feed.

GETTING AROUND
Birding methods: WALK.
A nature trail makes a loop through the site; a branch of this trail leads to Black Rock State Park.

DIRECTIONS: This site is about a mile southwest of the center of Thomaston. To get there from the intersection of Routes 109 and 6, go west on Route 109 for 0.4 mile, and left at the driveway just past the high school buildings. Park in the lower lot. The trail starts on the right, off the driveway just above this lot.

THOMASTON/WATERTOWN:
BLACK ROCK STATE PARK/FLOOD CONTROL AREA

HABITATS
FOREST: hardwoods, hardwoods/white pine, hardwoods/hemlock, white pine/hemlock, white pine, hemlock, flood plain, mountain laurel;
OPEN TERRESTRIAL: short grass and shrubby field, edge;
LAKE/POND: ponds, mud flat (intermittent), seasonal pools;
RIVER/STREAM: perennial and seasonal streams; herbaceous, shrubby and wooded streambelts;
Marsh/swamp/bog: herbaceous and shrub marsh, shrubby and wooded edges;
Other: hawk watching site, rocky slope, ledge, cliff.
Black Rock State Park occupies 439 acres in a valley just below the Black Rock Dam. The flood control area includes another 300-plus acres above the dam. The valley floor includes a flood plain forest, ponds, small pockets of marsh, and a variety of forested, open terrestrial and streambelt habitats. The dam provides a view of the valley.

SEASONS/BIRDS
SPRING MIGRATION: water birds, marsh birds, shore birds, LAND BIRDS;
NESTING SEASON: land birds;
FALL MIGRATION: water birds, marsh birds, shore birds, LAND BIRDS;
Winter: land birds.
This is a very good site in which to look for land birds during migration. In the spring, the highlights are osprey, and lots of thrushes, vireos and warblers. There is a good variety of the nesting species you would expect to find in this diverse assemblage of habitats - northern forest species including solitary vireo, Blackburnian and yellow-rumped warblers, edge species including brown thrasher and indigo bunting, and streambelt species including least flycatcher and Louisiana waterthrush. In addition, green-backed heron occurs in spring, summer and fall, great egret in the fall, and great blue heron in the spring and fall. Spotted and solitary sandpipers and both yellowlegs occur during migration. Broad-winged hawk occurs in spring, summer and fall, and red-tailed hawk, great horned and barred owls are here all year. The fall migration is really good for thrushes and warblers in September, and sparrows in October and November. The dam provides a good spot from which to watch the fall hawk migration.

GETTING AROUND
Birding methods: CAR, WALK, BIKE, SKI.
Several driveways lead through some of the park and flood control area, and there are trails through the remaining portions, and also through nearby state forest and conservation land. The state park is crowded in summer, and an admission fee is charged. The flood control area is open to hunting.

DIRECTIONS: This state park, dam and flood control area lie about two miles southwest of the center of Thomaston.

To get to the main entrance to Black Rock State Park, from the intersection of Routes 6 and 109, go west (southward) on Route 6 for 0.4 mile to the park entrance on the right. Trails start from here and lead into parts of the park. In addition, across Route 6 from the park entrance, there is a trail that makes a loop through the Mattatuck State Forest.

To get to the dam from the intersection of Routes 109 and 6 in Thomaston, go west on Route 109 for 0.8 mile to a driveway that leads to the dam on the left.

To get to the flood control area, continue west on Route 109 for another 1.0 mile to a driveway on the left that leads into the flood control area.

TORRINGTON: JOHN A. MINETTO STATE PARK

HABITATS

MARSH/SWAMP/BOG: cattail, sedge and shrub marsh; shrub swamp, shrubby hardwood swamp, hardwood swamp; open water, dead wood, shrubby and wooded edges;

OPEN TERRESTRIAL: short grass, mixed herbaceous and shrubby fields; shrubby and wooded edges;

Lake/pond: ponds, short grass, mixed herbaceous, hardwoods, white pine and hemlock shores;

River/stream: stream, with streambelts of shrubs, hardwood and hemlock;

Forest: mixed hardwoods, white pine/hardwoods, white pine, hemlock, spruce plantation, mountain laurel.

This 678-acre area was formed by a flood control dam at the south end of a two mile long bottomland. The area contains a variety of habitat types, including a rich wetland/streambelt system with open water and an extensive shrub marsh. Periodic flooding prevents succession and holds the wetlands in a somewhat stable situation. This wetland area is bordered by reverting fields, shrubby edges, and by hillsides covered with varied deciduous and conifer woodlands. Part of the area is a developed park centered around several small ponds.

SEASONS/BIRDS

SPRING MIGRATION: WATER BIRDS, MARSH BIRDS; SHORE BIRDS; LAND BIRDS;

NESTING SEASON: water birds, marsh birds, LAND BIRDS;

FALL MIGRATION: water birds, marsh birds, shore birds, LAND BIRDS;

Winter: land birds.

The wide variety of habitats at this site provides some of the best birding in northwestern Connecticut throughout the year, but especially during the spring migration; (summer and fall can also be very good). The best birding area is from the entrance driveway south to the dam.

The spring migration may start here as early as mid-March, and is fully underway by mid-April. Water birds are the first to arrive - wood duck, mallard, black duck, blue-winged teal, ring-necked duck and hooded merganser are regular migrants. Marsh bird migrants include great blue and green-backed herons and Virginia rail, and there is usually a variety of shore birds, including spotted and solitary sandpipers, both yellowlegs, woodcock and snipe. Sometimes, among the land bird migrants are olive-sided flycatcher, Swainson's thrush and rusty blackbird, as well as a slew of warblers. Osprey often can be seen in trees out in the marsh in spring and fall.

Nesters include many wetland species: wood duck and other dabblers, hooded merganser, Virginia rail, green-backed heron, willow and alder flycatchers, northern waterthrush and swamp sparrow (lots of them). Edge species nesters also abound, and include yellow warbler (many), least flycatcher and warbling vireo. Among the many other nesters are several woodpecker species including yellow-bellied sapsucker.

The fall migration includes most of the same species as those that come in the spring. Highlights are swallows (in August), great egret (in August and September), a variety of warblers in early September, and many sparrows in October. In winter, look for sharp-shinned and Cooper's hawks, northern shrike (occasional), winter wren, hermit thrush and cedar waxwing.

GETTING AROUND
Birding methods: car, WALK, bike, ski.
The best part of this site (the southern portion from the entrance down to the dam) can be birded most effectively by walking an abandoned road that goes along the edge of the wetland. There is another abandoned road that can be walked in the northern part of the park, as well as trails throughout. Some of the good habitats can be seen from a car on the park driveways. The dam at the south end of the park looks down on the pond. The wetlands at the north end can be seen from the Route 272 bridge. The driveway is closed in winter, but the park may be entered on foot.

DIRECTIONS: This area is about eight miles northwest of Torrington. From the intersection of Routes 272 and 4, go north on Route 272 for 3.9 miles to the dam on the right, and for another 1.0 mile to the park entrance, also on the right, and for another 0.7 mile to the bridge over the wetland. (There is a place to park on the right north of the bridge.)

TORRINGTON: STILLWATER POND

HABITATS
FOREST: hardwoods, hardwoods/white pine, hardwoods/hemlock, white pine;
Lake/pond: pond, shore of hardwoods and white pine;
River/stream: perennial and seasonal streams, shrubby and wooded streambelts;
Marsh/swamp/bog: shrub marsh;
Other: rocky slope.
This is a recent addition to the Connecticut state park system. Its 210 acres consists of Stillwater Pond and the forest along the eastern shore, which is composed of white pine, hemlock and hardwoods in various combinations, on level ground along the shore of the pond, and on a rocky hillside back from the shore.

SEASONS/BIRDS
Spring migration: water birds, land birds;
Nesting Season: land birds;
Fall Migration: water birds, land birds;
Winter: land birds.

This is a good site in which to look for migrating and nesting land birds, especially for northern species. Nesters include winter wren, yellow-bellied sapsucker, hermit thrush, solitary vireo, and a variety of warblers - black-throated green, black-throated blue, blackburnian, yellow-rumped and pine. The water birds that occur on the pond are mostly common species - Canada goose, mallard, ring-necked duck, common and hooded mergansers (the latter three species in migration).

GETTING AROUND
Birding methods: car, walk.

There are several places along Route 272 where it is possible to pull off and scan the pond. In addition, there is one woods road that goes through the forest near the eastern pond shore, and several smaller trails that lead from it.

DIRECTIONS (see Map 40): This site is immediately northwest of the city of Torrington. To get there from the intersection of Routes 272 and 4, go north on Route 272 for 1.1 miles, right on Stillwater Terrace for 0.2 miles to the dam at the south end of the pond, and for another 0.1 mile to a woods road on the left into the forest along the eastern shore of the pond. It is also possible to continue north on Route 272 for a short distance to several pulloff areas that provide views of the western shore of the pond.

TORRINGTON: SUNNYBROOK STATE PARK/PAUGNUT STATE FOREST

HABITATS
MARSH/SWAMP/BOG: sedge, cattail and shrub marsh, shrub swamp, shrubby hardwood swamp, dead wood, open water, edges of tall grass field, hardwoods, white pine and hemlock;
RIVER/STREAM: streams, fast and slow water, streambelts intermittently herbaceous, marshy, shrubby and wooded (hardwoods, white pine and hemlock);
FOREST: hardwoods, hardwoods/white pine, hardwoods/hemlock, white pine/hemlock, scattered spruce and tamarack, mountain laurel;
OPEN TERRESTRIAL: tilled, short grass, tall grass, mixed herbaceous and shrubby fields; shrubby and wooded edges; cedar and juniper;
Lake/pond: ponds, marshy, shrubby and wooded shores.

Together, these two highly productive areas of over 2,000 acres include most of the upland and wetland habitat types found in northwestern Connecticut. Sunnybrook State Park occupies over a mile of a narrow valley that includes a pond, the East Branch of the Naugatuck River, its streambelt and varied wetlands. Up on the west side of the valley, there are two ponds and associated wetlands, shrubby openings, and varied forest habitats. The Paugnut State Forest lies immediately to the east across the state highway, and includes another wetland and a large forested area.

SEASONS/BIRDS
SPRING MIGRATION: water birds, marsh birds, shore birds, LAND BIRDS;
NESTING SEASON: water birds, marsh birds, LAND BIRDS;
FALL MIGRATION: water birds, marsh birds, shore birds, LAND BIRDS;
Winter: land birds.

As one would expect in an area that includes so many types of habitat, a very wide diversity of bird species occurs here. All seasons except winter are great, and the best periods are late April through late July, and from early September through mid-October.

During the spring migration, it is possible to see a wide variety of water, marsh, shore and land birds, including such uncommon species as olive-sided flycatcher. For many birders, the highlight of this area in the spring (starting in late April) is the wave of warblers that move along the streambelt.

Nesters include all of the standard species that belong in these habitats, including: Virginia rail, willow and alder flycatchers, and several woodpeckers. Predictably, there are many northern species: yellow-bellied sapsucker, Canada, black-throated green, black-throated blue and Blackburnian warblers, and northern waterthrush. For some years, there has been an active great blue heron nesting heronry that can be seen very well from one of the trails (see below under "Getting Around"). However, the herons now nest in another swamp, but still come here to feed. The fall is a good time to look along the edges for migrating land birds, especially warblers and sparrows. In winter, there are a few year-round residents (including red-tailed hawk, great horned and barred owls and red-breasted nuthatch). Winter finches are a possibility in flight years. Pine grosbeaks have been seen in the apple trees, crossbills and siskins in the spruces, and redpolls in the birches.

GETTING AROUND:
Birding methods: car, WALK, bike, ski.

An abandoned auto road, woods roads and trails go through Sunnybrook State Park, and provide a good way to bird this area on foot. Starting at the parking area near the entrance, there is an abandoned auto road that runs down the bottom of the valley, and provides easy walking through prime streambelt habitat. There is a network of trails that goes up the west side of the valley. To reach these trails, go south on the abandoned road for about 0.1 mile almost to the bridge; a trail starts on your right, and leads to other trails. These trails lead up to two wetlands and to the heronry. They are rough in places. The dam at the south end of Sunnybrook Park provides a place from which to look over the nearby habitats in the valley floor. In Paugnut State Forest, there are several woods roads and trails, and also a little-used vehicle road that can be driven most of the year. In addition, there is a wetland on the east side of Newfield Road and about 0.1 mile north of the Sunnybrook Park entrance. It can be seen from Newfield Road.

DIRECTIONS (see Map 40): These areas are about three miles northwest of Torrington. **To get to Sunnybrook State Park** from Route 8 at Torrington, take exit 44, go west on Route 4 for 0.5 mile, right on North Main Street for 0.5 mile, and left on Newfield Road for 1.2 miles to the East Branch Dam on the left and for an additional 1.2 miles to the park entrance on the left.

To get to Paugnut State Forest, after turning off North Main Street onto Newfield Road (see above), follow Newfield Road for 0.8 mile, and turn right on Guerdat Road. This road passes intermittently through Paugnut State Forest for 2.9 miles (bear right at the first two forks), until it intersects with Starks Road. For most of its length, Guerdat Road is gravel and is quite rough in places.

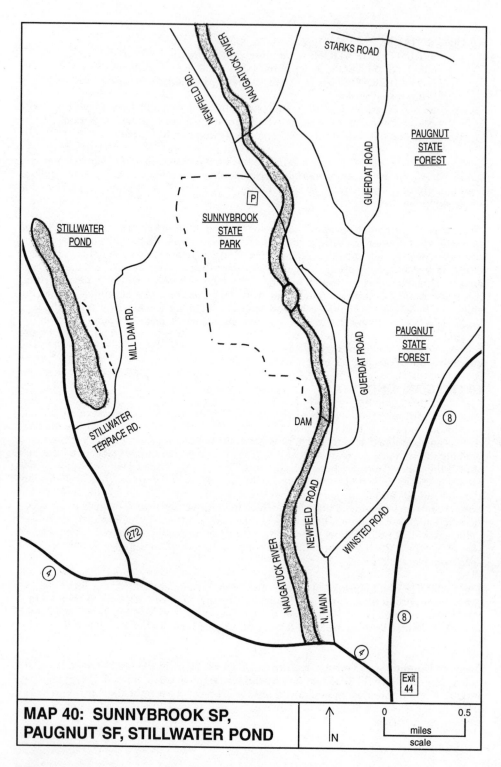

**MAP 40: SUNNYBROOK SP,
PAUGNUT SF, STILLWATER POND**

N

0   miles   0.5
scale

TORRINGTON/WINCHESTER: BURR POND STATE PARK

HABITATS
FOREST: hardwoods, hardwoods/white pine, hardwoods/hemlock, hemlock, conifer plantation, mountain laurel;
Lake/pond: lake, shallow water, coves, islands, hemlock and hardwoods/hemlock shore;
River/stream: perennial and seasonal streams, slow and fast water, waterfall, wooded streambelts;
Open terrestrial: short grass and shrubby fields, shrubby and wooded edges;
Marsh/swamp/bog: shrubby hardwood swamp;
Other: rocky slope.

Burr Pond State Park consists of two blocks that are near one another but not contiguous. The main area includes Burr Pond and the forest that surrounds it, and the other nearby area is the Taylor Brook Campground. Burr Pond is a lake with lots of coves, points and islands. Hemlock is the dominant tree species in the forest that surrounds the pond, and there are several areas in which there is a dense shrub layer of mountain laurel.

SEASONS/BIRDS
SPRING MIGRATION: water birds, LAND BIRDS;
NESTING SEASON: LAND BIRDS;
FALL MIGRATION: water birds, LAND BIRDS;
Winter: land birds.

There is a nice mix of land bird migrants in the spring and fall, and also a few water birds. Among the land bird nesters are a number of northern species, including solitary vireo, black-throated green warbler, and black-throated blue warbler (the latter is abundant in the areas with a mountain laurel understory). In winter, there is very little bird activity, except for a few resident species.

GETTING AROUND
Birding methods: car, WALK.

Several trails and a woods road provide opportunities for good birding on foot, through the hemlock forest and around the pond. In addition, a limited amount of the habitat areas can be seen from your car. In summer, there is an entrance fee, and the main parts of the park and campground get crowded. But there are quiet, outlying areas that you can reach by trail.

DIRECTIONS: This site is three to four miles south of the center of Winsted. From Route 8 exit 46, go west on Pine Woods Road for 0.3 mile, left on Winsted Road for 1.0 mile, and right on Burr Mountain Road. In 0.3 mile, there is a woods road on the left; this can be walked for several miles, and can be used to get to the trail around Burr Pond. In another 0.2 mile, the entrance to the main part of the park is on the left. In another 0.3 mile, a boat launch and parking area is on the left. The trail around the pond can be started from this area. An easier walk can be had by continuing on Burr Mountain Road to its intersection with Peck Road, which goes into the Taylor Brook Campground area, and can be birded on foot or by car.

WARREN: EEL POND

HABITATS

MARSH/SWAMP/BOG: cattail, mixed herbaceous and shrub marsh; shrub swamp; shrubby and hardwood edge, deadwood;
Lake/pond: pond, shallow water.

This is a large, shallow pond. Emergent shrubs occupy much of the open water within the pond, and varied marshes and swamps occur along the shoreline.

SEASONS/BIRDS

Spring migration: water birds, marsh birds, shore birds, land birds;
Nesting season: water birds, marsh birds, shore birds, land birds;
Fall migration: water birds, marsh birds, shore birds, land birds;
Winter: land birds.

There is something to see here throughout the spring, summer and fall. During the spring migration, water birds are the main attraction, and there are also some marsh, shore and land bird migrants to look at. Olive-sided flycatcher has been seen here. Nesting species include green-backed heron, Virginia rail, spotted sandpiper, kingfisher, pileated woodpecker, yellow-bellied sapsucker, willow and least flycatchers, tree swallow, northern waterthrush, yellow warbler, yellowthroat and swamp sparrow. Great blue heron comes here to feed. The fall migration is much like the spring migration. Winter is pretty quiet.

GETTING AROUND

Birding methods: car.

Most of this wetland can be seen from the wide shoulder of the highway. Traffic on the road can be heavy; it is best to come here in the early morning.

DIRECTIONS: Eel Pond is in Warren, seven or eight miles west of Litchfield. From Warren at the northern intersection of Routes 341 and 45, go west on Route 341 for 0.6 mile to a wide shoulder on the right, from which the pond is visible.

WARREN: WYANTENOCK STATE FOREST (WOODVILLE BLOCK)

HABITATS

FOREST: hardwoods, hardwoods/white pine, hardwoods/hemlock;
MARSH/SWAMP/BOG: sedge, mixed herbaceous and shrub marshes; shrub, shrubby hardwood and hardwood swamps; dead wood;
Lake/pond: pond, shore of wetlands and woods;
Open terrestrial: shrubby field;
River/stream: streams, with swampy, shrubby and wooded streambelts;
Other: rocky slope, ledge.

This is the largest block of a 3,220-acre state forest. It occupies very hilly, rugged terrain with rocky outcrops. Its forest communities include hardwoods, hemlock and white pine in various combinations. Part of the forest is managed, and contains areas that have been clearcut and are in various stages of succession, from shrubby fields to young hardwoods with a dense shrub understory. This site also contains a pond near the road, and several smaller beaver ponds. Several wetlands are scattered about as small pockets surrounded by forest.

SEASONS/BIRDS

SPRING MIGRATION: water birds, marsh birds, shore birds, LAND BIRDS;
NESTING SEASON: water birds, marsh birds, shore birds, LAND BIRDS;
FALL MIGRATION: water birds, marsh birds, shore birds, LAND BIRDS;
Winter: land birds.

Spring, summer and fall are all good at this site. There is a nice migration of warblers and other land birds in May and again in September; common species of water, marsh and shore birds occur here as spring and fall migrants and also as nesters. Over 100 species of birds have shown evidence of nesting at this site. Nesting land birds include a number of northern forest-dwelling species that you would expect in these forest communities: goshawk, yellow-bellied sapsucker, winter wren, hermit thrush, solitary vireo, black-throated blue, Canada and black-throated green warblers, and northern waterthrush. Other nesting species include many of the standard Connecticut forest and wetland species. Winter is pretty quiet.

GETTING AROUND

Birding methods: WALK.

A network of trails and logging roads goes through the area and provide plenty of opportunity to bird on foot. You can make a loop by starting at the entrance and taking right forks, thereby going past the wetlands that are in back of the pond, and ending on Route 341 by the pond. This state forest is a popular hunting area.

DIRECTIONS: This block of the state forest is about five miles southwest of Litchfield. To get there from the intersection of Routes 202 and 341 west of Litchfield, go west on Route 341 for 1.0 mile to a pull-off and trailhead on the right, just short of the pond, or for another 0.3 mile to the entrance and parking area, also on the right.

WASHINGTON: HIDDEN VALLEY RESERVATION

HABITATS

FOREST: hardwoods, hardwoods/hemlock, hemlock;
Open terrestrial: tilled, short grass, tall grass, mixed herbaceous and shrubby fields; shrubby and hardwood edges, hardwood hedgerows;
River/stream: river, streams, wooded streambelts;
Other: hawk watching site.

This site - the Hidden Valley Reservation - is a section of the Steep Rock Reservation, although it is geographically separate from it. And Hidden Valley itself has two very different sides, in terms of habitat. The west side is forested with a hemlock/hardwoods combination, and includes the Shepaug River, Bee Brook, their confluence, and the streambelt of each. The east side, as it borders on Sabbaday Lane, is open farm country, with a variety of fields, edges and hedgerows.

SEASONS/BIRDS

SPRING MIGRATION: LAND BIRDS;
NESTING SEASON: LAND BIRDS;
FALL MIGRATION: LAND BIRDS;
Winter: land birds.

The spring and fall migrations are both very good, especially for warblers in May and September in the wooded habitats. Nesters on the west side include such species as goshawk, yellow-bellied sapsucker, Louisiana waterthrush, black-throated green and worm-eating warblers. The more open farm country of the east side is a good place to look for indigo bunting, least flycatcher, warbling and yellow-throated vireos. The east side also has a high point which overlooks a large expanse of open fields, and would make a good fall hawk watching site.

GETTING AROUND
Birding methods: CAR, WALK.
There are a number of places at which it is possible to bird from your car or near to it. However, the Hidden Valley Preserve has a very extensive network of trails, with a map of them posted at the Bee Brook (western) entrance. (The map is also available by calling 868-9131.)

DIRECTIONS: This site is located in the northern part of Washington. To get to the forested west side of the preserve from the intersection of Routes 47 and 202, go south on Route 47 for 1.8 miles to a parking area on the left. A foot bridge leads across Bee Brook to the preserve entrance and the posted trail map. To get to the more open east side of the preserve, continue south on Route 47 for another 1.0 mile, left on Route 109 for 1.0 mile, and left on Sabbaday Lane. During the next 0.9 mile, several woods roads lead into the preserve from the left side of Sabbaday Lane.

WASHINGTON: SHEPAUG RIVER LOOP

HABITATS
RIVER/STREAM: river, fast shallow water; streambelt of shrubs, hardwoods, hardwoods/hemlock, hemlock; hemlock ravine;
FOREST: hardwoods, hardwoods/hemlock, hemlock, mountain laurel;
Open terrestrial: short grass, tall grass and shrubby fields, hardwood edges and hedgerows;
Marsh/swamp/bog: hardwood swamp.
Other: rocky slope.
This loop trip follows the Shepaug River for much of the way, but passes through three very different habitat areas. Initially it goes through open farm country, past the confluence of the Shepaug and Bantam Rivers, then climbs along one side of a deep hemlock ravine through which the Shepaug River tumbles, and finally rejoins the Shepaug above the ravine where it is flatter and calmer.

SEASONS/BIRDS
SPRING MIGRATION: LAND BIRDS;
NESTING SEASON: LAND BIRDS;
FALL MIGRATION: LAND BIRDS;
Winter: land birds.
The best season at this site is the spring migration, especially along Romford Road. The fall migration is also good, especially by the farm fields along Whittlesey Road, that provide a place from which to watch the hawk migration. Red-tailed hawk occurs here all year, and harrier in the spring and fall. Nesters include many northern species such as yellow-bellied sapsuckerr, brown creeper, hermit thrush, solitary vireo, black-throated green, black-throated blue, yellow-rumped and Canada warblers; as well as broad-winged hawk, barred and screech owls, pileated woodpecker, yellow-throated vireo and most of the basic forest-dwellers and

edge/open country species. In winter, the diversity is much lower, but there is still a good chance of seeing residents including golden-crowned kinglet, red-tailed hawk, and possibly long-eared owl or saw-whet owl.

GETTING AROUND
Birding methods: car, WALK, bike.
Whittlesey and Romford Roads are dirt, lightly used, and ideal for birding on foot, or by bike when the road is firm. Birding from your car requires some compromises: there are few pulloffs, and the roads may be muddy in late fall, winter and early spring. The surrounding land is private.

DIRECTIONS: This site is in the northernmost part of Washington. It is a triangular loop trip, with Romford Road forming one leg and Whittlesey Road the second. Route 202 forms the third leg, and provides a way back to the starting point. Start at the intersection of Route 202, Route 341 and Romford Road. Go south on Romford Road along the Shepaug River, right on Whittlesey Road, and right again on Route 202 back to the starting point. The total distance is about five miles.

WASHINGTON: STEEP ROCK RESERVATION

HABITATS
FOREST: hardwoods, white pine, hemlock, hardwoods/white pine, hardwoods/hemlock, white pine/hemlock, flood plain;
RIVER/STREAM: river, fast water, slow water; streambelt of hemlock and hardwoods, perennial and seasonal streams, hemlock ravine;
Open terrestrial: short grass and shrubby fields, shrubby and hardwood edges;
Other: rocky slope, rocky outcrops.
This reservation encloses a four- to five-mile stretch of the lovely Shepaug River, and includes almost all types of forest habitat found in Connecticut's Western Uplands, as well as the river, streambelt habitats and shrubby fields. Steep Rock is a rock outcrop which overlooks the valley of the Shepaug River. The high-sided ravine through which the river flows forms a cold microclimate, and provides suitable conditions for northern flora and fauna.

SEASONS/BIRDS
SPRING MIGRATION: LAND BIRDS;
NESTING SEASON: LAND BIRDS
FALL MIGRATION: LAND BIRDS;
Winter: land birds.
This dramatic river valley has produced high species counts over the years. Both migrations are good, with spring offering more easily perceived excitement - May and June are the best months to visit this site; early fall (September) is also quite good. Nearly 100 species nest here, including a number of northerners such as goshawk, brown creeper, winter wren, yellow-bellied sapsucker, red-breasted nuthatch, hermit thrush, solitary vireo, black-throated green, Canada and Blackburnian warblers. Other nesting species include warbling, yellow-throated and red-eyed vireos, gnatcatcher, both waterthrushes, worm-eating warbler, and (in and near the power line and its edges), brown thrasher, golden-winged and prairie warblers, and (in the hemlock ravine) Acadian flycatcher. In past years, whip-poor-will has also been a probable nester in this valley. Pileated woodpecker, great horned and barred owls are residents throughout the year.

GETTING AROUND
Birding methods: CAR, WALK, bike, ski.

A dirt road (rough at times and closed to cars in winter) goes downstream along the east bank of the river through varied woodland habitat and eventually to a power line. Also, starting at the reservation entrance, there is a trail that goes downstream along the west bank of the river. This trail connects with a network of trails that pass through northern hardwood / conifer habitat. One of these trails leads to the top of Steep Rock.

HOW TO GET THERE: This reservation is in Washington Depot. To get to the main entrance, from the center of Washington Depot at the intersection of Route 47, Route 109 and River Road, go south on River Road, downstream along the west bank of the Shepaug River for 1.4 miles to a point at which the hardtop road bends to the right, and there is a dirt road to the left. Turn left into the reservation entrance. To get to a point that looks down on the ravine with a trail that goes down into it, start in Roxbury Station at the intersection of Routes 199 and 67, go north on Route 199 for 3.2 miles, and left on Curtis Road for 0.3 mile to the dead end.

WASHINGTON: WEANTINOGUE LAND TRUST WETLAND

HABITATS
MARSH/SWAMP/BOG: mixed herbaceous and shrub marsh, shrub swamp, shrubby hardwood swamp, dead wood, open water, seasonal pools;
FOREST: hardwoods;
River/stream: stream, shrubby and hardwood streambelt.

This rather small site (15-20 acres) consists of a wetland that contains a variety of habitat types, and is bordered by a hardwood forest.

SEASONS/BIRDS
SPRING MIGRATION: water birds, marsh birds, shore birds, LAND BIRDS;
NESTING SEASON: water birds, marsh birds, LAND BIRDS;
FALL MIGRATION: water birds, marsh birds, shore birds, LAND BIRDS;
Winter: land birds.

This area has a wide variety and nice numbers of standard species for these types of habitat. The spring migration includes some marsh birds (great blue and green-backed herons), some shore birds (spotted and solitary sandpipers), plus lots of warblers and flycatchers. Birds that nest here include wetland-oriented species such as wood duck, green-backed heron, swamp sparrow; southern species such as red-bellied woodpecker; and many others, including yellow-bellied sapsucker, kingbird, least flycatcher and warbling vireo. For fall migrants, birding along the corridor formed by Romford Road works well, and early fall (September) is best. In winter, look for lingering migrants and a few residents such as red-bellied woodpecker.

GETTING AROUND
Birding methods: CAR, WALK, BIKE.

Romford Road is lightly traveled, and suitable for birding from a car, on foot or by bike. Nearby roads to the north (Romford, Turner and Hinkle Roads) are also suitable for birding in the same ways. Much of the habitats can be seen from the road, and if necessary, the Weantinogue Land Trust property (designated by signs) on the west side of Romford Road can be entered on foot. Other land is private.

DIRECTIONS: This site is in the northeastern part of Washington, three or four miles east of Washington Depot. To get there from the intersection of Routes 109 and 47 in Washington Depot, go east on Route 109 for 2.3 miles, left on Romford Road for 0.3 mile to the beginning of the Weantinogue Land Trust property on the left. For the next half mile or so, Romford Road runs north along the wetland, until it intersects with Turner and Hinkle Roads.

WASHINGTON/WARREN/KENT: LAKE WARAMAUG

HABITATS
LAKE/POND: lake, deep water; shore of hardwoods, short grass and residential developmenmt;
MARSH/SWAMP/BOG: shrub marsh;
Open terrestrial: short grass and shrubby field, edge;
Forest: hardwoods, hardwoods/white pine, hardwoods/hemlock;
River/stream: stream, wooded streambelt.
This is a large lake (680 acres) that is quite deep in places, and has a very irregular shape with many points and coves. The shoreline is mostly developed with private residences, but also includes a state park that has large areas of lawn along the shore. There also is a small but very productive shrub marsh beside the lake.

SEASONS/BIRDS
SPRING MIGRATION: gulls, WATER BIRDS, LAND BIRDS;
Nesting season: LAND BIRDS;
FALL MIGRATION: gulls, WATER BIRDS, LAND BIRDS;
Winter: gulls, water birds, LAND BIRDS.
This site is best known as a good place to see large numbers and an interesting variety of migrating water birds, especially in the early spring, late fall, and periods of winter when it is not iced-over. (Forget water birds in the summer; the lake is crowded and heavily used by boats.) A less well known attribute of this site is a shrub marsh near the lake (Ash Swamp) that provides interesting birding. In the spring and fall, the Lake Waramaug area is good for the standard land bird migrants. In the nesting season, it boasts all of the vireo species that breed in Connecticut (red-eyed, warbling, solitary, white-eyed, yellow-throated), plus a typical mix of other species. It has become a destination of birders doing the Christmas Bird Count, and in recent years has produced green-winged teal, saw-whet owl, and both Carolina and winter wrens.

GETTING AROUND
Birding methods: CAR.
A road follows the entire shoreline, and provides numerous intermittent views of the water and of shoreline habitats, but stopping is difficult along much of the way. The state park includes a section of shoreline open to the public; an entrance fee is charged in summer.

DIRECTIONS: Lake Waramaug is in western Connecticut, about ten miles north of New Milford. From New Preston, at the western intersection of Routes 45 and 202, go north on Route 45 for about a mile, until Lake Waramaug appears to the left of Route 45. From this point it is possible to make an eight mile counterclockwise loop along the shore of the lake by bearing left at each of several intersections. Ash Swamp is near Waramaug State Park at the west end of the lake.

WINCHESTER: CRYSTAL LAKE

HABITATS
Lake/pond: lake, deep water, wooded shore, shrubby islands;
Forest: hardwoods, white pine and hemlock in various combinations;
River/stream: perennial stream, wooded streambelt.
Crystal Lake is a public water supply reservoir, protected by an undeveloped, wooded shore.

SEASONS/BIRDS
Spring migration: water birds, land birds;
Nesting Season: land birds;
Fall Migration: water birds, land birds;
Winter: land birds.
This is an easy one-stop site at which to look for water birds; it can be quite good, but sometimes there is nothing. The best times to check are late October through November, and from ice-out in March to mid-April. Hooded merganser and ring-necked duck are often present, and there is also a chance of seeing common goldeneye, bufflehead, lesser scaup, canvasback, common merganser and pied-billed grebe.

GETTING AROUND
Birding methods: car.
Much of the lake can be seen from the roadside. The public is not permitted on the land around the lake, so stay on the road shoulder.

DIRECTIONS: This lake is about two miles west of the city of Winsted. In Winsted, at the intersection of Routes 263 and 44, go west on Route 263 for 1.8 miles to where the lake is visible on the right. Park by the roadside in a little pulloff on the right.

WINCHESTER: HIGHLAND LAKE

HABITATS
LAKE/POND: lake, deep water, shallow water, shore of shrubs, hardwood, white pine and hemlock, and almost entirely developed with residences.
This is a rather long and narrow lake with a densely developed shoreline. There are small areas of wooded and shrubby shore between the houses. It has three parts - Third Bay at the south end, Second Bay in the middle, and First Bay at the north end. There are some shallow areas near the south end of Third Bay, but most of Highland Lake is deep - up to 59 feet at one point in Second Bay.

SEASONS/BIRDS
Spring migration: water birds, marsh birds, shore birds, land birds;
Nesting season: land birds;
FALL MIGRATION: WATER BIRDS, marsh birds, shore birds, land birds.
Winter: gulls, water birds, land birds.
The main reason for a visit to Highland Lake is to see the water birds that drop in here during the spring and fall migrations. The best times for water birds are: early spring from ice-out (usually March) until boating activity begins (usually April); late fall, after the boats are put away (usually November) until freeze-up (usually late December, but sometimes there is open water for periods during the winter). The shallow water in the south end of the lake, in Third Bay, usually has the greatest species diversity. In the shallow water, there are often dabbling ducks here - pintail, gadwall, wigeon and coot. In deeper areas, you may see

ring-necked duck, both scaups, bufflehead, goldeneye and hooded merganser. Up north in the Second and First Bays, there are usually not many birds, but those that occasionally occur are apt to be interesting - common loon, pied-billed and horned grebe and common merganser all have been seen. The lake is drawn down in the fall (usually September), and sometimes the exposed mud in Third Bay attracts a variety of shore birds: spotted, solitary, least, and pectoral sandpiper; both yellowlegs, snipe and killdeer have all occurred here. Great blue heron sometimes feeds along the shore. Pipit has been seen in October and November, and snow bunting in November and December.

GETTING AROUND
Birding methods: car.
There can be interesting birds on the lake, but the birding is difficult and frustrating. West Wakefield Boulevard provides better views than other roads - it follows the shore of Highland Lake for almost three miles, with intermittent views of the water, but very limited opportunities to pull of the road and stop. The boat launch area at the north end of Wakefield Boulevard is the best place to stop to see First Bay. A small pulloff near Sucker Brook Road affords views of part of Third Bay. Another view of this bay can be had from the Taylor Brook section of Burr Pond State Park.

DIRECTIONS: Highland Lake is immediately south of the center on Winsted. The simplest way to get there is from Route 8 exit 46; go west on Pine Woods Road, (the name changes to Highland Lake Road and then Mountain Road) for 1.4 miles to an intersection, at which go right on Mountain Road for another 0.2 mile, and left on West Wakefield Boulevard. This road follows the shore of Highland Lake for 2.8 miles until it it intersects with West Lake Street at the boat launch and parking area. (At the 1.1 mile point on West Wakefield Boulevard, you pass Sucker Brook Road on the left; it leads to the nearby Sucker Brook Flood Control Area, described elsewhere in this chapter under Winchester.)

WINCHESTER: MAD RIVER DAM/FLOOD CONTROL AREA

HABITATS
OPEN TERRESTRIAL: mixed herbaceous and shrubby fields, shrubby and hardwood edges;
RIVER/STREAM: stream, fast and slow water, shrubby and hardwood streambelt;
MARSH/SWAMP/BOG: shrub swamp, shrubby hardwood swamp;
Forest: hardwoods, hardwoods/white pine, hardwoods/hemlock;
Lake/pond: pond, shrubby and hardwood shore; seasonal pools;
Other: hawk watching site.
This area consists of a flood control dam and the valley of the Mad River upstream. It was the Mad River - a placid little stream which hardly lives up to its name in normal times - which carried away much of Winsted's business district in the flood of 1955. The valley above the dam contains a variety of habitats, including several bodies of water, several streams and associated streambelt habitats, shrubby fields, several wetlands, and various forest communities.

SEASONS/BIRDS
SPRING MIGRATION: shore birds, LAND BIRDS;
NESTING SEASON: LAND BIRDS;
FALL MIGRATION: shore birds, LAND BIRDS;
Winter: land birds.

The spring and fall migrations are both very good here; warblers and other land birds abound in May and September. In the late fall, a variety of sparrows feed in the shrubs. During the nesting season, this bottomland streambelt attracts species that nest in shrubs and edges, along water, and also a number of both northern and southern forest-dwellers. Nesters include: spotted sandpiper, kingfisher, least and willow flycatchers, rough-winged swallow, brown thrasher, solitary, warbling and yellow-throated vireos, yellow and chestnut-sided warblers, indigo bunting, field sparrow and junco. Great blue heron comes in to feed.

GETTING AROUND
Birding methods: CAR, WALK, bike, ski.
There are hardtop and dirt roads and a number of trails through most parts of this area. The vehicle roads are not plowed in winter. Hunting is allowed in fall and winter.

DIRECTIONS: This area is immediately west of Winsted.

To get to the flood control dam from Winsted at the intersection of Routes 44 and 263, go west on Route 44 for 1.6 miles to a parking area by the dam on the left.

To enter the eastern portion of the flood control area, continue west on Route 44 for another 0.8 mile, and turn left onto a road that descends to the bottom of the valley where there are several other roads and a number of trails. This area is subject to flooding in the spring, and the road is not plowed in winter.

To reach the western portion of the flood control area, continue west on Route 44 for another 0.2 mile, and turn left on Rugg Brook Road. At 0.1 mile from Route 44, immediately after crossing the stream, there is a parking area on the left, from which several trails can be reached.

WINCHESTER: PLATT HILL STATE PARK

HABITATS
OPEN TERRESTRIAL: tilled, short grass, tall grass and shrubby fields, shrubby and wooded edges;
Forest: hardwoods, hardwoods/white pine, hardwoods/hemlock, mountain laurel;
Other: hawk watching site.
This small hilltop park contains a nice diversity of habitats, and provides a sweeping view of the surrounding Litchfield Hills. Several acres of white pine and red oak forest on the summit have an understory of mountain laurel, and are surrounded by highbush blueberry and other shrubs, farmland and reverting fields.

SEASONS/BIRDS
SPRING MIGRATION: LAND BIRDS;
NESTING SEASON: LAND BIRDS;
FALL MIGRATION: LAND BIRDS;
Winter: land birds.
The spring and fall migrations are both good here, for a variety of warblers and other land birds, as well as for hawks passing overhead in the fall. In addition, there are some interesting nesting species. Magnolia, yellow-rumped, Blackburnian and black-throated green war-

blers nest in the white pines and hemlock on the hilltop, black-throated blue and Canada warblers in the mountain laurel understory, and Nashville warbler in the nearby blueberry bushes. There are also a number of open country and edge species in the nearby active and abandoned farmland: kestrel, indigo bunting, brown thrasher, bobolink and meadowlark. Bluebird and tree swallow nest in houses that have been placed nearby (on private property). Raven and great horned owl are in the area all year. Redpoll has been seen in some winters.

GETTING AROUND
Birding methods: car, walk.
The park driveway provides access to or views of all the habitats in this small area.

DIRECTIONS: This park is about two miles southeast of Winsted. From Winsted at the intersection of Routes 44 and 263, go south on Route 263 for 1.5 miles, and left on Platt Hill Road for 1.5 miles to the park entrance on the left.

WINCHESTER: RUGG BROOK

HABITATS
MARSH/SWAMP/BOG: sedge, cattail, mixed herbaceous and shrub marsh; shrub, shrubby hardwood and hardwood swamp; dead wood;
RIVER/STREAM: perennial and seasonal streams, hardwood, hardwood/hemlock streambelt;
FOREST: hardwoods, hardwoods/white pine, hardwoods/hemlock, white pine, hemlock, mountain laurel;
Open terrestrial: shrubby field, edge;
Lake/pond: lake, deep water, shores of hardwoods, white pine, hemlock and mixtures;
Other: rocky slope, ledge.
This site includes the entire four mile length of Rugg Brook. Near its source, it feeds several wetlands, then provides the main flow for the Rugg Brook Reservoir, and finally runs down to the Mad River as a swift, rocky stream. For almost all of this distance, it flows through northern forest communities of hardwoods, white pine, hemlock, and combinations of these species, with extensive areas of mountain laurel understory. Other interesting vegetation is present - heaths characteristic of bogs, and also rhododendron maximum (native, or an escapee?).

SEASONS/BIRDS
SPRING MIGRATION: water birds, marsh birds, shore birds, LAND BIRDS;
NESTING SEASON: water birds, marsh birds, LAND BIRDS;
FALL MIGRATION: water birds, marsh birds, shore birds, LAND BIRDS;
Winter: land birds.
Many of the birds that occur in this stream valley as migrants or nesters are northern species, in keeping with the northern character of the habitat. The migrations are good, especially in the spring, when land birds move along the corridor of the streambelt. Also during both spring and fall migrations, wood duck, hooded and common mergansers can be seen on Rugg Brook Reservoir. Nesting species include: spotted sandpiper, woodcock, broad-winged hawk, yellow-bellied sapsucker, red-breasted nuthatch, alder, willow and great crested fly-

catchers, brown creeper, hermit thrush, solitary vireo, junco, white-throated sparrow, and many warblers - Nashville, magnolia, black-throated blue, Canada, black-throated green, Blackburnian, yellow-rumped, and both northern and Louisiana waterthrushes. Great blue heron comes to the wetland to feed in spring, summer and fall. In winter, species seen (or heard) for the most part are the year-round residents, including barred and great horned owls, turkey, yellow-bellied sapsucker, pileated, downy and hairy woodpeckers. All of the winter finches have been seen in invasion years.

GETTING AROUND

Birding methods: car, WALK, bike.

The habitats described above lie along Rugg Brook Road and Old Waterbury Turnpike. The former is hardtop and usable all year. Old Waterbury Turnpike is a dirt road that runs for three miles between its intersection with Rugg Brook Road at the north end, and its intersection with Route 263 near the center of Winchester at the south end. The marsh/swamp areas described above lie along this road, one near the north end, some in the middle, and one near the south end. The Old Waterbury Turnpike is not maintained in winter, and may be muddy and unusable by cars or bikes during periods in the early spring. However, it provides good birding on foot at almost any time, and the southern and largest of the wetlands is a walk of only half a mile from Route 263.

DIRECTIONS: This site is two miles west of Winsted. From the intersection of Routes 44 and 263 in Winsted, go west on Route 44 for 1.8 miles, and left on Rugg Brook Road for 1.1 miles, along Rugg Brook and the east shore of the Rugg Brook Reservoir to a fork in the road. The right fork is the Old Waterbury Turnpike, described above.

When the Old Waterbury Turnpike is usable by cars, drive right at the fork. At 0.3 mile and at 1.6 miles, you reach small wetlands that are visible from the road. Starting at 1.8 miles, a large wetland lies to the right, and can be reached by short trails. At 2.2 miles, the road crosses this wetland, which can be seen well from the road. After going past some open fields, the Old Waterbury Turnpike ends at Route 263 in the center of Winchester.

To get back to the center of Winsted from the center of Winchester, go east on Route 263 for four or five miles.

When the Old Waterbury Turnpike is not usable by cars, you can reach the smaller, northern wetland by parking at the fork of Rugg Brook Road and the Old Waterbury Turnpike, and walking 0.3 mile south on the Old Waterbury Turnpike (the right fork). To reach the larger, southern wetland, from the fork of Rugg Brook Road and Old Waterbury Turnpike, continue driving south on Rugg Brook Road (the left fork) for 1.5 miles, right on Route 263 for 1.2 miles, and right at the Winchester post office on Old Waterbury Turnpike for a short distance until you find a safe place to park. From here, walk for less than 0.5 mile to the southern wetland. Another alternative is to walk all the way through on the Old Waterbury Turnpike from one end to the other, a distance of about three miles. This is well worth the time in May, June and September.

WINCHESTER: SILAS HALL POND

HABITATS

MARSH/SWAMP/BOG: sedge, mixed herbaceous and shrub marsh; shrub, shrubby hardwood, hemlock and mixed conifer swamp; black spruce bog; marshy, shrubby and wooded edges;

FOREST: hardwoods, hardwoods/hemlock, hemlock, mountain laurel;

Lake/pond: pond, shallow water, shore of bog, sedge, mixed herbaceous and shrub marsh, shrub swamp, hemlock swamp, dead wood;

River/stream: stream, fast water, hardwood and hemlock streambelt;

Other: rocky slope.

Silas Hall Pond is a little gem of boreal wilderness hidden among the woodlands of northern Winchester. While it cannot be billed as a major birding site, it is a beautiful representation of a type of ecosystem that is very uncommon in Connecticut. Its position in a hollow at a high elevation (1,280') causes it to have a microclimate that usually occurs much farther north, and to support boreal types of vegetation. Northern hardwoods mixed with hemlock cover the hillsides around the pond, with a sphagnum bog around part of the shore, sedge and shrub marsh, shrub swamp and dead wood covering the remainder. The pond itself is beaver-controlled and quite shallow.

SEASONS/BIRDS

SPRING MIGRATION: water birds, LAND BIRDS;

NESTING SEASON: water birds, LAND BIRDS;

Fall migration: water birds, land birds;

Winter: land birds.

During both migrations and the nesting season, this is a good place in which to look for northern forest bird species: yellow-bellied sapsucker, hermit thrush, solitary vireo, black-throated green, black-throated blue, Blackburnian, yellow-rumped, Canada and Nashville warblers, northern waterthrush and junco, as well as least and great crested flycatchers, all of which nest at this site. In the spring, summer and fall, there are occasionally water birds including wood duck and hooded merganser. During the same period, great blue herons from a nearby heronry occasionally come to feed at the pond.

GETTING AROUND

Birding methods: WALK, boat.

There is a trail that leads from the town road down a wooded hill to the shore of the pond. Those willing and able to carry a canoe down to the pond will be rewarded for their effort. Do not worry about crowds at this site - it is visited infrequently.

DIRECTIONS: Silas Hall Pond is about five miles west of Winsted. From the western intersection of Routes 44 and 8 in Winsted, go west on Route 44 for 3.3 miles, left on the Danbury Quarter Road (aka Grantville Station Road) for 1.6 miles, left on Grantville Road (aka Yates Road) for 1.4 miles to the beginning of the trail on the right. The trailhead is difficult to see; it is 0.2 miles beyond (south of) a more visible blocked-off dirt pulloff area on the right. The trail goes down the hill, bearing slightly to the right, for a total distance of about 0.3 mile.

WINCHESTER: SUCKER BROOK DAM/FLOOD CONTROL AREA

HABITATS

OPEN TERRESTRIAL: tall grass, mixed herbaceous and shrubby fields, shrubby and wooded edges;
Marsh/swamp/bog: shrub swamp, shrubby hardwood swamp;
Forest: hardwoods and hemlock, alone and in combination;
Lake/pond: pond, shrubby shore;
River/stream: stream, shrubby and hardwood streambelt;
Other: hawk watching site, dam.

This flood control area is small, but it has a good mixture of bottomland habitat types, including wooded areas, reverting fields, a pond, a stream and a swamp. The dam provides a place from which to view the bottomlands and parts of nearby Highland Lake.

SEASONS/BIRDS

SPRING MIGRATION: shore birds, LAND BIRDS;
Nesting season: land birds;
FALL MIGRATION: shore birds, LAND BIRDS;
Winter: land birds.

The spring migration is good, and the fall migration even better. Shrubby field species are the specialty here. White-throated sparrows are abundant in October; often mixed in with them are white-crowned, Lincoln's, fox, and other sparrow species. Osprey occurs in spring and fall. The species that nest here are a nice assortment of standard species, plus rough-winged swallow that nests in the dam spillway drainpipes, and cliff swallow that nests under the bridge near the dam. Swamp sparrow and willow flycatcher nest in the wetlands of the valley. Great horned owl, turkey and pileated woodpecker are residents that can be seen in winter as well as other seasons. Snow bunting occurs in late fall and winter. Redpoll and siskin have been seen during some winters.

GETTING AROUND

Birding methods: car, walk.

It is possible to park at the end of the dam at a point that overlooks the bottomland and a bay of Highland Lake. A hundred yards of rough walking puts you down in the bottomland where it is possible to walk about among the habitats. This area is open to hunting.

DIRECTIONS: This area is immediately southwest of Winsted. To get there from Winsted at the intersection of Routes 263 and 44, go south (or east) on Route 263 for 1.5 miles, slant left on Platt Hill Road for 0.2 mile and left on Sucker Brook Road for 0.9 mile to the dam and flood control area on the right.

WOODBURY: VAN VLECK SANCTUARY

HABITATS
MARSH/SWAMP/BOG: cattail, sedge, mixed herbaceous and shrub marsh; shrub and shrubby hardwood swamp;

OPEN TERRESTRIAL: tilled, short grass, tall grass and shrubby fields, shrubby and wooded edges;

LAKE/POND: pond, shallow water, shore of mixed herbaceous marsh, shrubs, hardwoods;

FOREST: hardwoods, mixed conifers;

River/stream: perennial and seasonal streams, shrubby and wooded streambelts.

This sanctuary, managed by the Flanders Nature Center, consists of 130 acres of managed and natural habitats, including varied deciduous and conifer forest communities, a pond, a variety of wetlands, mowed and reverting fields.

SEASONS/BIRDS
SPRING MIGRATION: water birds marsh birds, shore birds, LAND BIRDS;

NESTING SEASON: water birds, marsh birds, LAND BIRDS;

FALL MIGRATION: water birds, marsh birds, LAND BIRDS;

Winter: land birds.

While this site cannot boast of any really uncommon species, it has a nice diversity and good numbers of the standard land bird migrants and nesters, particularly thrushes, vireos, and warblers. There are also some water birds (including pied-billed grebe in migration), and some marsh birds (including Virginia rail that occurs as both nester and migrant).

GETTING AROUND
Birding methods: WALK, ski.

Three miles of trails go throughout the area. The nature center has a trail map, and conducts guided nature walks.

DIRECTIONS: This sanctuary is about five miles north of the village of Woodbury, and about eight miles west of Waterbury. To get there from the center of Woodbury at the intersection of Routes 6 and 317, go north (eastbound) on Route 6 for 1.3 miles, left on Flanders Road for 3.0 miles, right on Church Hill Road for 0.3 miles to the sanctuary, with parking on the right and the visitor center on the left.

WOODBURY: WHITTEMORE SANCTUARY

HABITATS
FOREST: hardwoods, white pine and hemlock, alone and in various combinations, mixed conifers, mountain laurel;
Marsh/swamp/bog: hardwood and hemlock swamps, bog;
Lake/pond: ponds, seasonal pools;
River/stream: perennial and seasonal streams.
This sanctuary is managed by the Flanders Nature Center, also in Woodbury. It consists largely of hilly terrain, with varied hardwood communities and white pine groves in the upland areas, as well as several groves of white and Norway spruce near the wetlands. The preserve includes a number of small swamps, and a bog that is in the process of reverting to swamp.

SEASONS/BIRDS
SPRING MIGRATION: water birds, shore birds, LAND BIRDS;
NESTING SEASON: LAND BIRDS;
FALL MIGRATION: water birds, marsh birds, shore birds, LAND BIRDS;
Winter: land birds.
There are no really unusual species at this site in migration or during the nesting season, but there is a nice diversity of standard species, and there are lots of them. Land birds include such northerners as brown creeper, winter wren, Canada and yellow-rumped warblers, and northern waterthrush. Great blue heron and spotted sandpiper are here spring, summer and fall, and solitary sandpiper in migration.

GETTING AROUND
Birding methods: WALK.
There are several trails and a discontinued road that make it possible to reach all of the main habitat areas in this sanctuary. A trail map is available at the nature center at the nearby Van Vleck Sanctuary, described elsewhere in this chapter.

DIRECTIONS: This sanctuary is in Woodbury, about eight miles west of Waterbury. To get there from the center of Woodbury at the intersection of Routes 6 and 317, go south (westbound) on Route 6 for 1.0 mile, and left on Route 64 for 2.5 miles to the sanctuary entrance on the left.

Chapter 7

Middlesex County

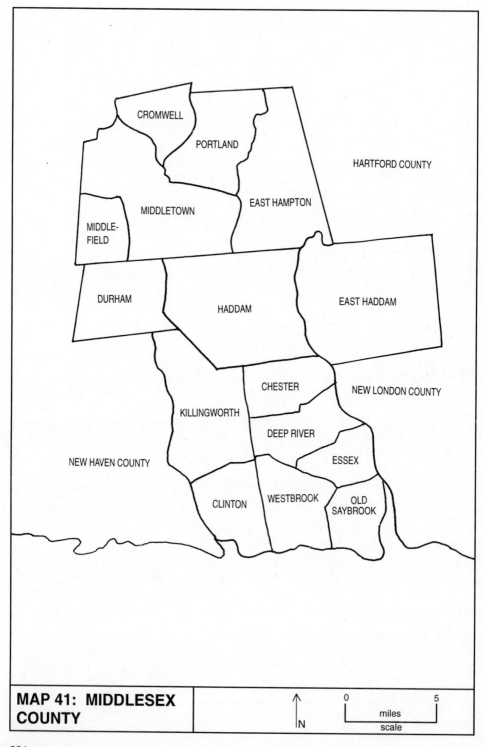

CROMWELL

PORTLAND

HARTFORD COUNTY

EAST HAMPTON

MIDDLETOWN

MIDDLE-
FIELD

DURHAM

HADDAM

EAST HADDAM

CHESTER

NEW LONDON COUNTY

KILLINGWORTH

DEEP RIVER

NEW HAVEN COUNTY

ESSEX

CLINTON

WESTBROOK

OLD
SAYBROOK

**MAP 41: MIDDLESEX
COUNTY**

N

0   5

miles
scale

TABLE 5: HABITATS AND SEASONS AT MIDDLESEX COUNTY SITES

Habitats / Seasons	FOREST	OPEN	MARSH	LAKE	RIVER	COAST	OTHER	SPRING	NEST	FALL	WINTER
Tour of the Lower Connecticut River	○	○	●		●			●	○	●	●
Tour of Old Saybrook						●		●	●	●	●
Chester: Cedar Lake	○		○	○			○	○	○	○	○
Chester: Chester Creek		●			●			●	○	●	●
Chester: Chester-Hadlyme Ferry Landing	○	○	○		●			○	○	○	●
Chester et al: Cockaponset SF	●	○	●	○	○		○	●	●	●	○
Clinton: Hammock River Marsh						●		●	○	●	○
Cromwell: Cromwell Meadows WMA	○	●	●	○	○			●	●	●	○
Deep River: Pratt Cove			●		●			●	○	●	○
Deep River: Town Dock					●			○	○	○	●
Deep River et al: Messerschmidts WMA	○	○	○	●	○			●	○	●	○
Durham: Durham Meadows WMA	○	○	●		○			●	●	●	○
East Haddam: Bahsan Lake	○		○	○			○	●	●	●	○
East Haddam: Chapman Pond	○	○	●		●		○	●	●	●	●
East Haddam: Devil's Hopyard SP	●		○		●			●	●	●	○
East Haddam: Gillette Castle SP	●	○		○	●			●	●	●	○
East Haddam: Lake Hayward	○		●	○				○	○	○	○
East Haddam: Moodus Reservoir	○	○	○	●				●	○	●	○
East Haddam: Salmon Cove Landing	○		○		●			●	○	●	○
East Hampton: Hurd SP	●	○	○	○	●		○	●	●	●	○
East Hampton: Pine Brook	○	○	●	●	○			●	●	●	○
East Hampton: Salmon River SF	●	○	○	○	●			●	●	●	○
Essex: Steamboat Dock			○		●			●	○	●	●
Essex: Turtle Creek Wildlife Sanctuary	●		●	○	○			●	○	●	●
Haddam: Camelot		○			●			●	○	●	●
Haddam: Haddam Meadows SP	○	●	●		●			●	○	●	●
Haddam: Haddam Neck	○	●	●	○	●			●	●	●	●
Haddam: Higganum Reservoir SP	○	○	○	○	○		○	●	○	●	○
Killingworth: Chatfield Hollow SP	●	○	●	○	●			●	●	●	○
Middlefield: Higby Mountain	○						●	○	○	○	○
Middlefield: Lyman Orchards	○	●	●	○	○			●	●	●	●
Middlefield: Wadsworth Falls SP	●				●			●	○	○	○
Middletown: Asylum Reservoirs	●	●	○	○	○		○	●	●	●	○
Middletown: Dripps Road	○						○	○	○	○	○
Middletown: NU Maromis WMA	●	○	○	○	○		○	●	●	●	○
Middletown: River Road	○	●	●		○	○		●	○	●	○
Old Saybrook: North Cove						●		●	○	●	○
Old Saybrook: Plum Bank Marsh/Beach						●		●	○	●	●
Old Saybrook: Saybrook Point						●		●	○	○	●
Old Saybrook: South Cove						●		●	○	●	●

Habitats
- ● very good example
- ○ present, but not as significant

Seasons
- ● excellent during this season
- ○ less good during this season

TABLE 5: HABITATS AND SEASONS AT MIDDLESEX COUNTY SITES (2)

Habitats ● very good example ○ present, but not as significant Seasons ● excellent during this season ○ less good during this season	HABITATS							SEASONS			
	FOREST	OPEN	MARSH	LAKE	RIVER	COAST	OTHER	SPRING	NEST	FALL	WINTER
Portland: Helen Carlson WMA	○		●	○	○		○	●	●	●	○
Portland: Wangunk Meadows/Gildersleeve Island	○	●	●		●			●	○	●	○
Westbrook: Salt Meadow Unit/McKinney NWR	○	○				●		●	●	●	●
Westbrook: Town Beach						●		●	○	●	●

BIRDING IN MIDDLESEX COUNTY

Middlesex County is located in the south-central part of Connecticut, and is bordered on the west by New Haven County, on the north by Hartford County, on the east by New London County, and on the south by Long Island Sound. It is crossed by three major highways - I-95, I-91, and State Route 9.

The People

Middlesex County has a population of 148,850 (sixth largest of the state's eight counties), and a land area of 373 square miles (the smallest of the counties) giving it a population density of 399 people per square mile. This density is about the same as New London and Tolland Counties, twice that of Litchfield and Windham Counties, and about one-third that of Fairfield, Hartford and New Haven Counties. The rate of population growth has been rapid during recent decades - second only to that of Tolland County. Middlesex is one of Connecticut's less affluent counties.

The Land

During the northern half of its course through our state, the Connecticut River flows southward in the broad Central Valley. However, at about the middle of the state (near "Middletown"), the river cuts to the southeast, leaves the Central Valley, and passes through a narrow valley to Long Island Sound. Middlesex County includes most of this narrow valley, much of the hilly country on either side of it, and a small portion of the Central Valley to the west of it. The southern part of the county lies on the relatively flat land of the Coastal Slope, and includes a section of the coast.

Most of the countryside is characterized by hills of moderate steepness, and includes several very steep trap rock ridges which run north/south. Elevations range from sea level to about 750', with the highest elevations occurring in the northeast corner of the county. Middlesex County is largely forested by central zone hardwoods, and is 10% in farmland. The climate of Middlesex County is moderated by proximity to the coast, so that winters tend to be milder and summers cooler than is the case farther inland.

The valley of the Connecticut River that passes through Middlesex County is for the most part bounded by steep hillsides, but has a narrow flood plain that contains a series of rich wetland and riparian forest habitats.

Middlesex County occupies a small section of the Long Island Sound coastline that is near the midpoint of the Connecticut coast. Tides and the intertidal zone are moderate in this part of the coast - greater than those of New London County, but smaller than those of Fairfield and New Haven Counties.

Public Areas and Birding Sites

Although cities and densely populated areas are not far away, there are quite large areas within Middlesex County which are relatively undisturbed, and some of which are protected. Within the county are 11 state parks, two state forests, several wildlife sanctuaries and DEP wildlife management areas, and a number of town docks, ferry landings and other public facilities that provide birding opportunities.

For birders, Middlesex County has several types of habitat that are especially rewarding.

First, there is the Lower Connecticut River itself. Each year it becomes a wintering area for bald eagle, other raptors and a variety of water birds. Several of the Middlesex County sites in Chester, Deep River, East Haddam, Essex, Haddam and Old Saybrook provide a view of the river and an opportunity to see these birds. Wetland habitats along the river in these same towns are good places to visit throughout the year to look for a variety of water, marsh and land birds, depending on the season. Several of these sites include fresh water tidal marshes, a rich and uncommon type of habitat.

Compared with New London, New Haven and Fairfield Counties, Middlesex has quite a short coastline, and access to coastal sites is often limited. However, there are several coastal sites in Clinton, Westbrook and Old Saybrook that have public access and include a variety of habitat types - intertidal zones, rocky coast, barrier beaches, coves, high and low salt marshes, brackish marshes and coastal forest. These habitat types are well represented at Plum Bank Marsh and South Cove in Old Saybrook, Salt Meadow in Westbrook and the Hammock River Marsh in Clinton.

Inland, Middlesex County includes several of the state's first-class birding areas - notably Devil's Hopyard and Gillette Castle in East Haddam, Hurd State Park in East Hampton, Durham Meadows in Durham, Chatfield Hollow State Park in Killingworth, Cromwell Meadows in Cromwell, Haddam Meadows and Haddam Neck, both in Haddam.

Seasons for Birding

Birding in Middlesex County can be an all-season activity. The intersection of the coastal flyway and Connecticut River flyway cause both spring and fall migrations to be interesting. There are good inland sites in which to look for nesting species. And, unlike inland areas in which the choices for birders diminish in winter, sites in Middlesex County on the coast and along the lower Connecticut River become a focus of interest every winter for birders across the state. The birding sites in Middlesex County share a relatively mild climate, and possess several types of coastal habitat, together with a diversity of inland habitats - particularly wetland and forested areas. It is not surprising, then, that a number of species can be found in Middlesex County more easily than in most other parts of Connecticut.

Spring migration is really good in Middlesex County, since there is a reliable passage of migrants along this section of the coast and also up the Connecticut River Valley. Early in the spring (March and early April), focus on water birds at coastal sites in Old Saybrook and Westbrook; along the Connecticut River at Chester, Deep River, Essex, Haddam Meadows and Cromwell Meadows. Also in March, look in South Cove for Bonaparte's gull, together (occasionally) with black-headed and little gulls. A little later, look for migrating and arriving waders and other marsh birds at many of these same sites. In addition, migrating snipe can be seen at Wangunk Meadows in Portland and Haddam Meadows. Still later (April and May), migrating shore birds can be seen at Plum Bank Marsh, Hammock River Marsh, Salt Meadow and South Cove. During this same period, look for migrating land birds along forest and shrubby edges at almost any of the sites on the coast and along the Connecticut River, as well as inland at sites such as Devil's Hopyard, Hurd State Park and Chatfield Hollow State Park.

Nesting Season. Many sites in Middlesex County provide suitable nesting habitat for a variety of land birds. Good sites are Hurd State Park, Haddam Meadows, Devil's Hopyard, the Cockaponset State Forest in Chester and Haddam, Cromwell Meadows, Durham Meadows and Chatfield Hollow State Park. In forest habitats, worm-eating and hooded warblers can be found at a number of sites, including Cockaponset State Forest, Devil's Hopyard, and Hurd State Park. Acadian flycatcher and cerulean warbler both nest at Devil's Hopyard and Gillette Castle. Common species of water birds nest at Durham Meadows, Cromwell Meadows, Haddam Neck, and Chapman Pond in East Haddam. For marsh birds, go to Durham Meadows, Cromwell Meadows or Chapman Pond. At two inland wetland sites - Cromwell Meadows and Durham Meadows - look for American and least bitterns (probable or confirmed as nesters), and for sora, moorhen and king rail, all three of which are inconsistent nesters at these two sites. There are several osprey nests at coastal marshes in Old Saybrook, Clinton and Westbrook. To see waders during the nesting season, look at the Plum Bank Marsh where several species come to feed. For black-crowned night heron and glossy ibis, try Salt Meadow, Plumb Bank Marsh and South Cove.

The fall migration. In the fall, as in the spring, Middlesex County receives the benefit of being at the intersection of two major migration routes - along the coast, and down the Connecticut River. In the main, the same sites that were good in the spring are the ones to head for in the fall, but the timing is reversed - look for shore birds early (in August and September), marsh birds and land birds a little later (in September, October and November, depending on the species), and water birds later still (in October and November). A greater number of migrating raptors pass by this area in the fall than in the spring - sites in the Saybrook Point area can be good for hawk watching, especially in September. Gilette Castle provides an excellent view of the Connecticut River, and of birds travelling along it. Many open terrestrial habitats at sites such as Haddam Meadows and Lyman Orchards are great for sparrows in the fall.

Winter. To many birders, Middlesex County is best known as an area to go to in winter to see water birds, bald eagle and possibly other raptor species. The main action at this time of year is at sites on the coast and along the lower Connecticut River, where the largest concentration of bald eagles in Connecticut occurs each winter, together with many wintering water birds. Rough-legged hawk sometimes can be seen at Plum Bank Marsh and - by looking across the river - from Saybrook Point and the Essex dock. Look for short-eared owl at Plum Bank Marsh and South Cove. Go to South Cove in late winter and early spring, and look carefully among the Bonaparte's gulls for black-headed and little gulls, which are sometimes present. For water birds, the best bets are Saybrook Point, South Cove and the Essex Steamboat Dock. If you want to see bald eagle as well as water birds, add in the Salmon Cove Boat Landing, the Chester-Hadlyme Ferry Landing, and the Deep River Town Dock. (See "Tour of the Lower Connecticut River"). Boat trips up the river can be arranged at the waterfront in Old Saybrook. The mild climate of Middlesex County causes land birds to linger during the winter at many sites in habitat appropriate for the species.

Sources of Information and Help

There is one local bird club located in Middlesex County - the Mattebeseck Audubon Society. Many places to eat or spend the night can be found, especially in coastal towns along Route 1.

TOUR OF THE LOWER CONNECTICUT RIVER

THE TOUR. This is an automobile tour of a section of the lower Connecticut River that is tidal fresh water; the tour goes from north to south, downstream along the west shore of the river from Haddam to Essex, at which point the river starts to be influenced by salt water. This tour provides access to points from which the river can be viewed, and also to areas that have good habitat along the shore. The tour is best in the late fall, winter and early spring, when migrating water birds are on the river, but the habitats along the shore can be good at other times as well. The tour is about 20 miles long (one way) and links the following sites, all of which are discussed in greater detail in separate site descriptions:
> **Haddam: Haddam Meadows State Park**
> **Haddam: Camelot**
> **Chester: Chester-Hadlyme Ferry Landing**
> **Chester: Chester Creek**
> **Deep River: Pratt Cove**
> **Deep River: Town Dock**
> **Essex: Steamboat Dock**

For a tour of the coastal portion of the Connecticut River, see "Tour of Old Saybrook". See also separate descriptions of additional sites along the Connecticut River in Middlesex and New London Counties, and upstream in Hartford County.

HABITATS
> **RIVER/STREAM:** river, slow deep water, wooded and shrubby streambelt, wooded islands, fresh water tidal creeks, mud bars;
> **MARSH/SWAMP/BOG:** fresh water tidal marsh, brackish marsh, wet meadow, mixed herbaceous and shrub marshes, shrub, shrubby hardwood and hardwood swamps;
> **Open terrestrial:** short grass, tall grass and shrubby fields, shrubby and wooded edges, vine tangles and thickets;
> **Forest:** hardwoods, hardwoods/hemlock, flood plain.

This tour covers a portion of the Connecticut River that is above the reach of salt water, but still within the influence of tides. As a result, the riverine marshes along this section that are above Essex are tidal fresh water - an uncommon type of wetland that contains unique and rich ecosystems. Along the shore of the river there is a wide variety of terrestrial habitats, including flood plain and upland forests as well as shrubby fields and other open areas.

SEASONS/BIRDS
> **SPRING MIGRATION:** WATER BIRDS, marsh birds, shore birds, LAND BIRDS;
> **Nesting season:** water birds, land birds;
> **FALL MIGRATION:** WATER BIRDS, marsh birds, shore birds, LAND BIRDS;
> **WINTER:** WATER BIRDS, LAND BIRDS.

Birding along this stretch of the Connecticut River is best during the period mid-October to mid-April. During the late fall, winter and early spring, a wide variety of water birds can be seen on the river, including black duck, common goldeneye, bufflehead, ring-necked duck, common and hooded mergansers. During this same period, bald eagle and other raptors such as red-tailed and red-shouldered hawks use the river for migration or local movement. Other land birds that are attracted to the mild environment along the river shores include lingering migrants and resident species such as Carolina wren. In March it is possible to see both the earliest of the spring migrants and lingering winter species. As the spring progresses (and again in the fall), the river becomes a major travel route for both water and land bird migrants. In addition, terrestrial habitats in Haddam Neck State Park and Pratt Cove are worth visiting during the spring, summer and fall.

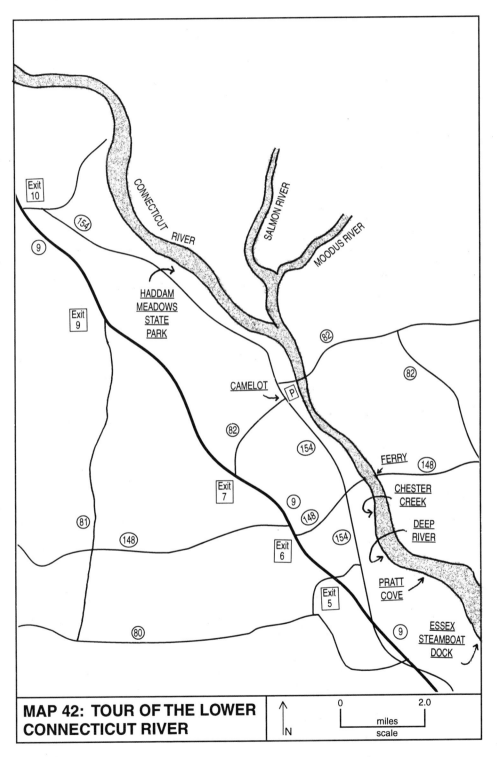

MAP 42: TOUR OF THE LOWER CONNECTICUT RIVER

0   2.0

miles

scale

N

GETTING AROUND
Can be birded by: CAR, walk, bike, boat.
Most of this tour can be done by automobile, but there is also the opportunity to walk through or bike past the habitats in Haddam Meadows State Park, and to explore Chester Creek and Pratt Cove by boat.

DIRECTIONS (see Map 42): The starting point is in Middletown on Route 9.

To get to Haddam Meadows State Park from Route 9, take exit 10, at the end of the exit ramp go south (right) on Route 154 for 4.6 miles to the park entrance on the left.

To get to Camelot from Haddam Meadows State Park, continue south on Route 154 for another 3.8 miles, left on Route 82 for 0.5 mile, and right just before the bridge over the Connecticut River into the parking area that overlooks the river.

To get to the Chester-Hadlyme Ferry Landing from Camelot, return via Route 82 to Route 154, and go south on Route 154 for another 3.2 miles, left on Route 148 for 0.7 mile to the landing at the river.

To get to Chester Creek from the Chester-Hadlyme ferry landing, return to the intersection of Routes 154 and 148, go south on Route 154 for 0.7 mile, left on Railroad Avenue for 0.7 mile to the DEP observation platform on the shore of the creek near where it flows into the Connecticut River.

To get to the Deep River Town Dock from Chester Creek, return to Route 154 and continue south for 1.9 miles to Deep River; left on River Street for 0.8 mile to the town dock.

To get to Pratt Cove from the Deep River Town Dock, return to Route 154 and go south for 0.1 mile, left on Essex Street for 0.5 mile, cross railroad tracks and a small bridge to a parking area on the right just past the bridge and next to the water.

To get to the Steamboat Dock at Essex from Pratt Cove, return to Route 154 again and continue south for 3.3 miles to Centerbrook, go left on West Avenue at the light, and follow signs to Essex. From the rotary in the village center, go east on Main Street for several blocks to where the street ends at the river. Turn into Steamboat Dock parking area.

This is the end of the tour. For sites on the lower, salt water section of the Connecticut River, refer elsewhere in this chapter to the Old Saybrook Tour, and to individual sites in the towns of Old Saybrook and across the river in Old Lyme, New London County.

TOUR OF OLD SAYBROOK

THE TOUR: Four sites that are located near each other in Old Saybrook can be reached by taking this driving tour of less than ten miles. The tour is usually done in late fall, winter and early spring when migrating water birds are present, but there is also much to see during the late spring, summer and early fall, when marsh, shore and land birds are present. All of the sites on this tour are discussed in greater detail in separate site descriptions. They are:
Plum Bank Marsh and Beach
South Cove
Saybrook Point
North Cove

HABITATS

COASTAL: Long Island Sound, rocky shore, tidal cove, marshy and wooded shore, high and low salt marsh, tidal creek, mud flat, sandy beach, sand flat, offshore rocks, coastal forest.

These four sites include just about all of the major types of coastal habitat.

SEASONS/BIRDS

SPRING MIGRATION: GULLS, TERNS, WATER BIRDS, MARSH BIRDS, SHORE BIRDS, LAND BIRDS;

NESTING SEASON: GULLS, TERNS, MARSH BIRDS, shore birds, land birds;

FALL MIGRATION: GULLS, TERNS, WATER BIRDS, MARSH BIRDS, SHORE BIRDS, LAND BIRDS;

WINTER: GULLS, WATER BIRDS, LAND BIRDS.

Among the sites on this tour, there is something to see at any season.

GETTING AROUND

Birding methods: CAR, walk, bike.

These habitats can be seen from your car or very near it. Most of the roads are suitable for biking (Route 1 being the exception). All property around the viewpoints is private and should not be entered. A spotting scope is desirable.

DIRECTIONS (see Map 43): The starting point for this tour is I-95 exit 66. Go south on Spencer Plain Road (Route 166) for 0.3 mile, left on Route 1 for 1.3 miles, and right on Route 154 (Great Hammock Road).

To get to Plum Bank Marsh and Beach, follow Great Hammock Road for 1.3 miles to the Old Saybrook Town Beach on the right, and a wide shoulder on which to park on the left. Plum Bank Marsh is on the left and can be seen from this parking area. Plum Bank Beach is on the right, and can be reached by walking through the town beach parking lot. (Parking within this town park is restricted to town residents during the summer.)

To get to South Cove, follow Route 154 (along the coast with good views of Long Island Sound) for another 2.4 miles, and park on a wide shoulder on the right just short of the causeway over South Cove. The cove can be seen by walking over the causeway.

To get to Saybrook Point, follow Route 154 for another 1.0 mile to the point at which Route 154 makes a sharp turn to the left. To reach Saybrook Point, jog a short distance right then left. Observe local regulations when parking your car.

To get to North Cove, follow Route 154 for another 0.6 mile, right on North Cove Road for 0.3 mile to a parking area overlooking North Cove.

To get to another point on South Cove, go back to Route 154 and follow it for another 0.5 mile, left on Maple Avenue for 0.2 mile, and left on Soundview Avenue for 0.2 mile to the landing on the shore of South Cove.

To get back to I-95, return to Route 154 and follow it north across Route 1 until you see signs to I-95.

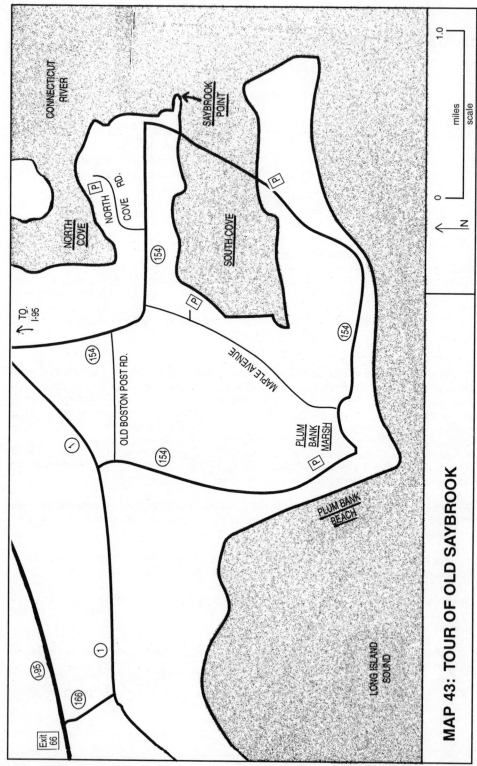

CONNECTICUT
RIVER

SAYBROOK
POINT

NORTH P
COVE RD.

NORTH
COVE

SOUTH COVE

154

TO
I-95

154

P

154

OLD BOSTON POST RD.

MAPLE AVENUE

154

1

154

PLUM
BANK
MARSH

P

PLUM BANK
BEACH

1

1-95

166

Exit
66

LONG ISLAND
SOUND

N

0   miles   1.0

scale

MAP 43: TOUR OF OLD SAYBROOK

CHESTER: CEDAR LAKE

HABITATS
Lake/pond: lake, deep water, shallow water, marshy, shrubby and wooded shore;
Marsh/swamp/bog: shrub marsh, shrub swamp;
Forest: hardwoods, mountain laurel;
Other: rocky slope.

This is a fairly small lake (68 acres) with a largely wooded shore, a portion of which has not been developed. At the north end by the public landing, there is a shrub marsh/shrub swamp that supports a variety of food-bearing shrubs including buttonbush, sweet pepperbush and highbush blueberry. Some red maple trees are starting to invade the wetland, and there are standing dead trees nearby. The surrounding forest is largely hardwoods, with rocky slopes and lots of mountain laurel.

SEASONS/BIRDS
Spring migration: water birds, marsh birds, land birds;
Nesting season: land birds;
Fall migration: water birds, marsh birds, land birds;
Winter: land birds.

The spring and fall migrations are the most active periods at this site (osprey occurs during both periods). In addition, a good variety of nesting species can be found in the woods near the landing at the north end. The habitat there is just right for worm-eating and hooded warblers.

GETTING AROUND
Birding methods: car, walk.

Most of the lake can be seen from various points along Cedar Lake Road and from the boat landing. A trail that follows the north and east shore of the lake starts at the boat landing.

DIRECTIONS: This lake is located several miles west of the center of Chester, and about ten miles north of the coast. To get there from Route 9 exit 6, go west on Route 148 for 1.5 miles, and right on Cedar Lake Road. This road follows the west shore of the lake, and there are several places where you can pull over to view the water. At the north end of the lake, follow signs to the right to reach the public boat landing.

CHESTER: CHESTER CREEK

HABITATS
RIVER/STREAM: fresh water tidal creek, shrubby and hardwood streambelt;
MARSH/SWAMP/BOG: fresh water tidal wetland (herbaceous and shrub marsh, shrub swamp, shrubby hardwood swamp).

Chester Creek flows into the lower Connecticut River in the section that is tidal, but fresh water. Chester Creek is one of several fresh water tidal marshes along the lower Connecticut River which include very diverse ecosystems that are enriched by tidal action. As Chester Creek approaches the Connecticut River, it flows in a streambelt composed partly of hardwoods and partly of shrubs, thickets and vine tangles.

SEASONS/BIRDS
SPRING MIGRATION: WATER BIRDS, MARSH BIRDS, shore birds, land birds;
Nesting season: water birds, marsh birds, land birds;
FALL MIGRATION: WATER BIRDS, MARSH BIRDS, shore birds, land birds;
WINTER: water birds, land birds.

This site can provide good birding throughout the year - the best periods are March through early April, and late October through early December. During the spring, summer and fall, water birds and marsh birds including waders and rails frequent the marsh, and land birds can be seen in the thickets along the sides of the creek. Water birds occur here during the spring and fall migrations, and also in winter, because the creek contains areas of fresh water that are kept open when inland marshes are frozen.

GETTING AROUND
Birding methods: car, BOAT, wheelchair.

This is an ideal site to explore by boat, but be careful to time the tides correctly (Chester Creek is about an hour and a half later than Saybrook Point). A portion of the creek can be seen from Route 154 just south of the intersection with Route 148. Another part can be seen from a DEP overlook platform that is wheelchair-accessible.

DIRECTIONS: Chester Creek is contained almost entirely within the town of Chester, on the west side of the Connecticut River about ten miles north of Long Island Sound. From the intersection of Routes 154 and 148, go south on Route 154 for 0.7 mile, left on Railroad Avenue for 0.7 mile to the DEP observation platform on the shore of the creek near where it flows into the Connecticut River.

CHESTER: CHESTER-HADLYME FERRY LANDING

HABITATS
RIVER/STREAM: river; slow, deep water, shrubby, hemlock and hardwood streambelt;
Forest: hardwoods, hardwoods/hemlock;
Marsh/swamp/bog: shrub marsh;
Open: mixed herbaceous and shrubby fields, shrubby edges.

This is the landing of a seasonal ferry on the west shore of the lower Connecticut River. From the landing, you can see a stretch of the river, as well as woods across the river on the hillside of Gillette Castle State Park. There is also a nearby small marsh and meadow at which land birds occur throughout the year.

SEASONS/BIRDS
Spring migration: water birds, shore birds, land birds;
Nesting season: land birds;
Fall migration: water birds, shore birds, land birds;
WINTER: WATER BIRDS, LAND BIRDS.

The spring and fall migrations are good at this site, especially for water birds and osprey, but it is best in winter. At that time, bald eagles can regularly be seen perching on the hillside across the river, or moving up and down the river. Other raptors including red-shouldered and red-tailed hawks, accipiters, kestrel and turkey vulture also use the river as a route for local movement during the winter, and for migration in spring and fall. Water birds including common merganser, goldeneye and great cormorant can be seen from the landing in winter. Mild winter conditions along the shores of the river attract Carolina and winter wrens, and white-throated sparrow.

GETTING AROUND

Birding methods: car.

The main limitation of this site as a birding area is that all the land surrounding the landing and the road to it is private, thus limiting your mobility. The landing on this west side should not be used during the summer, since parking is very tight when the ferry is in operation. There is more parking at the landing across the river (described in the New London County chapter under "Lyme: Chester-Hadlyme Ferry Landing").

DIRECTIONS: This ferry crosses the Connecticut River about 12 miles north of Long Island Sound. To reach this landing on the western shore, from Route 9 in Chester take exit 6 and go east on Route 148 for 3.1 miles to the ferry landing.

CHESTER/HADDAM ET AL: COCKAPONSET STATE FOREST

HABITATS

FOREST: hardwoods, hardwoods/hemlock, mountain laurel, conifer plantations;
MARSH/SWAMP/BOG: shrub marsh, shrub swamp, shrubby hardwood swamp, hemlock swamp, white cedar swamp;
Open terrestrial: shrubby fields, shrubby and wooded edges;
River/stream: perennial streams, seasonal streams, shrubby and wooded streambelts;
Lake/pond: ponds, hardwood and hemlock shores;
Other: rocky slope, ledges.

The Cockaponset State Forest is made up of a number of parcels of both natural and managed habitats which lie in six Connecticut towns, and which total over 15,000 acres. Most of the areas are forested, and contain a variety of woodlands, including extensive areas that have a dense understory of mountain laurel and other shrubs. There are many areas of steep, rocky slopes, ledges and rock outcrops. A powerline which passes through the block that is in Chester and Haddam (described here) provides lots of shrubby fields, as well as shrubby and wooded edges. There are also beaver ponds, a reservoir, varied marshes and swamps. Among these habitats are many areas of berry-producing trees and shrubs such as cedars, dogwoods and autumn olive.

SEASONS/BIRDS

SPRING MIGRATION: LAND BIRDS;
NESTING SEASON: LAND BIRDS;
FALL MIGRATION: LAND BIRDS;
Winter: land birds.

Large numbers of the standard woodland bird species can be found in these areas during the spring and fall migrations, the nesting season, and also into the early winter. Of all the seasons, May-June is probably best, since it offers the birder spring migrants, nesters and year-round residents. Early winter can also be good, as both resident species and lingering migrants are attracted by the bountiful berry crop that can be found in many of these areas. Breeding species include red-shouldered and broad-winged hawks, pileated woodpecker;

southern species such as Carolina wren and hooded warbler; northerners including black-throated green warbler; and open- and edge-habitat species such as prairie and blue-winged warblers. Worm-eating warbler nests on the forested, rocky hillsides.

GETTING AROUND

Birding methods: car, WALK, bike.

A number of roads and trails go through some, but not all, parts of the forest. Some of the roads are unpaved, rough, and better walked than driven. Trail maps of the Chester/Haddam portions are available at ranger headquarters. The Connecticut Walk Book also has a trail map of parts of the forest. This is a good site in which to look for nesting species, because this state forest does not become crowded in summer as do most state parks.

DIRECTIONS (see Map 44): The parts of the forest that are in Chester and Haddam lie on either side of Route 9 just west of the Connecticut River, ten to fifteen miles southeast of Middletown.

To get to ranger headquarters, from Route 9 take exit 8, at the end of the exit ramp go east on Beaver Meadow Road for 0.6 mile, and right on Ranger Road for 0.1 mile to the headquarters building.

To enter the north portion of the parcel, from Route 9 take exit 8, at the end of the exit ramp go east on Beaver Meadow Road for 0.2 mile, and left on Hubbard Road. This road initially goes through private land but then passes through the forest for almost a mile until it reaches the edge of the forest at an underpass beneath Route 9. There are two woods roads that head north through the forest from Hubbard Road before you reach the Route 9 underpass.

To enter the middle portion of the parcel, from Route 9, take exit 8 and go west on Beaver Meadow Road. Initially there is a short stretch of private land, but after that the forest is on the left (south or east) side of the road until the intersection with Parker Hill Road, 2.6 miles from Route 9. Several roads and trails lead from Beaver Meadow Road into the forest. At 2.0 miles from Route 9, there is a beaver pond/shrub marsh on the southeast side of the road, with a trail to the pond that starts at a wide shoulder on the road.

To go through more of the middle portion of the parcel, go left on Parker Hill Road for 0.6 mile, at which point enter the state forest by going straight ahead, off the hardtop onto a dirt road - Old County Road. This road goes through the forest for 1.4 miles, until it intersects with Filley Road. Go left on Filley Road for another several miles through the forest.

To go through still more of the middle portion of the forest, start at Route 9 exit 6, go west on Route 148 for 1.5 miles, and right on Cedar Lake Road. It passes through the forest for several miles, and leads to several other auto and woods roads that also go through the forest.

Another access to the middle portion of the forest can be taken by starting at the intersection of Routes 148 and 145 just west of Cedar Lake. Go west on Route 148 for 0.7 mile to a woods road on the right (north). This woods road can be walked through the forest; it connects with other woods roads.

To get to the "cedar swamp" portion of the forest, start at Route 9 exit exit 6, go west on Route 148 for 0.3 mile, left on Baker Road for 0.5 mile, and left again on Cedar Swamp Road. This road passes through the forest and areas of wooded swamp for the next 1.5 miles.

To get to another separate parcel in Haddam, from Route 9 take exit 7, go north on Route 82

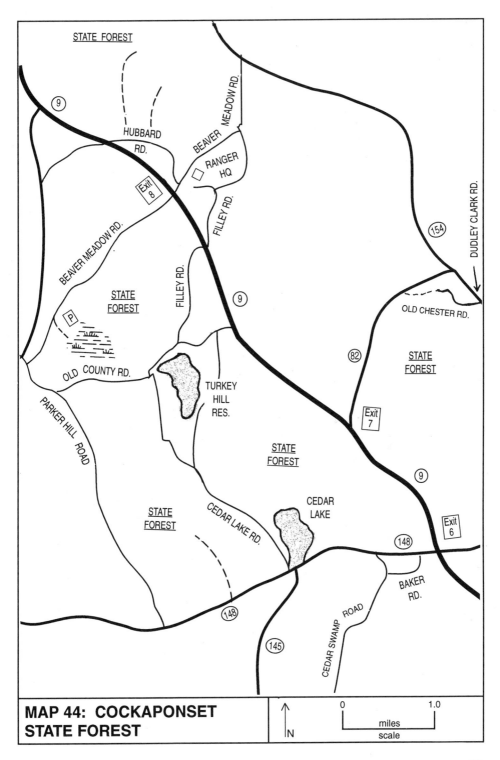

MAP 44: COCKAPONSET STATE FOREST

N
0 — 1.0
miles
scale

for 2.3 miles (the forest is on your right), right on Route 154 for 0.4 mile, right on Dudly Clark Road for 0.1 mile, and right onto Old Chester Road for 0.7 mile to a dead end where the road is blocked (but the blocked portion continues through the forest). This is a nice stretch of road to bird on foot.

Seven separate blocks of the forest are in Madison (New Haven County), about fifteen miles east of New Haven. They are one to four miles west of Route 79, and three to eight miles south of Route 80. From the center of North Madison, at the intersection of Routes 79 and 80, go south on Route 79 for 0.1 mile, and turn right on Opening Hill Road. Starting at 2.2 miles, parts of the forest lie intermittently on one side or the other of this road for the next 2.3 miles as it goes south, parallel to Route 79 (look for state forest markers on trees by the roadside). At 4.5 miles from its intersection with Route 79, Opening Hill Road intersects with Nortontown Road. A number of other town roads in this area lead to other parts of the forest. Topographic maps or a county atlas with large scale maps that show state forests are required to locate all of these parcels.

CLINTON: HAMMOCK RIVER MARSH

HABITATS
COASTAL: high salt marsh, tidal creek, salt pannes, shrubby and wooded edges. The Hammock River winds through this salt marsh, and the whole area is visible from a town road.

SEASONS/BIRDS
SPRING MIGRATION: water birds, MARSH BIRDS, SHORE BIRDS, land birds;
Nesting season: marsh birds, shore birds, land birds;
FALL MIGRATION: water birds, MARSH BIRDS, SHORE BIRDS, land birds;
Winter: land birds.
There are birds to see here throughout the year. It is a good site at which to see willet and waders during the nesting season, osprey in the spring, summer and fall, and harrier in the fall and winter.

GETTING AROUND
Birding methods: car.
The marsh can be viewed from the bridge, but watch out for fast-moving traffic.

DIRECTIONS: This site is half a mile from the coast, and a mile south of the Clinton village center. From I-95 exit 64, go south on Route 145 for 2.0 miles, left on Route 1 for 0.2 mile, and right on Beach Park Road for 0.4 mile to the bridge over the Hammock River, from which the marsh can be seen. There is a shoulder on which to park at the far end of the bridge on the left side of the road.

CROMWELL: CROMWELL MEADOWS WILDLIFE MANAGEMENT AREA

HABITATS

MARSH/SWAMP/BOG: fresh water tidal marsh (vegetation of sedge, cattail and shrubs); shrub, shrubby/hardwood and hardwood swamp; hardwood edge;
OPEN TERRESTRIAL: short grass and shrubby fields, edges;
River/stream: stream, shrubby and wooded streambelt;
Forest: flood plain;
Lake/pond: seasonal pools.

Cromwell Meadows lies between the Connecticut River and Mattabasset River and is within a backwater of both. It consists of 496 acres of varied wetlands, open terrestrial habitats and flood plain forest. Because the Connecticut River is tidal even this far from Long Island Sound, the wetlands include a freshwater tidal marsh that contains the wide variety of vegetation typical of that type of habitat.

SEASONS/BIRDS

SPRING MIGRATION: WATER BIRDS, MARSH BIRDS, SHORE BIRDS, LAND BIRDS;
NESTING SEASON: water birds, marsh birds, LAND BIRDS;
FALL MIGRATION: WATER BIRDS, MARSH BIRDS, SHORE BIRDS, LAND BIRDS;
Winter: water birds, land birds.

The position of this marsh in a major river valley, together with the rich habitats that it contains, produce conditions that are favorable for the occurrence of migrants, nesters and winter residents; it has something to offer during all seasons, but especially spring, summer and early fall. The spring migration of water birds is best in late March, and in April there is a chance of seeing migrating snipe. Probable nesting species include American and least bitterns, as well as sora and Virginia rail. Many green-winged teal, pintail and wood ducks also nest here. In the early fall, water birds are the main attraction, and at this time it is also possible to see moorhen in migration. In winter, this is a good site in which to look for lingering land birds.

GETTING AROUND

Birding methods: walk.

Unfortunately, as a birding area Cromwell Meadows suffers several drawbacks. A nearby elevated highway is noisy and the area near it is littered; in the fall the area is heavily hunted (except on Sundays); in the spring, it is often flooded. A path overlooks the marsh. Walking is very wet in the spring. Mosquitoes and ticks are numerous. Lock your car.

DIRECTIONS: This area is on the west side of the Connecticut River, one to two miles north of Middletown. To get there from Middletown at the intersection of Routes 9 and 66, go north on Route 9 for 1.0 mile to exit for Route 99 (Cromwell and Rocky Hill), north on Route 99 for 0.4 mile, left on South Street for 0.9 miles, and left through the tunnel under Route 9 to the entrance and parking.

DEEP RIVER: PRATT COVE

HABITATS

RIVER/STREAM: fresh water tidal creek, shrubby and wooded streambelt;
MARSH/SWAMP/BOG: fresh water tidal marsh, (mixed herbaceous vegetation), shrubby and wooded edge.

Pratt Cove contains a fresh water tidal marsh and creek on the west side of the lower Connecticut River. This unusual type of habitat contains a very diverse ecosystem that is enriched by tidally induced nutrients from the river. The vegetation is composed of a wide variety of emergent and aquatic plants, including wild rice, cattail, pickerelweed, arrowheads, impatiens and many more species. Elevated areas within the marsh support a high diversity of shrubs and other terrestrial plants. As the creek in Pratt Cove approaches the Connecticut River, it leaves the marsh and flows through a streambelt composed partly of hardwoods and partly of shrubs, thickets and vine tangles.

SEASONS/BIRDS

SPRING MIGRATION: WATER BIRDS, MARSH BIRDS, shore birds, land birds;
Nesting season: water birds, marsh birds, land birds;
FALL MIGRATION: WATER BIRDS, MARSH BIRDS, SHORE BIRDS, land birds;
Winter: water birds, land birds.

This site can provide good birding throughout the year; the best periods are March through early April, and late October through early December. During the spring, summer and fall, water birds and marsh birds including waders and rails frequent the marsh, and land birds can be seen in the thickets along the sides of the creek. During the spring and fall migrations, water bird species include ringneck, canvasback, pintail, gadwall and both teals. In winter, black duck, mallard and bufflehead are attracted to areas of fresh water in the cove that are kept open when other inland wetlands are frozen. Bald eagle occasionally occurs at the cove in winter.

GETTING AROUND

Birding methods: car, BOAT.

This is an ideal site to explore by canoe, in order to observe the birds, other animals and plants in this unusual habitat. One-half to one mile of the creek can be paddled, but avoid low tide (tide times at Pratt Cove are about one and a half hours later than at Saybrook Point). A portion of the creek and marsh can be seen from the bridge over the creek, near where you park.

DIRECTIONS: This site is on the west side of the lower Connecticut River, about ten miles north of Long Island Sound. From Route 9, take exit 4, go north on Route 154 for 1.7 miles, right on Essex Street for 0.5 mile, cross railroad tracks and a small bridge to parking on the right just past the bridge next to the water.

DEEP RIVER: TOWN DOCK

HABITATS

RIVER/STREAM: river, slow water, mud flat, wooded island, wooded streambelt.

This site provides a view of the lower Connecticut River, and of Eustasia Island in the river. The river is tidal at this point, and mud flats are exposed at low tide.

SEASONS/BIRDS
Spring migration: water birds, shore birds, land birds;
Nesting season: water birds, land birds;
Fall migration: water birds, marsh birds, shore birds, land birds;
WINTER: WATER BIRDS, LAND BIRDS.
Winter is the most interesting time at this site, because of the water birds that use this portion of the lower Connecticut River - species including pied-billed grebe, bufflehead, canvasback and common merganser. Also in winter, several raptor species use the river as an avenue for local movement - they include bald eagle, red-shouldered and red-tailed hawks, and (infrequently) golden eagle. During the spring and fall migrations, the mud flats near the dock attract shore birds and waders.

GETTING AROUND
Birding methods: car.
The river and mud flats can be seen from the dock; the surrounding land is private.

DIRECTIONS: This site is in Deep River, about five miles north of Essex. In Deep River, at the intersection of Routes 154 and 80, go east on River Street for 0.8 mile to the Deep River town dock.

DEEP RIVER/WESTBROOK:
MESSERSCHMIDTS WILDLIFE MANAGEMENT AREA

HABITATS
LAKE/POND: lake, shrubby and hardwood shore;
Forest: hardwoods, groves of conifers;
Open terrestrial: shrubby field, edge;
River/stream: small stream;
Marsh/swamp/bog: hardwood swamp, shrub swamp.
Messerschmidts Pond is the centerpiece of this 421-acre wildlife management area, which also encompasses some of the land surrounding the pond (really a lake), and an area of woodland east of the lake.

SEASONS/BIRDS
SPRING MIGRATION: WATER BIRDS, land birds;
Nesting season: water birds, land birds;
FALL MIGRATION: WATER BIRDS, marsh birds, land birds;
Winter: land birds.
This is a good site at which to look for water birds during the spring and fall migrations - especially in March and November. Species that may be seen include bufflehead, goldeneye, common and hooded mergansers. Later in the spring and earlier in the fall, migrating land birds occur in the shrubs and woods along the shore of the lake and in the woods to the east of the lake.

GETTING AROUND
Birding methods: car, walk.

The lake can be scanned from roadside viewpoints on both the west and east shores (see below). Several trails go through parts of the area on the east side of the lake.

DIRECTIONS: This area lies on the Deep River / Westbrook town line, about five miles north of the coast.

To get to a viewpoint on the west shore of the pond: from I-95, take exit 64 and go north on Route 145 for 3.4 miles to a point where Messerschmidts Pond is visible on the right. It is possible to park and view the lake from here.

To get to a viewpoint and enter the habitat on the east side of the pond: from I-95, take exit 64 and go north on Route 145 for 2.6 miles, right on Cross Road for 0.5 mile, and left on Winthrop Road. The wildlife management area lies on both sides of this road, the lake to the west (left), and forest habitats to the east (right).

DURHAM: DURHAM MEADOWS WILDLIFE MANAGEMENT AREA

HABITATS
MARSH/SWAMP/BOG: sedge, cattail and shrub marsh; shrub, shrubby hardwood and hardwood swamp, dead trees;
Forest: hardwoods;
Open terrestrial: tilled and shrubby fields, shrubby edges;
River/stream: stream, shrubby and wooded edges.
This 556-acre area includes the rich bottomland of the Coginchaug River that contains varied wetlands and both tilled and reverting fields.

SEASONS/BIRDS
SPRING MIGRATION: WATER BIRDS, MARSH BIRDS, SHORE BIRDS, LAND BIRDS;
NESTING SEASON: WATER BIRDS, MARSH BIRDS, shore birds, LAND BIRDS;
FALL MIGRATION: WATER BIRDS, MARSH BIRDS, SHORE BIRDS, LAND BIRDS;
Winter: land birds.
The species variety throughout the year makes birding this site worth the effort that is required. During the spring migration, it is possible to see a variety of shore birds, including snipe, both yellowlegs, solitary and spotted sandpipers. Nesting species include Canada goose, mallard, black duck, wood duck, blue-winged teal, American bittern (a possible nester), least bittern, moorhen, sora, Virginia and king rails, as well as a nice variety of land birds. The fall migration is similar to the spring migration. In winter, the species variety is not great, but what there is may be interesting - it is possible to see harrier, northern shrike (infrequently), and lingering land birds.

GETTING AROUND
Birding methods: walk.
There is a trail that goes north into this area from the parking spot (see below), but it is overgrown and movement is difficult. In the spring, it may be very wet. In the fall, since this is a popular hunting area, caution is advised. Ticks are a problem throughout the warm months.

DIRECTIONS: This area is at Durham Center, about five miles south of Middletown.

Access to the southern part of the area may be reached from Durham Center at the intersection of Routes 17 and 77; go south (westward) on Route 17 for 0.5 mile to the point at which the road crosses a stream; the wildlife management area is on the north (right) side of the road, with space to park.

Access to the northern parts of the area may be reached by starting just north of Durham Center at the intersection of Routes 68 and 17. Go west on Route 68 for 0.4 mile to the point at which Route 68 crosses the Coginchaug River. The wildlife management area lies on each side of the road near this point.

EAST HADDAM: BASHAN LAKE

HABITATS
　　Forest: hardwoods;
　　Lake/pond: lake, cove, deep water, wooded island, wooded shore;
　　Marsh/swamp/bog: shrub marsh, shrub swamp, shrubby hardwood swamp, hardwood swamp;
　　Other: rocky slope.
This site includes a boat landing that overlooks a cove and part of the main portion of Bashan Lake. The forest around the landing area includes many berry-producing species of shrubs and trees. There is a dense understory of mountain laurel, dogwoods, blueberry and southern species such as sweet pepperbush. The mile-long dirt road (Ballahack Road) that leads to the landing area passes through a hardwood forest with boulder-strewn hillsides.

SEASONS/BIRDS
　　SPRING MIGRATION: water birds, LAND BIRDS;
　　NESTING SEASON: LAND BIRDS;
　　FALL MIGRATION: water birds, LAND BIRDS;
　　Winter: land birds.
The standard variety of water birds occur here in migration - November and March are the best months. However, the land birds that occur in the forest near the landing area are the real attraction. This is especially the case during the spring and fall migrations, when a nice variety of forest-dwelling species may be seen. The berry crop of the forest understory near the landing attracts migrants from late summer until early winter. Among the interesting nesting species are hooded warbler (in the laurel near the landing), and worm-eating warbler (on the hillsides by Ballahack Road).

GETTING AROUND
　　Birding methods: car, walk, bike ski.
Ballahack Road provides potentially good birding by car, walking, biking or skiing. But stay on the road - most of the surrounding land is private. At the landing there are woods that can be birded from the parking area, or by walking several short trails, one of which leads to the shore of the lake.

DIRECTIONS: This lake lies about three miles north of the village of East Haddam. To get there from the intersection of Routes 82 and 151, go a few yards south of the intersection on Route 151, and turn east (left) on Mt. Parnassus Road for 2.5 miles, left on Ballahack Road for 1.1 miles to the landing on the shore of Bashan Lake.

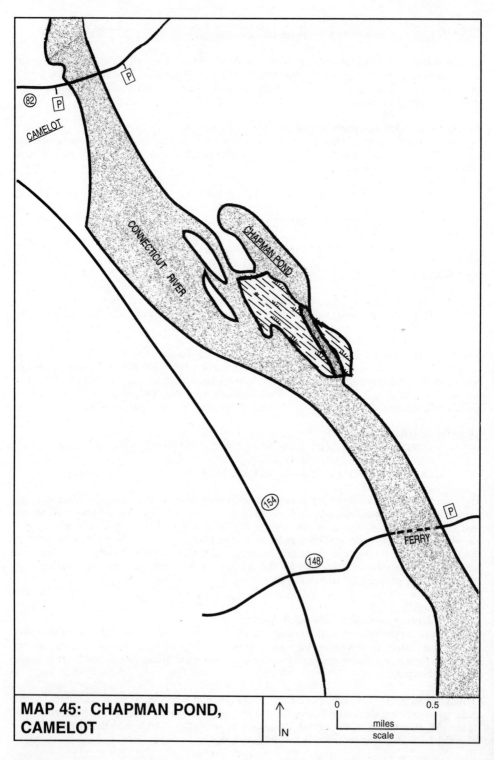

MAP 45: CHAPMAN POND, CAMELOT

N

0   miles   0.5
         scale

EAST HADDAM: CHAPMAN POND

HABITATS
RIVER/STREAM: river, fresh water tidal cove, tidal creek, streams with fast water, hardwood and hemlock streambelts and ravines;
MARSH/SWAMP/BOG: fresh water tidal marsh (sedge, cattail and mixed herbaceous vegetation);
Forest: hardwoods, hemlock, flood plain;
Open terrestrial: shrubby field;
Other: cliff/ledge.

Chapman Pond is an ecologically rich and unique area which supports a wide diversity of plants, birds and other animals. The pond itself lies in a small flood plain on the eastern shore of the Connecticut River, in a section of the river that is tidal but above the influence of salt water from Long Island Sound. The pond is connected to the river by two tidal creeks. Chapman Pond contains a tidal fresh water marsh similar to other sites along the lower Connecticut River. Its ecosystems are enriched by nutrients carried into the marsh by the tidal flow of the Connecticut River. The vegetation of the marsh is composed of a wide variety of emergent plants, including wild rice, cattails, pickerel weed and many species of sedges and rushes. The pond lies in a flood plain that is covered by red and silver maples, cottonwoods, ash, other hardwoods, and a dense understory of alders, willows, spicebush and other shrubs. An upland forest of hardwoods and hemlock covers the hillsides above the pond.

SEASONS/BIRDS
SPRING MIGRATION: WATER BIRDS, MARSH BIRDS, SHORE BIRDS, LAND BIRDS;
NESTING SEASON: WATER BIRDS, MARSH BIRDS, LAND BIRDS;
FALL MIGRATION: WATER BIRDS, MARSH BIRDS, SHORE BIRDS, LAND BIRDS;
WINTER: WATER BIRDS, LAND BIRDS.

The combination of aquatic and terrestrial habitats, together with the richness and diversity of the vegetation in and around Chapman Pond supports an exciting variety of bird species throughout the year. The spring and fall migrations bring many species of water birds including mallard, black duck, both teals, gadwall, American wigeon, ring-necked duck, canvasback, greater scaup and all three mergansers. Migrating marsh birds include great blue and green-backed herons; least sandpiper is among the shore bird migrants. In addition, many species of land birds may be seen in the habitats around the pond as they migrate along the Connecticut River Valley. Osprey hunts the pond during spring, summer and fall. Nesting land bird species include red-shouldered hawk, great horned, barred and screech owls, bobwhite and swamp sparrow. In the late fall, the mild riverine climate, together with the food provided by many berry-producing shrubs near the pond, cause such land bird migrants as hermit thrush and cedar waxwing to linger into early winter. Tides and currents keep the pond from freezing during most winters, and it is a favorite hunting and roosting area for bald eagle.

GETTING AROUND
Birding methods: boat.

To reach this site, it is necessary to use a boat. Use of a canoe requires careful planning, because the current and tidal flow of the river can be very strong, especially when both flow together downstream. Also, the creeks from the river into the pond can best be done with the tide, rather than against it. (To estimate the time of tides at this point on the river, add two hours to the tide time at Old Saybrook.) Motor boat wakes are a hazard in summer. Once at the pond, there are trails to walk through the surrounding woods. The area is hunted in the fall, so that a Sunday trip is advised.

DIRECTIONS (see Map 45): Chapman Pond is on the east shore of the Connecticut River, about fifteen miles upstream from Long Island Sound, and about one and a half miles downstream from the Route 82 bridge over the river at the East Haddam village center. To get to Chapman Pond from the eastern end of the bridge, go east on Route 82 for a few yards, and turn right on a road that leads to a large parking area. Put your canoe in here, and go south along the east bank of the river for about a mile and a half to the first of two tidal creeks that lead into the pond. A second creek that leads into Chapman Pond is another half mile plus downstream. It is longer, more winding, and the more interesting way to enter the pond. An alternate approach to this more southern creek is start your trip and launch your boat at the Chester/Hadlyme ferry (Route 148) at the landing on east side of the river in East Haddam. This leaves you with a trip of about a mile up the river to the creek into Chapman Pond.

EAST HADDAM: DEVIL'S HOPYARD STATE PARK

HABITATS
FOREST: hardwoods, hardwoods/hemlock, hemlock;
RIVER/STREAM: stream, fast water, hemlock ravine, wooded streambelt;
Marsh/swamp/bog: shrub swamp.
This 860-acre park encompasses a section of the valley of the Eight Mile River, several miles from where it flows into the Connecticut River, and not far inland from Long Island Sound. Habitat within the park includes a rocky brook that flows through a steep-sided ravine, a hemlock-dominated forest in and near the ravine, mixed hardwoods dominated by oaks and hickories farther up the hillsides of the valley, and a shrub swamp.

SEASONS/BIRDS
SPRING MIGRATION: LAND BIRDS;
NESTING SEASON: LAND BIRDS;
FALL MIGRATION: LAND BIRDS;
Winter: land birds.
The spring and fall migrations of warblers, vireos and numerous other land bird species is outstanding in this park. Nesting species include both southerners such as Acadian flycatcher, cerulean and hooded warblers, and such northerners as solitary vireo and black-throated green warbler. Other species that occur at this site include red-shouldered hawk, both cuckoos and worm-eating warbler. Orange-crowned warbler and Philadelphia vireo have been reported here during the fall migration.

GETTING AROUND
Birding methods: car, walk.
The park driveway goes by much of the wooded and streambelt habitats, and there are also several trails.

DIRECTIONS: This park is in East Haddam, about five miles south of Colchester. There are many ways to reach it, all of them confusing. Approaching from the south offers the advantages of relative simplicity in route finding, and the approach road follows the Eight Mile River up its beautiful ravine. Start at the intersection of Routes 82 and 156, about four miles east of Hadlyme. Go east on Route 82 for 0.2 mile, and turn north (left) on a road which is without a sign at this point, but which becomes Hopyard Road. This road follows the river for over three miles into the park.

EAST HADDAM: GILLETTE CASTLE STATE PARK

HABITATS
RIVER/STREAM: river, hardwood and hemlock streambelt;
FOREST: hardwoods, hardwoods/hemlock, flood plain;
Open terrestrial: short grass field, shrubby edge;
Lake/pond: small pond.
This former private residence is perched high on a hill overlooking the Connecticut River. The 184-acre grounds of the park include an upland forested area surrounding the castle building, steep, wooded hillside that leads down to the river's edge and a flood plain forest along the river. (This hillside can also be seen from the Chester-Hadlyme Ferry landings on both sides of the river - see under Chester, Middlesex County, and Lyme, New London County).

SEASONS/BIRDS
SPRING MIGRATION: water birds, LAND BIRDS;
NESTING SEASON: LAND BIRDS;
FALL MIGRATION: water birds, LAND BIRDS;
Winter: water birds, land birds.
The spring migration of warblers and other land bird species can be very good. Nesting species include southerners such as Acadian flycatcher and hooded warbler. In winter, bald eagles are sometimes seen as they fly over the river or perch in trees along the shore. Water birds occur on the river in late fall, winter and early spring.

GETTING AROUND
Birding methods: car, walk.
By standing at the castle building, you get a good view of birds travelling along the river, and also have the pleasure of looking down on warblers in the tops of trees on the hillside below you. A park driveway leads to a parking area near the castle. Trails that go throughout the park start on either side of the driveway at a point 0.2 mile from the entrance. There is an admission charge to enter the castle during the warm months; however, the park grounds are open without charge all year.

DIRECTIONS: This state park is on the east bank of the Connecticut River about 12 miles north of Long Island Sound. To get there from the center of East Haddam at the intersection of Routes 82 and 149, go east on Route 82 for 2.8 miles, right on River Road for 1.6 miles to park entrance on the right.

EAST HADDAM: LAKE HAYWARD

HABITATS
MARSH/SWAMP/BOG: bog (herbaceous and shrubby vegetation), hardwood/white pine shore.
Forest: hardwoods, hardwoods/white pine;
Lake/pond: pond, shore of bog and marsh; lake, hardwood and shrubby shore.
At the northern end of Lake Hayward, there is a small pond that has a sphagnum bog along its shore. It is one of the few remaining in Connecticut, and very easily seen from a town road. The lake itself has a shoreline that is mostly developed but with some natural (shrubby and hardwood) areas.

SEASONS/BIRDS
    Spring migration: water birds, marsh birds, land birds;
    Nesting season: land birds;
    Fall migration: water birds, marsh birds, land birds;
    Winter: land birds.

The bog along the shore of the pond, as well as the woods that surround the bog, offer the possibility, during the spring and fall migrations, of seeing a nice diversity of woodland vireos and warblers, as well as yellow-bellied and olive-sided flycatchers, white-throated sparrow and junco. Common moorhen is listed as a probable nester at this site. On Lake Hayward itself, look for the standard mix of water bird migrants during November and March.

GETTING AROUND
    Birding methods: car, boat.

The bog and small pond off the northern end of Lake Hayward can be seen from the side of Lake Shore Road (park off the road on the wide shoulder). Part of Lake Hayward can be seen from the public boat landing at its north end, and a boat can be launched from here. (This does not connect with the pond and bog, however.)

DIRECTIONS: Lake Hayward is in the extreme northeast corner of East Haddam, about five miles south of Colchester. To get there from the intersection of Routes 16 and 2, go west on Route 16 for 0.1 mile, left on Cabin Road for 1.4 miles to a stop sign; bear right on Lake Hayward Road for 1.4 miles to a fork in the road. To get to the bog, bear right at the fork on Lake Shore Road for 0.1 mile to where the bog is visible on the right. To get to the landing on Lake Hayward, bear left at the fork on East Shore Road for 0.2 mile to the boat landing on the right.

EAST HADDAM: MOODUS RESERVOIR

HABITATS
    LAKE/POND: Lake, deep water, shallow water, coves, mixed herbaceous, shrubby and hardwood shores;
    Open terrestrial: tilled, tall grass and shrubby fields, shrubby and wooded edges;
    Marsh/swamp/bog: cattail, mixed herbaceous and shrub marsh, shrub swamp, dead-wood;
    Forest: hardwoods.

This reservoir is irregular in shape, with lots of coves that contain areas of emergent vegetation and other rich wetlands. There are also nearby areas of productive open terrestrial habitats, including shrubby fields and edges. Many blueberry and other berry-producing shrubs are present in these areas.

SEASONS/BIRDS
    SPRING MIGRATION: WATER BIRDS, marsh birds, LAND BIRDS;
    Nesting season: land birds;
    FALL MIGRATION: WATER BIRDS, marsh birds, LAND BIRDS;
    Winter: land birds.

A mix of the standard water bird migrants can be seen at this site in the spring and fall - including mallard, black duck, wood duck, ring-necked duck and pied-billed grebe. November and March are the best months for seeing these species. Migrating land birds may be seen along the shores and in nearby areas of shrubs. Osprey and bald eagle are also possible during migration.

GETTING AROUND

Birding methods: car, walk, boat.

There are several points at which it is possible to see portions of the reservoir, including two boat landing sites (see "Directions" below). In addition, there is a quiet dirt road (Beebe Road, see below) that allows you to walk past two marshy coves of the reservoir and through areas of dense shrubs.

DIRECTIONS (see Map 46): This reservoir lies about four miles northeast of the village of East Haddam. To get to a boat landing at the north end of the reservoir, from East Haddam, at the intersection of Routes 149 and 82, go north on Route 149 for 6.0 miles, right on Mott Lane for 0.1 mile, and right for 0.1 mile to the boat landing, from which a cove of the reservoir can be seen. To get to a second boat landing, go back to the intersection of Mott Lane and Route 149, left (west) on Route 149 for 0.4 mile, left on Falls Bashan Road for 0.8 mile, left on Colchester Turnpike for 0.7 mile, and right on Launching Area Road for 0.2 mile to the landing. To get to a causeway across the reservoir, go back up Launching Area Road to Colchester Turnpike, right on Colchester Turnpike for 0.3 mile to the causeway and park on a road shoulder on the right at the far end. To get to Beebe Road, continue on Colchester Turnpike for another 0.5 mile, and turn right on Beebe Road. During the next 1.3 miles, this road crosses two marshy coves and passes through areas of dense shrubs.

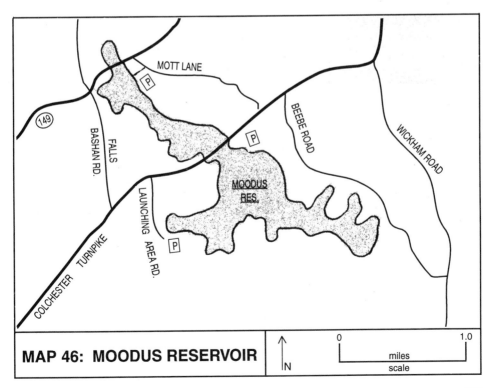

MAP 46: MOODUS RESERVOIR

EAST HADDAM: SALMON COVE BOAT LANDING

HABITATS
RIVER/STREAM: fresh water tidal river and cove, slow water, mud flat, shrubby and wooded streambelt;
Forest: hardwoods, hardwoods/hemlock, flood plain;
Marsh/swamp/bog: shrub marsh, shrub swamp, shrubby edge.
This boat landing is located on the east shore of the lower Connecticut River, at the mouth of a tidal cove that is fed by the Salmon and Moodus Rivers. The cove contains marshes and mud flats, and much of the shoreline is covered with the shrubby edge of a flood plain forest. The boat landing provides a view of the lower end of the cove and of the Connecticut River.

SEASONS/BIRDS
SPRING MIGRATION: gulls, WATER BIRDS, marsh birds, shore birds, LAND BIRDS;
Nesting season: , water birds, land birds;
FALL MIGRATION: gulls, WATER BIRDS, marsh birds, shore birds, LAND BIRDS;
WINTER: gulls, WATER BIRDS, LAND BIRDS.
At this site, you can look for birds in the cove and its surrounding marshes, and also on the Connecticut River and its nearby shoreline of flood plain forest. The wide variation in habitat types makes it possible to see an interesting species diversity within a rather small area. Its position on the lower Connecticut River produces active spring and fall migrations - especially in March and November for water birds, and during April and October for land birds. In winter, the landing area is a good spot from which to look for water birds on the Connecticut River, for lingering land birds in the woods and shrubby edges, and for bald eagle flying along the river or perched in trees on the shore.

GETTING AROUND
Birding methods: car.
It is necessary to stay within the landing area because the surrounding property is private.

DIRECTIONS (See Map 48): Salmon Cove enters the Connecticut River from the east about 15 miles north of Long Island Sound. To get to the boat landing from the center of East Haddam at the intersection of Routes 149 and 82, go north on Route 149 for 1.2 miles to a small road on the left marked by a state boat launch area sign; the road leads to the landing in 0.1 mile.

EAST HAMPTON: HURD STATE PARK

HABITATS
FOREST: hardwoods, hardwoods/hemlock, hemlock, flood plain, mountain laurel;
RIVER/STREAM: river, sand bar; stream, shrubby and wooded streambelt, hemlock ravine;
Marsh/swamp/bog: hardwood swamp, small patches of shrubby hardwood swamp;
Open terrestrial: shrubby field, shrubby and wooded edge;
Lake/pond: seasonal pools;
Other: cliff/ledge, rocky slope.

Hurd Park occupies high land on the east side of the Connecticut River, the hillside down to the river, and a strip of flood plain forest along it- a total area of 884 acres. The upper part of the park is wooded, has mountain laurel thickets, rocky outcrops and the upper end of a ravine which drops through steep ledges to the river. The portion of the park along the river includes flood plain forest; there are shrubby clearings and pockets of wooded swamp in the northern portion of the park near Route 151.

SEASONS/BIRDS
SPRING MIGRATION: WATER BIRDS, shore birds, LAND BIRDS;
NESTING SEASON: LAND BIRDS;
FALL MIGRATION: water birds, marsh birds, shore birds, LAND BIRDS;
WINTER: WATER BIRDS, LAND BIRDS.

For land birds, this site is best during the spring migration and the nesting season. It can be especially good for migrating warblers during the period late April through late May. Nesting species include hooded and worm-eating warblers; barred owl and pileated woodpecker are residents. Water birds and bald eagle can be seen on the river in the late fall, winter and early spring.

GETTING AROUND
Birding methods: car, WALK, bike, ski.
A driveway goes through much of the upper part of the park, and there are numerous trails that go through the woods and down to the river.

DIRECTIONS: Hurd Park lies just southeast of Middletown, but on the opposite (east) side of the river. To get there from Cobalt (just east of Middletown) at the intersection of Routes 151 and 66, go south on 151 for 2.5 miles to Hurd Park Road. Starting at this point, several woods roads and trails on the right lead into the park. To reach the park entrance, turn right on Hurd Park Road and go for 0.6 mile to the park entrance on the right.

EAST HAMPTON: PINE BROOK

HABITATS

MARSH/SWAMP/BOG: cattail, mixed herbaceous and shrub marsh; shrub and shrubby hardwood swamp, deadwood; shrubby and wooded edges;
LAKE/POND: pond, shrubby and hardwood shore;
Forest: hardwoods;
Open terrestrial: shrubby field, vine tangles and thickets;
River/stream: stream, wooded streambelt.

This is a large inland wetland system that includes a wide spectrum of very productive habitats. At the north end (visible from Route 16), there is a mix of marsh, swamp, open terrestrial and forest habitats that grade from one to another. There are areas of dense vine tangles and thickets, as well as berry-producing shrubs such as silky dogwood, winterberry and arrowwood, along with southern species such as greenbriar and bayberry. At the southern end of this wetland (visible from Terp Road), is a large beaver-controlled pond with shrubby and hardwood shores, an outflow stream with a wooded streambelt, and more areas of dense shrubs and thickets.

SEASONS/BIRDS

SPRING MIGRATION: WATER BIRDS, marsh birds, shore birds, LAND BIRDS;
NESTING SEASON: water birds, marsh birds, LAND BIRDS;
FALL MIGRATION: WATER BIRDS, marsh birds, shore birds, LAND BIRDS;
Winter: land birds.

The spring and fall migrations are excellent at this site. The profusion of berry-producing shrubs attracts a variety of passing fall land bird migrants, and cause many to linger into early winter. Other migrants include pied-billed grebe, mallard, black duck, wood duck, hooded merganser, bufflehead, ring-necked duck, harrier and great blue heron. There is also a good variety of nesters and residents, including several southern species. Standing deadwood in the pond and at the outflow attracts a variety of woodpeckers - downy, hairy, pileated, flicker and red-bellied (the latter in large numbers). Among the warblers that nest here are chestnut-sided and hooded, possibly worm-eating, and also Louisiana waterthrush. Red-shouldered hawk and barred owl are also nesters. In addition, this wetland includes the kind of habitat in which sora and Virginia rail are likely to nest.

GETTING AROUND

Birding methods: car

It is possible to see the northern (marsh/swamp) portion of this wetland from Route 16. However, the traffic is heavy and the road shoulder is narrow. For these reasons, it is best to visit early in the morning. The southern (pond/outflow) portion can be viewed from the end of a quiet residential street. There are no trails, and much of the property surrounding the roads is private.

DIRECTIONS: This site is on Route 16 in East Hampton, between Middletown and Colchester. To get to the northern portion of the wetland, from the intersection of Routes 16 and 66, go east on Route 16 for 0.5 mile and park on a wide shoulder on the right, just past the place from which the wetland can be seen from the highway. To get to the southern portion of the wetland, from the intersection of Routes 16 and 66, go east on Route 16 for 0.2 mile, right on Hog Hill Road for 0.9 mile, and left on Terp Road for 0.5 mile to the dead end, from which the pond and its outflow can be seen.

EAST HAMPTON: SALMON RIVER STATE FOREST (COMSTOCK BRIDGE)

HABITATS
RIVER/STREAM: river, hemlock and hardwoods streambelt, stream, wooded streambelt, hemlock ravine;
FOREST: hardwoods, hardwoods/hemlock, hemlock/white pine, hemlock, white pine, sand plain, cedar, mountain laurel;
Open terrestrial: short grass and shrubby fields, edges;
Lake/pond: small ponds, seasonal pools;
Marsh/swamp/bog: shrub and hardwood swamps in pockets.
The Salmon River State Forest occupies over 6,000 acres in several towns which are in four of Connecticut's eight counties. The Comstock Bridge section is a relatively small part of the forest, but one that includes a number of productive streambelt, open and woodland habitats. It is narrow, and encloses a stretch of the Salmon River as it passes through a steep-sided ravine. The woods have extensive areas of dense mountain laurel understory.

SEASONS/BIRDS
SPRING MIGRATION: LAND BIRDS;
NESTING SEASON: LAND BIRDS;
FALL MIGRATION: LAND BIRDS;
Winter: land birds.
This is a good site in which to look for woodland species during the spring and fall migrations. Nesters include southern species such as red-bellied woodpecker, Carolina wren and worm-eating warbler, and there are areas of suitable nesting habitat for Acadian flycatcher and hooded warbler.

GETTING AROUND
Birding methods: car, walk.
It is possible to follow dirt roads (very rough in places) for three miles along the top of the ravine, through state forest and other currently undeveloped (but private) land. Numerous woods roads and trails lead through the forest, but in using them, be careful not to enter private property.

DIRECTIONS: This site is in East Hampton, about five miles west of Colchester. To get there from Route 2 at Colchester, take exit 18 and go west on Route 16 for 6.1 miles to Gulf Road on the left. Gulf Road runs southwest near the Salmon River, and passes intermittently through parts of the state forest for the next 1.5 miles to a fork. At this point bear right onto Stockberger Road which runs close to the ravine, through land that is in part private. In 1.8 miles, Stockberger Road ends at a hardtop road. A right turn will take you to Route 151, several miles north of Moodus.

ESSEX: STEAMBOAT DOCK

HABITATS
RIVER/STREAM: river, slow water, island, sand bar, shrubby and wooded streambelt;
Marsh/swamp/bog: brackish tidal marsh (mixed herbaceous vegetation).
A large and productive section of the lower Connecticut River can be seen from this wharf at the river's edge. It is possible to see the marshes (albeit distantly) across the river in Lyme on

the east shore (on Notts Island and at Elys Ferry), and also to see marshes in Essex along the west shore (upstream at Great Meadow and downstream on Thatchbed Island).

SEASONS/BIRDS
SPRING MIGRATION: gulls, WATER BIRDS, LAND BIRDS;
Nesting season: water birds;
FALL MIGRATION: gulls, WATER BIRDS, marsh birds, LAND BIRDS;
WINTER: gulls, WATER BIRDS, LAND BIRDS.

This site is a good place from which to look for water birds in the fall, winter and spring. The river usually stays ice-free during the winter; species that commonly occur include red-breasted and common mergansers, both scaups and canvasback. It is also possible to see a variety of raptors - migrating hawks in the fall, and, especially in winter, bald eagles perched along the shore and in flight, as well as harrier, rough-legged hawk and short-eared owl hunting over the marshes across the river.

GETTING AROUND
Birding methods: car.

It is necessary to stay right at this small access to the river's edge, since other parts of the shoreline are developed and privately owned. A telescope is really necessary to get good looks at birds at the marshes along the river.

DIRECTIONS: This location is on the waterfront in the village of Essex. From the rotary in the village center, go east on Main Street for several blocks to where the street ends near the shore of the river. The parking area and dock are through the stone pillars on the left side of the circle.

ESSEX: TURTLE CREEK WILDLIFE SANCTUARY

HABITATS
FOREST: hardwoods, hardwoods/hemlock, hemlock, mountain laurel;
MARSH/SWAMP/BOG: fresh water tidal marsh;
Lake/pond: pond, hardwood shore;
River/stream: fresh water tidal cove; stream, herbaceous, shrubby and wooded streambelt.

This 89-acre sanctuary is situated on a point of land that separates Essex South Cove from the main channel of the lower Connecticut River. Much of the sanctuary is deciduous forest dominated by oaks mixed with hemlock, and there is an extensive understory of mountain laurel. There is a fresh water pond, a tidal marsh bordering Turtle Creek, and a stretch of the shore of South Cove. At this time, (late 1995) the hemlocks are dying from effects of the wooly adelgid, and will probably soon be gone. Replanting with white pines and other ever-greens is occurring now.

SEASONS/BIRDS
SPRING MIGRATION: WATER BIRDS, marsh birds, shore birds, LAND BIRDS;
Nesting season: water birds, marsh birds, land birds;
FALL MIGRATION: WATER BIRDS, marsh birds, shore birds, LAND BIRDS;
WINTER: WATER BIRDS, land birds.

The variety of habitat types, and the placement of this site near the mouth of the Connecticut River, make it a very productive birding area - 173 species have been seen from the trails of the sanctuary. A wide variety of migrating warblers and other land birds can be seen in spring and fall, and views of Essex South Cove make a trip in late fall, winter and early spring worthwhile for water birds and possibly bald eagle and harrier.

GETTING AROUND
Birding methods: walk.

There are several trails that lead through the woods, past the pond and marsh, and to the shore of South Cove. The road that goes to the sanctuary entrance becomes private past that point, and should not be driven.

DIRECTIONS (see Map 47): This site is on the west side of the Connecticut River about five miles north of Long Island Sound, between the villages of Essex and Old Saybrook. To get there from Route 9 exit 2, go north on Route 154 for 0.7 mile, right on Watrous Point Road for 0.3 mile to the sanctuary entrance on the left.

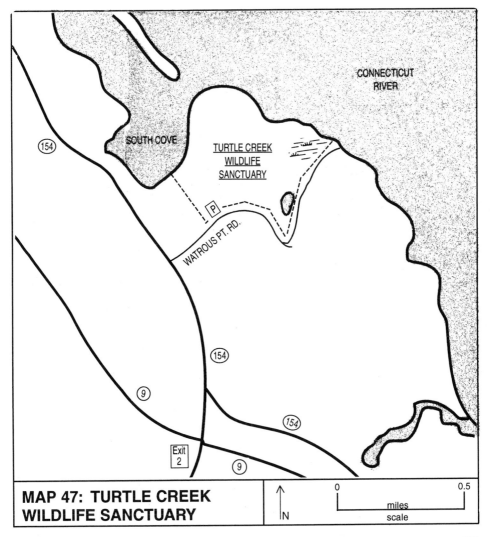

MAP 47: TURTLE CREEK
WILDLIFE SANCTUARY

HADDAM: CAMELOT

HABITATS
RIVER/STREAM: river; deep, slow water, hardwood streambelt, wooded islands;
Open terrestrial: short grass field.
This site (also known as "Marine Park") provides access to the shore of the Connecticut River in a section that is tidal fresh water. Chapman Pond is about a mile downstream on the other side of the river.

SEASONS/BIRDS
SPRING MIGRATION: WATER BIRDS, land birds;
Nesting season: land birds;
FALL MIGRATION: WATER BIRDS, land birds;
WINTER: WATER BIRDS, LAND BIRDS.
This site is an easy way to get a chance of seeing water birds and possibly bald eagle during the spring and fall migrations and in winter. In addition, osprey fly along the river in migration and sometimes in summer.

GETTING AROUND
Birding methods: car.
From the parking area, it is a walk of only a few yards to the shore of the river. This is private land, so be sure that your presence is not unwelcome to those in charge.

DIRECTIONS (see Map 45): This site is on the west bank of the Connecticut River directly across from the village of East Haddam and about fifteen miles upstream from Long Island Sound. The entrance to the parking area in on the south side of Route 82, at the west end of the bridge over the Connecticut River.

HADDAM: HADDAM MEADOWS STATE PARK

HABITATS
OPEN TERRESTRIAL: short grass, tall grass and shrubby fields, shrubby and wooded edges, vine tangles and thickets;
RIVER/STREAM: river, slow water, shrubby and hardwood streambelt;
MARSH/SWAMP/BOG: wet meadow, mixed herbaceous and shrub marsh; shrub, shrubby hardwood and hardwood swamp; seasonal open water;
Forest: hardwoods, flood plain.
This 175-acre park lies along the west shore of the Connecticut River, and provides a view of the river. It also includes a long strip of varied wetlands that lie along an old railroad line, as well as a variety of open fields and edges.

SEASONS/BIRDS
SPRING MIGRATION: WATER BIRDS, marsh birds, shore birds, LAND BIRDS;
Nesting season: water birds, land birds;
FALL MIGRATION: WATER BIRDS, marsh birds, shore birds, LAND BIRDS;
WINTER: WATER BIRDS, land birds.
The spring migration is especially good here, with a variety of migrating water birds and

land birds. Wood duck and ring-necked duck are especially numerous in March. Several blackbird species occur throughout the spring, osprey frequently flies past, and snipe sometimes occurs in the wet meadow during April. The fall migration is also worthwhile, and includes those same species plus a variety of sparrows in the late fall. Several land bird species (mainly berry- and seed-eaters) are attracted by relatively mild conditions along the river, and linger here into the winter. Throughout the winter, this is a good site from which to look for water birds on the river, as well as bald eagle and other raptors in terrestrial habitats near the river.

GETTING AROUND
Birding methods: car, walk, bike.
Park driveways go along open and edge habitats and near the shore of the river for over a mile. These driveways make it possible to bird from your car, and also provide an easy way to walk or bike through the main part of the park.

DIRECTIONS: This site is about ten miles southeast of Middletown, on the west shore of the Connecticut River. From the village of Higganum at the intersection of Routes 154 and 81, go south on Route 154 for three miles to the park entrance on the left.

HADDAM: HADDAM NECK

HABITATS
RIVER/STREAM: river, cove, slow water, deep water, shallow water, shrubby and wooded streambelt, mud flat, sand flat;
OPEN TERRESTRIAL: shrubby field, edge;
MARSH/SWAMP/BOG: sedge marsh, cattail marsh, shrub marsh, shrub swamp, shrubby hardwood swamp;
Forest: flood plain, hardwoods, hardwoods/hemlock, hemlock, laurel understory, vine tangles and thickets;
Lake/pond: small pond, wooded shore.
This site lies along the eastern shore of the Connecticut River, and overlooks both a section of the river and also Salmon Cove (see also East Haddam: Salmon Cove Boat Landing). The site includes a nuclear power plant warm water discharge canal that flows into the Connecticut River and keeps an area ice-free all winter. The shore of the river includes flood plain forest, and near it is an area that is succeeding from shrubby fields to hardwood forest. There are also shrubby fields along a power line. A service road goes between the discharge canal (west of the road), and a nice backwater wetland (east of the road). Also, there is a nature trail near the main power plant buildings.

SEASONS/BIRDS
SPRING MIGRATION: gulls, WATER BIRDS, marsh birds, shore birds, LAND BIRDS;
NESTING SEASON: water birds, LAND BIRDS;
FALL MIGRATION: gulls, WATER BIRDS, MARSH BIRDS, shore birds, LAND BIRDS;
WINTER: WATER BIRDS, LAND BIRDS.
There are birds to see at this site throughout the year. During the early spring, a variety of

water birds can be seen on the river, in the flooded riverine forest and in Salmon Cove. Throughout the spring a variety of land birds pass through, particularly harrier, bald eagle, osprey, vireos, warblers and sparrows. Shore birds (primarily greater yellowlegs, solitary and spotted sandpipers) can be seen feeding on the mud flats. In summer, a nice mix of species nest here, including several of the southern species normally found in a flood plain forest, and also shrubby field and edge species. Among the nesters are: white-eyed, warbling, red-eyed and yellow-throated vireos, many warblers including worm-eating, prairie and hooded, indigo bunting and brown thrasher. Bobwhite is a year-round resident. The fall migration is especially good, and includes most of the species that occur in the spring, with species that move south along the Connecticut River very evident - particularly water birds, broad-winged hawk and waders. In winter, a good variety of water birds can be seen on the open water of the river and cove, and lingering land birds stay to feed on the berries in the shrubby areas. Also in winter, bald eagles often perch on trees along the discharge canal to feed on the fish that occur in the warm water.

GETTING AROUND
Birding methods: car, walk, bike.

The habitats described above lie within a wildlife management area, and birding is permitted outside of the power plant facility itself. A paved road follows the discharge canal, and there are several places to park along it. Several trails start at the end of this road, and go through other habitat areas. An easy way to bird this site (and to avoid the legions of ticks that wait for you along the trails) is to park at the first parking area and walk down the rest of the road. In winter, bald eagles perch in the trees along the canal, so observe them from within your car to avoid disturbing them. In addition, there is a nature trail that starts at the Northeast Utilities Environmental Education Center, to which there is a sign. This trail goes through forest with mountain laurel, and is very good for migrating warblers in the spring.

DIRECTIONS (see Map 48): This site is on the east shore of the Connecticut River about 15 miles north of Long Island Sound and about one mile north of the village of East Haddam. To get to it from the center of East Haddam at the intersection of Routes 149 and 82, go north on Route 149 for 3.2 miles, left on Route 151 for 4.3 miles, left on Haddam Neck Road for 1.0 mile, left on Quarry Hill Road for 1.3 miles, left on Cove Road for 0.7 mile to a fork in the road at a power substation. Follow a road that goes to the right of the substation for 0.7 mile, left at the end of this road onto a road that goes along the power plant cooling canal for 0.9 mile, and ends at a parking area where the cooling canal enters the Connecticut River. This spot is within sight of Salmon Cove in East Haddam. To reach the nature trail that starts near the main power plant buidings, from Route 151, take Haddam Neck Road, and go left at a fork onto Injun Hollow Road to the plant parking area.

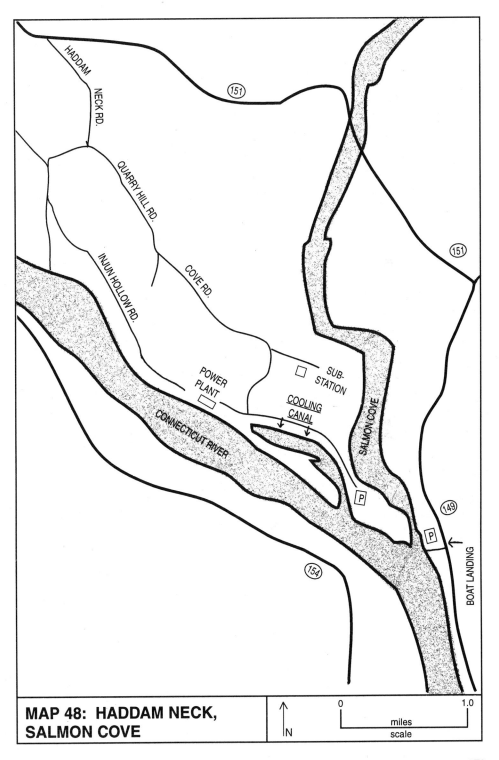

MAP 48: HADDAM NECK, SALMON COVE

N

0   1.0
miles
scale

HADDAM: HIGGANUM RESERVOIR STATE PARK

HABITATS
Forest: hardwoods, hardwoods/hemlock, shrubby thickets;
Open terrestrial: shrubby field, shrubby edges;
Lake/pond: pond, shallow and deep water, shore of shrub marsh, shrub swamp, shrubs, hardwoods and hardwoods/hemlock;
River/stream: stream, shrubby and wooded streambelt;
Marsh/swamp/bog: shrub marsh, shrub swamp;
Other: gravel bank.

This is not a large site, but it has lots of shrubs, thickets and edges, composed of greenbriar, bayberry and other berry-producing plants. These areas lie around a pond with small areas of wetlands on its shoreline, and also surround an old gravel bank that is becoming overgrown.

SEASONS/BIRDS
SPRING MIGRATION: water birds, LAND BIRDS;
Nesting season: water birds, land birds;
FALL MIGRATION: water birds, LAND BIRDS;
Winter: land birds.

This is a nice place in which to look for land birds. Expect to find the standard mix of woodland and edge species. This site is worth a visit during migration, in the spring for warblers, and in the fall when a variety of berry-eaters come here to feed.

GETTING AROUND
Birding methods: car, walk, bike.

The park driveway can be driven, walked or biked (although it is not very long), and there is a trail that goes through the woods from the end of the driveway.

DIRECTIONS: This park is in Haddam, about five miles southeast of Middletown. To get there from Route 9 exit 9, go north on Route 81 for 0.6 mile, left on Dish Mill Road and immediately right on the park driveway that leads through the park and ends in 0.5 mile at the old gravel bank.

KILLINGWORTH: CHATFIELD HOLLOW STATE PARK

HABITATS
FOREST: hardwoods, white pine and hemlock alone and in combination; cedars;
RIVER/STREAM: stream, hardwood streambelt;
MARSH/SWAMP/BOG: shrub swamp, shrubby/hardwood swamp, hardwood swamp;
Open terrestrial: short grass and shrubby fields, shrubby edges;
Lake/pond: two ponds with short grass, shrubby and hardwood shores.

This park is composed of 356 acres of developed, managed and natural areas, and includes rich and varied avian habitats. A rocky stream, its wooded streambelt and a shrub swamp are in the center of the park.

SEASONS/BIRDS
SPRING MIGRATION: water birds, marsh birds, LAND BIRDS;
NESTING SEASON: water birds, LAND BIRDS;
FALL MIGRATION: water birds, marsh birds, LAND BIRDS;
Winter: land birds.
This is a nice area to bird anytime during the warm months. The spring warbler migration is especially good, as you would expect of a wooded stream valley not far from the coast - pine warblers are vocal in the mature white pines. Many of the species that nest here feed in the wooded streambelt. Among the nesters are northern woodland species such as Blackburnian and Canada warblers. Other nesters include: broad-winged and red-shouldered hawks, barred owl, pileated woodpecker, purple martin, worm-eating warbler.

GETTING AROUND
Birding methods: car, walk, bike.
This park is a good place for birders who need to stay in or near their car. There also are trails that offer pleasant walking for those so inclined. In addition, it is one of the few sites in Connecticut in which there is a boardwalk that goes through a swamp. The boardwalk provides an excellent way to observe birds, other animals and plants.

DIRECTIONS: Chatfield Hollow State Park is six or seven miles inland from the Connecticut shoreline, north of Hammonasset Beach State Park in Madison. To get there from the village of Killingworth at the intersection of Routes 80 and 81, go west on Route 80 for 1.5 miles to the park entrance on the right.

MIDDLEFIELD: HIGBY MOUNTAIN

HABITATS
Forest: hardwoods;
OTHER: cliff/ledge, hawk watching site.
Higby Mountain is a trap rock ridge that affords spectacular views of Connecticut's central lowlands to the west. Except for the top of the ridge, the area is largely wooded with hardwoods of various ages.

SEASONS/BIRDS
Spring migration: land birds;
Nesting season: land birds;
Fall migration: land birds;
Winter: land birds.
The top of the ridge provides a good place from which to watch migrating hawks - in spring as well as fall. It also allows you to look down on warblers and other migrants that feed in treetops. Because this is a ridge, fall is better than spring for such species.

GETTING AROUND
Birding methods: walk.
There is a trail which is moderately rough and steep, and reaches the top of the ridge from the edge of the highway in about 0.4 mile.

DIRECTIONS: Higby Mountain is about five miles west of Middletown. To get there from I-91, take exit 18 and go east on Route 66 for 1.5 miles to the point at which Route 66 ceases being a divided highway. A broad shoulder on which to park and the beginning of the trail are visible on the north side of the highway at this point.

MIDDLEFIELD: LYMAN ORCHARDS

HABITATS
MARSH/SWAMP/BOG: wet meadow, sedge, cattail, mixed herbaceous and shrub marsh; shrub, shrubby hardwood and hardwood swamp;
OPEN TERRESTRIAL: tilled, short grass, tall grass and shrubby fields; edges;
Forest: hardwoods, flood plain;
Lake/pond: pond, shrubby and marshy shore;
River/stream: stream, shrubby, wetland and wooded streambelt.
This site (also known as "Miller Road") is part of an extensive wetland system that lies along the Coginchaug River. The site described here includes a wide variety of wetland and terrestrial habitats. The high productivity of the area is due in large part to the interface of wetland and open terrestrial habitats.

SEASONS/BIRDS
SPRING MIGRATION: water birds, marsh birds, shore birds, LAND BIRDS;
NESTING SEASON: water birds, marsh birds, LAND BIRDS;
FALL MIGRATION: water birds, marsh birds, shore birds, LAND BIRDS;
WINTER: LAND BIRDS.
The diversity and productivity of the habitats within this site is reflected in the impressive number of bird species that occur here. Spring and fall are exceptional; summer and winter are also good. Each season offers a wide variety of standard species as well as the possibility of seeing a number of uncommon species. The spring migration includes such uncommon species as snipe (March/April) and rusty blackbird. Species that nest in the area include Virginia rail, green-backed heron, woodcock, white-eyed vireo, orchard oriole, meadowlark, bobolink, Savannah sparrow, red-bellied woodpecker, Carolina wren and great horned owl. Blue-winged teal, sora and moorhen are considered possible nesters. The fall migration is similar to the spring migration with the addition of a wide variety of sparrows, and berry-eaters such as thrushes and cedar waxwing. In winter, this is a good place to look for raptors such as harrier, roughlegged, red-tailed, Cooper's and sharp-shinned hawks, and northern shrike (irregular), plus lingering berry-eaters and sparrows.

GETTING AROUND
Birding methods: car, walk.
A lightly travelled town road goes around the north side of the wetlands at this site, and provides good views. (Route 147, which goes along the south side, has heavy traffic.) The habitats are on private property, so stay on this road. The ease with which this fine area can be viewed makes it a good alternative to nearby Durham Meadows, which has similar habitat diversity, but is much more difficult to enter and move about.

DIRECTIONS: This site is about five miles southwest of Middletown. In Middlefield, at the southern intersection of Routes 147 and 157, go southeast on Route 147 for 0.4 mile, and left on Miller Road. You can now make a 2.3 mile loop around the edge of the wetlands by turning right at each of two opportunities - from Miller Road onto Cherry Hill Road and then onto Route 147 again. This will take you back to the starting point at Route 147 and Miller Road. The best parking spot is on Miller Road by the Coginchaug bridge.

MIDDLEFIELD: WADSWORTH FALLS STATE PARK

HABITATS
FOREST: hardwoods/hemlock, hardwoods/white pine, hemlock;
RIVER/STREAM: stream, fast water, hemlock and hardwoods streambelt, hemlock ravine.
Most of this 267 acre park is forested, and it includes a steep-sided hemlock ravine, through which the Coginchaug River flows.

SEASONS/BIRDS
SPRING MIGRATION: LAND BIRDS;
Nesting season: land birds;
Fall migration: land birds;
Winter: land birds.
This is a nice site in which to observe the spring migration. Nesters include a variety of woodland species that are standard for Connecticut.

GETTING AROUND
Birding methods: walk.
There is a trail system that leads through the park.

DIRECTIONS: The park lies at the western edge of the city of Middletown. To get there from the intersection of Routes 66 and 157 in Middletown, go south on Route 157 for 1.6 miles to the park entrance on the left. A trail map is posted at the entrance.

MIDDLETOWN: ASYLUM RESERVOIRS

HABITATS
FOREST: hardwoods, hardwoods/white pine, white pine, mixed conifers, cedar, mountain laurel;
OPEN TERRESTRIAL: tilled, mixed herbaceous, short grass, tall grass and shrubby fields; shrubby edges, vine tangles;
Lake/pond: ponds; shores of herbaceous, shrub and cattail marsh, shrubs and woods;
River/stream: streams, shrubby and wooded streambelts;
Marsh/swamp/bog: cattail, mixed herbaceous and shrub marsh;
Other: rocky slopes.
This area includes three small reservoirs that are surrounded by a variety of forest and open habitats that include lots of mountain laurel, a cedar grove, a power line, shrubby areas, vines and berry-producing shrubs.

SEASONS/BIRDS
SPRING MIGRATION: water birds, LAND BIRDS;
NESTING SEASON: water birds, LAND BIRDS;
FALL MIGRATION: water birds, LAND BIRDS;
Winter: land birds.
The main attraction at this site is a variety of standard woodland and open habitat land bird species, during migration and the nesting season. Hooded warbler nests in mountain laurel thickets, and worm-eating warbler on the rocky hardwood slopes. Great horned owl and red-tailed hawk are residents. It is also possible to see some water birds on the reservoirs, most often during migration.

GETTING AROUND
Birding methods: CAR, WALK.

Quiet back roads lead through the terrestrial habitats and past the reservoirs, and provide good birding either from your car or on foot. This area does not get crowded in summer. Much of the land surrounding the roads is private.

DIRECTIONS (see Map 49): This area is a mile or two southeast of the city of Middletown, and lies between Route 9 and the Connecticut River, very near River Road and the NU Maromis Wildlife Management Area, both also in Middletown and described elsewhere in this chapter.

To get to the Asylum Reservoirs from Route 9 exit 11, at the end of the ramp go east for 0.2 mile, right on Saybrook Road (Route 154) for 0.3 mile, and left on Brooks Road. **To get to Reservoir #3,** go 0.4 mile on Brooks Road, and left on Training Hill Road for 0.2 mile to Reservoir #3 on the right, and a cedar grove just beyond where the road passes near the reservoir. **To get to Reservoir #1,** go back to Brooks Road and continue (left) on it for another 0.1 mile, left on Cedar Lane for 0.8 mile to Reservoir #1 on the right, together with tall grass and shrubby fields. (In addition, Cedar Lane provides good birding on foot.) **To get to Reservoir #2,** go back to Brooks Road and continue (left) on it for another 0.3 mile to Reservoir #2 on the left. **To get to another pond (Hubbard Pond) and go through a variety of terrestrial habitats,** make the following loop: continue on Brooks Road for still another 1.2 miles (through mountain laurel where hooded warblers have nested), right on Maromis Road for 0.7 mile, right on Bear Hill Road for 2.0 miles (past Hubbard Pond) back to Brooks Road. A left on Brooks Road will take you back to Saybrook Road, near your starting point.

MIDDLETOWN: DRIPPS ROAD

HABITATS
Forest: hardwoods;
Other: rocky slope.

In this site, a hardwood forest on a rocky hillside extends along both sides of a small country road.

SEASONS/BIRDS
Spring migration: land birds;
Nesting season: land birds;
Fall migration: land birds;
Winter: land birds.

Go to this site during both migrations for a mix of woodland land birds, and also during the nesting season for possible worm-eating warbler (the rocky hardwoods hillside is good nesting habitat for this species).

GETTING AROUND
Birding methods: car, walk.

This quiet back road can be driven or walked; the habitat can be seen well from the road.

DIRECTIONS (see Map 49): This site is a couple of miles southeast of the city of Middletown, and just south of the NU Maromis Wildlife Management Area. From Route 9 exit 10, at the end of the ramp, go north (left) on Route 154 (Saybrook Road) for 0.6 mile, and right on Dripps Road. In a few yards, there is a wide shoulder on the left on which to park, if you are going to bird Dripps Road on foot. The next half mile or so goes through the habitat described above.

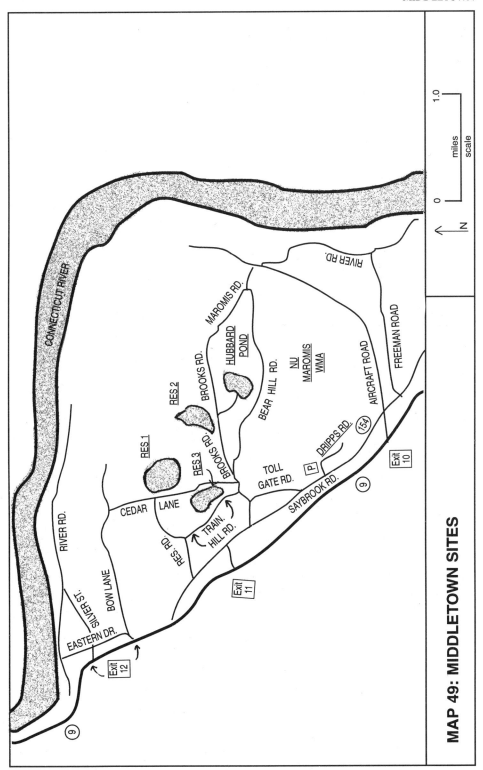

MAP 49: MIDDLETOWN SITES

379

MIDDLETOWN: NU MAROMIS WILDLIFE MANAGEMENT AREA

HABITATS
FOREST: hardwoods, hardwoods/hemlock, hemlock, mixed conifers, cedars, vine tangles, mountain laurel;
Open terrestrial: shrubby field, shrubby edge;
Lake/pond: pond, shore of shrubs, shrub swamp and hardwoods;
River/stream: streams, wooded streambelts, hemlock ravine;
Marsh/swamp/bog: shrub swamp;
Other: rocky slope.

This large, managed wildlife area occupies hilly, mostly wooded terrain next to the Connecticut River. It contains a variety of rich habitats including hardwood forest with a dense understory of mountain laurel and thickets of other shrubs, hemlock ravines, and shrubby openings. (With the expected demise of hemlocks, the character of this forest will change radically.)

SEASONS/BIRDS
SPRING MIGRATION: LAND BIRDS;
NESTING SEASON: LAND BIRDS;
FALL MIGRATION: LAND BIRDS;
Winter: land birds.

This is a good area in which to look for a standard mix of woodland birds - migrants in the spring and early fall, and nesters in the spring and summer. Worm-eating and hooded warblers may well nest here - there is suitable habitat for each of these species. In winter, there are a few resident land birds; owls (probably saw-whet, possibly long-eared) roost in the cedars.

GETTING AROUND
Birding methods: CAR, WALK, bike.

Several quiet country roads, both paved and gravel, run through this area, and they can be driven or walked. In addition, there are several woods roads for walking.

DIRECTIONS (see Map 49): This area is immediately south of the city of Middletown, and lies between Route 9 and the Connecticut River, very near the Asylum Reservoirs and River Road, both described elsewhere in this chapter under Middletown. To get to the NU Maronis Wildlife Management Area from Route 9 exit 10, at the end of the exit ramp go straight through the intersection onto Aircraft Road. Starting 1.0 mile after the intersection, and continuing for the next mile, Aircraft Road goes through the wildlife management area. To reach other parts of the wildlife area, continue on Aircraft Road for a total distance of 2.2 miles from the intersection at the end of the Route 9 exit 10 ramp, and go right on River Road for 1.1 miles through the area. Or, continue on Aircraft Road for another 0.1 mile, and go left on Maromis Road. (If you then go left off of Maromis Road onto Bear Hill Road or onto Brooks Road, you will reach the Asylum Reservoirs and can make a loop back to Route 9 (see the Asylum Reservoirs site description).

MIDDLETOWN: RIVER ROAD

HABITATS
OPEN TERRESTRIAL: short grass, tall grass, mixed herbaceous and shrubby fields, shrubby edges;
Forest: hardwoods, hardwoods / hemlock, flood plain;
River/stream: river, slow water, hardwood streambelt;
Lake/pond: small pond, shrubby and wooded shore.
There are several types of open terrestrial habitat along this road. The Connecticut River, although nearby, is easily seen only from one point along the road.

SEASONS/BIRDS
SPRING MIGRATION: gulls, water birds, LAND BIRDS;
Nesting season: land birds;
FALL MIGRATION: gulls, water birds, LAND BIRDS;
Winter: gulls, water birds, land birds.
Open habitat land birds are the main attraction at this site. Nesters include bobolink, meadowlark, kestrel and red-tailed hawk. There is a variety of migrants, particularly white-crowned, Savannah and various other sparrows in the fall. Osprey migrates along the river in spring and fall, and bald eagle is a possibility in the fall, winter and spring. A few water birds also occur on the river in fall, winter and spring.

GETTING AROUND
Birding methods: car, walk.
The road passes through the open terrestrial habitats, and they can be seen either from your car or by walking.

DIRECTIONS (see Map 49): This area is immediately southeast of the city of Middletown. It lies between Route 9 and the Connecticut River, and just north of the Asylum Reservoirs and the NU Maromis Wildlife Management Area, both in Middletown and described elsewhere in this chapter. **From Route 9 southbound,** take exit 12, go east on Silver Street for 0.1 mile, left on Eastern Drive for 0.4 mile to River Road. Go north (left) on River Road for a short distance to get a view of the river, or go south (right) on River Road for about two miles in order to go through the terrestrial habitats. **From Route 9 northbound,** take exit 12, at the end of the exit ramp go north (straight ahead) on Eastern Drive for 0.9 mile to River Road, and proceed as above.

OLD SAYBROOK: NORTH COVE

HABITATS
COASTAL: salt water tidal cove.
This is a nice cove habitat, but there is no intertidal mud and little marsh.

SEASONS/BIRDS
SPRING MIGRATION: gulls, terns, WATER BIRDS, land birds;
Nesting season: gulls, terns, land birds;
FALL MIGRATION: gulls, terns, WATER BIRDS, land birds;
Winter: gulls, water birds, land birds.

This is a good site at which to look for water birds during the spring migration (especially March), and the fall migration (October into December). Winter can also be good if there is open water. Osprey is often present in spring, summer and fall, as well as harrier and bald eagle in late fall, winter and early spring. The lack of marsh and intertidal mud precludes the occurrence of marsh and shore birds.

GETTING AROUND
Birding methods: car.
Most of the cove can be seen from the parking area. The surrounding land is all private.

DIRECTIONS (see Map 43): This site is near the coast at Old Saybrook. From I-95 exit 66, go south on Spencer Plain Road (Route 166) for 0.4 mile, left on Route 1 for 1.3 miles, right on Route 154 for 0.1 mile, left (straight, really) off Route 154 and onto Old Boston Post Road for 0.8 mile, right on Route 154 for 0.9 mile, left on North Cove Road for 0.3 mile to a parking area on the left that overlooks North Cove.

OLD SAYBROOK: PLUM BANK MARSH AND BEACH

HABITATS
COASTAL: high salt marsh, tidal creek, ditches, mud flats; sandy beach with gravel deposits, sand flats, offshore rocks, Long Island Sound.
There is a large salt marsh on the inland side of Route 154, and a sandy beach between Route 154 and Long Island Sound.

SEASONS/BIRDS
SPRING MIGRATION: gulls, terns, WATER BIRDS, MARSH BIRDS, SHORE BIRDS, land birds;
Nesting season: gulls, terns, marsh birds, shore birds, land birds;
FALL MIGRATION: gulls, terns, WATER BIRDS, MARSH BIRDS, SHORE BIRDS, LAND BIRDS;
WINTER: WATER BIRDS, land birds.
The marsh on one side of the road and the beach on the other cause this site to be a kind of double-header that has something to offer throughout the year.

Plum Bank Marsh is an especially good site at which to look for the species that favor high salt marsh habitat, such as glossy ibis, which feed here during the spring, summer and fall. During the spring and fall migrations, the marsh also attracts dabbling ducks, a good variety of marsh birds, shore birds, osprey, red-tailed hawk and harrier. Nesting species include clapper rail, willet, osprey and purple martin. The fall migration is similar to spring migration. In winter, look for red-tailed hawk, roughlegged hawk and short-eared owl.

Across the road, on Long Island Sound near the beach, there are water birds during the fall, winter and spring (late October through late April is the best period). From here, it is possible to see both loons, horned grebe, oldsquaw and all three scoters.

GETTING AROUND
Birding methods: car
The marsh can be viewed from the wide shoulder of Route 154, and Long Island Sound from the Old Saybrook Town Beach across the road. (Parking within this town park is restricted to town residents during the summer.)

DIRECTIONS (see Map 43): This site is on the coast at Old Saybrook. From I-95 exit 66, go south on Spencer Plains Road (Route 166) for 0.3 mile, left on Route 1 for 1.3 miles, right on Route 154 (Great Hammock Road) for 1.3 miles to the Old Saybrook Town Beach on the right, and a wide shoulder on which to park on the left. Plum Bank Marsh is on the left and Plum Bank Beach is on the right.

OLD SAYBROOK: SAYBROOK POINT

HABITATS
> **COASTAL:** rocky shore, tidal river, and (in the distance) high and low salt marshes, sandy beach, coastal forest.

This is a developed peninsula that overlooks the Connecticut River as it enters Long Island Sound. It also provides a view across the river of Great Island and Griswold Point in Old Lyme.

SEASONS/BIRDS
> **SPRING MIGRATION:** gulls, terns, WATER BIRDS, marsh birds, land birds;
> **Nesting season:** gulls, terns, land birds;
> **Fall migration:** gulls, terns, water birds, marsh birds, land birds;
> **WINTER:** gulls, WATER BIRDS, LAND BIRDS.

This site comes into its own in winter, when you can count on seeing water birds nearby on the river, and have a good chance of seeing a bald eagle, harrier or rough-legged hawk at the marshes across the river. Osprey can be seen here in the spring, summer and fall.

GETTING AROUND
> **Birding methods:** car.

The parking area is just a few feet from points that overlook the river. In order to look for raptors over the marshes across the river and water birds on the river, a spotting scope is essential.

DIRECTIONS (see Map 43): This site is on the coast at Old Saybrook. From I-95 exit 66, go south on Spencer Plain Road (Route 166) for 0.3 mile, left on Route 1 for 1.3 miles, right on Route 154 (Great Hammock Road) for 4.7 miles to the point at which Route 154 makes a sharp turn to the left. Saybrook Point is straight ahead (take a short jog to the right). Observe local regulations when parking your car.

OLD SAYBROOK: SOUTH COVE

HABITATS
> **COASTAL:** salt water tidal cove, intertidal mud, marshy and wooded shore.

This site consists largely of cove habitat, but has areas of mud flats and salt marsh along the shore.

SEASONS/BIRDS
SPRING MIGRATION: gulls, WATER BIRDS, MARSH BIRDS, shore birds, land birds;
Nesting season: gulls, water birds, marsh birds, land birds;
FALL MIGRATION: gulls, WATER BIRDS, MARSH BIRDS, SHORE BIRDS, land birds;
WINTER: WATER BIRDS; land birds.

The main attraction at this site is a wide variety of water birds, especially during the spring and fall migrations (March and November are best). Species frequently seen during both migrations include black duck, pintail, gadwall, wigeon, green-winged teal, shoveler, bufflehead, goldeneye, ringneck, canvasback, both scaup, all three mergansers, pied-billed and horned grebes. Also present during migration are shore birds and marsh birds, including snowy and great egret, little blue heron, black-crowned night heron and glossy ibis. Many of these waders also feed in the cove during the summer. Osprey is present during spring, summer and fall. Winter can be good for water birds if the cove does not freeze, and raptors (including bald eagle, harrier and short-eared owl) are occasionally seen here in winter. Large flocks of Bonaparte's gull, sometimes with little gull and black-headed gull among the group, have been seen here.

GETTING AROUND
Birding methods: car, walk.

The cove can be seen by walking over the causeway from where you park, or from your car at the viewpoint on the west shore. Walking the causeway makes it possible to get closer looks at the birds in the cove.

DIRECTIONS (see Map 43): This site is near the coast at Old Saybrook.

To get to a viewpoint at the causeway across South Cove, from I-95 exit 66, go south on Spencer Plain Road (Route 166) for 0.3 mile, left on Route 1 for 1.3 miles, right on Route 154 (Great Hammock Road) for 3.7 miles to the beginning of the causeway over South Cove. Park on a wide shoulder on the right just short of the causeway.

To get to a viewpoint on the west shore of South Cove, continue on Route 154 for another 2.1 miles, left on Maple Avenue for 0.2 mile, and left on Soundview Avenue for 0.2 mile to the landing on the shore of South Cove.

PORTLAND: HELEN CARLSON WILDLIFE SANCTUARY AND VICINITY

HABITATS
MARSH/SWAMP/BOG: mixed herbaceous and shrub marsh; shrub and shrubby hardwood swamp; bog;
Forest: hardwoods, hardwoods/white pine, vine tangles;
Lake/pond: pond, shore of varied wetlands; lake, shore of shrubs, hardwoods, white pine;
River/stream: stream, hardwood and shrub streambelt;
Other: rocky slope, boulder field.

The centerpiece of the Carlson Sanctuary is a varied wetland that surrounds a small pond. The wetland includes a shrub marsh (principally buttonbush) and the remnant of a bog with areas of vegetation typical of bogs - pitcher plant, leatherleaf and other heaths. A forested hillside near the wetland includes a rocky slope that levels out as a boulder field. The sanctuary is contiguous to a part of the Meshomasic State Forest and near to the Portland Reservoir. This combination provides each of the parts with the advantages of size, habitat diversity, and a quality of isolation. The nearby Portland Reservoir has a shore of shrubs, hardwoods and white pine.

SEASONS/BIRDS
SPRING MIGRATION: water birds, marsh birds, LAND BIRDS;
NESTING SEASON: water birds, LAND BIRDS;
FALL MIGRATION: water birds, marsh birds, LAND BIRDS;
Winter: land birds.

You can expect to find a nice variety of standard woodland and wetland-oriented land birds, during both migrations and as nesters. Osprey occurs here in migration, and a pair of red-shouldered hawks have been seen in the spring. The rocky slope near the pond in the sanctuary provides suitable nesting habitat for worm-eating warbler. In winter, look for the usual resident land bird species in the sanctuary and state forest. Red-tailed hawk can be seen at any time of year. During the spring and fall migrations, water birds occur on the sanctuary pond and on the Portland Reservoir. Also, rough-winged swallows nest in drain pipes at the dam of the reservoir.

GETTING AROUND
Birding methods: WALK.

In the sanctuary, there is a trail that makes a loop of about one half mile around the pond and wetland. It includes a boardwalk over part of the wetland (with a section that was flooded at the time of our visit). In addition, a number of trails lead into Meshomasic State Forest from the sanctuary trail and from surrounding town roads.

DIRECTIONS: The Carlson Sanctuary is in Portland, about five miles northeast of Middletown. From the northern intersection of Route 17 and Route 17A with Sage Hollow Road, go east on Sage Hollow Road for 0.3 mile, right on Rose Hill Road for 0.2 mile, left on Cox Road for 1.2 miles, left on South Road for 0.4 mile. Park under the large spruce tree on the right. The trail around the pond and wetland in the sanctuary starts at this point, and ends about 0.2 mile north on South Road.

To get to one of the trails into the state forest and an overlook of Portland Reservoir, continue north on South Road for another 0.4 mile, right on Marlborough Turnpike for 0.3 mile to the trail on the right, and for another 0.1 mile to the reservoir overlook.

PORTLAND: WANGUNK MEADOWS (LOWER SECTION)
GILDERSLEEVE ISLAND

HABITATS
OPEN TERRESTRIAL: tilled, short grass, tall grass and mixed herbaceous fields; shrubby and hardwood edges; seasonal pools;
MARSH/SWAMP/BOG: wet meadow; fresh water tidal marsh, vegetation of mixed herbs and shrubs;
RIVER/STREAM: river, deep water, island, streambelt of shrubs, hardwoods;
Forest: hardwoods, flood plain, shrubby edges.

Wangunk Meadows is a large bottomland that lies along the east shore of the Connecticut River. The lower, southern section of the Meadows is described here. The upper, northern section is described in the Hartford County chapter under "Glastonbury: Wangunk Meadows (Upper Section)". Both sections are shown on Map 14.

Also described as part of this site is Gildersleeve Island that lies in a nearby stretch of the Connecticut River (you pass it on the way to Wangunk Meadows). The island is covered by flood plain forest with a wooded and shrubby shoreline, and the river at this point is deep and slow.

The lower section of Wangunk Meadows that lies next to the parking area (see "Directions" below) is composed mostly of large fields that are either tilled or mowed as part of a farming operation. Given typical spring rainfall, in March and April parts of these fields contain areas of wet meadow, herbaceous marsh and seasonal pools. The fields are bordered by hardwood forest with shrubby edges.

SEASONS/BIRDS

SPRING MIGRATION: WATER BIRDS, marsh birds, SHORE BIRDS, LAND BIRDS;
Nesting season: land birds;
FALL MIGRATION: WATER BIRDS, marsh birds, SHORE BIRDS, LAND BIRDS;
Winter: water birds, land birds.

The river by Gildersleeve Island is apt to have water birds during the fall, winter and spring - typically mallard, black duck, common and hooded mergansers. In winter, bald eagles sometimes perch on the trees along the island's shore.

The fields in the southernmost section of Wangunk Meadows are excellent during the spring migration, especially if there has been enough rainfall to create seasonal pools. This can be one of the best areas of wet meadow habitat in Connecticut, and is a prime site in which to look for snipe in April. The habitat is also good for migrating sora and moorhen. During both spring and fall migrations, a wide variety of shore birds have often been seen here, including (in addition to snipe), both yellowlegs, spotted, least and pectoral sandpipers. When there are rain pools during migration, look also for blue-winged and green-winged teal, pintail, gadwall and wigeon. The spring and fall swallow migrations can be impressive, as can the migrations of blackbirds (including rusty blackbird). Migrating sparrows usually present an interesting species diversity during April, October and November. Pipit passes through in early spring and late fall. From late fall through early spring, this is a good site in which to look for horned lark and snow bunting.

Land birds that nest here include a number of open habitat species, as well as southerners such as red-bellied woodpecker and Carolina wren. In addition, a variety of raptors frequently occur at various times during the year - kestrel in spring, summer and fall; peregrine falcon, merlin and osprey in spring and fall; harrier in fall, winter and spring; rough-legged hawk, bald eagle and short-eared owl in winter.

GETTING AROUND

Birding methods: car, walk.

A section of the Connecticut River and the east shore of Gildersleeve Island can be seen from the pulloff on Route 17A (see "Directions" below). The southern portion of the lower section of Wangunk Meadows can be seen from the parking area (see "Directions" below), but effective birding requires walking into or along the edge of the field. The ownership of this area is in dispute at the time of writing, so that it is important to observe any signs that may prohibit public access. Farming activity may preclude entering the lower area during the nesting season. At present, the issue of property ownership rules out walking from the lower section of Wangunk Meadows up to the upper section, but this may change.

DIRECTIONS (see Map 14): This area is immediately north of the Gildersleeve section of Portland. To get to a viewpoint on the Connecticut River opposite Gildersleeve Island, from the intersection of Routes 17A and 66, go north on Route 17A for 2.3 miles to a pulloff on the left. To get to a parking area at the lower section of Wangunk Meadows, continue on Route 17A for another 0.3 mile to the parking area on the left.

WESTBROOK: SALT MEADOW UNIT OF MCKINNEY NWR

HABITATS
    COASTAL: high salt marsh, shrub marsh, tidal creek, intertidal mud, wooded edges, coastal forest;
    Forest: young and mature hardwoods, mixed conifers;
    Open terrestrial: short grass and shrubby fields, wooded edge.
This wildlife refuge is a former estate which overlooks the Menunketesuck River Marsh. The inland area includes reverting fields and deciduous upland forest. Closer to the marsh is an area of coastal forest that has a richly developed layer of shrubs and thickets, plus lots of standing dead trees. The marsh itself is large and relatively unspoiled. A tidal river and two smaller tidal creeks flow through it, and one of these passes along the edge of the refuge. The tidal river forms a projection of coastal habitats into upland areas, with rich interfaces.

SEASONS/BIRDS
    SPRING MIGRATION: WATER BIRDS, MARSH BIRDS, SHORE BIRDS, LAND BIRDS;
    NESTING SEASON: marsh birds, shore birds, LAND BIRDS;
    FALL MIGRATION: WATER BIRDS, MARSH BIRDS, SHORE BIRDS, LAND BIRDS;
    WINTER: water birds, marsh birds, LAND BIRDS.
This site offers an exciting mix of coastal and upland birding throughout the year. During the spring, summer and fall, it is a good place to look for a variety of waders, particularly species that occur in high salt marshes such as glossy ibis, as well as great blue heron, great egret, little blue heron and black-crowned night heron. The spring and fall migrations are good for marsh birds such as clapper rail and shore birds such as willet on the marsh, as well as land birds in the woods and fields. In the summer, this is a good place in which to avoid the crowds at most public areas of this size, and to observe a wide variety of nesting and resident species, particularly osprey and various woodpeckers. Winter is also good - the river and creeks offer sheltered open water for black duck, other water birds and great blue heron, and the dense understory of the woods provides shelter for lingering and wintering land birds including woodpeckers, hermit thrush, fox sparrow and golden-crowned kinglet. Harrier is also a possibility in late fall, winter and early spring.

GETTING AROUND
    Birding methods: walk, ski.
From the entrance, stay on the main trail which goes past the administration building and through upland and coastal forest straight down to the edge of the marsh, a distance of

about one-half mile. The trail then bends to the left, goes along the edge of the marsh, bends left again, passes through upland forest and then reverting fields, and brings you back to your starting point - a counterclockwise loop of about two miles. There are a number of side trails that enable you to lengthen or shorten this walk. The trails are also suitable for cross-country skiing in winter.

DIRECTIONS: The refuge is located about a mile inland from Long Island Sound, and about a mile west of the center of Westbrook. To get there from I-95, take exit 64, go south on Route 145 for 0.2 mile, and left on Old Clinton Road for 1.0 mile to the refuge entrance on the right.

WESTBROOK: TOWN BEACH

HABITATS
COASTAL: Long Island Sound, sandy beach, intertidal sand, island.
This is a town beach that provides a view of Long Island Sound. Menunketesuck Island can be seen in the distance offshore.

SEASONS/BIRDS
SPRING MIGRATION: gulls, terns, WATER BIRDS, marsh birds, SHORE BIRDS;
Nesting season: gulls, terns, shore birds;
FALL MIGRATION: gulls, terns, WATER BIRDS, marsh birds, SHORE BIRDS;
WINTER: gulls, WATER BIRDS, shore birds.
This site is a good place to see a variety of water birds on the Sound in the late fall, winter and early spring (the best period is October through April). During this period, it is possible to see greater scaup, bufflehead, common goldeneye, all three scoters, both loons, horned and (occasionally) red-necked grebes. Dunlin, sanderling and ruddy turnstone are often present in the spring and fall, and sometimes in winter, along with purple sandpiper. During the spring, summer and fall, it is possible to see oystercatcher, which nests on Menunketesuck Island.

GETTING AROUND
Birding methods: car, walk.
This is town property with restrictions on parking, so that it is necessary to stay in or near your car, and observe any regulations that are in effect at the time of your visit. Bring a scope if you plan to look for oystercatchers.

DIRECTIONS: This site is on the coast, in the village of Westbrook. From I-95 exit 65, go south on Route 153 for 0.5 mile, right on Route 1 for 0.5 mile, left on Seaside Avenue for 0.8 mile to the Westbrook Town Beach on the left.

Chapter 8

New Haven County

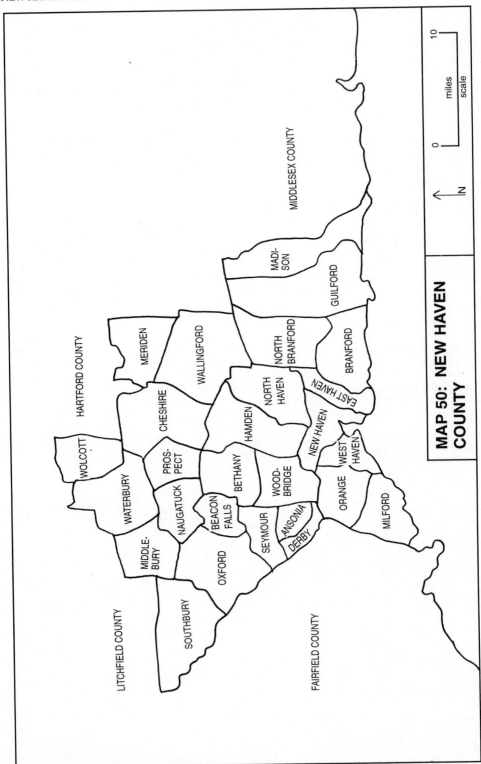

MAP 50: NEW HAVEN COUNTY

NEW HAVEN COUNTY

TABLE 6: HABITATS AND SEASONS AT NEW HAVEN COUNTY SITES

Habitats ● very good example ○ present, but not as significant Seasons ● excellent during this season ○ less good during this season	FOREST	OPEN	MARSH	LAKE	RIVER	COAST	OTHER	SPRING	NEST	FALL	WINTER
Tour of New Haven County Reservoirs	●	○	○	○	○		○	●	●	●	○
Tour of New Haven Harbor						●		●	○	●	●
Ansonia: Ansonia Nature Center	○	●	○	○				●	○	●	○
Bethany: Lake Chamberlain	○	●	○	○	○			●	●	●	○
Branford: Branford Supply Ponds	○		○	○	○		○	●	○	○	○
Branford: Jarvis Marsh						●		○	○	○	○
Branford et al: Lake Saltonstall	○	○	○	●	○			●	○	●	○
Cheshire: Broad Brook Reservoir	○	○		●				●	○	●	○
Cheshire: Canal Park		○	○		●			●	○	●	○
Cheshire: Quinnipiac Audubon Society Sanctuary	●	●	○		○			●	○	●	○
Derby: Osbornedale SP/Kellogg Envir. Center	●	●		○	○			●	●	●	○
Guilford: Great Harbor et al	○					●		●	●	●	○
Guilford: Westwoods Preserve	●	○	○	○	○		○	●	●	●	○
Guilford/Madison: East River Marsh						●		●	●	●	○
Hamden: Sleeping Giant State Park	●		○	○	○		○	●	●	●	○
Hamden/Cheshire: Brooksvale Park	●	○	○		○			○	○	○	○
Hamden et al: West Rock Ridge/Lake Wintergreen	●	●		●	○		○	●	●	●	○
Madison: Hammonasset Beach SP	○	●		○	○	●		●	○	●	●
Madison: Lake Hammonasset	●	○		○	○			○	○	○	○
Madison: Middle Beach Road						●		●	○	●	○
Meriden: West Peak SP/Hubbard Park	●	○		○	○		●	●	●	●	○
Middlebury: Sperry Sanctuary	●		●	○				●	●	●	○
Milford: Gulf Pond/Gulf Beach						●		●	●	●	●
Milford: Merwin Point/Beach Avenue						●		●	○	●	●
Milford: Milford Pt./Wheeler Wildlife Area		○				●		●	●	●	●
Milford: Silver Sands SP/Charles Island		○				●		●	○	●	○
Milford et al: Oyster River						●		●	○	●	●
Milford et al: Oyster River Marsh						○		○	○	○	○
Naugatuck et al: Naugatuck SF	●	○		○	●		○	●	●	●	○
New Haven: East Shore Park et al						●		●	○	●	○
New Haven: Lighthouse Point Park	●	●				●		●	○	●	○
New Haven: Long Wharf						●		●	○	●	●
New Haven et al: East Rock Park	●	○	○	○	○		○	●	○	●	○
North Branford: Big Gulph	○	○		○	○		○	○	○	○	○
Orange: Racebrook Rec. Area	●	●	○		○		○	●	●	●	○
Oxford: Jackson Cove Park	○			○				○	○	○	○
Oxford: Towantic Pond/Larkin SP Trail	○	○	○	○				○	○	○	○
Oxford et al: Southford Falls SP	●	○	○	○	○			○	○	○	○
Southbury: Crook Horn Road	○	●	○	○			○	●	○	●	●
Southbury: George C. Waldo SP	●	○	○	●	○			●	●	●	○

TABLE 6: HABITATS AND SEASONS AT NEW HAVEN COUNTY SITES (2)

Habitats ● very good example ○ present, but not as significant Seasons ● excellent during this season ○ less good during this season	FOREST	OPEN	MARSH	LAKE	RIVER	COAST	OTHER	SPRING	NEST	FALL	WINTER
Southbury: Janie Pierce Park	●	○	●	●	○			●	○	●	○
Southbury: Shepaug Dam/River Road	●	●	○	●	●		○	●	●	●	●
Southbury: Southbury Training School Pond	○	○	○	●	○			●	○	●	○
Southbury/Oxford: Kettletown SP	●	○		○	○		○	●	○	●	○
Wallingford: Community Lake	○	●	○	○	○			●	●	●	○
Wallingford: Wharton Brook SP	○	○		○	○			○	○	○	○
Waterbury: Rifle Range Pond	○	○	○	●			○	●	○	●	○
West Haven: Prospect Beach/Bradley Point		○				●		●	○	●	●
West Haven: Sandy Point						●		●	○	●	●
West Haven: West Haven Boat Ramp						●		●	○	●	●
West Haven: West River						●		●	○	●	●
West Haven: West Shore Beach						●		●	○	●	●
West Haven/Orange: Maltby Lakes	●			●				●	○	●	○
Wolcott: Peterson Park/Mattatuck Trail	○	○	○		○			●	○	●	○
Wolcott: Scoville Reservoir			○	●				●	○	●	○
Woodbridge: Community Garden	○	●	●	○	○			●	○	●	○
Woodbridge: Konolds Pond			○	●				●	○	●	○

BIRDING IN NEW HAVEN COUNTY

New Haven County is located in the south-central part of Connecticut, and is bounded on the west by Fairfield County, on the north by Litchfield and Hartford Counties, on the east by Middlesex County, and on the south by Long Island Sound. It is crossed by five major highways: I-84, I-91, I-95, State Route 8, and the Wilbur Cross Parkway.

The People

New Haven County has a population of 819,470 (it is Connecticut's third most populous county, behind Fairfield and Hartford), and a land area of 610 square miles (the fifth largest county), giving it a population density of 1,343 people per square mile, a close second to Fairfield County. In recent decades, it has had a relatively slow rate of population growth - about the same as Fairfield and Hartford Counties. In terms of overall affluence, New Haven is about average among Connecticut counties.

The Land

New Haven County occupies parts of three of Connecticut's ecological regions - the Central Valley, the Coastal Slope, and the Western Uplands.

The southern section of the Central Valley reaches Long Island Sound at the city of New Haven. The otherwise rather flat land in the valley is broken by several steep north-south trap rock ridges, including East Rock and West Rock.

The land near the shoreline on either side of the Central Valley is part of the Coastal Slope. It drops down to sea level at a moderate rate of about 50' per mile, includes gentle hills of 50'-100' in height, and ends at an irregular coastline that is characterized by alternating points and coves. This section of the coast is about midway up Long Island Sound, so that the tides and intertidal areas are moderate - they tend to be greater than those of New London and Middlesex Counties to the east, but not as large as those along the coast of Fairfield County to the west.

The northwestern part of New Haven County lies in the Western Uplands - an area of steep hills and valleys. This area is bounded on the west by the Housatonic River, which passes through a steep-sided valley for most of its course along the western side of New Haven County.

Elevations in New Haven County range from sea level to about 1,000', with the highest elevations in the Western Uplands ecoregion in the western and northwestern parts of the county. Most of this area is forested by Central Zone hardwoods mixed with white pine and hemlock. About 7% of the county is in farmland. The climate in areas near the coast is relatively mild, with cooler summers, milder winters and less precipitation than at higher elevations inland.

Public Areas and Birding Sites

The diverse topography of New Haven County produces varied and interesting opportunities for birding. It includes a section of the coast that has birding sites that are unsurpassed elsewhere in Connecticut (and, one is tempted to say, elsewhere in New England). It also includes inland areas that offer unspoiled forest habitats, a major river, numerous lakes and ponds, plus a variety of other types of wetland.

The portions of New Haven County near and to the west of the city of New Haven are heavily industrialized. The shoreline to the east of the city is occupied by less dense residential development, with several important areas of avian habitat protected in a relatively natural state. Most of the inland areas of the county are less densely populated.

Within New Haven County there are 15 state parks, one state forest, a national wildlife refuge, several water supply lakes and surrounding watersheds (see "Regional Water Authority" later in this section), and numerous nature centers, sanctuaries, town parks and recreation areas. These public areas are distributed throughout the county, in both rural and urban areas. In fact, two that offer excellent birding are right within the cities of Milford and New Haven/West Haven. Anywhere in the county, you are within easy reach of a first-class birding site. And almost anywhere along the county's coastline, there are places where members of the public can reach the water.

New Haven County, and particularly the Greater New Haven and Milford urban areas, exemplify the degree to which it is possible to preserve excellent avian habitats amid high-density development - thanks in large part to the efforts and resources of dedicated conservationists, in both public and private organizations.

The best-known birding sites in New Haven County are those along the coast. These include several of the most outstanding birding sites in Connecticut: Milford Point/Wheeler Wildlife Area (also known as Nells Island) in Milford, New Haven Harbor in West Haven and New Haven, Lighthouse Point Park in New Haven, and Hammonasset Beach State Park in Madison. Inland sites include a nice variety of habitat types: there are forest habitats at Sleeping Giant State Park in Hamden, West Rock Park in Hamden/Woodbridge, Waldo State Park in Southbury and Naugatuck State Forest in Naugatuck/Beacon Falls; there are open and edge habitats at Osborndale State Park in Derby and Shepaug Dam in Southbury; riverine habitats at Shepaug Dam; lake and pond habitats at reservoirs in several towns (see "Tour of New Haven County Reservoirs").

Regional Water Authority. This organization is a non-profit public agency, the purpose of which is to provide drinking water to South Central Connecticut. It owns and manages a number of properties in New Haven County that total over 20,000 acres. Most of these properties include a reservoir and the surrounding uplands. Among them are seven that are included in this guide:
>Bethany: Lake Bethany
>Bethany: Lake Chamberlain
>Branford/East Haven: Lake Saltonstall
>Madison: Lake Hammonasset
>North Branford: Big Gulph
>Orange: Racebrook Recreational Area
>West Haven/Orange: Maltby Lakes

These areas all have good avian habitats and trail systems. They are secured by locked gates and require a permit to enter. With the permit comes the combination for the locks on the gates. In addition to the fact that these areas contain good habitat, they are particularly good as birding sites for several reasons. Once inside the gate, the only people you are likely to encounter are others who have also received a permit. The areas do not become crowded even during the summer, as do many state parks, so they are good places to visit during the nesting season. And for each, there is a detailed trail map, provided with your permit (see Chapter 12: "Sources of Additional Information").

Seasons for Birding

New Haven County offers really good birding all year long. Migrants travel along the coast, through the county's main river valleys (Housatonic, Naugatuck and Quinnipiac), and along ridge lines such as those formed by East Rock and West Rock. Near and within these land forms is a diversity of upland and aquatic habitats that attract a wide variety of both migrating and nesting bird species. Low and mild areas near the coast attract some southerners among the typical Connecticut species that occur there. In addition, a few northern species are among those that occur in higher inland areas. Winter is perhaps the most interesting season, because of New Haven County's superb coastal sites. An impressive variety of water birds can be seen along the coast, and also up the Housatonic and other rivers, which have ice-free portions during most winters. Over the years, New Haven County has produced far more than its share of sightings of birds that are uncommon, irregular and rare in Connecticut, and such sightings often occur at Milford Point, New Haven Harbor, Hammonasset or Lighthouse Point, and most often during the fall migration or winter.

Spring migration. Start your spring birding in March, looking for water birds and early land bird arrivals. For water birds, look first in coastal sites such as Milford Point and Gulf Pond in Milford, New Haven Harbor and Hammonasset. Land birds arrive near bodies of ice-free water as early as March, and later along edges and open habitats. As spring progresses and water bodies open up, move up the Housatonic River to sites such as River Road below the Shepaug Dam in Southbury, and to the reservoirs (see "Tour of New Haven County Reservoirs"). At this time of year, these sites are good places to look for green-winged teal, pintail, gadwall, shoveler, American wigeon, canvasback and common goldeneye. But also keep visiting coastal sites, because loons, grebes, scoters and brant continue to travel northward along the coast into May. Marsh birds and osprey arrive and / or pass through starting in late March and continuing through April and May. Also during this period, migrating shore birds pass along the coast - in increasing numbers as the spring progresses. The best sites overall for both marsh birds and shore birds are Milford Point / Nells Island and Hammonasset; especially good for marsh birds are Great Harbor Marsh and East River Marsh; and especially good for shore birds are the mud flats at sites along the western shore of New Haven Harbor. From late April through May, migrating warblers can be seen in good diversity and numbers at sites such as East Rock and West Rock, Osbornedale Park and Naugatuck Forest.

Nesting season. New Haven County's diversity of habitat types and the varying elevations at which they occur provide the environment for a wide diversity of nesting species. Terns are certainly a New Haven County specialty; least and common terns nest at Milford Point, Sandy Point in West Haven and at Hammonasset. The largest roseate tern colony in Connecticut nests on Faulkner's Island off Guilford, and these birds often congregate off Milford Point in August. Water birds that nest in the county include gadwall at Nells Island and other sites, black duck at Nells Island and Hammonasset, wood duck at a number of inland water bodies such as Konolds Pond in Woodbridge. To see nesting waders, take your scope to Silver Sands Park at Milford, and scan the rookery on Charles Island offshore. At nearby Nells Island, you can get a closer look at these waders (and in fact, all or most of the wader species that occur in Connecticut) as they feed in the marsh. Both black-crowned and yellow-crowned night herons nest at Nells Island. There is now also a heron rookery at Tuxis Island, and many of the birds that nest there come to Hammonasset to feed. Great Harbor Marsh and East River Marsh are also good for waders during the nesting season. For nesting clapper rail, try either Nells Island or Hammonasset. Nesting oystercatcher has been visible from the Meigs Point area of Hammonasset. Piping plover nests near the least terns at Milford Point, Sandy Point and Hammonasset. Osprey nests at Hammonasset, Guilford, Gulf Pond and Nells Island. It is possible to see a nice diversity of nesting land bird species at both coastal and inland sites. Naugatuck State Forest and Waldo State Park both have a good variety of forest species. Purple martin occurs at a number of sites, including Hammonasset and the East River Marsh. Go to Shepaug Dam to see Connecticut's largest nesting colony of cliff swallows (as well as all the other swallow species that occur in the state except martin). Worm-eating warbler nests at Osbornedale Park, Waldo Park, West Peak/Hubbard Parks in Meriden, and the Naugatuck State Forest. Nesting hooded warbler can be found at Osbornedale Park and the Naugatuck Forest. Sharp-tailed and seaside sparrows nest at Hammonasset and Nells Island. Orchard oriole nests at several sites, including Osbornedale Park and Shepaug Dam. Monk parakeets are becoming increasingly abundant at a few sites in Connecticut; they often congregate near the Court Street landing by Nells Island.

Fall migration. Three of Connecticut's best sites throughout the fall migration are on the coast of New Haven County: Milford Point and Hammonasset are arguably the best all-around sites, with Lighthouse Point not far behind. The fall migration begins in July with the passage of shore birds along the coast. During August, Milford Point provides a kind of double-header, because as the shore birds are passing through, large numbers of terns congregate over the gravel flats prior to their migration. These flocks often also include black skimmer, Forster's and black terns. Shore birds also feed on the mud flats at Sandy Point and other sites in western New Haven Harbor. Milford Point and Hammonasset both continue to be interesting in September and October as marsh birds, later-moving shore birds and land bird migrants travel along the coast - often including uncommon species. To catch the early warbler migration, go to sites with ridges, such as West Rock and Naugatuck State Forest. Lighthouse Point is best known as a site from which to watch the fall hawk migration, but it also seems routinely to provide a very wide variety of other species, especially later-migrating sparrows and warblers such as chat, orange-crowned and yellow-rumped. Hammonasset can also be very interesting during the fall migration - vesper and Lincoln's sparrows, dicksissal, Lapland longspur, meadowlark and pipit have all occurred there during migration. Water birds start to arrive and/or pass through in October and November. They can be seen at inland lakes, but the coast offers more variety and bigger numbers, especially later in the fall. The best sites are Milford Point/Nells Island, Gulf Pond, western New Haven Harbor and Hammonasset.

Winter. For winter birding, you just can't beat the coast of New Haven County, and once again, the top sites are western New Haven Harbor, Hammonasset, Milford Point/Nells Island and Gulf Pond. Water birds are the main attraction, with a great variety of dabbling and diving ducks, loons and grebes. Go to sites along western New Haven Harbor from Oyster River to West River, and look carefully at groups of American wigeon for the occasional Eurasian wigeon. Redhead is sometimes present in the upper harbor. The New Haven County coast is a good area to look for raptors - harrier and rough-legged hawk hunt the marshes and open habitats at Hammonasset, Silver Sands Park and Nells Island; look for owls (sometimes including short-eared, long-eared and snowy) at Hammonasset, Sandy Point and Milford Point. Snow bunting, Lapland longspur and a variety of lingering land bird species occur in open areas and shrubs at sites along the coast.

Sources of Information and Help

The best source of up-to-date birding information, guidebooks and other supplies is the Audubon Shop in Madison. In addition, there are several environmental/nature centers with offices that are open most days: the new Environmental Center at Milford Point, the Kellogg Environmental Center in Derby, and the Ansonia Nature Center in Ansonia. The nature center at Hammonasset Beach State Park is open during the warm months. The Eagle Observation Area at Shepaug Dam in Southbury has a naturalist on site whenever the facility is open (certain days during the winter; a reservation is required to enter the area). There are also four bird clubs that are based in New Haven County, that are best reached by mail: the New Haven Bird Club in New Haven (the largest and most active of the four), the Menunketuck Audubon Society in Guilford, the Naugatuck Valley Audubon Society in Derby, and the Quinnipiac Valley Audubon Society in Wallingford.

The coastal part of New Haven County has all of the amenities a traveller could want. Inland areas, especially the northwestern part of the county, have services in the main towns, but often not between them.

TOUR OF NEW HAVEN COUNTY RESERVOIRS

THE TOUR: This tour includes three reservoirs (Lakes Bethany, Watrous and Dawson) that lie quite close to one another in Bethany and Woodbridge and can be easily linked in a driving tour. A fourth reservoir, Lake Chamberlain in Bethany, is not far away, but is difficult to link on a tour with the others, so it is discussed in a separate site decription. This tour is about 16 miles round trip, beginning and ending on the Wilbur Cross Parkway. The sites on this tour, in the order they are reached, are:

> **Bethany: Lake Bethany**
> **Woodbridge: Lake Watrous**
> **Woodbridge: Lake Dawson**

HABITATS

> **FOREST:** hardwoods, hardwoods/white pine, white pine, hardwoods/hemlock, hemlock, mixed conifers including tamarack, shrubby understory;
> **Open terrestrial:** mixed herbaceous and shrubby fields, wooded edges;
> **Lake/pond:** lakes, shores of cattail and shrub marshes, shrubs, hardwoods, white pine and hemlock in various combinations;
> **River/stream:** streams, fast water, hemlock ravine, shrubby and wooded streambelts;
> **Marsh/swamp/bog:** hardwood swamp;
> **Other:** cliffs and ledges.

Each of the lakes have shores that are mostly wooded but also include areas of shrubs and small pockets of marsh. The land around Lake Bethany is composed of a wide variety of multi-aged forest habitat types, plus open terrestrial habitats associated with a power line. The West River passes through the southern part of the Lake Bethany area, and forms a steep-sided hemlock ravine. The cliffs and ledges of the steep western side of West Rock Ridge lie to the east of Lakes Watrous and Dawson.

SEASONS/BIRDS

> **SPRING MIGRATION:** water birds, LAND BIRDS;
> **NESTING SEASON:** LAND BIRDS;
> **FALL MIGRATION:** water birds, LAND BIRDS;
> **Winter:** land birds.

Water birds occur on each of these reservoirs - mostly ring-necked duck and other common migrants in spring and fall. However, it is land birds that are the real attraction of this tour. The spring and fall migrations bring a nice mix of the standard woodland and open habitat migrants, but the most interesting period is the nesting season, when a number of open and edge habitat species breed in the shrubby areas along the power line. It is not unusual to see indigo bunting, brown thrasher and prairie warbler on territories near each other. Hooded and worm-eating warblers also nest in appropriate forest habitats. In September and October, migrating hawks can be seen across Lake Watrous riding the updrafts of West Rock Ridge.

GETTING AROUND
Birding methods: CAR, WALK, ski.
Many of the good habitats on this tour can be seen from your car or near it. In addition, there are over three miles of trails within the Lake Bethany area, for which a Regional Water Authority permit is required, and for which their trail map is very useful. These trails form a network that goes through or past all of the significant habitats within the area. However, if you do not have a permit, it is also very rewarding to bird by walking or driving along several of the town roads that are part of this tour. Although the land on either side of the roads is private, the roads themselves are public.

DIRECTIONS (see Map 51): This area is in Bethany and Woodbridge, five to ten miles north of New Haven. From the Wilbur Cross Parkway, exit 59, go north on Route 69 for 5.6 miles, and right on Hatfield Hill Road.

To reach trails near Lake Bethany, follow Hatfield Hill Road for 0.5 mile to the south shore of Lake Bethany on the left. Two trails that go along the lake shores start here on either side of the lake.

To bird by car or on foot along town roads and also reach an access to additional trails, continue on Hatfield Hill Road for another 0.3 mile to Downs Road, and turn left (north). Downs Road can be driven north for 1.1 miles, and walked for a considerable distance farther. At 0.8 mile north of the intersection of Downs and Hatfield Roads, Hoadley Road goes off to the left. It can be driven for 0.6 miles to another entrance to Lake Bethany trails, and birded by car or on foot still farther. These roads pass through forest habitats (mostly hardwoods and hardwoods/white pine, with rocky outcrops) - all good birding country.

For some more birding along town roads, return to the intersection of Downs and Hatfield Hill Roads, and drive south on Downs Road for 1.2 mile to an overlook point at the north end of Lake Watrous. Continue south on Downs Road for another 1.0 mile to Route 69, left on Route 69 for 0.6 mile to an overlook point at the north end of Lake Dawson. Almost all of your route on Downs Road takes you through worthwhile birding habitat.

To return to the Wilbur Cross Parkway, continue south on Route 69.

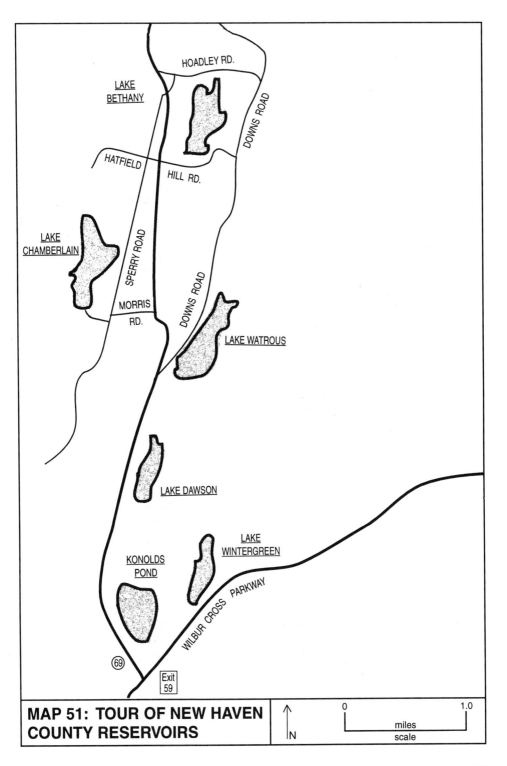

MAP 51: TOUR OF NEW HAVEN COUNTY RESERVOIRS

TOUR OF NEW HAVEN HARBOR

THE TOUR: This tour goes entirely around the shore of New Haven Harbor, from west to east - starting in the eastern part of Milford and ending in the eastern part of New Haven. Taken together, the sites that are included in the tour contain almost all of the types of coastal habitat that occur in Connecticut.

The tour links the sites that are listed below, and provides directions that will enable you to go from one to another. For those who do not want to do the entire tour, it is possible to go to one or several of these sites or to do a segment of the tour, such as just the west shore (Merwin point through Long Wharf) or just the east shore (East Shore Park through Lighthouse Point Park). Because of the position of the sun (especially in winter), the visibility is best from the east shore of the harbor in the morning, and from the west shore in the afternoon. (However, the tour is run from west to east, because this involves making right turns into and out of the sites - easier and safer than left turns.) The sites, in the order that they are reached on the tour, are as follows:

      Milford: Merwin Point/Beach Avenue
      Milford: Oyster River Marsh
      West Haven/Milford: Oyster River
      West Haven: West Shore Beach at St. John's By The Sea
      West Haven: Prospect Beach/Bradley Point
      West Haven: Sandy Point
      West Haven:West Haven Boat Ramp
      West Haven: West River (Kimberly Avenue Bridge)
      New Haven: Long Wharf
      New Haven: East Shore Park/Fort Hale Park/Morris Cove
      New Haven: Lighthouse Point Park

Each of these sites is described in detail elsewhere in this New Haven County chapter, alphabetically by town.

HABITATS

      COASTAL: rocky shore, point, breakwater, sand, gravel and cobble beach, dunes, mud, sand and gravel flats, gravel bar, tidal cove, tidal creek, salt and brackish water tidal river, tide pool, high and low salt and brackish marshes, coastal forest, New Haven Harbor, Long Island Sound.

New Haven Harbor is an estuary that contains a wide variety of coastal habitat types - a large cove of Long Island Sound (New Haven Harbor itself), a peninsula, rocky shores, beaches, salt and brackish marshes, tidal creeks, intertidal areas of mud, sand and gravel, and a sand spit that extends halfway across the harbor.

SEASONS/BIRDS

      SPRING MIGRATION: GULLS, TERNS, WATER BIRDS, MARSH BIRDS, SHORE BIRDS, LAND BIRDS;
      Nesting season: gulls, terns, water birds, marsh birds, shore birds, land birds;
      FALL MIGRATION: GULLS, TERNS, WATER BIRDS, MARSH BIRDS, SHORE BIRDS, LAND BIRDS;
      WINTER: GULLS, WATER BIRDS, shore birds, LAND BIRDS;

New Haven Harbor is one of the truly outstanding coastal birding areas in New England. The spectrum of coastal land forms and habitat types that are concentrated in the sheltered estuary of the harbor attracts a wide variety of bird species. The spring and fall migrations are perhaps the most interesting seasons, because during those times it is possible to see a great species variety of all of the bird groups that occur here - gulls, terns, water birds, marsh birds, shore birds and land birds. Winter is also exciting, because sites in New Haven Harbor are among the best in New England for seeing winter specialties among species of loons, grebes, ducks and gulls. Even summer does not have to be a down time, because waders that nest on several of the nearby offshore islands can be seen as they come to shoreline sites to feed.

Throughout the year, all of the species that one would hope to see in these types of coastal habitat occur at New Haven Harbor. In addition, over the years, many uncommon species and a few rarities have been seen at various points along the harbor shore. The list is long, but includes the following:

gulls: glaucous, Iceland, lesser black-backed, little, black-headed, Bonaparte's and laughing (try Long Wharf or Oyster River in winter and early spring);

terns: Caspian, royal, black and roseate (Long Wharf is good in the warm seasons);

water birds: red-necked and western grebes, Eurasian wigeon, Barrow's golden-eye, common and king eider (in winter at West River and several sites that look at the Harbor or Sound);

shore birds: Wilson's plover, Hudsonian and marbled godwits, spotted redshank, Baird's, upland, buff-breasted and purple sandpipers, all three phalaropes, American avocet (most species in spring and fall, especially at Sandy Point and Long Wharf);

land birds: golden eagle, gyrfalcon, snowy owl, western kingbird, lark bunting, lark sparrow (most species in fall at Lighthouse Point and winter at Sandy Point).

GETTING AROUND

Birding methods: CAR, walk.

Most of the sites that are part of this tour can be reached by car; several require very short walks, and only one requires a significant amount of effort - Sandy Point must be walked (up to a mile) to be fully explored. Also, there are several beaches that can be walked, and are seen more completely by doing so.

DIRECTIONS (see Map 52): The sites on this tour are listed below in the order in which they occur as you go clockwise around the harbor, from west to east.

The tour starts just east of the center of Milford, at the western intersection of Routes 162 and 1.

To get to Merwin Point/Beach Avenue in Milford, go east on Route 162 for 4.1 miles, bear right (not sharp right) on Chapel Street for 0.4 mile, right on Kings Highway for 0.2 mile, left on Beach Avenue for 0.1 mile to Merwin Point. **Before entering Beach Avenue,** park as best you can on a side street and walk to the point. Then continue north on Beach Avenue, making right turns as necessary, as Beach Avenue follows the coast intermittently for 0.6 mile to a small town park between Wall Street and Bonsilene Street. Park here and walk to the beach.

To get to Oyster River Marsh in West Haven, from the town park on Beach Avenue, go left on Bonsilene Street for 0.1 mile, right on Route 162 for 0.2 mile, and left on Anderson Avenue for 0.1 mile to where the marsh is visible on both sides of the road.

To get to the mouth of the Oyster River in West Haven, from Anderson Avenue at the Oyster River Marsh, return to Route 162 (New Haven Avenue) and go east for 0.2 mile to the bridge over the Oyster River. Park just beyond (east of) the bridge.

To get to West Shore Beach/Saint John's By The Sea in West Haven: at the traffic light just east of the Oyster River, go right on Ocean Avenue for 1.1 miles and park in an area on the right, across the road from a church (Saint John's By The Sea).

To get to Prospect Beach/Bradley Point in West Haven from Saint John's By The Sea, continue north on Ocean Avenue along the shore for 1.0 mile to parking at Prospect Beach, and for another 0.3 mile to parking at Bradley Point.

To get to Sandy Point in West Haven, from Bradley Point, continue north on the road that follows the shore (under several different names), zig-zagging as necessary, for 1.8 miles to parking on the right at the base of Sandy Point.

To get to the West Haven Boat Ramp in West Haven, from the Sandy Point parking area, turn right onto Beach Avenue and almost immediately bear right onto First Avenue for 0.4 mile; at stop sign turn right into parking for the boat ramp.

To get to the West River in West Haven, from the Boat Ramp, continue north on First Avenue for 0.8 mile, right on Elm Street/Kimberly Avenue for 0.2 mile, left at the traffic light to the dead end at the river.

To get to Long Wharf in New Haven, from the site at the West River, go back to Kimberly Avenue, turn left and enter I-95 northbound; go a short distance and get off at exit 46; immediately turn onto Frontage Road and follow it for about 100 yards to a parking area on the right that overlooks the harbor and mud flats.

To get to East Shore Park/Fort Hale Park/Morris Cove in New Haven from Long Wharf, get back on I-95 northbound, take exit 50 and follow the exit ramp for 0.2 mile; go right on Woodward Avenue (which becomes Fort Hale Park Road) for 1.2 miles to one of the entrances to East Shore Park on the right. To reach Fort Hale Park, continue south on Woodward Avenue for an additional 0.3 to 0.9 mile. During this section of the road Fort Hale Park is on the right. To reach Morris Cove, continue on Woodward Avenue to its end, right on Townsend Avenue which runs along the shore of Morris Cove starting in 0.2 mile.

To get to Lighthouse Point Park in New Haven from Morris Cove, continue south on Townsend Avenue for 0.4 mile, right on Lighthouse Road for 0.6 mile to the park entrance.

Lighthouse Point is at the tip of the eastern shore of New Haven Harbor; this completes the tour of the harbor. Retrace your route back up to I-95 exit 50.

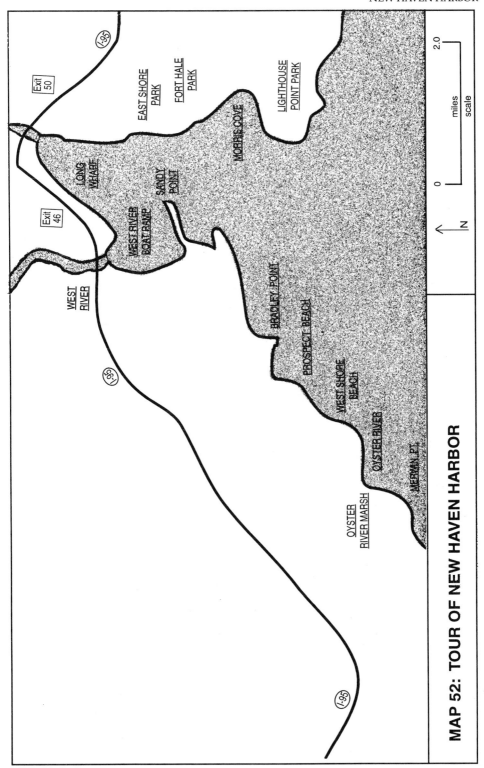

MAP 52: TOUR OF NEW HAVEN HARBOR

EAST SHORE PARK

FORT HALE PARK

MORRIS COVE

LIGHTHOUSE POINT PARK

LONG WHARF

SANDY POINT

WEST RIVER BOAT RAMP

Exit 50

Exit 46

I-95

WEST RIVER

I-95

BRADLEY POINT

PROSPECT BEACH

WEST SHORE BEACH

OYSTER RIVER

MERWIN PT.

OYSTER RIVER MARSH

N

0   2.0

miles
scale

ANSONIA: ANSONIA NATURE CENTER

HABITATS
OPEN TERRESTRIAL: short grass, tall grass, mixed herebaceous and shrubby fields; shrubby and wooded edges;
Forest: hardwoods, cedars;
Lake/pond: pond, marshy and shrubby shore;
Marsh/swamp/bog: mixed herbaceous and shrub marsh, hardwood swamp.

This site is former farmland that is in a state of rapid succession. It now consists largely of reverting fields and young second-growth hardwoods surrounding a recreation area of mowed playing fields.

SEASONS/BIRDS
SPRING MIGRATION: LAND BIRDS;
Nesting season: land birds;
FALL MIGRATION: LAND BIRDS;
Winter: land birds.

This is a good site for the spring and fall migrations of land birds. It can be excellent when there is a "fallout" of migrants because the vegetation is low and the birds are easy to see. Nesters include such open and edge habitat species as Carolina wren, blue-winged warbler, white-eyed vireo and brown thrasher. In addition, both cuckoos have been seen here. In the late fall, look for sparrows including white-crowned and white-throated. In winter, the presence of shrubs with berries causes some migrants to linger.

GETTING AROUND
Birding methods: walk.

There is a good network of trails; those near the nature center (at the entrance) are easy, but the others are rough.

DIRECTIONS: This site is very near the city of Ansonia. In Ansonia, at the intersection of Routes 243 and 115, go east on Route 243 for 1.7 miles, left on Benz Street for 1.0 mile (stay on Benz Street as it jogs right then left), right on Milan Street for 0.2 mile to the nature center.

BETHANY: LAKE CHAMBERLAIN

HABITATS
OPEN TERRESTRIAL: short grass, tall grass, mixed herbaceous and shrubby fields; edges;
Lake/pond: lake, deep water, exposed sand and gravel shoreline, shrubby, marshy and wooded shores;
Forest: hardwoods, hardwoods/white pine, hardwoods/hemlock, white pine/hemlock, mixed conifers (mostly tamarack and cedar);
River/stream: stream, mixed herbaceous and shrubby streambelt;
Marsh/swamp/bog: hardwood swamp.

There is a rich diversity of terrestrial habitats in the area near this lake. In addition to the varied conifer and deciduous woodlands, there is a spectrum of open field habitat types, ranging from mowed lawns to reverting shrubby fields. The lake (a reservoir) has a shore that is mostly wooded (hardwoods, white pine and hemlock in various combinations), but also has areas of shrubs and small marshes.

SEASONS/BIRDS

SPRING MIGRATION: water birds, marsh birds, shore birds, LAND BIRDS;
NESTING SEASON: LAND BIRDS;
FALL MIGRATION: water birds, marsh birds, shore birds, LAND BIRDS;
Winter: land birds.

This is an excellent site, in which a variety of land bird species occur. The spring and fall migrations of warblers and sparrows are especially good. In the fall, also look for a variety of water birds. Osprey occurs in the spring and fall, and the hawk migration can be pretty good. Nesters include such standard species as Carolina wren, bluebird, tree swallow (lots of them), rough-winged swallow, yellowthroat, yellow and prairie warblers and indigo bunting. Wild turkey may be seen at any time of year.

GETTING AROUND

Birding methods: car, WALK, ski.

This area can be entered only with a Regional Water Authority Recreation Permit; with the permit comes a detailed trail map of the area (see Chapter 12: "Sources of Additional Information"). There is a trail network that includes over five miles of trails that offer easy walking and in some cases skiing. Enter RWA land only through the designated gate; there are also service roads on which the public is not permitted. In addition, it is also worthwhile to bird by car or on foot along several of the nearby town roads.

DIRECTIONS (see Map 51): This site is about ten miles north of New Haven. From the Wilbur Cross Parkway exit 59, go north on Route 69 for 4.2 miles, left on Morris Road for 0.6 mile, and left on Sperry Road for 0.1 mile to the entrance on the right.

BRANFORD: BRANFORD SUPPLY PONDS

HABITATS

Forest: hardwoods, hardwoods / white pine, white pine, mountain laurel;
Lake/pond: ponds, shores of shrubs, hardwoods and white pine;
River/stream: seasonal streams;
Marsh/swamp/bog: shrubby hardwood swamp;
Other: rocky slope, rock outcrops.

When you are by the tranquil ponds and woods in this small town park, it is difficult to realise that I-95 and intense development are close by. The park contains two small ponds with points and coves, and shores that are dominated by white pine together with some hardwoods. The surrounding forest is also made up of white pine and hardwoods, with areas of mountain laurel understory.

SEASONS/BIRDS

SPRING MIGRATION: water birds, LAND BIRDS;
Nesting season: water birds, land birds;
Fall migration: water birds, land birds;
Winter: land birds.

The spring migration is the best season at this site. At that time, there is a good variety of land birds in the woods and pond shores, plus a few water birds, often including wood duck, ring-necked duck and hooded merganser. The standard mix of forest species nest here. Osprey can often be seen hunting the ponds.

GETTING AROUND
Birding methods: car, walk.
The park driveway goes between these two ponds, and provides views of parts of both of them. There are several trails near the ponds and through the woods. There are almost always at least a few people in the park, and it gets quite crowded on weekends and in warm weather.

DIRECTIONS: This park is at the northern edge of the center of Branford, several miles east of New Haven. From I-95 exit 54, go south on Cedar Street for 0.2 mile, left on Main Street (Route 1) for 0.7 mile, and left on Chestnut Street for 0.4 mile to the park entrance.

BRANFORD: JARVIS MARSH

HABITATS
COASTAL: low salt marsh, tidal creek, coastal forest.
This is a sheltered, low salt marsh that is surrounded by coastal forest.

SEASONS/BIRDS
Spring migration: water birds, marsh birds, shore birds, land birds;
Nesting season: marsh birds, land birds;
Fall migration: water birds, marsh birds, shore birds, land birds;
Winter: water birds, land birds.
Spring, summer and early fall are the most interesting seasons at this marsh. During this period, you can watch activity by osprey at a clearly visible nest platform, and look for waders that come to the marsh to feed.

GETTING AROUND
Birding methods: car.
Most of the marsh can be seen from two overlook points on the state road.

DIRECTIONS: This site is in the southeastern corner of Branford, and extends from the coast half a mile inland. Starting at the Branford/Guilford town line, follow Route 146 west for 0.5 mile to a pulloff on the right, or 0.7 mile to a pulloff on the left.

BRANFORD/EAST HAVEN: LAKE SALTONSTALL

HABITATS
LAKE/POND: lake, deep water, wooded shore; seasonal pools;
Marsh/swamp/bog: shrub, shrubby hardwood and hardwood swamps;
Forest: hardwoods, hardwoods/white pine, white pine, mixed conifers;
Open terrestrial: shrubby field;
River/stream: perennial streams, seasonal streams.
This is a long, narrow reservoir that is surrounded by varied forest habitats. It is deep, and there often is open water well into winter. In addition, the road to the entrance (Hosley Avenue) runs along a series of forested wetlands and a conifer plantation. There is also a field in a late stage of succession from shrubs to young hardwoods.

SEASONS/BIRDS
SPRING MIGRATION: WATER BIRDS, LAND BIRDS;
Nesting season: land birds;
FALL MIGRATION: WATER BIRDS, LAND BIRDS;
Winter: water birds, land birds.

This is a good site at which to look for migrating water birds; spring is very good, and fall even better. Winter may also be good when there is open water, as there often is. Among the many species that you may expect to see are canvasback, both scaups, American and occasionally Eurasian wigeons, and sometimes tundra swan. Osprey is present in the spring and fall, and bald eagle in winter. Land birds in the woods along the shore by Hosley Avenue add to the interest at all seasons, and in the warm months include a standard variety of woodland nesters. This could be a good place to look for winter finches in incursion years.

GETTING AROUND
Birding methods: car, WALK, ski.

This area can be entered only with a Regional Water Authority Recreation Permit; with the permit comes a detailed trail map which is really necessary (see Chapter 12: "Sources of Additional Information"). There are many service roads into the area, but only two are open to the public (with a permit). Within the area, there are thirteen miles of trails; some offer easy walking, others more challenging hiking, and some can be skied. Some of these trails lead to or follow the lake shore, others go through the forest. Hosley Road is public, and can be birded without a permit.

DIRECTIONS: This lake lies on the Branford / East Haven town line, and is two to five miles north of Long Island Sound. **From I-95 eastbound**, take exit 51 onto Route 1 (eastbound) for 1.7 miles, and left on Holsey Avenue. **From I-95 westbound**, take exit 52 onto Route 100 south for 1.0 mile (at 0.4 mile, Route 100 turns sharp left), right on Route 1 (eastbound) for 0.3 mile, and left on Hosley Avenue. Follow Hosley Avenue for 1.9 miles to an entrance on the left into RWA land around Lake Saltonstall. In another 1.0 mile on Hosley Avenue, there is a second entrance on the left into RWA land. In addition, there is good birding along Hosley Avenue starting at 0.9 mile from Route 1 and continuing for the next two miles to the second entrance. (Stay on the road - the surrounding land is not open to the public.)

CHESHIRE: BROAD BROOK RESERVOIR

HABITATS
LAKE/POND: lake, shallow water, deep water, wooded and shrub marsh shore;
Open terrestrial: shrubby field, shrubby and wooded edges;
Forest: hardwoods, hardwoods / white pine, white pine.

This is a long, narrow reservoir, with an irregular shoreline that is largely wooded and has some areas of shrubs and shrub marsh. The water tends to stay ice-free into early winter.

SEASONS/BIRDS
SPRING MIGRATION: WATER BIRDS, land birds;
Nesting season: water birds, land birds;
FALL MIGRATION: WATER BIRDS, marsh birds, land birds;
Winter: water birds, land birds.

A good variety of water birds can be seen at this site during the fall and spring migrations. From late October into December, and again during March, species to expect include ring-necked duck, common goldeneye, canvasback, coot, common and hooded mergansers. A variety of dabbling duck species occur somewhat earlier in the fall and later in the spring. Nesting species include mallard and wood duck, and in the surrounding forest, pine warbler as well as redstart and a variety of other standard species.

GETTING AROUND
Birding methods: car, walk.

Two areas of the reservoir can be seen from roads (see "Directions" below). However, these go through water department land which is off-limits to the public, so stay on the roads. Also, note that the traffic is heavy during weekday rush hours.

DIRECTIONS: This reservoir is about five miles southwest of Meriden. To go across the middle of the reservoir, from the eastern intersection of Routes 68 and 70, go north on Route 70 for 0.8 mile, and right on Reservoir Road for 0.7 mile, to the point at which the road passes across the reservoir. (This is the better of the two viewpoints - the habitats are richer and the traffic is lighter.) To reach the south end of the reservoir, in Cheshire at the eastern intersection of Routes 68 and 70, go east on Route 68 for 1.3 miles to the point at which the south end of the reservoir can be seen. Exercise caution in parking along these roads.

CHESHIRE: CANAL PARK

HABITATS
RIVER/STREAM: perennial stream, shrubby and wooded streambelt, seasonal stream;
Marsh/swamp/bog: shrub swamp, shrubby hardwood swamp, hardwood swamp;
Open terrestrial: shrubby field, shrubby edge.

This park, also known as "Lock 12 Historical Park" is a rather narrow strip that encompasses a section of an old canal. The habitats include a stream (Willow Brook) that runs in the canal bed, together with strips of wetland along the stream, and a streambelt of young second-growth hardwoods, together with berry-producing shrubs, vines and thickets.

SEASONS/BIRDS
SPRING MIGRATION: water birds, LAND BIRDS;
Nesting season: water birds, land birds;
FALL MIGRATION: water birds, LAND BIRDS;
Winter: land birds.

This is a good place to observe the spring and fall migrations of land birds. Nesters include warbling vireo and other species that you would expect in this kind of streambelt habitat, plus some southerners such as red-bellied woodpecker and Carolina wren. Green-backed heron and woodcock also nest at this site. A visit in winter can be worthwhile, because the berries on the vines by the stream, plus the feeders at nearby houses cause migrants to linger, and wintering species to come in to feed. Several common species of water birds are here most of the year. Screech, barred and great horned owls are year-round residents.

GETTING AROUND
Birding methods: WALK, BIKE, SKI, WHEELCHAIR.

A level paved path goes parallel to the canal for almost three miles (from the parking area at the entrance, 1.8 miles to the north and 1.1 miles to the south), and it makes for easy going through the habitat areas. The entire path can be used by wheelchair. During the warm months, the park tends to get crowded on weekends and weekday evenings.

DIRECTIONS: This park is in Cheshire, midway between New Haven and Waterbury. To get there from the intersection of routes 42 and 10, go west on Route 42 for 1.1 miles to the park entrance on the left.

CHESHIRE: QUINNIPIAC AUDUBON SOCIETY SANCTUARY

HABITATS
    FOREST: hardwoods, flood plain;
    OPEN TERRESTRIAL: herbaceous and shrubby fields, vine tangles, thickets;
    River/stream: river, deep, slow water, wooded and shrubby streambelt, streams;
    Marsh/swamp/bog: small pockets of shrubby hardwood swamp.
This site lies along the Quinnipiac River. The main attraction for birders is the variety of streambelt and other terrestrial habitats - both open and wooded. Much of the area is in a state of succession, from fields to young second-growth forest. The overgrown fields contain areas of sumac and groves of cedars, as well as a rich variety of berry- and seed-bearing shrubs; the woodland includes stands of beeches.

SEASONS/BIRDS
    SPRING MIGRATION: LAND BIRDS;
    Nesting season: land birds;
    FALL MIGRATION: LAND BIRDS;
    Winter: land birds.
This is an excellent birding area, and well worth the difficulties involved (see "Getting Around" below). The spring migration of land birds is especially good, and May is the best month. Nesters include a nice mix of the species you would expect to find in these habitats such as cedar waxwing, gnatcatcher and tanager, and southerners such as Carolina wren and red-bellied woodpecker. The fall migration is also good, especially September and October when berry- and seed-eaters come in to feast on the vines and shrubs. In winter, this vegetation, together with the mild river valley climate, attract lingering berry-eating migrants, plus the usual year-round residents.

GETTING AROUND
    Birding methods: walk.
There is a figure-eight loop trail that provides somewhat rough walking. Poison ivy is a problem, plus the usual ticks and seasonal mosquitoes.

DIRECTIONS: This site lies midway between Waterbury and Meriden. To get there from the intersection of Routes 10 and 691, go south on Route 10 for 0.2 mile, left on East Johnson Avenue for 1.2 miles over the Quinnipiac River to South End Road. Go left on South End Road for 0.1 mile to a small parking area on the left. The sanctuary is not well marked, and lies between this parking area and the Quinnipiac River, which is a short distance to the west. The sanctuary can be entered by walking from the back of the parking area a short distance west through the woods until you meet a marked trail that goes down to the river. Or, you can walk from the north side of the parking area for a short distance through the woods until you meet a trail that runs behind the house just north of the parking area.

DERBY: OSBORNDALE STATE PARK/KELLOGG ENVIRONMENTAL CENTER

HABITATS
OPEN TERRESTRIAL: short grass, tall grass and shrubby fields; shrubby and wooded edges;
FOREST: hardwoods, vine tangles and thickets;
Lake/pond: ponds with grassy and marshy shores;
River/stream: perennial and seasonal streams, wooded streambelts.
This site includes a visitor center (The Kellogg Environmental Center) and a contiguous 350-acre state park (Osbornedale). The land of the park is former farmland that now includes lots of successional growth - open fields becoming shrubby fields, and shrubby fields succeeding to young second-growth hardwoods. The hardwood forest is characterized by a dense understory, filled with vine tangles and thickets.

SEASONS/BIRDS
SPRING MIGRATION: LAND BIRDS;
NESTING SEASON: LAND BIRDS;
FALL MIGRATION: LAND BIRDS;
Winter: land birds;
This is an excellent site to visit during the spring migration for the chance to see a wide variety of land birds, particularly warblers as well as open-habitat and edge species. The fall migration is also excellent, and offers a good chance of seeing a variety of raptors and sparrows. Nesting species include worm-eating warbler, white-eyed vireo and orchard oriole. In early winter, there are usually some lingering migrants among the berry-producing shrubs. A number of resident species can be seen throughout the year, including great horned owl.

GETTING AROUND
Birding methods: car, WALK.
There are a number of paved and gravel roads and paths that provide easy walking, as well as trails that are more demanding; the terrain is hilly, and some trails are in poor condition. Limited areas can be seen from your car. Trail maps are available at the Environmental Center, and their use is recommended.

DIRECTIONS: This site is about two miles northwest of the center of Derby. **To get to the Kellogg Environmental Center,** from Derby at the intersection of Routes 34 and 8, go northwest on Route 34 for 1.5 miles, right on Cedric Avenue for 0.2 mile to Hawthorne Avenue, and left on Hawthorne Avenue for 0.3 mile to the entrance on the left. Get a map of Osbornedale State Park here. (It is possible to walk into Osbornedale State Park on trails that start at the center.) **To get to the main entrance of Osbornedale State Park** from the Kellogg Environmental Center, return to Hawthorne Avenue, and go east for 0.5 mile, and left on Chatfield Street for 0.4 mile to the park entrance on the left.

GUILFORD: GREAT HARBOR/LOST POND/LEETES ISLAND/ISLAND BAY

HABITATS
COASTAL: low brackish marsh, low and high salt marsh, brackish tidal pond, tidal creeks, mud flats, tidal pools, rocky coast, cove, gravel and cobble beach, rocky island, coastal forest;
Forest: hardwoods, hardwoods/hemlock.

This is a very productive cluster of sites that contain just about every type of coastal habitat. Great Harbor is a brackish low tidal marsh that is surrounded by coastal forest, and cut through by several tidal creeks. There is an area of open water at the upper end. Just upstream of Great Harbor, and connected to it by a short tidal creek, is Lost Pond - a brackish tidal pond that is composed largely of open water, and surrounded by upland hardwood forest. Half a mile to the west is Leetes Island Marsh - a high salt marsh that drains into Island Bay, a cove of Long Island Sound with a rocky coastline, a beach and an island.

SEASONS/BIRDS
SPRING MIGRATION: gulls, TERNS, WATER BIRDS, MARSH BIRDS, SHORE BIRDS, LAND BIRDS;
NESTING SEASON: gulls, TERNS, MARSH BIRDS, LAND BIRDS;
FALL MIGRATION: gulls, TERNS, WATER BIRDS, MARSH BIRDS, SHORE BIRDS, LAND BIRDS;
Winter: water birds, land birds.

Taken together, these areas provide an excellent opportunity to see a great diversity of bird species, especially during the period from mid-April through late November. During migration, there are lots of dabbling ducks and shore birds to be seen. Also during migration, white-eyed vireo, many warblers and a variety of other land birds are attracted to the dense understory of the coastal forest along the edges of the marshes. All of the waders that occur in Connecticut can be seen in the marshes, especially during July and August. Clapper rail nests in the Great Island marshes; osprey also nests here, and can be seen in spring, summer and fall. A host of shore birds feed on the mud flats during both migrations. In winter, there are usually present a variety of dabbling ducks, and several raptor species. Harrier hunts the marsh in the fall, winter and spring, and lingering land bird migrants can be seen feeding on the berries of the shrubs at the edge of the coastal forest.

GETTING AROUND
Birding methods: car, walk, boat.

Most of these habitats can be seen well from the roads described below. In addition, a trail follows part of the shore of Great Harbor. It is also possible to explore Lost Pond by boat.

DIRECTIONS (see Map 53): These areas lie two miles southwest of Guilford center. The following directions take you to each of the four sites in sequence. Start from I-95, exit 58; go south on Route 77 for 1.0 mile to the south end of the Guilford town green.

To reach the south end of Great Harbor, from the south end of the Guilford town green go right on Route 146 for 1.3 miles to the point at which Route 146 passes under a railroad line; bear left on Sachems Head Road for 0.6 mile, right at a fork at Colonial Road for 0.1 mile to a wide shoulder on the right, just before the road forks again. A trail leads to the edge of the marsh and follows the shore.

To get to the north end of Great Harbor, go back up to the intersection of Sachem Head Road and Route 146, go left on Route 146 for 0.5 mile to where Route 146 passes the north end of the Great Harbor (on your left), from which point almost the entire marsh can be seen. Park on a wide shoulder on the right immediately after crossing over the water.

To reach Lost Pond, from the point at the north end of Great Harbor described above, go another 0.1 mile on Route 146 to a point at which there is a shoulder on the right at which to park, and a short trail on the right to the shore of Lost pond.

To reach the north end of Leetes Island Marsh, continue west on Route 146 for 0.4 mile to a point at which the marsh is visible on the left, and there is a wide shoulder on the right on which to park.

To get to Island Bay and the south end of Leetes Island Marsh, continue west on Route 146 for another 0.3 mile, left on Shell Beach Road for 0.1 mile, and right for a few yards on a road that leads to a parking area on the shore of Island Bay.

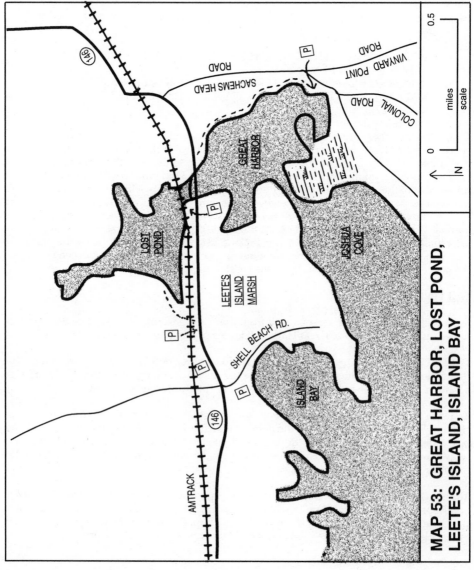

MAP 53: GREAT HARBOR, LOST POND, LEETE'S ISLAND, ISLAND BAY

GUILFORD: WESTWOODS PRESERVE

HABITATS
FOREST: hardwoods, hardwoods/hemlock;
Open terrestrial: shrubby field;
River/stream: perennial and seasonal streams, wooded streambelts;
Marsh/swamp/bog: shrub marsh, shrub and shrubby hardwood swamp;
Lake/pond: ponds, wooded shores;
Other: ledge, rocky outcrop.
This preserve has 1,000 acres of varied habitat, including a variety of upland and bottomland forest types, ridges, hilltops, wetlands and several ponds. Most of these habitats can be reached by an extensive trail system (that also enables you to reach Great Harbor and Lost Pond, both described separately under Guilford).

SEASONS/BIRDS
SPRING MIGRATION: LAND BIRDS;
NESTING SEASON: LAND BIRDS;
FALL MIGRATION: LAND BIRDS;
Winter: land birds.
The spring and fall migrations bring a good mix of woodland species, particularly vireos and warblers. Nesting species include pileated woodpecker, Carolina wren, worm-eating warbler, orchard oriole and scarlet tanager. Great horned, barred and screech owls are year-round residents of the preserve.

GETTING AROUND
Birding methods: WALK.
There are six entrances to the preserve trail system, and over 40 miles of trails within it. The best way to find the trailheads and to use the trail system is to get a preserve map. These maps are available in Guilford at the tax collector's office, the town hall, the police station, and also at Bishop's Apple Orchard store. The large size of this preserve and the extensive trail system keeps it from getting crowded, even on summer weekends, so that it is a good place to bird during the nesting season.

DIRECTIONS: The Westwoods Preserve lies two miles west of the center of Guilford. One of the preserve entrances can be reached from I-95 exit 57 by going east on Route 1 for 0.5 mile, right on Peddlers Road for 1.1 miles to a small parking area on the left. Bishop's Apple Orchard store can also be reached from I-95 exit 57, and going east on Route 1 for 0.6 mile (0.1 mile past Peddlers Road) to the store on the left.

GUILFORD/MADISON: EAST RIVER MARSH

HABITATS
COASTAL: high salt marsh, tidal river, tidal creek, intertidal mud, salt pannes, marsh pools, Long Island Sound, mud and gravel bars, intertidal rocks, rocky coast, shrubby and wooded edges, coastal forest, groves of cedars.
This is one of the largest and finest salt marshes in Connecticut. It lies on both sides of the East River and extends upstream from Long Island Sound for several miles. Within the marsh are many varied habitats, and on its edges and extending into it are wooded islands, areas of shrubs and meadows.

SEASONS/BIRDS
SPRING MIGRATION: gulls, terns, WATER BIRDS, MARSH BIRDS, SHORE BIRDS, LAND BIRDS;
NESTING SEASON: gulls, TERNS, water birds, MARSH BIRDS, SHORE BIRDS, LAND BIRDS;
FALL MIGRATION: gulls, TERNS, WATER BIRDS, MARSH BIRDS, SHORE BIRDS, LAND BIRDS;
Winter: water birds, land birds.

An impressive variety of species may be seen at this site at any season. During the spring migration, water birds include brant and a variety of dabbling ducks; various waders are present, including glossy ibis; there is a good variety of shore birds; and land birds often include osprey, merlin and peregrine falcon. During the warm months, many species of waders are present, and there is an exceptional variety of terns that feed at the mouth of the East River - common, least, Forster's, roseate and black all have all been seen here (Faulkner's Island with its tern colony is not far offshore). During the nesting season, you may see oystercatcher, willet, various waders, osprey and purple martin. The fall shore bird migration is even better than the spring migration, and frequently includes both yellowlegs, western, least, pectoral and white-rumped sandpipers. In winter, it is not unusual to see harrier and short-eared owl.

GETTING AROUND
Can be birded by: car.
There are four points around the edge of this marsh that are public and can be reached by car. Part of the marsh can be seen from each of them.

DIRECTIONS (see Map 54): The East River Marsh lies on the coast one mile southeast of the center of Guilford. A starting point for reaching all four of the points from which the marsh can be seen is I-95 exit 61. The following route goes around the edge of the marsh to these four points.

To get to the **southeastern edge of the marsh at the Neck River,** go south on Route 79 for 0.6 mile, right on Route 1 for 1.6 miles, left on Neck Road for 1.3 miles, and right down a short access road to a parking area at the edge of the marsh.

To get to the **southern edge of the marsh at the confluence of the Neck River and East River,** go back up the access road, turn right and follow this road around to the right for 0.8 miles to a boat launch and parking area at the edge of the marsh at the confluence of the Neck and East Rivers.

To get to the **northwestern edge of the marsh known as Guilford Sluice,** return to Route 1 and go west on Route 1 to its intersection with Route 146; go left on Route 146 for 0.8 mile, left on South Union Street for 0.6 mile, left on Sawpit Road for 0.1 mile to a dead end that overlooks the marsh. Caution: fast-moving trains use the tracks just ahead.

To get to the **western edge of the marsh at the mouth of the East River,** return to Route 146 and go west to the intersection with Route 77. At this intersection, go south (left) on Whitfield Avenue for 0.3 mile, bear right on New Whitfield Avenue for 0.9 mile to the mouth of the East River.

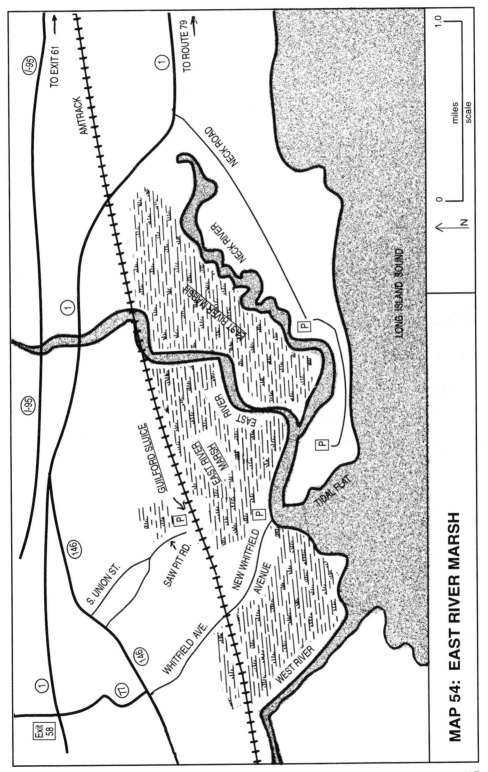

MAP 54: EAST RIVER MARSH

HAMDEN: SLEEPING GIANT STATE PARK

HABITATS
> **FOREST:** hardwoods, hardwoods/hemlock, mountain laurel;
> **River/stream:** stream, wooded streambelt;
> **Marsh/swamp/bog:** shrub and hardwood swamp;
> **Lake/pond:** ponds;
> **Other:** cliff and ledge.

This park consists of about 1,500 acres, including upland habitats of ledges, talus slopes, mixed hardwood forest and thickets of mountain laurel, as well as bottomlands that contain streambelt habitats, and patches of hardwood swamp and shrub swamp.

SEASONS/BIRDS
> **SPRING MIGRATION:** LAND BIRDS;
> **NESTING SEASON:** LAND BIRDS;
> **FALL MIGRATION:** LAND BIRDS;
> **Winter:** land birds.

Spring and fall are very good times at this site for seeing the basic assortment of land bird migrants, including several raptor species and a variety of warblers. The nesting season is also worthwhile, because the habitat in this park is large enough to attract forest-interior species such as wood thrush, red-eyed vireo, ovenbird and scarlet tanager, in addition to worm-eating and hooded warblers, and a standard mix of other woodland nesters.

GETTING AROUND
> **Birding methods:** WALK, ski.

There several access points to the park, and 27 miles of trails that form an intricate network and lead to every part of it. Some of these trails are quite rough, but there are also easy ones. A trail map is available at the park entrance, and is useful. The park has many visitors during the warm months, but is large enough so that parts of it are not crowded.

DIRECTIONS: This park is about ten miles north of New Haven. To get there from I-91, take exit 10 onto Route 40; follow it for 2.6 miles, turn right (north) on Route 10 for 1.4 miles, and right on Mt. Carmel Avenue for 0.3 mile to the park entrance on the left. To reach another access, continue north on Route 10 for another 0.6 mile past Mt. Carmel Avenue, and turn right on Tuttle Avenue. The park is on the right (east) side along the section of Tuttle Avenue from 0.2 to 0.8 miles from Route 10.

HAMDEN/CHESHIRE: BROOKSVALE PARK

HABITATS
> **FOREST:** hardwoods, hardwoods/white pine, hardwoods/hemlock, white pine, hemlock, cedars;
> **Open terrestrial:** short grass, tall grass and shrubby fields, shrubby edges;
> **River/stream:** stream, wooded streambelt;
> **Marsh/swamp/bog:** hardwood swamp.

This 400-acre town park is a pleasant area that includes woodlands and a couple of fields. There are many small areas of habitat types that intermingle.

SEASONS/BIRDS

Spring migration: land birds;
Nesting season: land birds;
Fall migration: land birds;
Winter: land birds.

As a birding site, this park is nice, but not exceptional. During both migrations and the nesting season, you can find a standard mix of land bird species. In winter, look in the cedars for screech owl and possibly other owl species.

GETTING AROUND

Birding methods: walk.

Woods roads and trails lead to the habitats, and a trail map is posted near the main parking area. The park is crowded during the summer.

DIRECTIONS: This park is about ten miles north of New Haven, on the Hamden/Cheshire town line. To get there from I-91, take exit 10 onto Route 40, follow it for 2.6 miles, turn right (north) on Route 10 for 3.0 miles, left on Brooksvale Avenue for 1.0 mile to the park entrance on the left.

HAMDEN/WOODBRIDGE: WEST ROCK RIDGE/LAKE WINTERGREEN

HABITATS

FOREST: hardwoods, hardwoods/white pine, hardwoods/hemlock, mixed conifers, mountain laurel;
OPEN TERRESTRIAL: mixed herbaceous field, shrubby field including cedar, edge;
LAKE/POND: lake; barren, shrubby, mixed herbaceous, hardwood shore;
River/stream: perennial and seasonal streams, shrubby and wooded streambelts;
Other: cliff/ledge, rocky slope, hawk watching site.

West Rock is a seven-mile long trap rock ridge that rises to a height of over 500 feet above the surrounding land, abruptly on its west side, less so on the east side. It is believed to have been formed by the same geologic event that formed East Rock and other smaller trap rock ridges in the New Haven area. These formations lie at the south end of a system of north/south-oriented basaltic ridges that extends northward through Connecticut's central lowlands. West Rock Ridge State Park occupies about 1,500 acres along the top, slopes and base of the ridge, including Lake Wintergreen at the foot of the east side of the ridge. There is a wide diversity of wooded and open habitats associated with this ridge. Habitats include ledge, talus slope, forest communities of hardwoods, white pine, hemlock and mixed conifers alone and in various combinations, with mountain laurel and other shrubs in the understory, plus shrubby fields that are succeeding to hardwoods and mixed conifers.

SEASONS/BIRDS

SPRING MIGRATION: water birds, marsh birds, shore birds, LAND BIRDS;
NESTING SEASON: LAND BIRDS;
FALL MIGRATION: water birds, marsh birds, shore birds, LAND BIRDS;
Winter: land birds.

West Rock Ridge is an extraordinary area in terms of the number of unusual plant and animal species that occur there. More than 220 species and subspecies of birds have been reported at this site. The ridge itself is an exciting area throughout the spring, summer and fall. During the migrations, there is a nice mix of land birds, and in the fall, the ridge is a spectacular site from which to watch the hawk migration. Nesters include all of the standard species for this mix of forest and open habitats, plus white-eyed vireo, chat, hooded and worm-eating warblers, whip-poor-will, woodcock, red-tailed hawk, great horned and screech owls.

Lake Wintergreen is not notable for water birds (some common species occur here during the spring and fall migrations), but more than makes up for it in land birds. The habitats around the shore are extremely good for land birds during the spring migration; as many as 28 warbler species (including yellow-throated) as well as vireos and other migrants have been seen here on a single visit. Migrating greater yellowlegs, spotted and solitary sandpipers feed along the barren shore of the lake. Green-backed heron nests by the lake. Other sightings have included white-winged crossbill and rough-legged hawk in winter.

GETTING AROUND
Birding methods: car, walk, ski.

A paved road goes up the east side of the ridge and along the top. It is closed to vehicles in winter, but can be walked at all times of year. There are also trails throughout the park on the east slope of the ridge and along the ridge top. A trail map can be obtained at the entrance station of Sleeping Giant State Park, described in this chapter under Hamden. Lock your car.

DIRECTIONS (see Map 55): This is a long, narrow state park that lies immediately north of New Haven, and straddles the line that divides Woodbridge and the southern part of Hamden.

To get to a road to the top of the ridge and trails up the southern part of it, from New Haven at the northern intersection of Whalley Avenue and Route 10 (Fitch Street), go north on Route 10 for 0.7 mile to the Southern Connecticut College campus and pedestrian overpass, left on Wintergreen Avenue (aka Wilmot Avenue) for 0.6 mile. At this point, to stay on Wintergreen Avenue, jog left across a short connector road, then right for 0.3 mile to a stop sign. Turn left on Brookside Avenue and go for 0.2 mile to a hardtop road on the left that can be driven to the top of the ridge, except in winter, when it is barred but can be walked.

To get to Lake Wintergreen and trails up the northern part of the ridge, continue on Brookside Avenue for another 1.2 miles, left on Main Street for 0.2 mile to the park entrance on the left.

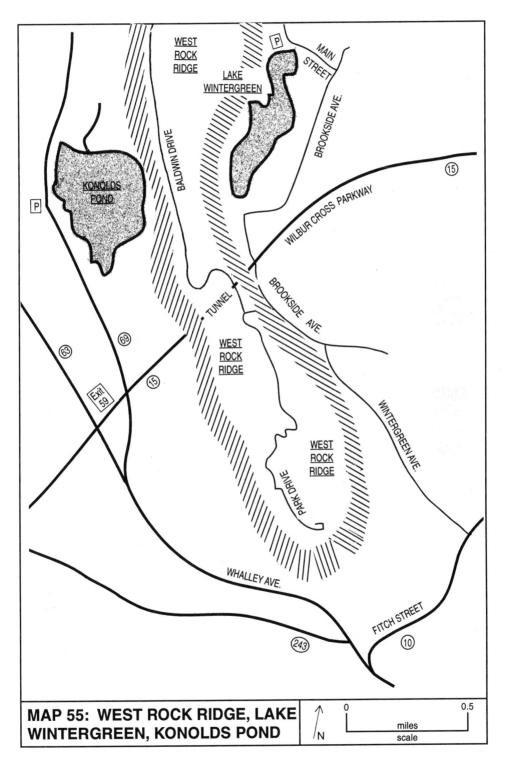

MAP 55: WEST ROCK RIDGE, LAKE WINTERGREEN, KONOLDS POND

N

0   miles   0.5
scale

MADISON: HAMMONASSET BEACH STATE PARK

HABITATS

> **COASTAL:** high and low salt marsh, tidal cove, tidal creek, mud flat, sandy beach, dunes, rocky coast, breakwater, Long Island Sound, brackish pools;
> **OPEN TERRESTRIAL:** short grass and shrubby fields;
> **Forest:** coastal forest, cedar, pitch pine, hardwoods;
> **Lake/pond:** fresh water pond, seasonal pools, grassy and mixed herbaceous shore;
> **River/stream:** river.

This 1,000-acre park occupies a peninsula that extends into Long Island Sound and forms the west side of Clinton Harbor. It benefits both from its geographical position as a coastal peninsula, and from the rich diversity of habitats that it contains. Hammonasset Park contains almost every type of coastal habitat found in Connecticut, and one could profitably spend days exploring the park. Anywhere you go is worthwhile, and any time of year can be very good, but the best times are fall, winter and spring. As a way to start getting to know the park, the route outlined below under "Directions" is suggested as a simplified overview of the highlights.

SEASONS/BIRDS

> **SPRING MIGRATION:** GULLS, TERNS, WATER BIRDS, MARSH BIRDS, SHORE BIRDS, LAND BIRDS;
> **Nesting season:** GULLS, TERNS, water birds, MARSH BIRDS, shore birds, LAND BIRDS;
> **FALL MIGRATION:** GULLS, TERNS, WATER BIRDS, MARSH BIRDS, SHORE BIRDS, LAND BIRDS;
> **WINTER:** GULLS, WATER BIRDS, marsh birds, shore birds, LAND BIRDS;

This is a four-star, all-season birding site. Many would argue that Hammonassett, together with Milford Point, are Connecticut's best all-around coastal birding areas. In addition to a broad spectrum of the species that you would expect to see at a good coastal site, Hammonasset regularly offers species that are not usually found elsewhere in Connecticut; over the years Hammonasset has produced an impressive list of rarities and "firsts" for the state. Among the highlights (some seen often, others rarely):

> gannet
> American bittern
> little egret (a Eurasian cousin of snowy egret)
> white-faced ibis (present in the park as this is being written)
> tundra swan
> possible nesting by harrier
> three of the four falcons that occur in Connecticut
> all eight of Connecticut's owls
> lesser golden plover
> upland, Baird's and buff-breated sandpipers
> whimbrel, Hudsonian and marbled godwits
> black skimmer, royal and Forster's terns
> lark and clay-colored sparrows

Notable confirmed nesters include: least and common terns, oystercatcher, clapper rail, piping plover, willet, osprey, sharp-tailed and Savannah sparrows.

Like Milford Point, the peninsula on which Hammonasset lies acts as a land trap during the fall migration (it can be really good for the hawk migration in October), and as a landfall for spring migrants.

Hammonasset is best during the migrations (especially fall) and winter, but is certainly worth a visit even in summer, in spite of the hordes of non-birders who are present.

GETTING AROUND
Birding methods: CAR, WALK, BIKE.
Hammonasset offers excellent birding from your car, on foot or by bike. Park roads and trails lead to virtually all of the habitat areas. In the summer, the park is crowded and there is an admission charge, but anyway, the birding is best during the rest of the year. Some areas are posted as restricted during the nesting season.

DIRECTIONS (see Map 56): This park lies on the Connecticut shore between Madison and Clinton. To get there from I-95, take exit 62, turn south at the end of the ramp and go 1.5 miles to the park entrance. The route that is described below starts just inside the park at the rotary and takes you around the park for a distance of four miles. Set your trip odometer to zero at the rotary; the mileages in the directions indicate the total distance of the route from your starting point at the rotary.

Swan Pond area. At the rotary, go west (right). Swan Pond on the right at 0.1 mile is good early in the fall migration for shore birds, and later for water birds including pied-billed grebe, ruddy duck, wigeon, gadwall and others. There is a trail that goes in back of the pond past shrubs (look for sparrows in October and November), and into an area of cedars (look for various owls at almost any time of year).

Fields past Swan Pond. Continue past Swan Pond to the end of the driveway (0.5 mile). The fields on the right are good for shore birds - in August and early September, look for upland and buff-breasted sandpipers, and from September through November look for lesser golden and black-bellied plovers. Also in these fields, look for meadowlark and pipit in spring and fall, longspur and snow bunting in the fall, winter and spring, and horned lark all year.

Bath house and picnic shelter area. At the end of the driveway that you have followed past Swan Pond, take two left turns to reverse your direction so that you are headed back toward the rotary. On your right is a marsh (0.6 mile) - look here for seaside and sharp-tailed sparrows in August and September. Also on your right is a shrubby ditch - a variety of migrating sparrows occur here in October and November. Continue past the paved West Beach parking lot to the dirt/grass parking area (1.0 mile). The pitch pines in back of this area sometimes have winter finches (both crossbill species have been seen here). When there are rain pools near this area during the spring, summer and fall, look around them for gulls and shore birds (possibly including buff-breasted, Baird's and upland sandpipers).

Rotary area. Continue on the driveway back to the rotary, go straight through it on the main park driveway (follow sign to East Beach and Meigs Point) past the pavillion to an area of berry-producing shrubs and cedars (1.2 to 1.4 miles) that is good for a variety of migrating land bird in the fall (especially sparrows in October and November), and lingering berry-eating land birds into winter.

Meigs Point marsh. Continue on the main park driveway past the East Beach parking area and pavillion to two pulloffs on the right (at 1.8 and 2.0 miles) opposite a high salt marsh on the left. Clapper rail, sharp-tailed and seaside sparrows all breed here, and may be seen if you are patient (and lucky). Shore birds can sometimes be seen during migration, and waders during spring, summer and fall, especially at high tide. During the period October through March, harrier, short-eared owl and snowy owl are sometimes present, hunting the marsh.

Meigs Point. Continue on the park driveway past the Meigs Point Nature Center and take the next right into the Meigs Point parking area (2.4 miles). Look in the surrounding areas of high salt marsh and grass for sharp-tailed and seaside sparrows and clapper rail, all of which breed here. Walk back along the driveway past an area of bayberry bushes, looking for land birds. In October and March there is a chance of seeing chat, palm, pine and orange-crowned warblers in these shrubs. The areas of marsh near this driveway can be good for migrating shore birds in spring and fall, and for waders and shore birds including American bittern and whimbrel in spring, summer and fall.

From the Meigs Point parking area, you can walk a few feet south to an observation platform that overlooks Long Island Sound, a breakwater, the beach and dunes. The platform provides a good place from which to look for water birds (often including one or more of the scoters and sometimes king eider), during the period October through March; purple sandpiper at the breakwater in winter; oystercatcher and osprey in spring, summer and fall. Also from here, you can get on a trail that goes along the coast to the east (left as you face Long Island Sound), and gives you views of the Sound, the beach, dunes and a large salt marsh that lies behind the dunes.

Meigs Point Nature Center. Now go back to the park driveway, and enter the large paved parking lot across the road by the Meigs Point Nature Center building (2.6 miles). Go to the back of this lot, and drive (or walk if the driveway is barred) down the road that leads past open fields, shrubs and a salt marsh. Look in the open fields for sparrows during October and November, for short grass species (longspur, snow bunting et al) from October through April.

Cedar Island Trail. When you reach the parking area beyond the fields (2.8 miles), you will see some woods north of the parking area (immediately behind the picnic shelter). This is a wooded peninsula that extends into the marsh toward Cedar Island with a trail that goes down its entire length. The peninsula acts as a land trap for migrants, and also provides good views of the marsh. Birding from the trail is especially good for shore birds during the periods April/May and August/September; for osprey, sharp-tailed and seaside sparrows and clapper rail during spring, summer and fall; for crabs and other marsh life anytime during warm weather.

Willard Island. This is the wooded area northwest of the parking area (to your left as you face the picnic shelter from the parking area). A trail that leads to a network of trails within Willard Island can be reached from the northwestern part of the parking area. Willard Island includes hardwoods and cedar, with lots of shrubs, vine tangles and thickets. Bird these trails for chat and other land bird migrants during the spring and especially September, October and November, and for several owl species during the period October through March. The far end of the wooded area of Willard Island has an observation platform that overlooks another part of the tidal marsh and a part of the Hammonasset River. This is a good place from which to look for shore birds in spring and fall, and raptors throughout the year.

End of tour. Continue around on the park driveway back to the rotary (4.0 miles), and from there to the park exit. This will give you another look at some of the habitats you saw earlier on this tour.

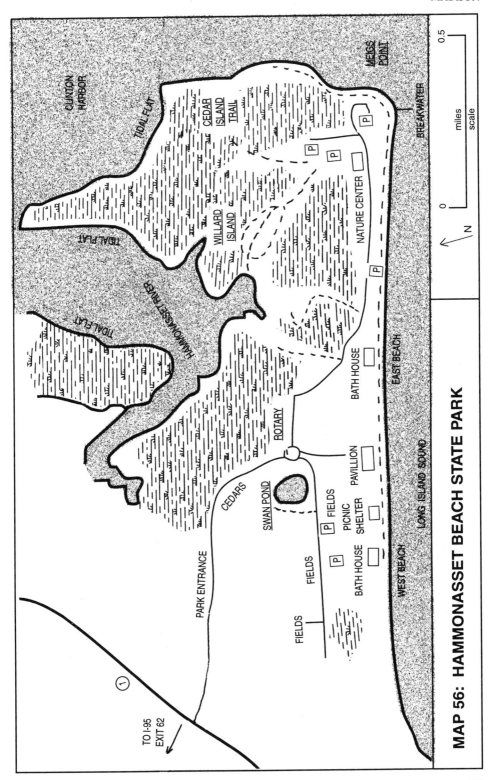

MAP 56: HAMMONASSET BEACH STATE PARK

MADISON: LAKE HAMMONASSET

HABITATS
FOREST: hardwoods, hardwoods/hemlock, hemlock;
Lake/pond: lake, wooded shore;
Open terrestrial: shrubby fields;
River/stream: stream, wooded streambelt.
This site consists of a lake (a dammed section of the Hammonasset River) that is used as a reservoir, together with the surrounding forest - a mix of hardwoods and conifers. The level of the reservoir varies with water use, and is usually low in the summer.

SEASONS/BIRDS
Spring migration: water birds, land birds;
Nesting season: land birds;
Fall migration: water birds, land birds;
Winter: land birds.
It is possible to see a nice variety of standard woodland birds at this site - during the spring and fall migrations, and also during the nesting season. Both northern and southern species occur here. This is one of the few sites in southern Connecticut at which black-throated green warbler has nested over the years (look in the hemlocks). Other nesters include Louisiana waterthrush and hooded warbler. In the spring and fall, in addition to Canada goose and mallard, there are usually a few ring-necked ducks to be seen on the lake.

GETTING AROUND
Birding methods: walk.
This area can be entered only with a Regional Water Authority Recreation Permit; with the permit comes a detailed trail map of the area (see Chapter 12: "Sources of Additional Information"). A nine-mile trail network goes entirely around the lake. This area does not get crowded, so that it is a good area in which to bird during the nesting season.

DIRECTIONS: Lake Hammonasset lies on the Madison/Killingworth town line, about seven miles north of Long Island Sound. In Madison, from the intersection of Routes 80 and 79, go east on Route 80 for 1.5 miles to the entrance on the left. This point is at the south end of the lake.

MADISON: MIDDLE BEACH ROAD

HABITATS
COASTAL: rocky shore, sand beach, tidal creek, Long Island Sound, island with rocky and shrubby shore; offshore rocks.
This road goes along the shore of Long Island Sound for 1.3 miles, with several places that provide views of or access to the Sound. Tuxis Island, about one half mile offshore, is wooded with a rocky and shrubby shore.

SEASONS/BIRDS
SPRING MIGRATION: gulls, terns, WATER BIRDS, marsh birds, shore birds, land birds;
Nesting season: gulls, terns, marsh birds, land birds;
FALL MIGRATION: gulls, terns, WATER BIRDS, marsh birds, shore birds, land birds;
Winter: gulls, water birds, shore birds, land birds.

This is primarily a site from which to view Long Island Sound for water birds in migration and winter (scoters are fairly regular during the period November-April). Offshore, Tuxis Island is used as a rest and nesting area by waders including snowy egret, green-backed heron and black-crowned night heron. Short eared owl has been seen on the island during some winters. Purple sandpiper often occurs on the offshore rocks in winter.

GETTING AROUND
Birding methods: car, walk.
Drive along this road, or park at a small town park and walk along the sidewalk. Access to the park is restricted during warm months. A scope is needed to see birds on Tuxis Island.

DIRECTIONS: This stretch of coastline lies on the south side of the village of Madison. In the center of Madison, at the intersection of Routes 1 and 79, go south (that is, west) on Route 1 for 0.2 mile, left on Island Avenue for 0.5 mile until it becomes Middle Beach Road and turns left to run along the coast.

MERIDEN: WEST PEAK STATE PARK/HUBBARD PARK

HABITATS
FOREST: hardwoods, hardwoods/white pine, hardwoods/hemlock, white pine, hemlock, mountain laurel;
Open terrestrial: short grass field, shrubby and wooded edge;
Lake/pond: lake, ponds, barren, grassy and wooded shores;
River/stream: perennial and seasonal streams, wooded streambelts;
OTHER: cliff, ledge, rocky slope, rocky summit, hawk watching site.
Hubbard Park is a small municipal park on the south side of Route 691. It is fully developed, and contains mowed lawns, groves of trees and a small pond. These habitats can be worth exploring at certain seasons, but the main value of Hubbard Park to the birder is that it provides access to the best parts of West Peak State Park.

From Hubbard Park you can enter West Peak State Park by walking a pedestrian access road that goes under Route 691 to the state park on the north side of the highway. This pedestrian road goes through forest communities of hardwoods, white pine and hemlock in various combinations, with a shrub layer of mountain laurel in many areas. The pedestrian road passes near a lake (Merimere Reservoir) and small ponds, all with wooded shores. As the road climbs toward the high part of the ridge, it goes along a wooded rocky hillside and into a dry upper slope forest of hardwoods and hemlock.

At the top of the ridge are two summits - West Peak and East Peak. They form the western end of the Hanging Hills of Meriden; at 1,024 feet above sea level, West Peak is the high point of the highest of Connecticut's trap rock ridges. The views are spectacular - you can see as far as Long Island Sound to the south and western Massachusets to the north.

SEASONS/BIRDS
SPRING MIGRATION: water birds, LAND BIRDS;
NESTING SEASON: LAND BIRDS
FALL MIGRATION: water birds, LAND BIRDS;
Winter: land birds.

The main attraction of this area for birders is the great variety and numbers of migrating and nesting land birds that can be found here in the spring, summer and fall.

Hubbard Park does produce some water birds - on the pond there are tame ducks most of the year and migrants in the fall (usually bufflehead, ruddy duck and occasionally shoveler). Lots of warblers and other land birds move through the groves of oaks and other hardwoods in this park during the spring and fall migrations. Rough-winged swallow nests at the outlet of the pond.

West Peak Park can provide exciting birding for migrants and nesters throughout the spring, summer and fall. Much of the best birding is on either side of the pedestrian access road that leads into West Peak Park from Hubbard Park. Worm-eating warbler nests on the rocky slopes near the road; black-throated green warbler throughout the forest; hooded warbler in the laurel thickets, and cerulean warbler also nearby. Gnatcatcher, kingfisher, green-backed heron and wood duck are among the other nesters in the park. The summits of West Peak and Castle Craig provide good places from which to watch the fall hawk migration.

GETTING AROUND
Birding methods: car, WALK.
It is possible to drive through much of Hubbard Park. The park roads that lead to the summits of West Peak and East Peak have been blocked but can still be walked. The best birding can be had by walking the pedestrian road that leads from Hubbard Park into West Peak Park, and up the park driveway to the summits of West Peak and East Peak. However, this is a walk of well over a mile (one way), and all uphill. Stay on the access road - copperhead snake is fairly common among the rocks.

DIRECTIONS (see Map 57): These two parks lie immediately northwest of Meriden on either side of Route 691.

To enter Hubbard Park: from Route 691 take exit 4, at the end of the exit ramp go east on West Main Street for 0.8 mile, and left into Hubbard Park.

To enter West Peak Park by walking from Hubbard Park: start as above, and take the Hubbard Park driveway to the back (north) side of the park to the pedestrian access road that passes under Route 691 to the southern part of West Peak Park. This road passes through forest habitats described above until it intersects with Percival Park Road; turn left and walk up the drive to near the summits of West Peak and East Peak.

To go directly to the park driveway that goes through the northern part of West Peak Park to the summits: from exit 5 on Route 691, go north on Route 71 for 1.5 miles, left on Butler Street for 0.2 mile, and left on Park Drive. Park Drive is blocked 0.9 mile from Butler Street. It leads to Maloney Canal Road and Percival Park Road, which can be walked to West Peak and East Peak.

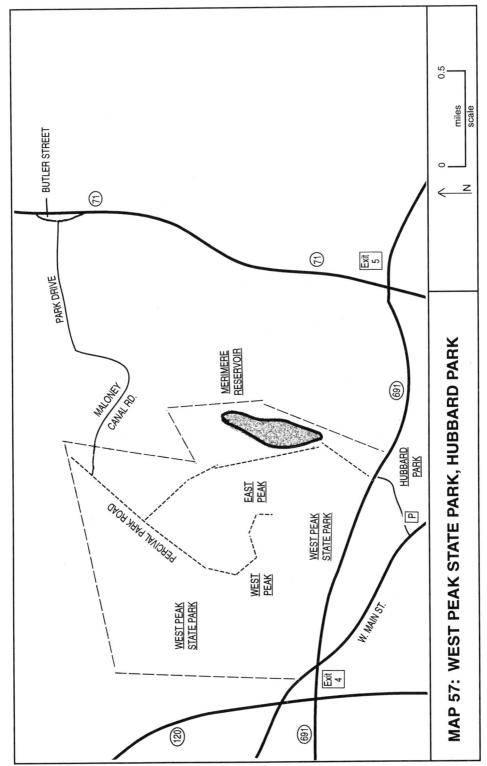

MAP 57: WEST PEAK STATE PARK, HUBBARD PARK

MIDDLEBURY: SPERRY SANCTUARY

HABITATS
FOREST: white pine, hardwoods/white pine, hardwoods/hemlock, mixed conifers, hardwoods;
MARSH/SWAMP/BOG:mixed herbaceous and shrub marsh; shrub and shrubby hardwood swamp; shrubby and wooded edges;
Lake/pond: pond, shallow water, marshy shore.
Sperry Pond is the centerpiece of this site; the richest avian habitats are the wetlands and forest that surround it.

SEASONS/BIRDS
SPRING MIGRATION: water birds, marsh birds, shore birds, LAND BIRDS;
NESTING SEASON: water birds, marsh birds, LAND BIRDS;
FALL MIGRATION: water birds, marsh birds, shore birds, LAND BIRDS;
Winter: land birds.
This is a good all-season birding site, especially for land birds. Spring provides the best birding, with a good mix of land bird migrants augmented by great blue and green-backed herons, woodcock, spotted and solitary sandpipers. There are also some common water bird species - principally Canada goose, mallard and wood duck. It is a also good site to visit during the nesting season, because it does not become crowded, and offers a good mix of the species you would expect in these habitats. The fall migration is similar to that in the spring, plus an occasional post-breeding wanderer great egret. While winter does not offer the species variety of other seasons, it does offer quality - this is a good place in which to look for raptors, particularly saw-whet owl. (It was here that a boreal owl was seen several winters ago.) In fact, this is a good site for raptors at all seasons: great horned owl, red-tailed and broad-winged hawks all nest here.

GETTING AROUND
Birding methods: walk.
Park on Route 63, and walk a short trail that goes to the pond, with branches that go through the woods.

DIRECTIONS: This sanctuary is located immediately west of the city of Waterbury, and just south of the New Haven/Litchfield County line. To get there from I-84 exit 17, go north on Route 63 for 1.5 miles to two stone pillars on the left, through which a woods road leads into the sanctuary. There is a wide shoulder on Route 63 on which to park.

MILFORD: GULF POND/GULF BEACH

HABITATS
COASTAL: Long Island Sound; cobble, gravel and sand beach, tidal pond, low salt marsh, high salt marsh, mud flat, tidal creek, coastal forest.
This is a tidal pond that is sheltered behind a barrier beach. The pond has extensive mud flats, a marsh along much of the shore, and behind the marsh, a coastal forest. The beach provides a look at Long Island Sound.

SEASONS/BIRDS
SPRING MIGRATION: gulls, terns, WATER BIRDS, MARSH BIRDS, SHORE BIRDS, land birds;
NESTING SEASON: gulls, terns, MARSH BIRDS, LAND BIRDS;
FALL MIGRATION: gulls, terns, WATER BIRDS, MARSH BIRDS, SHORE BIRDS, land birds;
WINTER: gulls, WATER BIRDS, shore birds, land birds.

Depending on the season and tide stage, Gulf Pond can offer an impressive variety and fine views of dabbling ducks, waders and shore birds. During the spring and fall migrations, look for shore birds in the pond on the mud flats at low tide. In the spring, summer and early fall, waders that nest on nearby Charles Island and other islands in the Sound come here to feed. Osprey, clapper and king rails all nest here. From mid-September to mid-April, look on the pond at high tide for ducks including canvasback, redhead (occasional) and Eurasian wigeon (occasional). In winter, look on the Sound off the beach where oldsquaw often occurs. Also in winter, there are sanderlings and dunlins on the beach, and sometimes glaucous and Iceland gulls are in the area.

GETTING AROUND
Birding methods: car.
The north end and middle of Gulf Pond can be seen well from the sidewalk on Buckingham Avenue. Park as safely as you can. The south end of the pond can be seen - and the beach can be reached - from Gulf Street, where there is parking (restricted to local residents from May through September). A spotting scope is helpful.

DIRECTIONS: Gulf Pond is in Milford, on Long Island Sound. **To get where you can see the north end and the middle of Gulf Pond from I-95 northbound,** take exit 40; at the end of the ramp turn right on Old Gate Lane for 0.7 mile; right on New Haven Avenue for 0.6 mile; left on Buckingham Avenue for 0.5 mile to Gulf Pond. **To get where you can see the north end and the middle of Gulf Pond from I-95 southbound,** take exit 40; at the end of the ramp left on Woodmont Road for a few yards; right on Old Gate Lane for 1.0 mile, right on New Haven Avenue for 0.6 mile; left on Buckingham Avenue for 0.5 mile to Gulf Pond.

To get to the south end of Gulf Pond and to Gulf Beach, continue on Buckingham Avenue for 0.2 mile; take the first right for 0.9 mile; right on Gulf Street for 0.1 mile to pond, beach and parking.

MILFORD: MERWIN POINT/BEACH AVENUE

HABITATS
COASTAL: rocky shore, point, gravel beach, tidal cove, Long Island Sound.
This small rocky point on the western shore of New Haven Harbor provides a place from which to look at the open water of the harbor and of Long Island Sound. It also has some gravel beach.

SEASONS/BIRDS
SPRING MIGRATION: GULLS, TERNS, WATER BIRDS, shore birds;
Nesting season: gulls, terns;
FALL MIGRATION: GULLS, TERNS, WATER BIRDS, shore birds;
WINTER: GULLS, WATER BIRDS, shore birds.

Merwin Point is a good place to see any of the many species of gulls, terns and water birds that occur in New Haven Harbor. Like most of the other sites in the harbor, it is is best during the period early November to late March. Water birds, including both dabbling ducks and diving species, occur during those three seasons (both loons and occasionally king eider are seen here); gulls of various species are here all year, and terns in the warm months. In winter, purple sandpiper is frequently seen.

GETTING AROUND
Birding methods: car, walk.
There are short walks to the water's edge from where you can park.

DIRECTIONS (see Map 52): This point is in Milford, on the west shore of New Haven Harbor. In Milford, at the eastern intersection of Routes 162 and 1, go east on Route 162 for 4.1 miles, bear right (not sharp right) on Chapel Street for 0.4 mile, right on Kings Highway for 0.2 mile, left on Beach Avenue for 0.1 mile to Merwin Point. Before entering Beach Avenue, park as best you can on a side street and walk to the point. To get to additional viewpoints of Long Island Sound, continue north on Beach Avenue as it follows the coast intermittently for 0.6 mile to a small town park between Wall Street and Bonsilene Street. Park here and walk to the beach.

MILFORD: MILFORD POINT/WHEELER WILDLIFE AREA (NELLS ISLAND)

HABITATS
COASTAL: Long Island Sound; brackish tidal river; tidal creeks; high and low salt marsh; intertidal flats of mud, sand, gravel and cobble; offshore bars of sand, gravel and cobble; beach of sand, gravel and cobble; dunes; shrub thickets; tide pools; edges of herbs, shrubs and coastal forest;
Open terrestrial: shrubby field.
Milford Point lies in the estuary of the Housatonic River. It is a sand spit which extends into the river as it enters Long Island Sound. The point itself is a barrier beach with sand dunes, grasses, low shrubs and, at its landward end, hardwoods. On the south side, facing Long Island Sound, is a breakwater and an extensive area of bars and flats.

Immediately north of the sand spit, and lying in its shelter, is an 800-acre tidal marsh - the largest in Connecticut which has been left in a natural condition, free of drainage ditches. The marsh, part of which is known as Nells Island, is included in the Charles E. Wheeler Wildlife Area. A part of the marsh lies next to a rich coastal forest composed of hardwoods, cedars, shrub thickets and an old reverting field with cedar and shrubs.

This site exemplifies the highly productive synergy that can occur among the avian habitats in an estuary in which there are areas for feeding, nesting and resting. Directly across the river in Stratford are Great Meadows, Long Beach and Short Beach, and just offshore is Charles Island. Taken together, these sites constitute one of the three finest avian areas along the coast of Connecticut (the others are Hammonasset Park and the sites in the estuary of the Connecticut River at Old Lyme).

SEASONS/BIRDS

SPRING MIGRATION: GULLS, TERNS, WATER BIRDS, MARSH BIRDS, SHORE BIRDS, LAND BIRDS;
NESTING SEASON: gulls, TERNS, water birds, MARSH BIRDS, shore birds, land birds;
FALL MIGRATION: GULLS, TERNS, WATER BIRDS, MARSH BIRDS, SHORE BIRDS, LAND BIRDS;
WINTER: GULLS, WATER BIRDS, shore birds, LAND BIRDS.

Taken together, these sites are unsurpassed in Connecticut for seeing a wide variety of birds in all of the species groups. It is safe to say that Milford Point provides the possibility of seeing any of the gulls, terns, water birds, shore birds, marsh birds and land birds that occur with any regularity along the Connecticut coast. In addition, over the years, an impressive number of uncommon species have been seen here. The most exciting seasons are the spring and fall migrations; however, Milford Point is also unsurpassed as a site in which to bird during the winter, and a variety of interesting species nest here.

Gulls can be seen all year and terns during the warm months, especially from the beach near the visitor center; least tern nests on the beach and sandbars. Water birds can also be seen from the beach all year, but the variety is greatest from November through April; gadwall nests in the marsh. During the spring and fall migration, the variety of shore birds on the flats and bars off the beach is impressive, especially at low tide; piping plover nests on the beach, and oystercatcher on sandbars offshore. Waders come in to feed during the spring, summer and fall at low and mid-tides on the flats and bars, and also in the marsh; clapper rail nests in the marsh. Looking for land birds at Milford Point can also be very rewarding. Horned lark nests here, and large numbers of passerines pause here during the spring and fall migrations. In winter, the sandspit is a good place to look for land birds - including snow bunting, horned lark, longspur, Ipswich sparrow, and lingering migrants. A variety of raptors regularly occur here, especially in fall and winter. All four of the falcons and all eight of the owls that occur in Connecticut have been seen at Milford Point; rough-legged hawk is sometimes present in winter.

GETTING AROUND

Birding methods: car, WALK, boat, wheelchair.

The Connecticut Audubon Coastal Center is located at the base of Milford Point off Seaview Avenue. There is a $3.00 charge to enter the building. At the site of this center, there is an observation platform that overlooks the marsh, and a second that overlooks the beach, Long Island Sound and intertidal flats offshore. Both of these platforms and the center building itself are wheelchair-accessible. It is possible to walk west along the beach for about one half mile to a third platform that is placed on the higher center portion of the sandspit, and provides a view over the marsh and also westward along the point to its end. These three platforms provide a way to see all of the habitats on the point, as well as the southern portion of the Nells Island marsh without disturbance to the birds that use these areas. A scope is very helpful.

The eastern edge of the Nells Island marsh and a contiguous coastal forest can be reached by going to the boat launch at Court Street, where good habitat surrounds the small open grassy area which is used for parking. It is also possible to explore the marsh by boat from this point. It is important when planning a trip by boat to take into account the strong tidal currents in the creeks that go through the marsh (for tide times, refer to Table 1). Two other places on town roads provide views of the northern part of the marsh, and of the Housatonic River (see "Directions" below).

DIRECTIONS (see Map 58): These areas are on the Connecticut shore between Milford and Stratford.

To get to the Milford Point visitor center: from I-95, take exit 34 and go 0.1 mile south to Route 1; left on Route 1 for 0.3 mile; right on Lansdale Road for 0.3 mile; right on Milford Point Road for 1.9 winding miles; right on Seaview Avenue for 0.3 mile to the visitor center driveway on the right. The trails to the beach and observation platforms start here.

To get to the boat launch site at Court Street: proceed as above from I-95 to Milford Point Road and follow it for 1.5 miles; right on Court Street for 0.2 mile to a dead end and the entrance to the boat launch site.

To get views of the northwestern part of the marsh and the Housatonic River: from I-95, take exit 34 and go 0.1 mile south to Route 1; right on Route 1 for 0.9 mile, left on Rivercliff Drive for a few yards, right on Housatonic Drive for 0.3 mile, and right on Edgemont Road for 0.1 mile to the deadend at the shore of the Housatonic River. From here, you can see a section of the river and the northern part of the marsh. To get a better view of the marsh, return to Housatonic Drive and go an additional 0.3 mile, right on Sailors Lane for 0.1 mile to the deadend at the edge of the marsh.

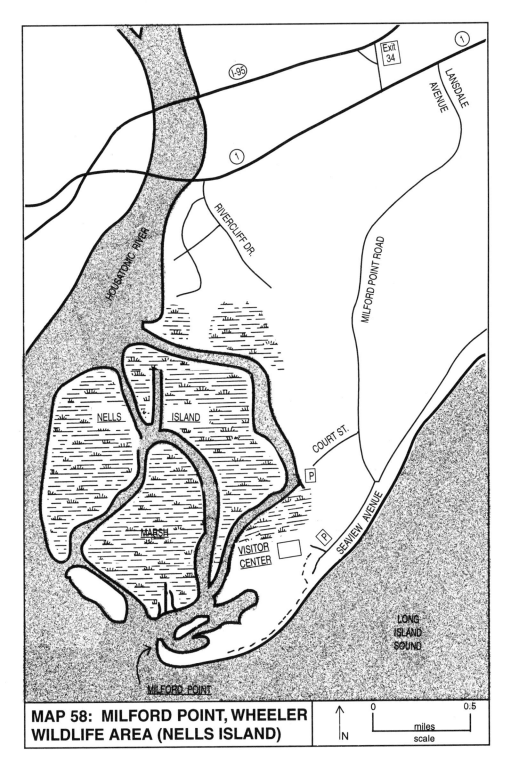

MAP 58: MILFORD POINT, WHEELER WILDLIFE AREA (NELLS ISLAND)

scale

0   miles   0.5

N

MILFORD: SILVER SANDS STATE PARK/CHARLES ISLAND

HABITATS
COASTAL: sandy beach, shrubby edge; disturbed high salt marsh, brackish, herbaceous (phragmites) and shrub marsh, salt pannes, pools, tidal creeks; mud, sand and gravel flats, gravel bar, rocky shore; Long Island Sound, island with herbaceous, shrubby, wooded and rocky shores;
Open terrestrial: short grass, tall grass and shrubby fields.

Silver Sands Park occupies a bulge on the Connecticut coast. In this small area, hemmed in by development, and marred by dumping of toxic wastes in the past, there is an extraordinary variety of coastal habitats. The proximity of the marshes at Milford Point and Stratford Great Meadow enhances the productivity of the habitats at Silver Sands. The park includes a beach that backs on a tidal marsh, and overlooks an extensive intertidal area of mud, sand and gravel. Also from the beach, you can see Charles Island, about half a mile offshore. The various marsh habitats lie just behind the beach, and the open fields further inland, immediately north of the service road.

SEASONS/BIRDS
SPRING MIGRATION: gulls, terns, WATER BIRDS, MARSH BIRDS, SHORE BIRDS, land birds;
Nesting season: gulls, terns, water birds, marsh birds, land birds;
FALL MIGRATION: gulls, terns, WATER BIRDS, MARSH BIRDS, SHORE BIRDS, LAND BIRDS;
Winter: gulls, WATER BIRDS, shore birds, land birds.

There is something to see at Silver Sands at any time of year. The spring and fall migrations bring the greatest variety, but summer and winter are also good, for quite different reasons. Water birds can be seen on the nearby waters of Long Island Sound throughout the fall, winter and spring, with the species mix varying somewhat by season. Herons and egrets feed on the large intertidal areas just off the beach in the spring, summer and fall, and there is a heronry of nesting waders on Charles Island. A wide variety of shore birds feed on the beach and intertidal areas during migration, while sanderling and dunlin occur here in winter. Several species of hawks occur during migration, particularly red-tail, kestrel and harrier, and this is an excellent place to look for wintering rough-legged hawk. In October and November, look for sparrows in the shrubby fields north of the service road.

GETTING AROUND
Birding methods: car, walk.

The park driveway goes to the beach and overlooks the intertidal areas and part of the marsh behind the beach. The service road passes by the shrubby fields north of the beach and marsh. All of the area can be seen by walking about half a mile. Charles Island is off-limits during the nesting season.

DIRECTIONS: This park is on the coast at the city of Milford, and a mile or two east of Milford Point and Stratford Great Meadows. To get there from I-95 exit 34, go left on Route 1 for 1.0 mile, right on Route 162 for 0.6 mile, right on Robert Treat Parkway (which becomes Surf Avenue) for 0.9 mile, and right on East Broadway for 0.6 mile to the eastern edge of the park. You can park at this point and walk into the area. It is also possible to reach the west end of the park by continuing on East Broadway (which becomes the Silver Sands Service Road) as it curves to the right and then to the left through the park and past the shrubby fields for 0.7 mile to another small parking area and the beginning of a trail, both on the left side of the road.

MILFORD/WEST HAVEN: OYSTER RIVER

HABITATS
COASTAL: rocky coast, salt water tidal cove, tidal creek, gravel, sand and mud flats, gravel bar, cobble, gravel and sand beach, tide pool, Long Island Sound.
This is a small cove where the Oyster River enters Long Island Sound. A great variety of habitats occur within it - it is a kind of miniature estuary that contains many of the habitat types typical of larger estuaries. It is very productive as a birding site, considering its small size.

SEASONS/BIRDS
SPRING MIGRATION: GULLS, terns, WATER BIRDS, marsh birds, shore birds, land birds;
Nesting season: gulls, terns, water birds, marsh birds, land birds;
FALL MIGRATION: GULLS, terns, WATER BIRDS, marsh birds, shore birds, land birds;
WINTER: GULLS, WATER BIRDS, land birds.
The concentration of rich estuarine habitats attracts a wide variety of gulls, water birds and shore birds. The highlights of this site are the gulls and dabbling ducks in fall, winter and early spring - occasionally including several uncommon gull species and Eurasian wigeon. In the spring and fall there are also shore birds; in the warm months terns feed here. The best period is from late October to late April.

GETTING AROUND
Birding methods: car.
This entire site can be seen from the shore, only a few feet from the parking area.

DIRECTIONS (see Map 52): This site is on the coast at the eastern edge of Milford, at the West Haven line. To get there from Milford at the western intersection of Routes 1 and 162, go east on Route 162 for 5.4 miles to the point at which Route 162 goes over a bridge and passes a small cove and beach where the Oyster River enters Long Island Sound. There is a place to park on the right side of the road just across the bridge.

MILFORD/WEST HAVEN: OYSTER RIVER MARSH

HABITATS
Coastal: high salt marsh, tidal creek, mud flats, coastal forest.
This sheltered high salt marsh is cut through by a tidal creek (the Oyster River), that is bordered by mud flats. The marsh is surrounded by a coastal forest.

SEASONS/BIRDS
Spring migration: water birds, marsh birds, shore birds, land birds;
Nesting season: marsh birds, land birds;
Fall migration: water birds, marsh birds, shore birds, land birds;
Winter: water birds, land birds.
This marsh is best in spring and fall, when it is a good site at which to look for marsh birds, as well as some dabbling ducks. In summer, black-crowned night heron and other waders come here to feed. In winter, there are dabbling ducks and sometimes harrier.

GETTING AROUND
Birding methods: car.
Most of this marsh can be seen from the sides of the road.

DIRECTIONS (see Map 52): This site is on the Milford/West Haven line, about a mile inland from the western shore of New Haven Harbor. To get there from the western intersection of Routes 162 and 1 in Milford, go east on Route 162 for 5.2 miles, and left on Anderson Avenue for a short distance to the point at which the marsh is visible on both sides of the road.

NAUGATUCK/BEACON FALLS: NAUGATUCK STATE FOREST

HABITATS
FOREST: hardwoods, hardwoods/white pine, white pine, hardwoods/hemlock, hemlock, cedar, mixed conifers, mountain laurel;
RIVER/STREAM: river, perennial and seasonal streams, fast water, shrubby and wooded streambelts, hemlock ravines;
Open terrestrial: shrubby field, edge;
Lake/pond: small ponds, shrubby and wooded shores;
Other: sand bank, gravel bank, cliff/ledge, rocky slope.
This, the 2,000-plus acre Hunters Mountain area of the Naugatuck State Forest lies on the steep and rocky sides of the Naugatuck Valley. Most of the area is forested, with an equal mix of deciduous woods and conifer forest. Forest communities include areas of pure old-growth hemlock. There are also areas of mountain laurel, ledges and talus slopes, streams with rocky gorges, hemlock ravines, small ponds, reverting fields, a power line right of way, and the west bank of the Naugatuck River. Many parts of this forest have been burned over at various times, so that succession is in varying stages.

SEASONS/BIRDS
SPRING MIGRATION: water birds, marsh birds, shore birds, LAND BIRDS;
NESTING SEASON: water birds, LAND BIRDS;
FALL MIGRATION: water birds, marsh birds, shore birds, LAND BIRDS;
Winter: land birds.
The wide variety of high quality inland habitats in the Nuagatuck Forest, together with its position in a major river valley, cause it to be a really good birding area. Over the years, 162 species have been seen here, including a number that are uncommon in the state. Forest-dwelling species are the specialty, but also present are a number of open-habitat and edge species, plus a few water, marsh and shore birds. This site is especially good during the spring migration, and provides the opportunity to see, in addition to all of the species you would expect in these habitats, less common species including such warblers as Cape May, bay-breasted, blackpoll, hooded, black-throated green, worm-eating, Canada, Wilson's and northern waterthrush, as well as olive-sided flycatcher and ruby-crowned kinglet. In the fall, species that have been seen here have included Connecticut warbler and gray-cheeked thrush. Nesters include a number of uncommon and interesting species. Some of them are northerners that find congenial habitat in the hemlock ravine and other cool microclimates at this site: hermit thrush, solitary vireo, winter wren, goshawk and black-throated green warbler. Southerners such as Acadian flycatcher, pine, worm-eating and hooded warblers

can be found nesting nearby. Other nesters include open- and edge-habitat species that occur in the power line and reverting fields within the site: brown thrasher, prairie warbler, indigo bunting and field sparrow. Eleven species of raptor occur at this site, seven of which are year-round residents. Osprey is a regular spring and fall migrant, and bald eagle is pretty regular during December-March.

GETTING AROUND

Birding methods: car, walk.

There are auto roads, woods roads and trails that you can take through the main habitat areas in this forest. In your auto, you can make a loop trip past the power line, through the Spruce Brook hemlock ravine, and through other forest habitats. If you walk, there is a network of trails and woods roads that lead to most parts of the forest.

DIRECTIONS (see Map 59): The Naugatuck State Forest lies between the cities of Naugatuck and Beacon Falls. The Naugatuck River and Route 8 run side by side along the bottom of the narrow Naugatuck Valley, and the Hunter's Mountain block of the forest occupies the hills on the western side of the valley. From Route 8, take exit 26, go north on Route 63 for 0.3 mile, left on Scott Street for 0.1 mile, and left on Lewis Street. Keep going straight, onto Hunters Mountain Road and follow it up a long steep hill. The state forest and productive habitats lie along the road in the section from 1.3 to 2.1 miles from the Lewis Street/Scott Street intersection.

To drive through the forest, on Hunter's Mountain Road at 1.6 miles from the Lewis Street/Scott Street intersection, turn left. This road takes you across a power line with shrubby field and edge habitats, through the Spruce Brook hemlock ravine, continues out through deciduous woods, past gravel banks to the southern entrance to the Hunter's Mountain block of the forest.

To make a walking loop through the forest, follow Hunter's Mountain Road for 1.9 miles from the Lewis Street/Scott Street intersection to a blocked-off dirt road on the right. By walking this road (take left turns at forks in the trail), it is possible to do a three-mile counterclockwise loop through a variety of the best habitats in this site. It leads through deciduous forest, past two ponds, across the power line, into the Spruce Brook hemlock ravine, and eventually back to your starting point.

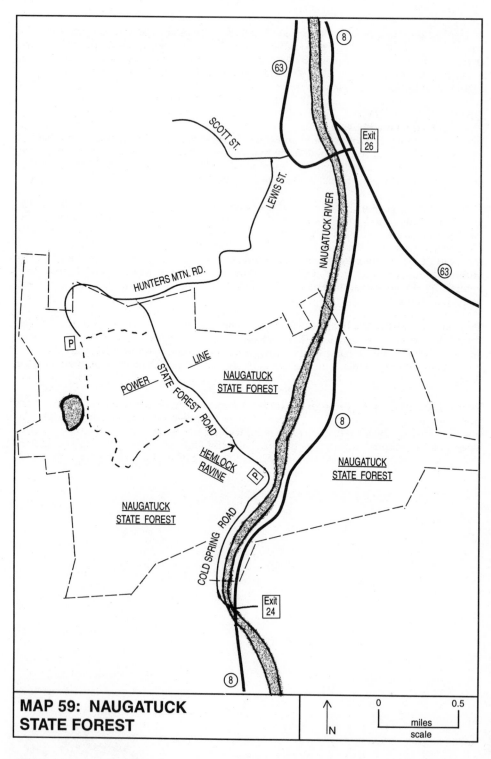

MAP 59: NAUGATUCK STATE FOREST

NEW HAVEN: EAST SHORE PARK/FORT HALE PARK/MORRIS COVE

HABITATS
COASTAL: rocky shore, tidal cove.
These three contiguous city parks occupy over a mile and a half of the eastern shore of New Haven Harbor, and provide good views of it.

SEASONS/BIRDS
SPRING MIGRATION: gulls, terns, WATER BIRDS, land birds;
Nesting season: gulls, terns;
FALL MIGRATION: gulls, terns, WATER BIRDS, LAND BIRDS;
WINTER: gulls, WATER BIRDS.
This is a good area during the fall, winter and spring for seeing any of the many water bird species that occur in the harbor. In addition, this coastline is a place to watch for hawks during the fall migration (but nearby Lighthouse Point is better).

GETTING AROUND
Birding methods: car, walk.
In places (Morris Cove), the shore can be seen from your car, and at other points, can be reached by short paths.

DIRECTIONS (see Map 52): These parks are about three miles from the center of New Haven, on the eastern shore of New Haven Harbor a short distance north of Lighthouse Point. **To get to these parks from I-95 northbound:** take exit 50 and follow the exit ramp for 0.2 mile; go right on Woodward Avenue (which becomes Fort Hale Park Road) for 1.2 miles to one of the entrances to East Shore Park on the right. To reach Fort Hale Park, continue south on Woodward Avenue for an additional 0.3 to 0.9 mile. During this section of road, Fort Hale Park is on the right. To get to Morris Cove, continue south on Woodward Avenue to its end, right on Townsend Avenue which runs along the shore of Morris Cove starting in 0.2 mile. **To get to these parks from I-95 southbound:** take exit 51 onto Frontage Road and go 0.9 mile; left on Woodward Avenue for 1.3 miles to the entrance to East Shore Park. To get to Fort Hale Park and Morris Cove, proceed as above.

NEW HAVEN: LIGHTHOUSE POINT PARK

HABITATS
COASTAL: rocky point, rocky shore, tidal cove, breakwater, sand and gravel beach, tidal creek, mixed herbaceous salt marsh, mud flat, Long Island Sound;
OPEN TERRESTRIAL: short grass and shrubby fields, shrubby and wooded edges;
FOREST: hardwoods, vine tangles and thickets.
This park is on the peninsula that forms the east side of New Haven Harbor. It is small - only 84 acres - but offers more birding per acre than almost anywhere else in Connecticut. The point lies in the path of the coastal migration route and is also an important land trap where migrants pause before continuing south. Its habitats, while good in themselves, owe their extreme productivity to their position at the end of this peninsula.

SEASONS/BIRDS

SPRING MIGRATION: gulls, terns, WATER BIRDS, marsh birds, shore birds, LAND BIRDS;

Nesting season: gulls, terns, water birds, marsh birds, land birds;

FALL MIGRATION: gulls, terns, WATER BIRDS, marsh birds, SHORE BIRDS, LAND BIRDS;

Winter: gulls, water birds, land birds.

Over the years, more than 200 bird species have been seen at Lighthouse Point, including many species that are uncommon in Connecticut. During the fall migration, for almost any bird group, Lighthouse Point is one of the best birding sites in the state. It is best known as a site from which to watch the fall migration of hawks and other land birds, especially during the period from early September through October, and with the wind coming from the northwest. A daily fall hawk watch has been maintained here since 1978, and species count records have been kept during that time. Almost all of the raptor species that occur in Connecticut have been seen here in recent years, including all four falcons and eight owl species. Throughout the fall, winter and spring, it is possible to see all of the water bird species that occur in New Haven Harbor, as well as a wide variety of land birds. The fall shore bird migration is especially good. In addition, many species of gulls, terns and marsh birds occur here at various seasons.

GETTING AROUND

Birding methods: car, walk.

It is possible to see many of the passing migrants from the parking area. There are also short paths to the shore, and trails through the nearby woods and wetlands. A fee is charged during the summer.

DIRECTIONS (see Map 52): This park is on the east side of New Haven Harbor, four miles south of the center of New Haven. **To get there from I-95 northbound:** take exit 50 and go straight ahead for 0.3 mile to the second traffic light; right on Townsend Avenue for 1.7 miles; right on Lighthouse Road for 0.6 mile to the park entrance. **To get there from I-95 southbound:** take exit 51 onto Frontage Road and go 0.9 mile; left on Townsend Avenue for 1.8 miles; right on Lighthouse Road for 0.6 mile to the park entrance.

NEW HAVEN: LONG WHARF

HABITATS

COASTAL: tidal cove, mud flat.

This site overlooks the west shore of upper part of New Haven Harbor. At low tide, there is an extensive mud flat within a few yards of the parking area.

SEASONS/BIRDS

SPRING MIGRATION: gulls, terns; WATER BIRDS, marsh birds, shore birds, land birds;

Nesting season: terns, water birds;

FALL MIGRATION: gulls, terns; WATER BIRDS, MARSH BIRDS, SHORE BIRDS, land birds;

WINTER: GULLS, WATER BIRDS, shore birds, land birds.

The mudflat at Long Wharf is where many uncommon and rare species have been seen. The shore bird migrations are exciting, and routinely offer all or most of the standard species, with a good chance of seeing something unusual among them - especially in the fall. Sightings over the years have included pectoral, white-rumped and western sandpipers, red knot and lesser golden plover. Raptors, including merlin, peregrine and even gyrfalcon (very irregular) are attracted by the sight of such prey, and have been seen hunting here. A variety of water bird species typical of a cove environment are seen here during the late fall, winter and early spring, as well as terns in the warm months (sometimes including Forster's, royal and Caspian), and various gulls at any time (sightings have included black-headed and lesser black-backed).

GETTING AROUND
Birding methods: car.
Here, it is simply a matter of finding a place to park in the area provided. In severe winter weather, you can look at the harbor from inside your car. Otherwise, lock it and hide valuables.

DIRECTIONS (see Map 52): This area lies along the north shore of New Haven Harbor just south of the center of the city.

From I-95 northbound, take exit 46 and immediately turn left onto Frontage Road, which runs along the shore past the mud flats. In about 100 yards there is a small parking area on the right side of the road overlooking the harbor.

From I-95 southbound, take exit 46, turn right onto Sargent Drive, right at the first intersection, pass under I-95, and right again onto Frontage Road. In 0.2 mile there is a small parking area on the left overlooking the harbor.

NEW HAVEN/HAMDEN: EAST ROCK PARK

HABITATS
FOREST: hardwoods, hemlock, flood plain, vine tangles and thickets;
Open terrestrial: short grass field;
Lake/pond: pond with wooded, shrubby and marshy shore;
River/stream: stream, slow water, shrubby and wooded streambelt;
Marsh/swamp/bog: cattail marsh;
Other: cliff, hawk watching site.
This 450-acre park includes a winding stream (the Mill River) that is bordered by cattail marsh, alder thickets, and moist flood plain hardwoods. Looming above this bottomland is a trap rock ridge, forested by mid- and upper-slope hardwoods and groves of hemlock.

SEASONS/BIRDS
SPRING MIGRATION: water birds, marsh birds, shore birds, LAND BIRDS;
Nesting season: water birds, marsh birds, land birds;
FALL MIGRATION: water birds, marsh birds, shore birds, LAND BIRDS;
Winter: water birds, land birds.
East Rock Park is one of the best sites in Connecticut to see migrating warblers. Thirty-seven species and two subspecies have been seen here, including worm-eating, golden-winged, Lawrence's, Brewster's, orange-crowned (fall), hooded and yellow-throated. Other land bird

migrants also pass through in impressive numbers and variety. This incredible seasonal activity is caused in part by the position of the park - it lies near the intersection of the coastal flyway and a river valley migration route.

The spectacular nature of the spring and fall migrations make it easy to overlook the fact that there is excellent birding here at other times - during the warm months marsh birds and some shore birds can be found near the Mill River, and there are also water birds there, especially during colder parts of the year. The upper part of the park, on top of the ridge, is a good place from which to watch migrating hawks. Do not leave valuables unattended in your car.

GETTING AROUND
Birding methods: car, walk.
There are a number of interconnecting trails through the bottomland by the Mill River, and an extensive trail system on the high ground of the ridge. It is also possible to bird from your car, along the driveway up to the top of the ridge.

DIRECTIONS: East Rock Park is about one mile northeast of the center of New Haven. To get there from I-91, take exit 6 to Willow Street at the end of the ramp. **To get to the northern part of the park,** go west on Willow Street for 0.8 mile, right on Whitney Avenue for 1.0 mile to the Eli Whitney Museum on the right. Park here and enter the trail system by walking across the covered bridge. **To get to the southern part of the park,** start as above, but go for 0.6 mile on Willow Street, right on Livingston Street for 0.5 mile to the intersection of Livingston Street and East Park Road. Park here and enter the trail system. **To get to the higher parts of the park,** instead of parking at this point, follow East Park Road to the right across the bridge and turn left on Farnum Drive which leads to the top of the ridge. On the way up, there is an overlook from which you can look down on warblers in the treetops.

NORTH BRANFORD: BIG GULPH

HABITATS
Forest: hardwoods/white pine, hardwoods/hemlock;
Open terrestrial: short grass and shrubby field, shrubby and wooded edges;
River/stream: streams, wooded streambelts;
Lake/pond: ponds, seasonal pools, wooded shores;
Other: rock outcrop, rocky slope.
This site lies in the valley of the Farm River, and includes the Totoket Ridge on the southeast side of the valley. It lies behind a large mowed playground next to the highway.

SEASONS/BIRDS
Spring migration: land birds;
Nesting season: land birds;
Fall migration: land birds;
Winter: land birds.
This is a nice place in which to see a standard mix of land bird migrants and nesting species. It is better than average for migrating warblers. Wild turkey is a resident.

GETTING AROUND
Birding methods: walk.
This is a Regional Water Authority property, accessible by permit only (see Chapter 12: "Sources of Additional Information"). There are more than seven miles of trails, some of which are rugged and steep, others flat and wide. The Regional Water Authority provides a trail map with trail descriptions to those who are given permits.

DIRECTIONS: This site is in North Branford, just south of the Wallingford town line. From the village of Northford at the intersection of Routes 17 and 22, go north on Route 17 for 2.2 miles to Northford Park on the right. Park here at the playground; Big Gulph area trails start from the south side (rear) of the playground area.

ORANGE: RACEBROOK RECREATION AREA

HABITATS
OPEN TERRESTRIAL: tall grass, mixed herbaceous and shrubby fields; shrubby and wooded edges;
FOREST: hardwoods, hardwoods/white pine, white pine, hemlock, mixed conifers, cedar;
River/stream: stream, shrubby streambelt;
Marsh/swamp/bog: shrubby hardwood swamp, wooded swamp (hardwoods, cedar and other conifers);
Other: sand and gravel.
This area contains a wide diversity of habitats. There is a spectrum of open areas, including a variety of fields and a little-used weedy gravel pit. The woodlands include young hardwoods and a variety of conifer mixtures. The stream is bordered by a streambelt of dense thickets, and the swamps contain a productive mix of tree species.

SEASONS/BIRDS
SPRING MIGRATION: LAND BIRDS;
NESTING SEASON: LAND BIRDS;
FALL MIGRATION: LAND BIRDS;
Winter: land birds.
This is an excellent area during the spring, summer and fall. The spring and fall migrations of land birds is extremely good, especially for warblers in the spring and sparrows in the fall. Ninety-three species are known to nest at this site. This group includes open habitat and edge species such as field sparrow, indigo bunting, prairie warbler, brown thrasher (those four species in relatively large numbers); also, white-eyed vireo (regular), and Brewster's warbler (irregular). Other nesters include pileated and red-bellied woodpeckers, brown creeper, red-breasted nuthatch and Carolina wren. In winter, look for lingering migrants and any of the residents that you would expect to see in these types of habitat. A variety of raptors can be seen here - broad-winged hawk, great horned and screech owls are nesters; and harrier, sharp-shinned and Cooper's hawks all occur here as migrants.

GETTING AROUND
Birding methods: walk, wheelchair.
This area can be entered only with a Regional Water Authority Recreation Permit; with the permit comes a detailed trail map of the area (see Chapter 12: "Sources of Additional Infor-

mation"). There is a well-maintained three-mile trail network that includes a wheelchair-accessible interpretive nature trail and a boardwalk that provides close views of wetland habitats. Other gravel pedestrian roads and trails provide easy walking. The area does not get crowded, even on summer weekends, so that it is a good place to do your birding during the nesting season.

DIRECTIONS: This site is about five miles west of New Haven. From the intersection of Routes 114 and 34, go north on Route 114 for 0.3 mile to the entrance on the right.

OXFORD: JACKSON COVE PARK

HABITATS
Lake/pond: lake, cove, deep water, wooded, grassy and sandy shore;
Forest: hardwoods, hardwoods/hemlock, hemlock, hardwoods/white pine.
This is a town park on the east shore of Lake Zoar, a dammed section of the Housatonic River, opposite the southern block of the Paugussett State Forest. It provides a view of the water and of the hillside on the opposite shore.

SEASONS/BIRDS
Spring migration: water birds, land birds;
Nesting season:
Fall migration: water birds, land birds;
Winter: water birds, land birds.
This is a site to use in the spring and fall, when looking for migrating water birds (common merganser, goldeneye and ring-necked duck are the most frequently seen). When there is open water during the winter (there usually isn't) these same species may be seen. Osprey hunts over the river when migrating in the spring and fall. Other land bird migrants move along the shore and edges of the park in the spring and fall. Bald eagle is pretty regular during the period November through March.

GETTING AROUND
Birding methods: CAR.
This is a one-look site, but nice and easy, and often rewarding. You can drive to the water's edge. The park is heavily used by town residents during the warm months, and non-residents are not welcome.

DIRECTIONS: This park is in Oxford, about ten miles southwest of Waterbury. To get there from I-84 exit 15, go south on Route 67 for 0.1 mile, turn right on Kettletown Road and keep going straight for about five miles as the road name changes to Maple Tree Hill Road and then Jackson Cove Road, and finally makes a dead end at the park.

OXFORD: TOWANTIC POND/LARKIN STATE PARK TRAIL

HABITATS
Lake/pond: pond, shallow water, marshy, shrubby and wooded shore;
Marsh/swamp/bog: shrub marsh, shrub swamp;
Forest: hardwoods, hardwoods/white pine, white pine;
Open terrestrial: short grass field, shrubby and wooded edges.
Towantic Pond is tucked away in a quiet hollow and is surrounded by natural areas. It is shallow, irregular in shape, and has an undeveloped shore with areas of shrub marsh, shrub swamp, shrubs, hardwoods and white pine. Between the pond and the trail there is a large wetland composed of shrub marsh and swamp. The trail itself is wide and grassy, and provides a strip of shrubby and wooded edge.

SEASONS/BIRDS
Spring migration: water birds, marsh birds, shore birds, land birds;
Nesting season: water birds, marsh birds, shore birds, land birds;
Fall migration: water birds, marsh birds, shore birds, land birds;
Winter: land birds.
This site provides an easy way to see a nice combination of water birds, marsh birds (including green-backed heron and Virginia rail), shore birds (solitary, spotted and least sandpipers), and many land birds: wetland-oriented species (including tree swallow, yellow warbler and swamp sparrow), edge species (including yellowthroat, prairie, blue-winged and chestnut-sided warblers), and forest-dwellers (including pewee, wood thrush, yellow-throated and red-eyed vireos, and pine warbler). The best times to visit are spring (early for migrating water birds, later for everything else) and fall (early for marsh, shore and land birds, later for water birds).

GETTING AROUND
Birding methods: WALK.
The Larkin State Park Trail runs near the west shore of Towantic Pond. It is wide and level, and provides easy walking through edge habitat and beside a wetland. The trail provides a good view of the near side of the pond, but a scope would help pick out more distant water birds. In order to reach the pond, it is necessary to walk about 0.3 mile on the trail. In addition, the trail can be walked for a considerable distance either north or south from Towantic Pond. It runs between Whittemore Glen State Park in Naugatuck and Kettletown Road in Southbury, a distance of about 11 miles. It is used by horseback riders.

DIRECTIONS: This site is in Oxford, several miles west of the city of Naugatuck. From the intersection of Routes 188 and 63, go west on Route 188 for 0.5 mile, left on Shadduck Road for 1.8 miles, right on Hill Road for 0.5 mile to a kind of asymmetrical intersection. Go almost straight across, and continue for another 1.0 mile, then turn right on Towantic Hill Road and go for 1.2 miles to an intersection and a parking area on the right. The trail crosses the road here; take it to the north (left) for about 0.3 mile to Towantic Pond.

OXFORD/SOUTHBURY: SOUTHFORD FALLS STATE PARK

HABITATS
> **FOREST:** hardwoods, hardwoods/white pine, hardwoods/hemlock, hemlock;
> **Open terrestrial:** short grass field, cedars, shrubby and wooded edges;
> **Lake/pond:** ponds, shores of short grass, shrubs and woods;
> **River/stream;** stream, fast water, wooded streambelt, hemlock ravine, seasonal streams;
> **Marsh/swamp/bog:** sedge, mixed herbaceous and shrub marsh; shrub and shrubby hardwood swamp.

This small (120-acre) park is composed of a nice mix of forest types, with a stream running through the woods and an adjacent irregularly-shaped pond. The site includes lots of edges and habitat interfaces.

SEASONS/BIRDS
> **Spring migration:** land birds;
> **Nesting season:** land birds;
> **Fall migration:** land birds;
> **Winter:** land birds.

This is a good site in which to look for a variety of land birds, especially warblers, during the spring and fall migrations. Acadian flycatcher nests in hemlocks by the stream. Other nesters include worm-eating and prairie warblers, Louisiana waterthrush and orchard oriole.

GETTING AROUND
> **Birding methods:** walk.

This is a nice place in which to bird on foot, as there is a well marked loop trail, including an observation tower.

DIRECTIONS: This park is on the Oxford/Southbury line, less than a mile south of the village of Southford. From I-84 exit 16, go south on Route 188 for 2.8 miles to the park entrance on the left, soon after the intersection with Route 67.

SOUTHBURY: CROOK HORN ROAD (STRAWBERRY PATCH)

HABITATS
> **OPEN TERRESTRIAL:** tilled, short grass, tall grass, mixed herbaceous and shrubby fields; shrubby edges;
> **Forest:** hardwoods;
> **Lake/pond:** pond, seasonal pools;
> **Marsh/swamp/bog:** shrub and shrubby hardwood swamp;
> **Other:** manure piles, brush dump, ditch.

At this site, the vegetation and habitats - both natural and artificial - provide a variety of berries, seeds and small rodents during the fall and winter.

SEASONS/BIRDS

SPRING MIGRATION: water birds, shore birds, LAND BIRDS;
Nesting season: land birds;
FALL MIGRATION: water birds, shore birds, LAND BIRDS;
WINTER: LAND BIRDS.

This is a good site at which to look for sparrows. During the spring migration, lots of sparrows and blackbirds pass through. However, the best time is during the period October-January, when the sparrows present may include vesper, white-crowned and Lincoln's. In addition, lark and LeConte's sparrows have been seen here. During the same period, large flocks of bluebirds and robins come in to feed. Pipit occurs here in the fall, and horned lark and snow bunting during the period November-March. A variety of raptors can be seen here from October through March (red-tailed and rough-legged hawks, all three accipiters, harrier, bald eagle and screech owl); red-shouldered hawk passes through in the spring.

GETTING AROUND

Birding methods: car, walk, bike.

This road is suitable for birding from your car, on foot, or by bicycle. The land on either side of the road is private. The area receives heavy agricultural use during the growing season.

DIRECTIONS: This area is just north of the center of Southbury, and about twelve miles southwest of Waterbury. In Southbury, at the northern intersection of Routes 67 and 6, go west on Route 67 for 0.2 mile, and left on Crook Horn Road. The best birding is about one mile down Crook Horn Road at the manure piles.

SOUTHBURY: GEORGE C. WALDO STATE PARK

HABITATS

FOREST: hardwoods, hardwoods/hemlock, hemlock;
LAKE/POND: lake, deep water, wooded shore;
River/stream: seasonal streams;
Open terrestrial: small tall grass field with cedars;
Marsh/swamp/bog: shrubby hardwood swamp, hardwood swamp.

This is a small (150 acre) and undeveloped state park that lies along the shore of Lake Lillinonah (a portion of the Housatonic River which has been dammed). The major habitats within the park include forest along the lake, together with interior forest communities.

SEASONS/BIRDS

SPRING MIGRATION: water birds, LAND BIRDS;
NESTING SEASON: LAND BIRDS;
FALL MIGRATION: water birds, LAND BIRDS;
Winter: land birds.

Considering the small size of this park, a surprising variety of species occur here. This is an especially good site for nesting forest-interior species, including red-shouldered hawk, barred owl, gnatcatcher, pileated woodpecker, wood thrush, veery, scarlet tanager, solitary, yellow-throated and red-eyed vireos, black-throated green and worm-eating warblers. Saw-whet owl is quite regular in the hemlocks.

GETTING AROUND
Birding methods: WALK.

There is one main trail that leads from the park entrance to the lake, and a few poorly-maintained side trails.

DIRECTIONS: This park is on the east side of Lake Lillinonah, about midway between Danbury and Waterbury, and about a mile north of the Shepaug Dam.

To get there from I-84 westbound: take exit 14, turn right at the end of the ramp and go a few yards to a traffic light; turn left on Main Street South which goes parallel to I-84 for 1.0 mile, at which point it turns sharply left and crosses over I-84. At the far end of this bridge, turn right on Fish Rock Road. Follow Fish Rock Road (which becomes River Road) for 3.0 miles, first bearing right and crossing back over I-84, and then following the east bank of the Housatonic River. (Do not turn left from River Road onto a bridge over the river.) Just before you reach the Shepaug Dam turn right on Purchase Brook Road and go for 0.9 mile to a barway on the left at a woods road leading into the forest. This is the park entrance.

To get there from I-84 eastbound: take exit 13 and go right on River Road for 3.0 miles as it follows the east bank of the river. Just before reaching the Shepaug Dam, turn right on Purchase Brook Road and go for 0.9 mile to a barway on the left. This is the park entrance.

SOUTHBURY: JANIE PIERCE PARK

HABITATS
FOREST: hardwoods, mountain laurel, scattered mixed conifers;

LAKE/POND: pond, shallow water, point, shore of herbaceous marsh, shrubs and hardwoods;

MARSH/SWAMP/BOG: cattail, mixed herbaceous and shrub marsh; shrub and shrubby hardwood swamp; dead wood;

River/stream; perennial stream, several seasonal streams, hardwood streambelts;

Open terrestrial: shrubby field.

This is a town park that surrounds a pond with varied wetlands nearby. The pond/wetland area is within a forest that is composed of hardwoods (mostly oaks). In addition to the edges created by the shore of the pond and the wetlands, there are very productive edges on either side of the driveway into the park, as it passes through the forest, areas of shrubs and a shrubby field.

SEASONS/BIRDS
SPRING MIGRATION: water birds, marsh birds, shore birds, LAND BIRDS;

Nesting season: water birds, land birds;

FALL MIGRATION: water birds, marsh birds, shore birds, LAND BIRDS;

Winter: land birds.

The spring migration is good for land birds, plus there are a few common species of water birds and an occasional great blue or green-backed heron. The nesting season occurs at a time when entrance to the park is restricted to Southbury residents. During the fall migration a wide variety of land birds pass through this park, including lots of warblers, thrushes and sparrows. As in the spring, there are a few of the standard water bird species and sometimes a great blue or green-backed heron or great egret. In winter, expect to see a few local resident species, including red-tailed and sharp-shinned hawks, great horned and screech owls. A red-headed woodpecker stayed here during the winter of 1994-95.

GETTING AROUND
Birding methods: car, walk.
There are two paths - one that follows the north shore of the pond, and goes between the pond and some nearby wetlands, and another that goes along the west side of the park through a larger wetland. The edges by the driveway can be birded by car or on foot. The park is restricted to use by town residents, and definitely should not be entered by outsiders during the period of heavy local use during the warm months. In addition, when the skating is good, the park receives frequent local use during the winter. In order to see the birds and avoid disturbing town residents, the best times to go here are late September, October, November and April.

DIRECTIONS: This site is about two miles north of the center of Southbury, and just south of the New Haven/Litchfield County line. To get there from the northern intersection of Routes 67 and 6, go north on Route 67 for 1.0 mile, and right on Transylvania Road for 0.5 mile to the park entrance on the right.

SOUTHBURY: SHEPAUG DAM/RIVER ROAD

HABITATS
RIVER/STREAM: river, fast and slow water; gravel bars; streambelt with areas that are marshy, shrubby, wooded and developed;
OPEN TERRESTRIAL: tilled, short grass, tall grass, mixed herbaceous and shrubby fields; shrubby and wooded edges, juniper hedgerows, cedars;
FOREST: hardwoods, hardwoods/white pine, hardwoods/hemlock, white pine, flood plain;
LAKE/POND: lake, deep water, wooded shore; pond, shore of shrub marsh; seasonal pools;
Marsh/swamp/bog: mixed herbaceous marsh (backwater of river), hardwood swamp;
Other: dam, rocky slope.
Shepaug Dam is a hydroelectric facility and recreation area on the Housatonic River. In winter, when power is being generated, there is an area of open water below the dam, even in the coldest weather. The area immediately around the dam includes a section of the Housatonic River, flood plain and upland forest, a steep wooded hillside, and a variety of fields and edges. Also included here is River Road, as it winds up from I-84 along the east (or north) bank of the Housatonic River (this stretch is known as Lake Zoar). It goes past flood plain and upland forests, a pond and agricultural fields.

In addition, the dam and the area immediately around it are within a larger area of over 5,000 acres of excellent habitat; this area includes George C. Waldo State Park, also in Southbury and described separately, the Paugussett State Forest (Northern Block) and several other nearby sites that encompass an area on the west (or south) side of the Housatonic River, above and below the Shepaug Dam. Sites across the river are described separately under Newtown in Fairfield County.

SEASONS/BIRDS
SPRING MIGRATION: gulls, WATER BIRDS, marsh birds, shore birds, LAND BIRDS;
NESTING SEASON: WATER BIRDS, marsh birds, shore birds, LAND BIRDS;
FALL MIGRATION: gulls, WATER BIRDS, marsh birds, shore birds, LAND BIRDS;
WINTER: gulls, WATER BIRDS, marsh birds, LAND BIRDS.

The Shepaug Dam is justly famous as the best site in inland Connecticut at which to see bald eagles in winter. The open water just below the dam attracts the eagles, which hunt for fish in this part of the river. They may arrive as early as December, and generally leave during March. In recent years, there have usually been five to ten eagles seen each day during this period, with 28 being the highest one-day count.

Shepaug Dam is a top birding site for other reasons as well. In winter, the open water downstream from the dam attracts not only bald eagle, but an interesting variety of water birds, including American wigeon, ring-necked duck, both scaups, common goldeneye, hooded and common mergansers, as well as additional species that are irregular or rare in occurrence. Gulls also occur here, including lesser black-backed and Iceland. In addition to bald eagle, other raptors occur here - harrier, goshawk, sharp-shinned, Cooper's and rough-legged hawks, and great horned owl.

Unusual species occur throughout the year in the habitats near the Shepaug Dam. Common merganser has been seen during the summer, and may nest in the area. Common loon, black-crowned night heron, great egret, double-crested cormorant, osprey and white-winged scoter have all occurred in summer as non-breeders. Confirmed nesters include orchard oriole, brown thrasher, prairie warbler, indigo bunting, both cuckoos, great horned and barred owls, and the largest cliff swallow colony in Connecticut.

For birding throughout the year, it is well to think of the Shepaug Dam and adjacent Housatonic River as part of a larger birding area that also includes George C. Waldo State Park, the Northern Block of the Paugussett State Forest, and other sites in Newtown on the west side of the Housatonic River. Within this large area, it is possible to find, as migrants, nesters or winter visitors, an impressive species variety that includes: 14 diurnal raptors, four owls, seven woodpeckers, six flycatchers, six swallows, five vireos, 28 warblers and 11 sparrows.

GETTING AROUND
Birding methods: CAR, WALK, bike.

During the winter when eagles are present, the Shepaug Dam Eagle Observation Area is open on specified days (Wednesday, Saturday and Sunday at the time of writing) by reservation only (call 1-800-368-8954); all activities are confined to the upper area at the observation building, and no one is allowed out of their vehicle between Purchase Brook Road and the upper parking lot. During the spring and fall, the Eagle Observation Area itself is not open to the public. During the summer (from Memorial Day until Labor Day), the entire area is open, but vehicles must park in the lower lot. In addition, the other nearby areas (Waldo Park, Paugussett Forest and other sites in Newtown) are open all year (with a few exceptions).

It is possible to drive along the Housatonic River on River Road for three miles, with birding opportunities along the way (but be careful; traffic is heavy and fast along this road). There are several trails that lead through habitats in the vicinity of the Shepaug Dam. Most of the habitats within Waldo State Park, the Paugussett Forest and other sites on the west side of the river can only be reached by trails.

DIRECTIONS (see Map 3): The Shepaug Dam is on the Housatonic River, about midway between Danbury and Waterbury.

To get to the Recreation and Eagle Observation Area from I-84 westbound: take exit 14, turn right at the end of the ramp and go a few yards to a traffic light; turn left on Main Street South which goes parallel to I-84 for 1.0 mile, at which point it turns sharply left and crosses over I-84. At the far end of this bridge, turn right on Fish Rock Road. Follow Fish Rock Road (which becomes River Road) for 3.0 miles, first as it bears right and crosses back over I-84, and then follows the east bank of the Housatonic River to the dam. (Do not turn left from River Road onto a bridge over the river.) At the end of River Road, near the dam, go through the first gate to the check-in vehicle (winter) or to the lower parking lot (summer). **To get to the Eagle Observation Area from I-84 eastbound:** take exit 13, go right on River Road and then proceed as above.

SOUTHBURY: SOUTHBURY TRAINING SCHOOL POND

HABITATS
LAKE/POND: pond, shrubby island, shore of short grass and shrubs;
Forest: white pine grove;
Open terrestrial: short grass, tall grass and mixed herbaceous fields, shrubby edge;
River/stream: streams, grassy and shrubby streambelts;
Marsh/swamp/bog: shrub swamp.
The centerpiece of this site is a pond - most of its shore is covered by shrubs, and there is a shrub swamp by the inlet. Nearby, there is a grove of white pines. Most of the rest of the area is lawn.

SEASONS/BIRDS
SPRING MIGRATION: WATER BIRDS, marsh birds, shore birds, land birds;
Nesting season: water birds, marsh birds, shore birds, land birds;
FALL MIGRATION: gulls, WATER BIRDS, marsh birds, shore birds, land birds;
Winter: gulls, water birds, land birds.
Water birds are the main attraction at this site. The best periods are in the early spring from ice-out until mid-April, and (even better) from mid-October to freeze-up. Early winter can be good as long as there is open water. Geese are a specialty at this pond; in addition to the usual Canada, snow goose is frequently here; greater white-fronted and blue-phase geese have been seen a number of times. Other water bird species that frequently occur include mallard, black, wood and ring-necked ducks, coot and hooded merganser. Great blue heron occurs in the spring and fall migrations, great egret sometimes in the fall, and green-backed heron is a nester. Spotted sandpiper and killdeer also nest here, and solitary sandpiper occurs in migration. This is also a good hawk spot: harrier, sharp-shinned and Cooper's hawks are seen in migration; bald eagle in winter and sometimes spring and fall. Throughout the year, look for great horned owl in the white pines.

GETTING AROUND
Birding methods: car.
Stay by your car in the parking area; the security guards do not want people wandering about. Use a scope to get good looks at birds on and near the pond.

DIRECTIONS: This site is about ten miles west of Waterbury. From I-84 exit 14, go north on Route 172 for 2.9 miles to where the pond is visible on the right, with parking just beyond, also on the right.

SOUTHBURY/OXFORD: KETTLETOWN STATE PARK

HABITATS
FOREST: hemlock, hardwoods/hemlock, cedar, white pine, hardwoods, flood plain;
Open terrestrial: short grass field, shrubby edge;
Lake/pond: lake, cove, deep water, wooded shore, beach;
River/stream: streams, hardwood and hemlock streambelts;
Other: rocky slope.
This park occupies 492 acres of hilly country on the east shore of Lake Zoar (a portion of the Housatonic River which has been dammed). Habitats include the deep water of Lake Zoar, a cove, wooded shoreline, various types of forest, a hemlock ravine, mowed open areas, and shrubby edges.

SEASONS/BIRDS
SPRING MIGRATION: water birds, LAND BIRDS;
Nesting season: land birds;
FALL MIGRATION: water birds, LAND BIRDS;
Winter: land birds.
The spring and fall migrations are the best seasons here. The water birds that occur on Lake Zoar are pretty much the common species, but land birds make a visit worthwhile. Bald eagle and other raptors occur here in spring and fall, along with a good variety of migrant thrushes, vireos, warblers and other land birds. The edges provide especially good birding for these migrants. Nesting species include worm-eating, black-throated green and prairie warblers, and Louisiana waterthrush. In winter, look in the cedars for owls - great horned, barred, screech and saw-whet (look on the ground beneath the cedars for pellets). Bald eagle and other land birds, including lingering migrants, can also be seen here in winter. The habitat is good for winter finches in years when they come to Connecticut.

GETTING AROUND
Birding methods: CAR, WALK, BIKE, SKI.
The park driveways go through most of the park. In addition, there are several service roads to walk, as well as a number of trails (that have steep ups and downs). In winter, the driveway is barred, but can be walked or skied. In summer, the park gets quite crowded, and there is an entrance fee.

DIRECTIONS: This park is on the east shore of the Housatonic River, about five miles south of Southbury. To get there from I-84 exit 14, go south and bear left onto Georges Hill Road; go south on it for 2.7 miles to the park entrance on the right.

WALLINGFORD: COMMUNITY LAKE

HABITATS
OPEN TERRESTRIAL: short grass and shrubby field, shrubby edge;
Lake/pond: pond, grassy and shrubby shore; seasonal pools;
River/stream; river, slow, deep water, mud banks, mixed herbaceous, shrubby and wooded streambelt;
Marsh/swamp/bog: mixed herbaceous and shrub marsh, shrub swamp;
Forest: flood plain.

This is a fine open space area right near the center of a city (Wallingford). It contains open and edge habitats interspersed with pockets of wetlands, one large and several smaller ponds, a river (the Quinnipiac) and riparian forest.

SEASONS/BIRDS
SPRING MIGRATION: water birds, marsh birds, shore birds, LAND BIRDS;
NESTING SEASON: water birds, marsh birds, shore birds, LAND BIRDS;
FALL MIGRATION: water birds, marsh birds, shore birds, LAND BIRDS;
Winter: land birds.

The variety of habitats cause a nice species diversity to occur here, including open and edge species, as well as wetland and wetland-associated species that are drawn by the ponds and their shores, the river and its streambelt. During the spring and fall migrations, a variety of edge-species pass through, and at this site they are easy to see. During May, there are lots of warblers in the riparian forest, as well as swallows and nighthawks that hunt over the water. Nesters include wood duck, green-backed heron, screech owl, spotted sandpiper, brown thrasher, willow flycatcher, white-eyed and warbling vireos, yellow warbler, yellowthroat, indigo bunting and orchard oriole. The fall migration usually brings a good variety of birds, especially sparrows.

GETTING AROUND
Birding methods: walk.

This is a town park that is open to the public. There are trails that lead north from the park, but they may be overgrown, muddy, and are loaded with ticks. There is also a path around the pond in similar condition.

DIRECTIONS: This park is on the western edge of Wallingford center, immediately east of the Wilbur Cross Parkway. **From the Parkway southbound,** take exit 65; at the end of the exit ramp, go south (left) on Route 150 for 0.6 mile to the entrance on the left. **From the parkway northbound,** take exit 65; at the end of the ramp, go south (right) on Route 150 for 0.1 mile to the entrance on the left.

WALLINGFORD: WHARTON BROOK STATE PARK

HABITATS
Forest: hardwoods, mixed conifers, cedar, pitch pine, sand plain;
Open terrestrial: short grass field, wooded edge;
Lake/pond: pond, shrubby and wooded shore;
River/stream: stream, shrubby and wooded streambelt.

Much of this 96-acre park is developed, with mowed grounds and widely separated groves of mature oaks and other deciduous trees, several groves of conifers, a pond and a small stream (Wharton Brook). The northern part of the park (to the left of the entrance) is wooded and includes a sand plain community of pitch pine, black and white oaks, and black cherry.

SEASONS/BIRDS

Spring migration: land birds;
Nesting season: land birds;
Fall migration: land birds;
Winter: land birds.

This is a nice place in which to see a standard mix of land birds, during migration and the nesting season. Nesting species include great horned owl, prairie warbler and orchard oriole. In winter, look in the cedars for screech and saw-whet owls.

GETTING AROUND

Birding methods: walk.

There are good trails and the walking is easy. However, the noise from a nearby highway does hinder birding by ear.

DIRECTIONS: This park is in Wallingford, midway between New Haven and Meriden. To get there from I-91, take exit 13 (which becomes the Wharton Brook Connector) for 0.9 mile, left on Route 5 for 0.4 mile to the park entrance on the left.

WATERBURY: RIFLE RANGE POND

HABITATS

LAKE/POND: pond, shallow water, shore of shrub and mixed herbaceous marsh, shrubs, hardwoods, hardwoods/white pine, deadwood;
Forest: hardwoods, hardwoods/white pine, white pine/hemlock, white pine, mountain laurel;
Open terrestrial: shrubby field, wooded edge;
Marsh/swamp/bog: small deadwood swamp (backwater of pond);
Other: cliff, ledges.

This site consists primarily of a shallow, beaver-influenced pond. The shoreline that surrounds it includes a great variety of habitat types, including varied forest communities with a mountain laurel shrub layer in places, and also shrubby fields and edges associated with a power line.

SEASONS/BIRDS

SPRING MIGRATION: water birds, marsh birds, shore birds, LAND BIRDS;
Nesting season: water birds, land birds;
FALL MIGRATION: water birds, marsh birds, shore birds, LAND BIRDS;
Winter: land birds.

The varied shoreline habitats around the pond cause this area to provide a nice variety of land bird species, especially during the spring and fall migrations. The spring migration includes a mix of the standard species that you would expect to see in these types of forest and open terrestrial habitats, plus some water birds, and great blue heron. Nesters include both northern and southern forest-dwelling species: Canada and black-throated green warblers, Carolina wren, red-bellied woodpecker and Louisiana waterthrush. Hooded warbler is a possibility. Among the edge and shrub dwellers known to nest here are indigo bunting, brown thrasher, prairie warbler and field sparrow. The fall migration is similar to the spring migration, with the addition of nighthawk and lots of tree, barn, bank and rough-winged swallows over the pond. Residents throughout the year include pileated woodpecker and both screech and great horned owls (in opposite ends of the area).

GETTING AROUND
Birding methods: car, walk.
One of the appeals of this site is the ease with which much of it can be seen. Parts of the pond and its surroundings can be seen from near your car; two fairly good trails offer ways to bird the interior of the area. They go past the southwest end of the pond and into the surrounding Mattatuck State Forest. Note that this area is open to hunting in the fall. Traffic is annoying during rush hours.

DIRECTIONS: This site lies just north of the city of Waterbury, almost on the Plymouth town line. To get there, start at the intersection of Route 262 and Thomaston Avenue, near the east bank of the Naugatuck River. Go in an easterly direction away from the river on Route 262 "north" (do not go north along the river on Route 262 "south"). Follow Route 262 for 0.3 mile to where Rifle Range Pond is visible on the right side of the road. There is a place to park on the left side.

WEST HAVEN: PROSPECT BEACH/BRADLEY POINT

HABITATS
COASTAL: sandy beach, rocky shore, rocky point, salt water tidal cove, mud flat, Long Island Sound;
Open terrestrial: short grass field, seasonal pools, shrubby edge.
This is a sandy beach and rocky point that overlook New Haven Harbor and Long Island Sound. There are extensive mud flats offshore, and often there are rain pools on the lawn that lies just behind the beach.

SEASONS/BIRDS
SPRING MIGRATION: gulls, terns, WATER BIRDS, marsh birds, SHORE BIRDS, land birds;
Nesting season: gulls, terns;
FALL MIGRATION: gulls, terns, WATER BIRDS, SHORE BIRDS, land birds;
WINTER: gulls, WATER BIRDS, shore birds, land birds.
This is known as a place to visit in the fall, winter and spring to see water birds and land birds, occasionally including horned lark, snow bunting and Lapland longspur. Offshore, red-throated loon and horned grebe are regular October-April. Inshore during the same period, American wigeon feeds along the rocks, and is occasionally joined by a Eurasian wigeon. During the spring and fall migrations, shore birds feed on the mud flat and at the rain pools (stilt sandpiper has been seen here). A variety of gulls are here all year.

DIRECTIONS: This site is in West Haven on the western shore of New Haven Harbor. To get there from Milford at the western intersection of Routes 1 and 162, go east on Route 162 for 5.4 miles to the point at which Route 162 passes a small cove and beach where the Oyster River enters Long Island Sound. At the traffic light, go right on Ocean Avenue and follow this road along the coast for 2.1 miles to parking at Prospect Beach, and for another 0.3 mile to parking at Bradley Point.

WEST HAVEN: SANDY POINT

HABITATS
COASTAL: sand spit, sandy beach, sand and mud flats, tidal cove, tidal creek, dunes, low salt marsh, tidal cove.

Sandy Point is a narrow, mile-long sand spit that extends halfway across New Haven Harbor, and includes a highly productive mix of habitat types. It also provides a place from which to view water birds in the harbor.

SEASONS/BIRDS
SPRING MIGRATION: GULLS, TERNS, WATER BIRDS, MARSH BIRDS, SHORE BIRDS, land birds;
Nesting season: gulls, terns, water birds, marsh birds, shore birds, land birds;
FALL MIGRATION: GULLS, TERNS, WATER BIRDS, MARSH BIRDS, SHORE BIRDS, LAND BIRDS;
WINTER: GULLS, WATER BIRDS, LAND BIRDS.

This is one of Connecticut's outstanding coastal areas, at which it is possible to see a great variety of gulls (various species at any time), terns (spring, summer and fall), water birds (fall, winter and spring), waders (spring, summer and fall), shore birds (spring and fall), and land birds (fall, winter and spring). Uncommon species among all these bird groups frequently occur here. Clapper rail and sharp-tailed sparrow nest in the marsh; piping plover and least tern nest on the beach and in the dunes. Snow bunting, Lapland longspur and horned lark are regular here mid-November through mid-March. Harrier, merlin and peregrine falcon have been seen during the fall, winter and spring, and snowy owl in winter. The best periods to visit this site are September to early December, and March through April, but winter is also good.

GETTING AROUND
Birding methods: car, WALK.

Parts of Sandy Point can be seen from the parking area by using a scope, but it really must be walked to be fully appreciated. During the nesting season, the dunes are fenced off to protect piping plover and least tern nests. At other times, the point can be walked to its end (about one mile). There are two options for walking. One is on the "inside", going due north from the parking lot, then east along the northern edge of the marsh and out to the upper part of the point. The other possibility is to walk south from the parking lot, then east over the creek, and along the "outer" beach on the south side of the point. At low tide, it is possible to make a big loop without getting too wet. During the period May to Labor Day, there is a parking fee.

DIRECTIONS (see Map 52): Sandy Point extends into New Haven Harbor from the west, about two miles south of the center of New Haven. To get there from I-95, take exit 44; follow the exit ramp onto Kimberly Avenue; go south on Kimberly Avenue for 0.5 mile; left on First Avenue for 1.1 miles to a parking area on the left, at the base of Sandy Point.

WEST HAVEN: WEST HAVEN BOAT RAMP

HABITATS
COASTAL: brackish tidal cove; gravel, sand and mud beach and mud flats.
This site overlooks a sheltered part of upper New Haven Harbor that has a short stretch of sand, gravel and mud beach, and exposed flats at low tide.

SEASONS/BIRDS
SPRING MIGRATION: gulls, terns, WATER BIRDS, marsh birds, SHORE BIRDS, land birds;
Nesting season: gulls, terns, water birds;
FALL MIGRATION: gulls, terns, WATER BIRDS, marsh birds, SHORE BIRDS, land birds;
WINTER: WATER BIRDS.
In the fall, winter and spring, look here for water birds. Although it is overrun with swans, it is still especially good for scaup, canvasback, common goldeneye and bufflehead. Also, in the spring and fall, it is a good site for shore birds.

GETTING AROUND
Birding methods: car.
It is possible to drive virtually to the edge of the water, from which point most of the cove can be seen. A scope is helpful.

DIRECTIONS (see Map 52): The West Haven Boat Ramp is on the western shore of New Haven Harbor about two miles south of the center of New Haven, and just north of Sandy Point. To get there from I-95, take exit 44; follow the exit ramp onto Kimberly Avenue; go south on Kimberly Avenue for 0.5 mile; left on First Avenue for 0.8 mile to the boat ramp on the left.

WEST HAVEN: WEST RIVER (KIMBERLY AVENUE BRIDGE)

HABITATS
COASTAL: brackish tidal cove, brackish tidal river.
This site overlooks a sheltered cove where the West River enters the upper end of New Haven Harbor.

SEASONS/BIRDS
SPRING MIGRATION: gulls, terns, WATER BIRDS;
Nesting season: gulls, terns;
FALL MIGRATION: gulls, terns, WATER BIRDS;
WINTER: gulls, WATER BIRDS.
From November to March, a nice variety of water birds occur here, often including canvas-back and redhead, and sometimes lesser scaup. Gulls and terns also feed here.

GETTING AROUND
Birding methods: car.
You can park your car virtually at the water's edge.

DIRECTIONS (see Map 52): The West River enters the northwestern part of New Haven Harbor about two miles south of the center of New Haven. To get there from I-95, take exit 44; follow the exit ramp onto Kimberly Avenue; go south on Kimberly Avenue for 0.3 mile to the first traffic light; turn sharp right onto a short road that reaches a dead end at the shore of the river by the Coast Guard Auxiliary Station.

WEST HAVEN: WEST SHORE BEACH/SAINT JOHN'S BY THE SEA

HABITATS
COASTAL: sandy beach, breakwater, rocky shore, tidal cove, Long Island Sound. This is a long sandy beach with breakwaters that overlooks New Haven Harbor and Long Island Sound.

SEASONS/BIRDS
SPRING MIGRATION: gulls, terns, WATER BIRDS, marsh birds, shore birds, land birds;
Nesting season: gulls, terns, marsh birds, land birds;
FALL MIGRATION: gulls, terns, WATER BIRDS, marsh birds, shore birds, land birds;
WINTER: WATER BIRDS, land birds.
This site is best in winter, but is also good in the spring and fall. The water birds that occur here include loons, grebes and occasionally Eurasian wigeon; in spring, summer and fall waders feed along the breakwaters; in the spring and fall, there are also some shore birds.

GETTING AROUND
Birding methods: car, walk.
It is possible to see a part of this stretch of coast from where you park; or you can walk the beach to get better looks.

DIRECTIONS (see Map 52): This site is on the western shore of New Haven Harbor in West Haven. To get there from Milford at the western intersection of Routes 1 and 162, go east on Route 162 for 5.4 miles to the point at which Route 162 passes a small cove and beach where the Oyster River enters Long Island Sound. At the traffic light, go right on Ocean Avenue for 1.1 miles and park in an area on the right, across the road from a church (Saint John's By The Sea).

WEST HAVEN/ORANGE: MALTBY LAKES

HABITATS
>**FOREST:** white pine, white pine/hemlock, mixed conifers, hardwoods, mountain laurel;
>**LAKE/POND:** ponds, shores of white pine, hemlock and conifer mixtures, exposed muddy bottom (occasional).

This site includes three connected reservoirs that have irregular shapes with bays and points, and undeveloped, wooded shores. In some years during the late summer and fall, the water levels of the reservoirs are drawn down and expose areas of mud along the shore.

SEASONS/BIRDS
>**SPRING MIGRATION:** WATER BIRDS, marsh birds, shore birds, LAND BIRDS;
>**Nesting season:** marsh birds, land birds;
>**FALL MIGRATION:** WATER BIRDS, MARSH BIRDS, shore birds, LAND BIRDS;
>**Winter:** land birds.

This site offers nice species variety during spring, summer and fall. The spring and fall migrations usually produce water birds including gadwall, wood duck, common and hooded mergansers; marsh birds including black-crowned night heron, little blue heron, great blue heron and great egret; land birds including a variety of woodland warblers and osprey. If the water levels of the reservoirs drop enough during the fall shore bird migration, a variety of shore bird species may come to feed at the exposed mud along the shores. Nesters include a good mix of land birds, including scarlet tanager and such northern species as magnolia warbler. In winter, look for winter finches in the conifers.

GETTING AROUND
>**Birding methods:** car, WALK.

This area can be entered only with a Regional Water Authority Recreation Permit; with the permit comes a detailed trail map of the area (see Chapter 12: "Sources of additional Information"). There is a four-mile network of trails to the pond shores and through the woods. Lack of crowds makes this a good area in which to bird during the nesting season.

DIRECTIONS: These ponds lie on the West Haven/Orange town line, north of the city of West Haven. It is best to approach from the east, from the intersection of Routes 34 and 122. Go west on Route 34 for 0.8 mile to the entrance and a parking area on the right.

WOLCOTT: PETERSON PARK/MATTATUCK TRAIL

HABITATS
>**Forest:** hardwoods, hardwoods/hemlock, cedar, mountain laurel, vine tangles and thickets;
>**Open terrestrial:** short grass field, shrubby and wooded edges;
>**River/stream:** perennial stream, seasonal streams, seasonal seeps; wooded streambelts;
>**Marsh/swamp/bog:** small shrubby hardwood swamp including seasonal pool.

Part of this rather small park is developed for recreation; the mowed playing fields of that portion of it are surrounded by wooded and shrubby edges that contain lots of berry-producing shrubs. Behind these edges there are varied hardwood and conifer forest habitats with mountain laurel thickets and greenbriar tangles, together with occasional stands of cedar. There is also a perennial stream (the Mad River) with a wooded streambelt (hardwoods and hardwoods/hemlock) plus several seasonal streams and seeps.

SEASONS/BIRDS
SPRING MIGRATION: LAND BIRDS;
Nesting season: land birds;
FALL MIGRATION: LAND BIRDS;
Winter: land birds.

A standard mix of land bird.species occur in this area during the spring and fall migrations and the nesting season. Nesters include great horned owl, red-bellied woodpecker, hermit thrush, Louisiana waterthrush, and possibly Canada warbler. Activity tapers off in winter, but sometimes there are enough remaining berries to attract lingering migrants during early winter.

GETTING AROUND
Birding methods: WALK.

The central part of this park can be birded by walking around the edges of the open playing fields. This park receives heavy recreational use, so that it is best to avoid weekends and evenings during the warm months. However, a bonus at this site is the Mattatuck Trail, that can be walked from the park through forest habitats north toward Plymouth. The main trail is in good condition, and there are several side trails that vary in condition. These trails provide a way to get away from the crowds.

DIRECTIONS: This park is in Wolcott, about five miles northeast of Waterbury. To get there from the intersection of Routes 69 and 322, go north on Route 69 for 0.3 mile, and left on Mad River Road for 0.3 mile to the park entrance on the right.

WOLCOTT: SCOVILLE RESERVOIR

HABITATS
LAKE/POND: lake, cove, point, island, shrubby and wooded shore;
Marsh/swamp/bog: shrub marsh, shrub, shrubby hardwood and hardwood swamp.

This reservoir has an irregular shape, with coves, points and islands. The shoreline is mostly wooded with shrubby sections and one wetland area on the east side.

SEASONS/BIRDS
SPRING MIGRATION: WATER BIRDS, marsh birds, shore birds, land birds;
Nesting season: water birds, land birds;
FALL MIGRATION: WATER BIRDS, marsh birds, shore birds, land birds;
Winter: land birds.

Migrating water birds are the attraction at this site, especially during the periods November/December and March/April. Common mergansers and ring-necked ducks are the most frequently seen, but there is always the potential for other species. Great blue and green-backed herons occur in the wetland just off the east shore in the spring and fall, and common land bird species can be seen during most of the year.

GETTING AROUND
Birding methods: car.
Birding this site is a matter of driving entirely around the reservoir, and stopping to view the water (and the wetland in one place) where it is possible to do so safely. There are no trails, and the public is not allowed on the land around the reservoir.

DIRECTIONS: This reservoir is in Wolcott about five miles northeast of Waterbury. To get there from Wolcott, at the intersection of Routes 69 and 322, go south on Route 69 for 1.7 miles, left on Nichols Road for 0.7 mile to the Woodtick Recreation complex where there is parking, and the south end of the reservoir can be seen. From here, you can either drive clockwise around the reservoir by taking right turns, or counterclockwise, by taking left turns. There are occasional places where you can pull off the road and view the water. At one point near the easternmost cove of the reservoir, you can look over the wetland that is across the road from the reservoir.

WOODBRIDGE: COMMUNITY GARDEN

HABITATS
OPEN TERRESTRIAL: tilled, short grass, mixed herbaceous and shrubby fields;
MARSH/SWAMP/BOG: shrubby hardwood swamp;
Forest: hardwoods;
Lake/pond: seasonal pools;
River/stream: seasonal streams.
This is a nice medium-sized open space conservation area. About half of it is various types of open terrestrial habitat, and the other half is a mix of shrubby hardwood swamp and hardwood forest. Consequently there is plenty of edge.

SEASONS/BIRDS
SPRING MIGRATION: shore birds, LAND BIRDS;
Nesting season: land birds;
FALL MIGRATION: shore birds, LAND BIRDS;
Winter: land birds.
The spring and fall migrations bring a nice variety of open country, edge and forest land bird species to this site. Seasonal pools in the tilled fields during the spring also attract shore birds. Breeding species include barred owl, prairie warbler and indigo bunting. Fall is really good for sparrows. Winter may produce lingering land birds.

GETTING AROUND
Birding methods: car, WALK.
The open fields can be viewed from a car, but the majority of the property, including a nice network of interconnecting trails, has to be travelled on foot.

DIRECTIONS: This site is in Woodbridge, several miles northwest of New Haven. In Woodbridge, from the intersection of Routes 114 and 63, head west (or south according to the sign) on Route 114 for 1.0 mile, left on Beecher Road for 0.2 mile to the area on the right.

WOODBRIDGE: KONOLDS POND

HABITATS
> **LAKE/POND:** pond, shallow water, marshy, shrubby and wooded shore;
> **Marsh/swamp/bog:** herbaceous and shrub marsh.

This shallow pond is being taken over by emergent plant growth and is rapidly succeeding to an herbaceous marsh. At the same time, the shrub marsh that occupies much of the shoreline is extending into the pond. At its present stage of succession, Konolds Pond is a very rich ecosystem.

SEASONS/BIRDS
> **SPRING MIGRATION:** WATER BIRDS, marsh birds, land birds;
> **Nesting season:** water birds, marsh birds, land birds;
> **FALL MIGRATION:** WATER BIRDS, marsh birds, land birds;
> **Winter:** land birds.

In spite of its drawbacks (see "Getting Around" below), Konolds Pond is an excellent place to see water birds, especially during the spring and fall migrations, with March/April and November being the best periods. Species that are often present include mallard, black duck, wood duck, gadwall, shoveler, both teals, common and hooded merganser. Green-backed heron is a nester; post-breeding great egret and great blue heron occur here in late summer and fall. A variety of land birds feed in the trees and shrubs around the shore of the pond throughout the spring, summer and fall.

GETTING AROUND
> **Birding methods:** car, walk.

Unfortunately, it is difficult and even somewhat dangerous to bird at Konolds Pond, because at present the only way to see the pond is from Route 69, a heavily travelled road with only one place to park at all safely. Hopefully, the expansion and restoration of West Rock Ridge State Park will improve this situation. The noise of traffic on the highway makes it difficult to bird by ear.

DIRECTIONS (see Map 55): Konolds Pond lies at the foot of the towering cliffs of the western face of West Rock Ridge, and is less than five miles northwest of the center of New Haven. To get to the pond from Route 15 (the Wilbur Cross Parkway), take exit 59 and go north on Route 69 for 1.1 miles where there is a wide shoulder on which to park on the west side of Route 69 (across the highway from the pond).

Chapter 9

New London County

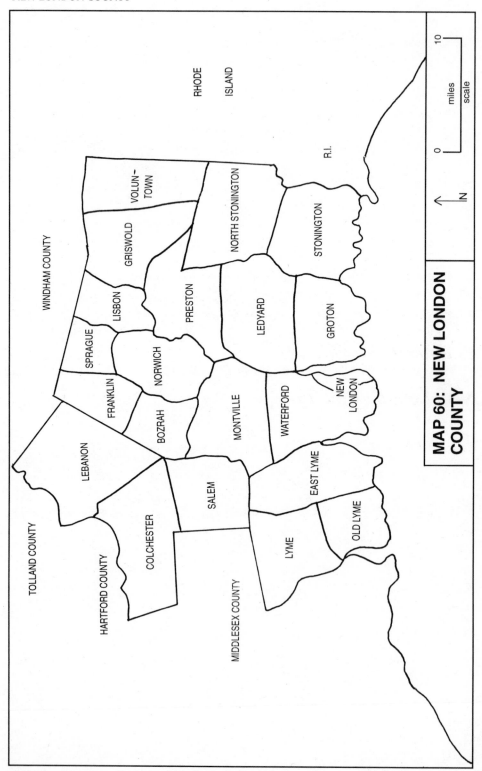

MAP 60: NEW LONDON COUNTY

TABLE 7: HABITATS AND SEASONS AT NEW LONDON COUNTY SITES

Habitats
- ● very good example
- ○ present, but not as significant

Seasons
- ● excellent during this season
- ○ less good during this season

	HABITATS							SEASONS			
	FOREST	OPEN	MARSH	LAKE	RIVER	COAST	OTHER	SPRING	NEST	FALL	WINTER
Tour of Old Lyme		○			○	●		●	●	●	●
Bozrah: Bear Hill WMA	○	●					○	●	○	●	○
Bozrah/Montville: Hopemead SP	○		○	○				○	●	○	○
Colchester: Babcock Pond WMA	○	○	●	●	○			○	○	○	○
East Lyme: Pattagansett Marshes						●		●	●	●	○
East Lyme: Rocky Neck SP	○	○				●		○	○	○	○
Franklin: Bailey's Ravine	●	○	○	○	●		●	○	○	○	○
Franklin: Franklin Swamp WMA	●	●	●	○	○		○	●	●	○	○
Griswold: Hopeville Pond SP	●			○				○	○	○	○
Groton: Avery Point		○				●		○	○	○	●
Groton: Bluff Point SP	○	●				●	●	●	●	●	●
Groton: Eastern Point						●		○	○	○	●
Groton: Haley Farm SP	○	●	○	○		●		●	○	●	○
Groton: Pequot Woods	●	○	○	○	○		○	○	○	○	○
Lebanon: Bartlett Brook WMA	○	●	●		○			●	○	●	○
Lebanon: Pease Brook WMA	●	●	○		○		○	●	●	●	○
Lebanon: Red Cedar Lake	●		○	●	○			●	●	○	○
Ledyard: Rose Hill WMA	○	●	○		○			●	●	●	○
Ledyard: Stoddard Hill SP	○	○		●				○	○	○	○
Ledyard et al: Poquetanuck Cove	○		●		●			○	○	○	○
Lyme: Chester/Hadlyme Ferry Landing	○	○	○	●				○	○	○	○
Lyme: Elys Ferry	○	○	○		○			○	○	○	○
Lyme: Hartman Park	●	●	●	○	○		○	●	●	●	●
Lyme: Lords Cove			●					●	●	●	●
Lyme: Nehantic SF	●		○	○	○			●	●	○	○
Lyme: Selden Cove/Selden Creek	●		●		●		●	●	●	●	●
Lyme: Whalebone Creek	○		●		●			●	●	●	●
Montville: Fort Shantok Park	○	●		○	●			●	●	●	●
Montville: Milo Light Preserve	●	○	○		○			○	○	○	○
New London: Connecticut Arboretum	●	●	○	○	●		○	●	●	●	○
North Stonington: Assekonk Swamp WMA	○	○	●	○				●	●	●	○
North Stonington: Patchaug SF	○	○		○	○			○	○	○	○
Old Lyme: Black Hall River	○				●	●		●	○	●	●
Old Lyme: DEP Marine Headquarters						○		○	○	○	○
Old Lyme: Four Mile River	○					○		○	○	○	○
Old Lyme: Griswold Point/Marsh						●		●	●	●	●
Old Lyme: Lieutenant River	○				○	○		●	○	●	○
Old Lyme: Smiths Neck/Great Island						●		●	●	●	●
Old Lyme: Smiths Neck Town Landing		●				●		●	○	●	○
Old Lyme: Watch Rock						●		●	●	●	●

TABLE 7: HABITATS AND SEASONS AT NEW LONDON COUNTY SITES (2)

Habitats ● very good example ○ present, but not as significant Seasons ● excellent during this season ○ less good during this season	HABITATS							SEASONS			
	FOREST	OPEN	MARSH	LAKE	RIVER	COAST	OTHER	SPRING	NEST	FALL	WINTER
Salem/Montville/Bozrah: Gardner Lake	○		○	●				○	○	○	○
Sprague: Waldo Tract	○	●	○		○		○	●	●	●	○
Stonington: Barn Island WMA	○	●	●			●		●	●	●	○
Stonington: Denison Pequotsepos NC	●	●	●	○	○			●	●	●	○
Stonington: Latimer Point						●		●	○	●	○
Stonington: Mystic River						●		●	○	●	●
Stonington: Stonington Point						●	○	○	○	○	○
Voluntown/Griswold: Patchaug SF	●	○	●	○	●		○	●	●	●	○
Waterford: Harkness SP/Goshen Cove		○				●		●	○	●	●
Waterford: Jordan Cove						●		○	○	○	○
Waterford: Millstone Point		○				●		●	○	●	○
Waterford: Waterford Beach Park		○				●		○	○	○	○

BIRDING IN NEW LONDON COUNTY

New London occupies the southeastern corner of Connecticut. It is bounded on the west by Middlesex County, on the north by Hartford, Tolland and Windham Counties, on the east by Rhode Island, and on the south by Long Island Sound. The major highways within it are I-95, I-395 and State Route 2.

The People

New London County has a population of 261,510 (#4 among Connecticut's eight counties, far below Hartford, Fairfield and New Haven), a land area of 669 square miles (third largest), giving it a population density of 393 people per square mile (#5 among the counties). New London's recent rate of population growth also ranks fifth among the counties. Outside of Lyme and Old Lyme, New London County is one of Connecticut's less affluent counties.

The Land

The southern third of New London County lies on Connecticut's Coastal Slope, and the northern two-thirds is part of the Eastern Uplands ecoregion. The rolling, hilly uplands are broken by many level to gently sloping valleys that lead down to the Coastal Slope. The Quinebaug and Shetucket Rivers flow from the north out of Windham County into New London County, where they join to form the Thames River that flows through a valley that is large, but without steep profile. Elevations in the county range from sea level along the coast and in the lower Thames River Valley up to 615' in the northeast corner of the county. Much of the land is forested by central hardwoods together with some white pine and hemlock; 17% of the county is in farmland.

The coast of New London County is more rocky than is the coast of counties to the west. It is also very irregular, with deep coves separated by prominant headlands and points. Tides are the smallest of any part of the Connecticut coast, with a range of less than three feet, compared with the range of over six feet that is typical of Fairfield County coastal areas. For this reason, New London County does not have intertidal areas as extensive as those farther west.

The climate of New London County along the coast is relatively mild, with cooler summers and milder winters than in inland areas of the county.

Public Areas and Birding Sites

New London County includes a great deal of public land - there are 15 state parks and three state forests, including 28,000-acre Patchaug, the largest in Connecticut. There are also numerous DEP wildlife management areas, of which eight are included as birding sites in this guide. In addition, there are many other public areas of interest to birders - town parks, nature sanctuaries, public landings on Long Island Sound and at other waterbodies.

The most densely developed areas of New London County lie along the coastline, and much of it is concentrated in the tri-city area of New London/Groton/Waterford. Along much of the rest of the coast, less dense residential development alternates with public natural areas. Inland, most of the countryside is still relatively open - some of it is farmland, but much of it is protected and open to the public. However, the Foxwood Casino in Ledyard has already had a profound impact on development and the character of that part of New London County, and this impact will undoubtedly increase with time.

For birders, by far the most important aspect of New London County is its coast on Long Island Sound, which at this eastern end of Connecticut, has an unspoiled quality suggestive of the coast of Maine. Several of Connecticut's best birding sites are at public areas on the coast of New London County - Barn Island Wildlife Management Area in Stonington, Bluff Point State Park and nearby Haley Farm, both in Groton. Each of these sites includes productive avian habitat, and also provides a view of a part of Long Island Sound that is a major migration corridor and wintering area for many water birds.

Another outstanding natural feature of New London County is the Lower Connecticut River, the valley through which it flows as it approaches Long Island Sound, and the estuary at Old Lyme, where it enters the Sound. This area includes an extraordinary constellation of superb coastal habitats - salt, brackish and fresh water tidal marshes, tidal creeks, mud flats and barrier beaches. And these habitats are in an area much of which is undeveloped and protected from future development. Several sites that include and provide access to these habitats are in Old Lyme: among them are Griswold Point and Griswold Marsh, Smiths Neck Landing and Great Island. Other fine sites are a short way up the river in Lyme; they include: Lords Cove, Selden Cove and Whalebone Creek.

However, the excellence of New London's coastal sites should not obscure the fact that there are fine inland areas as well.

The Patchaug State Forest in Voluntown lies at higher elevations in the northeastern part of the county, and provides suitable habitat for many forest-dwelling species, including northerners and species that require large areas of interior forest habitat. In addition, at nearby Hopeville Pond State Park there is one of Connecticut's finest sand plain forest communities.

The Patchaug State Forest also contains extensive wetlands, including two types of wetland that are uncommon in Connecticut: Atlantic white cedar swamp, and rhododendron swamp. The best single inland wetland in New London County is at Assakonk Swamp WMA in North Sonington.

Open terrestrial, shrub and edge habitats are well represented at Hartman Park in Lyme, Pease Brook Wildlife Management Area in Lebanon, Rose Hill WMA in Ledyard, as well as at Bluff Point State Park on the coast in Groton.

The Connecticut River, the Thames, the Shetucket, the Quinebuag and their tributaries provide bottomland and riparian habitat in an area of mild climate that attracts a rich diversity of bird life. The Connecticut Arboretum in New London and Waldo Tract in Sprague are good examples.

In a part of the state that is relatively flat overall, an abundance of ledge and cliff habitats can be found at one New London County site - Bailey's Ravine at Ayers Gap in Franklin.

Seasons for Birding

There is excellent birding at any time of year in New London County. The variety of habitats at sites throughout the county make for interesting birding during both migrations and the nesting season. Coastal sites provide interest during the winter, when there are fewer choices at inland areas. In addition, New London County can offer birders a good chance to see a number of species that are uncommon in other parts of the state.

Spring migration. Early in the spring (March and April), look for migrating water birds at sites along the coast (such as Avery Point, Eastern Point and Bluff Point, all in Groton, and Harkness Memorial Park and Goshen Cove in Waterford; and on major rivers (at sites such as the Mystic River in Stonington, Smiths Neck Landing, Great Island, the Lieutenant River, the Blackhall River and the Four Mile River, all in Old Lyme. A little later (April and May), look in both coastal and inland wetlands for the first marsh bird arrivals (try Bluff Point on the coast, and Assakonk Swamp inland in North Stonington). The peak of the shore bird migration occurs during May; go to sites along the coast such as Bluff Point in Groton, Great Island and Griswold Point in Old Lyme. In late April and May, migrating land birds can be seen almost anywhere, but in the early part of their migration focus on the edges of water bodies - along the coast and at ponds, marshes and rivers.

Nesting season. New London County offers a great diversity of nesting species. A variety of marsh birds nest at sites in the county, including sora, clapper and king rails, snowy egret, little blue heron, great egret, glossy ibis, least bittern and black-crowned night heron. These species nest at various coastal sites; Great Island in Old Lyme and Barn Island at Stonington are the best sites for most of them. Several shore bird species nest along the New London County coast. Willet nests at Barn Island and Great Island. Piping plover and least tern nest in a protected area at Griswold Point. Nesting oystercatcher can be seen at Bluff Point. Among nesting land birds, certainly the most easily seen is Osprey, and coastal marshes in New London County have the bulk of Connecticut's breeding population; the best view of the greatest number of nests is of Great Island from the state landing at Smiths Neck in Old Lyme. A nice variety of species that are typical for Connecticut, plus a number of southerners occur at sites along and near the coast that are at low elevations and have a mild climate. To find hooded warbler (in mountain laurel or sweet pepperbush) and worm-eating warbler (on rocky slopes), go to Hartman Park in Lyme. Look for chat in shrubby fields at Haley Farm or Bluff Point in Groton, or Barn Island in Stonington. Many pine warblers nest in the sand plain pitch pine community at Hopeville Pond State Park in Griswold. Numerous prairie warblers nest at Hartman Park, and at a number of other sites that have shrubby edges. For a mix of typical species for Connecticut plus some northerners, such as solitary vireo, Blackburnian and black-throated green warblers, go farther inland to sites at higher elevations in Patchaug Forest in Voluntown.

Fall migration. Early in the fall (late July through September) follow the migration of shore birds and waders at coastal marshes and mud flats like those at Griswold Point and Griswold Marsh, Great Island and Barn Island. Also in September, sites along the coast are excellent for watching migrating osprey, merlin, peregrine and other hawks; Griswold Point, Bluff Point and Haley Farm are especially good. Later in the fall (October, November and December), if you want to watch migrating water birds, terns and gulls, go to one of the points - Avery Point, Eastern Point, Stonington Point, Harkness Memorial, or Bluff Point.

Winter is not a down time in New London County. Water birds can be seen at almost any of the coastal sites, along with an interesting mix of gulls. Among water birds, red-necked grebe often occurs in winter in the lower part of the Thames River, and can sometimes be seen from Avery and Eastern Points. Sites on the Lower Connecticut River in Old Lyme and

Lyme are good places to look for dabbling ducks. But perhaps the best known winter birding in New London County is for bald eagle, because Connecticut's main population of eagles spends the winter along the Lower Connecticut River. They can be seen from sites in Lyme and Old Lyme, and on the other side of the river from sites in Middlesex County. Other raptors, including harrier, snowy and short-eared owls, sometimes occur at sites such as Barn Island and Harkness Park. Snow bunting and Lapland longspur sometimes also occur at these sites.

Sources of Information and Help

There are several good sources of information for birders in New London County. One that you can visit is Denison Pequotsepos Nature Center in Mystic (which serves as headquarters for the Pequot Audubon Society). The Potapaug Audubon Society can be reached by mail in Old Lyme. A map of the Patchaug State Forest can be obtained at forest headquarters.

There are plenty of places to eat or stay for the night in the shoreline communities of New London County, but inland there are large rural areas in which there are few facilities for the public. There are good campgrounds at Hopeville Pond State Park in Griswold and the Mount Misery Campground in the Patchaug State Forest in Voluntown. At each, during May you wake up to the songs of birds - pine warblers at Hopeville Pond, and northern waterthrush, black-throated green and hooded warblers at Mount Misery. There are also hoards of mosquitoes at the latter - hence the name and probably the abundance of birds.

TOUR OF OLD LYME

THE TOUR: Eight sites that are near each other on the east side of the lower Connecticut River in Old Lyme are included in this driving tour of less than ten miles. They are (in the order they are reached on the tour):
  DEP Marine Headquarters
  Lieutenant River
  Watch Rock
  Smiths Neck Town Landing
  Smiths Neck State Landing/Great Island
  Black Hall River
  White Sand Beach
  Four Mile River
Details for each of these sites are provided in separate site descriptions.

HABITATS
  COASTAL: tidal river, salt/brackish water, tidal creeks, estuaries, mud flats, high and low salt and brackish marshes, herbaceous, shrubby and wooded edges, white pine groves, deciduous coastal forest, sand and gravel beach, Long Island Sound;
  Open terrestrial: short grass and shrubby fields; shrubby and wooded edges;
  River/stream: river, marshy, shrubby and wooded streambelt;
All of the major types of coastal habitat are represented among the sites on this tour.

SEASONS/BIRDS
SPRING MIGRATION: gulls, terns, WATER BIRDS, MARSH BIRDS, SHORE BIRDS, LAND BIRDS;
NESTING SEASON: gulls, terns, WATER BIRDS, MARSH BIRDS, shore birds, land birds;
FALL MIGRATION: gulls, terns, WATER BIRDS, MARSH BIRDS, SHORE BIRDS, LAND BIRDS;
WINTER: gulls, WATER BIRDS, land birds.
Among the sites on this tour, there is something to see at any season.

GETTING AROUND
Birding methods: CAR, walk. bike.
This is basically a driving tour that gets you to places from which excellent coastal habitats can be seen from near your car. (The one exception is Watch Rock, which requires some easy walking.) In addition, the tour goes through an area that is ideal for biking, and offers the possibility of several fine boat trips (for details, see individual site descriptions).

DIRECTIONS (see Map 61): **This tour starts from I-95 exit 70, follows Route 156 eastward for about seven miles, and ends at I-95 exit 72.**

To get to DEP Marine Headquarters, from I-95 exit 70, go east (actually south at this point) on Route 156 for 0.5 mile, right on Ferry Road for 0.5 mile to the parking area for the facility. A platform that overlooks the Connecticut River is to the right of the parking area.

To get to the Lieutenant River, return to Route 156, and continue east (or south) for a few yards to a parking area on the right just before the bridge over the river. A short section of the river and the surrounding marsh can be seen from this parking area.

To get to Watch Rock and a trail that goes along the shore of a tidal cove and salt marsh, return to Route 156 and continue east (or south) for 0.9 mile to the intersection with McCurdy Road on the left and Noyes Road on the right. From this point, there are two ways to reach the site. **To reach the north end of the site by way of a shorter trail,** go left on McCurdy Road for 0.1 mile, left on a dirt road for 0.3 mile to a parking area. A short trail leads to the edge of the water. **To reach the south end of the site by way of a longer trail**, go right on Noyes Road for a few yards, right on Caulkins Road for a few yards, and right on Joel Road for 0.1 mile to the site entrance. A trail leads to the water in about 0.3 miles.

To get to Smiths Neck Town Landing, return to Route 156 and, from the intersection of Route 156, McCurdy Road and Noyes Road, continue east (or south) for 0.5 miles, right on Smiths Neck Road for 0.1 mile, right on a dirt road for 0.2 mile through shrubby fields and edges to its end at the landing. This landing overlooks a tidal creek and salt marsh.

To get to Smiths Neck State Landing/Great Island, return to Smiths Neck Road, and continue on it for 0.7 mile to its end at the landing. This point provides an excellent view of Great Island - a tidal creek, salt marshes and mud flats.

To get to the Black Hall River, return to Route 156, and continue east (or south) for 0.8 mile to where Route 156 crosses the Black Hall River. There are places to park at a marina on the left just west of the bridge or on a wide shoulder just east of the bridge. From the bridge, you get a good look at mud flats and salt/brackish marshes. In addition, just east of the bridge, a dirt road on the north (left) side of Route 156 leads in 0.3 mile to habitats along the shore of the Black Hall River upstream from the bridge.

To get to White Sands Beach, return to Route 156 and continue east for 0.1 mile, right on Old Shore Road, and right on White Sands Road for 0.3 mile to the beach parking area. This gives you a view of Long Island Sound, and also provides access to Griswold Point - a walk of about a half mile west (right) along the beach.

To get to Four Mile River, retrace your route back to Route 156 and continue east for 3.2 miles, right on Oak Ridge Drive for 0.3 mile, and right on the driveway to the landing for 0.2 mile to the parking area.

To get back to I-95, continue east on Route 156 for 1.4 mile, and turn left on the connector to I-95 exit 72.

BOZRAH: BEAR HILL WILDLIFE MANAGEMENT AREA

HABITATS
OPEN TERRESTRIAL: tilled, short grass, tall grass, mixed herbaceous and shrubby fields; orchard; shrubby and wooded hedgerows and edges;
Forest: hardwoods, pitch pine grove, cedar grove.
Other: manure pile.
The main feature of this 348-acre wildlife management area is farmland, with a variety of fields, hedgerows and edges. The area is managed by DEP to improve the habitat for agriculture/forest-associated wildlife species. Hay and other crops are grown in open fields, and shrubby fields are mowed periodically to arrest succession. Shrubby and wooded hedgerows and edges separate these open areas, and there are woods on the perimeter.

SEASONS/BIRDS:
SPRING MIGRATION: LAND BIRDS;
Nesting season: land birds;
FALL MIGRATION: LAND BIRDS;
Winter: land birds.
This is an excellent site in which to look for grassland and edge birds. The species vary by season, but there is something here throughout the year. In the early spring (April) and even more so in the late fall (October-November) there are many sparrows - including white-crowned, white-throated, field and song - attracted partly by the manure pile in the area. In spring, summer and fall, migrating and nesting bobolink, meadowlark, indigo bunting, blue-winged and prairie warblers are present. During the period late fall, winter and early spring, scan the fields for horned lark and snow bunting. Raptors also hunt over this area: kestrel in spring, summer and fall, harrier in fall, winter and spring, and red-tailed hawk all year.

GETTING AROUND
Birding methods: car, WALK, wheelchair.
Some (but not much) of the fields can be seen from the parking area. Walking is easy, over farm roads that go along the fields. The Connecticut DEP has upgraded the parking area and 4,000 feet of access roads and trails to meet standards of the Americans with Disabilities Act. The area is heavily hunted, so fall trips are best planned for Sundays.

HOW TO GET THERE: This site is about five miles west of Norwich. From Route 2 exit 23, go south on Route 163 for 1.2 miles, left on Bishop Road for 0.2 miles to the intersection just past the bridge; go straight across the intersection onto Bear Hill Road for 0.5 mile to a parking area that is surrounded by fields. This road may not be maintained in winter.

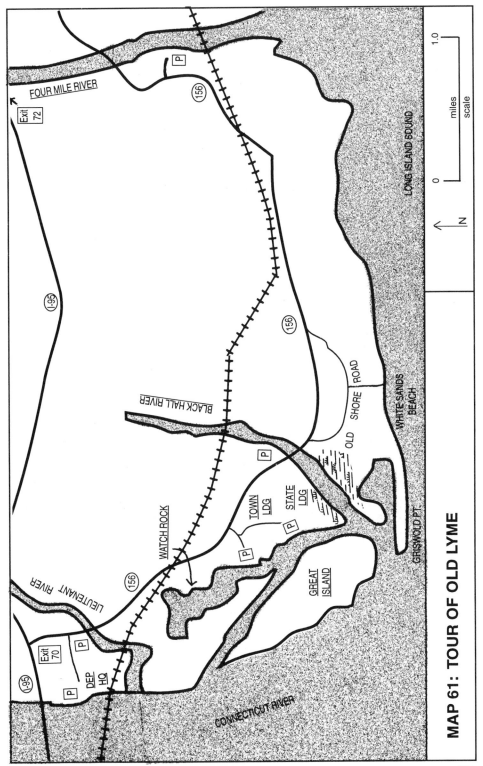

MAP 61: TOUR OF OLD LYME

BOZRAH/MONTVILLE: HOPEMEAD STATE PARK

HABITATS
Forest: hardwoods, mountain laurel;
Lake/pond: lake, wooded shore;
Marsh/swamp/bog: shrubby hardwood swamp, sweet pepperbush, mountain laurel.

This small (60-acre) park occupies a square area that lies between a town road and the east shore of Gardner Lake. It is covered by a hardwood forest and a shrubby hardwood swamp complex that has an understory of sweet pepperbush and mountain laurel.

SEASONS/BIRDS
Spring migration: water birds, land birds;
NESTING SEASON: LAND BIRDS;
Fall migration: water birds, land birds;
Winter: land birds.

Within this woodland, you can find a nice variety of standard forest-dwelling land birds, particularly during the nesting season. The best period for a visit is late April to late September. The mountain laurel and sweet pepperbush in the wetland provide suitable nesting habitat for hooded warbler. Water birds can be seen from the west side of the park, but are not an important reason for coming here.

GETTING AROUND
Birding methods: walk.

There is a well-maintained trail from the park entrance to the shore of Gardner Lake, a distance of perhaps half a mile, with views of the lake that are somewhat obscured by foliage.

DIRECTIONS: This park is about five miles west of the city of Norwich. From the intersection of Routes 82 and 354, go east on Route 82 for 0.5 mile, left on Doyle Road for 0.6 mile, left on Cottage Road for 0.8 mile to the park entrance on the left. (See also Salem et al: Gardner Lake.)

COLCHESTER: BABCOCK POND WILDLIFE MANAGEMENT AREA

HABITATS
LAKE/POND: pond, shallow water, deep water, shore of shrub marsh, shrubs and woods;
MARSH/SWAMP/BOG: mixed herbaceous and shrub marsh, shrub swamp, shrubby hardwood swamp;
Forest: hardwoods, hardwoods/white pine, young hardwoods/white pine with shrubby understory, sand plain;
Open terrestrial: short grass field, tall grass field, orchard, shrubby and wooded edges;
River/stream: stream, wooded streambelt.

This is a 1,208-acre DEP wildlife management area. Babcock Pond itself, which is on the south side of Route 16, has an undeveloped, largely wooded shore with areas of shrubs and shrub marsh on the shoreline. Across the road, on the north side of Route 16, is a small shrub and shrubby hardwood swamp, and a cemetery that is surrounded by a sand plain forest of hardwoods and white pine.

SEASONS/BIRDS
Spring migration: water birds, marsh birds, land birds;
Nesting season: water birds, marsh birds, land birds;
Fall migration: water birds, marsh birds, land birds;
Winter: land birds.
Although this cannot be billed as a premier birding area, there are birds to look for during most of the year. Water bird migrants and nesters include wood duck and hooded merganser. Great blue heron occasionally feeds in the wetland during spring, summer and fall. There is a greater species variety of land birds, especially during the spring migration. Nesting land birds include least flycatcher, yellow-throated vireo and prairie warbler. Woodcock are here during migration, and great horned owl all year.

GETTING AROUND
Birding methods: walk, boat, WHEELCHAIR.
This area has been developed by DEP for handicapped access. There are three parking areas with spaces for handicapped parking, and 4,000 feet of trails suitable for use by wheelchair. In addition, a handicapped-access waterfowl hunting blind was built, along with an inland marsh observation platform. Miles Standish Road is dirt and rough.

DIRECTIONS: This site is about four miles west of the center of Colchester. From Route 2 exit 18, go west on Route 16 for 3.0 miles to **Miles Standish Road** on the left, or for 3.3 miles to **the main entrance to the WMA** on the left, or for 3.5 miles to **a cemetery and small wetland,** both on the right.

Miles Standish Road runs along state land (hardwoods forest) on the right for 1.5 miles, with trails going off to the right into the woods and down to Babcock Pond, at 0.6 mile and at 1.4 miles.

The main entrance provides access to several trails, one of which goes to an observation platform on the shore of Babcock Pond.

The cemetery and small wetland on the right of Route 16 can be birded from within the cemetery and from Cemetery Road, next to it. Caution: Route 16 carries traffic that can be heavy and fast.

EAST LYME: PATTAGANSETT MARSHES

HABITATS
COASTAL: low salt marsh, high salt marsh, tidal creek, mud flat, estuary, shrubby edges, rocky shore, coastal forest.
This site is the estuary of the Pattagansett River, and it contains several islands, a shore occupied by high and low salt marshes, backed by shrubby edges and a coastal hardwood forest. The estuary is shallow and extensive mud flats are exposed at low tide.

SEASONS/BIRDS
SPRING MIGRATION: gulls, terns, WATER BIRDS, MARSH BIRDS, SHORE BIRDS, land birds;
NESTING SEASON: water birds, MARSH BIRDS, LAND BIRDS;
FALL MIGRATION: gulls, terns, WATER BIRDS, MARSH BIRDS, SHORE BIRDS, land birds;
Winter: water birds, land birds.

Although not as large or well known as several other sites along the Connecticut coast, this cove can offer almost the entire spectrum of tidewater bird species. The spring migration opens with the arrival of dabbling ducks (black, mallard, wigeon et al) and other water birds. The highlight of the spring occurs in April when male ospreys arrive to establish nests on the several platforms in the cove, and await the arrival of the females. (This is an excellent site at which to photograph or watch the entire osprey nesting/fledging cycle from a reasonably close viewpoint.) Also during the spring migration and throughout the summer, numerous marsh birds can be seen here, including great blue, little blue and green-backed herons, and black-crowned night heron. During the springtime passage of shore birds, it is possible to see almost any species that occurs along the Connecticut coast.

The fall migration resembles the spring migration, with the addition of raptors that pass by from time to time - sharp-shinned and Cooper's hawks, kestrel, merlin and peregrine falcon. In winter, there are some water birds in the cove, and again there is the potential for raptors, at this time principally red-tailed and rough-legged hawks, short-eared and snowy owls.

GETTING AROUND
Birding methods: car.
Old Black Point Road, which follows the east side of the cove, is a good place from which to observe life in the cove and surrounding marshes, including the osprey nesting platforms. All of the surrounding land is private and closely settled, so stay right on the road.

DIRECTIONS: This site lies along the west side of Black Point, on the Connecticut shore midway between New London and Old Saybrook. From I-95 exit 72, go south on the Rocky Neck Connector, east (left) on Route 156 for 2.4 miles, right on Black Point Road for 0.6 mile through a railroad underpass, right at the stop sign (still on Black Point Road) for 0.4 mile to another stop sign, right on Old Black Point Road for 0.5 mile until the marsh is visible on the right.

EAST LYME: ROCKY NECK STATE PARK

HABITATS
COASTAL: high and low salt marsh, salt water tidal creek, mud flats, sandy beach, rocky shore, Long Island Sound, coastal forest.
Open terrestrial: short grass field, scattered cedars, shrubby and wooded edge;
Forest: hardwoods, mountain laurel, shrubby edges.
This park has a nice combination of coastal habitats and inland habitats near the coast. It fronts on Long Island Sound, has a crescent beach and rocky point, and behind those areas there is a tidal marsh with a small mud flat, surrounded by shrubs and coastal hardwoods. Between the marsh and the beach is a large mowed field. Inland from these areas, there is hardwood forest with a mountain laurel shrub layer, more mowed fields in the camping area, and many cedars scattered about.

SEASONS/BIRDS
Spring migration: gulls, terns, water birds, marsh birds, shore birds, land birds;
Nesting season: gulls, terns, water birds, marsh birds, land birds;
Fall migration: gulls, terns, water birds, marsh birds, shore birds, land birds;
Winter: gulls, water birds, land birds .
There is a reason to come here at any season, even summer. In the spring, the park's coastal location enables it to offer water bird migrants on the Sound, and early land bird arrivals in

the terrestrial habitats. Marsh and shore birds are visible in the marsh, and there is an osprey nesting platform on it that usually provides interesting activity throughout the summer. The fall migration is a replay of that in the spring, with the addition of hawks migrating along the coast during September and October. In winter, look for water birds on the Sound, and snow bunting and horned lark in the mowed areas.

GETTING AROUND
Birding methods: CAR, WALK, BIKE.

Driveways go near most areas of the park, and provide really good looks at most of the habitats. The marsh is right next to the driveway between the entrance and the beach parking area. The beach is a short walk from the parking area. These same driveways provide an easy way to bird on foot or by bicycle. The park is popular and crowded during the warm months, and a fee is charged at that time. The rest of the year, you'll have the place almost to yourself. The campground opens earlier and closes later than others near coastal birding sites.

HOW TO GET THERE: Rocky Neck State Park is on the Connecticut shore midway between New London and Old Saybrook. From I-95, take exit 72, turn east on Route 156 and almost immediately turn right into the park entrance.

FRANKLIN: BAILEY'S RAVINE AT AYERS GAP

HABITATS
FOREST: hardwoods, hardwoods/hemlock, hemlock, cedar;
RIVER/STREAM: streams, swampy, shrubby and wooded streambelts, hemlock ravine;
Open terrestrial: tilled, short grass, mixed herbaceous and shrubby fields; wooded edges;
Lake/pond: pond; grassy, marshy and shrubby shore;
Marsh/swamp/bog: wet meadow, sedge marsh, shrubby hardwood swamp;
OTHER: ledge, cliff, rock outcrops, rocky slope.

This preserve lies on a steep, rocky hillside that is forested with hardwoods (dominated by chestnut oak) mixed with hemlock and scattered cedars. A stream descends steeply in a hemlock ravine through the eastern part of the preserve. Visible from the east side are tilled and short grass fields, a small pond and a wetland that includes a wet meadow and a sedge marsh.

SEASONS/BIRDS
Spring migration: land birds;
Nesting season: land birds;
Fall migration: land birds;
Winter: land birds.

This is a good area in which to look during the nesting season for a nice variety of woodland birds including a number of forest-interior species. Those present in the late spring, summer and early fall include scarlet tanager, yellow-throated and solitary vireos, black-throated green warbler and purple finch. Blue-winged warbler nests along the edges. The constant presence of turkey vultures suggests that they nest in the cliffs within the preserve.

GETTING AROUND
Birding methods: car, WALK.
Two town roads go along the boundaries of the preserve (Smith Road along the southwest side and Ayer Road along the southeast side). They are quiet and provide easy walking. Several trails go into the preserve - two start at the parking area and one at Ayer Road (that one goes up the hemlock ravine). Sections are steep and rocky.

DIRECTIONS: This site is in Franklin, about five miles northwest of the city of Norwich. From the intersection of Routes 207 and 32, go east on Route 207 for 1.5 miles to a pulloff on the left. The preserve lies on the hillside by the pulloff on the north side of Route 207. Smith Road, that goes along the southwest side of the preserve, is a few yards west of the parking area, and Ayer Road, which goes along the southeast side of the preserve, is a few yards east of the parking area.

FRANKLIN: FRANKLIN SWAMP WILDLIFE MANAGEMENT AREA

HABITATS
FOREST: hardwoods, hardwoods/hemlock;
OPEN TERRESTRIAL: tilled, short grass, tall grass and shrubby fields; shrubby and wooded hedgerows and edges, scattered cedars;
MARSH/SWAMP/BOG: shrub swamp, shrubby hardwood swamp, hardwood swamp;
Lake/pond: ponds, seasonal pools, shrubby and wooded shores;
River/stream: streams, slow water, swampy, shrubby and wooded streambelts;
Other: rocky slope.
This 452-acre area occupies a hollow in the rolling farm country of interior New London County. Much of it is covered by hardwood and hemlock forest, and it also includes extensive shrub and hardwood swamps, several slow-moving streams, a cemetery and farm fields divided by hedgerows.

SEASONS/BIRDS
SPRING MIGRATION: water birds, LAND BIRDS;
NESTING SEASON: LAND BIRDS;
Fall migration: land birds;
Winter: land birds.
This is a good site at which to look for a standard variety of forest land bird species, during both migrations and the nesting season. Those known to nest here include least flycatcher, pewee, gnatcatcher, red-eyed, solitary and yellow-throated vireos, black-throated green warbler, scarlet tanager, and a host of more common species.

GETTING AROUND
Birding methods: car, WALK.
It is possible to see some of the habitats from your car on roads that go through this area. In addition, there are a number of woods roads and trails that provide excellent opportunities for birding on foot. Parts of the area may be closed to the public at certain times of year; signs indicate when and where this is the case. It is also a popular hunting area.

DIRECTIONS: This area is about five miles northwest of Norwich. **To get to the main section** from the intersection of Routes 32 and 2 just west of Norwich, go north on Route 32 for 3.3 miles, right on Plains Road for 0.1 mile to the entrance and parking for the wildlife area on the right. **To get to the northern section of the area,** continue on Plains Road for 0.3 mile, left on Under The Mountain Road for 1.6 miles to Route 207. This stretch of road goes past farm fields, a cemetery, and the forested northern section of the wildlife management area. **To get to yet another section of the area,** do not turn left onto Under the Mountain Road, but stay on Plains Road; during the next mile it passes through more of the area.

GRISWOLD: HOPEVILLE POND STATE PARK

HABITATS
FOREST: hardwoods/white pine, hardwoods/hemlock, white pine, sand plain of pitch pine, white pine, hardwoods;
Lake/pond: pond, wooded shore.
This park includes an excellent example of a sand plain mixed forest community. The sand plain is quite large - it occupies much of the park's 554 acres, and is characterized by pitch pine, white pine, white oak and other hardwoods. The remainder of the park is also forested, with a portion near the pond developed for swimming and picnicking.

SEASONS/BIRDS
Spring migration: water birds, land birds;
Nesting season: land birds;
Fall migration: water birds, land birds;
Winter: land birds.
The migrating and nesting species that occur at this park include a nice mix of the forest-dwelling species that you would expect in this type of conifer-hardwood sand plain community. Among the nesters are pine warblers (lots of them!), brown creeper, gnatcatcher, yellow-throated vireo, black-throated green warbler, and broad-winged hawk. Some common species of water birds can be seen on the pond during the spring and fall migrations.

GETTING AROUND
Birding methods: car, walk, bike.
There is a park driveway, from which some of the habitat areas can be seen. In addition, there are access roads and trails that can be walked. In the summer, an entry fee is charged, and the park gets quite crowded.

HOW TO GET THERE: This park is located about ten miles east of Norwich. To get there from I-395 (Route 52), take exit 86 and go east on Route 201 for 1.4 miles to the park entrance on the right.

GROTON: AVERY POINT

HABITATS
COASTAL: Long Island Sound, rocky shore;
Open terrestrial: short grass field.
Avery Point is a rocky peninsula that extends into Long Island Sound east of the mouth of the Thames River, and provides a good view of the nearby water.

SEASONS/BIRDS
Spring migration: gulls, terns, water birds, shore birds, land birds;
Nesting season: gulls, terns;
Fall migration: gulls, terns, water birds, shore birds, land birds;
WINTER: gulls, WATER BIRDS, shore birds.
This point is a good site at which to look for water birds on Long Island Sound; it provides much the same birding opportunities as nearby Eastern Point. Winter is especially good for seeing a variety of water birds, often including brant, scoters, old squaw, gadwall and wigeon; many of the same species can be seen during the spring and fall migrations. In winter, also look for purple sandpiper feeding along the rocky shore.

GETTING AROUND
Birding methods: car, walk.
It is possible to park your car quite near to where you can see the rocky shore and the Sound. The area that includes the point is a UConn facility; be sure to follow regulations as to parking, as well as where you go by car or on foot.

DIRECTIONS: This point is on the coast at the south end of the city of Groton. From I-95 exit 85 (northbound) or exit 87 (southbound), go south on the Clarence B. Sharp Highway / Route 349. Follow Route 349 which separates from the Sharp Highway and later becomes Eastern Point Road (requiring a left turn at an intersection). At a total distance of about four miles from I-95, the road makes a bend to the left, Eastern Point Road and Route 349 end, and the entrance to Avery Point is on the right.

GROTON: BLUFF POINT STATE PARK

HABITATS
COASTAL: Long Island Sound, tidal river, estuary, salt water tidal cove, salt pond, sandy barrier beach, dunes, gravel bars, mud flats, high and low salt marsh, offshore rocks, rocky coast, coastal forest with shrubby edges;
OPEN TERRESTRIAL: shrubby field;
Forest: hardwoods, thickets and shrubby edges;
OTHER: rock outcrop, hawk watching site.
Bluff Point is a peninsula that extends for a mile into Long Island Sound, and is the last remaining large undeveloped portion of the Connecticut shore. It is bordered on the west by the Poquonock River and on the east by Mumford Cove. A ridge runs down the middle of the peninsula, and ends at a rock outcrop that offers a view of the nearby habitats and Long Island Sound. On the peninsula itself, there is upland forest, shrubby fields, thickets, shrubby and wooded edges. And surrounding this peninsula, there is just about every type of coastal habitat that occurs in Connecticut. On the west side there is a sheltered tidal river (the Poquonock) with an estuary that includes high and low salt marshes and mud flats. A mile-

long barrier beach extends most of the way across this estuary. To the south is Long Island Sound. And on the east side, there is a tidal cove (Mumford Cove) that offers more sheltered water and additional areas of mud flats. The peninsula itself is bordered by shrubby edges backed by coastal forest.

SEASONS/BIRDS

SPRING MIGRATION: GULLS, TERNS, WATER BIRDS, MARSH BIRDS, SHORE BIRDS, LAND BIRDS;

NESTING SEASON: gulls, TERNS, WATER BIRDS, MARSH BIRDS, shore birds, LAND BIRDS;

FALL MIGRATION: GULLS, TERNS, WATER BIRDS, MARSH BIRDS, SHORE BIRDS, LAND BIRDS;

WINTER: GULLS, WATER BIRDS, shore birds, LAND BIRDS.

Bluff Point is one of the best coastal birding sites in Connecticut. It includes a rich diversity of coastal and upland habitats, and is a classic coastal land trap. For these reasons, it can offer spectacular birding at any time of year. Over 200 species have been seen at this site, including a number that are uncommon in Connecticut: gulls including Iceland, glaucous, common black-headed and black-legged kittiwake; terns including roseate, Forster's and black skimmer; gannet; 30 species of water birds; many shorebirds, including oystercatcher, Hudsonian godwit, Baird's, purple and buff-breasted sandpipers; waders, including little blue heron; raptors, including peregrine falcon, short-eared and saw-whet owls; other landbirds, including both cuckoos, bobwhite, Swainson's and gray-cheeked thrushes, white-eyed and Philadelphia vireos, golden-winged, Nashville, Blackburnian, bay-breasted, black-poll, orange-crowned and mourning warblers, chat, and a variety of sparrows. Many of these uncommon species occur in migration, when Bluff Point acts as a landfall in the spring and a land trap in the fall. The result is that it attracts a wide species diversity and big numbers of individual birds. In the fall, the rock outcrop at the southern end of the peninsula is an excellent spot from which to watch the hawk migration. The little neck of woods just east of the driveway and immediately south of the railroad tracks can be exciting during the fall migration. There is a great diversity of nesting species, thanks to the variety of habitat types near one another. Among the more interesting nesting species are clapper rail, black-crowned night heron, osprey, orchard oriole, white-eyed vireo and bobwhite. Bluff Point is also a good place to see oystercatcher during the nesting season, afterwards during their post-breeding congregation, and finally as the fall migrants pass through. Winter is also exciting. From the southern portions of Bluff Point you may see: (on Long Island Sound) common and red-throated loons, red-necked and horned grebes, all three scoters, old squaw; (in the coves and estuary) bufflehead, common goldeneye, canvasback, red-breasted merganser; (on the beach or over the marshes) rough-legged hawk, short-eared owl; (on the beach or at the nearby airfield) horned lark and snow bunting.

GETTING AROUND

Birding methods: WALK, boat.

The main trail makes a two to three mile loop around the peninsula, and a number of side trails lead to most of the habitat areas. In addition, it is possible to launch a boat from the parking area, but the tides are strong, so time your trip with this in mind. This park does not get as crowded as others on the coast during the summer. Ticks are abundant.

DIRECTIONS (see Map 62): This park is on the coast one to two miles east of Groton. From I-95 take exit 88, go south on Route 117 for 1.1 mile, right on Route 1 for 0.3 mile, left on Depot Road for 0.3 mile, and right on a road which goes down under railroad tracks and reaches the park entrance, parking area and boat launch site in 0.4 mile. The trails start at the south edge of the parking area, and head east and south.

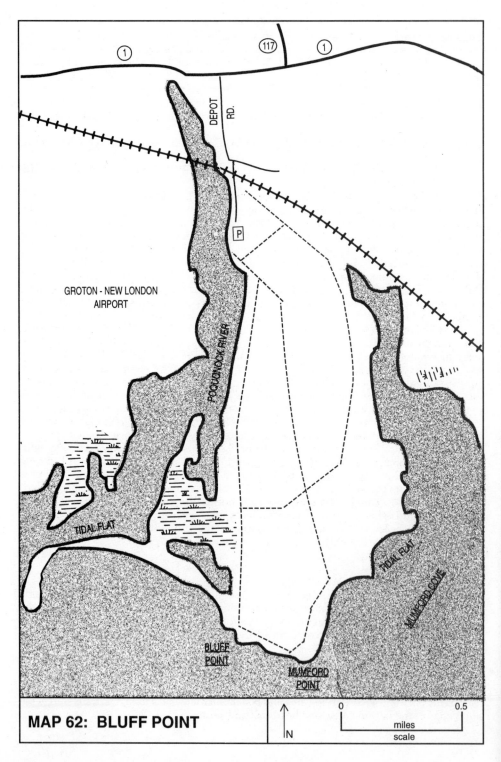

① 117 ① ①

DEPOT RD.

P

GROTON - NEW LONDON
AIRPORT

POQUONOCK RIVER

TIDAL FLAT

TIDAL FLAT

MUMFORD COVE

BLUFF
POINT

MUMFORD
POINT

MAP 62: BLUFF POINT

N

0   0.5
miles
scale

GROTON: EASTERN POINT

HABITATS
COASTAL: Long Island Sound, tidal cove, sand beach, rocky islands, river, deep water, rocky shore.
This is a rocky peninsula that extends into Long Island Sound at the mouth of the Thames River, and provides good views of both water bodies.

SEASONS/BIRDS
Spring migration: gulls, terns, water birds, shore birds;
Nesting season: gulls, terns;
Fall migration: gulls, terns, water birds, shore birds;
WINTER: gulls, WATER BIRDS, shore birds.
Eastern Point provides much the same birding opportunities as nearby Avery Point (described separately under Groton). Winter is especially good for seeing a variety of water birds, including brant, scoters, old squaw, gadwall and wigeon. Many of the same species can be seen during the spring and fall migrations. In winter, also look for purple sandpiper feeding along the rocky shore.

GETTING AROUND
Birding methods: car.
It is possible to park your car on public land quite near the shore on the point.

DIRECTIONS: This point is on the coast at the south end of the city of Groton. From I-95 exit 85 (northbound) or exit 87 (southbound), go south on the Clarence B. Sharp Highway / Route 349. Follow Route 349 which separates from the Sharp Highway and later becomes Eastern Point Road (requiring a left turn at an intersection). At a total distance of about three and a half miles from I-95, right on Tyler Avenue for 0.2 mile, left on Beach Road for 0.1 to the entrance on the right.

GROTON: HALEY FARM STATE PARK

HABITATS
COASTAL: salt water tidal cove, high and low salt marsh, coastal forest;
OPEN TERRESTRIAL: tall grass and shrubby fields, edges of shrubs and thickets;
Forest: hardwoods;
Lake/pond: pond, shore of shrubs and hardwoods;
Marsh/swamp/bog: shrub marsh, shrub swamp, hardwood swamp;
This is an abandoned 260-acre farm on one side of a tidal cove. In a rather small area, it provides an interesting combination of coastal and inland habitats. These habitats include tidal marshes and a tidal cove, fresh water marshes and swamps, mowed fields and reverting pastures with shrubby edges, shrub thickets, young post-agricultural hardwoods and a mature oak forest.

SEASONS/BIRDS
SPRING MIGRATION: WATER BIRDS, marsh birds, shore birds, LAND BIRDS;
Nesting season: water birds, marsh birds, land birds;
FALL MIGRATION: WATER BIRDS, MARSH BIRDS, shore birds, LAND BIRDS;
Winter: water birds, land birds.

Here is a chance to combine coastal and inland birding in one small site, and with birds to look for throughout the year. Water birds (principally dabbling ducks) are visible on the cove in fall, winter and spring; waders feed along the shore of the cove in spring, summer and fall. There is not enough exposed mud to attract many shore birds, but some do come here to feed, often including both yellowlegs. Land birds are here at all seasons. An osprey nesting platform is in a part of the preserve that overlooks the cove, and it provides a really good viewing opportunity (but don't get too close). A typical variety of edge and woodland species of land birds pass through as migrants and a number nest here (including white-eyed vireo and chat). Bobwhite is a resident. The open fields and marshes in this coastal location make Haley Farm an excellent site at which to look for migrating merlin and other hawks in both spring and fall. In winter, the mild coastal climate causes a variety of migrants to linger into winter.

GETTING AROUND
Birding methods: WALK, bike.

There are several interconnecting trails that go to all areas of the park. They are well maintained, and one is a wide cinder path that is used by a few local runners and bikers. Stay on the paths, as the underbrush is loaded with ticks.

DIRECTIONS: Haley Farm is located just north of Groton Long Point. To get there from I-95, take exit 88, go south on Route 117 for 1.1 miles, left on Route 1 for 1.0 mile, right on Route 215 for 0.6 mile, right on Brook Street for 0.5 mile, right on Haley Farm Road for 0.1 mile to the park entrance.

GROTON: PEQUOT WOODS

HABITATS
FOREST: hardwoods, mountain laurel;
River/stream: streams, slow water, shrubby and hardwoods streambelts;
Marsh/swamp/bog: shrub swamp, shrubby hardwood swamp, hardwood swamp;
Lake/pond: pond, shallow water, shore of shrub marsh, shrub swamp;
Open terrestrial: small clearing, tall grass, shrubby and wooded edge, cedar;
Other: rocky slope.

This town park occupies an interior wooded area that seems remote from the surrounding suburban development. It includes the wooded streambelt of a small, slow-moving stream. It is largely forested by mature hardwoods with a well-developed shrub layer that includes some mountain laurel and numerous areas of vine tangles and thickets. Low areas are composed of moist forest and hardwood swamp. Near the entrance, there is a shallow pond with lots of emergent vagetation and areas of marsh and swamp along the shore. Near the middle of the park, there is a small grassy clearing surrounded by shrubs, some cedars, and the forest of hardwoods. Also within the park are rocky hillsides covered by mid-slope hardwood forest. Its position near the coast gives this site a mild year-round climate.

SEASONS/BIRDS
Spring migration: land birds;
Nesting season: land birds;
Fall migration: land birds;
Winter: land birds.

This is a really nice, quiet place in which to look for a typical variety of woodland birds during any season. The park's coastal location brings good numbers of migrants in spring and fall. Nesting species include the standard hardwoods forest mix, plus some southern species, including red-bellied woodpecker and Kentucky warbler. Also, there is good nesting habitat for worm-eating warbler. Mild winters in this area produce a good population of year-round residents, augmented by lingering berry-eaters.

GETTING AROUND
Birding methods: WALK.
This park runs from Sandy Hollow Road on the north down to Route 1 on the south; it is over a mile north-south, and one half mile east-west. A trail makes a two-mile loop through the northern half of the park (another trail down to the southern end is proposed). The trail is rocky and wet in places.

DIRECTIONS: This park is about a mile northwest of the center of Mystic. From I-95 exit 89, go south on Allyn Street for less than 0.1 mile to the park entrance on the right.

LEBANON: BARTLETT BROOK WILDLIFE MANAGEMENT AREA

HABITATS
OPEN TERRESTRIAL: tilled and shrubby fields, shrubby and wooded edges;
MARSH/SWAMP/BOG: mixed herbaceous and shrub marsh, shrub and shrubby hardwood swamp;
Forest: hardwoods;
River/stream: perennial stream, wetland streambelt.
This is a managed State-owned property that consists of farm fields (usually planted in corn), surrounded by hardwood forest with dense shrubby edges. There is a nearby stream with a streambelt of varied marshes and swamps that have additional areas of shrubs.

SEASONS/BIRDS
SPRING MIGRATION: LAND BIRDS;
Nesting season: land birds;
FALL MIGRATION: LAND BIRDS;
Winter: land birds.
This is a good site in which to look for open- and edge-habitat species, as migrants and nesters. Species known to nest here include: white-eyed, yellow-throated and warbling vireos, bobwhite (probably released for hunting), chestnut-sided warbler and field sparrow. In the spring and late fall, the habitat is good for migrating sparrows, including vesper.

GETTING AROUND
Birding methods: walk.
There are several faint trails, but for birding, the best walking is around the edges of the fields. Hunting is permitted.

DIRECTIONS: This site is in Lebanon, three or four miles north of Colchester. From the intersection of Routes 16 and 207, go south on Route 16 for 1.4 miles to the entrance on the left. To get to another entrance from the intersection of Routes 16 and 207, go south on Route 16 for 0.8 mile, left on Goshen Hill Road for a little over a mile to the entrance on the right.

LEBANON: PEASE BROOK WILDLIFE MANAGEMENT AREA

HABITATS

OPEN TERRESTRIAL: tilled, short grass, tall grass, mixed herbaceous and shrubby fields, extensive stands of cedar and juniper, orchard, vine tangles and thickets, shrubby edges;

FOREST: hardwoods, hardwoods/white pine, cedar, shrub understory, vine tangles and thickets;

River/stream: perennial and seasonal streams, streambelts of shrubby hardwood swamp, shrubs and hardwoods;

Marsh/swamp/bog: shrubby hardwood and hardwood swamp in a strip along the streams;

Other: rocky slope.

This site includes very productive avian habitats. It is 207 acres in size, and consists of numerous patches of managed and early-stage reverting fields, extensive areas of shrubby bottomland, shrubby hardwood swamp, hardwood swamp and small streams. Also, there is open farmland that includes a grassy field with an old apple orchard. Because of the way that the area is managed, it includes succession in many stages, ranging from open, herbaceous fields to shrubs, thickets and young hardwood forest. The reverting fields and the forest understory contain extensive areas of berry-producing shrubs, including dogwoods, honeysuckle and spicebush. Grape vines, greenbrier and bittersweet tangles abound.

SEASONS/BIRDS

SPRING MIGRATION: LAND BIRDS;
NESTING SEASON: LAND BIRDS;
FALL MIGRATION: LAND BIRDS;
Winter: land birds.

This is a really good birding site because of the extensive areas of reverting habitats. It attracts a nice diversity of migrant and nesting land birds - with an emphasis on shrub- and edge-habitat species. Nesters include: edge-species such as brown thrasher, indigo bunting, white-eyed vireo and yellowthroat; woodland species such as gnatcatcher, and yellow-throated vireo, chestnut-sided and worm-eating warbler (the latter in the forested rocky slopes), and, in the sweet pepperbush, honeysuckle and greenbriars, hooded warbler. In addition, there are lots of ovenbirds. The fall migration brings a typical variety of land bird migrants in September, and numerous sparrows in October and November. In winter, there are a number of lingering berry-eaters that feed on the shrubs and cedars. All-season residents include red-bellied woodpecker, and, in some years barred owl, in other years great horned owl.

GETTING AROUND

Birding methods: WALK.

There is an extensive trail network. Hunting is permitted, so that late fall and early winter trips to find sparrows and other seed- and berry-eaters should be planned for Sundays. Trails are muddy in the spring.

DIRECTIONS: Pease Brook is about five miles northwest of Norwich. To get there from Route 2 exit 22, go north on Scott Hill road for 0.3 mile, straight across the intersection onto Waterman Road for 2.0 miles, and right on Turnpike road (dirt) for 0.4 mile to the entrance. This road is rough, and may be muddy and impassible by car at times, but can always be walked and provides good birding.

LEBANON: RED CEDAR LAKE

HABITATS
FOREST: hardwoods, hardwoods / white pine, hardwoods / hemlock;
LAKE/POND: lake, shore of hardwoods, hardwoods / white pine, hardwoods / hemlock, cedar, grass, shrubs, residential development;
River/stream: stream, shrubby hardwood swamp streambelt;
Marsh/swamp/bog: shrub swamp, shrubby hardwood swamp.
There is a new state-owned public area on the north shore of Red Cedar Lake that provides access to upland habitats near the lake. The lake itself is quite large, and has a shoreline that is mostly developed by residences.

SEASONS/BIRDS
SPRING MIGRATION: water birds, LAND BIRDS;
NESTING SEASON: LAND BIRDS;
Fall migration: water birds, LAND BIRDS;
Winter: land birds.
The terrestrial habitats are good for a standard variety of migrating and nesting woodland birds. Nesters include broad-winged hawk, red-bellied woodpecker, gnatcatcher and black-and-white warbler; among the migrants are yellow-rumped and various other warblers. The lake itself is worth checking for migrating water birds in the early spring after ice-out, and in the late fall and early winter until it becomes ice-covered.

GETTING AROUND
Birding methods: car, WALK.
There is nice walking on a few good trails. The lake can be seen from the parking area at the entrance.

DIRECTIONS: This site is in the southern tip of Lebanon, about five miles east of the village of Colchester. To get there from Route 2 exit 22, go north on Scott Hill Road for 0.3 mile, left on Colchester Road for 1.4 miles, left on Moween Road for 0.9 mile (bearing left at a fork to stay on Moween Road) to the entrance on the left.

LEDYARD: ROSE HILL WILDLIFE MANAGEMENT AREA

HABITATS
OPEN TERRESTRIAL: tilled, tall grass, mixed herbaceous and shrubby fields, shrubby and wooded edges; hedgerows;
Forest: hardwoods, cedar, dense shrub understory;
Marsh/swamp/bog: shrub marsh, shrub swamp;
River/stream: stream, shrubby streambelt.
This little-visited 412-acre site is a nice area of farmed and reverting open habitats. It includes a number of farm fields - some are tilled and others planted in hay and other grass crops. Surrounding these fields are dense shrubby edges and low areas of thickets. There are also scattered cedars and small swamps.

SEASONS/BIRDS
SPRING MIGRATION: LAND BIRDS;
NESTING SEASON: LAND BIRDS;
FALL MIGRATION: LAND BIRDS;
Winter: land birds.

The birds that occur here as migrants and nesters are the typical package of shrubby field and edge species - brown thrasher, white-eyed vireo, prairie and chestnut-sided warblers, indigo bunting, and also bobwhite (probably released for hunting). Hooded warbler nests in the woods. In the fall, look for warblers in September, and sparrows during October and November.

GETTING AROUND
Birding methods: car, walk.
There are vehicle roads through the area, and a number of woods roads and trails (some rather overgrown). Hunting is permitted, so plan fall trips for Sundays.

DIRECTIONS: This area is near Poquetanuck, six or seven miles southeast of Norwich. To get there from Poquetanuck at the intersection of Routes 117 and 2A, go south on Route 117 for 0.3 mile, and left on Rose Hill Road. This town road goes through the wildlife management area for most of the road's 1.4-mile length, and passes several access points into the area.

LEDYARD: STODDARD HILL STATE PARK

HABITATS
RIVER/STREAM: river, slow water, tidal cove, shores that are muddy, herbaceous, shrubby and wooded; stream, shrubby and wooded streambelt;
Open terrestrial: short grass field (lawn) with edges of shrubs and vine tangles;
Forest: hardwoods.
This is a small (55-acre) park that is located on the east shore of the Thames River where the river is wide and still, at the upper reaches of the tidal portion. It provides a look at the river itself, and also at a small cove that is within the park. The mowed park lawn is surrounded by edges of thickets and vine tangles.

SEASONS/BIRDS
Spring migration: water birds, marsh birds, shore birds, land birds;
Nesting season: water birds, land birds;
Fall migration: water birds, marsh birds, shore birds, land birds;
Winter: water birds, land birds.
This is a good add-on if you are in the area looking at other sites (the closest are Rose Hill Wildlife Management Area, also in Ledyard, and, across the Thames River in Montville, Fort Shantuck Park and Milo Light Preserve). Stoddard Hill Park is one of the few sites that provide a good opportunity to see water birds on the inland portion of the Thames River. Fall, winter and spring are all good. Most of the water birds to be seen are diving species on the river - greater and lesser scaup, redhead, canvasback, ring-necked duck, common goldeneye, bufflehead, and all three mergansers. Red-necked grebe has also been seen. In addition, some dabbling ducks including gadwall occur in the cove. The vine tangles and thickets around the edges of the park lawn attract edge-dwellers as migrants and nesters, and lingering berry-eaters in early winter.

GETTING AROUND
Birding methods: CAR, walk.
A driveway leads down to a parking area at the edge of the cove and near the shore of the

main part of the Thames River. From here, the cove can be seen well. To get a look at the river, take the short path from the parking area to the edge of the railroad tracks, but watch out for trains - this is a main line.

DIRECTIONS: This park is on the east shore of the Thames River about 7 miles south of Norwich. From the southern intersection of Routes 12 and 2A, go south on Route 12 for 1.8 miles to the park entrance on the right.

LEDYARD/PRESTON: POQUETANUCK COVE

HABITATS
> **RIVER/STREAM:** brackish tidal cove, marshy, wooded, shrubby and herbaceous shore; stream, hemlock ravine;
> **MARSH/SWAMP/BOG:** cattail, sedge and shrub marsh; shrub swamp;
> **Forest:** hardwoods, hemlock, pitch pine.

This is a long, narrow brackish-water cove that runs northeast from the upper tidal portion of the Thames River. While most of the shoreline is developed with small residences, there are also areas of wetlands along the shore, and a nature preserve that occupies 234 acres on the eastern shoreline.

SEASONS/BIRDS
> **Spring migration:** water birds, marsh birds, land birds;
> **Nesting season:** water birds, marsh birds, land birds;
> **Fall migration:** water birds, marsh birds, land birds;
> **Winter:** water birds, land birds.

This cove, together with the contiguous nature preserve, can be worthwhile throughout the year, including winter when there usually is open water.

GETTING AROUND
> **Birding methods:** car, WALK, BOAT.

There are several places on roads from which portions of the cove and the wetlands on its shore can be seen (see below). The nature preserve contains a 1.5 mile loop trail through wooded upland habitats. In addition, this is a good place to do your birding from a boat in order to gain access to wetlands along the eastern shore. At the top end of the cove, there is a small parking area and a place where a boat can be launched.

DIRECTIONS: This cove is on the east side of the Thames River about five miles south of Norwich. **To get a view of the lower part of the cove,** from the southern intersection of Routes 12 and 2A, go south on Route 12 for 0.8 mile to the bridge over the cove. There is a walkway over the bridge. **To reach the upper part of the cove,** from the northern intersection of Routes 2A and 12, go east on Route 2A for 1.2 miles to a parking area on the right at the upper end of the cove. On the way to this point, route 2A goes along the shore of the cove in several places, and provides a look at some of the wetlands. **To reach the nature preserve,** continue on Route 2A for a few yards past the parking area, and turn right on Cider Mill Road (which becomes Avery Hill Road) for 0.9 mile to the preserve entrance on the right.

LYME: CHESTER-HADLYME FERRY LANDING

HABITATS
RIVER/STREAM: fresh water tidal river, deep slow water, shrubby and wooded streambelt;
Forest: hardwoods, hardwoods/hemlock, flood plain;
Open terrestrial: mixed herbaceous and shrubby field, shrubby edge;
Marsh/swamp/bog: mixed herbaceous and shrub marsh.

This is a ferry landing on the east shore of the lower Connecticut River. From this location one can see a stretch of the river, and also the woods along the river shores. In addition, the ferry landing is within sight and hearing of the wooded hillsides of Gillette Castle State Park on the east side of the river just upstream. The road to the ferry landing goes along the side of the Whalebone Creek wetland, described separately.

SEASONS/BIRDS
Spring migration: water birds, land birds;
Nesting season: water birds, land birds;
Fall migration: water birds, land birds;
Winter: water birds, land birds.

During the fall, winter and spring, water birds and several raptor species use the river as a route for migration or local movement. Wintering bald eagles sometimes perch in the trees close to the landing and frequently feed along this section of the river. A fairly good variety of water birds can be seen here during the period November-March. Osprey is regular April-May and September-October.

GETTING AROUND
Birding methods: car.

This landing is larger than the one on the west side of the crossing, and can usually accomodate birders' cars. Take care not to disturb bald eagles that sometimes perch in the trees near the landing. This ferry landing provides a launching point for canoe trips to Whalebone Creek and Selden Cove.

DIRECTIONS (see Map 63): This ferry crosses the Connecticut River about eleven miles north of Long Island Sound. To reach this landing on the eastern shore, from the center of Hadlyme go west on Route 148 for 1.0 mile.

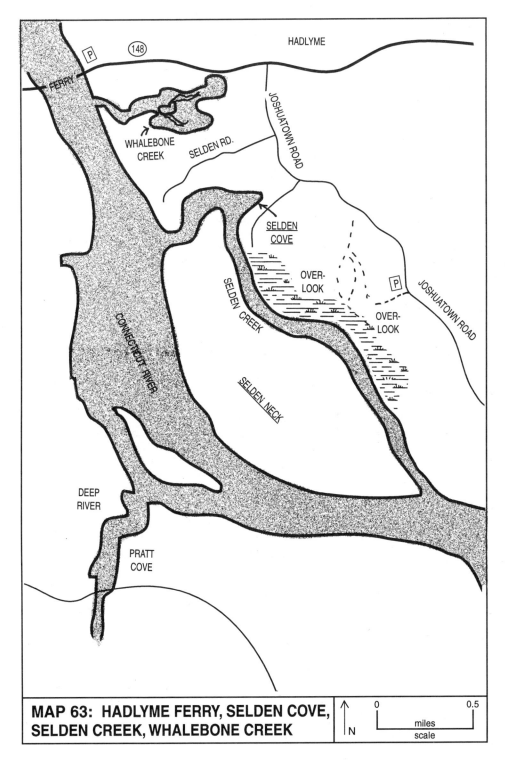

P (148)

FERRY

HADLYME

JOSHUATOWN ROAD

WHALEBONE CREEK

SELDEN RD.

SELDEN COVE

SELDEN CREEK

OVER-LOOK

P

OVER-LOOK

JOSHUATOWN ROAD

CONNECTICUT RIVER

SELDEN NECK

DEEP RIVER

PRATT COVE

MAP 63: HADLYME FERRY, SELDEN COVE, SELDEN CREEK, WHALEBONE CREEK

N

0 0.5
miles
scale

LYME: ELYS FERRY

HABITATS
River/stream: fresh water tidal river, deep slow water, wooded streambelt;
Forest: hardwoods, flood plain;
Marsh/swamp/bog: fresh water tidal marsh (cattail and mixed herbaceous vegetation, shrubby edge);
Open: short grass and tall grass fields, shrubby and hardwood edges, cedar.

This is a former ferry landing from which a section of the lower Connecticut River can be seen, as well as the Great Meadow marsh at Essex across the river. Elys Ferry Road, that leads to the landing, passes by the northern edge of the Lords Cove Marsh, hay fields and shrubby thickets.

SEASONS/BIRDS
Spring migration: water birds, marsh birds, shore birds, land birds;
Nesting season: water birds, marsh birds, land birds;
Fall migration: water birds, marsh birds, shore birds, land birds;
Winter: water birds, land birds.

Water birds occur on the river during the late fall, winter and early spring. During the same period, bald eagles move along the river and perch in trees on the shore; it is sometimes possible to see harrier and rough-legged hawk hunting over Great Meadow marsh across the river. The marsh, shrubby thickets and edges by Elys Ferry Road provide good habitat for marsh birds and land birds in spring, summer and fall.

GETTING AROUND
Birding methods: car.

The former ferry landing and the road leading to it are public, but all the surrounding land is private (and places to pull off are infrequent). A telescope is helpful for scanning the marsh across the river.

DIRECTIONS (see Map 64): This area is on the east shore of the Connecticut River, about seven miles north of Long Island Sound. From the east end of the Baldwin Bridge, over which I-95 crosses the Connecticut River, take exit 70 and go north on Route 156 for 3.4 miles, and left on Elys Ferry Road for 1.9 miles to its end at the river.

LYME: HARTMAN PARK

HABITATS
FOREST: hardwoods, mountain laurel;
OPEN TERRESTRIAL: shrubby field, scattered cedars, shrubby and wooded edges;
MARSH/SWAMP/BOG: shrub marsh, shrub swamp, shrubby hardwood swamp, dead wood, shrubby and wooded edges;
River/stream: streams, shrubby streambelts;
Lake/pond: pond, shrubby shore;
Other: rocky outcrop, rocky slope.

This site, sometimes referred to as "Gungy Road", is a large, diverse nature preserve. It consists of rich and varied habitats that lie for a mile along the east side of - yes - Gungy Road. Fortunately the best of this area has been preserved by creating Hartman Park. The northern portion consists of hardwood forest with a subcanopy composed of mountain laurel and other shrubs, together with occasional rocky slopes and outcrops. Then there is a large power line right of way that crosses Gungy Road. Within the power line cut, there are large areas of varied shrubs, scattered cedars, wetlands, a small pond and a small stream. Still farther south along the road, there is more forest, another wetland, and another pond. Much of the wetland areas are dominated by spicebush and sweet pepperbush.

SEASONS/BIRDS
SPRING MIGRATION: LAND BIRDS;
NESTING SEASON: LAND BIRDS;
FALL MIGRATION: LAND BIRDS;
Winter: land birds.

The diversity of habitats in this preserve produces excellent birding at almost any time of year, with the best period being from late April through November. During the nesting season, there is an abundance of standard species appropriate to each of the habitats within the preserve. In addition, look for red-shouldered hawk in bottomland woods and the power line cut, hooded and Kentucky warblers in the wetland areas that have spicebush and other shrubs; worm-eating warbler on the wooded rocky slopes, many gnatcatchers and scarlet tanagers throughout the woods; and, in the power line cut, edge species including white-eyed vireo, prairie warbler, indigo bunting and field sparrow. The power line is also an excellent area in which to look for migrating sparrows, especially in the late fall (October and November).

GETTING AROUND
Birding methods: CAR, WALK, BIKE.

Gungy Road does not carry much traffic, and has many pulloffs, so that it is good for birding from your car or on foot. A number of trails and woods roads go off from it, and there is a network of interconnecting trails that provide excellent opportunities to bird on foot. The vegetation in the power line cut is dense, loaded with ticks and walking is difficult, but this area can be seen nicely from Gungy Road.

DIRECTIONS: Hartman Park is about ten miles northwest of New London. From the point at which Route 82 passes under Route 11, go west on Route 82 for about 100 feet, left on Darling Road for 1.2 miles, and left on Gungy Road for 1.1 miles. From this point for the next mile, the Hartman Preserve lies on the east (left) side of the road.

LYME: LORDS COVE

HABITATS

MARSH/SWAMP/BOG: brackish low and high tidal marsh (mixed herbaceous vegetation), shrubby and wooded edges and shrubby high areas within the marsh. Lords Cove contains a brackish tidal marsh on the east side of the lower Connecticut River. It includes a diverse ecosystem that is enriched by fresh nutrients from the river that are brought into the marsh by the tides. The vegetation within the marsh is composed of a variety of emergent and aquatic plants, including cattails, bulrushes, rose mallow and (unfortunately) large areas of phragmites. Elevated areas within the marsh support a diversity of shrubs and other terrestrial plants.

SEASONS/BIRDS:

SPRING MIGRATION: WATER BIRDS, MARSH BIRDS, shore birds, land birds;
NESTING SEASON: water birds, MARSH BIRDS, land birds;
FALL MIGRATION: WATER BIRDS, MARSH BIRDS, SHORE BIRDS, land birds;
WINTER: WATER BIRDS, land birds.

This site can provide good birding throughout the year. Lords Cove is located near the intersection of two major migration corridors - the Connecticut River and the coast - so that a variety of water, marsh and land birds occur here in the spring and fall. Migrating water birds occur both within the marsh and on the river just outside of it. During the spring, summer and fall, marsh birds including waders and rails frequent the marsh, and land birds can be seen in the shrubs along the marsh edges and on higher areas within the marsh. In winter, water birds are attracted to areas of fresh water in Lords Cove that remain open when inland marshes are frozen.

GETTING AROUND

Birding methods: BOAT.

Lords Cove contains many creeks and openings, and a boat is the only way to explore it. There is a complex network of waterways within the marsh and it is easy to get lost, so that a compass and large scale map are necessary. Where to put a boat in is something of a problem; see "Directions" below for the best of some difficult alternatives. Also, it is necessary to time your trip for favorable tides. The tide times at Lords Cove are about 45 minutes later than times at Saybrook Point.

DIRECTIONS (see Map 64): Lords Cove is on the east shore of the Connecticut River four miles north of Long Island Sound. There are two boat access points which can be reached from I-95 exit 70 at the east end of the Baldwin Bridge which crosses the Connecticut River a mile south of Lord Cove.

Ferry Road Beach: There is a beach 0.5 mile south of the Baldwin Bridge from which a canoe or light outboard motor boat can be launched. This requires taking a boat upstream in the open water of the river for 1.5 miles to the mouth of the cove. From I-95 exit 70, go south on Route 156 for 0.5 mile, right on Ferry Road for 0.4 mile to the pulloff and beach on the right.

Pilgrim Landing: This town landing is on the east shore of the river, just north of the Baldwin (I-95) Bridge and about 0.5 mile downstream from the cove. The boat trip to the cove is largely sheltered by an island. However, the landing is intended for the use of town residents; keep this in mind when deciding whether your use of it would deny a resident a place to park. From I-95 exit 70, go north on Route 156 for 0.6 mile to the landing by the road on the left, opposite Calves Island.

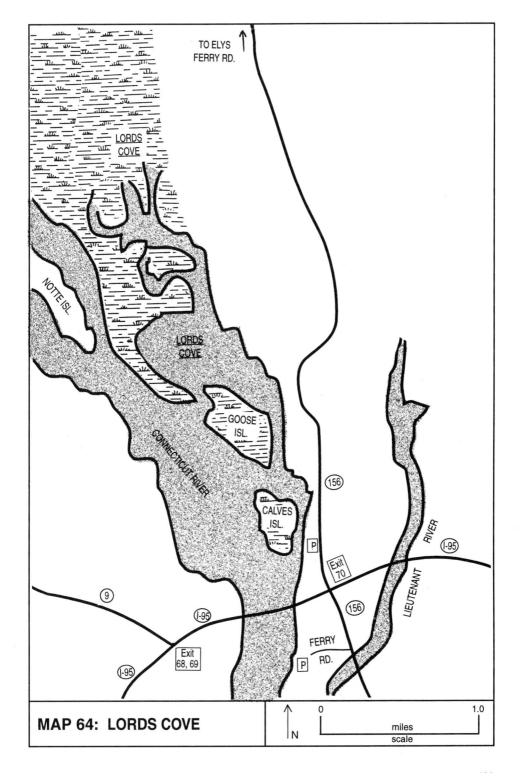

MAP 64: LORDS COVE

LYME: NEHANTIC STATE FOREST (TANEY HILL TRACT)

HABITATS
FOREST: hardwoods, hardwoods/hemlock, mountain laurel;
Lake/pond: ponds, shrubby and wooded shores;
River/stream: perennial and seasonal streams, wooded streambelts;
Marsh/swamp/bog: shrub, shrubby hardwood and hardwood swamps.
This block of the Nehantic State Forest is 1,000 acres in size, and consists of hardwoods dominated by white oak, areas of hemlocks, laurel thickets, hardwood swamps, small pockets of shrub and shrubby hardwood swamp, streams and two ponds (Norwich and Uncas Ponds).

SEASONS/BIRDS
SPRING MIGRATION: LAND BIRDS;
NESTING SEASON: LAND BIRDS;
Fall migration: land birds;
Winter: land birds.
In the spring, there is a nice variety of migrating land birds, particularly warblers. Nesting species include several southern species, such as Carolina wren and hooded warbler, as well as red-shouldered and broad-winged hawks, and many of the standard Connecticut nesters.

GETTING AROUND
Birding methods: CAR, WALK, BIKE.
Several roads and numerous trails go through the tract. A small road leads for several miles to Uncas and Norwich Ponds on the southeastern side of the forest.

DIRECTIONS: This part of the Nehantic State forest is in Lyme, seven to eight miles north of Long Island Sound and three miles east of the Connecticut River. From I-95 exit 70, go north on Route 156 for 3.8 miles to the entrance on the right.

LYME: SELDEN COVE/SELDEN CREEK

HABITATS
MARSH/SWAMP/BOG: fresh water tidal marsh (mixed herbaceous vegetation);
RIVER/STREAM: fresh water tidal river, cove and creek, slow deep water, shrubby and hardwood shore, perennial and seasonal streams, wooded streambelts;
FOREST: hardwoods, hardwoods/hemlock, hemlock, flood plain, mountain laurel;
OTHER: rock outcrop, hawk watching site.
Selden Cove is a sheltered tidal cove on the east shore of the lower Connecticut River, immediately north of Selden Neck (an island that lies against the east shore of the river). Selden Creek runs between this island and the mainland. This complex is an exceptional example of a fresh water tidal system that contain very fertile habitats which support rich food chains. Vegetation is very diverse, and includes pickerelweed, coontail, wild rice, arrow-arum and bulrushes.

SEASONS/BIRDS
> **SPRING MIGRATION:** WATER BIRDS, MARSH BIRDS, shore birds, LAND BIRDS;
> **NESTING SEASON:** water birds, MARSH BIRDS, LAND BIRDS;
> **FALL MIGRATION:** WATER BIRDS, MARSH BIRDS, shore birds, LAND BIRDS;
> **WINTER:** WATER BIRDS, LAND BIRDS.

This area provides an interesting birding experience at any time of year, and includes rocky promontories that allow you to look down on a tide marsh and observe its rich bird life. During the spring and fall migrations and the nesting season, a wide variety of water birds, waders, rails, other marsh birds and land birds occur in the cove, the creek, and the terrestrial habitats that surround them. Osprey hunts the cove in spring, summer and fall. Other raptors hunt the marsh that surrounds Selden Creek throughout the year. A variety of woodland species nest in the woods that you pass through on the way in to Selden Creek; these include black-throated green and hooded warblers. In winter, in addition to having a nice variety of water birds, Selden Cove often has bald eagles in trees along the shore, and, together with Whalebone Creek, it is a location at which golden eagles have been seen.

GETTING AROUND
> **Birding methods:** car, WALK, BOAT.

Selden Cove and the surrounding woods and hillsides can be seen from Selden Road, that unfortunately is surrounded by private land. The views from the road are somewhat distant. A far better way to see the cove is by boat, but if a canoe is to be used, that takes some careful planning in order to time the tides. (The tides here are about one hour thirty five minutes later than Saybrook Point.) The closest place at which a boat may be launched is the Chester-Hadlyme Ferry Landing, about a mile upstream. Do not use a boat during the period December-March, so as not to disturb bald eagles that may be present.

Overlooks that provide spectacular views of Selden Creek and the marsh around it can be reached by a walk of about half a mile through The Nature Conservancy Selden Creek Preserve on a good trail with some ups and downs, through forest habitats.

DIRECTIONS (see Map 63): Selden Cove is on the east side of the Connecticut River, about eleven miles north of Long Island Sound.

To reach Selden Cove by car, from the center of Hadlyme at the intersection of Route 148 and Joshuatown Road, go south on Joshuatown Road for 0.4 mile, and right on Selden Road for 0.6 mile to where it overlooks the cove.

To reach Selden Cove by boat, from the center of Hadlyme at the intersection of Route 148 and Joshuatown Road, go west on Route 148 for 1.0 mile to the ferry landing. Launch your boat from the landing, and go downstream along the east shore, past Whalebone Creek, for about a mile to Selden Creek on the left. It can be followed into Selden Cove, and on southward behind Selden Neck for about two miles, to where it re-enters the Connecticut River. (CAUTION: this is about three miles downstream of your starting point, and can be very difficult against the current. Consider doing only part of this trip, and retracing your route.)

To reach a rocky promontory that overlooks Selden Creek, start at the intersection of Joshuatown Road and Route 148, and go south on Joshuatown Road for 1.3 miles (past Selden Road and past the first Nature Conservancy trail on the right), to the second Nature Conservancy trail on the right, where there is a place to park. Follow the white-blazed trail for about one half mile to the overlook.

LYME: WHALEBONE CREEK

HABITATS
MARSH/SWAMP/BOG: fresh water tidal marsh (mixed herbaceous vegetation), tidal creek, mud flats, open water at high tide;
RIVER/STREAM: fresh water tidal river, cove and creek, slow water;
Forest: hardwoods, hardwoods/hemlock, flood plain.
This area is on the fresh water tidal section of the lower Connecticut River. It consists of a tidal creek that winds through a fresh water tidal marsh, through a wooded area and into a tidal cove. The marsh contains very diverse vegetation, dominated by wild rice.

SEASONS/BIRDS
SPRING MIGRATION: WATER BIRDS, MARSH BIRDS, SHORE BIRDS, LAND BIRDS;
NESTING SEASON: MARSH BIRDS, LAND BIRDS;
FALL MIGRATION: WATER BIRDS, MARSH BIRDS, SHORE BIRDS, LAND BIRDS;
WINTER: WATER BIRDS, LAND BIRDS;
Any time of year can be good in Whalebone Creek. During the period October through April, a variety of water birds occur here, including pintail, gadwall, wigeon and lots of black ducks. Wood duck and hooded merganser may be seen in the spring and fall. In the mid- to late spring, through the summer and into early fall, it is an excellent site in which to look for sora, and, especially in April/May and August/September, for waders, including great blue heron, great egret and black-crowned night heron. A variety of land birds occur in the shrubs and trees that surround the cove - migrants in spring and fall and nesters in spring, summer and fall. In winter, species such as hermit thrush and winter wren linger to feed on the remaining berries and get the benefit of the mild riverine climate. In the late fall, winter and early spring (and occasionally at other times), bald eagles perch in trees around the cove. Together with Selden Cove, this is one of the sites where golden eagles have been seen in some winters.

GETTING AROUND
Birding methods: car, BOAT.
There are two places from which to see parts of the area from town roads (see "Directions" below). A far better way to see this site is by boat, but the tides and river current must be taken into account when planning a trip by canoe (tides at Whalebone Creek are about one hour forty minutes later than tides at Saybrook Point). Do not use a boat during the period December-March, to avoid disturbing any eagles that may be present.

DIRECTIONS (see Map 63) Whalebone Creek is on the east shore of the Connecticut River, about eleven miles north of Long Island Sound.

To get a distant view of most of the cove: from the center of Hadlyme at the intersection of Route 148 and the Joshuatown Road, go south on Joshuatown Road for 0.1 mile to the high point from which the Whalebone Creek area can be seen at a distance on the right.

To reach the upper part of Whalebone Creek: from the center of Hadlyme at the intersection of Route 148 and the Joshuatown Road, go east on Route 148 for 0.2 mile to where the road passes close to the edge of the upper part of the cove. Some of the marsh and the coastal forest around it can be viewed from here. (Stay in your car if there are eagles nearby.)

To explore Whalebone Creek by canoe: if you can find a safe place to park that does not involve trespassing, a canoe can be launched from Route 148 where it goes along the northern part of the cove, as described above. An alternative is to put your boat in the Connecticut River at the Chester-Hadlyme ferry landing on the east shore of the river (to reach the landing from the center of Hadlyme at the intersection of Joshuatown Road and Route 148, go west on Joshuatown Road for 1.0 mile). This is several hundred yards upstream from where Whalebone Creek enters the river.

MONTVILLE: FORT SHANTOK PARK

HABITATS
OPEN TERRESTRIAL: short grass field, edges of shrubs, groves of cedars;
River/stream: river, deep slow water, wooded and shrubby streambelt; stream, wooded streambelt;
Forest: hardwoods, sand plain of hardwoods, white pine and pitch pine;
Lake/pond: pond, grassy, shrubby and wooded shore.
This 170-acre park is on the western shore of the Thames River, at the upper end of the tidal portion, where the river is wide and slow. It offers a nice mix of habitat types, including clumps of cedars in short grass fields.

SEASONS/BIRDS
SPRING MIGRATION: water birds, LAND BIRDS;
NESTING SEASON: LAND BIRDS;
FALL MIGRATION: water birds, LAND BIRDS;
Winter: water birds, land birds.
A good variety of open-country/edge species occur as nesters at this site (brown thrasher, bobwhite, indigo bunting, white-eyed and warbling vireos and prairie warbler). The spring and fall land bird migrations are also good. The presence of groups of cedars suggests that owls may roost here, especially in winter. In the fall, winter and spring, water birds can be seen on the river, but only at a considerable distance.

GETTING AROUND
Birding methods: car, walk.
Driveways and paths go throughout this park. What little walking is required is easy. One section of driveway provides a view of the river, and water birds can be seen at a distance from here. (A rail line runs along the shore of the river and prevents access to the shore itself.) The park is crowded on summer weekends.

DIRECTIONS: This park is on the west shore of the Thames River, about three miles south of Norwich. From I-395 exit 79A, go east on Route 2A for 0.6 mile, north (left) on Route 32 for 0.4 mile, right on Fort Shantok Road (which becomes Massapeag Side Road) for 1.3 miles to the park entrance on the left.

MONTVILLE: MILO LIGHT PRESERVE

HABITATS
FOREST: hardwoods, mountain laurel;
Open terrestrial: shrubby field, edges of shrubs and vine tangles;
River/stream: stream, wooded streambelt;
Marsh/swamp/bog: small shrub swamps.
This preserve consists of 338 acres of woodland, and borders on a small stream and power line. It is a good example of typical mixed hardwood forest.

SEASONS/BIRDS
Spring migration: land birds;
Nesting season: land birds;
Fall migration: land birds.
Winter: land birds.
During both migrations and in the nesting season, a standard mix of forest-dwellers together with edge and open country species occur at this site. Nesters include scarlet tanager, great-crested flycatcher, indigo bunting, brown thrasher and prairie warbler.

GETTING AROUND
Birding methods: WALK.
A nice, wide trail makes a loop of one to two miles through the woods and briefly along the power line.

DIRECTIONS: This preserve is about eight miles southwest of Norwich. From the intersection of Routes 163 and 82, go north on Route 163 for 0.3 mile, right on Herschler Road for 0.1 mile to a small parking area on the right.

NEW LONDON: CONNECTICUT ARBORETUM

HABITATS
FOREST: hardwoods, hardwoods/hemlock, conifer plantations;
OPEN TERRESTRIAL: short grass, tall grass and shrubby fields, shrubby edges; cedar, crabapple;
RIVER/STREAM: river, tidal cove, tidal marsh, shrubby and wooded streambelt; stream, hemlock ravine;
Lake/pond: pond, marshy shore;
Marsh/swamp/bog: shrub marsh, hardwood swamp;
Other: ledge, rocky slope.
The Connecticut College Arboretum is a 435-acre area of managed and natural habitats that surrounds the core of the college campus on the west, north and east sides. Much of it was once farmland (some had been farmed continuously since the mid-1600s), but farming gradually ceased over a period of years between 1910 and 1950, and much of the former farmland has reverted to hardwood forest of various ages. However, in some portions succession has been arrested and open habitats maintained by burn management, periodic mowing, and maintenance of power line and pipe line rights-of-way. Many species of trees and other plants native to Connecticut have been planted in the arboretum. Two areas within the

Arboretum - the Mamacoke Island Natural Area and the Bolleswood Natural Area - are not subject to management. The northeastern portion of the Arboretum lies along the Thames River, and includes a section of tidal river, a peninsula (Mamacoke Island), two coves and a marsh. Also within the arboretum there is a pond with a marshy shore and, in the Bolleswood section, a stream that runs through a hemlock ravine. The arboretum has been the site of numerous studies that have included examination of the effects on bird populations of changes in local and global habitats during the last 40 years.

SEASONS/BIRDS

SPRING MIGRATION: WATER BIRDS, marsh birds, LAND BIRDS;
NESTING SEASON: marsh birds, water birds, LAND BIRDS;
FALL MIGRATION: WATER BIRDS, marsh birds, LAND BIRDS;
Winter: water birds, land birds.

This is an excellent birding site throughout the spring, summer and fall, and good in the winter. Two hundred eighteen species have been seen at the Arboretum, including a handful of rare or very uncommon occurrences.

The spring migration starts in March with the arrival of woodcock at the open fields in the Bolleswood area. At about this time, resident great horned and barred owls become vocal, also in the Bolleswood area. Later, in April and May, waves of warblers come through, and it is possible to see as many as 20 species during a good morning. Species that have been seen include Kentucky and yellow-throated warblers, as well as summer tanager.

Eleven warbler species stay on to nest at the Arboretum. Hooded and worm-eating warblers do so in the southern part of the Bolleswood Natural Area. Open habitat species, including blue-winged and prairie warblers, orchard oriole and field sparrow nest in the managed open areas at Bolleswood and Arboretum Field. Acadian flycatcher and Louisiana warbler nest in the hemlock ravine in Bolleswood. During the summer, great blue heron, black-crowned night heron and osprey feed in the coves at the Mamacoke Island Natural Area.

The highlight of the fall migration is the arrival of many sparrow species (including white-crowned, white-throated, Savannah and Lincoln's) at the powerline right-of-way in the southern part of the Bolleswood Natural Area, and in other shrubby fields throughout the Arboretum.

During the late fall, winter and early spring, the action moves to the northeastern part of the Arboretum - along the Thames River, in the coves on either side of Mamacoke Island, and north along the river shore to Smith Cove. There is a sufficient variety of aquatic habitats in this area to attract a great diversity of water bird species: dabbling ducks including gadwall, wigeon, black duck and mallard; diving ducks including canvasback (sometimes many of them), both scaups, redhead, goldeneye and ring-neck; also pied-billed grebe, all three mergansers, and (infrequently) Eurasian wigeon. In winter, the terrestrial habitats of the Arboretum are relatively quiet, and are occupied primarily by common species of woodland residents.

GETTING AROUND

Birding methods: car, WALK.

The Arboretum is covered by a network of trails, most of which are well maintained. One trail follows the shore of the Thames River from the Mamacoke Natural Area north to Smith Cove. (Trail maps are available at the Williams Street entrance to the Arboretum). Some of the roads that go along or through the Arboretum are not heavily travelled and suitable for birding from your car, but others are too conjested or heavily used to do so.

DIRECTIONS (see Map 65): The Arboretum is located about one mile north of the city of New London. The larger western portion is located on the west edge of the Connecticut College campus, while the smaller eastern portion is immediately northeast of the campus. **From I-95 southbound,** take exit 84 to Route 32 at the end of the exit ramp. **From I-95 northbound,** take exit 83 and reach Route 32 by turning left at the first traffic light and right at the second. Once on Route 32, go north for 0.4 mile to a traffic light; left on Williams Street for 0.6 mile to the entrance of the western portion of the Arboretum on the left. To reach the eastern portion, continue north on Williams Street and turn right on Benham Avenue, which goes through part of the eastern section.

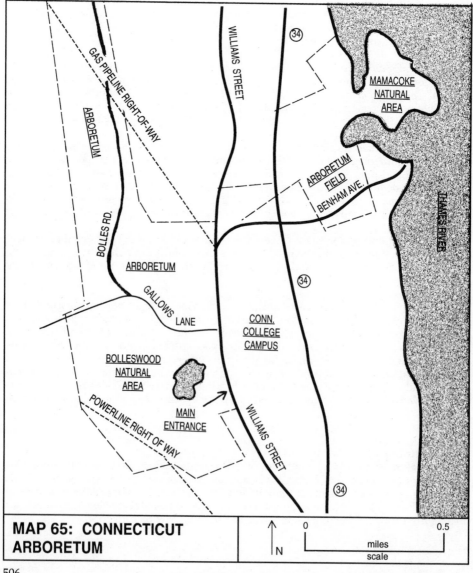

MAP 65: CONNECTICUT ARBORETUM

NORTH STONINGTON: ASSEKONK SWAMP WILDLIFE MANAGEMENT AREA

HABITATS

MARSH/SWAMP/BOG: sedge, cattail, mixed herbaceous and shrub marsh; shrub, shrubby hardwood and hardwood swamp, dead wood, shrubby and wooded edge; **Forest:** hardwoods, hardwoods/white pine, cedar, vine tangles, thickets, shrubby edges; **Open terrestrial:** short grass, mixed herbaceous and shrubby fields, shrubby and wooded edges; **Lake/pond:** pond, marshy and shrubby shore.

Much of this 698-acre site consists of a very large and beautiful wetland that includes almost every type of inland marsh and swamp habitat found in Connecticut, together with some open water. The remainder of the area is made up deciduous forest mixed with some white pine, with a dense shrub layer/understory of thickets and vine tangles, and shrubby edges. There are scattered clearings of reverting fields in the forest. The mowed playing fields of a local high school are contiguous.

SEASONS/BIRDS

SPRING MIGRATION: WATER BIRDS, MARSH BIRDS, shore birds, LAND BIRDS;
NESTING SEASON: water birds, MARSH BIRDS, shore birds, LAND BIRDS;
FALL MIGRATION: WATER BIRDS, MARSH BIRDS, shore birds, LAND BIRDS;
Winter: land birds.

An impressive variety of wetland-oriented bird species occur at this site during both migrations and the nesting season. In the spring, species that frequently occur here include wood duck, green-winged and blue-winged teals, gadwall and black duck; great blue heron; greater yellowlegs, spotted and solitary sandpipers; and also a nice variety of warblers and other land birds. Nesting species are known to include moorhen, and the habitat is just right for Virginia rail and sora. In addition, there are a number of shrub and edge species of landbirds, including brown thrasher, white-eyed vireo and orchard oriole. The fall migration is much like that in the spring, with the frequent addition of great egret and black-crowned night heron. In winter, look for resident and lingering land bird species.

GETTING AROUND

Birding methods: car, walk.

Trails and a woods road go through the woods in a portion of the southern and western parts of the area, and it is possible to reach the northern edge of the wetland from the high school playing fields (see "Directions" below). Hunting is permitted in the fall, so visit on Sundays during that time of year.

DIRECTIONS: This area is in the southeastern corner of Connecticut, six or seven miles north of Long Island Sound and about three miles west of the Rhode Island line.

To get into the forest habitats in the southern and western parts of the area, from the intersection of Routes 184 and 2 in North Stonington, go west on Route 184 for 1.8 miles to the North Stonington/Stonington town line (indicated by a sign on the highway). From this point, continue west on Route 184 for 0.2 mile to the third driveway on the right. Turn into the driveway, and bear right onto a dirt road that enters the area. It can be driven (but it is not plowed in winter) for 0.2 miles through forest habitats to a grassy parking area at the start of woods roads and trails.

To get to the northern edge of the wetland, from the intersection of Routes 184 and 2 in North Stonington, go west (northward) on Route 2 for 1.8 miles to the Wheeler High School. Park at the school athletic fields on the left side of the road and walk to the back of the fields. There are obscure paths through about 20 feet of shrubs and trees to the edge of the wetland.

NORTH STONINGTON: PATCHAUG STATE FOREST

HABITATS
Forest: hardwoods, hardwoods/hemlock, conifer plantations, shrubby and wooded edges, mountain laurel;
Open terrestrial: shrubby field, shrubby edge;
Lake/pomd: lake, deep water, wooded islands, wooded shore;
River/stream: streams, wooded streambelts.
This site is composed of two separate blocks of the Patchaug State Forest that lie near each other on either side of Wyassup Lake. Both are mostly forested with hardwoods, but the eastern block also includes an area of spruces and shrubby fields that have resulted from clearcutting. Lake Wyassup is composed of deep water, with a wooded and developed shore.

SEASONS/BIRDS
Spring migration: water birds, marsh birds, land birds;
Nesting season: marsh birds, land birds;
Fall migration: water birds, marsh birds, land birds;
Winter: land birds.
A typical mix of woodland birds occur in the state forest areas during the migrations and nesting season. In addition, nesting species include hooded warbler (in the sweet pepperbush), and worm-eating warbler. Several years ago, there was a great blue heron nesting colony on an island in Wyassup Lake. A few water birds stop at the lake during the late fall and early spring.

GETTING AROUND
Birding methods: car, WALK.
A certain amount of birding can be done from the roads that pass through the two state forest blocks; in addition, a number of woods roads and trails enter the forest from the road. There is a public landing at the lake. A scope would be helpful.

DIRECTIONS: This site is in North Stonington, four to five miles from the Rhode Island border. From the North Stonington village center at the intersection of Route 2 and Wyassup Road, go north on Wyassup Road for 3.4 miles to Wyassup Lake Road on the left. To get to Wyassup Lake and the western block of the state forest, go left on Wyassup Lake Road for less than a mile to the lake landing on the right, and the state forest on the left. To get to the eastern block of the state forest, do not turn left on Wyassup Lake Road, but continue on Wyassup Road for 0.6 mile. Starting at this point, and for the next 1.0 mile, the state forest is on both sides of the road. (Other blocks of the Patchaug State Forest are described under Voluntown/Griswold.)

OLD LYME: BLACK HALL RIVER

HABITATS

COASTAL: salt water and brackish tidal creek, mud flat, high and low salt and brackish marsh, mixed herbaceous vegetation; herbaceous, shrubby and wooded edges;

RIVER/STREAM: river, brackish and fresh water; hardwood, white pine and marshy streambelt;

Forest: hardwoods, white pine.

This site is part of the rich estuarine system of the Connecticut River just above Long Island Sound. It includes the lower section of the Black Hall River (above the Route 156 bridge) and its own estuary where it joins the Connecticut River (below the bridge). The river itself is tidal, but becomes brackish and then fresh as you go upstream. Its shore is partly wooded, with hardwoods and white pine, and partly bordered by small marshes. The estuary includes extensive mud flats surrounded by low and high salt marshes.

SEASONS/BIRDS

SPRING MIGRATION: gulls, WATER BIRDS, MARSH BIRDS, SHORE BIRDS, LAND BIRDS;

Nesting season: water birds, marsh birds, land birds;

FALL MIGRATION: gulls, WATER BIRDS, MARSH BIRDS, SHORE BIRDS, LAND BIRDS;

WINTER: WATER BIRDS, land birds.

This area includes habitats that are worth checking at any time of year. During the spring and fall, water birds come to the mud flats to feed - principally black duck, gadwall, hooded merganser and other shallow-water species, and they may also be seen here in winter. Waders come to the estuary to feed in the spring, summer and fall - especially great and snowy egrets, green-backed and little blue herons and black-crowned night heron. And a variety of shorebirds feed here at low tide as they pass through in migration. A standard mix of land birds occur during the spring, summer and fall in the terrestrial habitats that border the river and the marshes that are associated with it. Raptors are often present - harrier in the fall and spring, osprey in the spring, summer and fall, red-tailed hawk at any time, and a variety of other raptor migrants in the fall.

GETTING AROUND

Birding methods: car, walk, BOAT.

The two places described below can both be reached by car or on foot. In addition, the Black Hall River and its estuary can be explored by boat, given favorable tide conditions. Tide times are nearly the same at those at Saybrook Point. You can put a boat in the river just above the Route 156 bridge.

DIRECTIONS (see Map 66): This area is located in Old Lyme on the east shore of the Connecticut River near where it enters Long Island Sound. From I-95 take exit 70, go south on Route 156 for 2.7 miles to where Route 156 crosses the Black Hall River. From this bridge there is a good view to the south of the estuary and mud flat. There are places to park at the marina just east of the bridge or on a wide road shoulder just west of the bridge. Also, at the far end of the bridge, a dirt road on the left side of Route 156 leads in 0.3 mile to a cemetery and habitats along the shore of the Black Hall River upstream from the bridge.

OLD LYME: DEP MARINE HEADQUARTERS

HABITATS
Coastal: tidal river, brackish water, developed shore.
This is a wharf by the shore of the Connecticut River about three miles above where it enters Long Island Sound. From here, a section of the river can be seen very well.

SEASONS/BIRDS
Spring migration: gulls, terns, water birds;
Nesting season: gulls, terns, water birds;
Fall migration: gulls, terns, water birds;
Winter: gulls, water birds.
Birds on or moving along the river can be seen from here. While this section of river is not a bird concentration point, there is something going by most of the time.

GETTING AROUND
Can be birded by: car.
This wharf provides the public with a way to see this section of the river. Also, there are exhibits and rest rooms inside the DEP Headquarters building. You can park a few yards from the wharf. The public is not permitted to launch a boat from here.

DIRECTIONS (see Map 61): From I-95 exit 70, go south on Route 156 for 0.5 mile, right on Ferry Road for 0.5 mile to the parking area for DEP Marine Headquarters.

OLD LYME: FOUR MILE RIVER

HABITATS
Coastal: low and high brackish marsh, tidal creek, mud flats, shrubby and hardwood shore;
Forest: hardwoods, shrubby edge.
This is a state boat landing on a tidal creek a very short distance above Long Island Sound. From the landing, you get good close looks at the nearby tidal marsh, mud flats and the thickets along the edge of the marsh. Hardwood forest with a shrubby edge surrounds the parking area.

SEASONS/BIRDS
Spring migration: water birds, marsh birds, shore birds, land birds;
Nesting season: water birds, marsh birds, land birds;
Fall migration: water birds, marsh birds, shore birds, land birds;
Winter: water birds, land birds.
This site has something to offer during most of the year. A few water birds are usually present, especially in the late fall, winter and early spring. Shore birds can be seen as they feed on the mud flats during the spring and fall migrations. Marsh birds are here spring, summer and fall. And it is always worthwhile to look for land birds in the thickets along the marsh, and in the forest edges around the parking area.

GETTING AROUND
Birding methods: car, walk, boat.
You can drive right to the edge of the creek and marsh; limited walking is possible around the landing and parking areas. This is a place from which to start a boat trip, either up the creek or downstream and into Long Island Sound. However, time the tides carefully - at low tide the creek and the launching area are shallow, and at high tide, clearance under the railroad bridge downstream may be a problem. Tide times at the mouth of the Four Mile River are a few minutes ahead of the Saybrook Jetty.

DIRECTIONS (see Map 61): The Four Mile River divides Old Lyme from East Lyme just above Long Island Sound. From I-95 exit 72, at the end of the Rocky Neck State Park Connector, go west (right) on Route 156 for 1.4 miles, left on Oak Ridge Drive for 0.3 mile, and right on the driveway for 0.2 mile to the landing.

OLD LYME: GRISWOLD POINT/GRISWOLD MARSH

HABITATS
COASTAL: Long Island Sound, breakwater, salt and brackish tidal river, sand, gravel and cobble beach, dunes, tidal cove, intertidal mud, intertidal gravel, high and low salt marshes, herbaceous and shrubby edges, coastal forest, shrubby edges.
Griswold Point is the centerpiece of the rich and complex coastal habitat system that lies in the estuary of the Connecticut River. This entire area is unique in the Northeastern United States in that it lies at the mouth of a major river - a river that is longer and carries a greater volume of water than the Hudson - and yet with an estuary that is still in a largely natural and undeveloped condition. Griswold Point itself includes a barrier beach and dune system, in the shelter of which lies a shallow backwater cove that has extensive exposed mudflats at low tide, and is bordered by salt marshes.

SEASONS/BIRDS
SPRING MIGRATION: gulls, TERNS, WATER BIRDS, SHORE BIRDS, MARSH BIRDS, land birds;
NESTING SEASON: gulls, TERNS, SHORE BIRDS, MARSH BIRDS; land birds;
FALL MIGRATION: gulls, terns, WATER BIRDS, SHORE BIRDS, MARSH BIRDS, land birds;
WINTER: gulls, WATER BIRDS, LAND BIRDS.
Taken together, Griswold Point and the areas around it provide some of Connecticut's finest coastal birding, and it is excellent at any time of year. Early in the spring (March), the whole spectrum of Connecticut water bird species may be seen on Long Island Sound and also on the cove and Griswold Marsh behind the point. A little later (April and May), a wide variety of terns, marsh birds, shore birds and land birds pass in migration, or arrive to nest. Notable among the nesters are osprey, horned lark, least tern and piping plover (Griswold Point is one of only a handful of sites along the Connecticut coast where the latter two species nest). The early fall (September and October) brings with it the excitement of the raptor migration, occasionally including merlin, peregrine and harrier. Later (November), look for water birds once again on the Sound. In winter, this is one of the better sites on the coast at which to look for harrier, rough-legged hawk, snowy and short-eared owls.

GETTING AROUND
Birding methods: WALK, BOAT.

There is public access to Griswold Point from two directions. One is by boat from the state landing at Smiths Neck (a nice trip on sheltered water past good habitats), and the other is by walking west from White Sands Beach for about a mile. When doing this it is necessary to stay on public land, which means walking below the mean high tide line. The mainland at the base (east end) of Griswold Point is private property, and should not be entered under any circumstances. Once on Griswold Point, it is possible to walk much of its one mile length, but from April through August, it is necessary not to enter areas that are set aside and marked as piping plover and least tern nesting sites. (On the positive side, difficulty of access keeps the number of visitors to a tolerable level even during the summer.)

DIRECTIONS (see Map 66): To reach Griswold Point by boat, put in at the state landing at Smiths Neck (see directions under "Old Lyme: Smiths Neck State Landing"). From the landing, Griswold Point is the low land visible about a mile to the south. Use tide times for Saybrook Point as your guide.

You can reach Griswold Point by walking for about a mile west on White Sands Beach, during the period October through mid-April (access to the beach is restricted to Old Lyme residents during the rest of the year). To reach the beach from I-95 exit 70, go south on Route 156 for 2.8 miles (this is 0.9 miles past Smiths Neck Road), right on Old Shore Road for 0.5 mile, and right on White Sands Road for 0.3 mile to the beach parking area. From here, walk west along the beach for about a mile to the base (the eastern end) of Griswold Point. The beach offers a view of Long Island Sound and a chance to see water birds on it during the period from November to March.

OLD LYME: LIEUTENANT RIVER

HABITATS
Coastal: brackish and fresh water tidal creek, high and low salt and brackish marsh, coastal hardwood forest;
River/stream: brackish and fresh water tidal river, marshy, shrubby and wooded shore;
Forest: hardwoods.

This site includes the lower section of the Lieutenant River, both above and below the Route 156 bridge. From the bridge downstream, the river winds for a little less than a mile through salt marshes until it enters the Connecticut River about half a mile upstream from Great Island. Unfortunately, much of the marsh near the bridge has been taken over by phragmites. There are groves of coastal hardwoods along the edges of the marsh. From the bridge upstream, the Lieutenant River is still tidal for about two miles, and becomes brackish and then fresh as you go upstream. Its shore is partly wooded, mostly with hardwoods, and there are small marshes and areas of shrubs here and there.

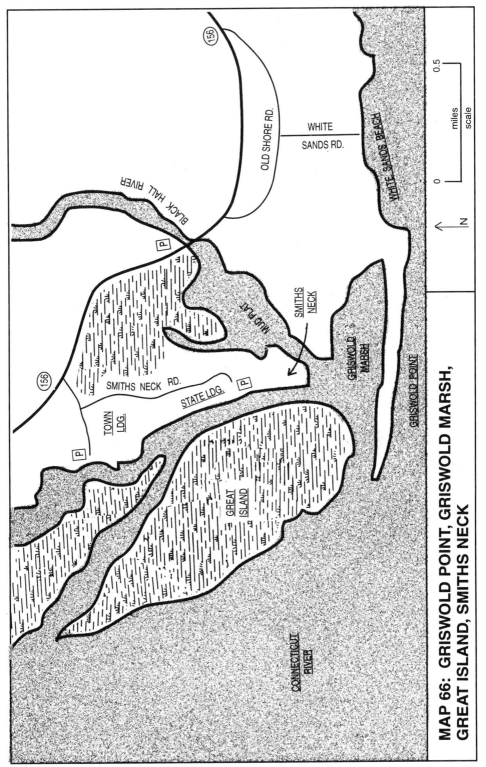

MAP 66: GRISWOLD POINT, GRISWOLD MARSH, GREAT ISLAND, SMITHS NECK

SEASONS/BIRDS

SPRING MIGRATION: WATER BIRDS, MARSH BIRDS, shore birds, land birds;
Nesting season: marsh birds, land birds;
FALL MIGRATION: WATER BIRDS, MARSH BIRDS, shore birds, land birds;
Winter: water birds, land birds.

This area can be good throughout the year. During the spring, summer and fall, waders feed along the shores of the river and in the marshes around it - great and snowy egrets, green-backed and little blue herons and black-crowned night heron; clapper rail nests in the marshes. During the fall, winter and spring, black duck, bufflehead, hooded merganser and other water birds feed and rest on the river. During this same period, a variety of raptors can be seen in the area - including harrier and red-tailed hawk (the latter is present all year). Where there are muddy river banks at low tide, shore birds occur during migration. There is a fair variety of land bird species to look for during both migrations and the nesting season in the terrestrial habitats along the river shore, mainly upstream of the Route 156 bridge.

GETTING AROUND

Birding methods: car, BOAT.

This is a site to look at briefly in passing, unless you have a boat to explore areas that cannot be seen from the road. A short stretch of the river can be seen from the parking area by Route 156 (see below). This is also a good place to put a boat in - it is possible to go up the river for a considerable distance, or to go downstream into the system of marshes and creeks near Great Island. Be sure to time your trip so that you have favorable tides. Tide times are about 30 minutes later than at Saybrook Point.

DIRECTIONS (see Map 61): This river flows from the east and north into the Connecticut River about two miles upstream from Long Island Sound. To reach the Lieutenant River from I-95 take exit 70, go south on Route 156 for 0.4 mile to the bridge over the river. There is a place to park on the right just before the bridge.

OLD LYME: SMITHS NECK STATE LANDING/GREAT ISLAND

HABITATS

COASTAL: high and low salt and brackish marshes, tidal creek, shrubby edges, coastal forest;

This landing is in the center of the system of rich coastal habitats in the Connecticut River estuary; it provides excellent views of some of them (Great Island and the salt marshes and mud flats near it), and is a good starting point to reach others by boat (see "Getting Around" below). Great Island is only a few yards from the state landing, across a tidal creek. It is composed of high and low salt marsh, and is cut through by a number of tidal creeks.

SEASONS/BIRDS

SPRING MIGRATION: gulls, terns, WATER BIRDS, SHORE BIRDS, MARSH BIRDS, LAND BIRDS;
NESTING SEASON: gulls, terns, water birds, MARSH BIRDS, shore birds, LAND BIRDS;
FALL MIGRATION: gulls, terns, WATER BIRDS, SHORE BIRDS, MARSH BIRDS, LAND BIRDS;
WINTER: WATER BIRDS, LAND BIRDS.

The habitats that are visible and / or accessible from the state landing can be exciting at any time of year. Water birds feed and rest on the tidal creek in front of the landing and on other nearby waters, during the period October through April. The species variety is often interesting, and can include green-winged teal, pintail, shoveler and gadwall. Waders and other marsh birds are present during the spring, summer and fall; species present may include American bittern, cattle egret, glossy ibis, yellow-crowned night heron, tricolored heron and little blue heron. Shore birds pass through during the spring and fall migrations, in large numbers and with an interesting species diversity. A number of willets nest here.

Among land bird species, osprey puts on the most visible performance. In 1995, there were 25 nest platforms visible from the landing, and 20 had parents attending nests. This is one of the best sites in Connecticut at which to watch the osprey nesting cycle, which starts with nest housekeeping by the males in April and ends with the southward migration of young and parents in late August and September. Other nesting land birds include sharp-tailed and seaside sparrows and marsh wren. Raptors are often common during the fall migration, sometimes including merlin and peregrine falcon. And in winter, Great Island is one of the best sites in Connecticut at which to look for rough-legged hawk.

GETTING AROUND
Birding methods: CAR, BOAT, WHEELCHAIR.
This is a good place to see coastal habitats from within or near your car, as the parking and launching areas provide excellent views of Great Island and other nearby coastal areas, and there is a wheelchair-accessible observation platform at the landing. It also can be a starting point for a boat trip to explore nearby coastal habitats: the Lieutenant River is just to the north, while Griswold Marsh, Griswold Point and the Black Hall River are less than a mile to the south. These nearby sites are described separately, also under Old Lyme. All of them can be reached through water that is sheltered, but subject to tidal currents. Use tide times for Saybrook Point as a guide for times at the state landing. Athough the landing is busy during the boating season, it is easy to get away from the crowds into the habitats nearby.

DIRECTIONS (see Map 66): This area is located in Old Lyme on the east shore of the Connecticut River as it enters Long Island Sound. From I-95 take exit 70, go south on Route 156 for 1.9 miles, right on Smiths Neck Road for 0.8 mile to its end at the state landing.

OLD LYME: SMITHS NECK TOWN LANDING

HABITATS
COASTAL: tidal creek, high and low salt marsh, brackish marsh, mud flats, coastal forest;
OPEN TERRESTRIAL: shrubby field, shrubby edges.
This town landing is half a mile up the coast from the Smiths Neck State Landing, and is also within the estuary of the Connecticut River. The landing itself is on the shore within a small coastal forest and overlooks a tidal creek and a salt marsh. The dirt driveway that leads to it goes through reverting fields with shrubby edges.

SEASONS/BIRDS
SPRING MIGRATION: WATER BIRDS, MARSH BIRDS, shore birds, land birds;
Nesting season: water birds, marsh birds, land birds;
FALL MIGRATION: WATER BIRDS, MARSH BIRDS, shore birds, land birds;
Winter: water birds, land birds.

This site has something to offer at any time of year. Water birds feed and rest on the tidal creek in front of the landing during the period November through March; species include green-winged teal, pintail, shoveler and gadwall. Waders and other marsh birds are present during the spring, summer and fall; species present may include great and snowy egrets, glossy ibis, black-crowned and yellow-crowned night herons. Shore birds pass through during the spring and fall migrations. Among land bird species that can be seen as they hunt the marshes, osprey is present during the spring, summer and fall, harrier in the spring and fall, and rough-legged hawk in winter (occasional). Other raptor species pass by frequently during September and October. White-eyed vireo and bobwhite nest in the shrubby field next to the driveway.

GETTING AROUND
Birding methods: car.

This is a good place to see coastal habitats from within or near your car - the parking area provides a view of a tidal creek and nearby salt marshes. The driveway to the landing may not be plowed in winter. The landing is not far from several other coastal sites - the Lieutenant River is just to the north, while Griswold Marsh, Griswold Point and the Black Hall River are about a mile to the south. If you plan a boat trip to any of these sites, put your boat in at the Smiths Neck State Landing.

DIRECTIONS (see Map 66): This site is located in Old Lyme on the east shore of the Connecticut River about a mile above where it enters Long Island Sound. From I-95 take exit 70, go south on Route 156 for 1.9 miles, right on Smiths Neck Road for 0.1 mile, right on a dirt road for 0.2 mile to its end at the landing.

OLD LYME: WATCH ROCK

HABITATS
COASTAL: tidal cove, high and low salt and brackish marsh, tidal creek, mud flat, coastal forest.

This is another site that lies within the Connecticut River estuary. It overlooks a small tidal cove and creek at the north end of the Great Island marsh, where there is an expansive area of mudflats exposed at low tide. It also includes a really nice coastal forest with heavy shrub growth in places, together with scattered cedars.

SEASONS/BIRDS
SPRING MIGRATION: WATER BIRDS, MARSH BIRDS, SHORE BIRDS, LAND BIRDS;
NESTING SEASON: water birds, MARSH BIRDS, shore birds, LAND BIRDS;
FALL MIGRATION: WATER BIRDS, MARSH BIRDS, SHORE BIRDS, LAND BIRDS;
WINTER: WATER BIRDS, land birds.

This is an excellent site at which to see a good variety and large numbers of water birds, especially dabbling ducks, in the fall, winter and spring (green-winged teal and gadwall are the most numerous). A variety of marsh birds are present in spring, summer and fall. At low tide during May and August, the mud flat is often teeming with migrating shore birds. Land birds are present at any time of year. Among the species that nest here are gadwall, osprey, clapper rail, white-eyed vireo, sharp-tailed and seaside sparrows.

GETTING AROUND
Birding methods: walk.
A trail follows the shore and goes through the coastal forest, providing excellent views of all the habitats at this site. A scope is necessary.

DIRECTIONS (see Map 61): This site is in Old Lyme, about two miles south of the Baldwin (I-95) Bridge over the Connecticut River. From I-95 exit 70 and go south on Route 156 for 1.4 miles. From this point, there are two ways to reach the site. **To reach the north end of the site by way of a shorter trail,** left on McCurdy Road for 0.1 mile, left on a dirt driveway for 0.3 mile to a parking area. A short trail leads to the edge of the water. **To reach the south end of the site by way of a longer trail,** right on Noyes Road for a few yards, right on Caulkins Road for a few yards, and right on Joel Road for 0.1 mile to the site entrance. A trail leads to the water in about 0.3 miles.

SALEM/MONTVILLE/BOZRAH: GARDNER LAKE

HABITATS
LAKE/POND: lake, deep water, shallow water, shrubby, wooded and partly developed shore, shrub marsh and shrub swamp along shore;
Marsh/swamp/bog: shrub marsh, shrub swamp;
Forest: hardwoods/hemlock.
This lake is quite large (487 acres), and over 40 feet deep at the south end near the boat launch. There are shallow areas and a marshy-swampy shoreline at the north end.

SEASONS/BIRDS
Spring migration: water birds, land birds;
Nesting season: land birds;
Fall migration: water birds, land birds;
Winter: water birds, land birds.
Migrating water birds during the early spring and late fall is pretty much the story at this site. Sometimes the deep area just north of the boat launch stays ice-free in early winter. Recreational boating activity rules out looking for water birds during the warm months. There are some land birds to look for along the wooded edges of the parking area.

GETTING AROUND
Birding methods: walk, BOAT.
The southern part of the lake can be viewed from the boat launch, but the marshy northern end is too far away (a little over two miles) even with a scope. This would be a good site at which to use a boat. (Motorboats up to 7 HP are permitted).

DIRECTIONS: This site is about six miles west of the city of Norwich. From the intersection of Routes 354 and 82, go north on Route 354 for 0.2 mile (past the driveway to the community park), and right on the driveway to the state boat launch. (See also Bozrah et al: Hopemead State Park.)

SPRAGUE: WALDO TRACT

HABITATS

OPEN TERRESTRIAL: tilled, short grass, tall grass, mixed herbaceous and shrubby fields, shrubby and wooded edges, scattered cedar;
River/stream: river, slow water, shrubby and wooded streambelt; stream, shrubby and wooded streambelt;
Forest: hardwoods, flood plain, dense shrub layer, shrubby edges;
Marsh/swamp/bog: mixed herbaceous and shrub marsh, shrub swamp;
Other: rocky slope.

This 75-acre site lies in the fertile valley of the Shetucket River. Most of it is in the bottomland of the valley, and consists of tilled farm fields, hayfields, shrubby reverting fields and shrubby edges. There is also flood plain forest, small pockets of wetlands, and the Shetucket River with a wooded streambelt. Part of the area is a rocky slope that forms one side of the valley.

SEASONS/BIRDS

SPRING MIGRATION: LAND BIRDS;
NESTING SEASON: LAND BIRDS;
FALL MIGRATION: LAND BIRDS;
Winter: land birds.

The specialty of this site is species that have an affinity for shrubby fields and edges; and large numbers of individual birds of these species are often present. Spring migrants and nesters include brown thrasher, white-eyed vireo, blue-winged and prairie warblers, field sparrow and indigo bunting. In summer, this is an ideal area in which to observe species that nest in open fields and edges. In addition, worm-eating warbler nests on the wooded, rocky hillside on the north side of Station Road just west of the Waldo Tract. During the fall migration, species seen in the spring are joined by a variety of sparrows (especially in October and November). Osprey uses the river as a migration corridor in the spring and fall. In winter bald eagles sometimes perch on trees overlooking the Shetucket River just below the dam.

GETTING AROUND

Birding methods: car, walk.

Park in the area provided at the entrance. A trail starts here and leads into the habitat areas. The rail line is active, and should not be walked. From your car, it is possible to see a portion of the habitats within the Waldo Tract, some of the rocky hillside on Station Road where worm-eating warblers nest, and the section of the Shetucket River where bald eagles perch and feed. However, all of these areas are better birded on foot (but stay in your car when eagles are present).

DIRECTIONS: The Waldo Tract is about six miles north of Norwich, on the New London County/Windham County line. To get there from I-395 (Route 52) just east of Norwich, take exit 83, go north on Route 97 for 6.1 miles, and, at the Sprague/Scotland Town line, left on

Waldo Road for 0.2 mile. Starting at this point and for the next 0.7 mile, the Waldo Tract is on the left. An entrance is at 0.6 mile. Then, continue on Waldo Road (which becomes Station Road) for 0.4 to 1.1 miles along a rocky hillside on the right (for nesting worm-eating warblers) and to the Shetucket River below the dam on the left (for wintering bald eagles).

STONINGTON: BARN ISLAND WILDLIFE MANAGEMENT AREA

HABITATS
COASTAL: Long Island Sound, tidal coves, tidal creeks, high and low salt marsh, mud flats, coastal forest;
OPEN TERRESTRIAL: shrubby fields, thickets, shrubby edges;
MARSH/SWAMP/BOG: cattail and mixed herbaceous marsh;
Forest: hardwoods.
This prime area contains a wide variety of habitat types - open water of Long Island Sound, a tidal cove, tidal marshes, brackish and fresh water ponds and marshes, coastal forest and large areas of shrubby field in various stages of succession.

SEASONS/BIRDS
SPRING MIGRATION: gulls, terns, WATER BIRDS, MARSH BIRDS, SHORE BIRDS, LAND BIRDS;
NESTING SEASON: gulls, terns, WATER BIRDS, MARSH BIRDS, shore birds, LAND BIRDS;
FALL MIGRATION: gulls, terns, WATER BIRDS, MARSH BIRDS, SHORE BIRDS, LAND BIRDS;
Winter: gulls, water birds, land birds.
A remarkable variety of bird species occur at Barn Island, including all the shore birds and all the waders that are seen in Connecticut, plus an impressive variety of land birds. The spring and fall migrations bring to the area a great variety of water birds, marsh birds, shore birds and land birds. Hawks which are migrating along the coast in the fall can be seen at the state landing and at areas of open marsh. Over the years, nesters have included several species that nest in only a handful of Connecticut sites - notably blue-winged teal, gadwall, least bittern, whip-poor-will, and chat. Other interesting nesting species include Virginia and clapper rails, bobwhite, willet, white-eyed vireo, thrasher, both cuckoos, martin, marsh wren, sharp-tailed and seaside sparrows. In recent summers there have been several active osprey nests on platforms in the tidal marshes. In winter, Barn Island is a good place to look on the tidal coves and creeks for water birds, including horned grebe, red-throated loon and common goldeneye. Look also for a variety of lingering land birds feeding in the shrubs and along edges. Harrier is a good possibility, and short-eared and snowy owls have occurred occasionally.

GETTING AROUND
Birding methods: car, WALK.
You can drive to the state landing which provides views of Long Island Sound and the tidal cove; there are also other habitat areas that can be reached by car. However, to do justice to this fine large area, it should be explored on foot, and there are a number of trails that make it possible. This area does not get as crowded as many state parks in the summer; hunting is allowed, so fall trips are best done on Sunday. Ticks are abundant much of the year.

DIRECTIONS (see Map 67): Barn Island lies on the Connecticut coast at Stonington, against the Rhode Island border. To get there, start at the intersection of Route 1 and Green Haven Road, about two miles northeast of the center of Stonington.

State landing, marsh and coastal forest areas: Turn onto Green Haven Road, immediately turn right on Palmer Neck Road and go for 1.7 miles to the state landing from which Long Island Sound and Wequetequock Cove can be viewed. Several hundred feet short of the launch parking area, trails go to the right and left. The trail to the right (west) leads through shrubs and thickets, while the trail to the left (east) passes through an area of coastal forest to tidal marshes and brackish ponds.

Stewart Farm Area: After turning from Route 1 onto Green Haven Road, go for 2.0 miles, right on Stewart Road for 0.4 mile to a dirt road on the right. This is the entrance to the Stewart Farm area. It has a mixture of weedy pastures and thicket-choked edges typical of abandoned farmland.

Brucker Farm Area: Continue on Stewart Road past the entrance to the Stewart Farm area for 0.5 mile to the entrance to the Brucker Farm, similar in habitat to the Stewart Farm.

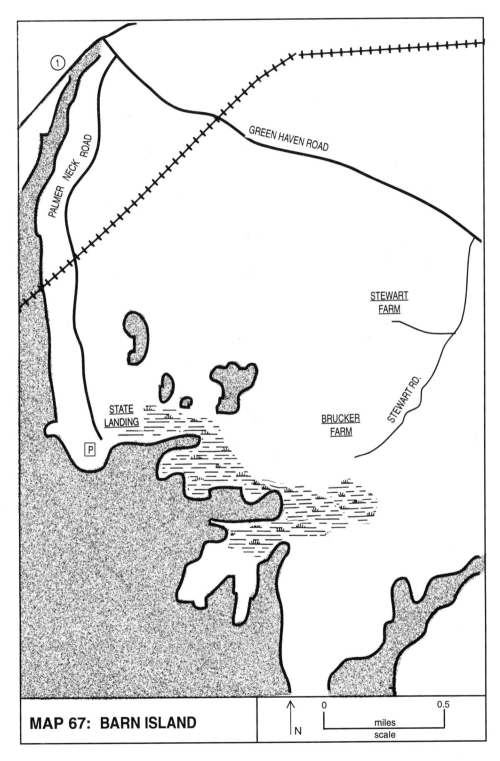

MAP 67: BARN ISLAND

PALMER NECK ROAD

GREEN HAVEN ROAD

STEWART FARM

STEWART RD.

BRUCKER FARM

STATE LANDING

P

N

0   miles   0.5
scale

STONINGTON: DENISON PEQUOTSEPOS NATURE CENTER

HABITATS
FOREST: hardwoods;
OPEN TERRESTRIAL: mixed herbaceous and shrubby fields, shrubby and wooded edges;
MARSH/SWAMP/BOG: shrub, shrubby hardwood and hardwood swamp;
Lake/pond: pond, shrubby shore; seasonal pools;
River/stream: seasonal streams.

The property of this nature center consists of 125 acres of managed habitat. It is a very productive site, especially considering its small size.

SEASONS/BIRDS
SPRING MIGRATION: LAND BIRDS;
NESTING SEASON: LAND BIRDS;
FALL MIGRATION: LAND BIRDS;
Winter: land birds.

There is a nice variety and good numbers of land birds at this site throughout the year, but especially in the spring, summer and fall. During the spring, you can count on seeing the standard mix of migrants. Nesters include Carolina wren, white-eyed vireo, barred owl, purple martin and many more common species. The fall migration brings warblers and other land birds in September, and a variety of sparrows in October and November. In winter, there are residents and lingering migrants such as hermit thrush and winter wren.

GETTING AROUND
Birding methods: WALK.

There are over four miles of well-maintained trails which provide access to all of the habitat areas. A trail map is available at the visitor center, and one is posted at the entrance.

DIRECTIONS: This nature center is located in the town of Stonington, about one mile north of the Mystic Seaport. From I-95 exit 90, go north on Route 27 for 0.4 mile, right on Jerry Brown Road for 1.1 miles, right on Pequotsepos Road for 0.5 mile to the entrance on the left.

STONINGTON: LATIMER POINT

HABITATS
COASTAL: tidal cove, mud flats, offshore rocks, high and low salt marsh, shrubby and hardwood edges; coastal forest, vine tangles and thickets, shrubby edges.

This site includes a half-mile stretch of country road that passes through a dense coastal forest with extensive areas of vine tangles and thickets. For a few yards, the road also goes along the shore of a tidal cove of Long Island Sound that is bordered by high and low salt marsh and shrubby edges.

SEASONS/BIRDS:
SPRING MIGRATION: gulls, terns, WATER BIRDS, MARSH BIRDS, SHORE BIRDS, land birds;
Nesting season: water birds, marsh birds, land birds;
FALL MIGRATION: gulls, terns, water birds, MARSH BIRDS, SHORE BIRDS, land birds;
Winter: water birds, land birds.

This site will provide you with interesting birding during all seasons. In the spring and fall, migrating water birds, marsh birds and shore birds feed in the cove, and the woods are a stopping place for large numbers of warblers that are traveling along the coast. Nesters include species drawn to dense shrubby areas, such as white-eyed vireo. Osprey can be seen hunting the cove during the spring, summer and fall. In winter, look for water birds on the cove, and resident and lingering land birds in the shrubs along the edges of the marsh and woods.

GETTING AROUND
Birding methods: car, walk.
Latimer Point Road is quiet and carries only infrequent local traffic. Therefore, it is suitable for birding from your car or on foot.

DIRECTIONS: This site is on the coast, about one mile east of the village of Mystic. From the intersection of Routes 1 and 27, go east on Route 1 for 0.9 mile, and turn right on Latimer Point Road. Starting immediately after the railroad tracks, and continuing for 0.4 mile, habitats on either side of the road are open to the public (do not be discouraged by the "keep out" sign just past the railroad tracks - private land does not begin until Latimer Point Road intersects with East Shore Road, 0.4 miles farther on).

STONINGTON: MYSTIC RIVER

HABITATS
COASTAL: salt and brackish tidal river and cove, herbaceous shore.
The Mystic River becomes wide in this section just above Mystic Seaport and the Mystic Harbor. Salt water is brought in as the tide rises, and brackish water goes through on the ebb tide.

SEASONS/BIRDS
SPRING MIGRATION: gulls, terns, marsh birds, WATER BIRDS, land birds;
Nesting season: gulls, terns, water birds, land birds;
FALL MIGRATION: gulls, terns, marsh birds, WATER BIRDS, land birds;
WINTER: gulls, WATER BIRDS.
This site provides an opportunity to see water birds up close, a nice contrast to the distant views that you sometimes have to settle for at coastal sites. It is best in late fall, winter and early spring, when it attracts both dabbling ducks (black duck, mallard and others), and divers (including canvasback, bufflehead and common goldeneye). Two osprey platforms on the western shore are usually attended and provide good looks during the spring, summer and fall. Terns are present during the warm months, and gulls all year.

GETTING AROUND
Birding methods: car, walk, BIKE.
The cove can be seen from a number of points along its shoreline, so that you can have the sun at your back. The route described below can certainly be done by car, would take quite a while to do on foot, but would be ideal on a bike.

DIRECTIONS: This site is in the southeastern corner of Connecticut about a mile north of Long Island Sound. The following route will take you entirely around the cove in a clockwise direction. From I-95 take exit 90, and go south on Route 27. In 0.4 mile on the right is the entrance to a cemetery from which the middle part of the cove can be seen. Continue south on Route 27 for another 1.4 miles, and right on Route 1 (Main Street) for 0.6 mile across the drawbridge over the Mystic River from which the lower part of the cove can be seen. At the far end of the bridge, go right on Gravel Street for several blocks along the river; then jog left onto Pearl Street and go north for several more blocks keeping to the river until Pearl Street leads to River Road. The latter follows the river most of the time for 3.0 miles, passes another cemetery that provides a view of the river, and takes you back to Route 27.

STONINGTON: STONINGTON POINT

HABITATS
COASTAL: Long Island Sound, rocky coast.
Other: hawk watching site.
This is a rocky point that extends into Long Island Sound, and provides an unobstructed view of the Sound.

SEASONS/BIRDS
Spring migration: gulls, terns, water birds;
Nesting season: gulls and terns;
Fall migration: gulls, terns, water birds, land birds;
Winter: gulls, water birds, shore birds.
Stonington Point is a good place from which to look for migrating hawks in the fall, and water birds in late fall, winter and early spring. Sightings have included horned grebe, both loons, brant, all three scoters, old squaw, common goldeneye and red-breasted merganser. Some years, gannet has been seen in the late fall. In winter, look for purple sandpiper feeding on the rocks.

GETTING AROUND
Birding methods: car.
A town road goes to a small parking area at the point.

DIRECTIONS: Stonington Point is at the southern end of the peninsula occupied by the village of Stonington. From I-95 exit 91, go south on Taugwank Road for 0.3 mile, left on North Main Street for 2.3 miles, left on Trumbull Avenue for 0.1 mile to stop sign, right on unmarked wide road over bridge for 0.3 mile, bear left onto Water Street and follow it for 1.0 mile to its end at the parking area on Stonington Point.

VOLUNTOWN/GRISWOLD: PATCHAUG STATE FOREST

HABITATS
FOREST: hardwoods, white pine and hemlock (alone and in various combinations); hardwood/white pine/pitch pine sand plain, flood plain;
RIVER/STREAM: stream, slow water, streambelts of mixed herbaceous marsh, hardwoods and hemlock;

MARSH/SWAMP/BOG: mixed herbaceous and shrub marsh; shrub, shrubby hardwood, hardwood, white cedar and rhododendron swamps;
Open terrestrial: short grass and shrubby fields;
Lake/pond: ponds, shallow water, marshy, shrubby and wooded shores;
Other: rocky slope, rocky summit.

This is the largest of Connecticut's state forests; its total area is 28,000 acres, and it consists of numerous separate parcels. These blocks make up most of the land area of Voluntown, and also occur in Griswold and North Stonington in New London County, and Sterling and Plainfield in Windham County.

This vast state forest contains almost every type of forest habitat found in Connecticut, plus numerous streams and streambelt habitats, ponds, and a variety of wetlands, including one of the small number of white cedar swamps that occur in Connecticut. Virtually all parts of this large state forest are worth exploring for birds of many species. For the sake of simplicity and brevity, two of the best areas have been selected and are described below. To get to other blocks of the forest, refer to Map 68.

Forest headquarters area and Rhododendron Sanctuary. The forest that surrounds the headquarters buildings and the Rhododendron Sanctuary is composed of white pine, hemlock, hardwoods and mixes of these species, with wooded and shrubby edges. There is also a large mowed field between the Rhododendron Sanctuary and a nearby camping area. The dominant plant species in the sanctuary are rhododendron and Atlantic white cedar - both uncommon in Connecticut. White cedar was once a common tree in New England, but is highly valued as a building material, and most have been cut down. Connecticut is at the northern edge of the range of rhododrendron, and it occurs only in isolated pockets. Hemlock and mountain laurel are also abundant in the swamp.

Patchaug River, Great Meadow Marsh and Beachdale Pond. The Patchaug River flows quietly through Great Meadow Marsh - a large wetland composed of mixed herbaceous marsh, shrub marsh, shrub swamp and white cedar swamp. It also leads to Beachdale Pond, which is shallow, filled with emergent vegetation, and surrounded by a marshy and shrubby shore.

SEASONS/BIRDS

SPRING MIGRATION: water birds, marsh birds, LAND BIRDS;
NESTING SEASON: water birds, marsh birds, LAND BIRDS;
FALL MIGRATION: water birds, marsh birds, LAND BIRDS;
Winter: land birds.

A great variety of species and large numbers of individual birds occur in these areas of this state forest. The nesting species of land birds include both northerners and southerners.

Forest headquarters area and Rhododendron Sanctuary. The woods near forest headquarters are a good area in which to look for a wide variety of migrating and nesting land birds, including such northern species as hermit thrush, solitary vireo, black-throated blue and black-throated green warblers, northern waterthrush and white-throated sparrow; as well as white-eyed vireo, hooded, worm-eating and pine warblers.

Patchaug River, Great Meadow Marsh and Beachdale Pond. During the spring, summer and fall, the Patchaug River, Great Meadow and Beachdale Pond attract water-oriented land bird species such as flycatchers, swallows, yellow warbler, and many others. Water birds (mostly dabbling ducks) and marsh birds (especially great blue and green-backed herons) are also present at these areas. Osprey nests in the marsh - an ususual occurrence this far inland.

GETTING AROUND

Birding methods: CAR, WALK, BIKE, BOAT, ski.

There are many miles of vehicle roads - both paved and dirt - that go through parts of the state forest and along its boundaries; most of them are quiet, little travelled, and suitable for birding from your car, on foot or by bike. In addition, there are many miles of woods roads and trails within the forest that are ideal for walking, and in many cases, skiing. The Patchaug River, Great Meadows and Beachdale Pond make a very nice canoe trip. A map of roads and trails through parts of the forest can be obtained at forest headquarters.

DIRECTIONS (see Map 68): The Patchaug State Forest is huge, irregular in shape, accessible from many separate points, and many parts of it are worthwhile for birding.

Forest Headquarters. To get to the largest block of the forest and to the headquarters office, start at the center of the village of Voluntown at the eastern intersection of Routes 49 and 165. Go north on Route 49 for 0.6 mile (over the Patchaug River and opposite the state landing), and left at the state forest sign to the headquarters building. (Detailed maps are available here.)

Rhododendron Sanctuary. Continue past the headquarters building, and go left at the fork, for a total distance from Route 49 of 0.7 mile to the trail to the Rhododendron Sanctuary on the right side of the large mowed field. (Many of the other roads lead through additional parts of the forest.)

Patchaug River, Great Meadow Marsh and Beachdale Pond. To start a canoe trip on the Patchaug River through the Great Meadow wetlands, put your boat in at the state landing; it is on Route 49 across the road from the entrance to the headquarters area of the forest (0.6 mile north of the eastern intersection of Routes 49 and 165). The Great Meadow wetlands are upstream (north) of the landing, and Beachdale Pond is a short distance downstream. (Another block of this state forest is described under North Stonington.)

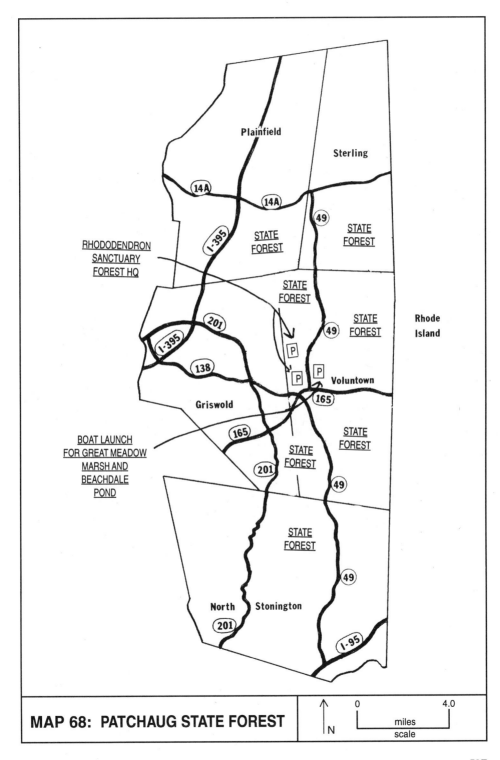

RHODODENDRON
SANCTUARY
FOREST HQ

BOAT LAUNCH
FOR GREAT MEADOW
MARSH AND
BEACHDALE
POND

Plainfield

Sterling

STATE FOREST

STATE FOREST

STATE FOREST

STATE FOREST

Rhode Island

Voluntown

STATE FOREST

Griswold

STATE FOREST

STATE FOREST

North Stonington

MAP 68: PATCHAUG STATE FOREST

N

0   4.0

miles
scale

WATERFORD: HARKNESS MEMORIAL STATE PARK/GOSHEN COVE

HABITATS
COASTAL: Long Island Sound, rocky coast, barrier beach, tidal pond, high and low salt marsh;
Open terrestrial: short grass field, shrubby field.
This former estate occupies a headland that extends into Long Island Sound, and, in a relatively small area, includes a variety of coastal and open terrestrial habitats. In addition, there are developed areas of the park - large shade trees, formal gardens and vast areas of lawn.

SEASONS/BIRDS
SPRING MIGRATION: gulls, terns, WATER BIRDS, shore birds, marsh birds, land birds;
Nesting season: terns, water birds, marsh birds, land birds;
FALL MIGRATION: gulls, terns, WATER BIRDS, shore birds, marsh birds, LAND BIRDS;
WINTER: WATER BIRDS, land birds.
This peninsula is especially good in the late fall, winter and early spring, when there are water birds to see on the Sound. Earlier in the fall, it is a pleasant place from which to watch raptors migrating along the coast. Water birds, shore birds and waders feed in Goshen Cove during the spring and fall (waders in summer as well), and they are easily seen from the park. There are two osprey nesting platforms in the park that are easily seen and often both are occupied. In summer there are lots of people in the park, but the ospreys don't seem to mind. In some years in the late fall, gannets have been seen over Long Island Sound from this site.

GETTING AROUND
Birding methods: car, walk.
Many of the habitat areas are visible from the park driveway and the others can be reached by a short walk. There is an admission charge during the summer.

DIRECTIONS: Harkness Park and Goshen Cove are located on Long Island Sound about five miles south of New London. From I-95 exit 74, go south on Route 161 for 3.1 miles, left on Route 156 for 3.0 miles, and right on Route 213 for 3.1 miles to the park entrance on the right. The driveway from the park entrance to the parking area overlooks Goshen Cove, the marsh, fields and thickets to the west (on the right as you enter). The point and Long Island Sound are straight ahead.

WATERFORD: JORDAN COVE

HABITATS
COASTAL: tidal cove, mud flats, high salt marsh, coastal forest.
This cove lies just east of Millstone Point, and contains several marine habitats. A coastal forest covers much of the shoreline of the cove. (Refer to the description of Millstone Point for information about access to this forest, and also to a place where Jordan Cove can be seen from Millstone Point.)

SEASONS/BIRDS
> **Spring migration:** gulls, terns, water birds, marsh birds, shore birds, land birds;
> **Nesting season:** gulls, terns, marsh birds, land birds;
> **Fall migration:** gulls, terns, water birds, marsh birds, shore birds, land birds;
> **Winter:** water birds, land birds.

The best times are the spring and fall migrations, when a variety of water, marsh, shore and land birds are present at various times. During the spring, summer and fall, waders come to the cove from other areas to feed, and osprey nests here. Land birds are present in the coastal forest at all seasons.

GETTING AROUND
> **Birding methods:** car.

There are two points with public access from which Jordan Cove can be seen, and both can be reached by car.

DIRECTIONS: This site is on the coast about five miles southwest of the city of New London. From I-95 exit 74, go south on Route 161 for 3.1 miles, left on Route 156 for 1.8 miles, right on Gardners Wood Road for 0.7 mile, left on Jordan Cove Road for 0.4 mile to the bridge over Jordan Cove, at which there is a wide shoulder on which to park in order to view the cove. For a second view, go another 0.1 mile, right on Shore Road for 0.7 mile, and right on Dock Street to a parking area on the shore.

WATERFORD: MILLSTONE POINT

HABITATS
> **COASTAL:** cove, salt pond, high salt marsh, Long Island Sound, rocky coast, coastal forest;
> **Open terrestrial:** shrubby field, shrubby edges.

This is a peninsula that extends into Long Island Sound between Jordan Cove on the east and the cove of the Niantic River on the west. The site includes a productive combination of coastal and open terrestrial habitats.

SEASONS/BIRDS
> **SPRING MIGRATION:** gulls, terns, water birds, MARSH BIRDS, shore birds, LAND BIRDS;
> **Nesting season:** gulls, terns, marsh birds, land birds;
> **FALL MIGRATION:** gulls, terns, water birds, marsh birds, shore birds, LAND BIRDS;
> **Winter:** gulls, water birds, land birds.

This is a good site for the spring and fall migrations of both coastal species and land birds. Marsh birds, including both black-crowned and yellow-crowned night herons occur here in the spring, summer and fall. The nature trail provides a good opportunity to look for migrating land birds in a coastal forest. During the nesting season, you can get good looks at osprey at a nesting platform on the point. Nearby along the power line, chat has nested in the shrubby fields.

GETTING AROUND
> **Birding methods:** car, WALK.

As you drive down to the point, you pass the beginning of a nature trail that follows the shore of Jordan Cove and goes through the coastal forest. Farther on, near the end of the point, there is a parking area at the environmental education center. It is possible to see some of the habitat areas from here. Also from the parking area, several trails go to the water and through the habitats on the point. The road to the parking area may not be plowed in winter. There are posted restrictions as to access to parts of this area, since it is a nuclear power plant owned by Northeast Utilities.

DIRECTIONS: This site is on the coast about five miles southwest of the city of New London. From I-95 exit 74, go south on Route 161 for 3.1 miles, left on Route 156 for 1.4 miles to the entrance to the Millstone Nuclear Power Plant on the right. Follow the access road for 0.8 mile, left at the fork for 0.3 mile to the nature trail on the left, and for an additional 0.4 mile to the parking area at the environmental education center at the point.

WATERFORD: WATERFORD BEACH PARK

HABITATS
COASTAL: tidal creek, barrier beach, dunes, low salt marsh, coastal forest;
Open terrestrial: short grass field, shrubby edge.
This is a small town park on the shore of Long Island Sound that includes a nice mix of coastal habitats.

SEASONS/BIRDS
Spring migration: gulls, terns, water birds, marsh birds, shore birds, land birds;
Nesting season: gulls, terns, land birds;
Fall migration: gulls, terns, water birds, marsh birds, shore birds, land birds;
Winter: gulls, water birds, land birds.
This small area provides a look at typical water bird and shore bird species during the spring and fall migrations. In winter, in addition to water birds on the Sound, there is an outside chance you may see one of the interesting raptor species that have occurred here over the years - rough-legged hawk, short-eared and snowy owls. Merlin has been seen in the fall and spring.

GETTING AROUND
Birding methods: car, walk.
Most of its habitats are visible from the driveway; the others can be reached by short trails. This park is closed to non-Waterford residents during the warm part of the year, but is open in the fall, winter and spring.

DIRECTIONS: This site is located just east of Harkness Park, on Long Island Sound about five miles south of New London. From I-95 exit 74, go south on Route 161 for 3.1 miles, left on Route 156 for 3.0 miles, and right on Route 213 for 3.5 miles to a stop sign just past the entrance of Harkness Park. Turn right at the stop sign and right again at the entrance to Waterford Beach Park. The park entrance leads to the tidal marsh.

Chapter 10

Tolland County

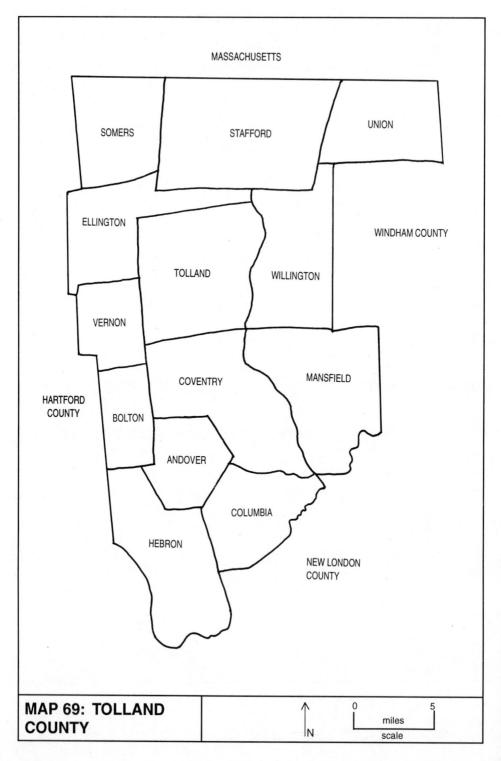

MAP 69: TOLLAND COUNTY

0 miles 5
scale

N

TOLLAND COUNTY   PAGE

TABLE 8: HABITATS AND SEASONS AT TOLLAND COUNTY SITES

Habitats ● very good example ○ present, but not as significant Seasons ● excellent during this season ○ less good during this season	FOREST	OPEN	MARSH	LAKE	RIVER	COAST	OTHER	SPRING	NEST	FALL	WINTER
Tour of Ponds in Tolland and Windham Counties	○	○		●	○			●	○	●	○
Andover: Bishop Swamp WMA	○	○	○	●	○			○	○	○	○
Andover: Nature Pond Conservation Area	○	○	○	○	○			○	○	○	○
Bolton: Bolton Lakes				●	○			●	○	●	○
Bolton: Bolton Notch Pond and State Park	●	○	○	●			○	●	○	●	○
Columbia: Mono Pond	○	○		○	○		○	○	○	○	○
Coventry: Coventry Lake (Wangumbaug Lake)			○	●	○			●	○	●	○
Coventry/Andover: Nathan Hale SF	●	●	●		○			●	●	●	○
Coventry/mansfield: Eagleville Pond			○	●	○			○	○	○	○
Ellington: Crystal Lake				●				○	○	○	○
Ellington/Tolland: Shenipsit Lake	●		○	●	○			●	○	●	○
Hebron: Gay City State Park	●	○	●	○	○			●	○	●	○
Hebron: Holbrook Pond	○	○	●	●	○			●	○	●	○
Mansfield: Horse Barn Hill	○	●	●	○	○			●	●	●	●
Mansfield: UConn: Mirror Lake		○		●	○			○	○	○	○
Mansfield: UConn: Parking Lot W	○	●	○	○				●	●	●	○
Mansfield: Pink Ravine	○	○	○	○	○			●	●	●	○
Mansfield: Schoolhouse Brook Park	●	○	○	○	○		○	●	●	●	○
Mansfield/Chaplin: Mansfield Hollow SP	●	●	●	●	●		●	●	●	●	○
Mansfield/Willington: Fenton River	●	●	○		●			●	●	●	○
Stafford: Ellithorpe FCA/Shenipsit SF	●	○	●	○	○		○	●	●	●	○
Stafford: Furnace Brook FCA	○	○	○	○	○		○	○	○	○	○
Stafford et al: Shenipsit SF	●	○	○	○	○		○	●	●	●	○
Tolland: Kollar WMA/Nye Holman SF	○	○	○		○			●	●	●	○
Union: Bigelow Hollow SP/Nipmuck SF	●		○	○	●			●	●	●	○
Union: Morse Meadow Pond	○		●	○				○	○	○	○
Union et al: Nipmuck SF	●	○	○	○	○			●	●	●	○
Vernon: Valley Falls Park/Belding WMA	○	●	○	○	●		○	●	●	●	○
Willington: Moss Conservation Area	●		○		○			●	●	●	○

BIRDING IN TOLLAND COUNTY

Tolland County is located in the north-central part of Connecticut, bounded on the west by Hartford County, on the north by Massachusetts, on the east by Windham County, and on the south by New London County. It is crossed by one major highway, I-84.

The People

Tolland County has a population of 130,470, (less than any other county but Windham), and a land area of 412 square miles (smaller than any other county but Middlesex). This gives it a population density of 317 people per square mile (less than any other county but Litchfield and Windham). Since 1960, Tolland County has had the fastest rate of growth of any county in Connecticut, but is one of the state's least affluent counties.

The Land

Most of Tolland County lies in Connecticut's Eastern Uplands ecoregion, with topography quite similar to the uplands of Windham County. The westernmost part of Tolland County lies in the Central Valley, and has topography that is similar to much of Hartford County. The uplands portion of Tolland County is rolling, hilly country, broken by many level to gently sloping valleys. Elevations range from 225' in the part of the county that is in the Central Valley, up to about 1,000' in the uplands. Forest communities are mainly central hardwoods mixed with white pine and hemlock. About 15% of the county is in farms. The climate is moderate, with hotter summers and colder winters typical of an inland area, compared with coastal areas. The lowest temperatures and highest precipitation occur at the higher elevations of the county.

Public Areas and Birding Sites

Tolland County is sandwiched between Connecticut's most populous county (Hartford) and the least populous county (Windham), and parts of Tolland County reflect each of these contrasting environments. In spite of its recent relatively rapid population growth, Tolland County still has large tracts of undeveloped land that is open to the public. Within the county, there are four state parks and four state forests, extensive open land that is owned by the University of Connecticut, several DEP wildlife management areas, several flood control areas, and a number of lakes and ponds to which there is public access. These areas include a nice diversity of habitats. There are large, unbroken forested areas, farms that are in use, and others that have been abandoned and are reverting to shrubby fields, young hardwood forest and edges. There are numerous marshes, swamps, rivers and streams with varied streambelts, and a variety of lakes and ponds. And these sites occur at various elevations. The result is a nice diversity of birds including both northern and southern species.

Tolland County's best area throughout the year is the cluster of sites in Mansfield, near the UConn campus. The second best (second only because it has relatively little action during the winter) is Mansfield Hollow State Park in Mansfield and Chaplin. Other good sites during the appropriate seasons are the Shenipsit and Nipmuck State Forests, the streambelt of the Fenton River in Mansfield and Willington, and several lakes and ponds, including Shenipsit Lake in Ellington and Tolland, Coventry Lake in Coventry, Bolton Lakes and Bolton Notch Pond, all in Bolton.

This chapter includes descriptions of certain blocks of Tolland County's larger state forests -

especially Shenipsit and Nipmuck - but there are other areas of these forests that are worth exploring. That would be best done with the aid of a large-scale map.

Seasons for birding

There is good birding in Tolland County throughout the year; the open habitats at Parking Lot W and Horse Barn Hill, both at UConn in Mansfield, keep winter from being the down season that it might otherwise be in an area that lacks coastal sites. Tolland County lures the birder not so much by the possibility of seeing rare or irregular species, as by the promise that you can see interesting and somewhat uncommon species with some regularity in certain habitats at known sites.

Spring migration. You have lots of choices in Tolland County. Early in the spring (just after ice-out, usually in March) go to Mansfield Hollow Lake in Mansfield Hollow State Park, or really any of the lakes and ponds that are described in this chapter, for migrating water birds. A little later (April), check the shores of these water bodies, as well as the edges of the fields in Mansfield for early land bird migrants. Still later (May), you can find migrating warblers at almost any of the sites - Schoolhouse Brook Park and appropriate habitats in Mansfield Hollow State Park are particularly good. During April and May, look for migrating snipe at Ibis Swale in Horse Barn Hill.

Nesting season. Again, you have lots of choices; where you should go depends on what species you are looking for. Owls (great horned, barred and saw-whet) can be found with some regularity in late winter/early spring along Pumping Station Road and Old Turnpike Road in the Fenton River area in Mansfield. To find open habitat species including kestrel, bluebird, bobolink, meadowlark and Savannah sparrow, the open fields at Horsebarn Hill and Parking Lot W are the best bets. For white-eyed vireo, worm-eating and Canada warblers, try the trail along the Fenton River. For a variety of northern species including solitary vireo, black-throated blue and black-throated green warblers, Bigelow Hollow State Park in Union and the Shenipsit State Forest in Stafford, Somers and Ellington have the right type of forest habitat. Also, for black-throated blue and Canada warblers, the Mountain Laurel Sanctuary in the Nipmuck State Forest in Union is a good place to look. Wetland-nesters, including Virginia rail and willow flycatcher, occur at Turnip Meadow in Mansfield Hollow State Park. Nesting great blue herons can be seen at the Ellithorpe Flood Control Area in Stafford.

Fall migration. As is the case during the spring migration, in the early fall (September and October) there are lots of good Tolland County sites at which to look for migrants (see sites listed for the spring migration). Later in the fall (October and November), try the open fields and edges at Parking Lot W and Horse Barn Hill for migrating sparrows (including Savannah, vesper, Lincoln's, white-crowned and occasionally grasshopper), as well as dicksissal, pipit, horned lark and meadowlark. Throughout the fall, look in these same areas for northern shrike, kestrel, harrier, sharp-shinned, Cooper's and red-tailed hawks. In October and November, check for snipe at Ibis Swale. Also in the late fall, check for migrating water birds on the lakes and ponds - especially Mansfield Hollow, Shenipsit, Coventry and those in Bolton.

Winter. In winter, the open habitats at Parking Lot W and Horse Barn Hill offer the possibility of seeing snow bunting, Lapland longspur, lingering berry-eating land birds, several hawk species, and northern shrike.

Sources of Information and Help

536

There are several good sources of information about birding in Tolland County. The Natchaug Ornithological Society has a mailing address in Mansfield Center. The State Museum of Natural History is located at UConn. Joshua's Trust manages a number of properties in Tolland and Windham Counties, including several that are listed as sites in this guide.

Tolland County includes built-up areas such as Vernon, Stafford Springs and several other town centers, at which there is no shortage of places to eat and stay for the night. However, there are also empty places in the county, where the birding is good, but the amenities are more difficult to find.

TOUR OF PONDS IN TOLLAND AND WINDHAM COUNTIES

THE TOUR: This driving tour is fairly short (about fourteen miles), but it provides views of four sites that lie in a cluster in eastern Tolland and western Windham Counties. In addition, the route of the tour goes right past Mansfield Hollow Lake. This large and very productive waterbody is not included on the tour, because to bird it requires several hours at the very least. However, if you have more time than the ponds tour requires, Mansfield Hollow Lake can easily be added. The sites included in the tour are listed below in the order that they are reached (they are not described separately):

> **Tolland County: Mansfield: Hansens Pond**
> **Windham County: Ashford: Knowlton Pond**
> **Windham County: Ashford: Leander Pond**
> **Tolland County: Mansfield: Mount Hope River**

HABITATS
> **LAKE/POND:** ponds, shallow and deep water, emergent vegetation; shores of pasture, shrubs and hardwoods; of marshes (sedge, cattail, mixed herbaceous, shrub), swamps (shrub, shrubby hardwood, hardwoods);
> **River/stream:** stream, shrubby and hardwood streambelt;
> **Open terrestrial:** tilled, short grass and shrubby field, cedars, shrubby and hardwood edges, vine tangles and thickets;
> **Forest:** hardwoods, mountain laurel.

These ponds vary widely in character and surroundings, and present interesting contrasts when seen in sequence.

Hansens Pond has both shallow and deep water, and a hardwood shore that is sparsely developed.

Knowlton Pond is composed of shallow water with much emergent vegetation, and an undeveloped shore of cattail, mixed herbaceous and shrub marsh, shrub swamp and hardwoods.

Leander Pond is also a shallow pond, with an undeveloped varied shore - pasture, cattail, sedge, mixed herbaceous and shrub marsh; shrub, shrubby hardwood and hardwood swamp, dead wood; shrubs and hardwoods. In the foreground of your view are short grass and shrubby fields, edges of shrubs, vine tangles and thickets.

Mount Hope River is a stream with slow and fast water, and a hardwood and shrubby streambelt.

SEASONS/BIRDS
SPRING MIGRATION: WATER BIRDS, marsh birds, land birds;
Nesting season: water birds, land birds;
FALL MIGRATION: WATER BIRDS, marsh birds, land birds;
Winter: land birds.

This tour has as its main focus migrating ducks and other water birds on the ponds (divers on Hansens Pond, and dabblers and ring-necked ducks on Knowlton and Leander Ponds). For that reason, it is best done in March and November, during the peak of the water bird migrations. A very good species variety and large numbers of water birds (especially ring-necked ducks) can be seen.

The tour also passes by habitat that attracts migrating marsh birds and land birds, so that there is activity later in the spring (especially May) and earlier in the fall (especially September). The most productive terrestrial habitats are the shores of the ponds (for migrating warblers), the fields next to Leander Pond (for edge-dwellers and seed- and berry-eaters) and the wooded streambelt of the Mount Hope River. Things are quieter during the summer, but some of the typical marsh and land bird species are present in pockets of suitable habitat. In winter, there may be some lingering land birds foraging among the shrubs.

Taken together, these varied habitats can provide excellent birding during the spring and fall migrations.

GETTING AROUND
Birding methods: CAR, walk.

This tour can be done entirely from within or near your car. Most of it follows little traveled country roads that are ideal for birding from your car or on foot. In addition, the stretch of Route 89 that passes near the Mount Hope River does provide an opportunity to bird while walking along the state highway, or on the town roads that it passes. During the entire tour, it is necessary to stay on the roads, because the surrounding land is private. Some of the views are distant, so that a scope is helpful.

DIRECTIONS (see Map 70): **The starting point for this tour is in Mansfield Center, at the intersection of Routes 89 and 195.**

To get to Hansens Pond, go north on Route 89 for 1.2 miles, left on Wormwood Hill Road for 1.7 miles to Hansens Pond on the right. (Shortly after starting at the intersection of Routes 89 and 195, Route 89 passes by Mansfield Hollow State Park and Lake.)

To get to Knowlton Pond from Hansens Pond, continue north on Wormwood Hill Road (bearing right at both forks) for 2.4 miles to a cove of Knowlton Pond on the left.

To get to Leander Pond from Knowlton Pond, continue of Wormwood Hill Road for another 0.3-0.4 mile to where you can see Leander Pond on the right. Find a safe place to park.

For another view of Knowlton Pond, from where you stopped at Leander Pond, continue on Wormwood Hill Road for another 0.2 mile to the intersection with Varga Road where Knowlton Pond can be seen to the left.

To complete the loop and return to your starting point, go east on Varga Road for 1.4 miles, and turn right on Route 89. In 5.9 miles, Route 89 intersects with Route 195 at the starting point of this tour. During this stretch, it intermittently comes close to the Mount Hope River and its hardwood streambelt. This route also passes Mansfield Hollow State Park and Lake once again, if you have time for more birding.

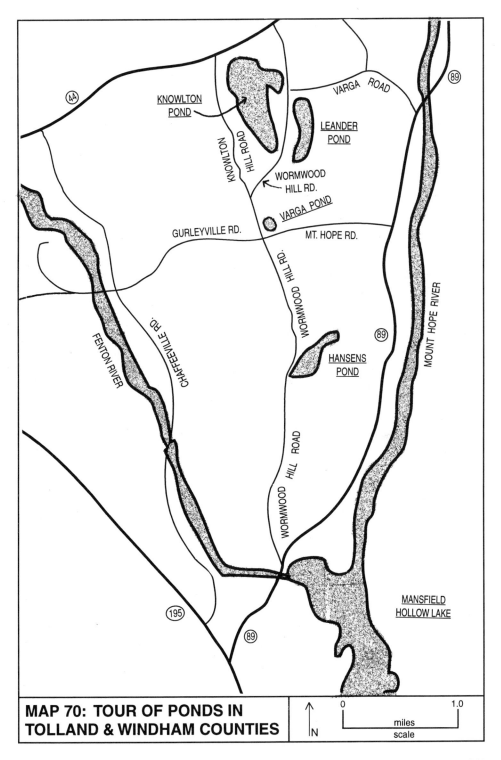

KNOWLTON POND

VARGA ROAD

LEANDER POND

KNOWLTON HILL ROAD

WORMWOOD HILL RD.

VARGA POND

GURLEYVILLE RD.

MT. HOPE RD.

WORMWOOD HILL RD.

FENTON RIVER

CHAFFEEVILLE RD.

MOUNT HOPE RIVER

HANSENS POND

WORMWOOD HILL ROAD

MANSFIELD HOLLOW LAKE

MAP 70: TOUR OF PONDS IN TOLLAND & WINDHAM COUNTIES

N

0   1.0

miles
scale

ANDOVER: BISHOP SWAMP WILDLIFE MANAGEMENT AREA

HABITATS
LAKE/POND: lake, shallow water, seasonal pools, shore of shrubby hardwood swamp and hardwoods, hardwood island;
Marsh/swamp/bog: cattail and shrub marsh, shrubby hardwood and hardwood swamp;
Open terrestrial: short grass, tall grass, tilled and shrubby fields;
Forest: hardwoods;
River/stream: perennial stream, seasonal streams.
In spite of its name, this site is more lake than swamp. There are areas of varied wetlands along the shore, backed by hardwood forest.

SEASONS/BIRDS
Spring migration: water birds, land birds;
Nesting season: water birds, land birds;
Fall migration: water birds, land birds;
Winter: land birds.
This site is worth checking during the spring and fall migrations, for a standard mix of land bird migrants plus a few water birds. Nesters include wood duck, red-tailed hawk, great horned and barred owls, woodcock and red-bellied woodpecker.

GETTING AROUND
Birding methods: car, walk, boat.
You can drive to the edge of the lake at a boat landing, and from here can see most of the lake, its island and shore. There is one woods road and several trails. Hunting is permitted in this area, and should be kept in mind when planning a fall trip.

DIRECTIONS: This site is in Andover, about six or seven miles southeast of Manchester. To get there from the intersection of Route 85 and I-384, go south on Route 85 for 4.3 miles, left on Daly Road for 0.8 mile, left on London Road (which becomes Boston Hill Road) for 1.3 miles, and right on Jorovaty Road for 0.7 mile to where the lake lies close to the right side of the road at a parking area and boat landing. From here, you can continue through state land by going another 0.6 mile on Jorovaty Road, and turning right on Gilead Road for 0.5 mile. During this stretch of road, several woods roads lead to the right toward the lake.

ANDOVER: NATURE POND CONSERVATION AREA

HABITATS
Marsh/swamp/bog: shrubby hardwood swamp;
Forest: hardwoods;
Open terrestrial: mixed herbaceous and shrubby field;
Lake/pond: pond, shrubby and hardwood shore; seasonal pools;
River/stream: seasonal streams.
This is a very small area that consists of a pond surrounded by shrubby hardwood swamp and hardwood forest. It is a nice place to stop at if you are nearby.

SEASONS/BIRDS

Spring migration: land birds;
Nesting season: land birds;
Fall migration: land birds;
Winter: land birds.

You can expect to find a standard mix of land birds during migration and the nesting season.

GETTING AROUND
Birding methods: car, walk.

You can park right at the edge of the pond; there are benches from which to observe life in and around the pond. In addition, there is a short trail that goes around the pond.

DIRECTIONS: This site is very near the village center of Andover. From Andover at the intersection of Routes 316 and 6, go south on Route 316 for 0.7 mile to the area on the left.

BOLTON: BOLTON LAKES

HABITATS
LAKE/POND: lakes, pond, deep and shallow water, shores of residences, hardwoods, hardwood/white pine, mountain laurel, other shrubs, shrub swamp, shrubby hardwood swamp;
River/stream: streams, wooded and shrubby streambelts.

Three closely connected lakes are included in this site. From south to north, and going upstream, they are: Lower Bolton Lake (178 acres of deep water), Middle Bolton Lake (115 acres of deep and shallow water), and Upper Bolton Lake (36 acres of shallow water). In the case of all three lakes, the shores are partly natural (hardwoods, hardwoods/white pine, shrubs) and partly developed.

SEASONS/BIRDS
SPRING MIGRATION: GULLS, WATER BIRDS, land birds;
Nesting season: water birds, land birds;
FALL MIGRATION: GULLS, WATER BIRDS, land birds;
Winter: gulls, land birds.

These lakes are good for gulls and water birds during the spring and fall migrations. Lower Bolton Lake offers the most variety and almost always has something interesting to look at during March and April, and again in October and November. Species to look for include common goldeneye, bufflehead, ring-necked duck, canvasback and common merganser. Gulls are usually also present. The middle and upper lakes usually have water birds, but not quite the species variety or number. The nesting season is much less interesting, but there are some land birds in the woods at the edge of the parking area between the upper and middle lakes. Species known to nest in the vicinity include broad-winged hawk, veery, red-eyed and warbling vireos, yellowthroat, ovenbird and towhee.

GETTING AROUND:
Birding methods: car.

There are two places from which the water of these lakes can be seen - one is a public boat landing at the south end of the Lower Lake, and the other is where a town road passes between the Middle and Upper Lakes. The surrounding land is private, so it is necessary to do your birding at these two places.

DIRECTIONS: These three lakes are located at Bolton Notch, about fifteen miles east of Hartford. To get to Lower Bolton Lake, from the eastern intersection of Routes 44 and 6, go east on Route 44 for 1.0 mile, and left on the driveway to the boat landing. To get to Middle and Upper Bolton Lakes, from the boat landing at the Lower Lake, continue east on Route 44 for another 0.4 mile, left on Tolland Road for 1.0 mile, left on Cedar Swamp Road for 0.6 mile, left on Vernon Branch Road for 0.4 mile to a parking area just past where the road passes between Middle Bolton Lake (on the left) and Upper Bolton Lake (on the right).

BOLTON: BOLTON NOTCH POND AND STATE PARK

HABITATS
> **LAKE/POND:** pond, shallow water, marshy, shrubby, wooded and rocky shore;
> **FOREST:** hardwoods, hardwoods/hemlock, white pine/pitch pine sand plain, mountain laurel;
> **Open terrestrial:** shrubby field, shrubby edge;
> **Marsh/swamp/bog:** mixed herbaceous, cattail and shrub marsh, shrub swamp;
> **Other:** ledge, rocky slope.

Bolton Notch Pond is rather small (15 acres), with water depths of three to six feet. The shore and the habitats next to it are quite varied. There is a small wetland, a sand plain that includes black oak, white pine and pitch pine, and more typical woodlands of hardwoods and hemlock. The pond lies next to Bolton Notch Park.

SEASONS/BIRDS
> **SPRING MIGRATION:** water birds, marsh birds, shore birds, LAND BIRDS;
> **Nesting season:** land birds;
> **FALL MIGRATION:** water birds, marsh birds, shore birds, LAND BIRDS;
> **Winter:** land birds.

This site is worth a visit at almost any season. The spring migration brings a good show of common water birds on the pond (usually wood duck and ring-necked duck), a nice variety of land birds in the surrounding habitats, plus an occasional great blue heron, solitary sandpiper and greater yellowlegs. Species known to nest here include wood duck, wood thrush, veery, cedar waxwing, worm-eating, yellow and pine warblers and oven bird. The fall migration is similar to that in the spring, but also includes a number of berry- and seed-eaters, such as hermit thrush, cedar waxwing, and a variety of sparrows. In late fall into winter, look also for golden-crowned kinglet, brown creeper, junco and tree sparrow.

GETTING AROUND
> **Birding methods:** walk.

The Shenipsit Trail follows the shore of the pond, leads to Bolton Notch State Park, and joins other trails that go through the area. There is traffic noise from the highway, and off-road vehicles are often present in good weather.

DIRECTIONS: This site is in Bolton Notch. To get to it from the traffic light at the eastern intersection of Routes 44 and 6, go west on Route 44 for 0.7 mile, off at the first exit, and in 0.1 mile right into the commuter parking lot. A path to Bolton Notch Pond can be reached from the northeastern (right rear) corner of the parking lot. Cut across to the gravel path close to the pond. The blue-blazed Shenipsit Trail follows the west and north sides of the pond and leads to Bolton Notch State Park.

COLUMBIA: MONO POND

HABITATS
Lake/pond: pond, deep and shallow water, wooded and developed shore, wooded and shrubby island;
Forest: hardwoods, hardwoods/white pine;
Open terrestrial: short grass and shrubby field, shrubby edges;
River/stream: stream, shrubby and wooded streambelt;
Other: dam.
This is a newly-acquired State DEP wildlife management area, that includes a 103-acre pond and 182 acres of woods and fields on one side of the pond.

SEASONS/BIRDS
Spring migration: water birds, land birds;
Nesting season: land birds;
Fall migration: water birds, land birds;
Winter: land birds.
The draw at this site is migrating water birds in the spring (ice-out to early April), and fall (late October through November). Ring-necked duck and hooded merganser are most frequent; sometimes also present are canvasback, lesser scaup and common goldeneye.

GETTING AROUND
Birding methods: car, walk.
This state wildlife management area is still in the development stage; signs have not yet been posted, nor have parking and access been provided. However, until that all happens, it is still possible to get a look at part of the pond from the dam at the north end.

DIRECTIONS: This site is in Columbia, about five miles southwest of Willimantic. To get there from the intersection of Routes 66 and 87 in Columbia, go west on Route 66 for 2.4 miles, left on Hunt Road for 1.7 miles to the dam on the right, that provides a look at the pond (although parking is difficult). Continue for another 0.4 mile and turn right on Pine Street. Somewhere in the next mile from the right side of Pine Street, it is believed that the state will provide access into the Wildlife Management Area.

COVENTRY: COVENTRY LAKE (WANGUMBAUG LAKE)

HABITATS
LAKE/POND: lake, deep water, cove, island, wooded and developed shore;
River/stream: perennial stream, wooded streambelt;
Marsh/swamp/bog: shrubby hardwood swamp.
This is a 378-acre lake with a shoreline that is almost completely occupied by residential development. The lake is quite deep (up to 36'), and for that reason it tends to freeze later in the fall than other nearby lakes and ponds.

SEASONS/BIRDS
SPRING MIGRATION: gulls, WATER BIRDS;
Nesting season:
FALL MIGRATION: gulls, WATER BIRDS;
Winter: gulls, water birds.
For seeing migrating water birds, Wangumbaug Lake is second only to the Mansfield Hol-

low Reservoir, among the lakes in Tolland County. Both the species variety and the number of individual birds is impressive on a typical day in March soon after ice-out, and again in the period November till the lake is frozen, in some years as late as January. Species that have been seen here include ring-necked duck, common goldeneye, bufflehead, both scaups, canvasback, redhead, hooded and common mergansers, coot, common loon, horned and pied-billed grebes. The entire focus at this site is on water birds in the spring and fall; boats in the summer, ice in the winter, and the highly developed shoreline mitigate against other seasons and bird groups.

GETTING AROUND
Birding methods: car, boat.
There are two places that are accessible to the public from which the water can be seen: one is a state boat launch site at the southeastern corner, and the other is a nearby cemetery that looks down on a cove. The land around each of these sites is private. The lake is large, and a scope is necessary to get good looks at distant water birds.

DIRECTIONS: This lake is in Coventry about five miles southwest of Storrs. From the intersection of Routes 31, 275 and Lake Street, go south on Lake Street for 0.2 mile to the cemetery entrance on the right, and for another 0.3 mile to the state boat landing, also on the right.

COVENTRY/ANDOVER: NATHAN HALE STATE FOREST

HABITATS
OPEN TERRESTRIAL: mixed herbaceous, short grass, tall grass, and shrubby fields, juniper, edges;
FOREST: hardwoods, white pine, hardwoods/hemlock, mixed conifers, cedar, mountain laurel;
MARSH/SWAMP/BOG: wet meadow, shrub marsh, shrub swamp, shrubby hardwood swamp, hardwood swamp, seasonal pools;
River/stream: stream, shrubby and wooded streambelt.
This park includes 1,296 acres of gently sloping terrain, which is largely wooded and also includes laurel thickets, varied wetlands, reverting fields, the Skungamaug River and streambelt habitats.

SEASONS/BIRDS
SPRING MIGRATION: LAND BIRDS;
NESTING SEASON: LAND BIRDS;
FALL MIGRATION: LAND BIRDS;
Winter: land birds.
This is a good site in which to look for a wide variety of land bird migrants and nesters that have an affinity for any of the diverse habitats in this state forest. Adding to the diversity of species is the fact that both northerners and southerners nest here. In total, 88 species have shown some evidence of breeding at this site. Among the forest-dwellers are broad-winged and red-shouldered hawks, barred owl, red-bellied woodpecker, yellow-throated vireo, hermit thrush and Canada warbler. Shrubby edge and shrubby wetland species include Carolina wren, white-eyed and warbling vireos, alder and willow flycatchers, prairie warbler, indigo bunting, swamp and field sparrows. And there are open fields to provide nest sites for bobolink and meadowlark. Louisiana waterthrush occurs along the Skungamaug River,

and northern waterthrush in the swamp.

GETTING AROUND
Birding methods: car, WALK.
Most of the habitat areas can be reached by trails that start at the entrance and also from nearby town roads. In addition, there are dirt and paved roads that go through the forest or along its boundaries and can either be walked or driven. (Seagraves Road is likely to provide the best birding.)

DIRECTIONS: This state forest is about six miles southwest of Storrs. To get to one access point from Bolton Notch at the eastern intersection of Routes 6 and 44, go east on Route 6 for 2.7 miles, and left on South Street (not South Road, which you pass on the way to South Street). The state forest lies on both sides of South Street in the segment that is 2.6 miles to 3.8 miles from the South Street/Route 6 intersection. The forest can also be entered from other roads. Within the forest, there are numerous woods roads, trails and clearings.

COVENTRY/MANSFIELD: EAGLEVILLE POND

HABITATS
LAKE/POND: pond, deep and shallow water, developed, shrubby, marshy and wooded shore, islands with shrubby and wooded shores;
Open terrestrial: shrubby field, shrubby edge;
River/stream: river, wooded streambelt;
Marsh/swamp/bog: shrub marsh, shrub swamp.
This is a stretch of the Willimantic River on which a dam has created a long, narrow pond, 80 acres in area and about a mile in length. Most of it is quite shallow, and there are several islands. The shores of the pond are largely developed. A free-flowing stretch of the Willimantic River and its hardwood streambelt can be seen just below the dam.

SEASONS/BIRDS
Spring migration: water birds, marsh birds, shore birds, land birds;
Nesting season: water birds, shore birds, land birds;
Fall migration: water birds, marsh birds, shore birds, land birds;
Winter: land birds.
This pond is worth checking for common species of migrating water birds during March/April, and again during October/November. Also during migration, a standard mix of land birds can be seen along the shores of the river and pond. Great blue and green-backed herons occasionally occur during migration. Nesters include a variety of common land birds plus Louisiana waterthrush and spotted sandpiper.

GETTING AROUND
Birding methods: car, walk, wheelchair, boat.
It is possible to park at the foot of the dam and walk a few yards to the top, from which the south end of the pond can be seen (a scope helps). A wheelchair-accessible path also goes to the top of the dam. From the parking areas (there are two), it is possible to look down on a portion of the Willimantic River below the dam. There is a path along the river that appears to be open to the public. It also appears permissible to put a boat in the pond from near the

dam.

DIRECTIONS: This pond lies between the centers of Coventry and Storrs. To get to the south end of the pond from the intersection of Routes 275 and 32, go west on Route 275 for 0.3 mile to either one of the two parking areas at either end of the dam. The trail along the river starts from near the parking area at the far (west) end of the dam.

ELLINGTON: CRYSTAL LAKE

HABITATS
LAKE/POND: lake, deep water, developed and wooded shore.
This is a fairly large (201-acre) lake, with almost entirely deep water and a largely developed shoreline.

SEASONS/BIRDS
Spring migration: gulls, water birds, land birds;
Nesting season: water birds, land birds;
Fall migration: gulls, water birds, land birds;
Winter: gulls, water birds.
The primary story here is water birds during peak periods of migration and into early winter until the lake freezes. Crystal Lake can sometimes be good, but is not consistent.

GETTING AROUND
Birding methods: car.
Much of the lake can be seen from several viewpoints on the lake shore. The land surrounding these points is all private, so be careful where you go. The lake and the surrounding areas are crowded and heavily used during warm weather.

DIRECTIONS: This lake lies between the centers of Ellington and Stafford Springs, at the intersection of Routes 30 and 140. To get there from this intersection, go north on Route 30 for 0.6 mile, right and immediately left onto West Shore Road for 0.1 mile to the boat landing on the right, and for 0.4 mile to a point where the lake can be seen from the side of the road. A third viewpoint can be reached by continuing on West Shore Road to where it rejoins Route 30, north (right) on Route 30 for 0.2 mile, right on Crystal Lake Road for a few yards to where the road passes by the lake. A fourth viewpoint can be reached by returning to the intersection of Routes 30 and 140, and going east on Route 140 for 0.5 miles to where the south end of the lake can be seen. (Stay on land that is not posted as private.)

ELLINGTON/TOLLAND: SHENIPSIT LAKE

HABITATS
LAKE/POND: lake, deep and shallow water, cove, island, wooded and developed shore;
FOREST: hardwoods, hardwoods/white pine, white pine, hardwoods/hemlock, mixed conifers;
Marsh/swamp/bog: shrub swamp, shrubby hardwood swamp;
River/stream: stream, shrubby and wooded streambelt.
This is a large lake with several coves and an island. It serves as a public water supply, and most of the shore is undeveloped.

SEASONS/BIRDS
SPRING MIGRATION: gulls, WATER BIRDS, land birds;
Nesting season: water birds, land birds;
FALL MIGRATION: gulls, WATER BIRDS, marsh birds, land birds;
Winter: water birds, land birds.
Migrating water birds in the spring and fall are the main attraction at this site. Early winter can also be good as long as there is open water on the lake. In addition, the roads that go around much of the lake provide easy and productive birding for land bird species during spring, summer and fall. Nesters include yellow-throated vireo, Canada warbler, plus many typical woodland species. Great horned owl is among the year-round residents.

GETTING AROUND
Birding methods: car, walk.
The roads around the lake are lightly used, pass through good woodland habitat and provide occasional views of the lake. They provide a pleasant and easy way to bird from your car or on foot. Much of the land on either side of the road is off-limits to the public.

DIRECTIONS: Shenipsit Lake straddles the Ellington/Tolland town line, and is immediately northwest of Tolland center, and northeast of Rockville center. Parts of the route described below follow the shore of the lake and also pass through good woodland habitats. Start in Tolland at the western intersection of Routes 74 and 30; go west on Route 74 for 0.3 mile, right on Shenipsit Lake Road for 1.8 miles, and left on Ellington Road (which becomes Snipsic Lake Road) for 1.6 miles to an overlook of the lake on the left. This is the end of the best portion of the road, but it can be followed for another mile or so to Route 83 in Ellington.

HEBRON: GAY CITY STATE PARK

HABITATS
FOREST: hardwoods, hardwoods/white pine, hardwoods/hemlock;
MARSH/SWAMP/BOG: shrub swamp, shrubby hardwood swamp, hardwood swamp, dead wood;
Open terrestrial: short grass and shrubby fields, shrubby and wooded edge;
Lake/pond: ponds; shores of hardwoods, varied wetlands and short grass fields; seasonal pools;
River/stream: perennial stream, slow water, seasonal streams, wooded streambelts.
This park includes 1,569 acres, largely wooded with hardwoods, alone and together with

white pine and hemlock. There is also a shrubby hardwood swamp, beaver ponds and a section of the Blackledge River. While no one type of habitat is outstanding, there are lots of small habitat areas with productive interfaces between them.

SEASONS/BIRDS

SPRING MIGRATION: water birds, marsh birds, LAND BIRDS;
Nesting season: water birds, land birds;
FALL MIGRATION: water birds, marsh birds, LAND BIRDS;
Winter: land birds.

The best times to bird at this site are March through May, and September through October. Good numbers of the standard mix of land bird species occur here in migration. A few water birds are present during the spring, summer and fall. The nesters are the species you would expect in these habitats, including southern species such as red-bellied woodpecker and gnat-catcher, as well as wood duck and Louisiana waterthrush. Residents include red-tailed hawk, great horned and barred owls.

GETTING AROUND

Birding methods: car, walk.

A park driveway and two town roads go through the park, and there is an extensive trail network; a trail map is available at the entrance gate. The park driveway is open to autos only during the warm months, but the trails can be used all year. During the summer, the park gets crowded, and an entry fee is charged.

DIRECTIONS: This park is about 12 miles east-southeast of Hartford. To get there from the intersection of Routes 85 and 94 in Hebron, go north on Route 85 for 2.0 miles to the park entrance on left.

HEBRON: HOLBROOK POND

HABITATS

LAKE/POND: pond, shallow water, shore of shrub marsh and hardwoods, seasonal pools;
MARSH/SWAMP/BOG: mixed herbaceous and shrub marsh; shrub, shrubby hardwood and hardwood swamps, open water, shrubby edge;
Forest: hardwoods, mixed conifers;
Open terrestrial: short grass, tall grass and shrubby fields;
River/stream: perennial stream, streambelt of shrubs and hardwood swamp, seasonal streams.

This is a secluded, shallow pond, 73 acres in size, with a wooded shoreline that is undeveloped and protected from development by the surrounding Salmon River State Forest. Along one shore of the pond there is a wetland composed of various types of marsh and swamp; there is also a beaver-controlled wetland along the driveway that leads to the lake.

SEASONS/BIRDS

SPRING MIGRATION: water birds, marsh birds, LAND BIRDS;
Nesting season: water birds, marsh birds, land birds;
FALL MIGRATION: water birds, marsh birds, LAND BIRDS;
Winter: land birds.

A good variety of land birds, common species of water birds and an occasional great blue and green-backed heron occur here - especially during the spring and fall migrations, but also during the nesting season. Nesting land birds reflect the mix of forest, open and wetland habitats - they include broad-winged hawk, barred owl, red-bellied woodpecker, white-eyed and warbling vireos, yellowthroat and yellow warbler.

GETTING AROUND

Birding methods: CAR, WALK, BOAT.

There is a long driveway (0.7 mile) that leads from the state highway to the pond, and this creates a nice edge along which to bird by car or on foot. Much of the pond can be seen from the state boat landing at the end of the driveway; the marsh on the far side of the lake can only be reached by boat. There is a trail that leads into the contiguous Salmon River State Forest.

DIRECTIONS: This site lies midway between the village centers of Hebron and Gilead, about ten miles east of Glastonbury. To get there from the center of Hebron at the intersection of Routes 85 and 66, go north (westward) on Route 85 for 0.7 mile to the entrance on the right.

MANSFIELD: HORSE BARN HILL

HABITATS

OPEN TERRESTRIAL: tilled, short grass, tall grass, mixed herbaceous and shrubby fields, shrubby edges, hedgerows;
MARSH/SWAMP/BOG: wet meadow, sedge, cattail and mixed herbaceous marshes;
Lake/pond: ponds, seasonal pools;
River/stream: stream, grassy streambelt;
Forest: hardwoods, patches of mixed conifers, cedars.

Horse Barn Hill is an open hilltop that provides broad views of the surrounding farmland. The habitats which the hill overlooks include tilled fields and pastures, woodlands with wooded and shrubby edges, and a swale in which there is a wet meadow and a marsh (Ibis Swale). It is one of the finest examples in Connecticut of open-country types of habitat.

SEASONS/BIRDS

SPRING MIGRATION: water birds, marsh birds, shore birds, LAND BIRDS;
NESTING SEASON: water birds, marsh birds, shore birds, LAND BIRDS;
FALL MIGRATION: water birds, marsh birds, shore birds, LAND BIRDS;
WINTER: water birds, LAND BIRDS.

This is an exceptionally good site at any time of year, and for almost any group of birds, but especially for species that occur in open habitats. During the spring migration, it is possible to see a variety of geese and ducks, marsh birds including great blue and green-backed herons, woodcock, snipe (in April), and a nice mix of forest land bird species. Nesting species include Virginia rail, woodcock, bluebird, meadowlark, bobolink, Savannah and swamp sparrows. During July and August there is often an impressive display of swallows, including tree, barn, bank and rough-winged. The fall migration brings many of the same species as are seen in the spring. In addition, Horse Barn Hill is notable for Canada and snow geese feeding in the fields, many blackbirds of various species, pipit, and, in October and November, a wide variety and large number of sparrows including Savannah, vesper, white-crowned, Lincoln's, grasshopper (occasional), and dicksissal (rare). In late fall, winter and early spring, you may see horned lark, snow bunting and Lapland longspur. This is also a good site from which to see raptors - harrier in the spring and fall, rough-legged hawk and short-eared owl (occasional) in the winter, and red-tailed hawk and kestrel throughout the year.

GETTING AROUND
Birding methods: CAR, WALK, BIKE.
Horse Barn Hill Road makes a loop through this site, and provides good views of the fields and wetlands, of the birds feeding in them or hunting over them. It has occasional pulloffs - park by the roadside, and not in parking areas that are designated for others. In places the viewing distances are great, so that a telescope is useful. The land on either side of Horse Barn Hill Road is open to the public for walking; be sure to close gates, avoid close encounters with livestock, and don't trample crops. Good birding can be had by walking edges between the fields and woods.

DIRECTIONS (see Map 71): Horse Barn Hill is in Mansfield, on the eastern edge of the UConn campus. To get there from the intersection of Routes 195 and 44, go south on Route 195 for 0.9 mile and left on Horse Barn Hill Road. This road makes a 1.4 miles loop clockwise around Horse Barn Hill; to return to Route 195 at the end of this loop, turn right on Gurleyville Road for 0.1 mile. To reach Ibis Swale, after turning onto Horse Barn Hill Road from Route 195, take the first right beyond the poultry houses. The marsh is on the right.

MANSFIELD: UCONN: MIRROR LAKE

HABITATS
LAKE/POND: pond, shrubby island, grassy shore;
Open terrestrial: short grass field;
River/stream: stream.
This small pond is part of the UConn campus. It is surrounded by lawn, includes a shrubby island, and has a very small outlet stream.

SEASONS/BIRDS
Spring migration: water birds, marsh birds, shore birds, land birds;
Nesting season: water birds, land birds;
Fall migration: water birds, marsh birds, shore birds, land birds;
Winter: water birds, land birds.
Although this is an unlikely-seeming pond for good birding, quite a variety of water birds have been seen here. The spring migration usually produces the standard mix of water bird species: Canada goose, mallard, black duck and wood duck, plus often something else among the dabbling ducks. Ring-necked duck and snow goose occasionally occur here, and (uncommonly) greater white-fronted goose. Regular spring migrants also include great blue and green-backed herons, killdeer and spotted sandpiper. The fall is a repeat of spring, plus an occasional great egret. There are usually some ducks present during the summer and also

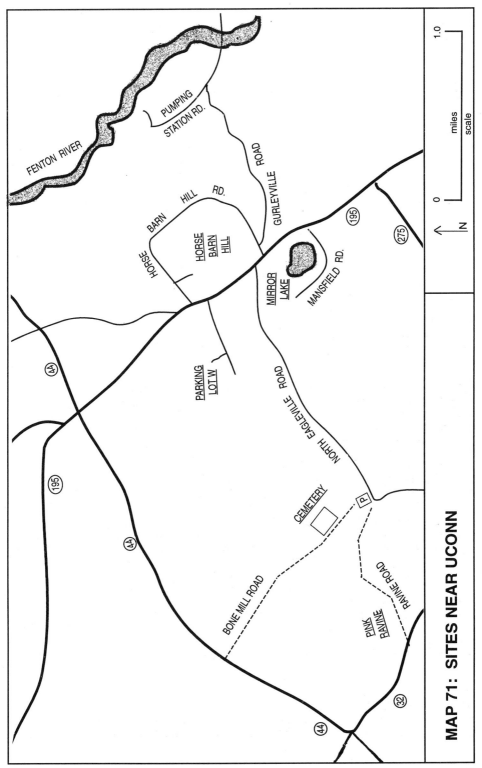

MAP 71: SITES NEAR UCONN

FENTON RIVER

PUMPING STATION RD.

GURLEYVILLE ROAD

HORSE BARN HILL RD.

HORSE BARN HILL

MIRROR LAKE

MANSFIELD RD.

195

275

PARKING LOT W

44

195

44

NORTH EAGLEVILLE ROAD

CEMETERY

P

BONE MILL ROAD

PINK RAVINE

RAVINE ROAD

32

44

N

0   miles   1.0
scale

in winter when there is open water.

GETTING AROUND
Birding methods: walk.
You need to get a parking permit from Traffic Services and must park where they direct you. From there, walk to the pond. A scope helps to see the birds across the pond.

DIRECTIONS (see Map 71): Mirror Lake is located on the UConn campus within sight of Route 195. From the intersection of Routes 195 and 44, go south on Route 195 for 2.0 miles and turn right on Mansfield Road. Mirror Lake is visible on the right. If you plan to park, first get a permit from Traffic Services (from the intersection of Routes 195 and 44, go south on Route 195 for 1.0 mile, and right at the driveway with the Traffic Services sign).

MANSFIELD: UCONN: PARKING LOT W

HABITATS
OPEN TERRESTRIAL: tilled, short grass, tall grass, mixed herbaceous and shrubby fields, shrubby and wooded edges;
Forest: hardwoods, hardwoods/white pine, mixed conifer plantations;
Lake/pond: pond, marshy and shrubby shore, seasonal pools;
Marsh/swamp/bog: cattail, mixed herbaceous and shrub marsh.
This site consists of large expanses of open fields and a wetland all of which are north and west of a parking lot. Together with Horse Barn Hill, it is one of the really outstanding open-habitat sites in eastern Connecticut. It includes a very productive variety of open terrestrial habitats that interface with woods and wetlands.

SEASONS/BIRDS
SPRING MIGRATION: water birds, marsh birds, shore birds, LAND BIRDS;
NESTING SEASON: water birds, shore birds, LAND BIRDS;
FALL MIGRATION: water birds, marsh birds, shore birds, LAND BIRDS;
Winter: land birds.
Every season is good at this site. The spring migration brings a mix of the standard water bird species - mostly Canada goose, mallard and black duck - plus great blue and green-backed herons, Virginia rail and sora. When springtime flooding produces seasonal pools, there can be a good variety of shore birds - spotted sandpiper, both yellowlegs, pectoral, least and spotted sandpipers, woodcock, snipe and killdeer. The land bird spring migration is also good, especially for warblers, sparrows, pipit, and raptors including harrier. The fall migration is even better, and often brings great egret and a wider variety of sparrows (often including Savannah, vesper, white-crowned, Lincoln's and occasionally grasshopper). The many species that nest at this site include kestrel (at the nearby buildings), red-tailed hawk, killdeer (that can be seen at the parking lot), bluebird, woodcock, bobolink, meadowlark, and Savannah sparrow. Winter can be good for land birds; among the species to look for are harrier, snow bunting and Lapland longspur.

GETTING AROUND
Birding methods: car, WALK.
Start by getting a parking pass for Lot W from Traffic Services. Some of these habitats can be

seen from the parking lot, but most require walking. There are several access roads that can be walked west and north from the parking lot through the open habitats to the woods.

DIRECTIONS (see Map 71): This site is on the UConn campus at Storrs in Mansfield. From the intersection of Routes 195 and 44, go south on Route 195 for 1.0 mile, right at the driveway with the Traffic Services sign, and right again into Lot W.

MANSFIELD: PINK RAVINE

HABITATS
River/stream: stream, fast water, shrubby, hardwood and hemlock streambelt, hemlock ravine;
Forest: hardwoods, hardwoods/hemlock, white pine, hardwoods/white pine, hemlock;
Open terrestrial: short grass, tall grass, mixed herbaceous and shrubby fields, scattered cedars, shrubby and wooded edges;
Marsh/swamp/bog: shrubby hardwood and hardwood swamps;
Lake/pond: pond, marshy, shrubby and wooded shore.
This site contains a variety of different types of habitat - a hemlock ravine, a pond with associated wetlands, a brook, farm fields and the cemetery, surrounded by shrubby and wooded edges, hardwood and conifer forest.

SEASONS/BIRDS
SPRING MIGRATION: water birds, marsh birds, shore birds, LAND BIRDS;
NESTING SEASON: LAND BIRDS;
FALL MIGRATION: water birds, marsh birds, shore birds, LAND BIRDS;
Winter: land birds.
The varied types of habitat at this site attract birds from all the major species groups. Both spring and fall migrations are good, and include some common water birds, great blue and green-backed herons, woodcock, as well as a good variety of land bird species. There also is a nice variety of nesters including red-shouldered hawk, barred owl, plus the standard mix of vireos, warblers and other woodland species, some edge-habitat species such as prairie and chestnut-sided warblers, streambelt and wetland species including both waterthrushes.

GETTING AROUND
Can be birded by: walk, bike.
There are dirt roads that cannot be driven, but provide good walking at any time of year, and can be biked when they are firm enough. Most of the land around the roads and cemetery is private, but some belongs to UConn. Be guided by the signs.

DIRECTIONS (see Map 71): This site is at the western edge of Mansfield, about a mile from the village of Mansfield Depot. To get there from the intersection of Routes 44 and 195, go south on Route 195 for 1.4 miles, and right on North Eagleville Road for 1.6 miles to where this road makes a sharp turn to the left. At this point, try to park safely by the barricade across Bone Mill Road. Follow Bone Mill Road down to the cemetery and to Ravine Road which goes to the left at the cemetery. Also, on the right, there is a trail that passes between the cemetery and the pond, and goes back into the woods.

MANSFIELD: SCHOOLHOUSE BROOK PARK

HABITATS
FOREST: hardwoods, hardwoods/hemlock, mixed conifers, mountain laurel;
Open terrestrial: short grass, mixed herbaceous and shrubby fields, apple orchard, shrubby and wooded edges;
River/stream: perennial streams, wooded streambelts, seasonal streams;
Marsh/swamp/bog: shrubby hardwood and hardwood swamp;
Lake/pond: ponds, shores of hardwoods and shrubby hardwood swamps; seasonal pools;
Other: ledges.

This is a town park that offers quite a good diversity of habitat types. It is partly post-agricultural land that has been left in a somewhat natural state, and partly second-growth woodland, including hardwood forest, mixed hardwood and conifer woodlands, conifer plantations and laurel thickets. Streambelt habitats, hardwood swamps, an orchard, managed and reverting fields, rocky ledges and two ponds are also present. The upper end (Bicentennial Pond) has been developed for recreational use, but the lower area is natural.

SEASONS/BIRDS
SPRING MIGRATION: water birds, marsh birds, LAND BIRDS;
NESTING SEASON: water birds, marsh birds, LAND BIRDS;
FALL MIGRATION: water birds, marsh birds, LAND BIRDS;
Winter: land birds.

Land birds are the big attraction at this site, and there are also a few of the standard species of water and marsh birds. The migrations are excellent, especially that in the spring. Ninety-eight species are believed to nest in the area, most of them within this park. Among those species are red-shouldered, red-tailed and broad-winged hawks, great horned and barred owls, brown creeper, worm-eating and prairie warblers, both waterthrushes, orchard oriole, wood duck and green-backed heron.

GETTING AROUND
Birding methods: walk, ski.

An extensive network of trails goes through the park. A trail map is posted at the entrance.

DIRECTIONS: This park is about two miles northwest of Mansfield Center. To get there from the intersection of Routes 195 and 89, go north on Route 195 for 0.6 mile, and turn left on Clover Mill Road. The park lies on one and sometimes both sides of Clover Mill Road for the next 1.1 miles; the park entrance is on the right 0.7 mile from the intersection of Clover Mill Road and Route 195.

MANSFIELD/CHAPLIN: MANSFIELD HOLLOW STATE PARK

HABITATS

FOREST: hardwoods, hardwoods/white pine, hardwoods/hemlock, white pine/hemlock, white pine and pitch pine sand plain, flood plain;

OPEN TERRESTRIAL: tilled, short grass, tall grass, mixed herbaceous and shrubby fields, shrubby and wooded edges;

LAKE/POND: lake, ponds and seasonal pools, mud flats, varied shorelines;

RIVER/STREAM: river, stream, slow water, fast water, shrubby and wooded streambelts;

MARSH/SWAMP/BOG: mixed herbaceous and shrub marsh, shrub swamp, shrubby hardwood swamp, hardwood swamp, white cedar swamp, black spruce and cranberry bogs;

OTHER: dam, levee; hawk watching site.

This site is a very productive area that includes many diverse habitats. This 2,320-acre park includes a large lake and flood control area; they are located just below the confluence of three rivers - the Natchaug, the Mt. Hope and the Fenton. The park's irregular shape follows the bounds of this complex watershed. In addition to the lakes, rivers and a number of streams, there are areas subject to seasonal flooding, seasonal pools in kettle holes, marshes, hardwood and shrub swamps, reverting fields, streambelt habitats, riparian forest, and a variety of upland woodlands. The most unique of this large site's habitats are the white pine and pitch pine sand plain communities, and the excellent examples of white cedar swamps and black spruce bogs. Mansfield Hollow Lake (a.k.a. Naubesatuck Lake) is a reservoir that is sometimes drawn down, and this exposes areas of mud flats. There is a dam and a long levee along the southwestern shore of Mansfield Hollow Lake - they look down on the water and seasonally-exposed mud flats of the lake, and on grassland habitats of the nearby Windham Community Airport.

SEASONS/BIRDS

SPRING MIGRATION: gulls, WATER BIRDS, MARSH BIRDS, SHORE BIRDS, LAND BIRDS;

NESTING SEASON: water birds, marsh birds, shore birds, LAND BIRDS;

FALL MIGRATION: gulls, WATER BIRDS, MARSH BIRDS, SHORE BIRDS, LAND BIRDS;

Winter: land birds.

For many, this is the best inland birding area in eastern Connecticut. It is easy to bird, and the wide diversity of habitats within this large area makes for varied and interesting birding at almost any time of year. The shrubby and wooded habitats along the lakes and rivers, together with the site's relatively low elevation, make it especially attractive to southern species of land birds. The migrations are very good for water birds; March and November are the best months. It is not uncommon, especially in the fall, to see ring-necked duck, both scaups, common goldeneye, bufflehead, canvasback, common loon and horned grebe. For migrating land birds, the periods April/May and September/October are best. Patches of wetlands among terrestrial habitats produce many small birding hot spots. Land birds that nest in the park include many wetland-oriented species, such as yellow warbler. Willow, alder and Acadian flycatchers all are nesters, as are pine warbler in stands of pine, and cerulean warbler in areas of flood plain forest. Whip-poor-will has nested in the park in past years. Green-backed heron, Virginia rail, killdeer, spotted sandpiper and woodcock are regular nesters. The levee and dam provide a good place to look for shore birds, as well as migrating hawks; also, uncommon gulls have been seen from here. In years when the reservoir is drawn down during the fall migration, some surprising shore bird species have been seen feeding on the mud, and also in the nearby grassland habitats of the airport - long-billed curlew, upland and buff-breasted sandpipers have all been reported. The airport is also where harrier and grasshopper sparrow occur regularly. Snipe have been seen in the park during

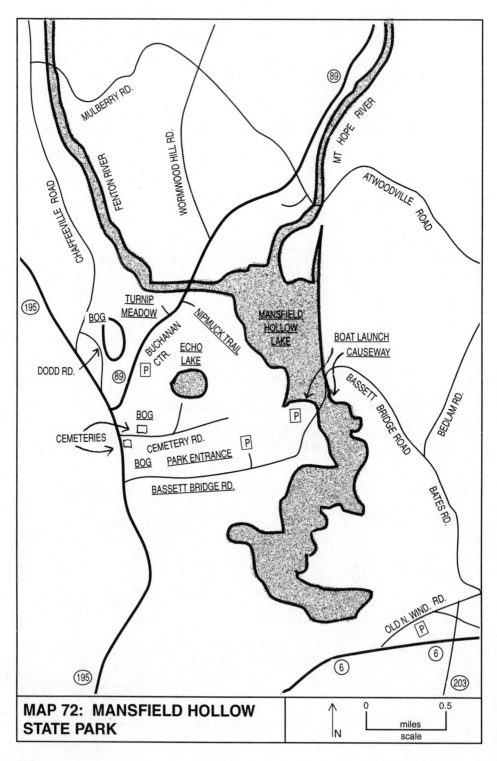

MAP 72: MANSFIELD HOLLOW STATE PARK

October and November. Nine species of hawks and owls are known to occur in the park.

GETTING AROUND
Birding methods: CAR, WALK, BIKE, SKI, BOAT.
This park is large and the networks of auto roads, woods roads and trails that surround and go through it are complex; but the rewards are great, and worth your time and effort. Many parts of the park can provide good birding. Those parts that can be reached by the routes described below are among the best, and represent a variety of habitat types. However, there are many other excellent areas and scattered pockets of good habitat in the park that are rewarding to explore. Many parts of the park can be seen adequately from near your car, but the better way is to use the extensive trail network that provides miles of good walking. Some of these trails are also suitable for skiing. In addition, this is an ideal site in which to do your birding from a canoe; there is a public landing on Mansfield Hollow Lake, from which you can explore a number of coves and rivers.

DIRECTIONS (see Map 72): This park lies just east of Mansfield Center, about six miles southeast of Storrs. The directions that follow will enable you to see many of the habitat areas from your car, to reach many others by taking trails that you pass along the way, and to start a boat trip from a public boat launch site.

To explore areas in the northeastern and northern parts of the park, start in Mansfield Center at the intersection of Routes 195 and 89.

1. There are two ponds and three bogs near this intersection that are worth checking for water birds, marsh birds, shore birds and land birds along their shores. **To get to two of the bogs,** go south on Route 195 for 0.2 mile, left on Cemetery Road for 0.4 mile, and left into New Mansfield Cemetery. From the back of this cemetery, you can get a view of one of the bogs. To see the second bog, walk back to Old Mansfield Cemetery that is at the corner of Cemetery Road and Route 195. The bog can be seen from the back of this cemetery. **To get to Echo Lake and an associated wetland,** continue east on Cemetery Road for another 0.1 mile, and go left on Echo Road to the dead end that is at the edge of the park. A trail leads through mature white pine forest to two ponds and a wetland composed of varied types of marsh and swamp. **To get to Chapins Pond and a third bog,** from the intersection of Routes 89 and 195, go north on Route 195 for 0.2 mile, and right on Dodd Road for 0.3 mile to where the pond and bog are visible on the right.

2. To reach the extreme northern part of the park along the Fenton River, (a good area for land birds from April through October, especially for warblers in May), from Mansfield Center at the intersection of Routes 89 and 195, go north on Route 195 for 0.4 mile, and right on the Chafeeville Road. Follow this road as it goes north near the Fenton River (on the right) for 1.9 miles to the intersection with Mulberry Road in Chafeeville at the northern end of the park. This stretch of road goes intermittently through both private land and public park land. There are places to pull off the road, and trails that lead to the right down to the river. Habitats include hardwood forest, hardwood swamp, occasional openings of tall grass, mixed herbaceous and shrubby fields.

To get to several areas in the northern and northeastern part of the park, start from Mansfield Center at the intersection of Routes 89 and 195, and go east (northward) on Route 89.

3. To get to the Bradley-Buchanan Woods area and a sand plain, go east (northward) on Route 89 for 0.3 mile to the Buchanan Center parking area on the right. A trail leads from the back of the parking area into the woods and to sand plain of white pine and pitch pine (pine warbler nests here).

4. To reach Turnip Meadow, go north on Route 89 for another 0.3 mile to an inconspicuous road on the left. Follow this for 0.1 mile to a parking area. The trail straight ahead leads across a levee and provides a view to the right of the upper end of a wetland known as Turnip Meadow. There is a network of trails that go throughout this area. Species that nest here include woodcock, willow and alder flycatchers; migrants seen here include snipe, short-billed dowitcher and pectoral sandpiper.

5. To get to a section of the Nipmuck Trail and the northern end of Mansfield Hollow Lake, continue north on Route 89 for another 0.2 mile to a driveway on the right to a parking area by athletic fields. From here, the Nipmuck Trail can be walked north along the Fenton River or south parallel to (but not next to) the shore of Mansfield Hollow Lake. The Nipmuck Trail leads to several other trails, including one that goes along the shore of the lake. Look in the spring and fall for land birds foraging in the trees along the shoreline. A good variety of land birds nest here, too.

6. To reach additional upland habitats in the northeastern part of the park, go another 0.4 mile north on Route 89 to Wormwood Hill Road on the left. It can be driven or walked, and leads to additional trails.

7. To reach trails in the northern part of the park, continue on Route 89 for another 0.6 mile past Wormwood Hill Road to Atwoodville Road on the right. The first section of this road and also Atwoodville Lane (a right turn) pass several trails which lead into good habitat areas, including a large wetland where Virginia rail has nested. Kingfisher, green-backed and great blue herons regularly feed here. This is a really good area for fall migrants.

To reach areas in the middle part of the park, also start in Mansfield Center at the intersection of Routes 195 and 89.

8. To reach the levee and Mansfield Hollow Dam, go south on Route 195 for 0.5 mile, left on Bassett Bridge Road for 0.7 mile, at which point the road crosses the levee, which can be walked south (right) to the dam, or north (left) for about half a mile. The levee and dam provide views down on the southeastern part of the lake. Look here for water birds in spring and fall, and for shore birds, especially in the fall when there may be exposed mud along the shore. The levee and dam also overlook the grassland habitats of the Windham Community Airport to the south. In addition, this is also a good place for watching hawks during the fall migration.

9. To reach the main park entrance, continue east on Bassett Bridge Road for another 0.2 miles to the park entrance on the left. In this area, there are large mowed fields that are surrounded by a white pine forest. Pine warblers nest in the pines, and migrants forage along the edges. Several trails start from here.

10. To reach a boat launching area and the causeway across the lake, continue east on Bassett Bridge Road for another 0.6 mile to the launch area on the left, and the causeway just beyond. This is a good place from which to look for water birds, especially during March and again in October and November. Species that have been seen here on a regular basis include ring-necked duck, canvasback, common goldeneye and bufflehead. Osprey is often seen here in the spring and fall. Several trails start from here.

To reach areas in the southern and eastern parts of the park, start at the intersection of Routes 6 and 203, near the southeastern corner of the park and Mansfield Hollow Lake.

11. To gain access to the southern part of the levee and the dam, from the intersection of Routes 6 and 203, go west on Route 6 for 0.4 mile to a parking area on the north (right) side of Route 6, from which there is access to the levee. The levee looks down on the shore of Mansfield Hollow Lake, the Windham Community Airport, and, to the south across Route 6, the Windham Bog (details about this unique habitat are included in the site description of it in the Windham County Chapter under the town of Windham).

12. To reach more trails that go into the southern part of the park, at the intersection of Routes 6 and 203, go north on Windham Center Road for a few yards, left on Spencer Lane for a few yards, and left again on Old North Windham Road for a few yards to a parking area. From here, a woods road goes into the park, and leads to other trails.

13. To get to Dianas Pool (off the left side of the map), from the intersection of Routes 6 and 203, go east on Route 6 for about two miles to the intersection of Routes 6 and 198, and go north (left) on Route 198 for 0.4 mile. Just before the bridge over the Natchaug River, go right on Dianas Pool Road for a few yards to a parking area on the left. From here, walk the trail down to the Natchaug River, which at this point is a rocky stream with fast water, pools and riffles that pass through a forest of hardwoods, white pine and hemlock. Sharp-shinned hawk, Acadian flycatcher and cerulean warbler nest in this area.

MANSFIELD/WILLINGTON: FENTON RIVER

HABITATS
RIVER/STREAM: stream; shallow, fast water, deep, slow water; shrubby, hardwood, hemlock and white pine streambelt;
FOREST: hardwoods, hardwoods/hemlock, hemlock, white pine/hemlock, spruce groves, mountain laurel;
OPEN TERRESTRIAL: mixed herbaceous, tall grass and shrubby fields, shrubby and wooded edges;
Marsh/swamp/bog: wet meadow, shrub marsh, shrub swamp, shrubby hardwood swamp, hardwood swamp.
This site consists of over seven miles of the Fenton River, together with the streambelt and bottomlands through which it flows. The habitats near the stream are diverse, and include moist mixed conifer/deciduous forest, wooded swamps, wet meadow, reverting fields and orchards.

SEASONS/BIRDS
SPRING MIGRATION: LAND BIRDS;
NESTING SEASON: LAND BIRDS;
FALL MIGRATION: LAND BIRDS;
Winter: land birds.
This is one of the best sites for land bird species in northeastern Connecticut - especially during the spring migration in May. The migration during the early fall is also good. In addition, because of the great variation of habitat types, there is a wide diversity of nesters, including both northern and southern species that can be heard singing near one another. Among the northern woodland nesters are goshawk, hermit thrush, solitary vireo, black-throated green, Canada and black-throated blue warblers (the latter two species in mountain

laurel). Southern nesters include Carolina wren, Acadian flycatcher, white-eyed vireo, and red-bellied woodpecker. Other woodland nesting species include red-tailed, red-shouldered and broad-winged hawks, great horned and barred owls, pileated woodpecker and Louisiana waterthrush. A variety of edge and open habitat species also nest in this streambelt, including woodcock, towhee, alder and willow flycatchers, chestnut-sided and yellow warblers. In winters of irruption years, crossbills, pine grosbeak and common redpoll have been seen.

GETTING AROUND
Birding methods: car, WALK.
Paved and dirt roads and the Nipmuck Trail go near and intermittently along the shore of this seven mile stretch of river. While it is possible to walk this entire length of river, it is more practical to do it in sections, as described below. Parts of the dirt roads are rough and seasonally impassable for cars, but provide good walking most of the year.

DIRECTIONS (see Map 73): This seven mile stretch of the Fenton River starts in Willington at Route 74, and ends in Mansfield at Chafeeville by the edge of the Mansfield Hollow State Park. Think of this stretch of river as having five segments that can be done separately or linked together. For convenience, they are treated separately below, and numbered one through five, north to south.

1. To reach the north end of segment #1: in Ashford at the intersection of Routes 74 and 44, go west on Route 74 for 3.8 miles, and left on Daleville Road. This road goes south along or near the Fenton River for about two miles, and provides intermittent views across private land. This section of the river includes a streambelt of hardwoods, hardwoods/hemlock and hemlock. The stretch near the Daleville School Road bridge is particularly good.

2. To reach segment #2: from Mansfield Four Corners at the intersection of Routes 44 and 195, go east on Route 44 for 1.6 miles (past one intersection with Old Turnpike Road), turn sharp right at the second intersection with Old Turnpike Road, go for 0.3 mile across the Fenton River to a small parking area on the left where the Nipmuck Trail crosses the road. Follow the Nipmuck Trail north along the Fenton River by going across Route 44. This section of the river includes a streambelt of hardwoods/hemlock with an understory of mountain laurel. Acadian flycatcher and goshawk occur in this section.

3. To reach segment #3: from the parking area described in the preceding paragraph, walk the Nipmuck Trail south along or near the Fenton River. This trail can be followed to the Gurleyville Road, which is about two miles to the south, and is described below. This is an excellent section of the river. The beginning of it goes through shrubby fields, old orchards and young hardwoods. Then it enters a streambelt of hardwoods and hemlock/hardwood forest with an understory of mountain laurel, and passes through shrubby hardwood and hardwood swamps. Barred owl, warbling and solitary vireos, Canada and black-throated blue warbler nest in this segment.

4. To reach segment #4: from Mansfield Four Corners at the intersection of Routes 195 and 44, go south on Route 195 for 1.5 miles, left on Gurleyville Road for 1.1 miles, and sharp left on Pumping Station Road (hard to see - looks like a driveway). This road continues through the habitat area for 0.9 mile until it reaches the Fenton River. (Shrubby streambelt, hardwood/hemlock streambelt, tall grass and shrubby field, shrubby edges, hardwood, white pine, hemlock and mixed conifer forest, mountain laurel.) In addition, you can continue on Gurleyville Road for another 0.2 mile to a small parking area on the left by the Fenton River at the Nipmuck trail. This trail can be followed northward through the habitat area - a streambelt of mixed conifers and mountain laurel. There is excellent birding along this seg-

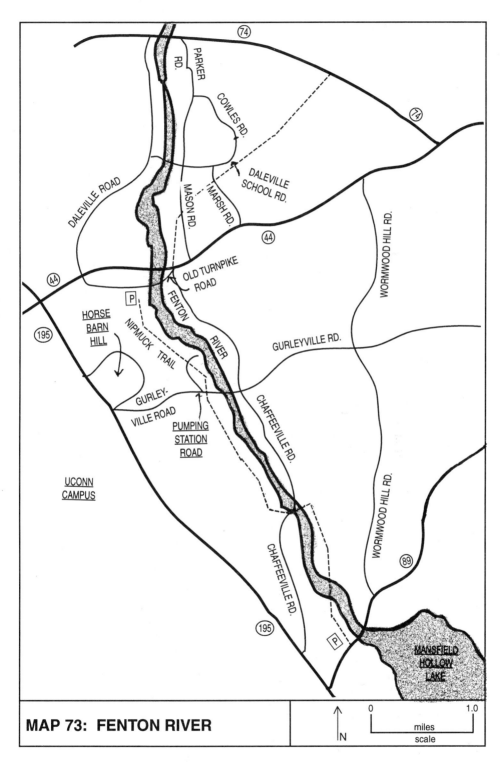

MAP 73: FENTON RIVER

ment from May through September.

5. To reach segment #5: proceed as above to the intersection of Gurleyville Road and Pumping Station Road, continue for another 0.1 mile to the clearing described above, and walk the Nipmuck Trail south. It eventually goes parallel to the Chaffeeville Road through an area of mature white pines, and then a mixed hardwoods/conifer forest for about four miles until it reaches a parking area on Route 89. An alternative is to continue for another 0.1 mile on Gurleyville Road, and turn south (right) on Chaffeeville Road. This road continues along or near the Fenton River for about four miles to Route 195 through a streambelt of hardwoods, white pine and shrubs within the Mansfield Hollow Flood Control Area and State Park (described separately).

STAFFORD: ELLITHORPE FLOOD CONTROL AREA/SHENIPSIT STATE FOREST

HABITATS
MARSH/SWAMP/BOG: mixed herbaceous, cattail and shrub marsh, shrub swamp, shrubby hardwood swamp, hardwood swamp, white pine swamp, hemlock swamp, dead wood;
FOREST: hardwoods, hardwoods/white pine, hardwoods/hemlock, hemlock;
Open terrestrial: mixed herbaceous and shrubby field, shrubby and wooded edges;
River/stream: perennial stream, streambelts composed of the wetland and upland habitat types listed above;
Lake/pond: pond, wetland and wooded shores as listed above;
Other: dike.
The 400-acre Ellithorpe Flood Control Area occupies a small valley above a dam, and includes a stream and the surrounding bottomland. Two-thirds of the area is made up of various types of wetland, and much of the remainder is woodland and edge. Just below the dam is Ginhott Point Pond. The contiguous block of the Shenipsit State Forest is composed of hardwoods, white pine and hemlock alone and in various combinations.

SEASONS/BIRDS
SPRING MIGRATION: water birds, marsh birds, shore birds, LAND BIRDS;
NESTING SEASON: water birds, marsh birds, shore birds, LAND BIRDS;
FALL MIGRATION: water birds, marsh birds, shore birds, LAND BIRDS;
Winter: land birds.
Taken together, these two contiguous areas are very productive. Their combination of wetland and forest habitats offer a nice species variety and good birding throughout most of the year. During the spring and fall migrations, both areas offer a diversity of land birds, common species of water birds, plus some marsh and shore birds. Species that nest in the wetland include black duck, wood duck, and land bird species that have an affinity for wetlands and edges, such as yellow warbler and common yellowthroat. In 1995 there were several great blue heron nests at the swamp. In addition, a nice variety of land birds nest in the nearby forest. Among these nesters are a number of northern species: hermit thrush, solitary vireo, black-throated blue, black-throated green, Blackburnian and Canada warblers, northern waterthrush, and white-throated sparrow.

GETTING AROUND
Birding methods: walk, car, bike.

The best way to see the flood control area is to walk along the dike; from it you can see the wetland habitats from an elevated position. The nearby block of the Shenipsit State Forest can be birded from your car or on foot by following a lightly-used but well-maintained dirt road. There are also woods roads and trails throughout this site.

DIRECTIONS: This area is a mile or two northwest of the center of Stafford. To get there from the western intersection of Routes 32 and 190, go north on Route 32 for 2.4 miles, left (west) on Diamond Ledge Road for 0.8 mile to an intersection just past a railroad bridge.

To reach the Ellithorpe Flood Control Area, turn right (north) at this intersection, and go for 0.1 mile to a parking area and barway on the right. From here, a path leads across railroad tracks to the dike. (Caution: the tracks are in use!)

To go through the nearby block of the Shenipsit State Forest, return to the intersection with Diamond Ledge Road near the railroad bridge, and this time go south (a left turn from Diamond Ledge Road). This road goes for 0.8 mile through the forest.

STAFFORD: FURNACE BROOK FLOOD CONTROL AREA

HABITATS
Forest: hardwoods/white pine, white pine;
Open terrestrial: short grass, mixed herbaceous and shrubby fields, edges;
Lake/pond: pond, shrubby, marshy and wooded shore;
River/stream: stream, shrubby and wooded streambelt;
Marsh/swamp/bog: mixed herbaceous and shrub marsh, shrub swamp, dead wood, shrubby and wooded edges;
Other: dike.

This flood control area is composed of varied wetlands and a pond in the bottom of a valley that is upstream of a dike.

SEASONS/BIRDS
Spring migration: water birds, land birds;
Nesting season: land birds;
Fall migration: water birds, land birds;
Winter: land birds.

This site offers a standard mix of the migrant and nesting species that you would expect in these habitats. However, surprises are always possible - a northern shrike was seen here in December 1995.

GETTING AROUND
Birding methods: walk.

Walking along the dike provides an excellent view of the habitats in the valley. In addition, there are woods roads and trails.

DIRECTIONS: This area in about five miles northwest of the center of Stafford. To get there from the intersection of Routes 190 and 30, go west on Route 190 for 0.1 mile, right on Old Springfield Road for 0.8 mile to the dike and parking on the right. To get to a second entrance, continue on Old Springfield Road for another 1.0 mile to the entrance and parking area, also on the right.

STAFFORD/SOMERS/ELLINGTON: SHENIPSIT STATE FOREST

HABITATS
> **FOREST:** hardwoods, white pine and hemlock, alone and in various combinations; pitch pine/white pine/hardwoods sand plain; mountain laurel;
> **Open terrestrial:** shrubby field, shrubby and wooded edges;
> **Lake/pond:** ponds, seasonal pools, shrubby and wooded shores;
> **River/stream:** perennial streams, seasonal streams, shrubby and wooded streambelts;
> **Marsh/swamp/bog:** shrub marsh, shrubby hardwood swamp, hardwood swamp;
> **Other:** observation tower, rock outcrop, rocky slope, sand pit.

This 6,198 acre state forest exists as a number of separate parcels quite near one another in Stafford, Somers and Ellington. The largest of these parcels (the subject of this site description) straddles the three towns. It is largely forested, but also includes a variety of marshes, swamps, streams, ponds and pools. The most prominent topographical feature is Soapstone Mountain that has an observation tower on its 1,061' summit. From the tower, you get a view of Connecticut's Central Lowlands and of the interface between the Lowlands and the Eastern Uplands.

SEASONS/BIRDS
> **SPRING MIGRATION:** LAND BIRDS;
> **NESTING SEASON:** LAND BIRDS;
> **FALL MIGRATION:** LAND BIRDS;
> **Winter:** land birds.

This large state forest attracts a nice mix of land bird species, including those that require areas of undisturbed interior-forest habitat. Both spring and fall migrations are good, and this site has the added advantage of the observation tower, from which migrating hawks may be seen - notably broad-wings in September. Nesters include such northern species as red-breasted nuthatch, hermit thrush, solitary vireo, Canada, black-throated green and black-throated blue warblers and junco. Other nesters include barred owl, worm-eating warbler, ovenbird, lots of towhees, plus a host of other species that typically nest in Connecticut forests.

GETTING AROUND
> **Birding methods:** car, walk, bike, ski.

There are vehicle roads that go through this block of the forest, and they are quiet enough to permit birding from your car or on foot. In addition, there are numerous woods roads and trails.

DIRECTIONS: The largest parcel of this fragmented state forest lies immediately west and south of the village of West Stafford, within five miles of the Massachusetts line. To get to it from the western intersection of Routes 190 and 30, go west on Route 30 for 2.3 miles to the forest entrance on the left (Sodom Road). Follow Sodom Road for 2.0 miles through the forest to the intersection with Gulf Road. Cross Gulf Road onto Soapstone Road, and follow it for 0.8 mile to a parking area near the top of Soapstone Mountain. Then, from the parking area, take Skye Road for 4.1 miles down the mountain (straight across the intersection with Parker Road on the right and Webster Road on the left) to Kibbe Road, at which go either left or right for 0.1 mile to Route 83. In addition, several of the side roads are worth exploring. A large scale topographic map is very helpful.

TOLLAND: KOLLAR WMA/NYE HOLMAN STATE FOREST

HABITATS
Forest: hardwoods, hardwoods/white pine, hardwoods/hemlock, white pine, flood plain, mixed conifers, mountain laurel;
Open terrestrial: mixed herbaceous and shrubby fields, edges;
River/stream: river, fast water, hardwoods and hemlock streambelt, small streams, wooded and shrubby streambelts;
Marsh/swamp/bog: shrubby hardwood swamp.
These two areas are very close to each other but are quite different in terms of habitat. Kollar, just north of Route I-84, is a 911-acre area managed by DEP for game birds (primarily ruffed grouse), and includes mixed herbaceous and shrubby fields, within a mostly forested area. Between the south side of the highway and the Willimantic River is a portion of the Nye-Holman State Forest. Habitats here are hardwoods, white pine, hemlock and other conifer forest mixtures, some flood plain forest along the river, and the river itself.

SEASONS/BIRDS
SPRING MIGRATION: LAND BIRDS;
NESTING SEASON: LAND BIRDS;
FALL MIGRATION: LAND BIRDS;
Winter: land birds.
These two areas taken together provide a nice site in which to look for a good variety of land birds - spring and fall migrants and also a standard mix of the nesting species you would expect to find in woodlands (including Canada warbler and broad-winged hawk), in open habitats (including prairie and chestnut-sided warblers) and along rivers (including king-fisher, bank and rough-winged swallows).

GETTING AROUND
Birding methods: car, walk.
Two roads that go along or through these areas are suitable for birding from your car or on foot. In addition, the Nye Holman Forest south of the highway has a barricaded road that can be walked down to the river. Within the Kollar area, north of the highway, it is possible to walk through the portion that includes shrubby fields. Unfortunately, I-84 is close enough to each of these areas to create traffic noise that is annoying. Kollar is a popular hunting area, so restrict your fall visits to Sundays.

DIRECTIONS: These two contiguous areas are three or four miles northeast of Tolland Center, and both can best be reached from I-84 exit 69. To get to the Kollar Wildlife Management Area, go west (or north) on Route 74 for 0.2 mile, right on North River Road for 1.2 miles, and left on Babcock Road for 0.1 mile to a parking area on the left. To get to this block of the Nye Holman State Forest from I-84 exit 69, go east (or south) on Route 74 for 0.6 mile, right on South River Road for 0.2 mile to the state forest entrance on the right.

UNION: BIGELOW HOLLOW STATE PARK/NIPMUCK STATE FOREST

HABITATS
FOREST: hardwoods/white pine, hardwoods/hemlock, white pine/hemlock, white pine, hemlock, conifer plantation, mountain laurel;
RIVER/STREAM: stream, fast water, hemlock ravine, wooded streambelt;
Lake/pond: ponds, shallow water, deep water, wooded shores;
Marsh/swamp/bog: shrub marsh, shrub swamp.
Bigelow Hollow State Park occupies 513 acres within one of the largest areas of unfragmented forest in Connecticut. A parcel of the Nipmuck State Forest lies along the east and west sides of the park, and part of the Yale Forest along the south side. As its name implies, the park lies in a "hollow" - a depression in the forest into which cold air settles. As a result, the park is a kind of southern outpost of Canadian Zone habitats.

SEASONS/BIRDS
SPRING MIGRATION: water birds, marsh birds, shore birds, LAND BIRDS;
NESTING SEASON: LAND BIRDS;
FALL MIGRATION: water birds, marsh birds, shore birds, LAND BIRDS;
Winter: land birds.
The spring and fall migrations are both very good, especially for warblers in May and early September. Nesters include such northern species as hermit thrush, winter wren, brown creeper, solitary vireo, northern waterthrush, yellow-rumped, Canada, black-throated green and Blackburnian warblers, white-throated sparrow and junco. Also among the nesters are broad-winged and red-shouldered hawks, and Louisiana waterthrush. Year-round residents include red-tailed hawk, great horned and barred owls. In winter during invasion years, look for crossbills, evening grosbeak and other finches.

GETTING AROUND
Birding methods: car, WALK, bike ski.
There is a network of trails throughout the park and the nearby Nipmuck and Yale forests. In addition, the park driveway runs for about two miles through the park, and affords access to much of the area (it is not plowed in winter).

DIRECTIONS: This park is in Union, near the Massachusetts border in the northeastern part of Connecticut. From I-84, take exit 73, go east on Route 190 for 2.0 miles, right on Route 171 (Bigelow Hollow Road) for 1.4 miles to park entrance on left. The Nipmuck State Forest lies on the north (left) side of Route 171, and the Yale Forest on the south (right) side of Route 171, both east and west of Bigelow Hollow State Park.

UNION: MORSE MEADOW POND

HABITATS
MARSH/SWAMP/BOG: shrub marsh, shrub swamp; white cedar bog with leatherleaf and blueberry;
Lake/pond: pond; shore of wetlands, shrubs, hardwoods, white pine and hemlock;
Forest: hardwoods, hardwoods/white pine, hardwoods/hemlock, white pine, hemlock;

This pond has a distinctly northern quality, more typical of Northern New England than Connecticut. Its open water area is about a quarter of a mile across, and there is an area of about the same size composed of a bog, with a few remaining white cedars, together with typical bog vegetation. The forest around the pond is composed of northern hardwoods, white pine and hemlock. Shrubs at the pond's edge include sweet pepperbush. (The road to Morse Meadow Pond passes Lost Pond, which is also worth a look.)

SEASONS/BIRDS
Spring migration: water birds, land birds;
Nesting season: water birds, land birds;
Fall migration: water birds, land birds;
Winter: land birds.

While this is not a birding hot spot, it does provide a good look at a bog - an uncommon type of habitat in Connecticut. It also offers the possibility of seeing northern species of land birds throughout the year, and migrating water birds during the spring and fall. Among the species that nest near the pond are red-breasted nuthatch, hermit thrush, solitary vireo, black-throated blue, yellow-rumped, Blackburnian and Canada warblers, northern waterthrush, purple finch, junco and white-throated sparrow.

GETTING AROUND
Birding methods: car, walk, BOAT.

In order to see the pond and bog/marsh area, it is necessary to walk a few yards through the woods. There is a trail from Route 171 to the shore at the south end of the pond, from which most of it can be seen. In addition, there is a pulloff from Route 171 opposite the bog and marsh at the north end. To reach the edge of the wetland, it is necessary to scramble down a steep bank. By far the better way is to launch a canoe at the south end; this will enable you to see the entire pond and get a close look at one of Connecticut's few bogs.

DIRECTIONS: Morse Meadow Pond is in Union, about five miles south of the Massachusetts line. To get there from I-84 exit 73, go east on Route 190 for 1.9 miles, and right on Route 171. When you have gone 2.3 miles on Route 171, bear right at an intersection in order to stay on Route 171; at 3.3 miles, Lost Pond is on the right; at 3.6 miles, the trail to the north end of Morse Meadow Pond is on the right; at 3.9 miles, the trail to the south end of Morse Meadow Pond is on the right.

UNION/STAFFORD/WILLINGTON: NIPMUCK STATE FOREST

HABITATS

FOREST: hardwoods, hardwoods/white pine, hardwoods/hemlock, white pine, hemlock, spruce plantations, mixed conifers, mountain laurel;
Open terrestrial: shrubby field, edge;
Lake/pond: ponds, deep water, shallow water, seasonal pools, hardwoods, white pine and hemlock shores;
River/stream: streams, wooded streambelts;
Marsh/swamp/bog: shrub swamp, shrubby hardwood swamp, hardwood swamp, white pine swamp, hemlock swamp.

This is a large state forest that has a quality of wilderness; several parcels in three towns total over 8,000 acres. Most of these areas are wooded, primarily with northern hardwoods in combination with some hemlock and white pine. There are also several types of swamps, as well as a variety of ponds, streambelt habitats and reverting fields.

SEASONS/BIRDS

SPRING MIGRATION: water birds, marsh birds, LAND BIRDS;
NESTING SEASON: water birds, marsh birds, LAND BIRDS;
FALL MIGRATION: water birds, marsh birds, LAND BIRDS;
Winter: land birds.

The spring and fall migrations are good in this vast state forest, but the real draw for birders is the nesting season for forest-dwelling land birds. Northern species are the specialty, including veery, hermit thrush, black-throated blue, yellow-rumped and Canada warblers and junco. Other nesters include red-shouldered and broad-winged hawks, yellow-throated vireo and ovenbird. Red-tailed hawk, great horned and barred owls are year-round residents. In recent years, there has been a nesting colony of great blue herons in one of the white pine swamps.

GETTING AROUND

Birding methods: car, walk, bike, ski.

There are numerous access points to the various blocks of this state forest. Many roads go through them, and most are suitable for driving, walking, biking or skiing. In addition, there are many woods roads and trails that can be walked. At the same time, there are many parts of the forest that are quite remote; getting off by yourself to bird quietly is not a problem here.

DIRECTIONS: It is difficult to decide where to begin exploring this large state forest, that has separate blocks in the towns of Union, Willington and Stafford. To properly explore the forest, it is best to use large scale (topographic) maps.

A good starting point is the Laurel Sanctuary. To get to it from I-84 exit 72, go north on Route 89 for 0.4 mile, left on Route 190 for 0.1 mile to the sanctuary entrance on the left. To get to nearby Morey Pond, go back to Route 190, go right (east) for 0.5 mile to the access trail on the right.

To get to another part of the forest, continue east on Route 190 for another 0.3 mile, left on Stickney Hill Road for 0.6 mile to state forest roads on left and right, or for 2.0 miles to Bear Den Road on the right, or for 3.8 miles to Skopec Road, also on the right. These roads all lead to parts of the forest, but may be rough and better walked than driven.

Another good part of the forest can be reached from the intersection of Routes 190 and 89, by going west on Route 190 for 1.2 miles to a state forest road on the left. This also affords views of Pinneys Pond, also on the left.

VERNON: VALLEY FALLS PARK/BELDING WILDLIFE MANAGEMENT AREA

HABITATS
RIVER/STREAM: perennial stream, hardwood, hemlock and shrubby streambelt, hemlock ravine, seasonal streams;
OPEN TERRESTRIAL: tilled, short grass, mixed herbaceous and shrubby fields, shrubby and hardwood edges, hedgerows;
Forest: hardwoods, hardwoods/hemlock, hemlock, red pine, mixed conifer groves, cedar;
Lake/pond: pond, sandy, shrubby and hardwood shore;
Marsh/swamp/bog: shrub swamp;
Other: cliff and ledges.

These two contiguous areas include and protect a portion of the streambelt of Railroad Brook (which becomes the Tankerhousen River). Valley Falls Park (a Vernon town park) is at the upstream end, and includes a small pond that is surrounded by fields and woods. The main feature of the park is a hemlock ravine that is just downstream from the pond, and includes a promontory of cliffs and ledges. The nearby Belding Wildlife Management Area includes Railroad Brook as it passes into more open farm country, with fields containing scattered areas of shrubs, cedars and other trees, and a shrubby streambelt.

SEASONS/BIRDS
SPRING MIGRATION: water birds, LAND BIRDS;
NESTING SEASON: water birds, LAND BIRDS;
FALL MIGRATION: water birds, LAND BIRDS;
Winter: land birds.

These areas are pleasant and worthwhile areas to visit at any time of year, even in the winter. You can expect to see a standard variety of land bird species in migration and during the nesting season. The habitat in the park provides the potential for nesting by northern species, worm-eating warbler and acadian flycatcher, although none have been confirmed as yet. Red-tailed hawk is a resident and evident throughout the year.

GETTING AROUND
Birding methods: car, walk.

It is possible to see the pond and some of the surrounding terrestrial habitats from the Valley Falls parking area. There are trails throughout the park, including one on the railroad bed that goes near the stream through the ravine. At the Belding Wildlife Management Area, the fields and some of the streambelt can be seen from the road. The surrounding land is private.

DIRECTIONS: This site is two to three miles southeast of Vernon. To get to the Belding WMA from the intersection of I-84 and Route 85 (at I-84 exit 66), go south on Route 85 for 0.6 mile, left on Valley Falls Road for 0.6 mile, and left on Bread Milk Road. This road leads through the Belding WMA and across Railroad Brook. To get to Valley Falls Park, continue on Valley Falls Road for another 0.3 mile to the park entrance on the right.

WILLINGTON: MOSS CONSERVATION AREA

HABITATS

FOREST: hardwoods, hardwoods/white pine, hardwoods/hemlock, white pine/hemlock, white pine, hemlock, spruces;

River/stream: streams, hardwoods and hemlock streambelts;

Marsh/swamp/bog: shrubby hardwood swamp, hardwood swamp.

This site, which is owned by the University of Connecticut, is largely wooded, and has areas of mixed conifers throughout the forest. It also includes a section of the Fenton River and the small surrounding valley. Habitats include almost every type of forest community that occurs in Connecticut (there is no sand plain or flood plain), as well as hemlock-dominated streambelt habitats along the river.

SEASONS/BIRDS

SPRING MIGRATION: LAND BIRDS;

NESTING SEASON: LAND BIRDS

FALL MIGRATION: LAND BIRDS;

Winter: land birds.

This is a really good birding area; the spring migration and the nesting season are especially productive. There is a wide variety of the species one would expect to find in these types of habitat. In addition, both northern and southern species nest here, including goshawk, broad-winged and red-shouldered hawks, Acadian flycatcher, junco, solitary vireo, black-throated green, black-throated blue and pine warblers. Residents include great horned, barred and screech owls.

GETTING AROUND

Birding methods: walk.

An abandoned dirt road (blocked and not driveable) goes through much of the area, and crosses the Nipmuck Trail.

DIRECTIONS: This area is in the southern part of Willington, about five miles north of the main UConn campus. To get there from Mansfield Four Corners at the intersection of Routes 320 and 195, go north on Route 320 for 1.6 miles and right on Eldridge Road. Follow Eldridge Road for 1.0 mile to an intersection, at which point the road becomes dirt and rough. Continue straight ahead on foot down to the Fenton River, which is within the conservation area, and to a network of abandoned roads and trails.

Chapter 11

Windham County

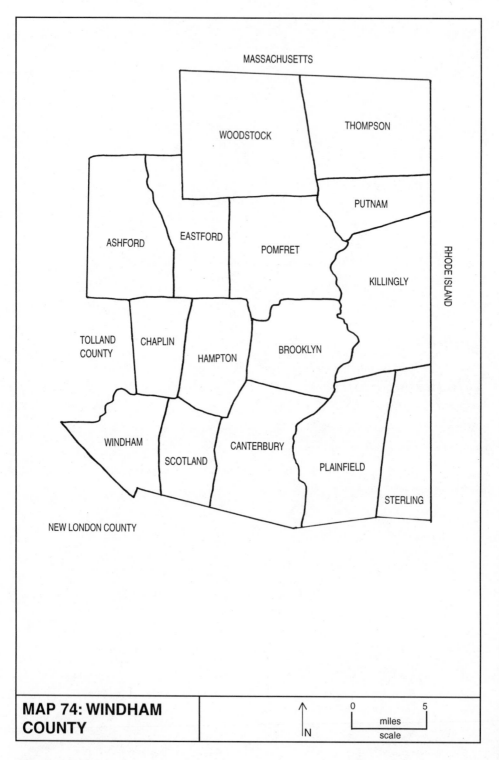

MAP 74: WINDHAM COUNTY

N

0 miles 5

scale

TABLE 9: HABITATS AND SEASONS AT WINDHAM COUNTY SITES

Habitats ● very good example ○ present, but not as significant Seasons ● excellent during this season ○ less good during this season	HABITATS							SEASONS			
	FOREST	OPEN	MARSH	LAKE	RIVER	COAST	OTHER	SPRING	NEST	FALL	WINTER
Tour of Lakes in Windham County	○	○	●	●	○			●	●	●	○
Ashford: Freidman Mem For/Bebbington Lane	○	○	○	○	○			○	○	○	○
Ashford: Natchaug State Forest	●		●	○	○			●	●	●	○
Ashford/Eastford: Boston Hollow	●	○	○	○	●		○	●	●	●	○
Canterbury et al: Quinebaug River WMA	○	●	○		●		○	●	●	●	○
Chaplin et al: Natchaug State Forest	●	○	●	●	○			●	●	●	○
Eastford: Westford Road Wetland		○	○	○				○	○	○	○
Eastford: Yale Forest Wetland	○		●	●	○			●	●	○	○
Hampton: Goodwin State Forest	●	○	●	●	○			●	●	●	○
Killingly: Tetrault Pond			●					○	○	○	○
Killingly/Sterling: Ross Marsh WMA	●	○	●	●	○			●	●	●	○
Pomfret: Mashamoquet Brook SP et al	●	●	●		●		○	●	●	●	○
Scotland: Pudding Hill WMA	○	○			○			○	○	○	○
Scotland: Rock Spring	●	○	○	○	○		○	●	●	○	○
Scotland: Talbot WMA	○	○	○		○			○	○	○	○
Thompson: Quaddick Reservoir et al	●	○	○	○	○			○	●	○	○
Thompson: West Thompson Lake	●	●	○	●	○		○	●	●	●	○
Windham: Windham Bog	○	○	●	○			○	●	○	●	○

BIRDING IN WINDHAM COUNTY

Windham County occupies the northeastern corner of Connecticut; it shares its northern border with Massachusetts, its eastern border with Rhode Island, is bounded on the west by Tolland County and on the south by New London County. It is crossed really by only one major highway (I-395) - I-84 barely nicks a corner of Windham County.

The People

Windham County has a population of 102,200, the lowest of Connecticut's eight counties, and less than one-eighth the population of Hartford County. With a land area of 515 square miles, it has a population density of 198 people per square mile, a little more dense than Litchfield County, and far less than Connecticut's six other counties. The largest cities in the county - Willimantic, Putnam and Danielson - have smaller populations than do suburban communities in more developed parts of the state. Growth has been slow - of Windham County's 15 towns, 11 have grown slowly or not at all in recent years. Most of the towns in Windham County are among Connecticut's least affluent.

The Land

Windham County lies in Connecticut's Eastern Uplands ecoregion. It is composed of gentle hilly terrain, broken by many gradually sloping valleys. The topography is moderate and lacking in sharp profile; elevations range between 400' and 800', except for the valleys of the Quinebaug and Natchaug Rivers, in which elevations are below 400'. The climate, compared with other areas of Connecticut, is cool but not cold; higher elevations in the north-central and west-central parts of the county have cooler temperatures and more precipitation than the lower areas in other parts of the county.

Most of Windham County is forested by central hardwoods, often mixed with white pine and hemlock. These woodland communities include areas that have distinctly northern characteristics - hardwoods combined with lots of white pine, hemlock and mountain laurel - and also communities of a more southern nature, particularly in the riparian forests along the county's many slow-moving rivers and streams. In addition, there are numerous occurrences of sand plain forest that support both white pine and pitch pine communities.

Windham County is richly endowed with the whole spectrum of wetland types that are typical of Connecticut, plus certain other wetland habitats that are uncommon elsewhere in the state. There are several fine examples of Atlantic white cedar swamp, black spruce bog and cranberry bog.

About 20% of Windham County is actively farmed, and in addition, there are many abandoned farms that contain various stages of reverting open habitats.

Public Areas and Birding Sites

Among Connecticut's eight counties, Windham has the most undeveloped land. Much of it is privately held, not open to the public, and has simply not yet been transformed by development. Fortunately however, a significant amount of the county's undeveloped land is both protected and open to the public. Much of this land lies within two contiguous state forests (Natchaug and Goodwin) and within a forest tract (Yale Forest) that is privately owned but open to the public. Additional protected areas include several water supply reservoirs, wildlife management areas, and land held by conservation organizations such as Joshua's Tract.

Northeastern Connecticut is almost unknown to many birders - the habitats of this region are less frequently visited and their avian populations less thoroughly studied than are those of other parts of the state. All of this represents an opportunity for birders, because good habitats are there - its just a matter of developing more information about them.

For forest habitats, the best area in Windham County is the Natchaug/Goodwin State Forest complex, most of which lies in Eastford, Chaplin and Hampton. High quality and varied wetland/riparian habitats occur in these two state forests, and also at Ross Marsh and the cluster of reservoirs, all in Killingly. Other excellent areas are the Mashamoquet Brook/Wolf Den Park complex in Pomfret, and Boston Hollow in Ashford.

Seasons for Birding

The main attraction of Windham County to birders is the great diversity of forest species that can be found during the spring, summer and fall. The wide range of habitat types within the county provides an interesting nesting season, with a great species diversity. Although Windham County does not have a coastline or major river valley to serve as an avenue to concentrate migration flights, both the spring and fall migrations are good. Winter offers fewer choices, but there are enough to make birding trips worthwhile.

Spring Migration. In March and April, starting as soon as there is open water, check the reservoirs in Killingly and other lakes and ponds for migrating water birds. In April and May, concentrate on land birds; in the absence of a major river valley, do your spring birding in smaller stream valleys, along the shores of small waterways and along other edges. Look for returning great blue heron, sora and Virginia rail at wetlands. Goodwin Forest and Boston Hollow can be really good in May for land birds.

Nesting Season. A wide diversity of land bird species nest in Windham County. Forest-dwellers are the most numerous; among the areas mentioned under "Public Areas and Birding Sites" above, it is possible to find all the standard species, plus many northerners including raven, black-throated blue warbler, northern waterthrush, and southerners, including Acadian flycatcher (look in Natchaug State Forest and Boston Hollow, both in Ashford), and cerulean warbler (at the Natchaug State Forest, in Chaplin et al). Wetland-oriented land bird species abound at the wetlands in areas mentioned in "Public Areas and Birding Sites" above. One of the best places in the state to observe nesting great blue herons is at the Yale Forest Wetland in Eastford. Great horned, barred and screech owl all nest at various sites in the county. Nesting open-country birds can be found at grassy and shrubby fields and edges at Wolf Den Park and several other sites. Bobolink and meadowlark nest at Wolf Den Park.

Fall Migration. Look for migrating water birds on the reservoirs in Killingly and other water bodies during October and November. For sparrows, go to the shrubby fields at Wolf Den; for other land bird migrants, bird edges and the corridors formed by streams and wide trails through forests. Goodwin Forest is especially good for this.

Winter. There are two main winter birding opportunities in Windham County. One is to look from town roads at farm fields for open country land bird species such as rough-legged and red-tailed hawks, horned lark, snow bunting and Lapland longspur. The second is to look among conifers in the state forests and other wooded sites for cross-bills, pine grosbeak and other winter finches.

Sources of Information and Help

Probably the most effective way to develop additional information about birds and birding sites in Windham County would be to contact the Natchaug Ornithological Society, or Joshua's Tract Conservation and Historical Trust. The visitor center at the Goodwin Forest in Hampton can provide information about trails and habitats within the forest.

When planning a birding trip to Windham County, it is well to remember that places to stay or even to eat are few and far between; the larger cities in the county do have some fast food restaurants. Wolf Den Park has a very nice campground amid excellent habitat.

TOUR OF LAKES, PONDS AND A RIVER IN WINDHAM COUNTY

THE TOUR: This driving tour provides looks at six water bodies that lie in a cluster in eastern Windham County in the town of Killingly. Like the "Tour of Lakes and Ponds in Tolland County", this tour is quite short - just under 12 miles. The sites that it includes are listed below in the order in which they are seen on the tour (they are not described separately):

> **Chase Reservoir**
> **Bog Meadow Reservoir**
> **Middle Reservoir**
> **Alva Chase Reservoir**
> **Killingly Pond**
> **Eddy Pray Reservoir**
> **Five Mile River**

HABITATS

> **LAKE/POND:** lakes and ponds, shores of wetlands, shrubs and woods;
> **MARSH/SWAMP/BOG:** shrub marsh, shrub swamp, shrubby hardwood swamp, white cedar swamp, cranberry bog;
> **River/stream:** streams with hardwood streambelts;
> **Forest:** hardwoods, hardwoods/hemlock, hemlock, white pine/hardwoods sand plain, flood plain;
> **Open terrestrial:** wooded and shrubby edges;

In a rather small area, this site contains a great variety of habitats: the reservoirs and ponds that are the focus of the tour, cranberry bogs, Atlantic white cedar swamps and other wetlands, the Five Mile River and several smaller streams with associated wooded streambelts, and quiet country roads that pass through productive terrestrial edge habitats.

SEASONS/BIRDS

> **SPRING MIGRATION:** WATER BIRDS, marsh birds, shore birds, LAND BIRDS;
> **NESTING SEASON:** water birds, marsh birds, LAND BIRDS;
> **FALL MIGRATION:** WATER BIRDS, marsh birds, shore birds, LAND BIRDS;
> **Winter:** land birds.

These varied and nearly contiguous wetlands provide a good diversity of the common species that you would expect to see in these types of habitat. During the spring and fall migrations, a nice variety and large numbers of water birds occur on the reservoirs and ponds -

especially ring-necked duck, but also good numbers of wood and ruddy ducks, and hooded merganser. In addition, many migrating land birds can be seen, especially along the shores of the ponds, by the edges of the roads, and in the flood plain forest along the Five Mile River. Birds that nest in this area include: wood duck, kingbird, yellow-throated vireo, yellow warbler, gnatcatcher and swamp sparrow. In winter, look for northern shrike, various owls and hawks.

GETTING AROUND
Can be birded by: CAR, WALK, bike.

There are places to park by each of the ponds and along the Five Mile River. Many of these parking spots give you really good looks at the water, and several provide close-up looks at Atlantic white cedar swamps and cranberry bogs - both uncommon habitat types for Connecticut. In addition, several of the roads (especially Pond Road, Quinns Hill Road and River Road) are quiet, pass through rich habitat, and are ideal for birding on foot . The surrounding land is private, so stay on the roads.

DIRECTIONS (see Map 75): This area is in the eastern part of Connecticut, near the Connecticut/Rhode Island state line. **The starting point for the tour is I-395 exit 93.**

To get to the Chase Reservoir, go east on Route 101 for 2.0 miles, left on Pratt Road for 0.3 mile and right on Pettingill Road for 0.1 mile to the reservoir on the left.

To get to Bog Meadow Reservoir, continue on Pettingill Road for 0.1 mile, east (left) on Route 101 for 1.2 miles, right on Bailey Hill Road for 0.1 mile, left on Bear Hill Road for 0.2 mile to where Bog Meadow Reservoir can be seen on both sides of the road.

To get to another part of Bog Meadow Reservoir, to Middle Reservoir and a cranberry bog, return to Route 101, turn right and continue east for another 0.4 mile to the causeway between Bog Meadow Reservoir on the right and Middle Reservoir on the left. The cranberry bog is just beyond the causeway on the left, near the shore of Middle Reservoir. An Atlantic white cedar swamp lies along the northern (distant) shore of Middle Reservoir.

To get to the Alva Chase Reservoir, continue east on Route 101 for 0.3 mile to a causeway that crosses the Alva Chase Reservoir.

To get to another part of Middle Reservoir, turn around and go back west on Route 101 for 0.2 mile, and turn north (right) on Pond Road which you reach just before the causeway that you came across between Middle Reservoir and Bog Meadow Reservoir. Pond Road passes near the white cedar swamp at the north end of Middle Reservoir.

To get to Killingly Pond, continue north on Pond Road for another 0.7 mile until you see Killingly Pond and associated wetlands on the right.

To get to the Eddy Pray Reservoir, continue on Pond Road (bearing left as it becomes Quinns Hill Road) for 0.7 mile until you see a small place to park on the right at the foot of the dike of the reservoir. White cedar and shrub swamp are visible on the left side of the road at this point.

To get to the Five Mile River, continue on Quinns Hill Road for another 0.4 mile, right on North Road for 2.4 miles, and left on River Road which follows the Five Mile River for 1.6 miles. (At the intersection of North and River Roads, there is a pond that is worth looking at.)

When you come to the end of River Road, keep heading west until you reach Route 21 (less than a mile), turn south (left) and this will bring you back to I-395 exit 93 in about five miles.

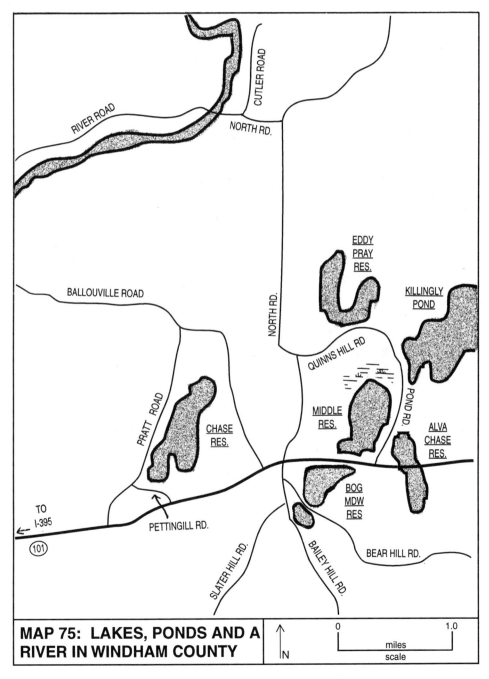

MAP 75: LAKES, PONDS AND A RIVER IN WINDHAM COUNTY

ASHFORD: FRIEDMAN MEMORIAL FOREST/BEBBINGTON LANE

HABITAT
Forest: hardwoods, vine tangles and thickets;
Open terrestrial: wooded and shrubby edges, tilled and shrubby fields;
Lake/pond: pond, hardwood shore;
River/stream: stream, hardwood streambelt;
Marsh/swamp/bog: mixed herbaceous marsh, shrubby hardwood swamp.
This is a 143-acre Joshua's Tract property that is mostly wooded, and includes a perennial stream with a hardwood streambelt, a small pond, and a shrubby/hardwood swamp that is visible just outside of the preserve. Bebbington Lane is a gravel country road that passes tilled and shrubby fields, varied wetlands and ponds.

SEASONS/BIRDS
Spring migration: land birds;
Nesting season: land birds;
Fall migration: land birds;
Winter: land birds.
Look for the typical variety of forest- and edge-dwelling land birds during the spring, summer and fall. Nesters include broad-winged hawk, woodcock, brown thrasher, hermit thrush, yellow-throated and warbling vireos, prairie warbler, Louisiana waterthrush, indigo bunting and field sparrow.

GETTING AROUND
Birding methods: car, WALK.
There is a trail that makes a loop of just under two miles through this property; it is hilly and sometimes wet in places. Good birding can also be had by walking along Bebbington Lane; if necessary, it can be driven. Stay on the road - the surrounding land is private.

DIRECTIONS: This site is in Ashford, about five miles northeast of Storrs. To get there from the intersection of Routes 89 and 44, go south on Route 89 for 1.4 miles, left on Bicknell Road for 0.6 mile, and left again on Bebbington Road for 0.2 mile to a small parking area and the preserve entrance on the right side of the road. (Bebbington Lane is on your right shortly before you reach the parking area.)

ASHFORD: NATCHAUG STATE FOREST

HABITATS
FOREST: hardwoods, hardwoods / white pine; hardwoods / hemlock, white pine / hemlock, mixed conifers;
MARSH/SWAMP/BOG: mixed herbaceous and shrub marsh; shrub, shrubby hardwood, hardwood, hemlock and white pine swamps; dead wood; open water;
Lake/pond: beaver pond, marshy, shrubby and wooded shore;
River/stream: river, perennial and seasonal streams, wooded streambelts.
Three blocks of the large Natchaug State Forest are within the town of Ashford (other blocks are described separately under Chaplin). The three blocks in Ashford are largely wooded and all three contain wetlands. Among the three areas, it is possible to find a wide variety of inland habitats typical of Windham County.

SEASONS/BIRDS
SPRING MIGRATION: water birds, marsh birds, LAND BIRDS;
NESTING SEASON: water birds, marsh birds, LAND BIRDS;
FALL MIGRATION: water birds, marsh birds, LAND BIRDS;
Winter: land birds.
The migration in the spring (May) and the early fall (September) are both excellent. During the nesting season, it is possible to find several species of marsh birds and a wide variety of land birds including both northern and southern species. Among the nesters are red-shouldered and broad-winged hawks, green-backed heron, Acadian flycatcher, brown creeper, hermit thrush, solitary and yellow-throated vireos, black-throated green warbler, both waterthrushes and purple finch. Great blue heron is a possible nester.

GETTING AROUND
Birding methods: car, WALK, bike.
Town roads go along and through parts of these areas, and a number of trails go through them. The roads that lead to the blocks of the forest described here provide good birding, but stay on the road - much of the surrounding land is private.

DIRECTIONS (see Map 76): These three blocks of the Natchaug State Forest are in a cluster ten to fifteen miles north of Willimantic. To get to them, a logical starting point is at Warrenville, at the intersection of Routes 44 and 89.

One block can be reached by going north on Route 89 for 1.0 miles, and left on Perry Hill Road. This road goes through parts of the forest intermittently for several miles. Trails lead into the forest from either side of the road.

A second block can be reached from the intersection of Routes 44 and 89 by going north on Route 89 for 1.1 miles, right on James Road for 1.6 miles and left on Horse Hill Road. The state forest is on the right side of Horse Hill Road intermittently for the next 1.1 miles. This part of the forest includes a fine beaver-controlled wetland.

To get to the third block of the forest, follow Horse Hill Road to the intersection with North Road, and turn left on North Road. The state forest is on the left side of North Road intermittently for the next mile.

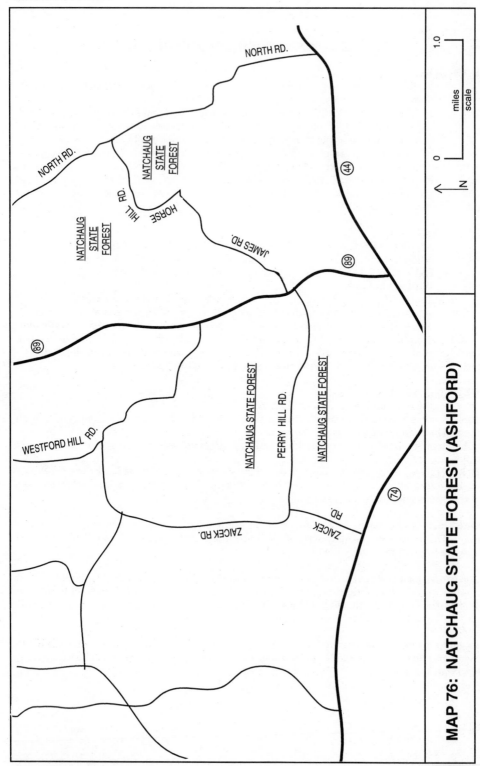

MAP 76: NATCHAUG STATE FOREST (ASHFORD)

ASHFORD/EASTFORD: BOSTON HOLLOW

HABITATS
FOREST: hardwoods, hardwoods/white pine, hardwoods/hemlock, hemlock, mountain laurel;
RIVER/STREAM: stream, shrubby, hardwood and hemlock streambelt;
Open terrestrial: tilled, short grass, tall grass and shrubby fields, shrubby edges;
Lake/pond: ponds, grassy and shrubby shores; seasonal pools;
Marsh/swamp/bog: sedge marsh, shrubby hardwood and hemlock swamp, dead wood;
Other: rock outcrop, rocky slope.

Boston Hollow lies within a 7,000-acre tract of forest owned by Yale University. The upper (southern) part of the ravine is rather broad and shallow and contains a swamp, but as it descends northward, the sides grow steeper and higher, and the swamp becomes a stream. This ravine acts as a cold trap, and contains northern hardwoods, hemlock, and other flora of a northern character. Finally, it emerges onto a lowland in which there are marshes, swamps, reverting fields and ponds.

SEASONS/BIRDS
SPRING MIGRATION: marsh birds, shore birds, LAND BIRDS;
NESTING SEASON: marsh birds, LAND BIRDS;
FALL MIGRATION: marsh birds, shore birds, LAND BIRDS;
Winter: land birds.

Boston Hollow is widely regarded as one of Connecticut's top inland birding sites. Because the ravine in Boston Hollow contains a cold microclimate, it attracts many species normally found north of Connecticut. In contrast, the bottomland hardwoods north of the ravine attract southerners. Spring is the high season of this site because of the warbler migration, with over 30 species occurring regularly. Migrating marsh birds and shore birds occur on Kinney Pond in the lowlands north of the ravine. Summer is also interesting, because of the wide variety of nesting species: red-shouldered and broad-winged hawks, barred owl, raven, gnatcatcher, Blackburnian, Canada, yellow-rumped, black-throated blue and black-throated green warblers, northern and Louisiana waterthrush, white-throated sparrow, junco, Acadian flycatcher and winter wren. Among nesting marsh birds are Virginia rail and great blue heron. Early fall can also be good; winter is quiet by comparison, but sometimes the forest is visited by winter finch species.

GETTING AROUND
Birding methods: CAR, WALK, bike.

This is one of the few hemlock ravines in Connecticut through which you can follow a quiet country road that provides excellent birding on foot or from your car. By following this road, you pass through the ravine (1.7 miles) and then go past the wetlands, fields and ponds that are in the lowlands north of the ravine for another several miles. In addition, a trail leads up the west side of the ravine to a high overlook. In winter and early spring, the road may not be usable by cars, but can still be walked.

DIRECTIONS (see Map 77): Boston Hollow is in Ashford, about ten miles south of the point at which I-84 enters Massachusetts. To get to Boston Hollow from I-84, take exit 72, go south on Route 89 for 4.0 miles to the intersection where Route 89 turns sharp right. Here, go straight ahead on Boston Hollow Road for 0.4 mile to the point at which the paved road turns right and Boston Hollow Road continues straight ahead as a dirt road. Go straight ahead on Boston Hollow Road for 1.7 mile through the ravine and into the lowlands, left on Axe Factory Road for 1.2 mile, right on Kinney Hollow Road for 3.0 miles, left on Route 190 for 1.3 miles to I-84 exit 73.

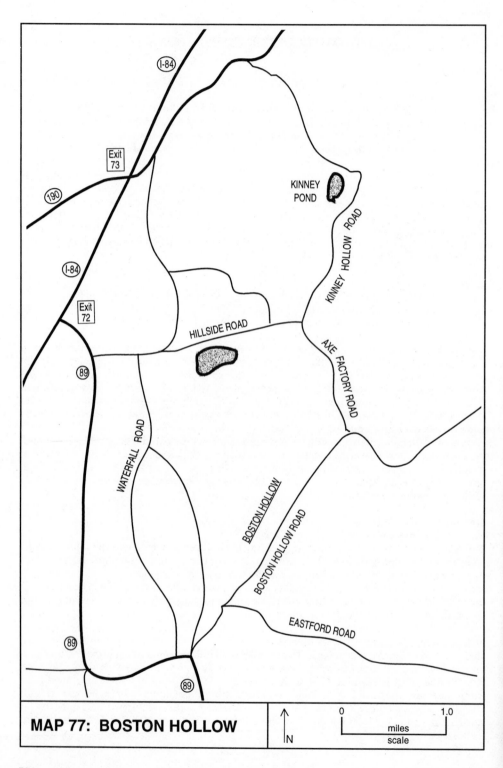

MAP 77: BOSTON HOLLOW

KINNEY POND

KINNEY HOLLOW ROAD

AXE FACTORY ROAD

HILLSIDE ROAD

WATERFALL ROAD

BOSTON HOLLOW

BOSTON HOLLOW ROAD

EASTFORD ROAD

I-84

Exit 73

190

I-84

Exit 72

89

89

89

N

0   1.0
miles
scale

CANTERBURY/PLAINFIELD: QUINEBAUG RIVER WMA

HABITATS

OPEN TERRESTRIAL: shrubby field, shrubby edge;
RIVER/STREAM: river, shrubby and wooded streambelts;
Marsh/swamp/bog: shrub swamp, shrubby hardwood swamp, hardwood swamp;
Forest: hardwoods, hardwoods/white pine, hardwoods/hemlock, conifer plantations, flood plain;
Other: steep dirt river embankments.

This 1,219-acre managed area extends along both sides of the Quinebaug River for about three miles. In addition to a variety of typical inland wetland and forest habitats, there are interesting blends of flood plain and open terrestrial habitats, including an area along the river that is a kind of flood plain shrubby field.

SEASONS/BIRDS

SPRING MIGRATION: marsh birds, LAND BIRDS;
NESTING SEASON: LAND BIRDS;
FALL MIGRATION: marsh birds, LAND BIRDS;
Winter: land birds.

During the spring and fall migrations, the river attracts osprey, occasionally bald eagle, and a good variety of other land birds. The varied habitats at this site attract a variety of nesters: shrubby field species of land birds such as prairie warbler, indigo bunting and orchard oriole, as well as kingfisher and bank swallow that nest in the river banks.

GETTING AROUND

Birding methods: car, walk.
Several roads and a number of trails go through the area.

DIRECTIONS: This area is in eastern Connecticut on the Canterbury/Plainfield line, six or seven miles west of the Rhode Island border. It follows the winding course of the Quinebaug River, and lies within the area bounded by Route 169 on the west, Route 205 on the north, and Route 14 on the south and east.

The southern part of the area can be entered near the intersection of Routes 14 and 14A. Park on the west side of Route 14 about 50 yards north (or east) of the intersection, and walk into the woods toward the river. The wildlife management area includes a narrow strip of land which runs upstream along the river from this point for about two miles.

The middle part of the area can be reached by starting at the intersection of Routes 14 and 14A, going north (or east) on Route 14 for 1.8 miles, and left on Sugar Brook Road for 0.6 mile to the edge of the area, at which point there are trails into the area.

To reach the northern part of the area, continue on Route 14 for another 1.5 miles (a total of 3.3 miles from the intersection of Routes 14 and 14A), and turn left onto Cady Lane (at the sign for the fish hatchery). Follow Cady Lane for 1.0 mile, past the hatchery to a point at which dirt roads can be walked straight ahead and to the right into the wildlife management area.

CHAPLIN ET AL: NATCHAUG STATE FOREST

HABITATS

FOREST: hardwoods, hardwoods/white pine, hardwoods/hemlock, white pine/hemlock, white pine, flood plain, mixed conifers, mountain laurel, sweet pepperbush and other shrubs, thickets;

MARSH/SWAMP/BOG: cattail, sedge, mixed herbaceous and shrub marsh; shrub, shrubby hardwood and hardwood swamp, dead wood; cranberrry bog; shrubby and wooded edges;

LAKE/POND: ponds; dead wood, wooded and shrubby islands, shores of mixed herbaceous and shrub marsh, shrub swamp, shrubs and hardwoods, seasonal pools;

River/stream: streams; streambelts of shrub swamp, shrubs and hardwoods; hemlock ravine;

Open terrestrial: shrubby field, shrubby edge.

The Natchaug State Forest is big (12,428 acres), and includes most types of inland habitat typical of eastern Connecticut, in a largely undisturbed natural setting. Most of the forest lies in two nearly contiguous blocks in the towns of Chaplin, Eastford, Hampton and Pomfret; that area is described here. Within this part of the forest are the Beaverdam Wildlife Management Area, Catden Swamp, the Hampton Reservoir, the Hale Wildlife Marsh, Maple Swamp and the Ledge Brook wetland. Another block of the forest is in Ashford; it is described earlier in this chapter. Still other blocks are in Hampton, Pomfret and Brooklyn.

Much of the area included in this site description consists of northern and central deciduous/conifer forest, and also includes the Natchaug River, a number of smaller streams, riparian forest, several hemlock ravines, ponds, marshes and swamps.

The Beaverdam Wildlife Management Area includes a large, shallow, beaver-influenced pond. Much of the pond is covered by emergent plant growth, and it has a shore of varied marshes, swamps, shrubs and hardwoods. The surrounding forest is composed primarily of hardwoods, and also of hardwoods mixed with some white pine and hemlock.

Catden Swamp is one of the largest and least disturbed shrub swamps in eastern Connecticut. It feeds a large, shallow pond with profuse emergent vegetation and a marshy shore (the northern part of the Hampton Reservoir). These wetlands lie within a forest of hardwoods, white pine and hemlock in various combinations, with several planted conifer groves. In many areas, these woods have a dense shrub layer of mountain laurel and various other shrubs.

The Hampton Reservoir lies downstream from Catden Swamp, and is composed of a large shallow pond with open water, emergent vegetation, a shrubby shore, areas of shrub marsh, shrub swamp, and shrubby hardwood swamp with standing dead trees, shrubby and wooded islands. The surrounding forest is composed of hardwoods and white pines with a rich shrub layer of mountain laurel, sweet pepperbush and blueberry. The immediate area also includes a red pine plantation and a stream with a shrubby and wooded streambelt.

Hale Wildlife Marsh is composed of a pond, surrounded by basically the same wetland, forest and shrub habitats as the Hampton Reservoir.

Maple Swamp, despite its name, is not now a hardwood swamp, but rather a mixed herbaceous and shrub marsh, with some areas of shrubby hardwood swamp and some open water; it is surrounded by hardwoods/white pine forest with an understory of mountain laurel.

The Ledge Brook wetland is composed of a large pond with lots of standing dead trees, associated wetlands, and is surrounded by a forest of hardwoods, white pine and hemlock with thickets of mountain laurel and sweet pepperbush.

SEASONS/BIRDS
SPRING MIGRATION: water birds, MARSH BIRDS, shore birds, LAND BIRDS;
NESTING SEASON: water birds, MARSH BIRDS, shore birds, LAND BIRDS;
FALL MIGRATION: water birds, marsh birds, shore birds, LAND BIRDS;
Winter: land birds.

The wooded portion of this state forest contains a wide variety of habitat types, and this is reflected in the diversity of bird species that occur here. Included among the nesters are both northerners in the upland forests (including solitary vireo and yellow-rumped warbler), and southerners down in the flood plain (including cerulean warbler). In winter, look for saw-whet owl in cedars along Pumpkin Hill Road (see "Several additional good habitat areas" under "Directions" below).

The Beaverdam Wildlife Management Area has a good variety of the migrants and nesters you would expect in these types of habitat. Spring, summer and early fall are good; by October, the action is pretty much over. Nesters include both northern and southern species: solitary vireo, Canada, Blackburnian, black-throated green, yellow-rumped and cerulean warblers, both waterthrushes, red-shouldered hawk, saw-whet and barred owls, great blue and green-backed herons, woodcock and spotted sandpiper. Several woodpecker species are here all year, and in winter, look for winter finches in years of southward irruption into Connecticut.

Catden Swamp provides excellent habitat for marsh birds, and nesting species include American bittern, Virginia rail and great blue heron. Among the other nesters are wood duck, great crested flycatcher, warbling vireo and swamp sparrow.

The Hampton Reservoir, the Hale Wildlife Marsh, and the habitats immediately surrounding both areas are especially good during the spring migration and in the nesting season. Nesting species include wood duck, great blue and green-backed herons, barred owl, pileated, red-bellied and hairy woodpeckers, great crested flycatcher, brown creeper, Carolina wren, gnatcatcher and swamp sparrow.

Maple Swamp is a good area at which to look for land birds throughout the year; for water birds and marsh birds during the spring, summer and fall.

The Ledge Brook wetland provides good habitat for a variety of wetland-oriented species as well as forest-dwellers that have an affinity for mountain laurel, sweet pepperbush and other berry-carrying shrubs. Among the known nesters are great blue heron, wood duck, pileated woodpecker and great crested flycatcher.

GETTING AROUND
Birding methods: CAR, WALK, BOAT, ski.

The main part of the forest has fourteen miles of paved roads and many woods roads and trails; a map is really necessary, and is available at park headquarters. Several of the roads and trails within the Natchaug State Forest lead south into the contiguous Goodwin State Forest. Some of the roads in these forests get soft and muddy in the spring, and are unsafe to use in winter. At the **Beaverdam WMA,** there are several trails, but much of the walking is quite difficult. Much of the pond can be seen from the parking area, or explored by boat. The auto roads that are near **Catden Swamp** are ideal for birding from your car or on foot. The **Hampton Reservoir and Hale Wildlife Marsh** can each be reached by car, and much of the ponds and associated wetlands can be seen well from where you park (the view from the

Hampton Reservoir dam is broad and spectacular). Hampton Reservoir is an interesting pond to explore by boat. **Maple Swamp** can be seen by parking on Paine Road. **The Ledge Brook wetland** can be seen from Route 44, but requires parking at a designated area on the north (opposite) side of the road. Traffic is fast and noisy.

DIRECTIONS: This part of the Natchaug State Forest is about 10 miles northeast of Willimantic. **To get to the main entrance and park headquarters,** from Phoenixville at the intersection of routes 198 and 44, go south on Route 198 for 2.7 miles, and left into the state forest entrance. This road leads to the forest headquarters buildings in 0.9 mile (maps can be obtained here); on the way there you pass other roads and trails that lead into the forest.

To get to the Beaverdam Wildlife Management Area, from the state forest entrance on Route 198, follow the driveway for 0.8 mile, right on Kingsbury Road for 0.1 mile to the Beaver Dam WMA entrance on the left.

To get to Catden Swamp, which lies just inside the eastern edge of the Natchaug State Forest in Eastford, start from the intersection of Routes 44 and 198, go south on Route 198 for 0.1 mile, left on General Lyon Road for 0.4 mile, and left on Pilfershire Road. In 1.1 miles, bear left at a fork, and at 2.3 miles, scan the wetland that is associated with Beaverdam Brook. At 3.2 miles, Pilfershire Road ends at Fayette Wright Road, on which turn right. Catden Swamp, a cattail marsh and other wetlands lie to the left of this road for much of its length of about two miles, until it ends at a hardtop road (Old Griffin Highway).

To get to the Hampton Reservoir, turn left on Old Griffin Highway for 0.4 mile, and left again on Kenyon Road for 0.7 mile to the driveway on the left.

To get to Hale Wildlife Marsh, continue north on Kenyon Road for 0.8 mile to where the pond and marsh is visible on the left.

To get to Maple Swamp, continue north on Kenyon Road (which becomes Stetson Road) for 0.1 mile, left on Fay Road for 0.8 mile, and left on Paine Road for 1.2 mile to where Maple Swamp is visible on the east (right) side of the road.

To get to the Ledge Brook wetland, continue north on Paine Road for 0.4 mile, left on Route 44 for 1.1 mile to the wetland on the left.

To return to the intersection of Routes 44 and 198 (your starting point), continue west on Route 44 for another 1.8 mile to Route 198.

Several additional good habitat areas can be reached by starting again at the intersection of Routes 198 and 44, and going south on Route 198 for about three miles. The forest lies intermittently on the left (east) side of the road, and can be entered at several points. At a point 3.8 miles from the intersection of Routes 44 and 198, go left on Morey Road, which goes through a part of the forest. For additional areas (not shown on the map), return to Route 198, and continue south for an additional 2.0 miles, and go right on Pumpkin Hill Road, which goes through a part of the forest.

Access to still more parts of the forest can be gained from the following points:

At the intersection of Routes 44 and 198, go east on Route 44. The forest is on both sides of the road intermittently for several miles.

Also from the intersection of Routes 44 and 198, go west on Route 44 for 0.9 to 1.2 miles. The forest is on both sides of the road for this brief stretch.

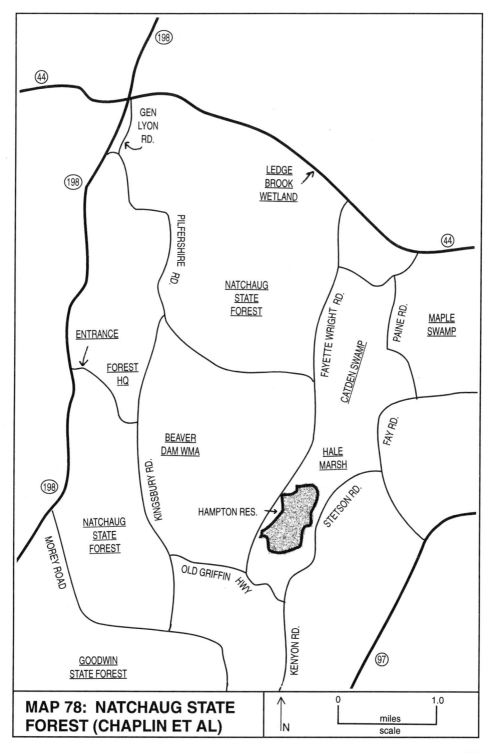

MAP 78: NATCHAUG STATE FOREST (CHAPLIN ET AL)

589

EASTFORD: WESTFORD ROAD WETLAND

HABITATS
Marsh/swamp/bog: cattail, sedge, mixed herbaceous and shrub marsh; shrub and shrubby hardwood swamp, dead wood, shrubby and white pine edge;
Lake/pond: pond, marshy shore;
Open terrestrial: short grass field, shrubby edge.
This is a medium-sized wetland that includes several types of marsh and swamp, together with some open water. A nearby cemetery provides open and edge habitat.

SEASONS/BIRDS
Spring migration: water birds, marsh birds, shore birds, land birds;
Nesting season: water birds, marsh birds land birds;
Fall migration: water birds, marsh birds, shore birds, land birds;
Winter: land birds.
Common species of water, marsh and land birds can be seen on this wetland during spring, summer and fall. Nesters include wood duck, kingbird, common yellowthroat, yellow warbler and redstart.

GETTING AROUND
Birding methods: car, walk.
Most of this wetland can be seen from a small parking area by the side of Westford Road. Birding the cemetery involves a short and easy walk. This site provides an effortless way to see a typical wetland, and is worth a stop if you are in the area.

DIRECTIONS: This wetland lies immediately west of the center of Eastford. From the intersection of Routes 198 and 44, go north on Route 198 for 1.8 mile, left on Westford Road for 0.5 mile to a parking area by the edge of the wetland on the left. The cemetery is directly across the road.

EASTFORD: YALE FOREST WETLAND

HABITATS
LAKE/POND: beaver pond, hardwood/white pine shore;
MARSH/SWAMP/BOG: shrub swamp, shrubby hardwood swamp, dead wood;
FOREST: hardwoods, white pine and hemlock, alone and in various combinations; mountain laurel;
River/stream: stream, wooded streambelt.
The centerpiece of this site is a pristine beaver-controlled wetland that includes open water, lots of standing dead trees, areas of swamp around the edge, all backed by a wooded shore. This wetland is tucked away amid a mature forest of northern hardwoods, white pine and hemlock.

SEASONS/BIRDS
SPRING MIGRATION: water birds, MARSH BIRDS, shore birds, LAND BIRDS;
NESTING SEASON: water birds, MARSH BIRDS, LAND BIRDS;
Fall migration: water birds, marsh birds, shore birds, land birds;
Winter: land birds.

The beaver pond and the areas of marsh, swamp and edge that are associated with it provide excellent habitat for a variety of land birds, as well as several species of water, marsh and migrating shore birds. One of the many nice features of this site is that it provides an excellent view of great blue heron nests (at least at the time of writing - but herons tend to move on after a few years in one heronry). Be careful not to disturb the herons while watching them. Other species that nest at or near the wetland include wood duck, green-backed heron, Acadian and great crested flycatchers and Louisiana waterthrush. Northern waterthrush is a possible nester. Species that nest in the surrounding forest include pileated woodpecker, brown creeper, black-throated green warbler and probably numerous other northern forest species (this remote area needs a more thorough bird inventory).

GETTING AROUND
Birding methods: car, walk.
The wetland can be seen well from French Road. The forest that surrounds the pond and through which Crystal Pond Road and French Road pass is part of the Yale Forest, and is open to the public. Several trails lead into it from both roads.

HOW TO GET THERE: This site is in Eastford, about fifteen miles northeast of Storrs. From the western intersection of Routes 171 and 198 at Kenyonville (just north of the village of Eastford), go west (or northward) on Route 171 for 1.3 miles, left on Crystal Pond Road for 0.8 mile, and right on French Road for 0.3 mile to the pond. Note: there are two Crystal Pond Roads that are left turns off Route 171; ignore the first one (in Woodstock) and take the second (in Eastford).

HAMPTON: GOODWIN STATE FOREST

HABITATS
FOREST: hardwoods, hardwoods/white pine, hardwoods/hemlock, white pine/hemlock, mixed conifers;
MARSH/SWAMP/BOG: cattail, mixed herbaceous and shrub marsh, shrub swamp, shrubby hardwood swamp, hardwood swamp, shrubby and wooded edges;
LAKE/POND: ponds, shallow water, emergent vegetation, marshy, swampy, shrubby and wooded shores;
Open terrestrial: short grass and shrubby fields, shrubby edge;
River/stream: perennial and seasonal streams, wooded streambelts.
This area consists of 1,820 acres of natural areas together with managed habitats of various types. Most of the area is forested, and there are also open areas, several ponds and varied wetlands. Pine Acres Pond is large (133 acres), shallow, choked with emergent vegetation and filled with stumps. It is surrounded by marshes and swamps, and a rich and varied wetland lies at the north end of the pond. Brown Hill Pond is a formerly beaver-controlled wetland that appeared at the time of writing to be undergoing some sort of management - the water was drawn down, and a dam was being built. It is surrounded by forest, and the shore is wooded, with hardwoods, white pine and mixes of them.

SEASONS/BIRDS
SPRING MIGRATION: water birds, marsh birds, shore birds, LAND BIRDS;
NESTING SEASON: water birds, marsh birds, LAND BIRDS;
FALL MIGRATION: water birds, marsh birds, shore birds, LAND BIRDS;
Winter: land birds.

In the forested part of this site, spring (May) and fall (late August, September and early October) are especially good for migrating warblers. In the Goodwin Forest as a whole, 95 species have shown evidence of breeding. Among the nesters are: hooded merganser, great blue heron, barred owl, great crested flycatcher, brown creeper, golden-crowned kinglet, yellow-throated, solitary and warbling vireos, magnolia, yellow-rumped, black-throated blue and Blackburnian warblers.

Pine Acres Pond and the habitats that surround it often have a good variety of birds - water birds on the pond, marsh birds in the wetland at the north end of the pond, and land birds on the edges and within the forest around the wetlands.

At Brown Hill Pond, common species of water and marsh birds can be seen on the pond itself during the warm months. Land birds such as kingfisher and flycatchers hunt from trees along the shore. Forest-dwellers occur in the woods along the trail.

GETTING AROUND
Birding methods: CAR, WALK, ski.

Several roads and many trails lead through the wooded part of this site. A pamphlet and trail map are available at the Conservation Center, near the entrance.

At Pine Acres Pond, there are trails that go along the edge of the pond and the associated wetland area. (A trail also goes over to Brown Hill Pond.) The parking area near the visitor center overlooks Pine Acres Pond, which can be scanned with a spotting scope. The dense emergent vegetation on the pond would make boating difficult.

At Brown Hill Pond, there is a short driveway that leads to the edge of the pond. Also from the driveway, a woods road leads through the forest on the west side of the pond.

Other trails lead off Potter Road, north of the Conservation Center.

DIRECTIONS: This area is mostly in Hampton, about five miles northeast of Willimantic. To get there from the intersection of Routes 6 and 97, go west on Route 6 for 1.4 miles, right at the entrance on Potter Road for 0.2 mile to the visitor center, parking area and driveway to the shore of **Pine Acres Pond** which is visible on the right. Driveways, woods roads and trails can be started or found from the visitor center. **To get to Brown Hill Pond,** return to the main forest entrance, go east (left) on Route 6 for 0.3 mile, left on West Old Route 6 for 0.4 mile to the pond and a dirt driveway on the left.

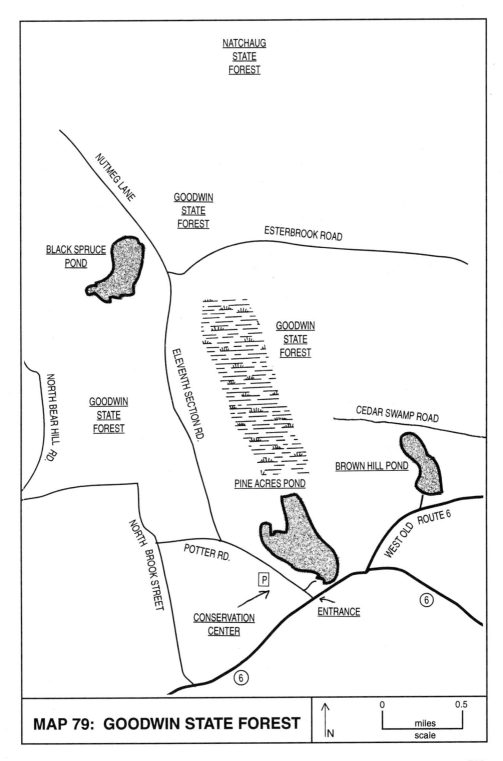

NATCHAUG
STATE
FOREST

NUTMEG LANE

GOODWIN
STATE
FOREST

ESTERBROOK ROAD

BLACK SPRUCE
POND

ELEVENTH SECTION RD.

GOODWIN
STATE
FOREST

NORTH BEAR HILL RD.

GOODWIN
STATE
FOREST

CEDAR SWAMP ROAD

BROWN HILL POND

PINE ACRES POND

WEST OLD ROUTE 6

NORTH BROOK STREET

POTTER RD.

P

CONSERVATION
CENTER

ENTRANCE

6

6

MAP 79: GOODWIN STATE FOREST

N

0   0.5
miles
scale

KILLINGLY: TETRAULT POND

HABITATS
MARSH/SWAMP/BOG: cattail, mixed herbaceous and shrub marsh; cranberry bog; shallow open water; shore with areas of shrubs, white pine, hardwoods/white pine. This wetland was once a cranberry bog, remnants of which are still visible. Through a process of succession, it has become an open marsh, and is apparently in the process of further transition to a pond.

SEASONS/BIRDS
Spring migration: water birds, marsh birds, land birds;
Nesting season: water birds, marsh birds, land birds;
Fall migration: water birds, marsh birds, land birds;
Winter: land birds.
This is a nice site at which to stop briefly if you are in the area. It is good for calling up sora and Virginia rail, and to look for common species of water, marsh and land birds that you would expect in these habitat types. Nesting species in the area include broad-winged hawk, kingbird, yellow-throated and warbling vireos, gnatcatcher, yellow warbler and swamp sparrow.

GETTING AROUND
Can be birded by: car.
From the parking area by the side of the road, you can look over the marsh. Traffic can at times be annoying.

DIRECTIONS: This pond is about two miles east of the city of Danielson. From I-395 exit 92, go east on the Danielson Pike for 1.2 miles, left on Cranberry Bog Road for 0.6 mile to Tetrault Pond and a place to park on the right.

KILLINGLY/STERLING: ROSS MARSH WILDLIFE MANAGEMENT AREA

HABITATS
MARSH/SWAMP/BOG: cattail, sedge, mixed herbaceous and shrub marsh, shrub swamp, shrubby hardwood swamp, wooded swamp, Atlantic white cedar swamp, cranberry bog, dead wood, wooded edge (hardwoods, white pine and hemlock in various mixes);
FOREST: hardwoods, hardwoods/white pine, hardwoods/hemlock, white pine;
LAKE/POND: pond, shallow water, shore of the wetland and forest types listed above;
Open terrestrial: shrubby field;
River/stream: stream; streambelt that is composed of woods and shrubby hardwood swamp.
This wildlife management area consists of 278 acres on either side of Quandock Brook and a large pond formed by damming the brook. The other habitats include varied wetlands (including an Atlantic white cedar swamp and a cranberry bog) around the pond and stream, areas of forest and open fields.

SEASONS/BIRDS
>   **SPRING MIGRATION:** WATER BIRDS, marsh birds, shore birds, LAND BIRDS;
>   **NESTING SEASON:** water birds, marsh birds, LAND BIRDS;
>   **FALL MIGRATION:** WATER BIRDS, marsh birds, shore birds, LAND BIRDS;
>   **Winter:** land birds.

This is a beautiful site in which to look for common wetland-oriented and forest species. Nesters include wood duck, mallard, hairy woodpecker, kingbird, hermit thrush, ovenbird, black-throated green and yellow warblers. Ring-necked duck occurs on the pond in migration. Other species of migrating water birds are likely.

GETTING AROUND
>   **Birding methods:** car, walk, boat.

The driveway within the area is 0.5 mile long, and provides a nice way to bird your way past forest, edge and wetland habitats, without traffic or disturbance of any kind. There is one nice trail that starts at the dam. A canoe would allow you to get a close look at the wetlands along the shore of the pond - especially the Atlantic white cedar swamp.

DIRECTIONS: The Ross Marsh Wildlife Area lies near the Rhode Island border about five miles southeast of Danielson. In Danielson, from Route I-395 exit 91, go east on Route 6 for 3.6 miles, right on Sawmill Hill Road for 1.5 miles to the entrance on the left, or for 1.8 miles, to the dam and the start of the trail also on the left.

POMFRET: MASHAMOQUET BROOK SP/WOLF DEN PARK/CAMPING AREA

HABITATS
>   **MARSH/SWAMP/BOG:** sedge, cattail and shrub marsh, standing deadwood;
>   **FOREST:** hardwoods, hardwoods/hemlock, hardwoods/white pine, hemlock, mountain laurel;
>   **OPEN TERRESTRIAL:** tilled, short grass, tall grass, mixed herbaceous and shrubby fields; shrubby and wooded edges; cedars;
>   **RIVER/STREAM:** stream, fast water, hardwood and hemlock streambelt;
>   **Other:** rocky slopes.

Taken together, these three contiguous areas offer a wide variety of habitat types, and include a gorgeous wetland.

Mashamoquet Brook Park occupies the valley of a small rocky stream. The surrounding land is rugged, and has bedrock ridges, glacial erratic boulders, and varied forest communities and laurel thickets.

The main attraction at the nearby **Wolf Den Camping area** is a large beaver-influenced wetland that contains a variety of herbaceous marshes. This area includes varied open terrestrial habitats.

At the south end of this site is **Wolf Den State Park.** This area is hilly and covered by deciduous forest dominated by oaks and white ash, with occasional groves of conifers.

SEASONS/BIRDS

SPRING MIGRATION: water birds, MARSH BIRDS, shore birds, LAND BIRDS;
NESTING SEASON: water birds, MARSH BIRDS, shore birds, LAND BIRDS;
FALL MIGRATION: water birds, marsh birds, shore birds, LAND BIRDS;
Winter: land birds.

The spring and fall migrations and the nesting season are all excellent in this area. Nesters include an impressive variety of species. Among the marsh birds are Virginia rail, great blue and green-backed herons. All five of the vireos that occur in Connecticut nest here, each in its own type of habitat. Nesting raptors include great horned, barred and screech owls, kestrel and broad-winged hawk. The abundance of fields and edges attract bobolink, meadowlark, prairie warbler, indigo bunting, field and Savannah sparrows. Other nesters include yellow-billed cuckoo, pileated woodpecker, hermit thrush, willow flycatcher and swamp sparrow.

GETTING AROUND

Can be birded by: car, WALK, bike, ski.

Park driveways go through each of these areas. In addition, there are many woods roads and trails, including a trail that connects the two parks.

DIRECTIONS: These three contiguous areas are in northeastern Connecticut, about five miles southwest of Putnam.

To get to Mashamoquet Brook State Park, from the intersection of Routes 44 and 101, go west on Route 44 for 1.0 mile to the park entrance on the left. A driveway goes along the stream through the park for 0.5 mile to a dead end. A trail leading south to Wolf Den Park starts at this point.

To get into the Wolf Den Camping Area, from the intersection of Routes 44 and 101, go east on Route 101 for about 100 feet and turn right (south) on Wolf Den Road for about one mile, and left into the camping area road.

To make a driving loop through Wolf Den Park, continue south on Wolf Den Road past the road to the camping area and keep bearing right. This route goes through a part of Wolf Den State Park, and passes a number of woods roads and trails on both sides of the road that lead into the park.

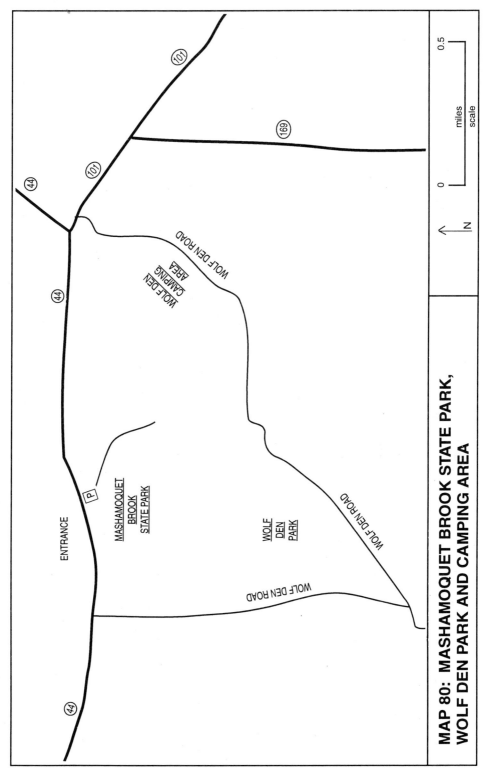

MAP 80: MASHAMOQUET BROOK STATE PARK, WOLF DEN PARK AND CAMPING AREA

SCOTLAND: PUDDING HILL WILDLIFE MANAGEMENT AREA

HABITATS
Open terrestrial: tilled, short grass, mixed herbaceous and shrubby fields, shrubby edges and hedgerows;
Forest: hardwoods, hardwoods/white pine, hemlock;
River/stream: river, slow water, shrubby and wooded streambelt.
This is a small area (135 acres) managed by the state primarily for hunting. It contains varied types of forest and open terrestrial habitats. The property is bounded on the east side by the Little River.

SEASONS/BIRDS
Spring migration: land birds;
Nesting season: land birds;
Fall migration: land birds;
Winter: land birds.
A variety of edge- and forest-dwelling land birds occurs in the front (west side) and middle of this area, together with species that are drawn to streambelts that can be found in the back (east) side of the area, by the Little River. The spring and fall migrations are both good. Whip-poor-will has been heard in this area.

GETTING AROUND
Birding methods: walk.
A farm/woods road and several trails go through the area. It is used for hunting in the fall, so time your visits accordingly.

DIRECTIONS: This area is in Scotland, about five miles east of Willimantic. To get there from the eastern intersection of Routes 97 and 14, go north on Route 97 for 1.2 miles to the area entrance on the right.

SCOTLAND: ROCK SPRING

HABITATS
FOREST: hardwoods, hardwoods/white pine;
Open terrestrial: shrubby field, shrubby and hardwood edge, scattered red cedar;
River/stream: perennial stream, slow water, shrubby and wooded streambelt; seasonal streams;
Marsh/swamp/bog: sedge and shrub marsh; shrub, shrubby hardwood and hardwood swamp;
Lake/pond: seasonal pools;
Other: rock outcrop.
This 445-acre Nature Conservancy preserve occupies a portion of the valley of the Little River, including a stretch of the river itself. Much of the uplands on the west side of the valley was once farmland, but is now covered with an oak-hickory hardwood forest with areas of mountain laurel. There are also shrubby fields surrounded by shrubs and young hardwoods. In the back (east side) of the preserve near the river, there is an aging red maple swamp with a shrub layer that includes sweet pepperbush. The preserve includes a rocky high point with good views.

SEASONS/BIRDS
> **SPRING MIGRATION:** LAND BIRDS;
> **NESTING SEASON:** LAND BIRDS;
> **Fall migration:** land birds;
> **Winter:** land birds.

This is a good site to see how bird species sort out according to habitat type. A variety of forest-dwelling land birds occur in the wooded portion of this preserve; species include red-shouldered hawk, pileated woodpecker, hermit thrush, cerulean and worm-eating warblers. Open- and edge-habitat species can be found near the clearings; these species include prairie, blue-winged and chestnut-sided warblers. In addition, species with a streambelt-wetland affinity inhabit the back (east side) of the preserve near the Little River; these species include flycatchers, hooded and yellow warblers, and swamp sparrow. The spring migration and the nesting season are the best times here.

GETTING AROUND
> **Birding methods:** WALK.

Trails and old farm roads make several loops through the area, one of three miles, and several shorter. One of the trails leads to the rocky overlook.

DIRECTIONS: This area is in Scotland, about five miles east of Willimantic. To get there from the eastern intersection of Routes 97 and 14, go north on Route 97 for 1.5 miles to the area entrance on the right.

SCOTLAND: TALBOT WILDLIFE MANAGEMENT AREA

HABITATS
> **Forest:** hardwoods, hardwoods/white pine, white pine;
> **Open terrestrial:** shrubby fields, shrubby edges;
> **River/stream:** stream, slow water; marshy, swampy and shrubby shore, wooded streambelt.
> **Marsh/swamp/bog:** shrub marsh, shrub swamp, shrubby hardwood swamp.

This 456-acre wildlife management area encloses sections of the streambelts of Merrick Brook (on the south side of Gager Road) and Beaver Brook (mostly on the north side). These streambelts have areas of shrubby wetlands that include sweet pepperbush. Much of the area is forested, with hardwoods and white pine. It is managed as a hunting area, and clearings (now shrubby fields) have been created for that purpose.

SEASONS/BIRDS
> **Spring Migration:** land birds;
> **Nesting season:** land birds;
> **Fall Migration:** land birds;
> **Winter:** land birds.

Forest- and edge-dwelling species of land birds occur here, with a good variety occurring in both the spring and fall migrations. Nesting species include pine warbler (in the white pines), and hooded warbler (in the sweet pepperbush).

GETTING AROUND
Birding methods: WALK.

A woods road provides easy walking. Hunting is allowed in the fall, so time your visits with this in mind.

DIRECTIONS: This area is in Scotland, about five miles east of Willimantic. To get there from the western intersection of Routes 97 and 14, go south on Route 97 for 0.4 mile, right on Gager Hill Road for 1.7 miles to the inconspicuous entrance and a parking area on the left. Most of the area lies on the south side of Gager Hill Road (the left side as you approached the area), and some on the north side, along the stream.

THOMPSON: QUADDICK RESERVOIR/STATE PARK/STATE FOREST

HABITATS
FOREST: hardwoods, hardwoods/white pine, hardwoods/hemlock, white pine; sand plain of mixed pitch pine, white pine and hardwoods;

Open terrestrial: short grass and shrubby fields, shrubby and wooded edges;

Lake/pond: lake, coves, islands; shore is wooded (white pine, hardwoods), partly developed, and has a sandy beach;

River/stream: stream, wooded streambelt;

Marsh/swamp/bog: shrub swamp, hardwood swamp.

Although small by comparison with other public areas in Windham County, this park and contiguous forest offer an excellent array of habitat types. Quaddick Park is based around a large body of water, (Quaddick Reservoir), some of which is developed for swimming, picnicking and boating. It has a very irregular shoreline, with points, coves and islands. The nearby Quaddick State Forest has a variety of forest types - mostly hardwoods/white pine.

SEASONS/BIRDS
Spring migration: water birds, land birds;

NESTING SEASON: water birds, LAND BIRDS;

Fall migration: water birds, land birds;

Winter: land birds.

The nesting season is the most interesting period at this site, because of the variety of species that are known to nest here, including: raptors (barred and screech owls, red-tailed and red-shouldered hawks), northern forest-dwellers (red-breasted nuthatch, hermit thrush, black-throated green, Canada and Blackburnian warblers), as well as gnatcatcher, brown creeper, scarlet tanager, great crested flycatcher and pine warbler (lots of the latter).

GETTING AROUND
Can be birded by: car, WALK, bike, ski, boat.

A nice feature of this site is that it provides easy birding - it is most effective on foot, but you can also do a lot from near your car. Small town roads go through and along the forest, and several woods roads go into it. You can also put a boat in the reservoir, and bird along the shore.

DIRECTIONS: This site is in the extreme northeastern corner of Connecticut, within a mile of Rhode Island and within three to five miles of Massachusetts.

To get to Quaddick State Park and Reservoir from I-395, take exit 97, go east on Route 44 for 1.5 miles, left on Thurber Road for 1.2 miles, right on Hill Road for 0.5 mile, right on Quaddick Road for 0.6 mile, left on Town Farm Road for 1.4 to the park entrance on the left.

To reach parts of Quaddick State Forest, from the park entrance go north (left) on Town Farm Road for 100' to a woods road on the right. Also, continue north on Town Farm Road for less than a mile to Baker Road. Woods roads lead into the forest on the right opposite Baker Road, and also off Town Farm Road farther north.

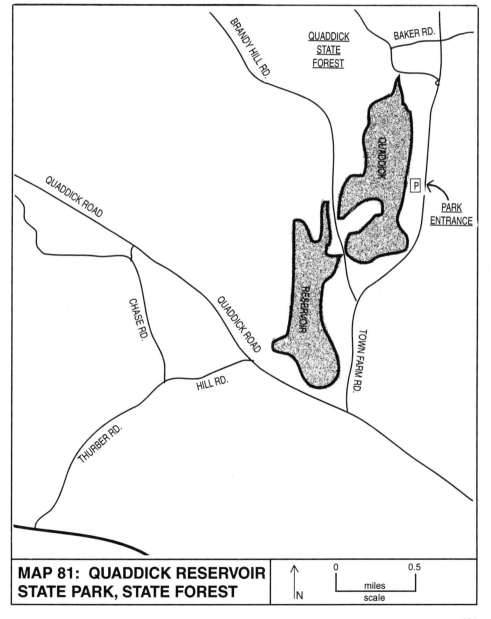

MAP 81: QUADDICK RESERVOIR STATE PARK, STATE FOREST

THOMPSON: WEST THOMPSON LAKE

HABITATS
LAKE/POND: lake; shrubby islands; shore of mixed herbaceous marsh, shrubs, white pine, hardwoods/white pine;
FOREST: hardwoods, hardwoods/white pine, mixed conifers, sand plain, flood plain;
OPEN TERRESTRIAL: short grass, mixed herbaceous and shrubby fields, cedars, shrubby edges;
River/stream: river, wooded streambelt, stream, wooded streambelt;
Marsh/swamp/bog: mixed herbaceous and shrub marsh; shrub, shrubby hardwood and hardwood swamp;
Other: dam.

This 1,950-acre area encompasses a portion of the gentle valley formed by the Quinebaug River. The principal features within this area are the West Thompson Flood Control Dam, West Thompson Lake which is impounded by it, and several miles of the Quinebaug River upstream of the lake. Surrounding these water bodies are varied forest habitats including sand plain and flood plain, as well as open terrestrial and wetland areas. The dam provides a broad view of the lake and surrounding habitats.

SEASONS/BIRDS
SPRING MIGRATION: water birds, marsh birds, shore birds, LAND BIRDS;
NESTING SEASON: water birds, LAND BIRDS;
FALL MIGRATION: water birds, marsh birds, shore birds, LAND BIRDS;
Winter: land birds.

Both migrations and the nesting season make a trip to this faraway site worthwhile. Common species of water birds occur on the lake in spring and fall, and the open, edge and forest habitats that surround the lake attract a variety of migrating and nesting land birds. Among the nesters are: (near the dam) rough-winged swallow; (among the shrubs and along the edges) indigo bunting, field sparrow, brown thrasher, white-eyed vireo and prairie warbler; (in the forested areas) wood duck, brown creeper, yellow-throated vireo, black-throated green warbler and purple finch.

GETTING AROUND
Can be birded by: car, WALK, SKI, boat.

Woods roads and trails reach many parts of the area, and it is possible to use a small boat in West Thompson Lake and the marsh just above it. Some of the woods roads are ideal for skiing. The top of the flood control dam provides open views of the reservoir and habitats at the south end of it.

DIRECTIONS: This area is in the very northeastern corner of Connecticut, within about five miles of both Massachusetts and Rhode Island.

To get to areas on the east side of West Thompson Lake, from the intersection of Routes 12 and 193 in West Thompson (near exit 98 of I-395), go west from that intersection on West Thompson Road for 0.3 mile, right on Reardon Road for 0.5 mile, and left on a park driveway that goes to the shore of West Thompson Lake and to several woods roads and trails that can be walked.

To get to areas on the west side of West Thompson Lake, from the intersection of Routes 12 and 193 in West Thompson, go west from that intersection on West Thompson Road for 0.9 mile across the top of the dam to a parking area. One woods road starts nearby, and other woods roads can be reached by continuing past the dam for another 0.4 mile, and turning right on Ravenville Road. There is a woods road on the right immediately after the turn, and others farther north on Ravenville Road.

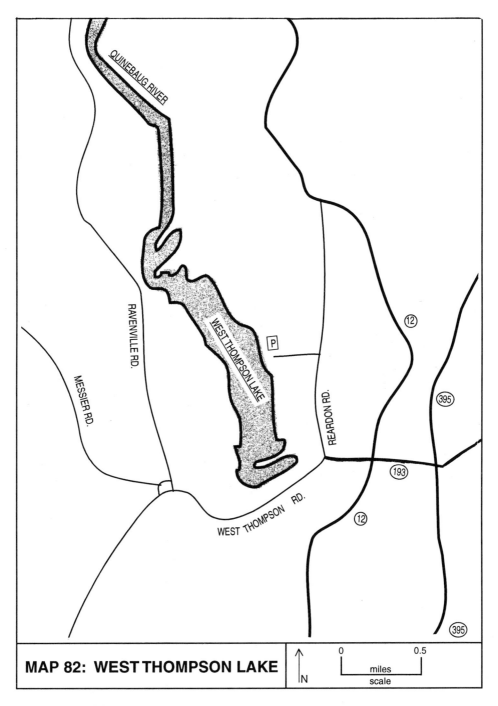

QUINEBAUG RIVER

RAVENVILLE RD.

MESSIER RD.

WEST THOMPSON LAKE

P

REARDON RD.

⑫

㊌

WEST THOMPSON RD.

⑫

⑲③

㊌

MAP 82: WEST THOMPSON LAKE

↑ N

0   0.5
miles
scale

WINDHAM: WINDHAM BOG

HABITAT

MARSH/SWAMP/BOG: white cedar and black spruce bog, shrub swamp;
Forest: hardwoods, hardwoods/hemlock; sand plain of white pine, pitch pine and scrub oak;
Open terrestrial: mixed herbaceous and shrubby field, wooded edge;
Lake/pond: pond, wooded shore;
Other: sandy areas.

This 89-acre preserve contains one of the few bogs in Connecticut - one that is especially unusual because it includes both white cedar and black spruce. Habitats include the bog itself, which has a mat of sphagnum moss, and a shrub layer of highbush blueberry, leather-leaf, swamp azalea and other peat-loving plants. In the middle of the preserve, there is a nearly inaccessible area of mature forest; around the periphery, there are young hardwoods. On the eastern side of the preserve, there is a sand plain forest, composed of white pine, pitch pine and scrub oak with patches of grassland and open sand. In the northwestern corner is a one-acre pond, probably a remnant of peat-mining operations.

SEASONS/BIRDS

SPRING MIGRATION: LAND BIRDS;
Nesting season: land birds;
FALL MIGRATION: LAND BIRDS;
Winter: land birds.

This site just recently became accessible to the public, so that its bird life has not been thoroughly studied. However, those familiar with the area say that the spring and fall migrations are both good, especially for a variety of warblers. An old railroad bed (now unused) provides habitat that should be attractive to edge-affinity species. Red-bellied woodpecker is known to nest here.

GETTING AROUND

Birding methods: car, WALK.

There is one place by the roadside that offers a view of the bog. By its nature, this site is difficult if not impossible to move about in, but an old railroad line crosses the southern portion of the site, and provides an easy way to bird on foot, with the advantage of having a few feet of elevation above the land nearby.

DIRECTIONS: This site is in Windham, immediately south of Mansfield Hollow State Park and the Windham Airport, and lies between Route 6 on the north and Route 203 on the east. To see part of the bog from a parking area on Route 6, start at the intersection of Routes 6 and 203, and go west on Route 6 for 0.3 mile to a pulloff on the south (left) side of the highway; the bog is visible from here. To walk through part of the bog on the railroad bed, go back east on Route 6 (back toward the Route 6/Route 203 intersection) for 0.2 mile to another pulloff, also on the south side of the highway. Park here, because there is nowhere to park at the beginning of the trail. Walk east on Route 6 for 0.1 mile to the Route 6/Route 203 intersection, right on Route 203 for 0.1 mile to the beginning of the trail on the right, opposite Beaver Hill Road.

Chapter 12

Sources of Additional Information

SOURCES OF ADDITIONAL INFORMATION

Birders in Connecticut are fortunate in having a well-developed network of organizations on which to rely for information, and for the opportunity to participate in activities that involve birds and other aspects of nature. In addition, there are several excellent references about avifauna in Connecticut, and a wealth of maps and field guides. The most important of the organizations and references are listed below, together with several suggestions for maps and trail guides.

ORGANIZATIONS, SERVICES AND STORES

National

National Audubon Society
Audubon Center in Greenwich
88 Field Point Road
Greenwich, CT 06830
203-661-9200
(Conservation and ornithology)

National Audubon Society
Northeast Audubon Center in Sharon
RR1, Box 171
Sharon, CT 06069
860-364-0520
(Conservation and ornithology)

Stuart B. McKinney National Wildlife Refuge
U. S. Fish and Wildlife Service
Box 1030
Westbrook, CT 06498
Tel: 203 399 2513
(Manages sites within the refuge, including Great Meadows/Long Beach, Milford Point/Nells Island, the Salt Meadow Unit, the Norwalk Islands, and other islands in Long Island Sound.)

State and Regional

Connecticut Ornithological Association
314 Unquowa Road
Fairfield, CT 06430
(Conservation and ornithology)

Connecticut Rare Bird Alert Phone
203-254-3665
(Reports of unusual bird occurrences)

Connecticut Department of Environmental Protection
Bureau of Outdoor Recreation
79 Elm Street
Hartford, CT 06106-5127
860-424-03014
(State conservation department)

Maps and Publications Division
79 Elm Street
Hartford, CT
860-424-3555
(Source of books and maps)

Franklin WMA
391 Route 32
North Franklin, CT 06254
860-642-7239

Sessions Woods WMA
P. O. Box 1550
Burlington, CT 06013-1550
860-675-8130

DEP Eastern District Area Hq.
209 Hebron Road
Marlboro, CT 06447
860-295-9523

DEP Western District Area Hq.
230 Plymouth Road
Harwinton, CT 06791
860-485-0226

Kellogg Environmental Center
Derby, CT
203-734-2513

Meigs Point Nature Center
Hammonasset Beach State Park
Madison, CT
203-245-8743

State Forest Headquarters
Cockaponset: 860-345-8521
Goodwin: 860-455-9534
Natchaug: 860-928-6121
Patchaug: 860-376-4075

Connecticut State Museum of Natural History
University of Connecticut U23
Storrs, CT 06269-3023
860-0486-4460
(Connecticut natural sciences)

Metropolitan District Commission (MDC)
(Water resources management)

  Barkhamsted Reservoir Area
  860-379-0938

  Goodwin/Hogback Dams
  860-379-6925

  Talcott Mountain Reservoir Area
  860-278-7850

Ct Audubon Society
(Conservation and ornithology education)

  Environmental Center and Administrative Offices
  118 Oak Street
  Hartford, CT 06115-1514
  860-527-8737

  Birdcraft Museum
  314 Unquoa Road
  Fairfield, CT 06430-5018
  203-259-0416

  Connecticut Audubon Coastal Center at Milford Point
  1 Milford Point Road
  Milford, CT 06460
  203-878-7440

  Fairfield Nature Center
  2325 Burr Street
  Fairfield, CT 06430-710
  203-259-6305

  Holland Brook Nature Center
  1361 Main Street
  Glastonbury, CT 06033-3105
  203-633-8402

The Nature Conservancy Connecticut Chapter
55 High Street
Middletown, CT 06457-3788
860-344-0716
(Conservation)

  Land Trust Service Bureau
  55 High Street
  Middletown, CT 06457-3788
  860-344-0716
  (Services for local land trusts)

Devil's Den Preserve
33 Pent Road, P. O. Box 1162
Weston, CT 06883
203-226-4991
(Preserve)

Sunny Valley Preserve
8 Sunny Valley Lane
New Milford, CT 06776-3321
860-355-3716
(Preserve)

Northeast Utilities
Community Relations (for all NU properties)
P. O. Box 270
Hartford, CT 06141-0270
1-800-286-5000
(Energy resources management)

Eagle Observation Area, Shepaug Dam
For Reservations: 1-800-368-8954

Connecticut Yankee Information and Science Center
362 Injun Hollow Road
Haddam Neck, CT 06424-3099
1-800-348-INFO

Connecticut Forest and Park Association
16 Meriden Road
Rockfall, CT 06481
(Conservation, publisher)

Connecticut River Watershed Council
1 Ferry Street
East Hampton, MA 01027
860-528-3588
(Watershed conservation)

Farmington River Watershed Association
749 Hopmeadow Street
Simsbury, CT 06070
860-658-4442
(Watershed conservation)

Housatonic Valley Association
Box 28
Cornwall Bridge, CT 06754
860-672-6678
(Watershed conservation)

Quinnipiac River Watershed Association
99 Colony Street, #9
Meriden, CT 06450
203-237-2237
(Watershed conservation)

Local

Fairfield County

Darien Audubon Society
P. O. Box 3313
Darien, CT 06820
(Local birding)

New Canaan Nature Center
144 Oenoke Ridge
New Canaan, CT 06840
203-966-9577
(Nature center)

New Canaan Audubon Society
Box 241
New Canaan, CT 06840
(Local birding)

Norwalk Seaport Association
Norwalk, CT
203-838-9444
(Arranges trips to Sheffield Island)

Hartford County

The Hartford Audubon Society
P. O. Box 270-207
West Hartford, CT 06127-0207
860-633-7135
Bird Information Line: 860-644-7343
(Local birding)

Roaring Brook Nature Center
712 Gracey Road
Canton, CT
860-693-0263
(Nature center)

The Wild Bird Center
The Shops at River Park
51 East Main Street
Avon, CT 06001
860-674-0855
(Birders' store)

Litchfield County

Eliot Pratt Education Center
Paper Mill Road
New Milford, CT
860-355-3137
(Nature center)

Flanders Nature Center
P. O. Box 702
Woodbury, CT 06978
203-263-3711
(Nature center)

Housatonic Audubon Society
RR1, Box 171
Sharon, CT 06069
(Local birding)

Litchfield Hills Audubon Society
P. O. Box 861
Litchfield, CT 06759
(Local birding)

Western Connecticut Bird Club
44 Church Street
Woodbury, CT 06798
203-263-2502
(Local birding)

White Memorial Foundation
Route 202
Litchfield, CT 06759
860-567-0857
(Nature center)

Middlesex County

Mattabeseck Audubon Society
P. O. Box 307
Middletown, CT 06457
(Local birding)

Saugatuck Valley Audubon Society
P. O. Box 684
Westport, CT 06881
(Local birding)

New Haven County

Ansonia Nature Center
10 Deerfield Road
Ansonia, CT 06401
203-736-9360
(Nature center)

The Audubon Shop
871 Boston Post Rd
Madison, CT 06443
1-800-776-5811
(Birders' store)

The Fat Robin
3000 Whitney Avenue
Hamden, CT 06518
203-248-7068
(Birders' store)

Lillinonah Audubon Society
P. O. Box 791
Southbury, CT 06488
(Local birding)

Menunketuck Audubon Society
P. O. Box 214
Guilford, CT 06437
(Local birding)

Naugatuck Valley Audubon Society
Box 371
Derby, CT 06418
(Local birding)

New Haven Bird Club
P. O. Box 9004
New Haven, CT 06532-0004
(Local birding)

Quinnipiac Valley Audubon Society
111 Mohawk Drive
Wallingford, CT 06492
(Local birding)

Recreation Department
Regional Water Authority
90 Sargent Drive
New Haven, CT 06511-9984
1-203-624-6671
Owns and manages a number of properties in New Haven County including several sites in this guide that require a permit to enter (for a list of sites, see Chapter 8: "New Haven County:

Birding in New Haven County"). The cost is $35 per year, less for seniors. To apply, call or write.

Waterbury Naturalist Club
77 West Ridge Drive
Waterbury, CT 06708
(Local birding)

New London County

Denison Pequotsepos Nature Center
P. O. Box 122
Mystic, CT 06355
860-536-1216
(Nature center)

Potapaug Audubon Society
Box 591
Old Lyme, CT 06371
(Local birding)

Tolland and Windham Counties

Joshua's Tract
Conservation and Historic Trust, Inc.
P. O. Box 4
Mansfield Center, CT 06250-0004
(Conservation, land management)

Natchaug Ornithological Society
P. O. Box 192
Mansfield Center, CT 06250
(Local birding)

BASIC REFERENCES

The Atlas of Breeding Birds of Connecticut, Bevier, Louis R., editor. 1994. State Geological and Natural History Survey of Connecticut, Department of Environmental Protection. A study that determined what bird species breed in Connecticut, and where in the state they breed.

Connecticut Birds, Zeranski, Joseph D. and Thomas R. Baptist. 1990. University Press of New England, Hanover, NH. Provides a current summary of knowledge of the occurrence of birds in Connecticut.

Field Checklist Birds of Connecticut, Connecticut Rare Records Committee, compiler. 1994. Connecticut Ornithological Association.

MAPS, ATLASES, TRAIL GUIDES

Connecticut Walk Book. Seventeenth edition, 1993. Connecticut Forest and Park Association. A complete guide to the major hiking trails in Connecticut.

Joshua's Tract Walk Book. Second edition, 1991. Joshua's Tract Conservation and Historic Trust. A field guide to Trust properties.

State of Connecticut, Official Tourist Map. Updated each year and distributed free at Interstate Highway rest areas and other public facilities. This is basically a highway map - it is easy to read, and has information about state-owned public areas.

Atlas of Connecticut Topographic Maps. Connecticut Department of Environmental Protection, Natural Resources Center. DEP Bulletin 17. Contains USGS maps covering all of Connecticut, reduced to 12"x16". Available from the DEP Maps and Publications Division.

Champion Map Books. 1994. Champion Map Corporation, 1-800-444-1072 x237. There are six of these books which together cover all of Connecticut in a large scale - about two inches to a mile. Available at many magazine sellers.

Glossary and Abbreviations

GLOSSARY

The intent of the guide is to provide the average birder with practical information that will be easy to use in the field. Scientific terms have been avoided when it was possible to provide accurate information without using them. Those words and terms that are not part of our daily vocabulary are defined below in this Glossary.

Some of the terms that have been used in the guide are familiar to many birders, but perhaps not to everyone. Examples are terms that refer to the occurrence and abundance of bird species, such as "common", "occasional" etc.

Other terms are used as a kind of shorthand - an abbreviated form of expression that serve as a convenience when conveying repetitive information in over 450 site descriptions. Examples are the terms that refer to groups of bird species, such as "water birds", "shore birds", etc. These groups are composed of species that occur in similar types of habitat, as they are usually seen by birders. They are not scientific terms, and in some cases do not conform to standard taxonomic arrangements.

Terms that refer to types of habitat, natural communities and ecological systems are defined and discussed in Chapter 2: "Using Habitats to Find Birds", and are not included in this glossary.

Seasonal occurrence, abundance and distribution of bird species.

Abundant: species so well distributed in such high numbers that it is almost certain to be seen in appropriate habitat during the appropriate time of year.

Common: species that is easily found in appropriate habitat during the appropriate time of year.

Uncommon: species that occurs every year, but it is not certain to be seen, because it occurs in low numbers, or with restricted distribution, or in restricted habitat.

Occasional: species that occurs in most years, but it is seen infrequently even in appropriate habitat and during the appropriate time of year, because it occurs in such low numbers.

Rare: species does not occur every year, and is very infrequently seen even in appropriate habitat and during the appropriate time of year, because of irregular occurrence, very low numbers, limited distribution and/or limited habitat usage.

Accidental: species that occurs in a given place only very infrequently and irregularly. Such occurrence may result from severe weather or may represent abberations in the movements of individual birds.

Local: generally seen only in very restricted habitats and areas.

Regular: the occurrence, distribution and relative abundance of a species in appropriate habitat and during the appropriate time of year varies little from one year to another.

Irregular: the occurrence or relative abundance of a species in appropriate habitat and during the appropriate time of year tends to vary from one year to another.

Irruptive species: comes to Connecticut during the winter in some years but not every year, apparently in response to the availability of food in northern areas.

Migrant: used in the guide to refer to a species that passes through Connecticut on its way to or from its breeding area.

Nester, or nesting species: reported as a probable or confirmed breeding species at the site being described by records of The Atlas of Breeding Birds of Connecticut, as updated through 1995.

Resident: species occurs in Connecticut throughout the year in appropriate habitat.

Winter visitor: comes to Connecticut during the winter, typically from breeding ranges north of Connecticut.

Terms that refer to bird groups. These groups are composed of species that occur in similar types of habitat, as they are usually seen by birders.

Water birds: species that typically occur swimming on open water, including: loons, grebes cormorants, swans, geese, ducks, mergansers and coot.

Dabbling ducks: duck species that typically feed in shallow water by dabbling or tipping up (such as black duck, wood duck, green-winged teal).

Diving ducks: duck species that typically feed in deeper water by diving for food (such as bufflehead, goldeneyes and scoters).

Marsh birds: species that typically occur amid the vegetation of marshes or swamps, (such as herons, bitterns, ibis, rails, moorhen).

Waders: long-legged marsh birds, such as herons, egrets and ibis.

Shore birds: species that typically occur on or near shores, at the shallow water or mud of marshes and swamps, or on fields, including: oystercatcher, plovers, sandpipers, godwits, woodcock, snipe, dowitchers, and related species.

Land birds: all remaining species that typically occur in terrestrial habitats.

Raptors: birds of prey, including hawks, eagles, vultures and owls.

Terms that relate to the breeding range, or geographical occurrence (usually of land birds):

Northern species (or northerner): species of birds whose breeding ranges lie mainly north or northwest of Connecticut, and which occur in Connecticut only in certain areas or types of habitat - typically inland at higher elevations. Some of these species are expanding their ranges southward. Examples of northern species include:

common merganser
yellow-bellied sapsucker
olive-sided flycatcher
common raven
red-breasted nuthatch
winter wren
golden-crowned kinglet
hermit thrush
solitary vireo
Blackburnian warbler
black-throated blue warbler
yellow-rumped warbler
Canada warbler
Nashville warbler
northern waterthrush
white-throated sparrow
dark-eyed junco

Southern species (or southerner): species of birds whose breeding ranges lie mainly south or southwest of Connecticut, and which occur in Connecticut only in certain areas or types of habitat - typically at lower elevations along the coast, in river valleys or in southern Connecticut. Some of these species are expanding their ranges northward. Examples of southern species include:

red-bellied woodpecker
Acadian flycatcher
Carolina wren
white-eyed vireo
yellow-throated warbler
worm-eating warbler
cerulean warbler
Kentucky warbler
hooded warbler
orchard oriole

Winter finch: members of the finch family that breed in boreal forests and move to Connecticut during some winters; notably:

evening grosbeak
pine grosbeak
common redpoll
pine siskin
red crossbill
white-winged crossbill.

Terms that relate to food:

> **Berry-eater (or frugivore):** species for which berries are a major item of diet when available, primarily in late summer, fall and winter. Berry-eaters include thrushes, cedar waxwing, mockingbird and many others.

> **Seed-eater:** species for which seeds are a major item of diet when available, primarily in fall and early winter. Seed-eaters include sparrows, chickadees, winter finches and other species.

Terms that relate to vegetation:

Trees: plants with a single woody stem (trunk) that extends several feet between the ground and the lowest branching point. Trees typically are taller than shrubs.

> **Hardwoods:** broad-leafed flowering trees that (in Connecticut) shed their leaves in the autumn.

> **Conifers:** trees that bear cones - including pines, spruces, firs and junipers.

Shrubs: plants with several woody stems rather than a single trunk. Shrubs typically are less tall than trees.

Herbs, herbaceous plants: plants that have stems that are fleshy, rather than the woody tissue of shrubs and trees. The stems generally die back at the end of each growing season.

Emergent plant: a herbaceous plant or shrub that grows in a water body with its roots in submerged soil, with stems that are partly under and partly above water, and leaves and flowers that are above water.

ABBREVIATIONS

Cty County
DEP Connecticut Department of Environmental Protection
FCA Flood Control Area
NC Nature Center
NWR National Wildlife Refuge
rec recreation
Res Reservoir
ROW Right-of-way
RWA Regional Water Authority (New Haven County)
sanct sanctuary
SF State Forest
SP State Park
WMA Wildlife Management Area

INDEX 1: SITES

Begins on Page(s)

Begins on Page(s)

INDEX 1: SITES Cont.)

Begins on Page(s)

Begins on Page(s)

INDEX 2: TOURS

INDEX 3: TOWNS

INDEX 3: TOWNS Cont.)

INDEX 3: TOWNS Cont.)

* No sites are included in the guide for these eleven towns.

ABOUT THE AUTHORS

Dave Rosgen is a professional wildlife biologist with a Bachelor of Science degree in Biological Sciences from the University of Connecticut, 1981. He founded the Connecticut Wildlife Services (CWS) in 1987 as a non-profit operation that provides wildlife inventories, censuses, research, management and educational services. CWS includes the on-going Connecticut Wildlife Atlas and the Connecticut Bluebird Restoration Project. Dave serves as director of all these projects. Since none of them generate income, he also works for Northeast Utilities as a Wildlife Biologist, environmental educator and park ranger. In addition, he teaches adult education classes, and is a certified law enforcement officer, fire fighter, hazardous materials technician and medical response technician. He was the principal consultant for Birds of Prey in Connecticut, and the Statewide Field Coordinator for The Connecticut Breeding Bird Atlas Project. At present, he lives in Watertown, Connecticut.

Gene Billings. Since retiring in 1984 from a career in the insurance business, he has pursued his interests in conservation and birding - as a writer (Birds of Prey in Connecticut), and through activities as a member of The Nature Conservancy, the Norfolk Land Trust, the Connecticut Ornithological Association, and other organizations. He lives in Norfolk, Connecticut.

TO BUY THIS GUIDE

This guide is sold in Connecticut at some book stores, a number of nature centers, and at the Audubon Shop in Madison. It may also be purchased directly from the authors by contacting:

> Gene Billings
> 28 Sunset Ridge
> Norfolk, CT 06058
> Tel: 860-542-5177